ATTACK ON TITAN
JUNIOR HIGH

3

SAKI NAKAGAWA

Based on "Attack on Titan" by
HAJIME ISAYAMA

Contents

PLANETARIUM
CAFÉ VENUS
CAT CAFÉ FLUFFY HOUSE

No Name

SCHEDULE FOR WEDNESDAY, AUGUST 8

LEVI

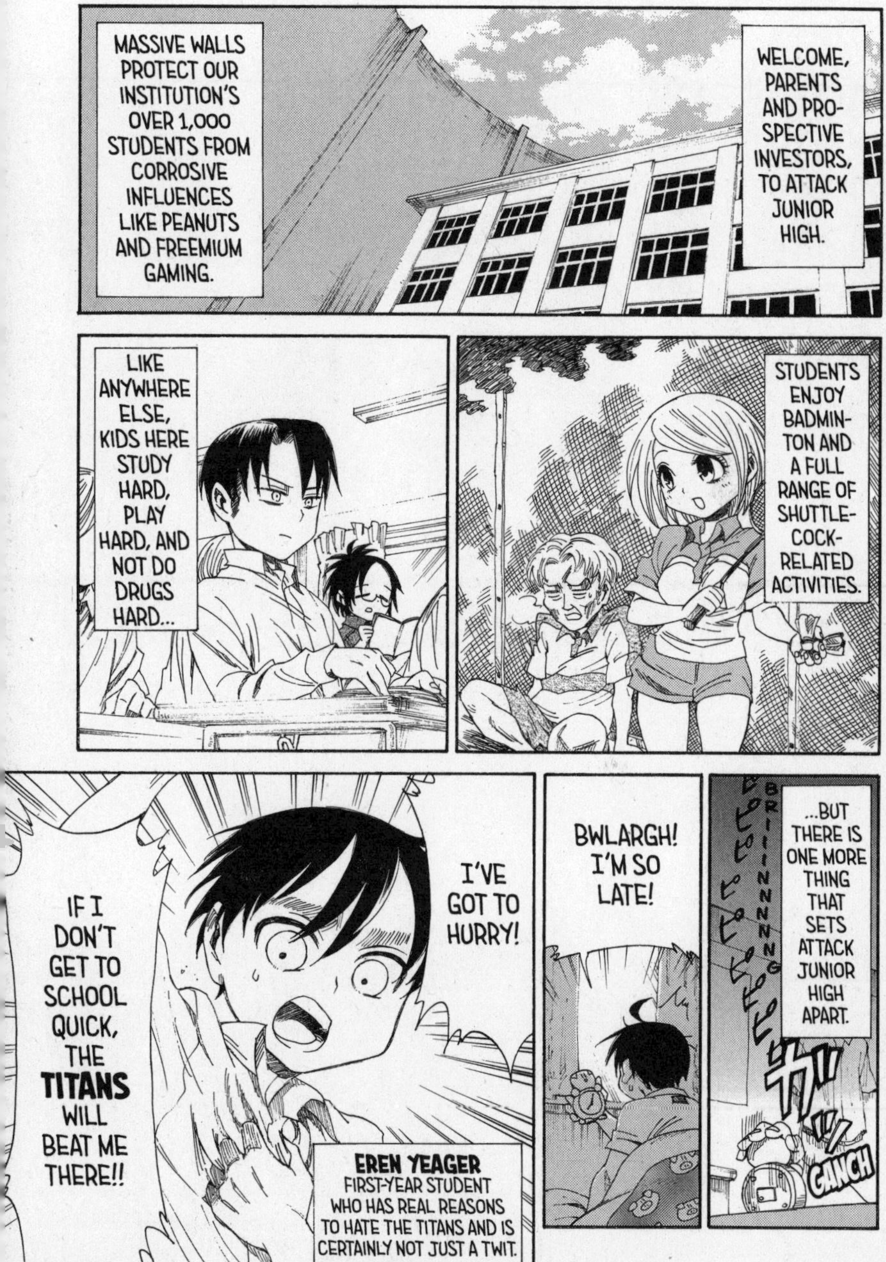
WELCOME, PARENTS AND PROSPECTIVE INVESTORS, TO ATTACK JUNIOR HIGH.
MASSIVE WALLS PROTECT OUR INSTITUTION'S OVER 1,000 STUDENTS FROM CORROSIVE INFLUENCES LIKE PEANUTS AND FREEMIUM GAMING.
STUDENTS ENJOY BADMINTON AND A FULL RANGE OF SHUTTLECOCK-RELATED ACTIVITIES.
LIKE ANYWHERE ELSE, KIDS HERE STUDY HARD, PLAY HARD, AND NOT DO DRUGS HARD...
...BUT THERE IS ONE MORE THING THAT SETS ATTACK JUNIOR HIGH APART.
BRIIINNNNNG
GANCH
BWLARGH! I'M SO LATE!
I'VE GOT TO HURRY!
IF I DON'T GET TO SCHOOL QUICK, THE **TITANS** WILL BEAT ME THERE!!
EREN YEAGER
FIRST-YEAR STUDENT WHO HAS REAL REASONS TO HATE THE TITANS AND IS CERTAINLY NOT JUST A TWIT.

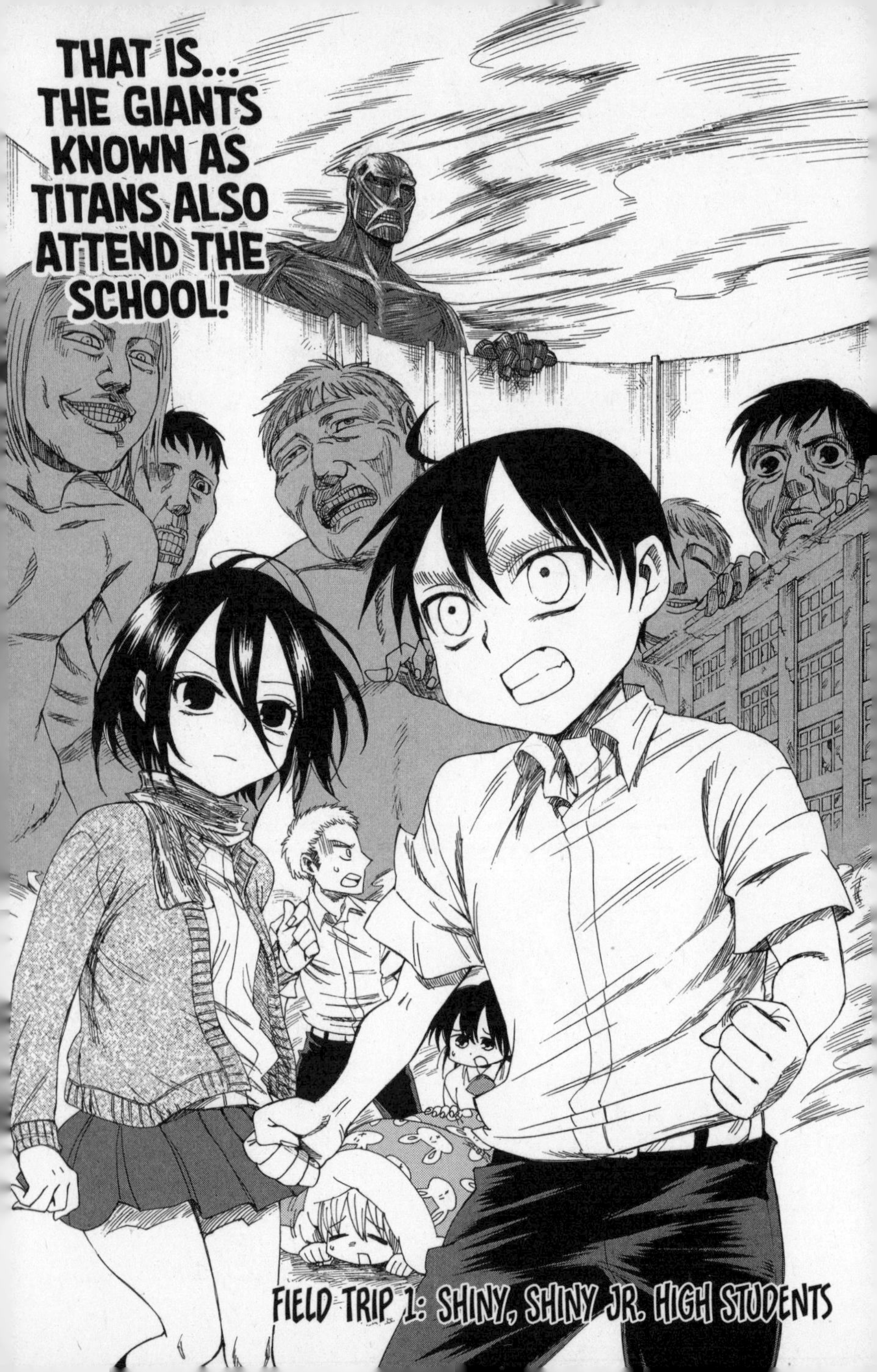
THAT IS... THE GIANTS KNOWN AS TITANS ALSO ATTEND THE SCHOOL!
FIELD TRIP 1: SHINY, SHINY JR. HIGH STUDENTS

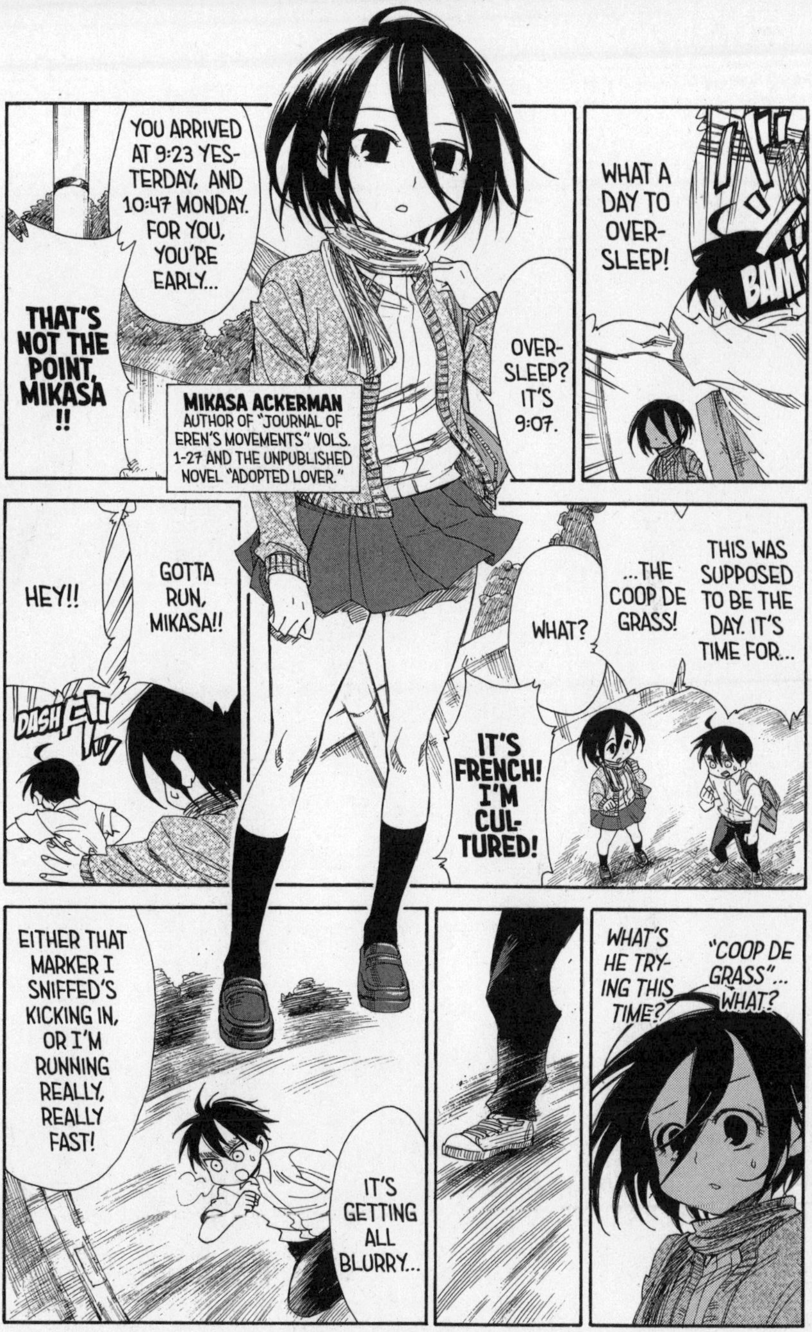

WHAT A DAY TO OVER-SLEEP!
BAM
OVER-SLEEP? IT'S 9:07.
YOU ARRIVED AT 9:23 YES-TERDAY, AND 10:47 MONDAY. FOR YOU, YOU'RE EARLY...
THAT'S NOT THE POINT, MIKASA!!
MIKASA ACKERMAN AUTHOR OF "JOURNAL OF EREN'S MOVEMENTS" VOLS. 1-27 AND THE UNPUBLISHED NOVEL "ADOPTED LOVER."
THIS WAS SUPPOSED TO BE THE DAY. IT'S TIME FOR...
...THE COOP DE GRASS!
WHAT?
IT'S FRENCH! I'M CUL-TURED!
GOTTA RUN, MIKASA!!
HEY!!
DASH
"COOP DE GRASS"... WHAT?
WHAT'S HE TRY-ING THIS TIME?
EITHER THAT MARKER I SNIFFED'S KICKING IN, OR I'M RUNNING REALLY, REALLY FAST!
IT'S GETTING ALL BLURRY...

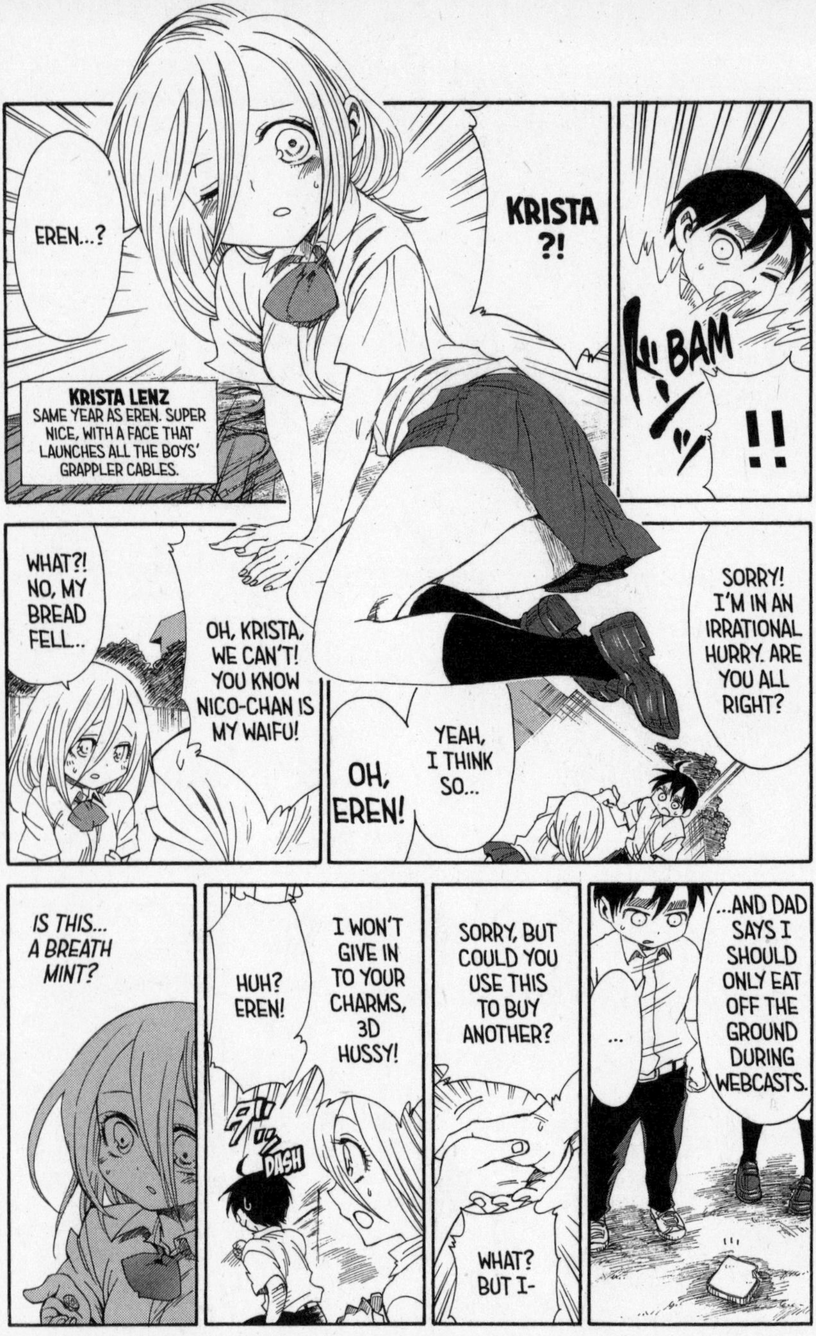
BAM
!!
KRISTA ?!
EREN...?
KRISTA LENZ
SAME YEAR AS EREN. SUPER NICE, WITH A FACE THAT LAUNCHES ALL THE BOYS' GRAPPLER CABLES.
SORRY! I'M IN AN IRRATIONAL HURRY. ARE YOU ALL RIGHT?
YEAH, I THINK SO...
OH, EREN!
OH, KRISTA, WE CAN'T! YOU KNOW NICO-CHAN IS MY WAIFU!
WHAT?! NO, MY BREAD FELL...
...AND DAD SAYS I SHOULD ONLY EAT OFF THE GROUND DURING WEBCASTS.
...
SORRY, BUT COULD YOU USE THIS TO BUY ANOTHER?
WHAT? BUT I-
I WON'T GIVE IN TO YOUR CHARMS, 3D HUSSY!
HUH? EREN!
DASH
IS THIS... A BREATH MINT?

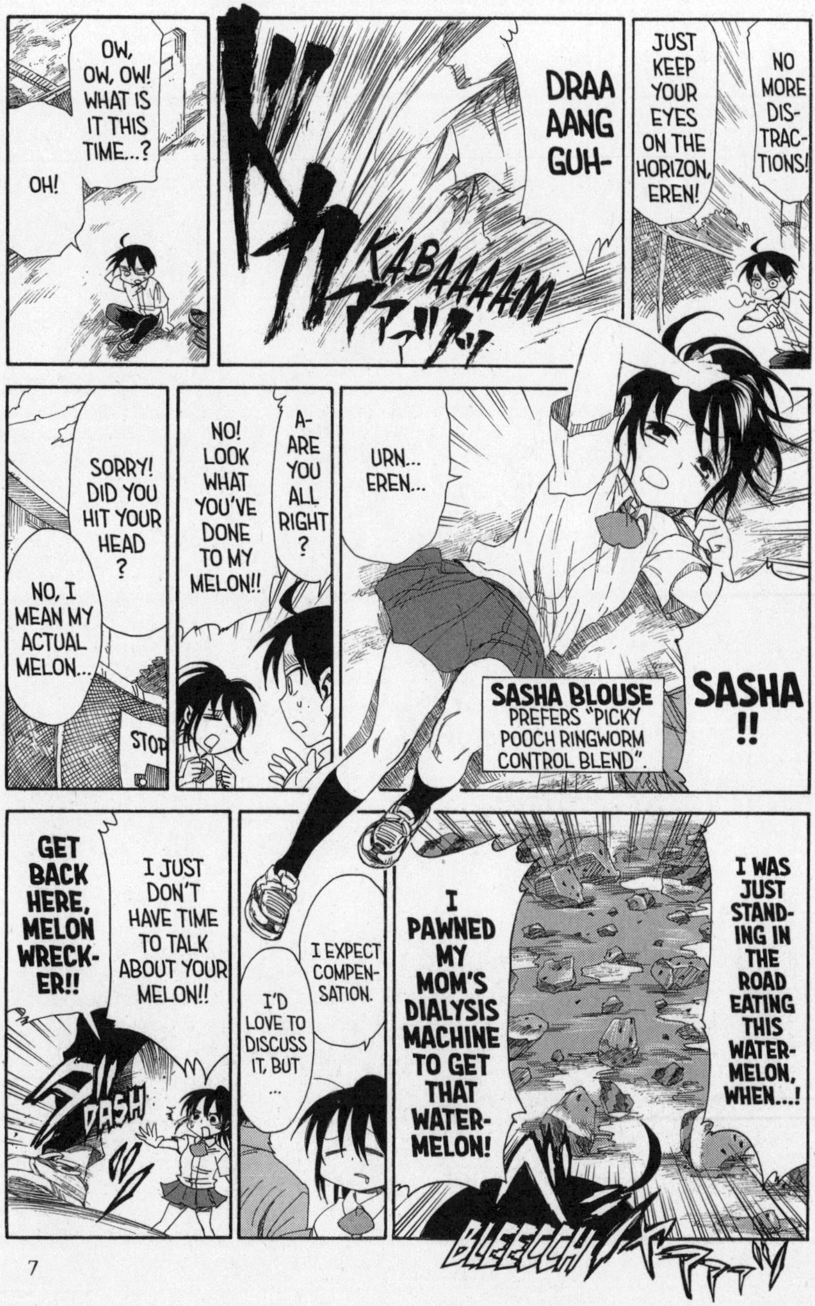
NO MORE DIS-TRAC-TIONS!
JUST KEEP YOUR EYES ON THE HORIZON, EREN!
DRAA AANG GUH-
KABAAAAAM
OW, OW, OW! WHAT IS IT THIS TIME...?
OH!
SASHA !!
URN... EREN...
SASHA BLOUSE PREFERS "PICKY POOCH RINGWORM CONTROL BLEND".
A- ARE YOU ALL RIGHT?
NO! LOOK WHAT YOU'VE DONE TO MY MELON!!
SORRY! DID YOU HIT YOUR HEAD?
NO, I MEAN MY ACTUAL MELON...
STOP
I WAS JUST STANDING IN THE ROAD EATING THIS WATER-MELON, WHEN...!
I PAWNED MY MOM'S DIALYSIS MACHINE TO GET THAT WATER-MELON!
BLEEECH
I EXPECT COMPEN-SATION.
I'D LOVE TO DISCUSS IT, BUT ...
I JUST DON'T HAVE TIME TO TALK ABOUT YOUR MELON!!
GET BACK HERE, MELON WRECK-ER!!
DASH

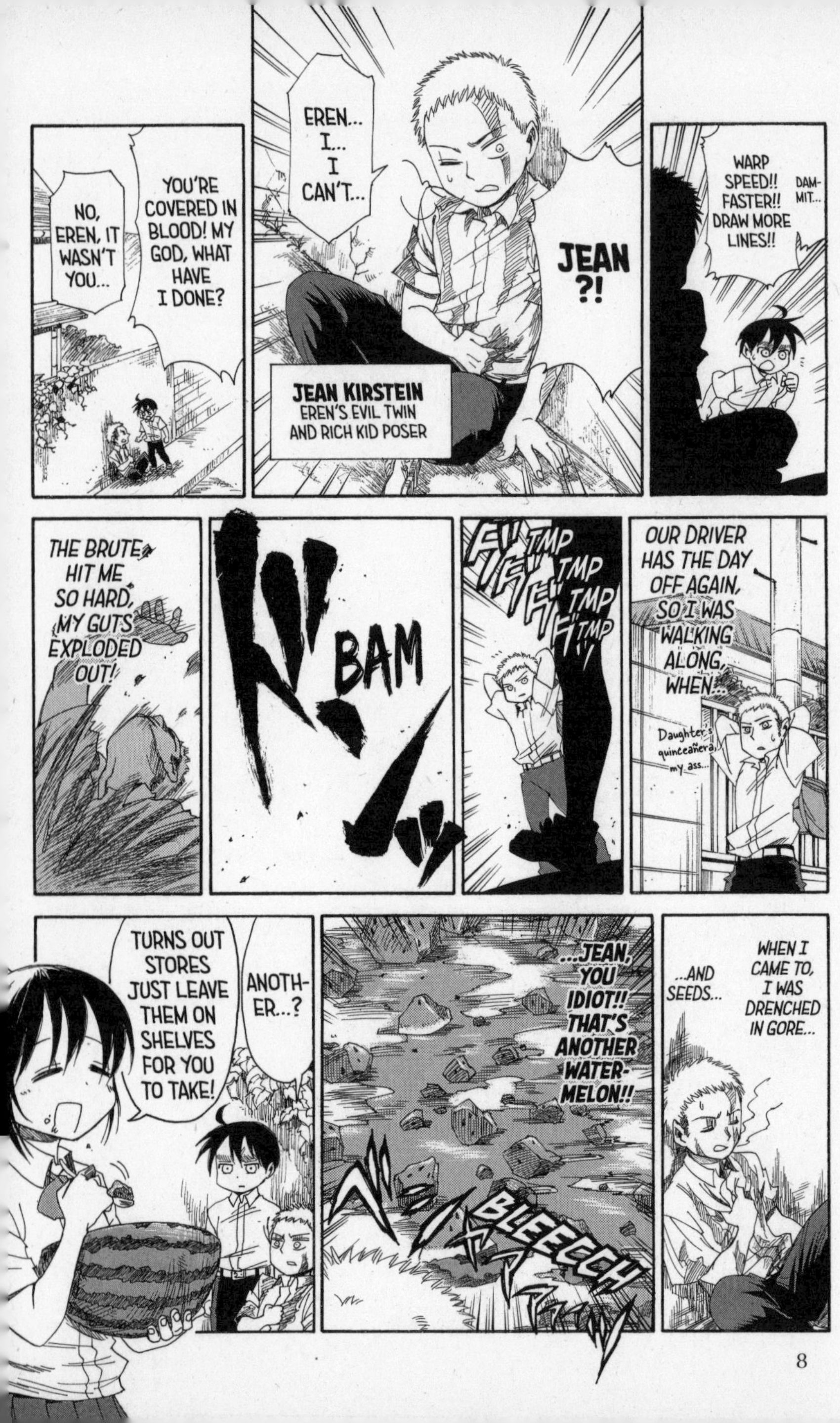
WARP SPEED!! FASTER!! DRAW MORE LINES!!
DAM-MIT...
EREN... I... I CAN'T...
JEAN ?!
JEAN KIRSTEIN
EREN'S EVIL TWIN AND RICH KID POSER
YOU'RE COVERED IN BLOOD! MY GOD, WHAT HAVE I DONE?
NO, EREN, IT WASN'T YOU...
OUR DRIVER HAS THE DAY OFF AGAIN, SO I WAS WALKING ALONG, WHEN...
Daughter's quinceañera, my ass...
TMP TMP TMP TMP
BAM
THE BRUTE HIT ME SO HARD, MY GUTS EXPLODED OUT!
WHEN I CAME TO, I WAS DRENCHED IN GORE...
...AND SEEDS...
...JEAN, YOU IDIOT!! THAT'S ANOTHER WATER-MELON!!
BLEEECH
ANOTH-ER...?
TURNS OUT STORES JUST LEAVE THEM ON SHELVES FOR YOU TO TAKE!

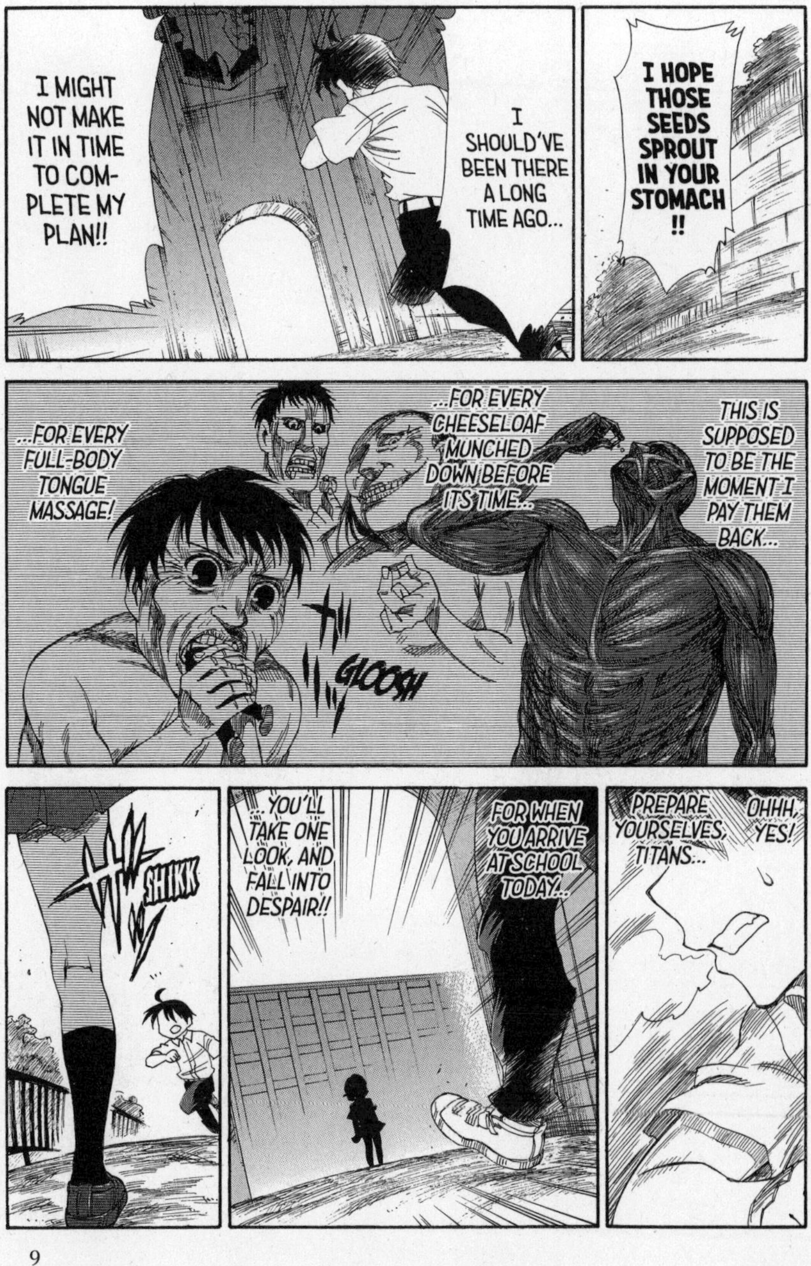
I HOPE THOSE SEEDS SPROUT IN YOUR STOMACH !!
I SHOULD'VE BEEN THERE A LONG TIME AGO...
I MIGHT NOT MAKE IT IN TIME TO COM-PLETE MY PLAN!!
THIS IS SUPPOSED TO BE THE MOMENT I PAY THEM BACK...
...FOR EVERY CHEESELOAF MUNCHED DOWN BEFORE ITS TIME...
...FOR EVERY FULL-BODY TONGUE MASSAGE!
GLOOSH
OHHH, YES!
PREPARE YOURSELVES, TITANS...
FOR WHEN YOU ARRIVE AT SCHOOL TODAY...
...YOU'LL TAKE ONE LOOK, AND FALL INTO DESPAIR!!
SHIKK

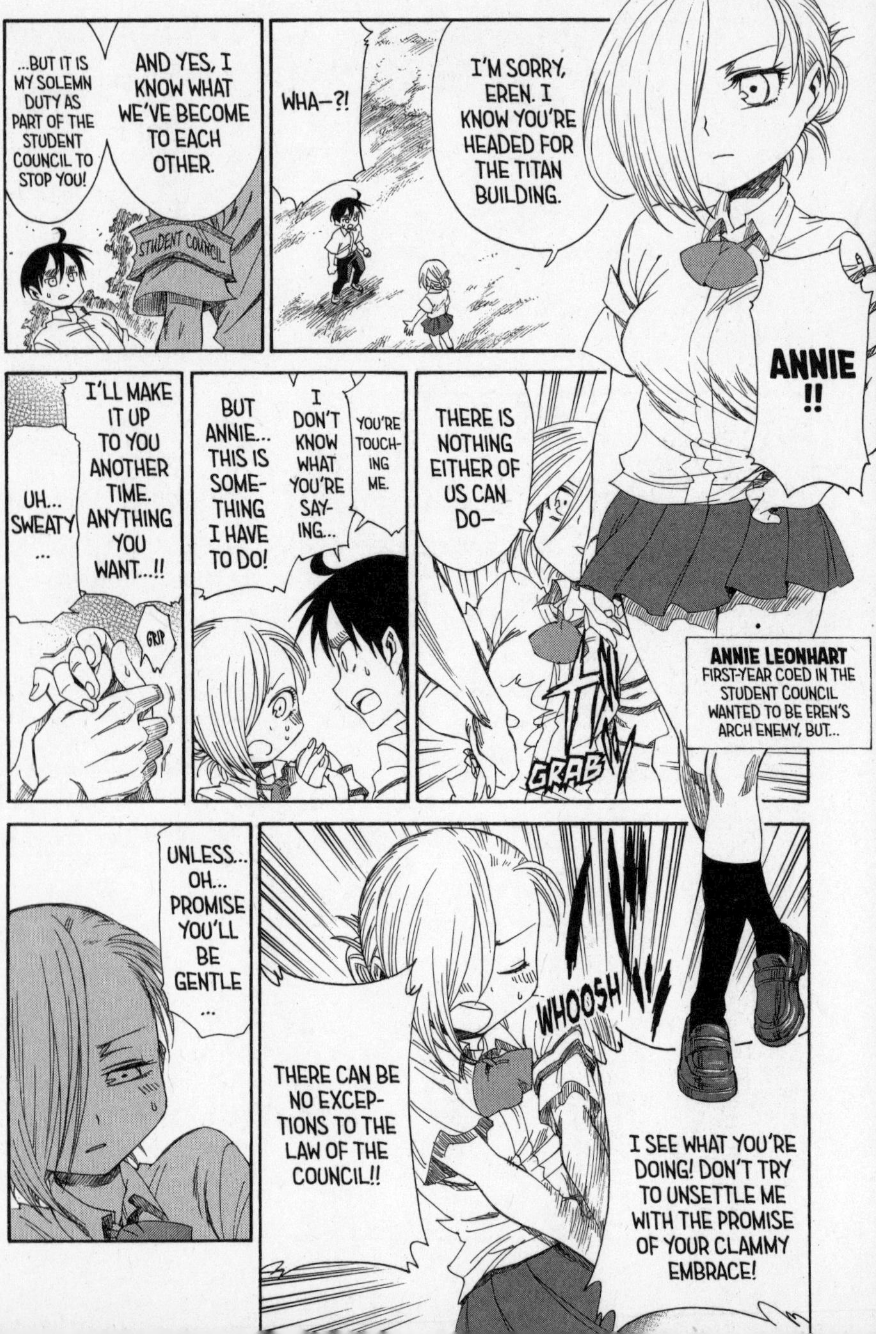
ANNIE!!
ANNIE LEONHART FIRST-YEAR COED IN THE STUDENT COUNCIL WANTED TO BE EREN'S ARCH ENEMY, BUT...
I'M SORRY, EREN. I KNOW YOU'RE HEADED FOR THE TITAN BUILDING.
WHA—?!
AND YES, I KNOW WHAT WE'VE BECOME TO EACH OTHER.
...BUT IT IS MY SOLEMN DUTY AS PART OF THE STUDENT COUNCIL TO STOP YOU!
STUDENT COUNCIL
THERE IS NOTHING EITHER OF US CAN DO—
GRAB
YOU'RE TOUCHING ME.
I DON'T KNOW WHAT YOU'RE SAYING...
BUT ANNIE... THIS IS SOMETHING I HAVE TO DO!
I'LL MAKE IT UP TO YOU ANOTHER TIME. ANYTHING YOU WANT...!!
UH... SWEATY...
GRIP
I SEE WHAT YOU'RE DOING! DON'T TRY TO UNSETTLE ME WITH THE PROMISE OF YOUR CLAMMY EMBRACE!
WHOOSH
THERE CAN BE NO EXCEPTIONS TO THE LAW OF THE COUNCIL!!
UNLESS... OH... PROMISE YOU'LL BE GENTLE...

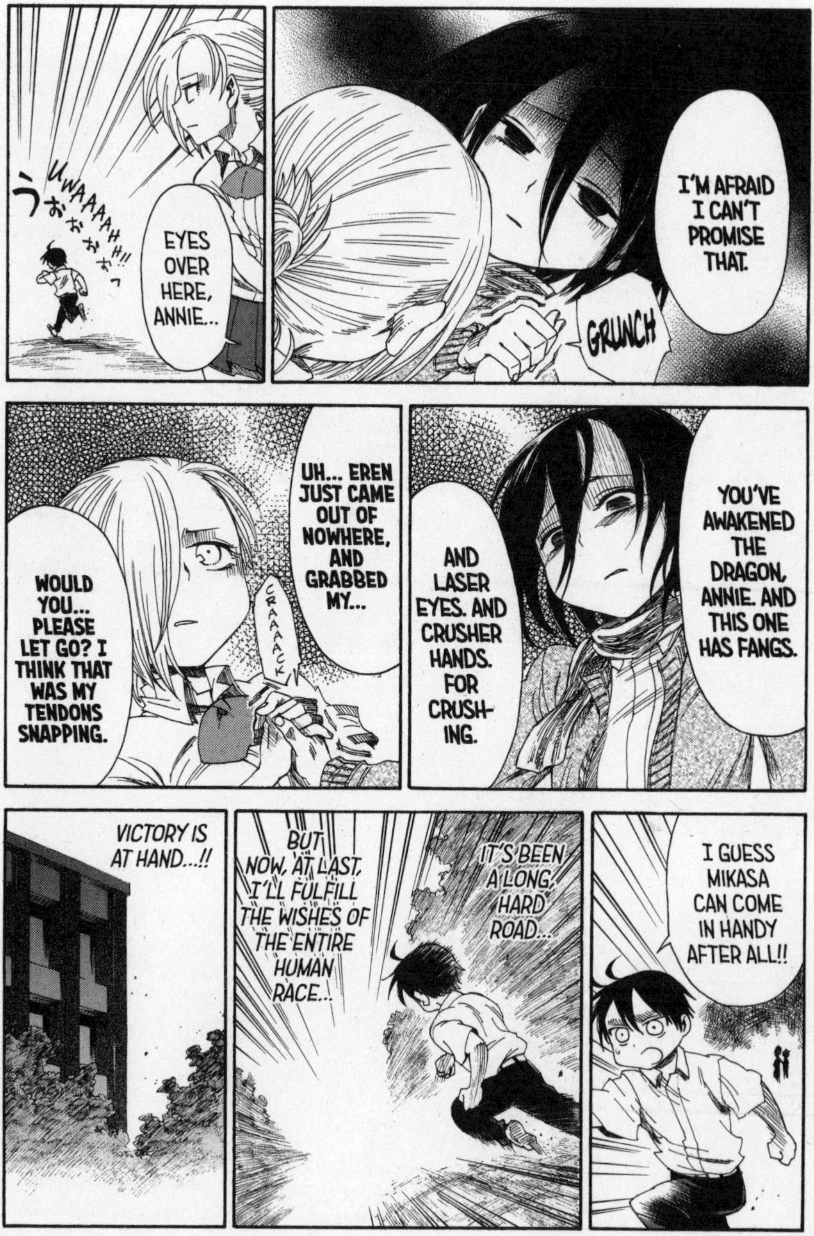
I'M AFRAID I CAN'T PROMISE THAT.
GRUNCH
UWAAAAAHH!!
うおおおおっ
EYES OVER HERE, ANNIE...
YOU'VE AWAKENED THE DRAGON, ANNIE. AND THIS ONE HAS FANGS.
AND LASER EYES. AND CRUSHER HANDS. FOR CRUSH-ING.
UH... EREN JUST CAME OUT OF NOWHERE, AND GRABBED MY...
CRAAAACK
WOULD YOU... PLEASE LET GO? I THINK THAT WAS MY TENDONS SNAPPING.
I GUESS MIKASA CAN COME IN HANDY AFTER ALL!!
IT'S BEEN A LONG, HARD ROAD...
BUT NOW, AT LAST, I'LL FULFILL THE WISHES OF THE ENTIRE HUMAN RACE...
VICTORY IS AT HAND...!!

DINNG
キーン
DONNG
コーン
DINNG
カーン
TITAN CLASSROOMS
MURMUR
ざわ
MURMUR
ざわ
KACHIK
パカッ

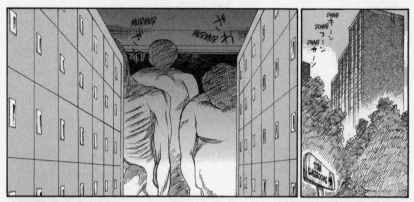

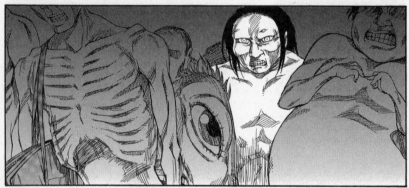

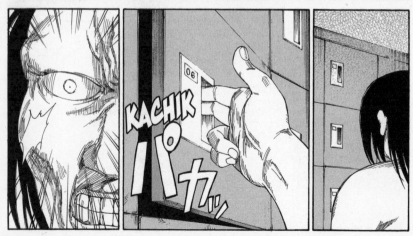

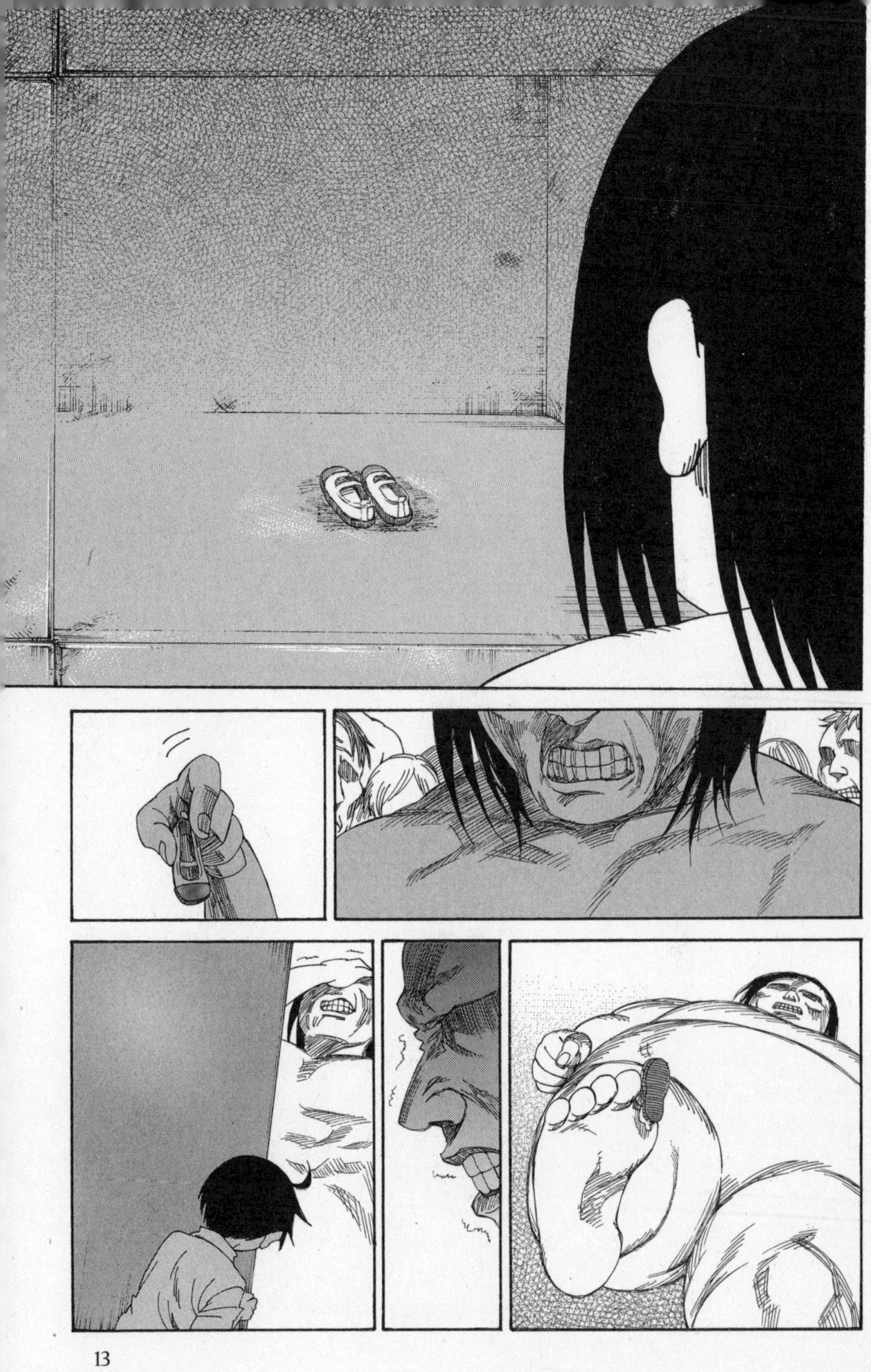

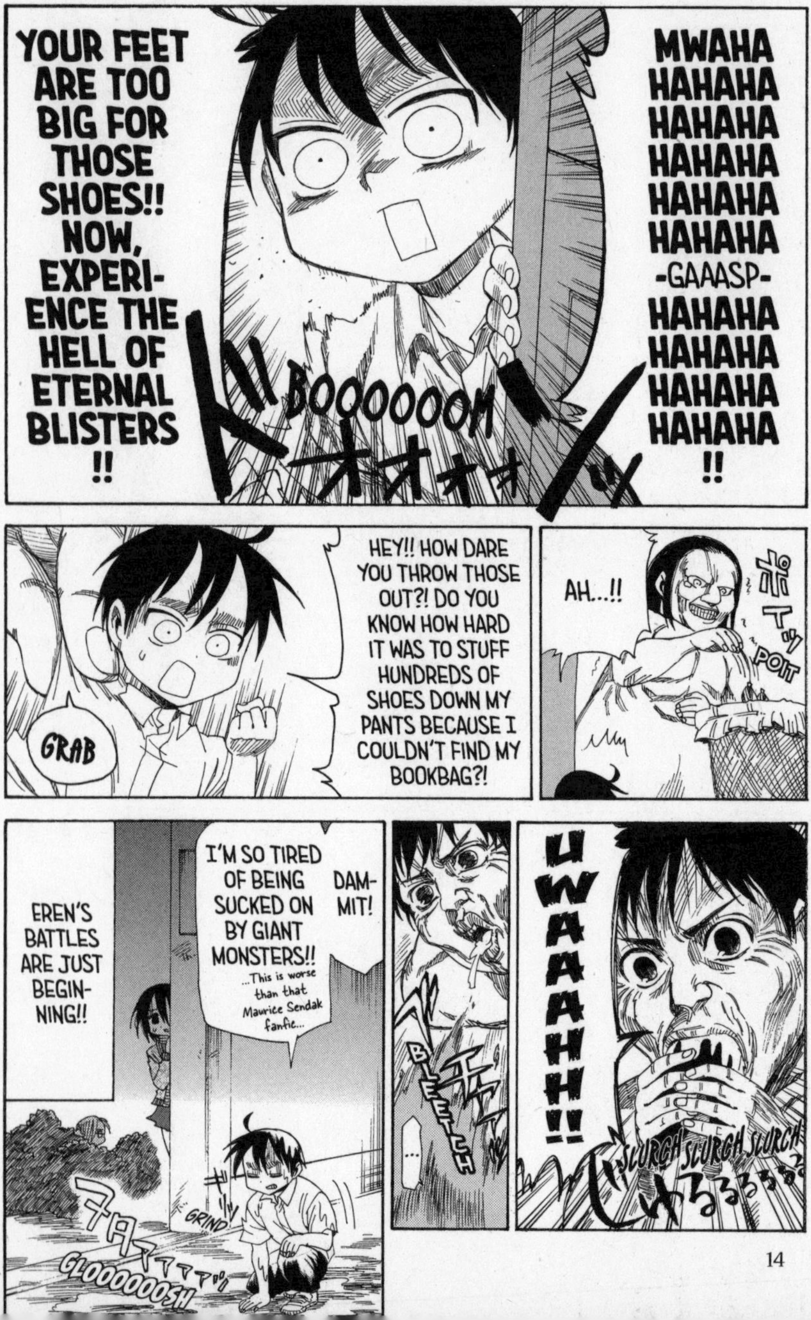
MWAHA HAHAHA HAHAHA HAHAHA HAHAHA HAHAHA -GAAASP- HAHAHA HAHAHA HAHAHA HAHAHA!!
YOUR FEET ARE TOO BIG FOR THOSE SHOES!! NOW, EXPERI-ENCE THE HELL OF ETERNAL BLISTERS!!
BOOOOOOM
AH...!!
POIT
HEY!! HOW DARE YOU THROW THOSE OUT?! DO YOU KNOW HOW HARD IT WAS TO STUFF HUNDREDS OF SHOES DOWN MY PANTS BECAUSE I COULDN'T FIND MY BOOKBAG?!
GRAB
UWAAAAHH!!
SLURCH SLURCH SLURCH
...
BLEETCH
DAM-MIT!
I'M SO TIRED OF BEING SUCKED ON BY GIANT MONSTERS!!
...This is worse than that Maurice Sendak fanfic...
EREN'S BATTLES ARE JUST BEGIN-NING!!
GRIND
GLOOOOOOSH

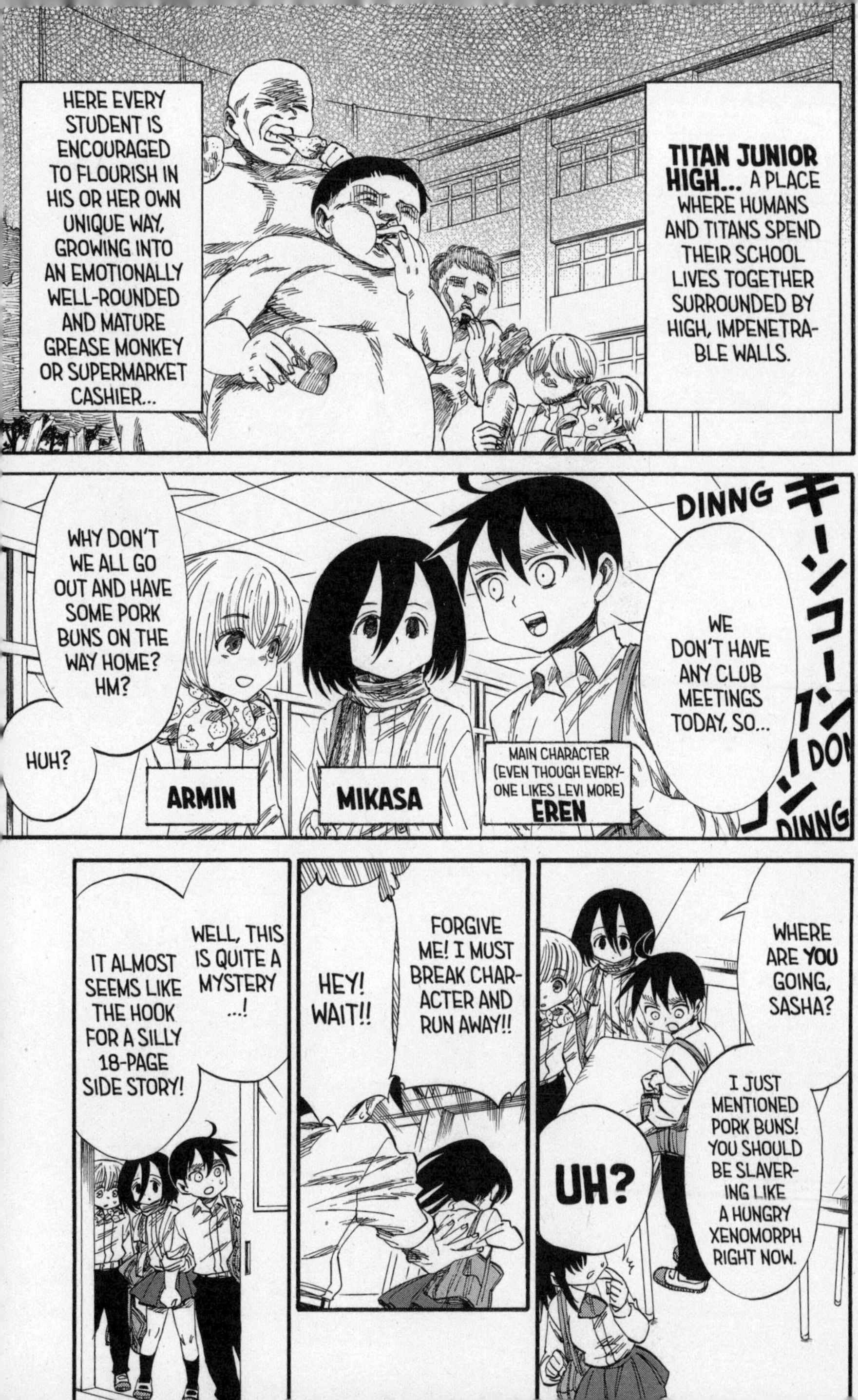
TITAN JUNIOR HIGH... A PLACE WHERE HUMANS AND TITANS SPEND THEIR SCHOOL LIVES TOGETHER SURROUNDED BY HIGH, IMPENETRABLE WALLS.
HERE EVERY STUDENT IS ENCOURAGED TO FLOURISH IN HIS OR HER OWN UNIQUE WAY, GROWING INTO AN EMOTIONALLY WELL-ROUNDED AND MATURE GREASE MONKEY OR SUPERMARKET CASHIER...
DINNG
キーンコーン
DINNG
WE DON'T HAVE ANY CLUB MEETINGS TODAY, SO...
MAIN CHARACTER (EVEN THOUGH EVERYONE LIKES LEVI MORE) EREN
MIKASA
WHY DON'T WE ALL GO OUT AND HAVE SOME PORK BUNS ON THE WAY HOME? HM?
ARMIN
HUH?
WHERE ARE YOU GOING, SASHA?
I JUST MENTIONED PORK BUNS! YOU SHOULD BE SLAVERING LIKE A HUNGRY XENOMORPH RIGHT NOW.
UH?
FORGIVE ME! I MUST BREAK CHARACTER AND RUN AWAY!!
HEY! WAIT!!
WELL, THIS IS QUITE A MYSTERY ...!
IT ALMOST SEEMS LIKE THE HOOK FOR A SILLY 18-PAGE SIDE STORY!

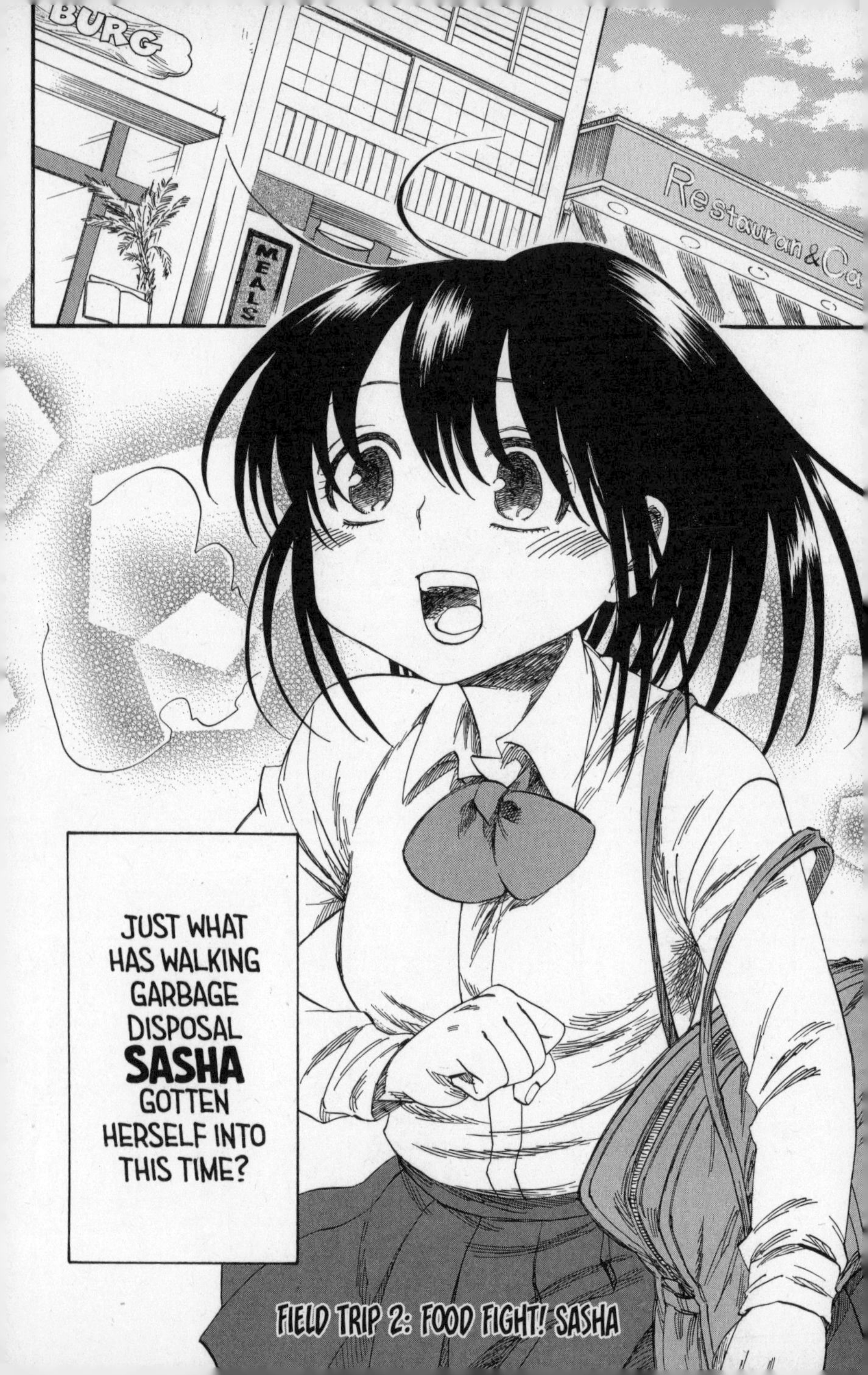
BURG
MEALS
Restauran&Ca
JUST WHAT HAS WALKING GARBAGE DISPOSAL SASHA GOTTEN HERSELF INTO THIS TIME?
FIELD TRIP 2: FOOD FIGHT! SASHA

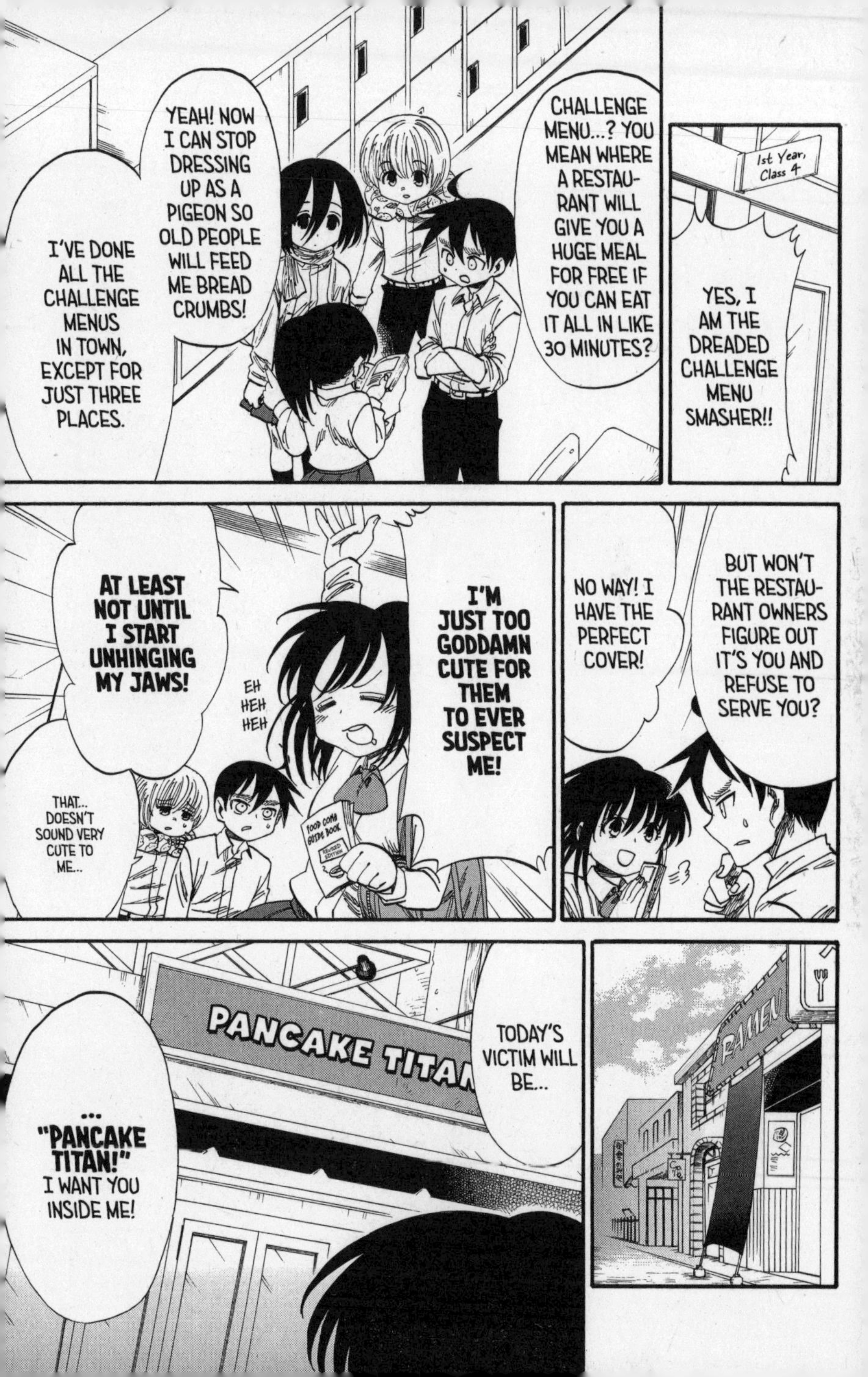
1st Year, Class 4
YES, I AM THE DREADED CHALLENGE MENU SMASHER!!
CHALLENGE MENU...? YOU MEAN WHERE A RESTAURANT WILL GIVE YOU A HUGE MEAL FOR FREE IF YOU CAN EAT IT ALL IN LIKE 30 MINUTES?
YEAH! NOW I CAN STOP DRESSING UP AS A PIGEON SO OLD PEOPLE WILL FEED ME BREAD CRUMBS!
I'VE DONE ALL THE CHALLENGE MENUS IN TOWN, EXCEPT FOR JUST THREE PLACES.
BUT WON'T THE RESTAURANT OWNERS FIGURE OUT IT'S YOU AND REFUSE TO SERVE YOU?
NO WAY! I HAVE THE PERFECT COVER!
I'M JUST TOO GODDAMN CUTE FOR THEM TO EVER SUSPECT ME!
AT LEAST NOT UNTIL I START UNHINGING MY JAWS!
EH HEH HEH
FOOD COMA GUIDE BOOK
REVISED EDITION
THAT... DOESN'T SOUND VERY CUTE TO ME...
RAMEN
TODAY'S VICTIM WILL BE...
PANCAKE TITAN
... "PANCAKE TITAN!" I WANT YOU INSIDE ME!

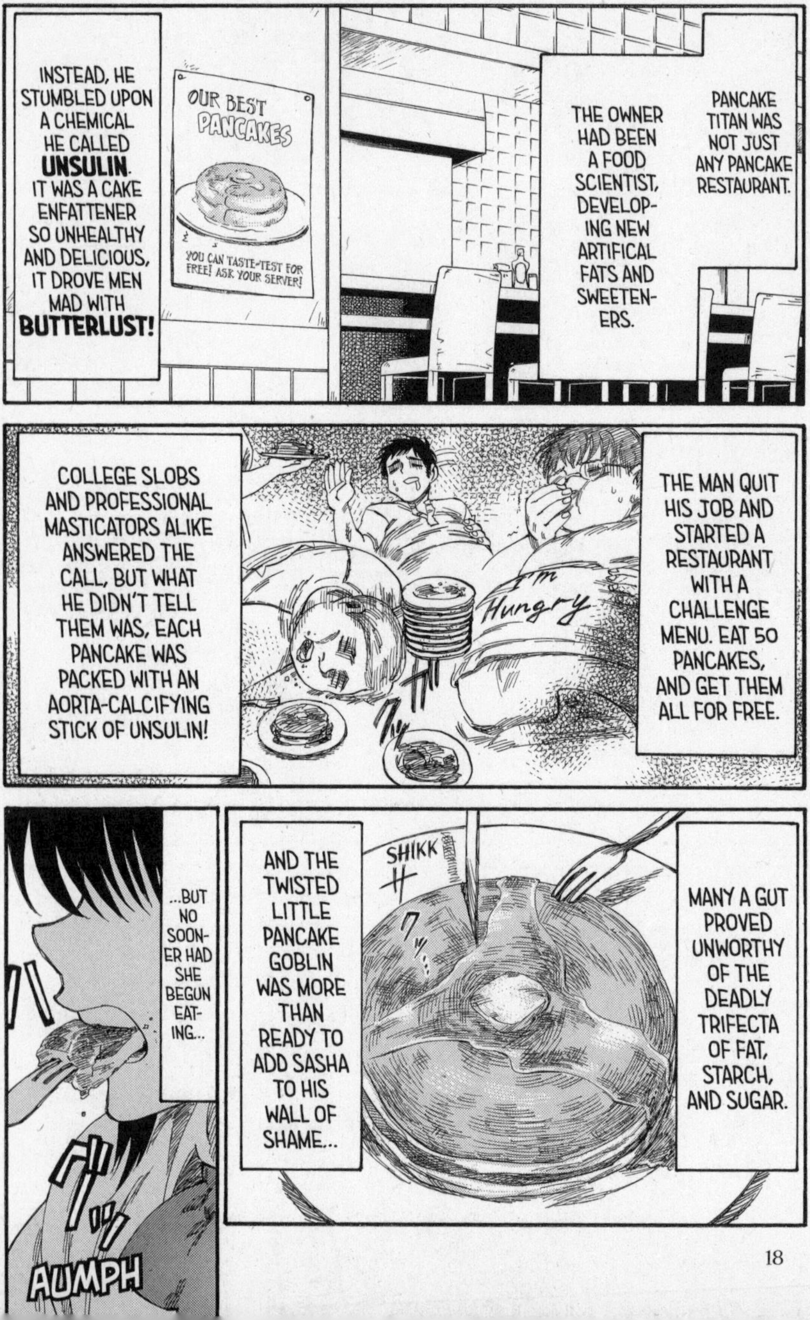
PANCAKE TITAN WAS NOT JUST ANY PANCAKE RESTAURANT.
THE OWNER HAD BEEN A FOOD SCIENTIST, DEVELOPING NEW ARTIFICAL FATS AND SWEETENERS.
OUR BEST PANCAKES
YOU CAN TASTE-TEST FOR FREE! ASK YOUR SERVER!
INSTEAD, HE STUMBLED UPON A CHEMICAL HE CALLED **UNSULIN**. IT WAS A CAKE ENFATTENER SO UNHEALTHY AND DELICIOUS, IT DROVE MEN MAD WITH **BUTTERLUST!**
THE MAN QUIT HIS JOB AND STARTED A RESTAURANT WITH A CHALLENGE MENU. EAT 50 PANCAKES, AND GET THEM ALL FOR FREE.
I'm Hungry
COLLEGE SLOBS AND PROFESSIONAL MASTICATORS ALIKE ANSWERED THE CALL, BUT WHAT HE DIDN'T TELL THEM WAS, EACH PANCAKE WAS PACKED WITH AN AORTA-CALCIFYING STICK OF UNSULIN!
MANY A GUT PROVED UNWORTHY OF THE DEADLY TRIFECTA OF FAT, STARCH, AND SUGAR.
SHIKK
AND THE TWISTED LITTLE PANCAKE GOBLIN WAS MORE THAN READY TO ADD SASHA TO HIS WALL OF SHAME...
...BUT NO SOONER HAD SHE BEGUN EATING...
AUMPH

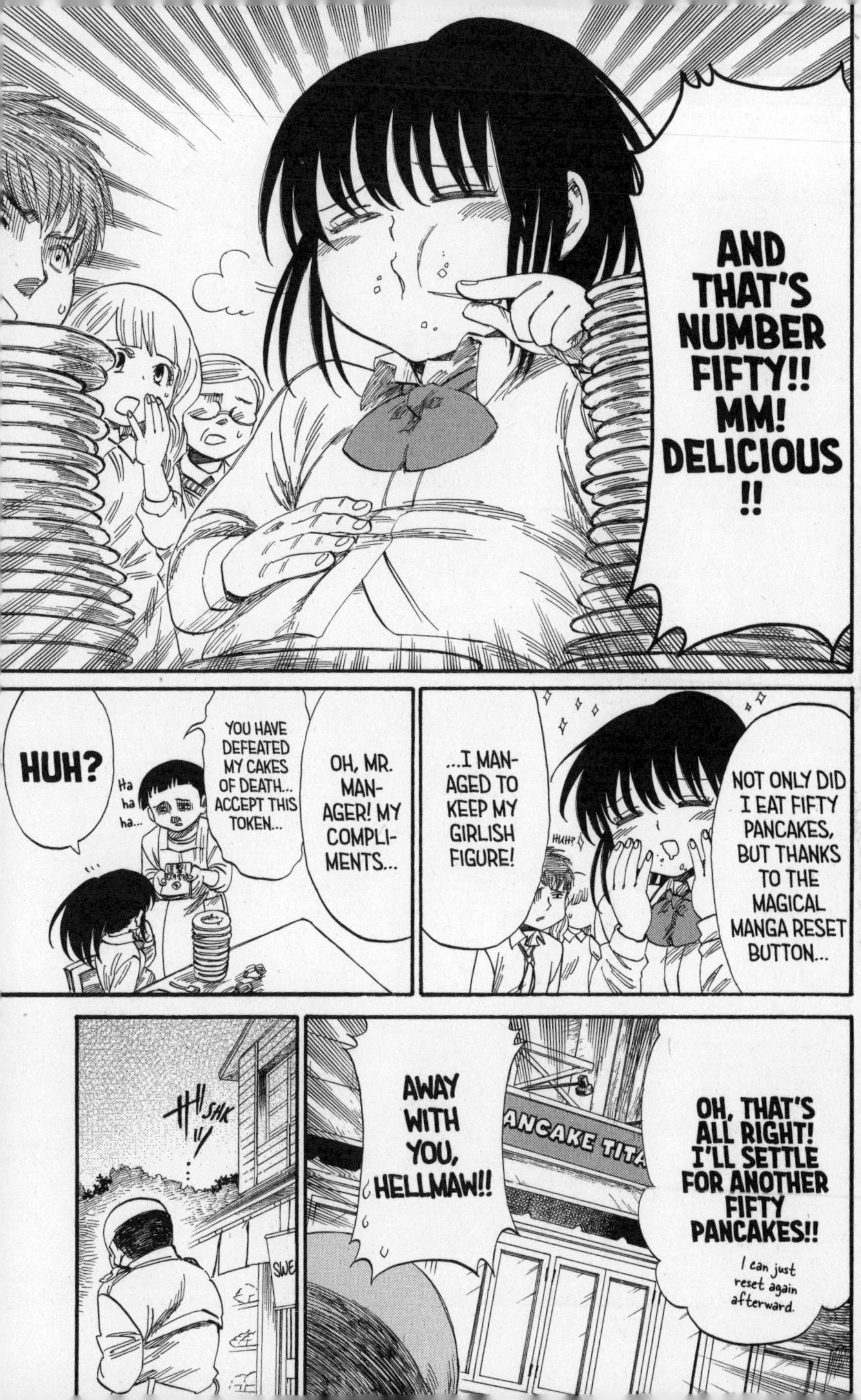
AND THAT'S NUMBER FIFTY!! MM! DELICIOUS !!
NOT ONLY DID I EAT FIFTY PANCAKES, BUT THANKS TO THE MAGICAL MANGA RESET BUTTON...
HUH?
...I MAN-AGED TO KEEP MY GIRLISH FIGURE!
OH, MR. MAN-AGER! MY COMPLI-MENTS...
YOU HAVE DEFEATED MY CAKES OF DEATH... ACCEPT THIS TOKEN...
Ha ha ha...
HUH?
OH, THAT'S ALL RIGHT! I'LL SETTLE FOR ANOTHER FIFTY PANCAKES!!
I can just reset again afterward.
ANCAKE TITA
AWAY WITH YOU, HELLMAW!!
SHK
SWE

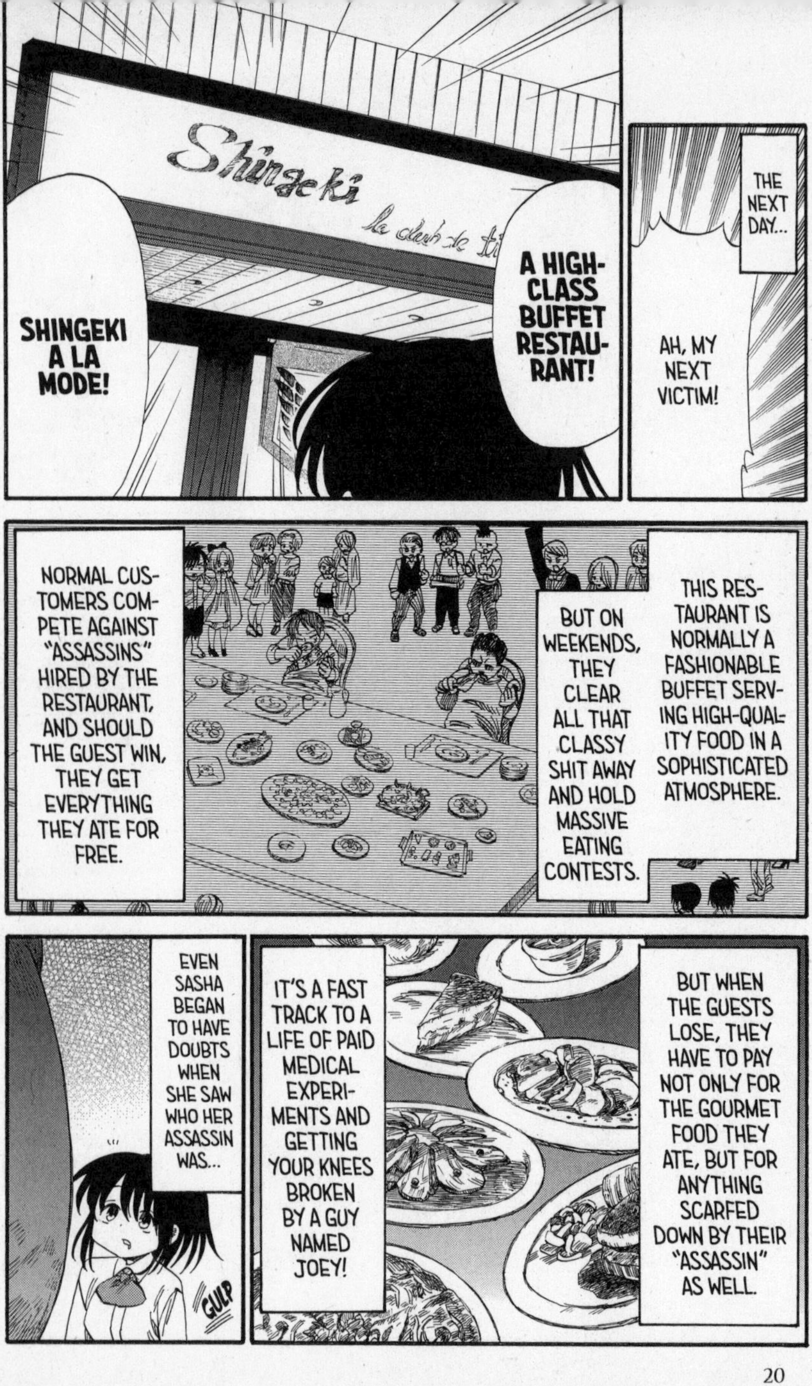
THE NEXT DAY...
AH, MY NEXT VICTIM!
Shingeki
A HIGH-CLASS BUFFET RESTAURANT!
SHINGEKI A LA MODE!
THIS RESTAURANT IS NORMALLY A FASHIONABLE BUFFET SERVING HIGH-QUALITY FOOD IN A SOPHISTICATED ATMOSPHERE.
BUT ON WEEKENDS, THEY CLEAR ALL THAT CLASSY SHIT AWAY AND HOLD MASSIVE EATING CONTESTS.
NORMAL CUSTOMERS COMPETE AGAINST "ASSASSINS" HIRED BY THE RESTAURANT, AND SHOULD THE GUEST WIN, THEY GET EVERYTHING THEY ATE FOR FREE.
BUT WHEN THE GUESTS LOSE, THEY HAVE TO PAY NOT ONLY FOR THE GOURMET FOOD THEY ATE, BUT FOR ANYTHING SCARFED DOWN BY THEIR "ASSASSIN" AS WELL.
IT'S A FAST TRACK TO A LIFE OF PAID MEDICAL EXPERIMENTS AND GETTING YOUR KNEES BROKEN BY A GUY NAMED JOEY!
EVEN SASHA BEGAN TO HAVE DOUBTS WHEN SHE SAW WHO HER ASSASSIN WAS...
GULP

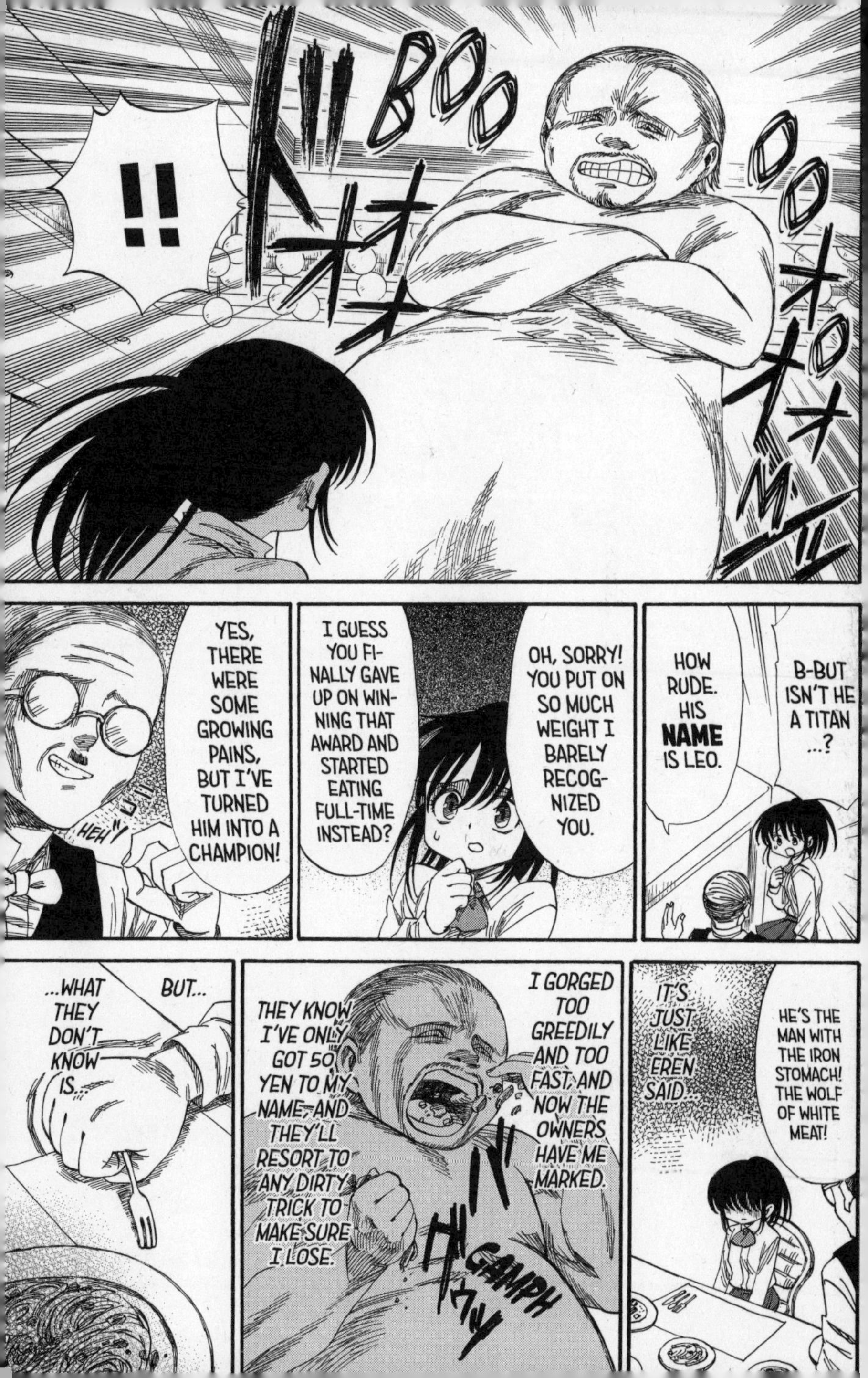
BOOOOOOM!!
!!
B-BUT ISN'T HE A TITAN ...?
HOW RUDE. HIS **NAME** IS LEO.
OH, SORRY! YOU PUT ON SO MUCH WEIGHT I BARELY RECOGNIZED YOU.
I GUESS YOU FINALLY GAVE UP ON WINNING THAT AWARD AND STARTED EATING FULL-TIME INSTEAD?
YES, THERE WERE SOME GROWING PAINS, BUT I'VE TURNED HIM INTO A CHAMPION!
HEH
HE'S THE MAN WITH THE IRON STOMACH! THE WOLF OF WHITE MEAT!
IT'S JUST LIKE EREN SAID.
I GORGED TOO GREEDILY AND TOO FAST, AND NOW THE OWNERS HAVE ME MARKED.
THEY KNOW I'VE ONLY GOT 50 YEN TO MY NAME, AND THEY'LL RESORT TO ANY DIRTY TRICK TO MAKE SURE I LOSE.
GAMPH
BUT...
...WHAT THEY DON'T KNOW IS...

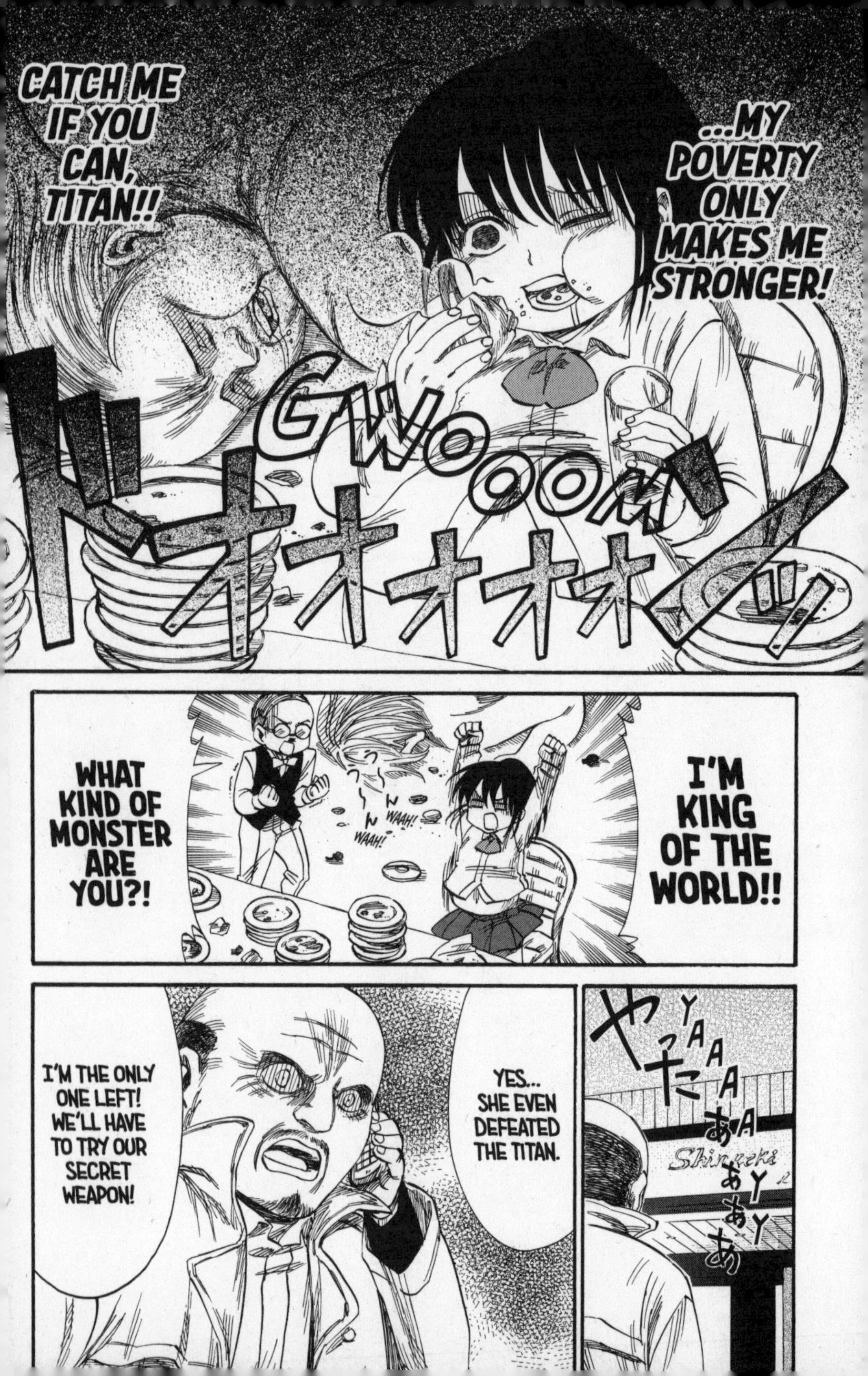
...MY POVERTY ONLY MAKES ME STRONGER!
CATCH ME IF YOU CAN, TITAN!!
GWOOOOM
ドオオオオンッ
I'M KING OF THE WORLD!!
WAAH!
WAAH!
WHAT KIND OF MONSTER ARE YOU?!
やったあああ
YAAAAAYY
YES... SHE EVEN DEFEATED THE TITAN.
I'M THE ONLY ONE LEFT! WE'LL HAVE TO TRY OUR SECRET WEAPON!

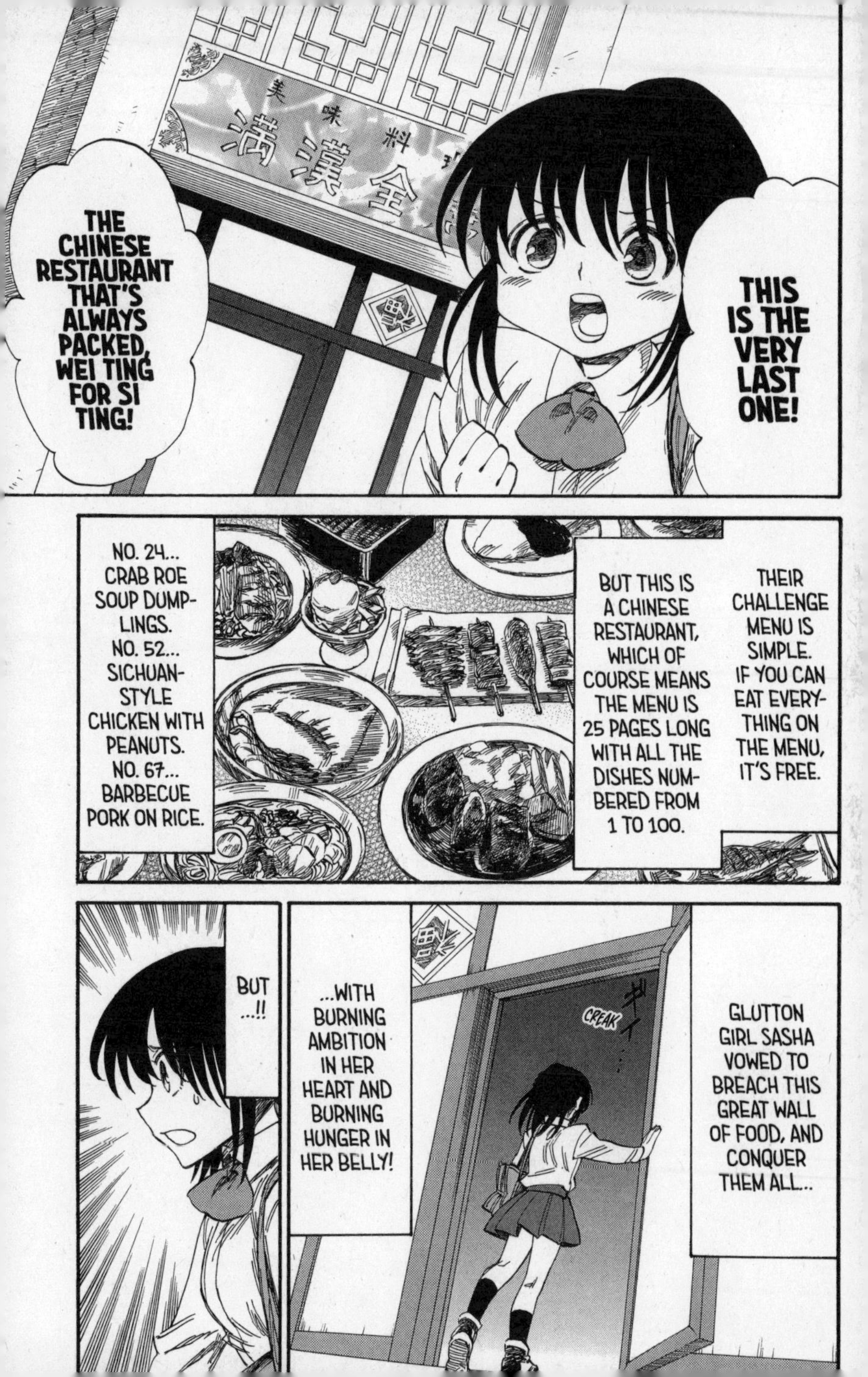
THIS IS THE VERY LAST ONE!
THE CHINESE RESTAURANT THAT'S ALWAYS PACKED, WEI TING FOR SI TING!
THEIR CHALLENGE MENU IS SIMPLE. IF YOU CAN EAT EVERY-THING ON THE MENU, IT'S FREE.
BUT THIS IS A CHINESE RESTAURANT, WHICH OF COURSE MEANS THE MENU IS 25 PAGES LONG WITH ALL THE DISHES NUM-BERED FROM 1 TO 100.
NO. 24... CRAB ROE SOUP DUMP-LINGS. NO. 52... SICHUAN-STYLE CHICKEN WITH PEANUTS. NO. 67... BARBECUE PORK ON RICE.
GLUTTON GIRL SASHA VOWED TO BREACH THIS GREAT WALL OF FOOD, AND CONQUER THEM ALL...
CREAK
...WITH BURNING AMBITION IN HER HEART AND BURNING HUNGER IN HER BELLY!
BUT ...!!

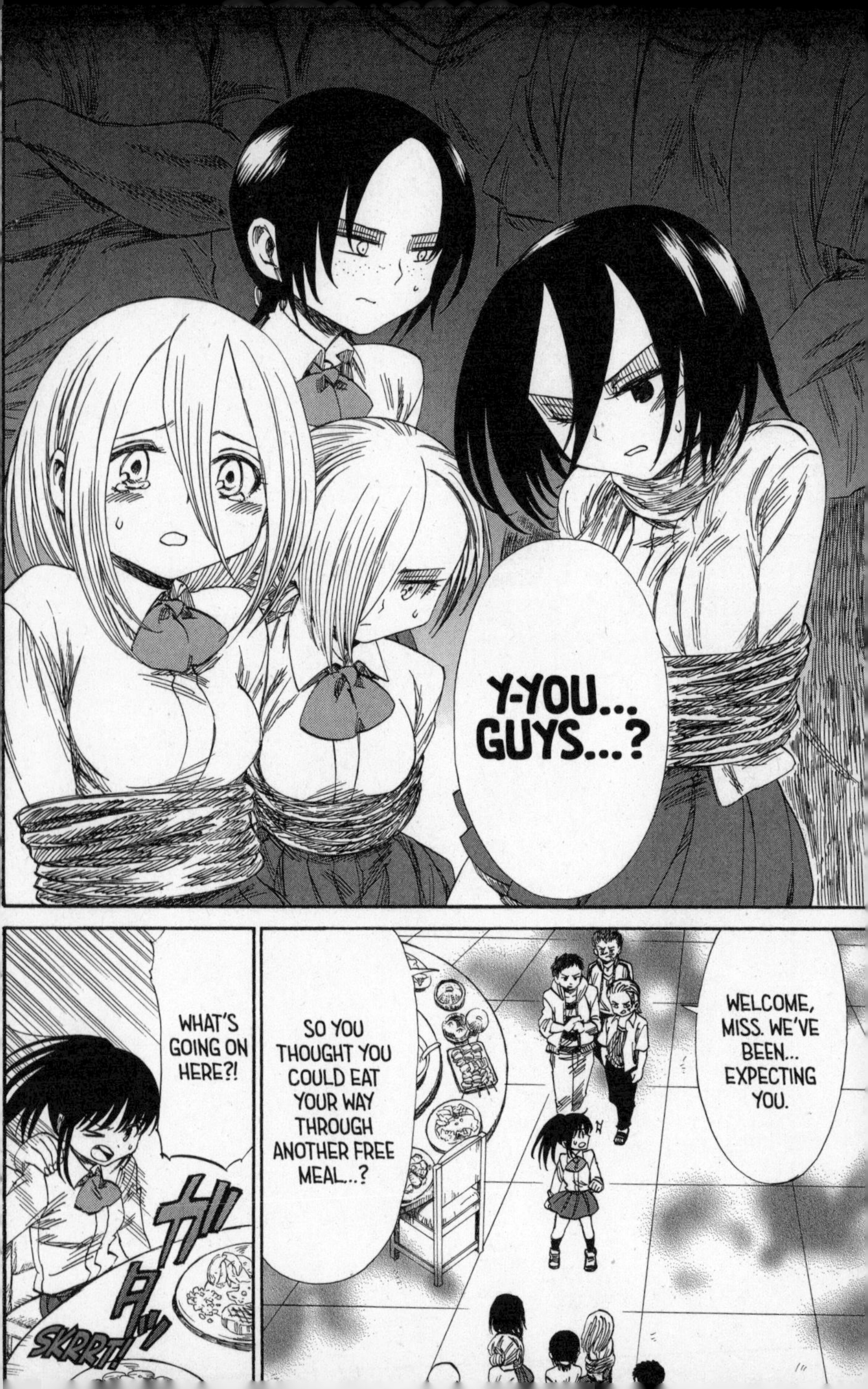
Y-YOU... GUYS...?
WELCOME, MISS. WE'VE BEEN... EXPECTING YOU.
SO YOU THOUGHT YOU COULD EAT YOUR WAY THROUGH ANOTHER FREE MEAL...?
WHAT'S GOING ON HERE?!
SKRRT!

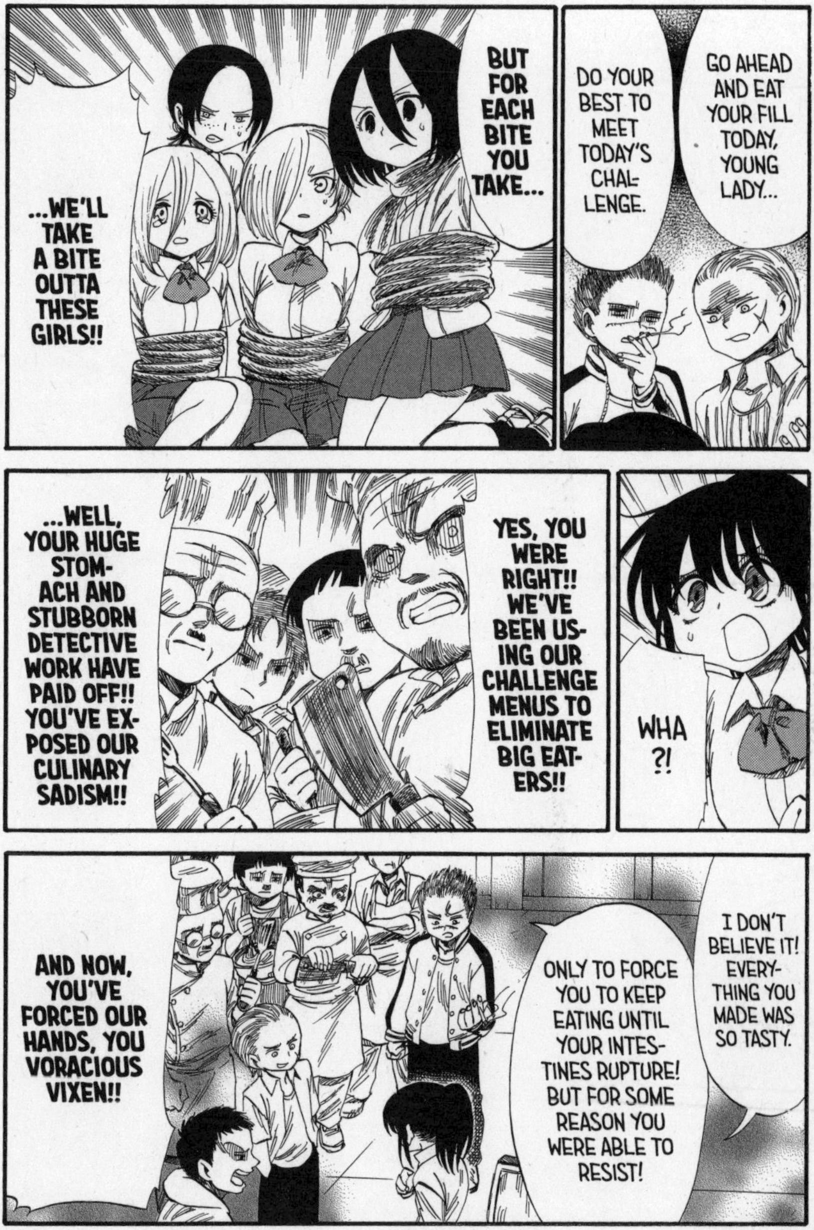
GO AHEAD AND EAT YOUR FILL TODAY, YOUNG LADY...
DO YOUR BEST TO MEET TODAY'S CHAL-LENGE.
BUT FOR EACH BITE YOU TAKE...
...WE'LL TAKE A BITE OUTTA THESE GIRLS!!
WHA ?!
YES, YOU WERE RIGHT!! WE'VE BEEN US-ING OUR CHALLENGE MENUS TO ELIMINATE BIG EAT-ERS!!
...WELL, YOUR HUGE STOM-ACH AND STUBBORN DETECTIVE WORK HAVE PAID OFF!! YOU'VE EX-POSED OUR CULINARY SADISM!!
I DON'T BELIEVE IT! EVERY-THING YOU MADE WAS SO TASTY.
ONLY TO FORCE YOU TO KEEP EATING UNTIL YOUR INTES-TINES RUPTURE! BUT FOR SOME REASON YOU WERE ABLE TO RESIST!
AND NOW, YOU'VE FORCED OUR HANDS, YOU VORACIOUS VIXEN!!

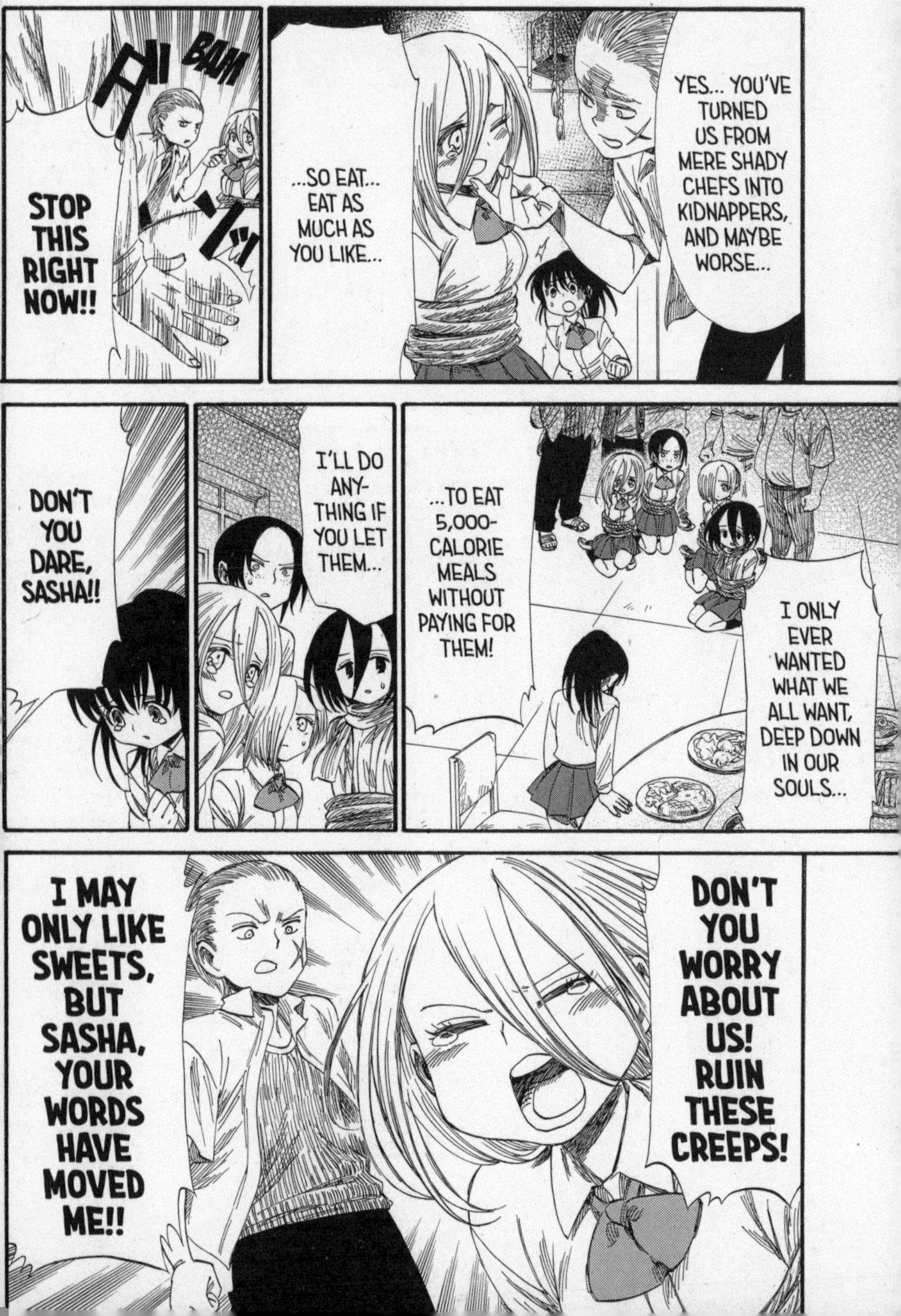
YES... YOU'VE TURNED US FROM MERE SHADY CHEFS INTO KIDNAPPERS, AND MAYBE WORSE...
...SO EAT... EAT AS MUCH AS YOU LIKE...
BAM
STOP THIS RIGHT NOW!!
I ONLY EVER WANTED WHAT WE ALL WANT, DEEP DOWN IN OUR SOULS...
...TO EAT 5,000-CALORIE MEALS WITHOUT PAYING FOR THEM!
I'LL DO ANY-THING IF YOU LET THEM...
DON'T YOU DARE, SASHA!!
DON'T YOU WORRY ABOUT US! RUIN THESE CREEPS!
I MAY ONLY LIKE SWEETS, BUT SASHA, YOUR WORDS HAVE MOVED ME!!

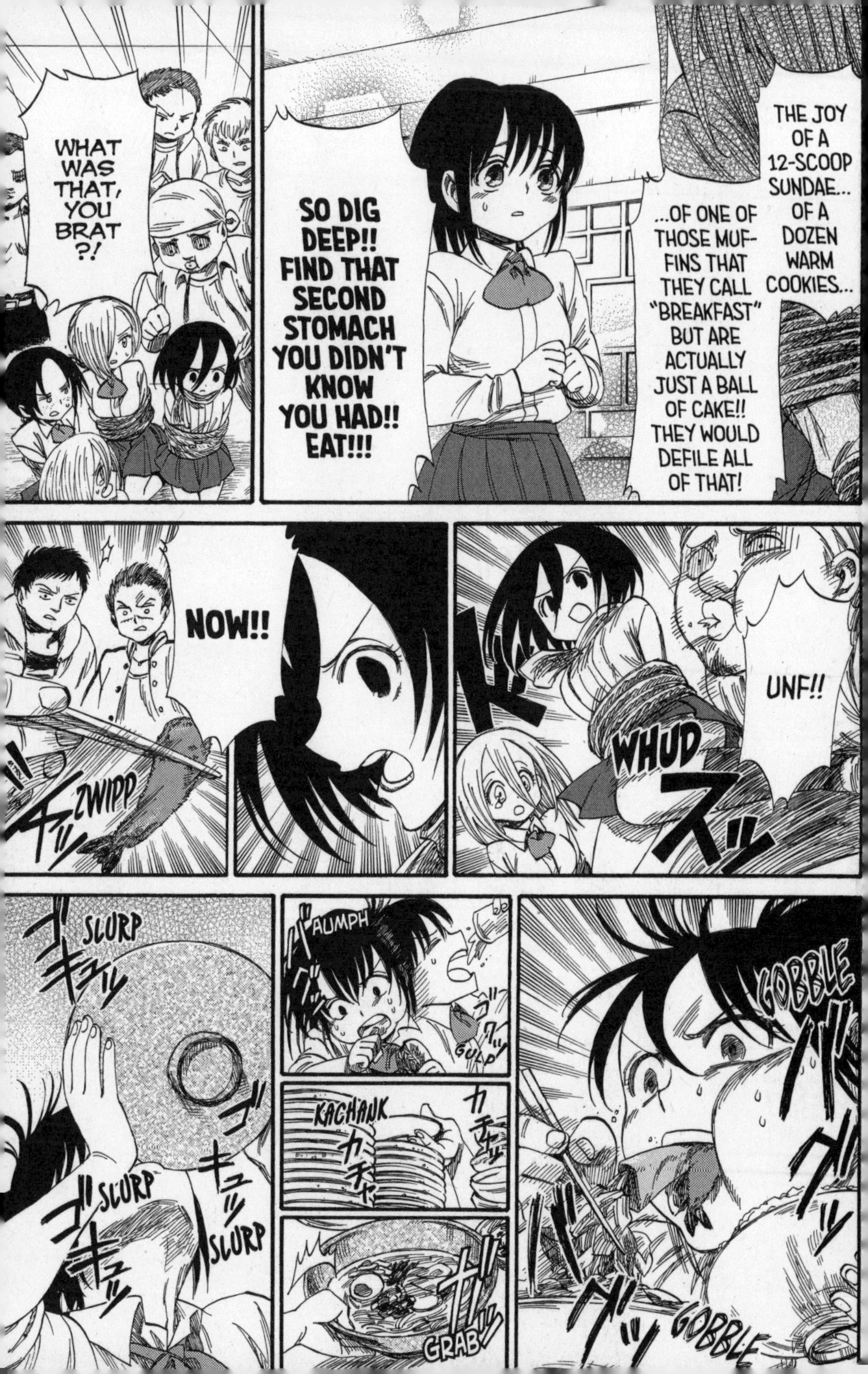
THE JOY OF A 12-SCOOP SUNDAE... OF A DOZEN WARM COOKIES...
...OF ONE OF THOSE MUF-FINS THAT THEY CALL "BREAKFAST" BUT ARE ACTUALLY JUST A BALL OF CAKE!! THEY WOULD DEFILE ALL OF THAT!
SO DIG DEEP!! FIND THAT SECOND STOMACH YOU DIDN'T KNOW YOU HAD!! EAT!!!
WHAT WAS THAT, YOU BRAT?!
UNF!!
WHUD
NOW!!
ZWIPP
GOBBLE
GOBBLE
AUMPH
GULP
KACHANK
GRAB
SLURP
SLURP
SLURP

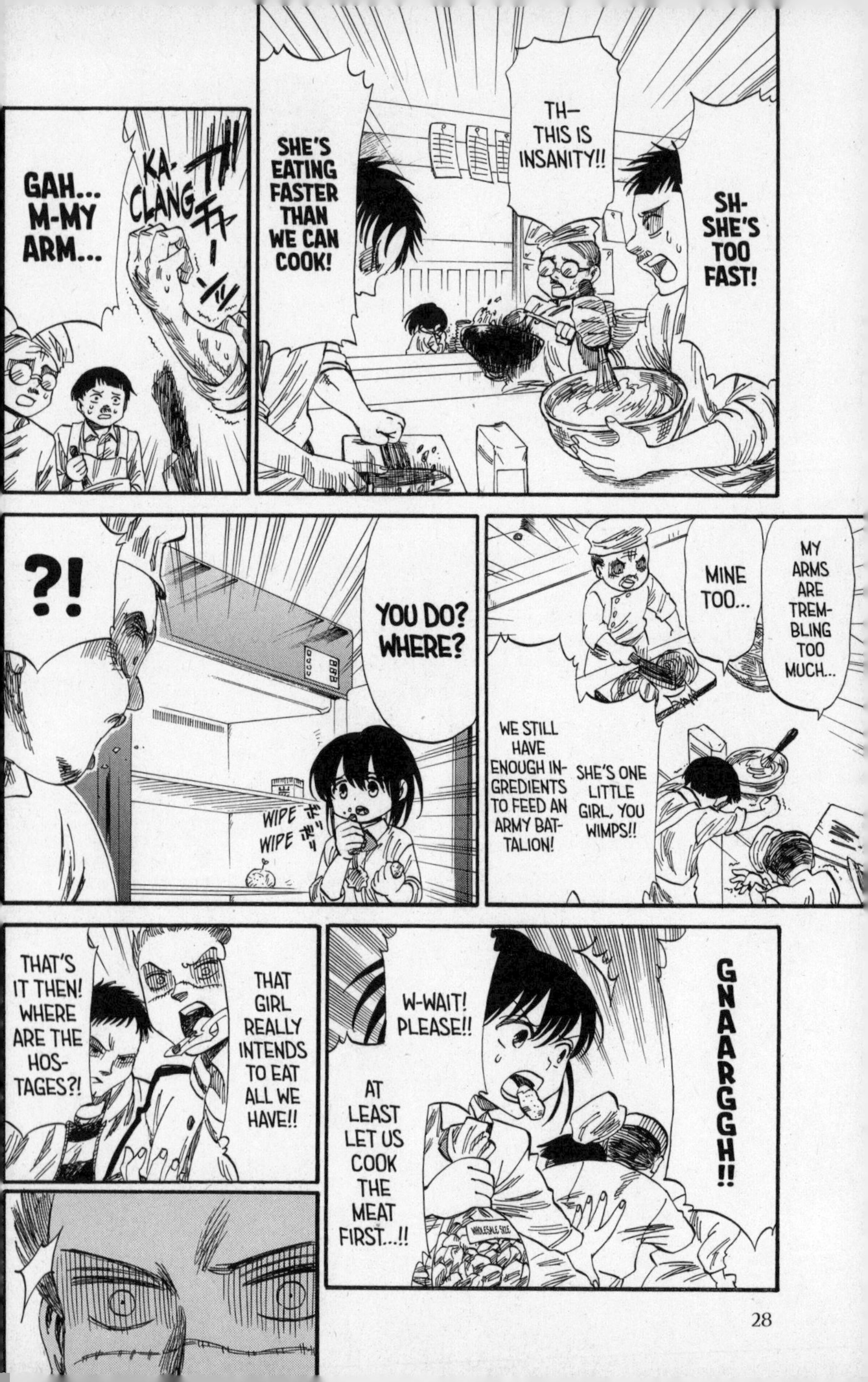
SH-SHE'S TOO FAST!
TH— THIS IS INSANITY!!
SHE'S EATING FASTER THAN WE CAN COOK!
KA-CLANG
GAH... M-MY ARM...
MY ARMS ARE TREM-BLING TOO MUCH...
MINE TOO...
SHE'S ONE LITTLE GIRL, YOU WIMPS!!
WE STILL HAVE ENOUGH IN-GREDIENTS TO FEED AN ARMY BAT-TALION!
YOU DO? WHERE?
?!
WIPE WIPE
GNAARGGH!!
W-WAIT! PLEASE!!
AT LEAST LET US COOK THE MEAT FIRST...!!
WHOLESALE SIZE
THAT GIRL REALLY INTENDS TO EAT ALL WE HAVE!!
THAT'S IT THEN! WHERE ARE THE HOS-TAGES?!

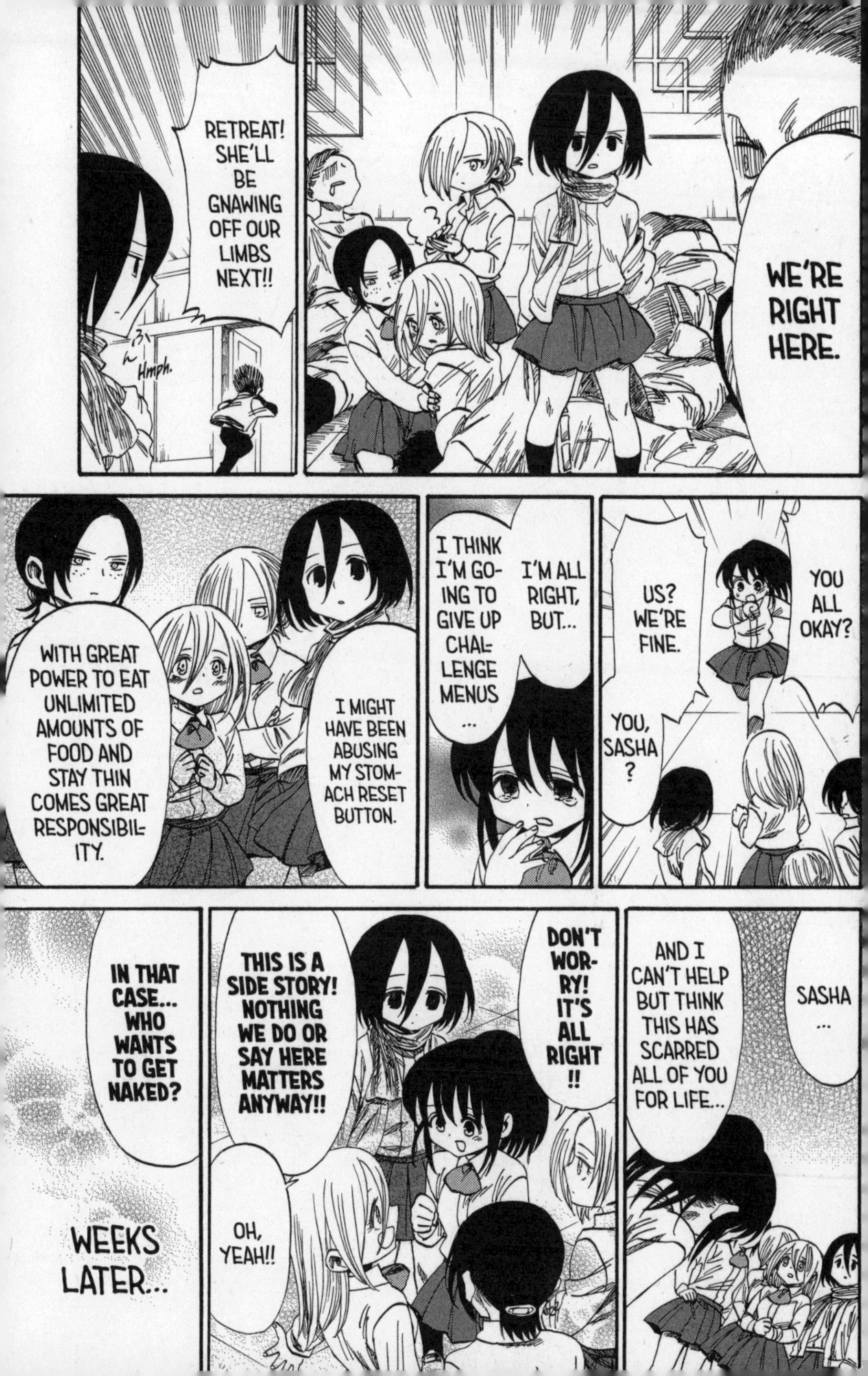
WE'RE RIGHT HERE.
RETREAT! SHE'LL BE GNAWING OFF OUR LIMBS NEXT!!
Hmph.
YOU ALL OKAY?
US? WE'RE FINE.
YOU, SASHA?
I'M ALL RIGHT, BUT...
I THINK I'M GOING TO GIVE UP CHALLENGE MENUS...
I MIGHT HAVE BEEN ABUSING MY STOMACH RESET BUTTON.
WITH GREAT POWER TO EAT UNLIMITED AMOUNTS OF FOOD AND STAY THIN COMES GREAT RESPONSIBILITY.
SASHA...
AND I CAN'T HELP BUT THINK THIS HAS SCARRED ALL OF YOU FOR LIFE...
DON'T WORRY! IT'S ALL RIGHT!!
THIS IS A SIDE STORY! NOTHING WE DO OR SAY HERE MATTERS ANYWAY!!
OH, YEAH!!
IN THAT CASE... WHO WANTS TO GET NAKED?
WEEKS LATER...

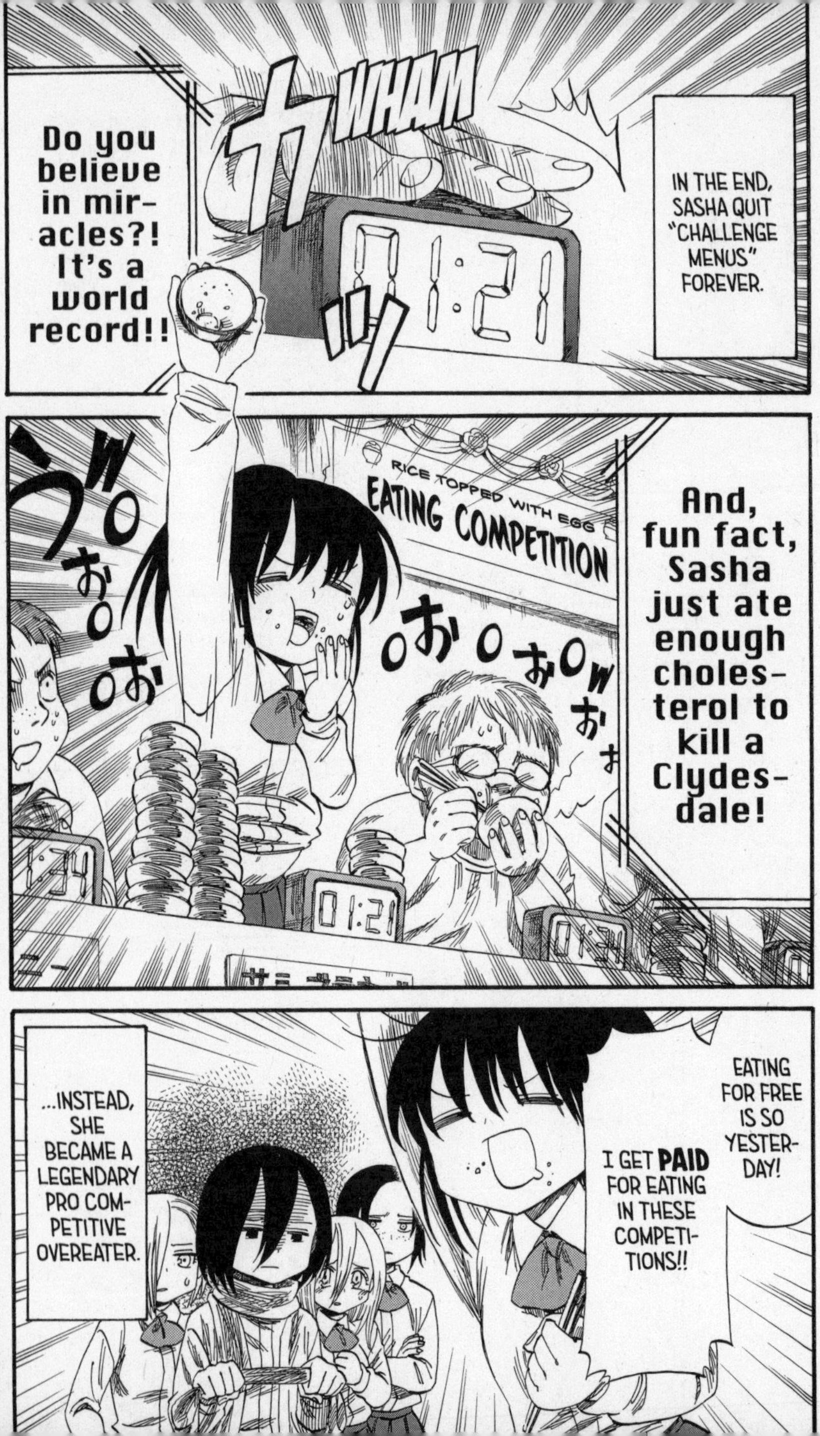
IN THE END, SASHA QUIT "CHALLENGE MENUS" FOREVER.
WHAM
01:21
Do you believe in miracles?! It's a world record!!
And, fun fact, Sasha just ate enough cholesterol to kill a Clydesdale!
RICE TOPPED WITH EGG
EATING COMPETITION
EATING FOR FREE IS SO YESTERDAY!
I GET PAID FOR EATING IN THESE COMPETITIONS!!
...INSTEAD, SHE BECAME A LEGENDARY PRO COMPETITIVE OVEREATER.

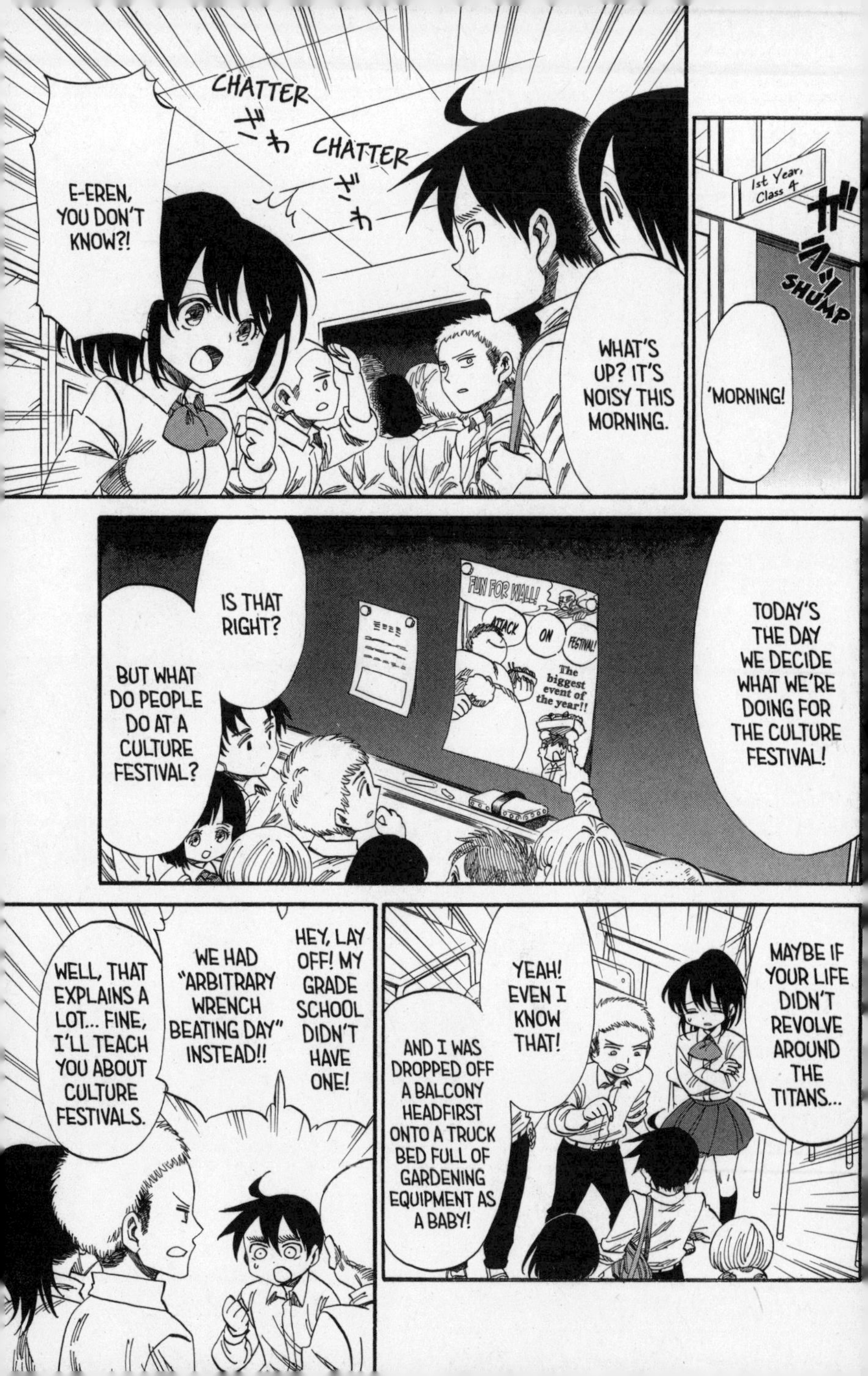
1st Year, Class 4
ガラッ
SHUMP
'MORNING!
WHAT'S UP? IT'S NOISY THIS MORNING.
CHATTER
ざわ
CHATTER
ざわ
E-EREN, YOU DON'T KNOW?!
TODAY'S THE DAY WE DECIDE WHAT WE'RE DOING FOR THE CULTURE FESTIVAL!
FUN FOR WALL!
ATTACK ON FESTIVAL!
The biggest event of the year!!
IS THAT RIGHT?
BUT WHAT DO PEOPLE DO AT A CULTURE FESTIVAL?
MAYBE IF YOUR LIFE DIDN'T REVOLVE AROUND THE TITANS...
YEAH! EVEN I KNOW THAT!
AND I WAS DROPPED OFF A BALCONY HEADFIRST ONTO A TRUCK BED FULL OF GARDENING EQUIPMENT AS A BABY!
HEY, LAY OFF! MY GRADE SCHOOL DIDN'T HAVE ONE!
WE HAD "ARBITRARY WRENCH BEATING DAY" INSTEAD!!
WELL, THAT EXPLAINS A LOT... FINE, I'LL TEACH YOU ABOUT CULTURE FESTIVALS.

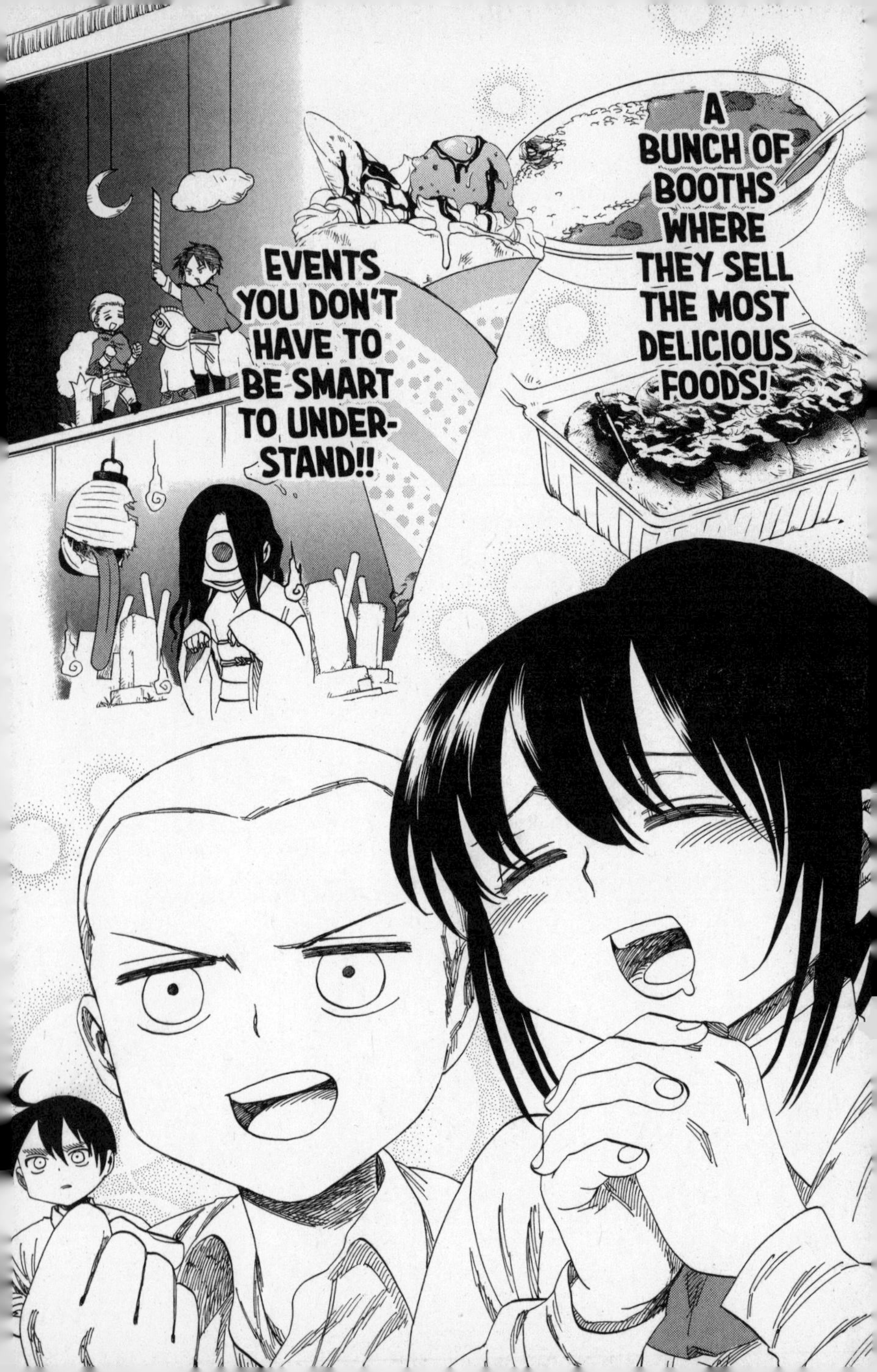
A BUNCH OF BOOTHS WHERE THEY SELL THE MOST DELICIOUS FOODS!
EVENTS YOU DON'T HAVE TO BE SMART TO UNDER-STAND!!

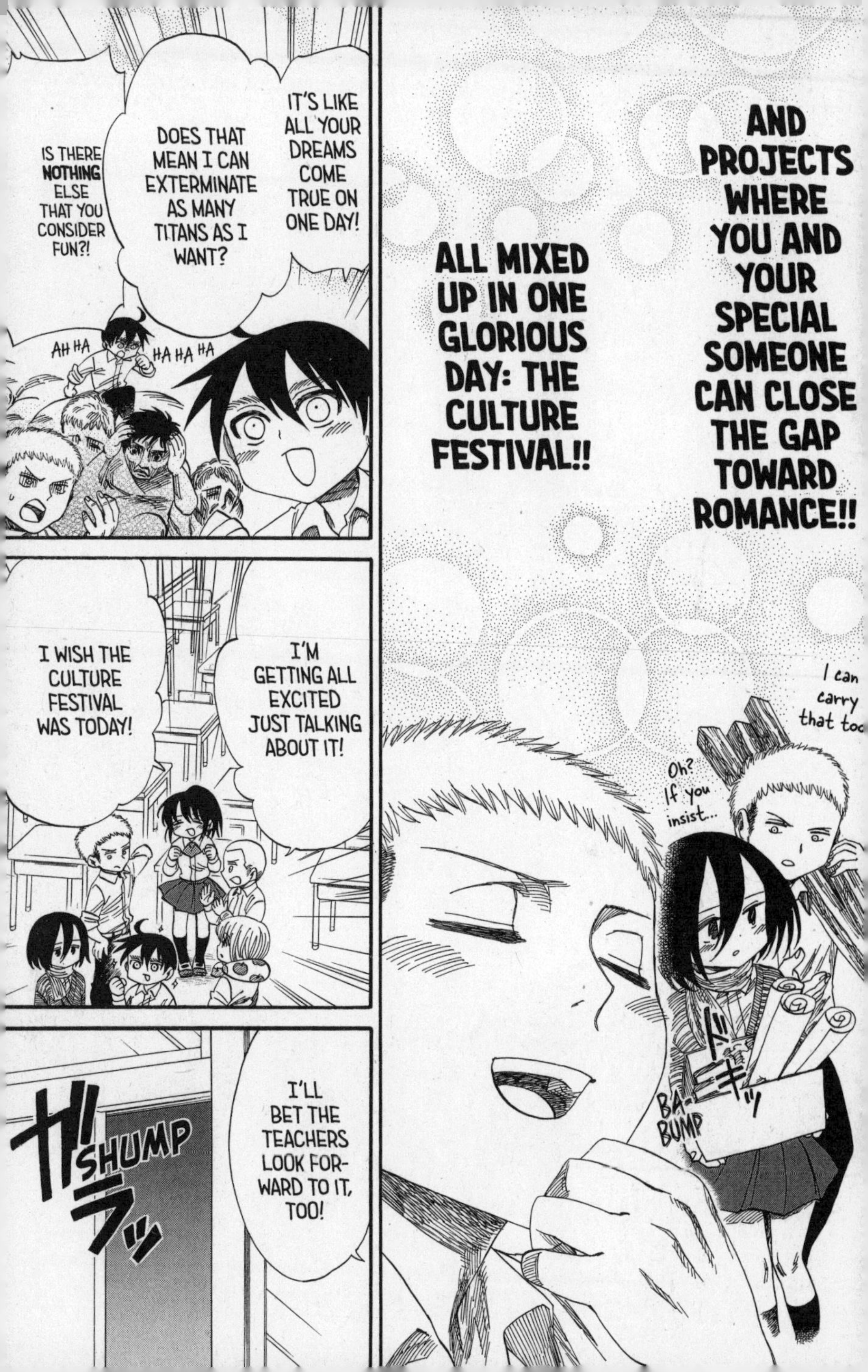
AND PROJECTS WHERE YOU AND YOUR SPECIAL SOMEONE CAN CLOSE THE GAP TOWARD ROMANCE!!
ALL MIXED UP IN ONE GLORIOUS DAY: THE CULTURE FESTIVAL!!
I can carry that too
Oh? If you insist...
BA-BUMP
IT'S LIKE ALL YOUR DREAMS COME TRUE ON ONE DAY!
DOES THAT MEAN I CAN EXTERMINATE AS MANY TITANS AS I WANT?
IS THERE NOTHING ELSE THAT YOU CONSIDER FUN?!
HA HA HA
AH HA
I'M GETTING ALL EXCITED JUST TALKING ABOUT IT!
I WISH THE CULTURE FESTIVAL WAS TODAY!
I'LL BET THE TEACHERS LOOK FOR-WARD TO IT, TOO!
SHUMP

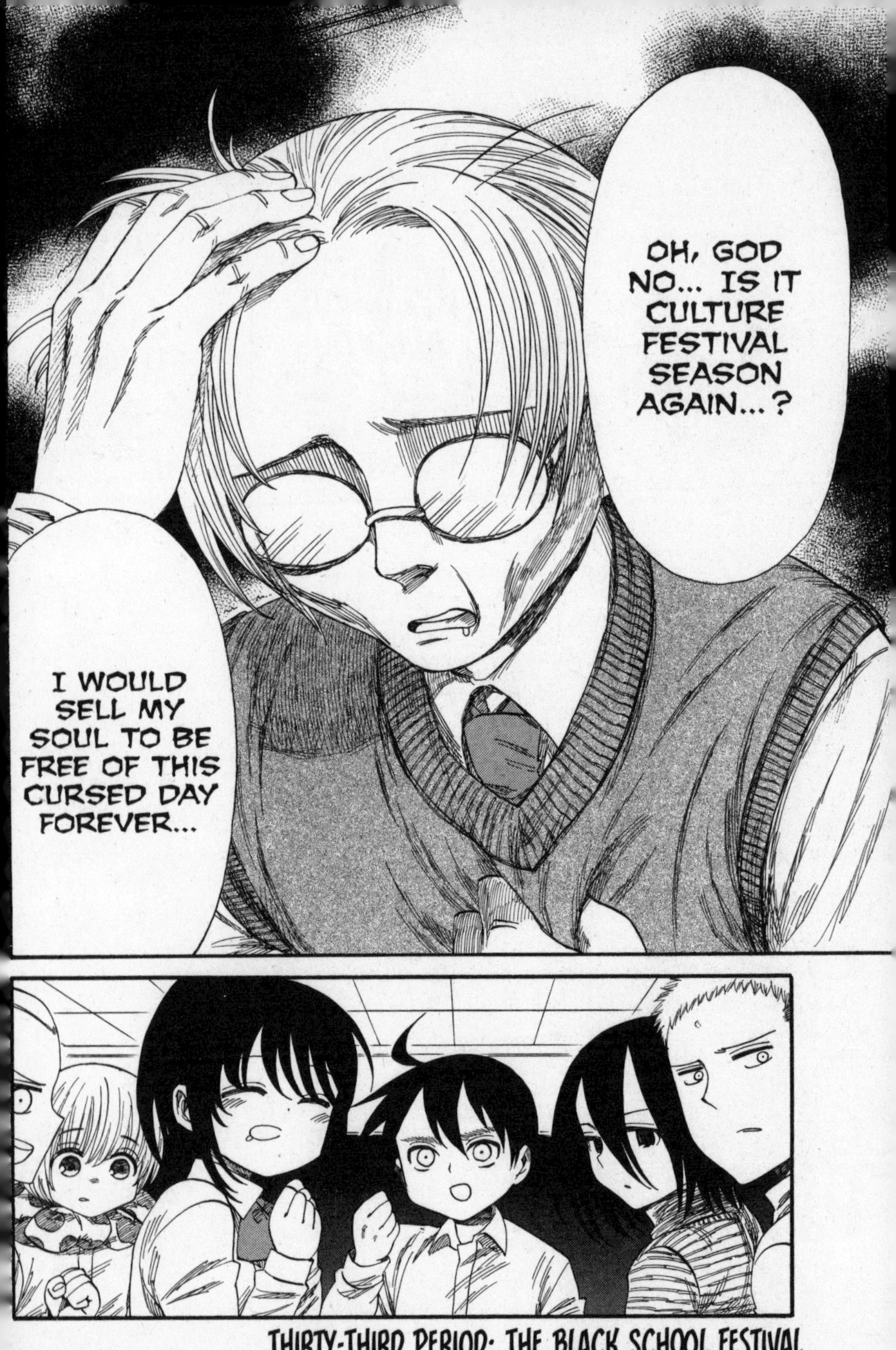
OH, GOD NO... IS IT CULTURE FESTIVAL SEASON AGAIN...?
I WOULD SELL MY SOUL TO BE FREE OF THIS CURSED DAY FOREVER...

THIRTY-THIRD PERIOD: THE BLACK SCHOOL FESTIVAL

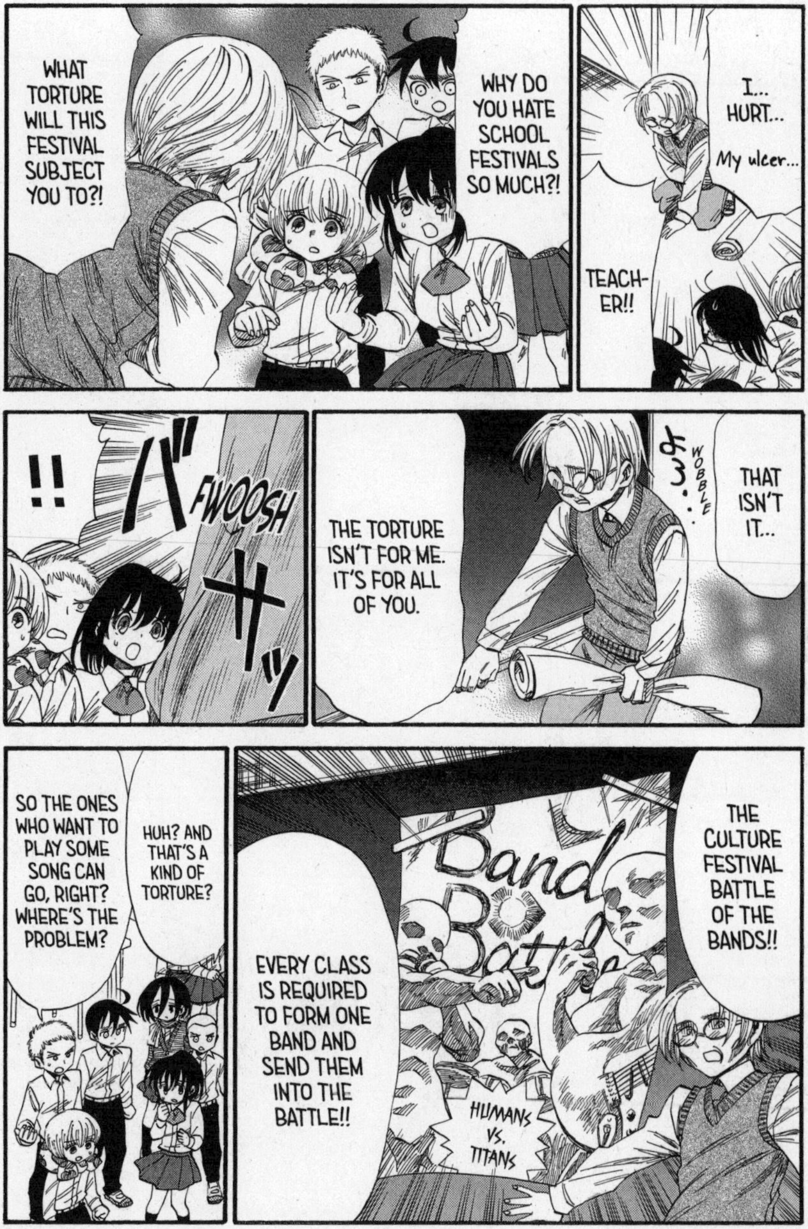
I... HURT...
My ulcer...
TEACHER!!
WHY DO YOU HATE SCHOOL FESTIVALS SO MUCH?!
WHAT TORTURE WILL THIS FESTIVAL SUBJECT YOU TO?!
よろ…
WOBBLE
THAT ISN'T IT...
THE TORTURE ISN'T FOR ME. IT'S FOR ALL OF YOU.
!!
バ
FWOOSH
サッ
THE CULTURE FESTIVAL BATTLE OF THE BANDS!!
Band Battle
EVERY CLASS IS REQUIRED TO FORM ONE BAND AND SEND THEM INTO THE BATTLE!!
HUMANS VS. TITANS
HUH? AND THAT'S A KIND OF TORTURE?
SO THE ONES WHO WANT TO PLAY SOME SONG CAN GO, RIGHT? WHERE'S THE PROBLEM?

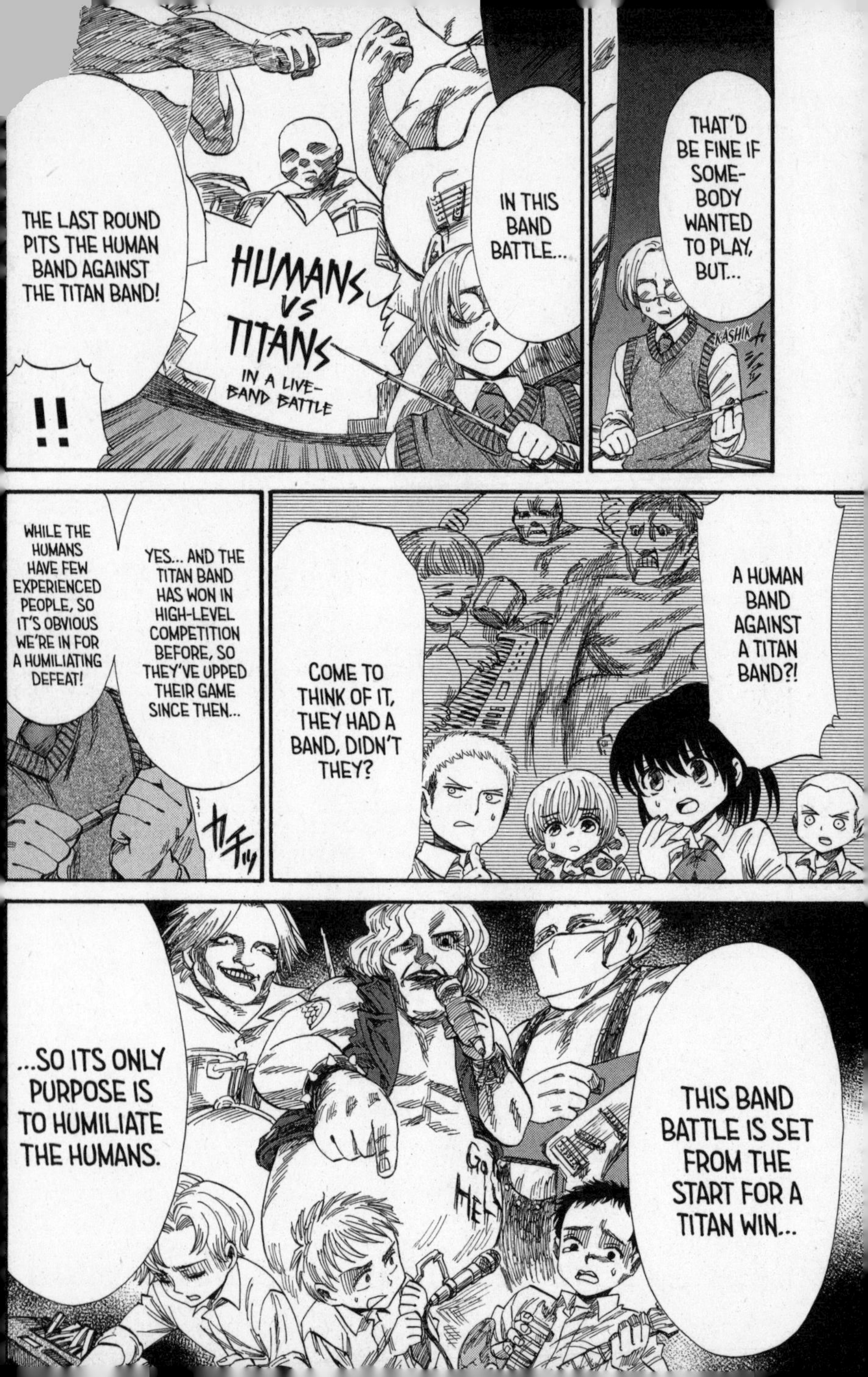
THAT'D BE FINE IF SOME-BODY WANTED TO PLAY, BUT...
KASHIK
IN THIS BAND BATTLE...
HUMANS VS TITANS
IN A LIVE-BAND BATTLE
THE LAST ROUND PITS THE HUMAN BAND AGAINST THE TITAN BAND!
!!
A HUMAN BAND AGAINST A TITAN BAND?!
COME TO THINK OF IT, THEY HAD A BAND, DIDN'T THEY?
YES... AND THE TITAN BAND HAS WON IN HIGH-LEVEL COMPETITION BEFORE, SO THEY'VE UPPED THEIR GAME SINCE THEN...
WHILE THE HUMANS HAVE FEW EXPERIENCED PEOPLE, SO IT'S OBVIOUS WE'RE IN FOR A HUMILIATING DEFEAT!
カチッ
THIS BAND BATTLE IS SET FROM THE START FOR A TITAN WIN...
...SO ITS ONLY PURPOSE IS TO HUMILIATE THE HUMANS.

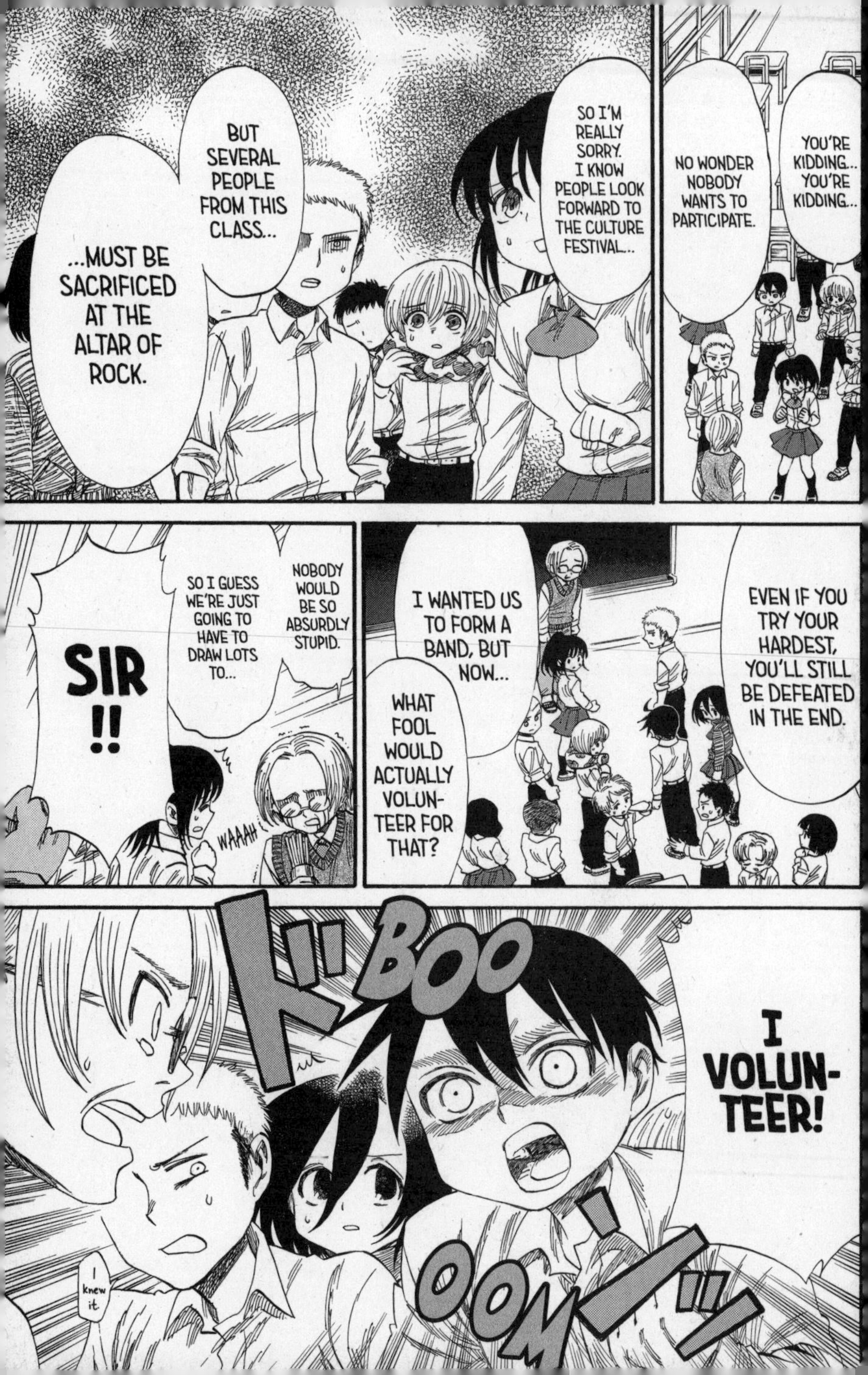
YOU'RE KIDDING... YOU'RE KIDDING...
NO WONDER NOBODY WANTS TO PARTICIPATE.
SO I'M REALLY SORRY. I KNOW PEOPLE LOOK FORWARD TO THE CULTURE FESTIVAL...
BUT SEVERAL PEOPLE FROM THIS CLASS...
...MUST BE SACRIFICED AT THE ALTAR OF ROCK.
EVEN IF YOU TRY YOUR HARDEST, YOU'LL STILL BE DEFEATED IN THE END.
I WANTED US TO FORM A BAND, BUT NOW...
WHAT FOOL WOULD ACTUALLY VOLUNTEER FOR THAT?
NOBODY WOULD BE SO ABSURDLY STUPID.
SO I GUESS WE'RE JUST GOING TO HAVE TO DRAW LOTS TO...
WAAAH
SIR !!
I VOLUNTEER!
K BOO
OOM
I knew it.

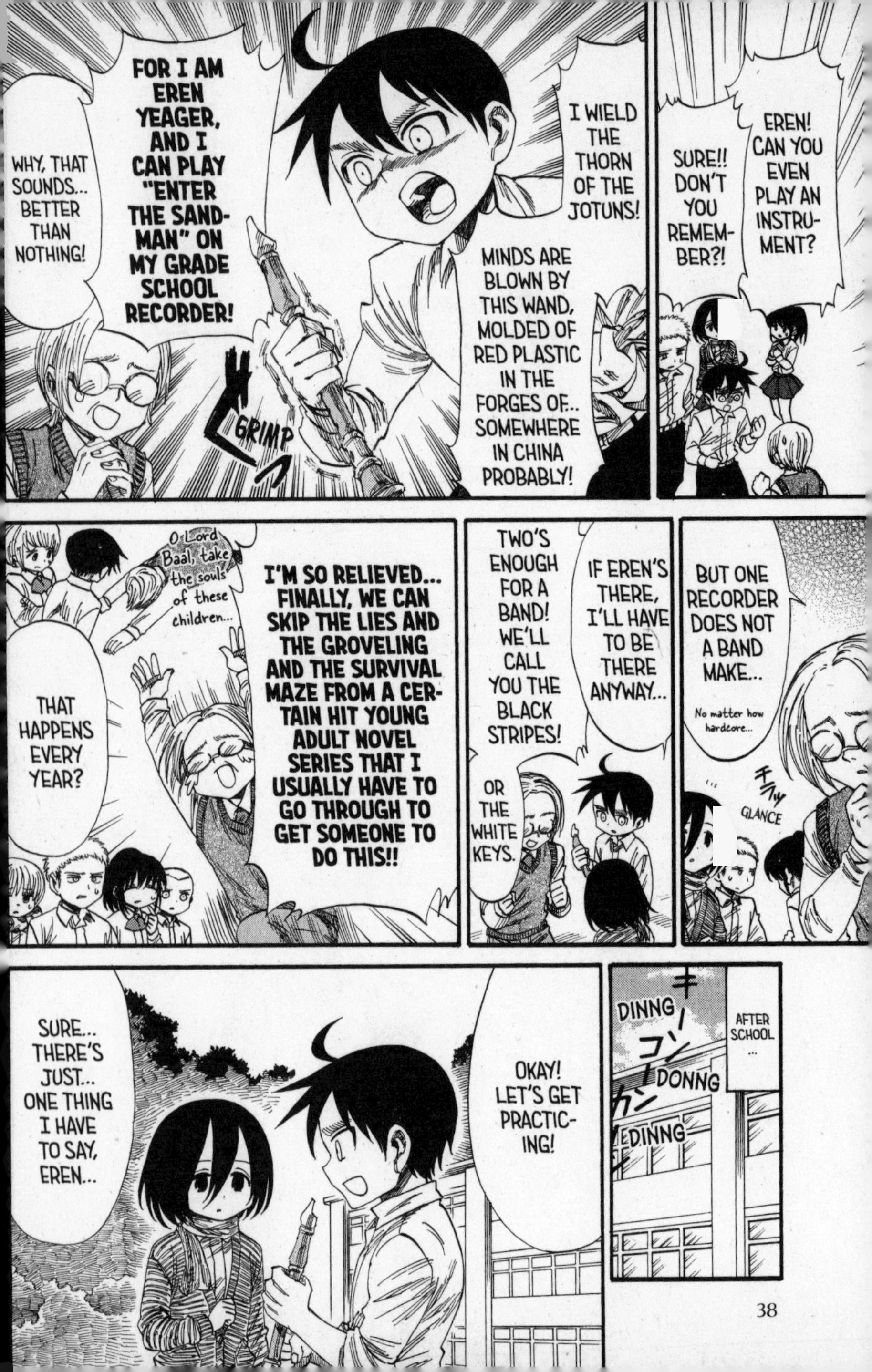

EREN! CAN YOU EVEN PLAY AN INSTRUMENT?
SURE!! DON'T YOU REMEMBER?!
I WIELD THE THORN OF THE JOTUNS!
MINDS ARE BLOWN BY THIS WAND, MOLDED OF RED PLASTIC IN THE FORGES OF.. SOMEWHERE IN CHINA PROBABLY!
FOR I AM EREN YEAGER, AND I CAN PLAY "ENTER THE SANDMAN" ON MY GRADE SCHOOL RECORDER!
GRIMP
WHY, THAT SOUNDS... BETTER THAN NOTHING!
BUT ONE RECORDER DOES NOT A BAND MAKE...
No matter how hardcore...
GLANCE
IF EREN'S THERE, I'LL HAVE TO BE THERE ANYWAY...
TWO'S ENOUGH FOR A BAND! WE'LL CALL YOU THE BLACK STRIPES!
OR THE WHITE KEYS.
I'M SO RELIEVED... FINALLY, WE CAN SKIP THE LIES AND THE GROVELING AND THE SURVIVAL MAZE FROM A CERTAIN HIT YOUNG ADULT NOVEL SERIES THAT I USUALLY HAVE TO GO THROUGH TO GET SOMEONE TO DO THIS!!
O Lord Baal, take the souls of these children...
THAT HAPPENS EVERY YEAR?
AFTER SCHOOL...
DINNG
DONNG
DINNG
OKAY! LET'S GET PRACTICING!
SURE... THERE'S JUST... ONE THING I HAVE TO SAY, EREN...

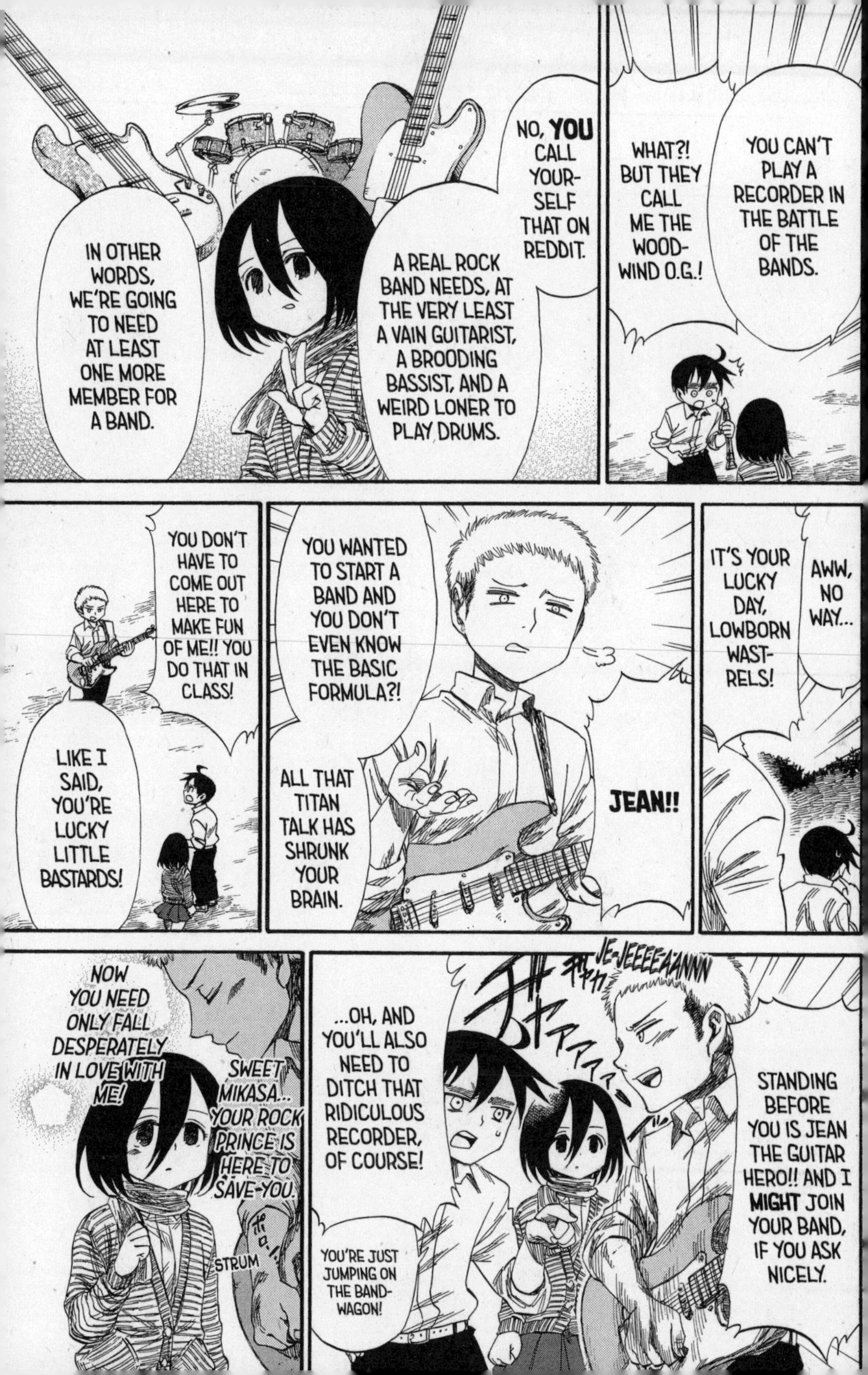
YOU CAN'T PLAY A RECORDER IN THE BATTLE OF THE BANDS.
WHAT?! BUT THEY CALL ME THE WOOD-WIND O.G.!
NO, **YOU** CALL YOUR-SELF THAT ON REDDIT.
A REAL ROCK BAND NEEDS, AT THE VERY LEAST A VAIN GUITARIST, A BROODING BASSIST, AND A WEIRD LONER TO PLAY DRUMS.
IN OTHER WORDS, WE'RE GOING TO NEED AT LEAST ONE MORE MEMBER FOR A BAND.
AWW, NO WAY...
IT'S YOUR LUCKY DAY, LOWBORN WAST-RELS!
JEAN!!
YOU WANTED TO START A BAND AND YOU DON'T EVEN KNOW THE BASIC FORMULA?!
ALL THAT TITAN TALK HAS SHRUNK YOUR BRAIN.
YOU DON'T HAVE TO COME OUT HERE TO MAKE FUN OF ME!! YOU DO THAT IN CLASS!
LIKE I SAID, YOU'RE LUCKY LITTLE BASTARDS!
JE-JEEEEAANNN
STANDING BEFORE YOU IS JEAN THE GUITAR HERO!! AND I **MIGHT** JOIN YOUR BAND, IF YOU ASK NICELY.
...OH, AND YOU'LL ALSO NEED TO DITCH THAT RIDICULOUS RECORDER, OF COURSE!
YOU'RE JUST JUMPING ON THE BAND-WAGON!
NOW YOU NEED ONLY FALL DESPERATELY IN LOVE WITH ME!
SWEET MIKASA... YOUR ROCK PRINCE IS HERE TO SAVE YOU.
STRUM

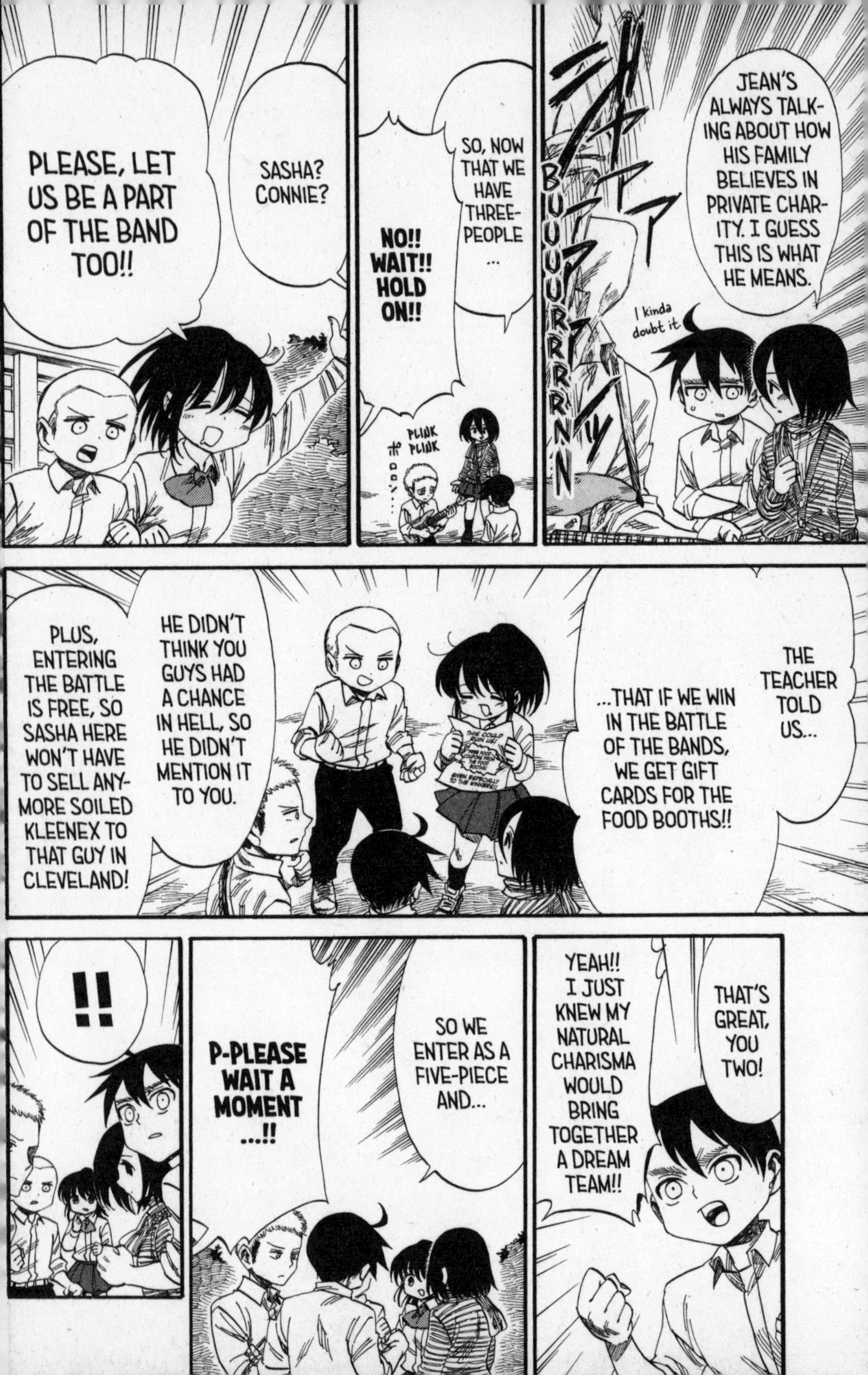
JEAN'S ALWAYS TALKING ABOUT HOW HIS FAMILY BELIEVES IN PRIVATE CHARITY. I GUESS THIS IS WHAT HE MEANS.
I kinda doubt it.
BUUUURRRRNN
SO, NOW THAT WE HAVE THREE-PEOPLE ...
NO!! WAIT!! HOLD ON!!
PLINK PLINK
SASHA? CONNIE?
PLEASE, LET US BE A PART OF THE BAND TOO!!
THE TEACHER TOLD US...
...THAT IF WE WIN IN THE BATTLE OF THE BANDS, WE GET GIFT CARDS FOR THE FOOD BOOTHS!!
THIS COULD RUIN US!
FREE FOOD COUPONS FROM THE FOOD BOOTHS!
GIVEN ESPECIALLY TO THE WINNERS!!
HE DIDN'T THINK YOU GUYS HAD A CHANCE IN HELL, SO HE DIDN'T MENTION IT TO YOU.
PLUS, ENTERING THE BATTLE IS FREE, SO SASHA HERE WON'T HAVE TO SELL ANY-MORE SOILED KLEENEX TO THAT GUY IN CLEVELAND!
THAT'S GREAT, YOU TWO!
YEAH!! I JUST KNEW MY NATURAL CHARISMA WOULD BRING TOGETHER A DREAM TEAM!!
SO WE ENTER AS A FIVE-PIECE AND...
P-PLEASE WAIT A MOMENT ...!!
!!

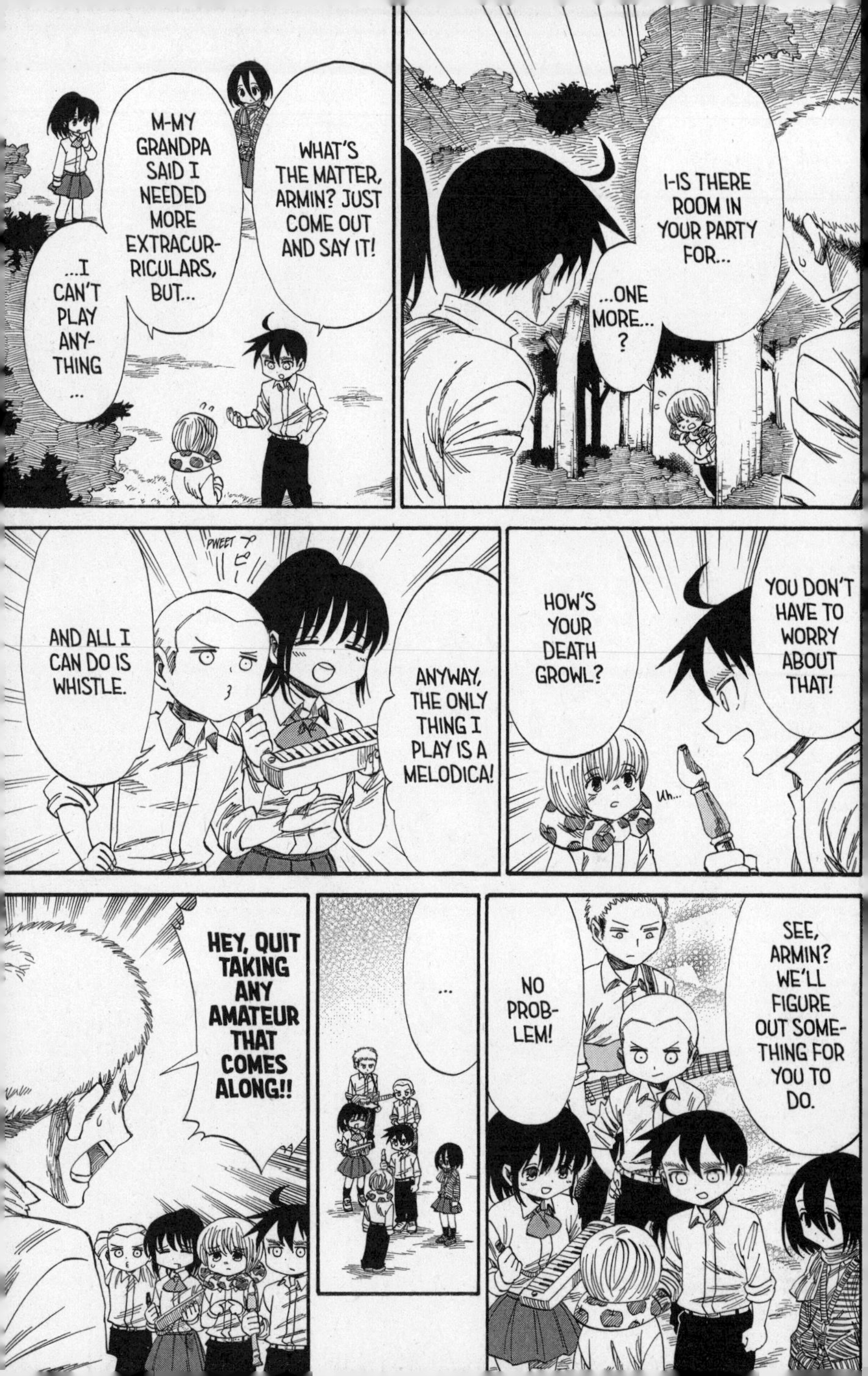
I-IS THERE ROOM IN YOUR PARTY FOR...
...ONE MORE...?
WHAT'S THE MATTER, ARMIN? JUST COME OUT AND SAY IT!
M-MY GRANDPA SAID I NEEDED MORE EXTRACURRICULARS, BUT...
...I CAN'T PLAY ANYTHING...
YOU DON'T HAVE TO WORRY ABOUT THAT!
HOW'S YOUR DEATH GROWL?
Uh...
ANYWAY, THE ONLY THING I PLAY IS A MELODICA!
PWEET
AND ALL I CAN DO IS WHISTLE.
SEE, ARMIN? WE'LL FIGURE OUT SOMETHING FOR YOU TO DO.
NO PROBLEM!
...
HEY, QUIT TAKING ANY AMATEUR THAT COMES ALONG!!

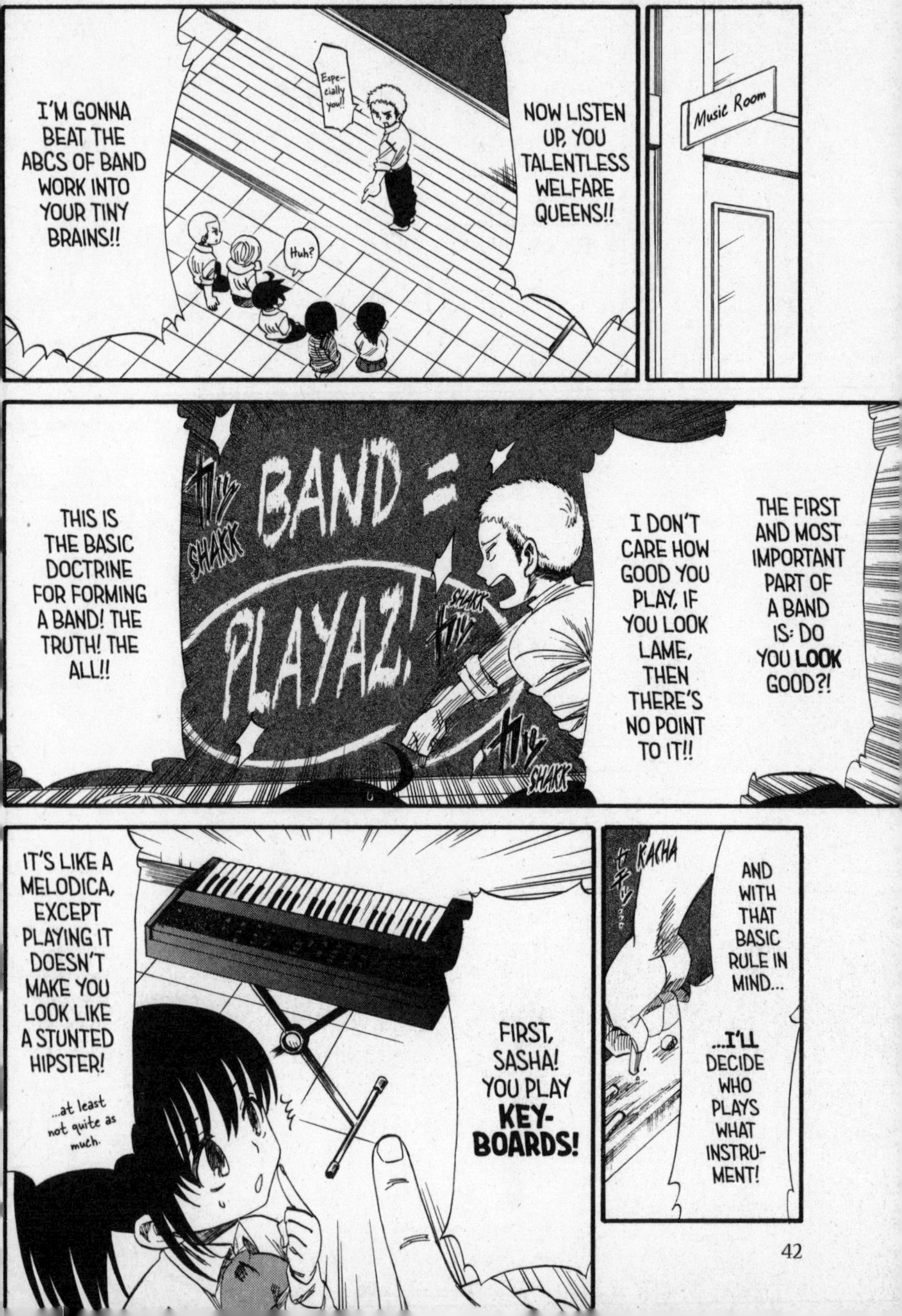
Music Room
NOW LISTEN UP, YOU TALENTLESS WELFARE QUEENS!!
Especially you!!
Huh?
I'M GONNA BEAT THE ABCS OF BAND WORK INTO YOUR TINY BRAINS!!
THE FIRST AND MOST IMPORTANT PART OF A BAND IS: DO YOU **LOOK** GOOD?!
I DON'T CARE HOW GOOD YOU PLAY, IF YOU LOOK LAME, THEN THERE'S NO POINT TO IT!!
SHAKK
SHAKK
SHAKK
BAND = PLAYAZ!
THIS IS THE BASIC DOCTRINE FOR FORMING A BAND! THE TRUTH! THE ALL!!
KACHA
AND WITH THAT BASIC RULE IN MIND...
...**I'LL** DECIDE WHO PLAYS WHAT INSTRUMENT!
FIRST, SASHA! YOU PLAY **KEY-BOARDS!**
IT'S LIKE A MELODICA, EXCEPT PLAYING IT DOESN'T MAKE YOU LOOK LIKE A STUNTED HIPSTER!
...at least not quite as much.

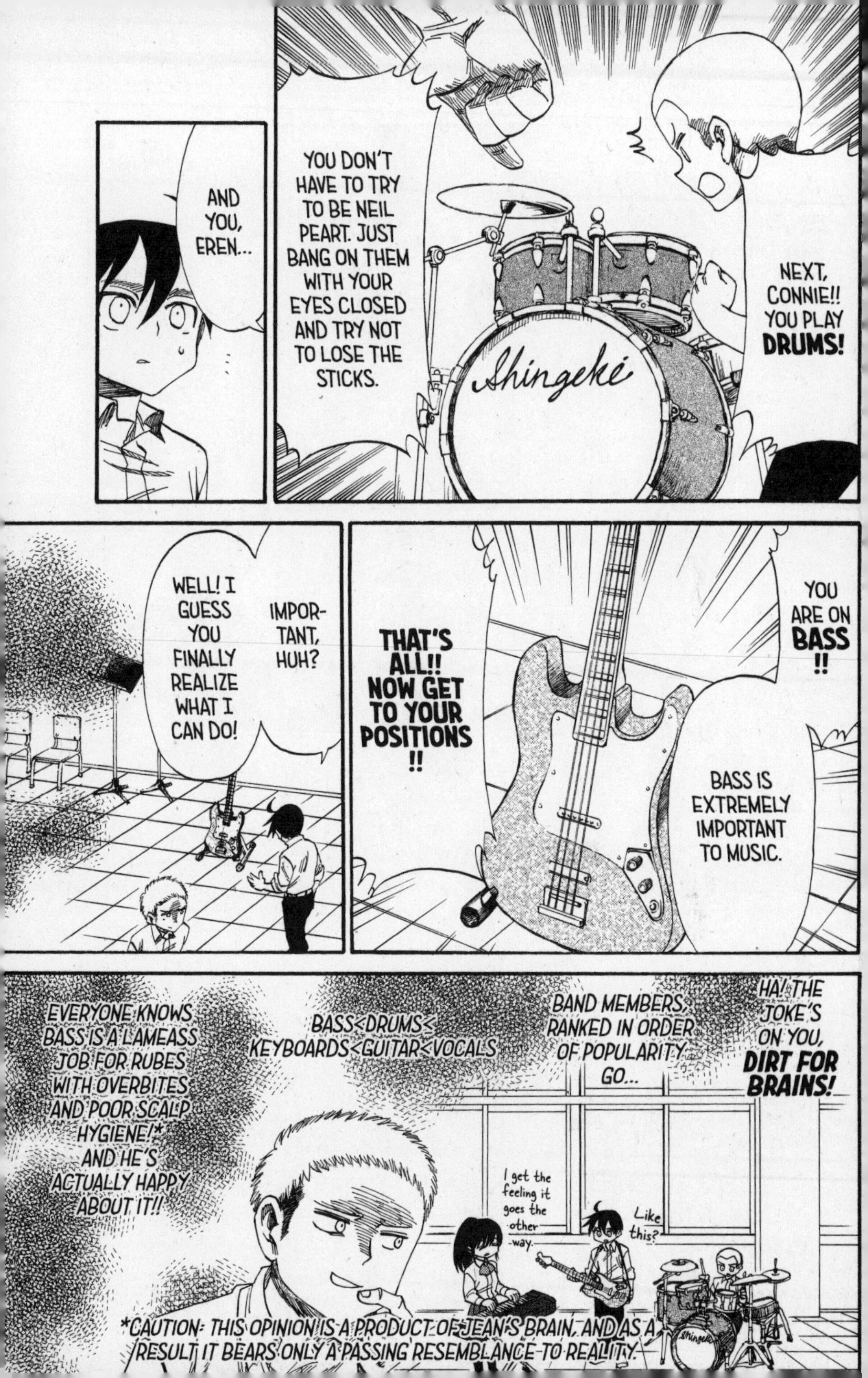
NEXT, CONNIE!! YOU PLAY **DRUMS!**
YOU DON'T HAVE TO TRY TO BE NEIL PEART. JUST BANG ON THEM WITH YOUR EYES CLOSED AND TRY NOT TO LOSE THE STICKS.
Shingeki
AND YOU, EREN...
YOU ARE ON **BASS!!**
BASS IS EXTREMELY IMPORTANT TO MUSIC.
THAT'S ALL!! NOW GET TO YOUR POSITIONS!!
IMPOR-TANT, HUH?
WELL! I GUESS YOU FINALLY REALIZE WHAT I CAN DO!
HA! THE JOKE'S ON YOU, **DIRT FOR BRAINS!**
BAND MEMBERS, RANKED IN ORDER OF POPULARITY GO...
BASS<DRUMS<KEYBOARDS<GUITAR<VOCALS
EVERYONE KNOWS BASS IS A LAMEASS JOB FOR RUBES WITH OVERBITES AND POOR SCALP HYGIENE!* AND HE'S ACTUALLY HAPPY ABOUT IT!!
Like this?
I get the feeling it goes the other way.
*CAUTION: THIS OPINION IS A PRODUCT OF JEAN'S BRAIN, AND AS A RESULT IT BEARS ONLY A PASSING RESEMBLANCE TO REALITY.

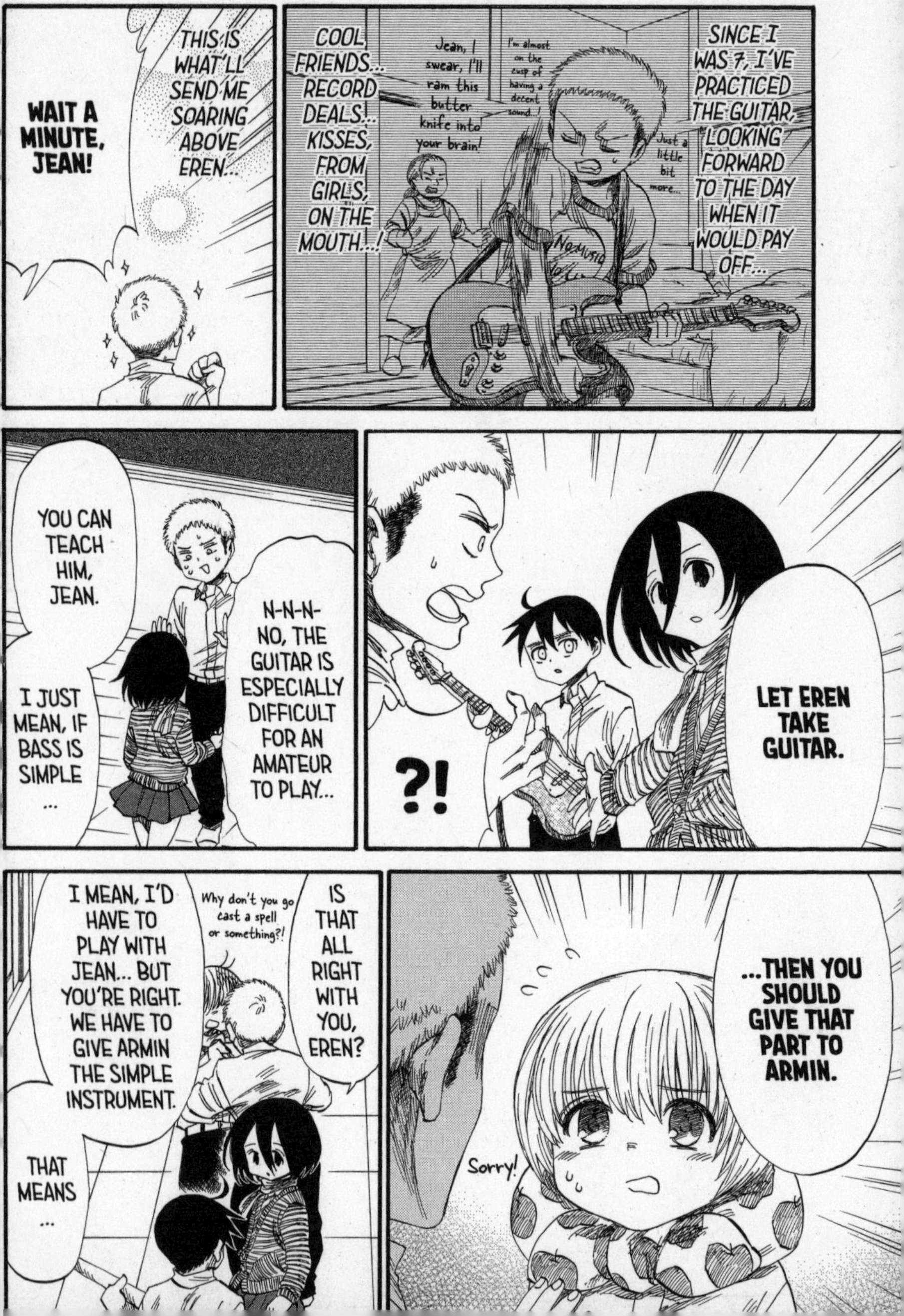
SINCE I WAS 7, I'VE PRACTICED THE GUITAR, LOOKING FORWARD TO THE DAY WHEN IT WOULD PAY OFF...
Just a little bit more...
I'm almost on the cusp of having a decent sound...!
Jean, I swear, I'll ram this butter knife into your brain!
COOL FRIENDS... RECORD DEALS... KISSES, FROM GIRLS, ON THE MOUTH...!
THIS IS WHAT'LL SEND ME SOARING ABOVE EREN...
WAIT A MINUTE, JEAN!
LET EREN TAKE GUITAR.
?!
N-N-N-NO, THE GUITAR IS ESPECIALLY DIFFICULT FOR AN AMATEUR TO PLAY...
YOU CAN TEACH HIM, JEAN.
I JUST MEAN, IF BASS IS SIMPLE...
...THEN YOU SHOULD GIVE THAT PART TO ARMIN.
Sorry!
IS THAT ALL RIGHT WITH YOU, EREN?
Why don't you go cast a spell or something?!
I MEAN, I'D HAVE TO PLAY WITH JEAN... BUT YOU'RE RIGHT. WE HAVE TO GIVE ARMIN THE SIMPLE INSTRUMENT.
THAT MEANS...

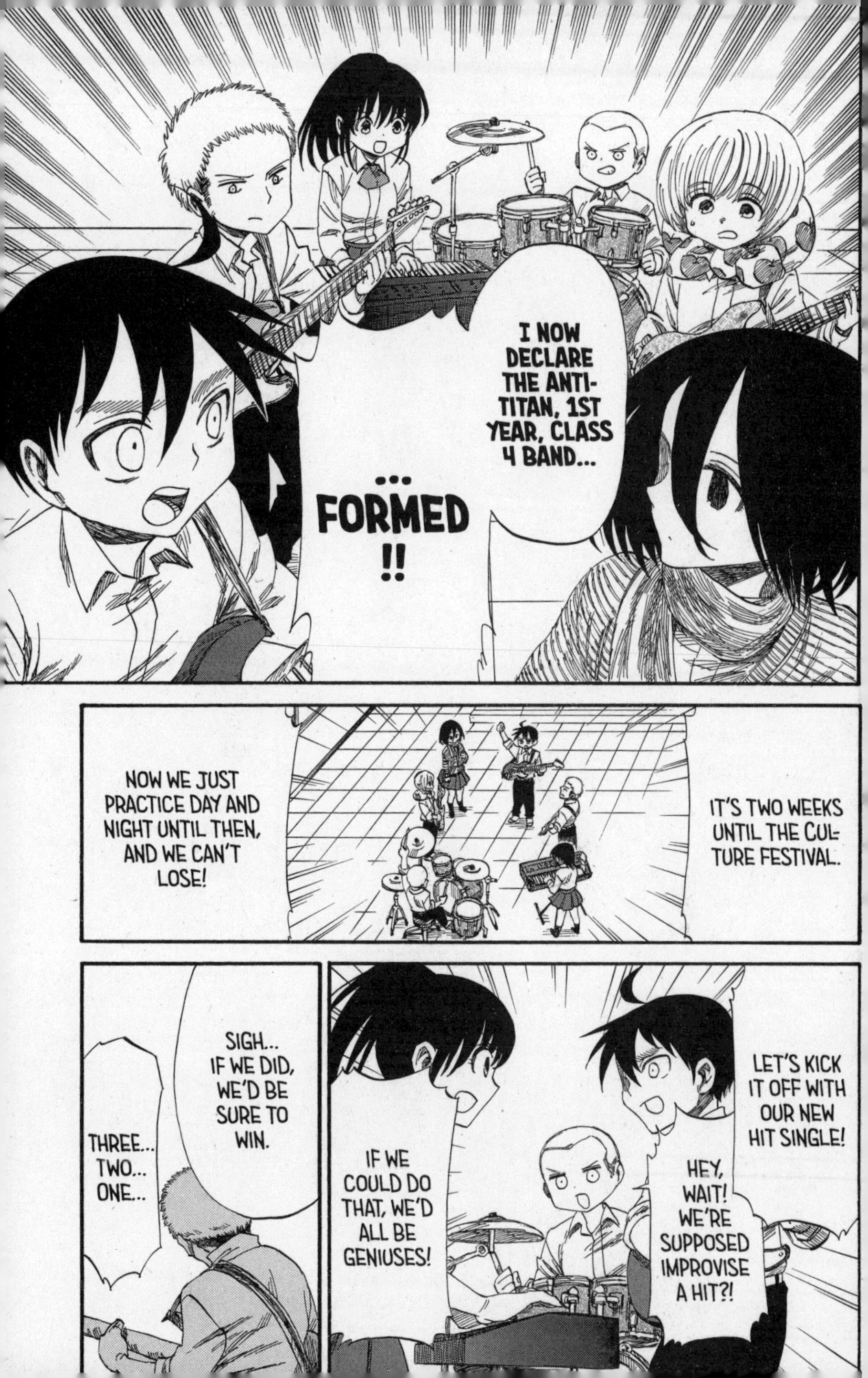
I NOW DECLARE THE ANTI-TITAN, 1ST YEAR, CLASS 4 BAND...
...FORMED!!
IT'S TWO WEEKS UNTIL THE CULTURE FESTIVAL.
NOW WE JUST PRACTICE DAY AND NIGHT UNTIL THEN, AND WE CAN'T LOSE!
LET'S KICK IT OFF WITH OUR NEW HIT SINGLE!
HEY, WAIT! WE'RE SUPPOSED IMPROVISE A HIT?!
IF WE COULD DO THAT, WE'D ALL BE GENIUSES!
SIGH... IF WE DID, WE'D BE SURE TO WIN.
THREE... TWO... ONE...

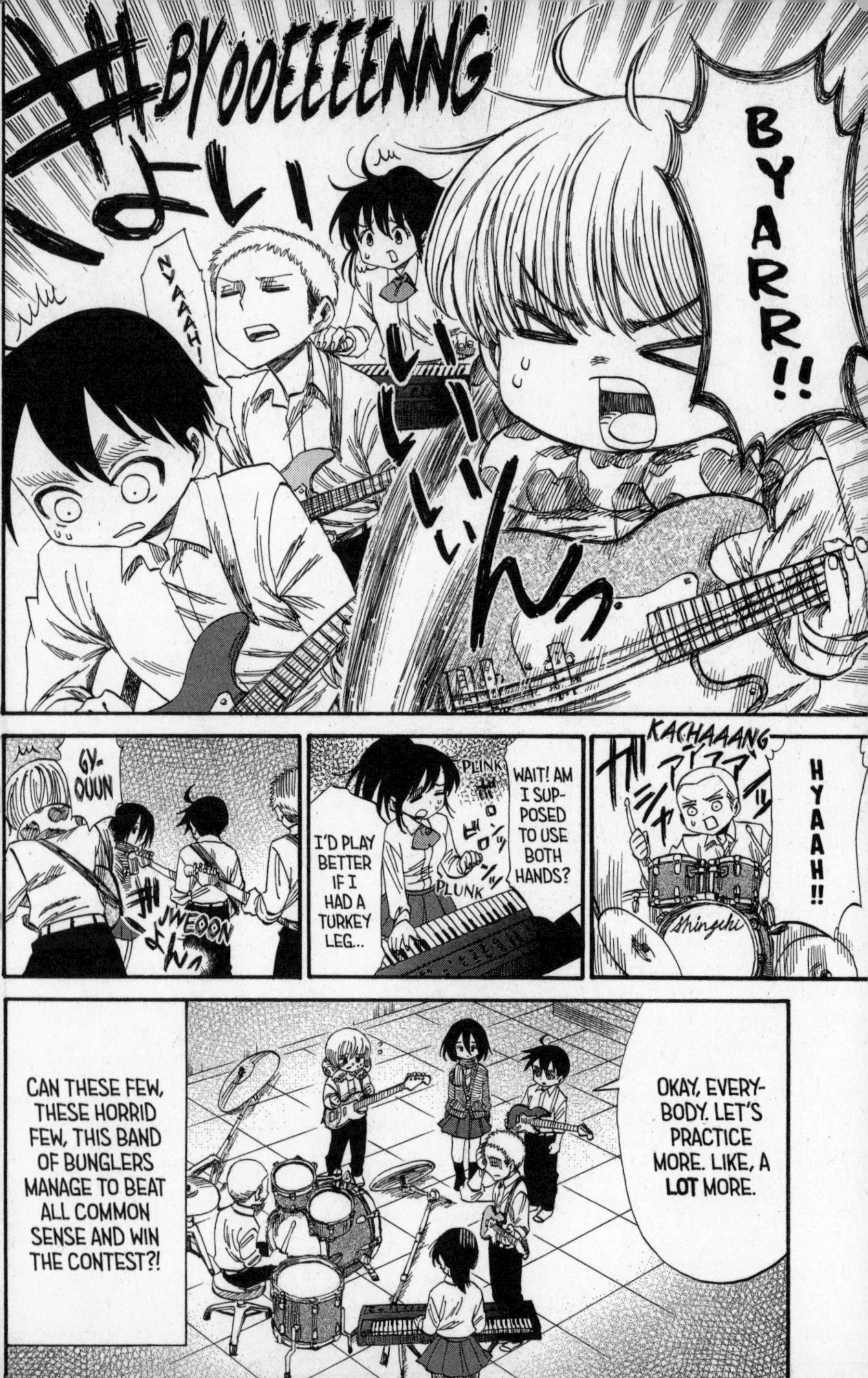
BYARR!!
BYOOEEEENNG
NYAAAH!
KACHAAANG
HYAAAH!!
Shingeki
WAIT! AM I SUP-POSED TO USE BOTH HANDS?
PLINK
PLUNK
I'D PLAY BETTER IF I HAD A TURKEY LEG...
GY-OUUN
JWEDON
OKAY, EVERY-BODY. LET'S PRACTICE MORE. LIKE, A **LOT** MORE.
CAN THESE FEW, THESE HORRID FEW, THIS BAND OF BUNGLERS MANAGE TO BEAT ALL COMMON SENSE AND WIN THE CONTEST?!

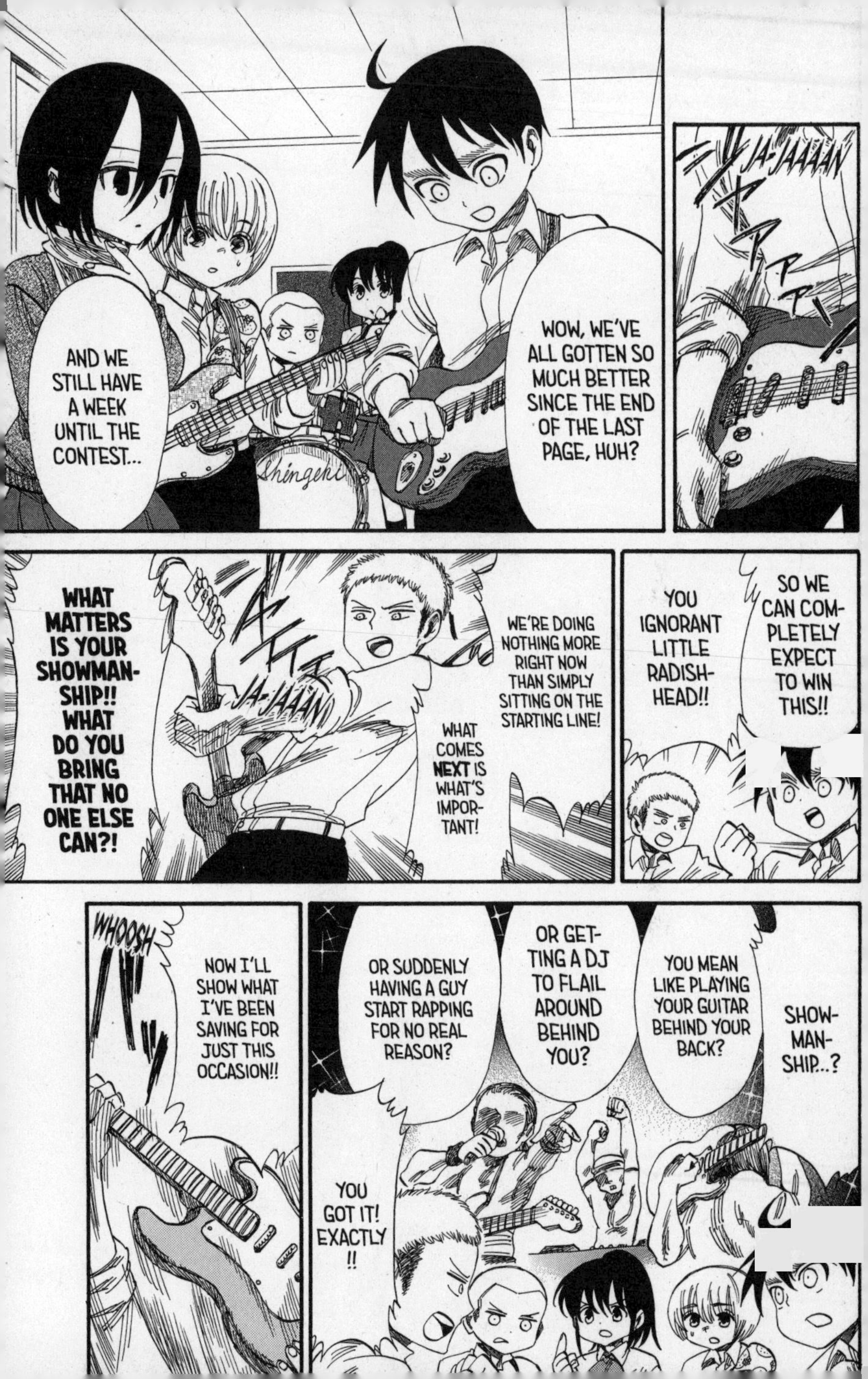
JA-JAAAAN
WOW, WE'VE ALL GOTTEN SO MUCH BETTER SINCE THE END OF THE LAST PAGE, HUH?
Shingeki
AND WE STILL HAVE A WEEK UNTIL THE CONTEST...
SO WE CAN COMPLETELY EXPECT TO WIN THIS!!
YOU IGNORANT LITTLE RADISH-HEAD!!
WE'RE DOING NOTHING MORE RIGHT NOW THAN SIMPLY SITTING ON THE STARTING LINE!
WHAT COMES **NEXT** IS WHAT'S IMPORTANT!
JA-JAAAN
WHAT MATTERS IS YOUR SHOWMANSHIP!! WHAT DO YOU BRING THAT NO ONE ELSE CAN?!
SHOWMANSHIP...?
YOU MEAN LIKE PLAYING YOUR GUITAR BEHIND YOUR BACK?
OR GETTING A DJ TO FLAIL AROUND BEHIND YOU?
OR SUDDENLY HAVING A GUY START RAPPING FOR NO REAL REASON?
YOU GOT IT! EXACTLY!!
WHOOSH
NOW I'LL SHOW WHAT I'VE BEEN SAVING FOR JUST THIS OCCASION!!

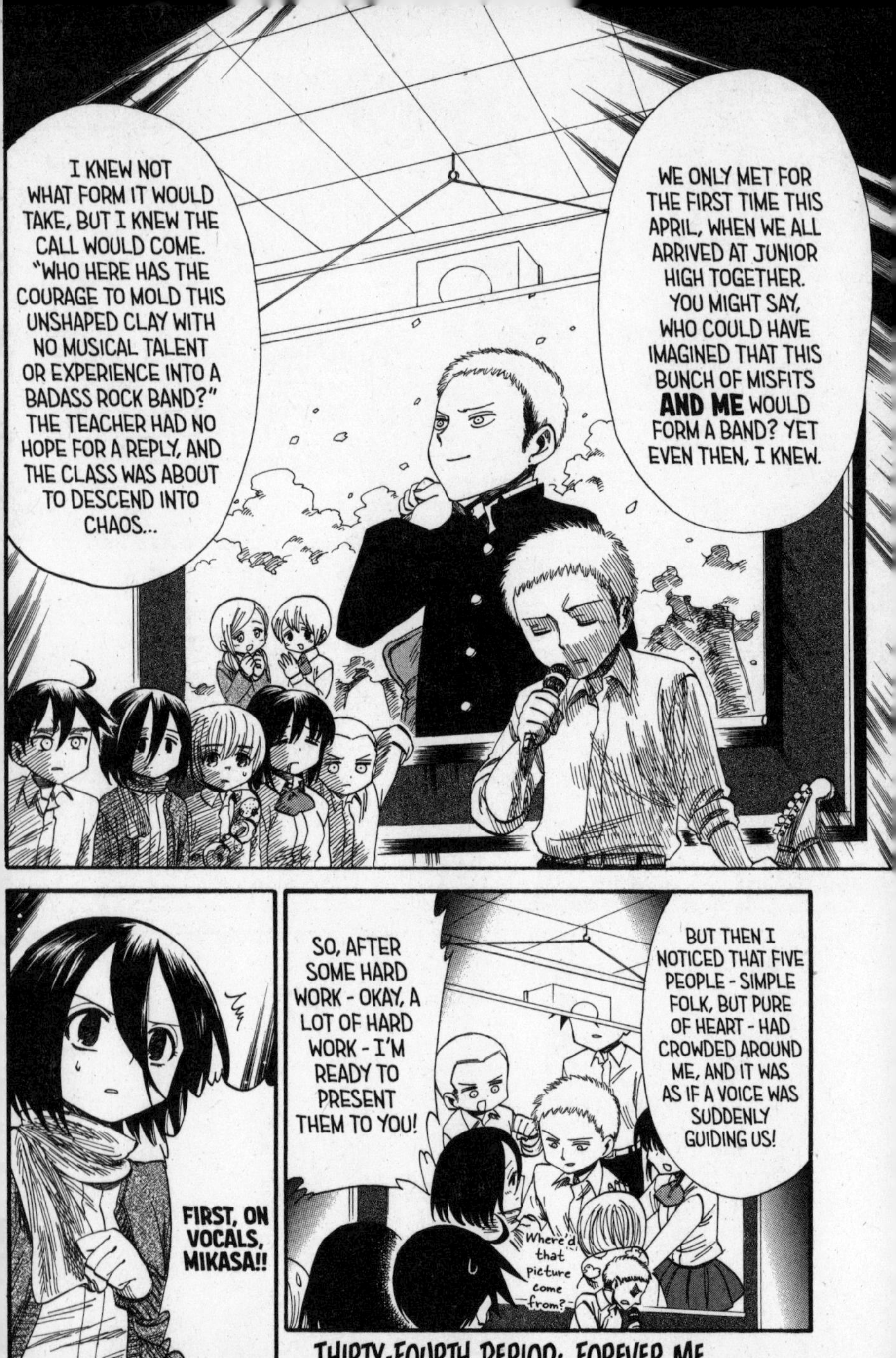
WE ONLY MET FOR THE FIRST TIME THIS APRIL, WHEN WE ALL ARRIVED AT JUNIOR HIGH TOGETHER. YOU MIGHT SAY, WHO COULD HAVE IMAGINED THAT THIS BUNCH OF MISFITS **AND ME** WOULD FORM A BAND? YET EVEN THEN, I KNEW.
I KNEW NOT WHAT FORM IT WOULD TAKE, BUT I KNEW THE CALL WOULD COME. "WHO HERE HAS THE COURAGE TO MOLD THIS UNSHAPED CLAY WITH NO MUSICAL TALENT OR EXPERIENCE INTO A BADASS ROCK BAND?" THE TEACHER HAD NO HOPE FOR A REPLY, AND THE CLASS WAS ABOUT TO DESCEND INTO CHAOS...
BUT THEN I NOTICED THAT FIVE PEOPLE - SIMPLE FOLK, BUT PURE OF HEART - HAD CROWDED AROUND ME, AND IT WAS AS IF A VOICE WAS SUDDENLY GUIDING US!
SO, AFTER SOME HARD WORK - OKAY, A LOT OF HARD WORK - I'M READY TO PRESENT THEM TO YOU!
Where'd that picture come from?
FIRST, ON VOCALS, MIKASA!!

THIRTY-FOURTH PERIOD: FOREVER ME

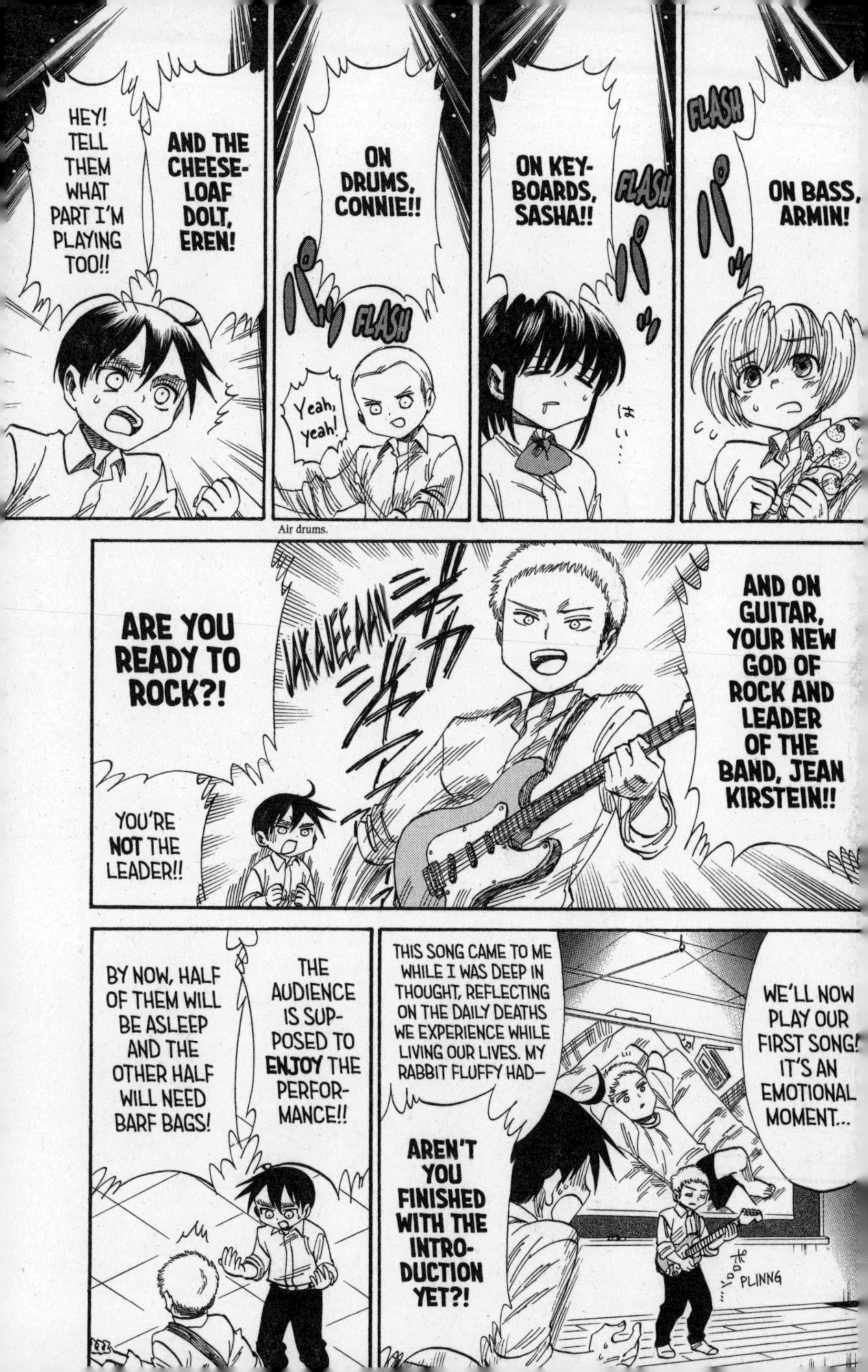
FLASH
ON BASS, ARMIN!
パッ
ON KEY-BOARDS, SASHA!!
FLASH
パッ
はい…
ON DRUMS, CONNIE!!
パッ
FLASH
Yeah, yeah!
AND THE CHEESE-LOAF DOLT, EREN!
HEY! TELL THEM WHAT PART I'M PLAYING TOO!!
Air drums.
AND ON GUITAR, YOUR NEW GOD OF ROCK AND LEADER OF THE BAND, JEAN KIRSTEIN!!
JAKAJEEAAN
ARE YOU READY TO ROCK?!
YOU'RE NOT THE LEADER!!
WE'LL NOW PLAY OUR FIRST SONG! IT'S AN EMOTIONAL MOMENT...
THIS SONG CAME TO ME WHILE I WAS DEEP IN THOUGHT, REFLECTING ON THE DAILY DEATHS WE EXPERIENCE WHILE LIVING OUR LIVES. MY RABBIT FLUFFY HAD—
AREN'T YOU FINISHED WITH THE INTRO-DUCTION YET?!
PLINNG
THE AUDIENCE IS SUP-POSED TO ENJOY THE PERFOR-MANCE!!
BY NOW, HALF OF THEM WILL BE ASLEEP AND THE OTHER HALF WILL NEED BARF BAGS!

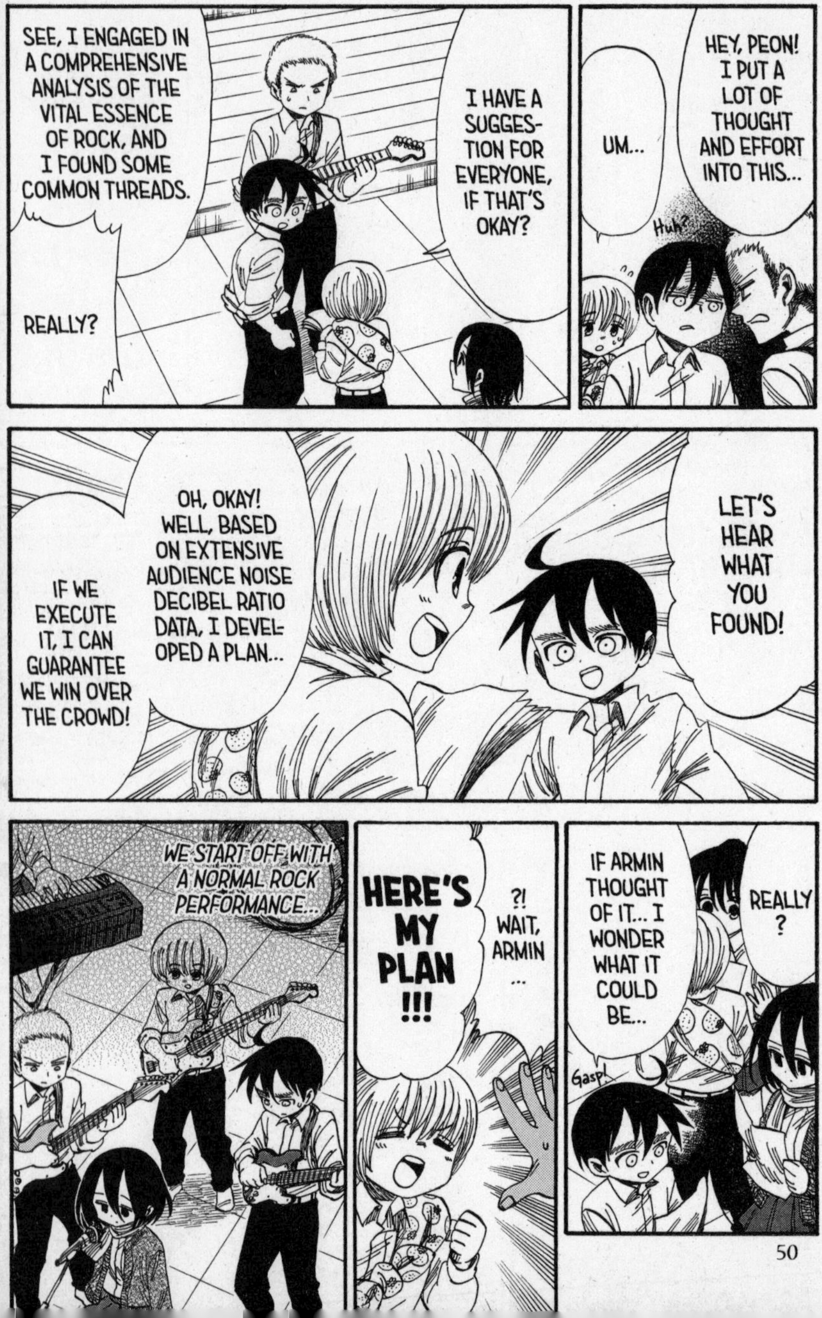
HEY, PEON! I PUT A LOT OF THOUGHT AND EFFORT INTO THIS...
UM...
Huh?
I HAVE A SUGGES-TION FOR EVERYONE, IF THAT'S OKAY?
SEE, I ENGAGED IN A COMPREHENSIVE ANALYSIS OF THE VITAL ESSENCE OF ROCK, AND I FOUND SOME COMMON THREADS.
REALLY?
LET'S HEAR WHAT YOU FOUND!
OH, OKAY! WELL, BASED ON EXTENSIVE AUDIENCE NOISE DECIBEL RATIO DATA, I DEVEL-OPED A PLAN...
IF WE EXECUTE IT, I CAN GUARANTEE WE WIN OVER THE CROWD!
REALLY?
IF ARMIN THOUGHT OF IT... I WONDER WHAT IT COULD BE...
Gasp!
?! WAIT, ARMIN ...
HERE'S MY PLAN !!!
WE START OFF WITH A NORMAL ROCK PERFORMANCE...

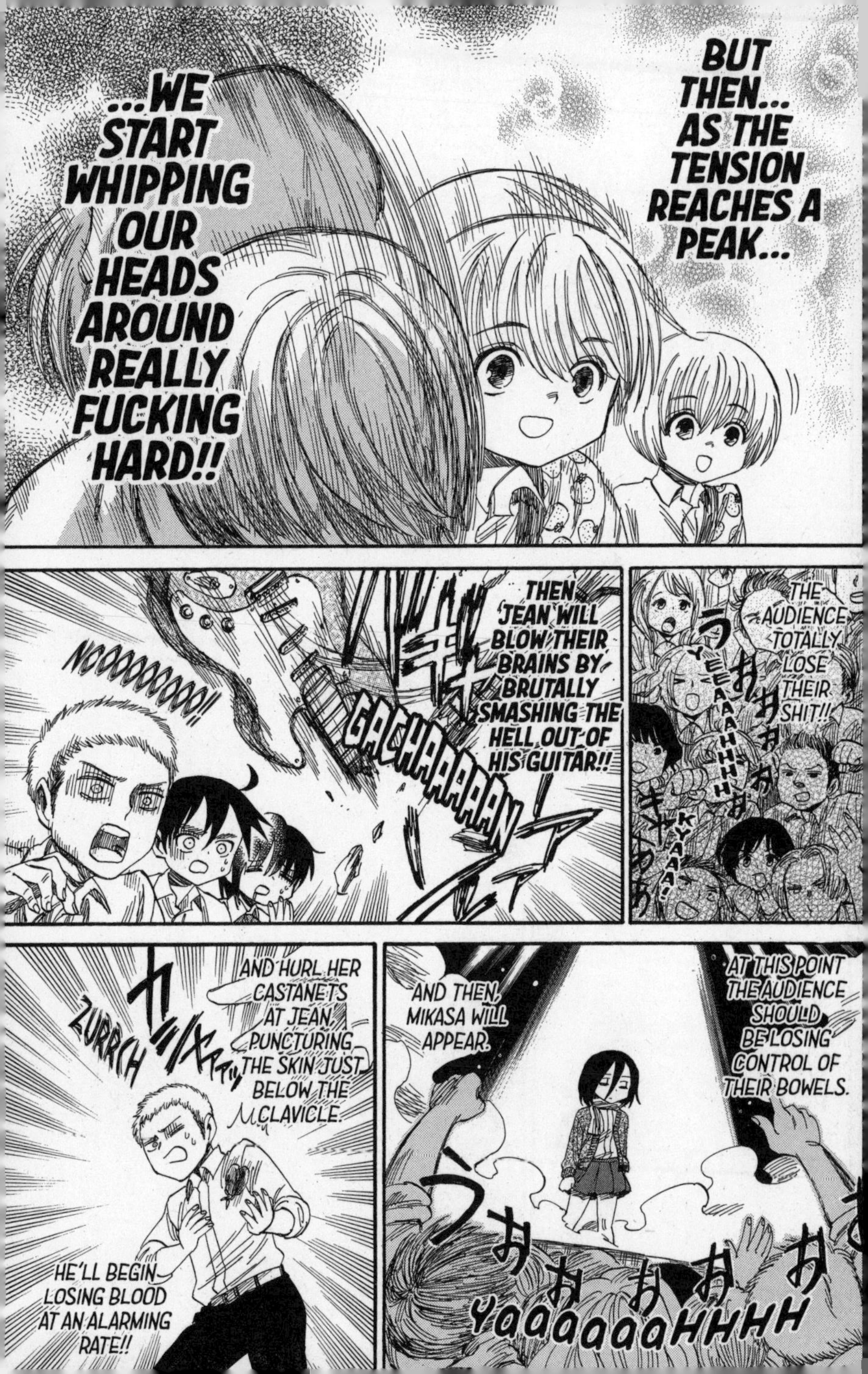

BUT THEN... AS THE TENSION REACHES A PEAK...
...WE START WHIPPING OUR HEADS AROUND REALLY FUCKING HARD!!
THE AUDIENCE TOTALLY LOSE THEIR SHIT!!
YEEAAAHHHH
KYAAAA!!
THEN JEAN WILL BLOW THEIR BRAINS BY BRUTALLY SMASHING THE HELL OUT OF HIS GUITAR!!
GACHAAAAAN
NOOOOOOOOOO!!
AT THIS POINT THE AUDIENCE SHOULD BE LOSING CONTROL OF THEIR BOWELS.
AND THEN, MIKASA WILL APPEAR.
YAAAAAAAHHHH
AND HURL HER CASTANETS AT JEAN, PUNCTURING THE SKIN JUST BELOW THE CLAVICLE.
ZURRCH
HE'LL BEGIN LOSING BLOOD AT AN ALARMING RATE!!

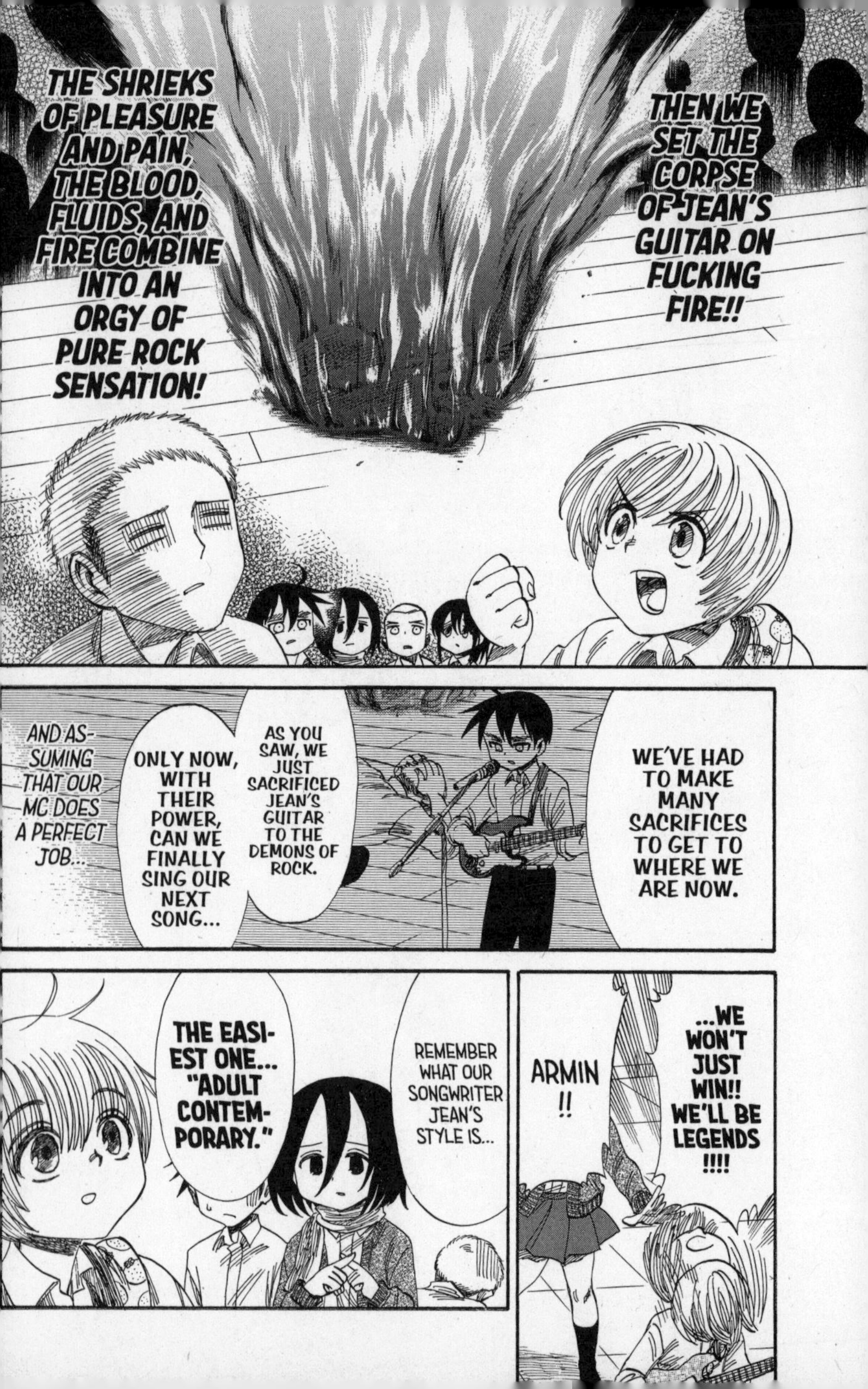

THEN WE SET THE CORPSE OF JEAN'S GUITAR ON FUCKING FIRE!!
THE SHRIEKS OF PLEASURE AND PAIN, THE BLOOD, FLUIDS, AND FIRE COMBINE INTO AN ORGY OF PURE ROCK SENSATION!
WE'VE HAD TO MAKE MANY SACRIFICES TO GET TO WHERE WE ARE NOW.
AS YOU SAW, WE JUST SACRIFICED JEAN'S GUITAR TO THE DEMONS OF ROCK.
ONLY NOW, WITH THEIR POWER, CAN WE FINALLY SING OUR NEXT SONG...
AND AS-SUMING THAT OUR MC DOES A PERFECT JOB...
...WE WON'T JUST WIN!! WE'LL BE LEGENDS !!!!
ARMIN !!
REMEMBER WHAT OUR SONGWRITER JEAN'S STYLE IS...
THE EASI-EST ONE... "ADULT CONTEM-PORARY."

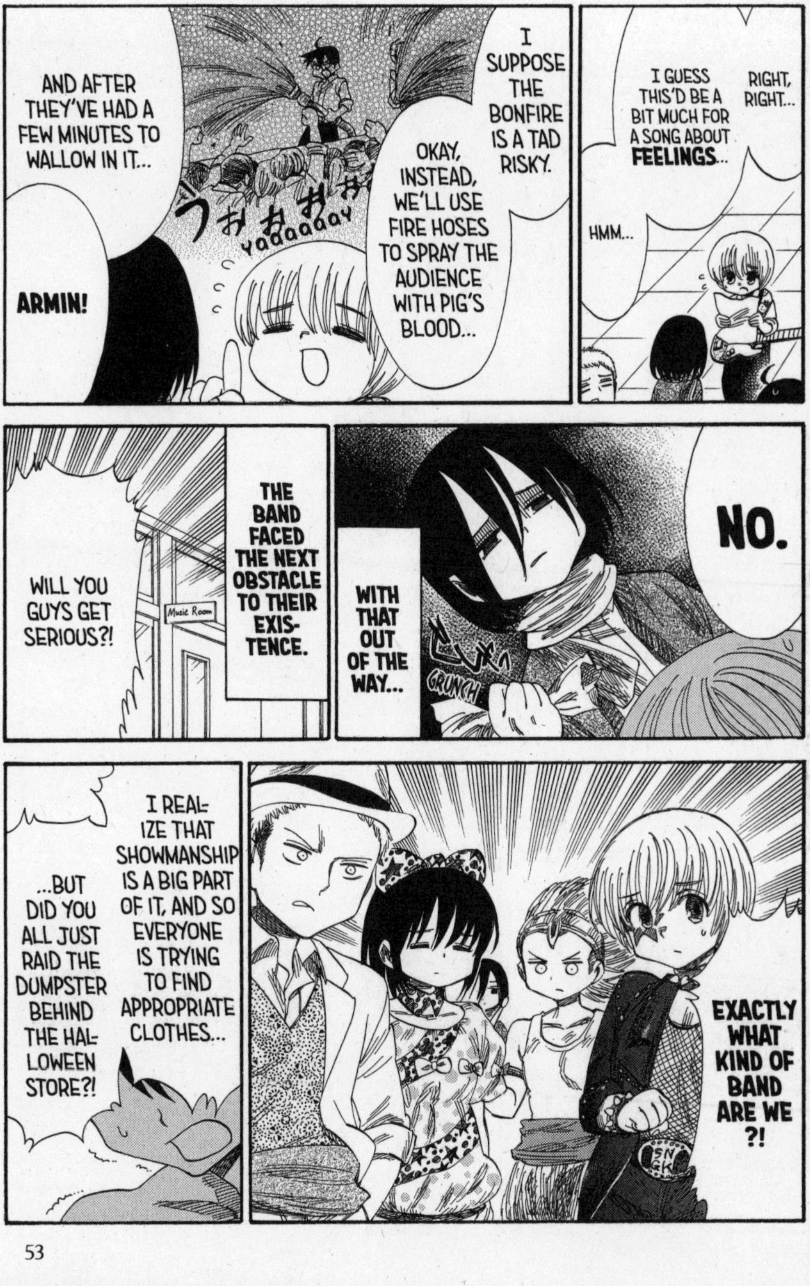
RIGHT, RIGHT...
I GUESS THIS'D BE A BIT MUCH FOR A SONG ABOUT FEELINGS...
HMM...
I SUPPOSE THE BONFIRE IS A TAD RISKY.
OKAY, INSTEAD, WE'LL USE FIRE HOSES TO SPRAY THE AUDIENCE WITH PIG'S BLOOD...
うおおお
yaaaaaay
AND AFTER THEY'VE HAD A FEW MINUTES TO WALLOW IN IT...
ARMIN!
NO.
GRUNCH
WITH THAT OUT OF THE WAY...
THE BAND FACED THE NEXT OBSTACLE TO THEIR EXISTENCE.
Music Room
WILL YOU GUYS GET SERIOUS?!
EXACTLY WHAT KIND OF BAND ARE WE ?!
I REALIZE THAT SHOWMANSHIP IS A BIG PART OF IT, AND SO EVERYONE IS TRYING TO FIND APPROPRIATE CLOTHES...
...BUT DID YOU ALL JUST RAID THE DUMPSTER BEHIND THE HALLOWEEN STORE?!

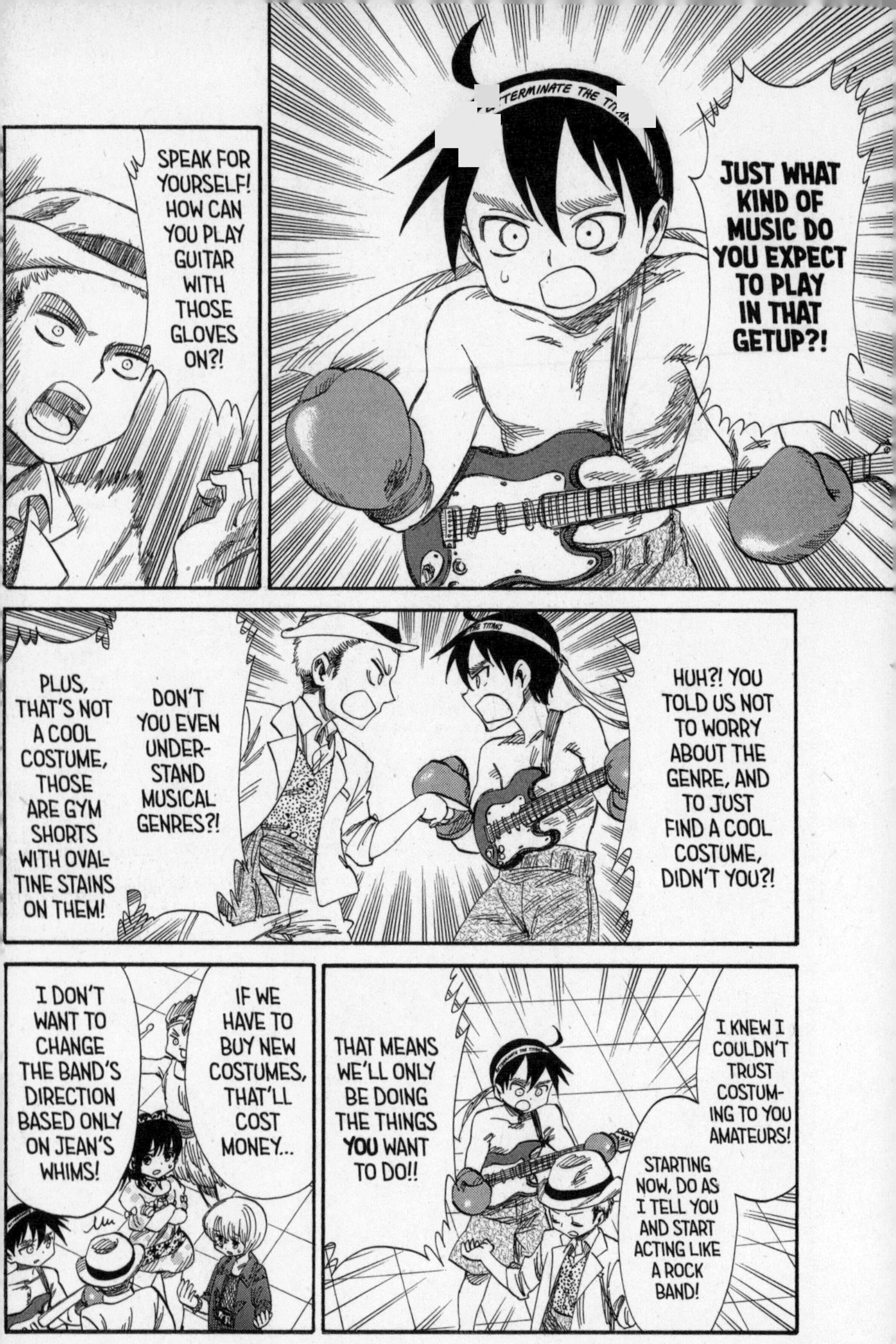
JUST WHAT KIND OF MUSIC DO YOU EXPECT TO PLAY IN THAT GETUP?!
SPEAK FOR YOURSELF! HOW CAN YOU PLAY GUITAR WITH THOSE GLOVES ON?!
HUH?! YOU TOLD US NOT TO WORRY ABOUT THE GENRE, AND TO JUST FIND A COOL COSTUME, DIDN'T YOU?!
DON'T YOU EVEN UNDER-STAND MUSICAL GENRES?!
PLUS, THAT'S NOT A COOL COSTUME, THOSE ARE GYM SHORTS WITH OVAL-TINE STAINS ON THEM!
I KNEW I COULDN'T TRUST COSTUM-ING TO YOU AMATEURS!
STARTING NOW, DO AS I TELL YOU AND START ACTING LIKE A ROCK BAND!
THAT MEANS WE'LL ONLY BE DOING THE THINGS **YOU** WANT TO DO!!
IF WE HAVE TO BUY NEW COSTUMES, THAT'LL COST MONEY...
I DON'T WANT TO CHANGE THE BAND'S DIRECTION BASED ONLY ON JEAN'S WHIMS!

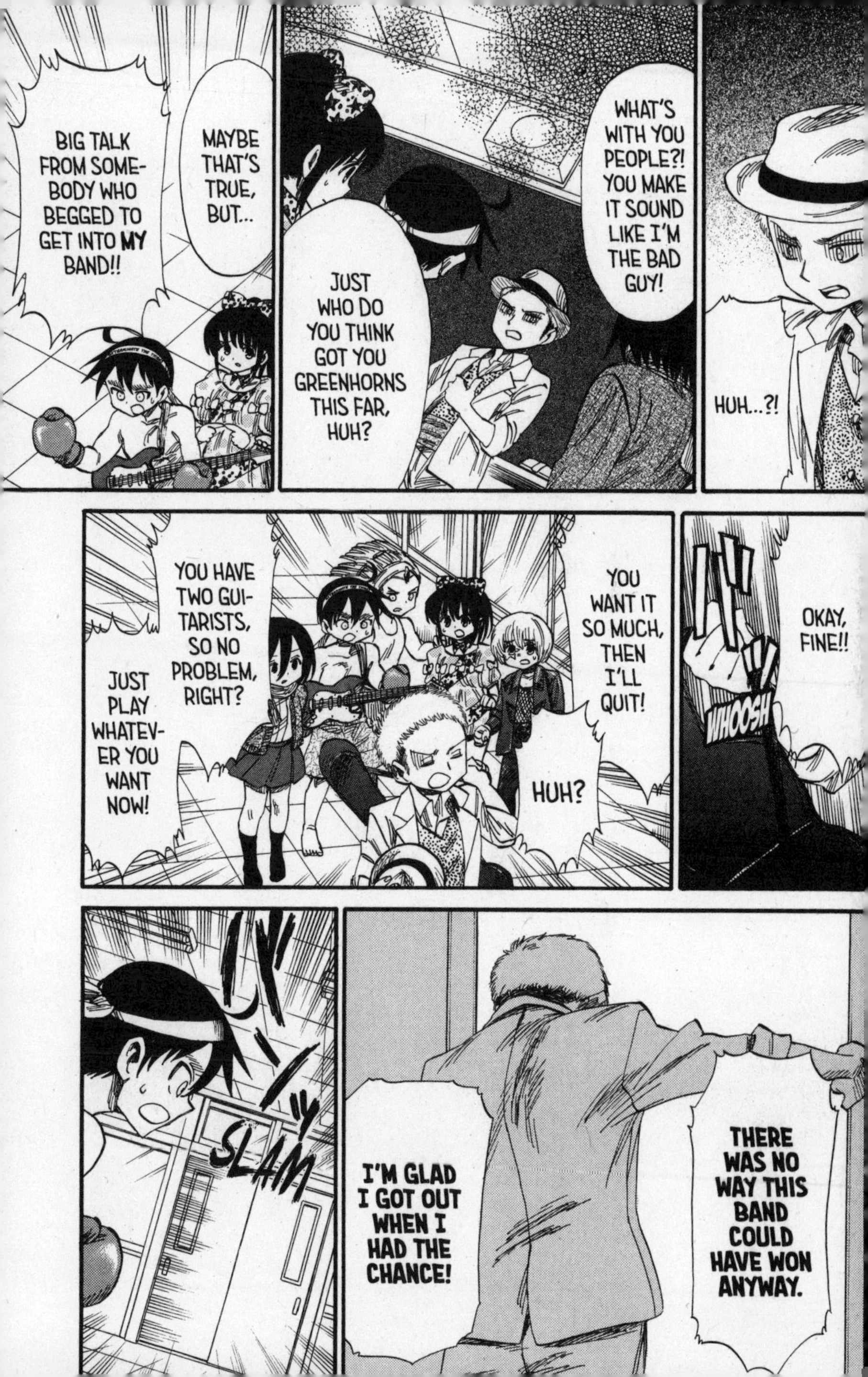
HUH...?!
WHAT'S WITH YOU PEOPLE?! YOU MAKE IT SOUND LIKE I'M THE BAD GUY!
JUST WHO DO YOU THINK GOT YOU GREENHORNS THIS FAR, HUH?
MAYBE THAT'S TRUE, BUT...
BIG TALK FROM SOME-BODY WHO BEGGED TO GET INTO MY BAND!!
OKAY, FINE!!
WHOOSH
YOU WANT IT SO MUCH, THEN I'LL QUIT!
HUH?
YOU HAVE TWO GUI-TARISTS, SO NO PROBLEM, RIGHT?
JUST PLAY WHATEV-ER YOU WANT NOW!
THERE WAS NO WAY THIS BAND COULD HAVE WON ANYWAY.
I'M GLAD I GOT OUT WHEN I HAD THE CHANCE!
SLAM

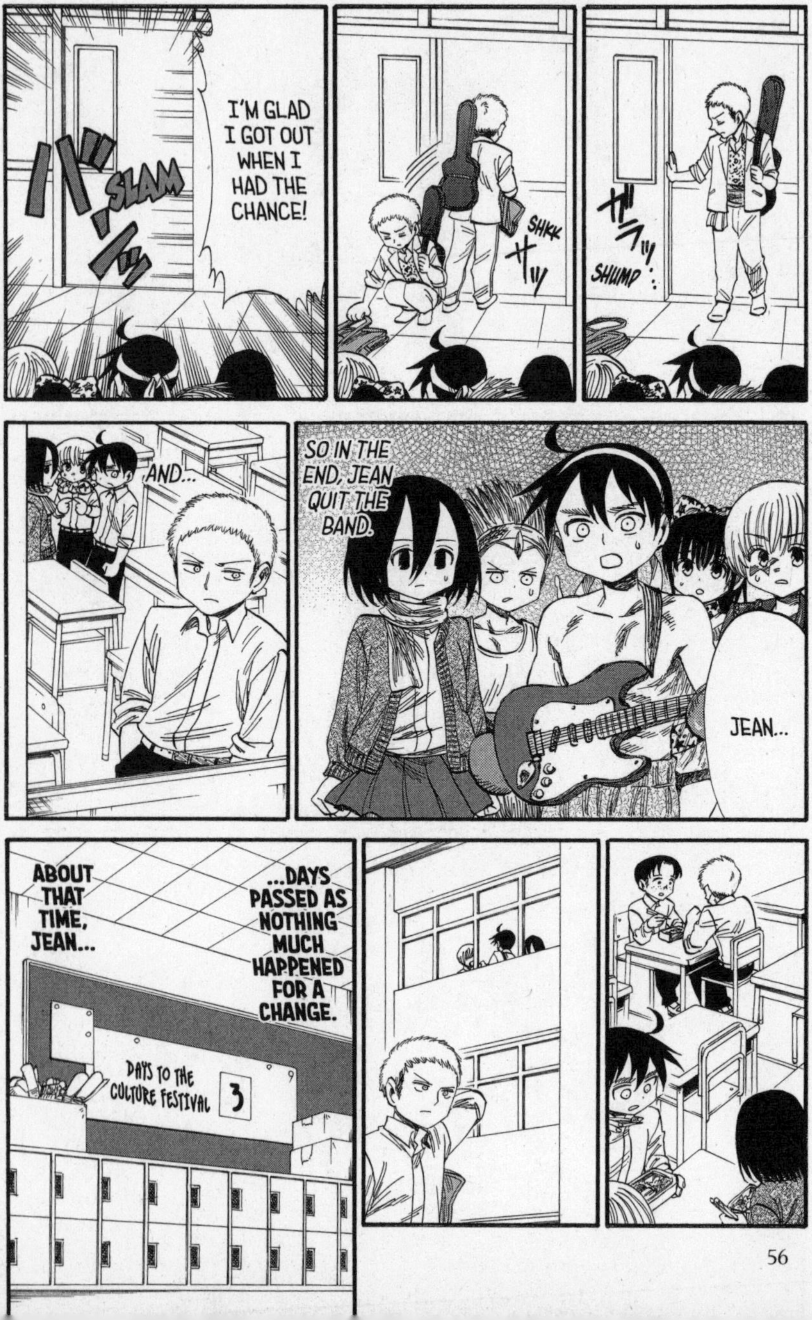
ガラッ
SHUMP
サッ
SHKK
I'M GLAD I GOT OUT WHEN I HAD THE CHANCE!
SLAM
SO IN THE END, JEAN QUIT THE BAND.
JEAN...
AND...
...DAYS PASSED AS NOTHING MUCH HAPPENED FOR A CHANGE.
ABOUT THAT TIME, JEAN...
DAYS TO THE CULTURE FESTIVAL 3

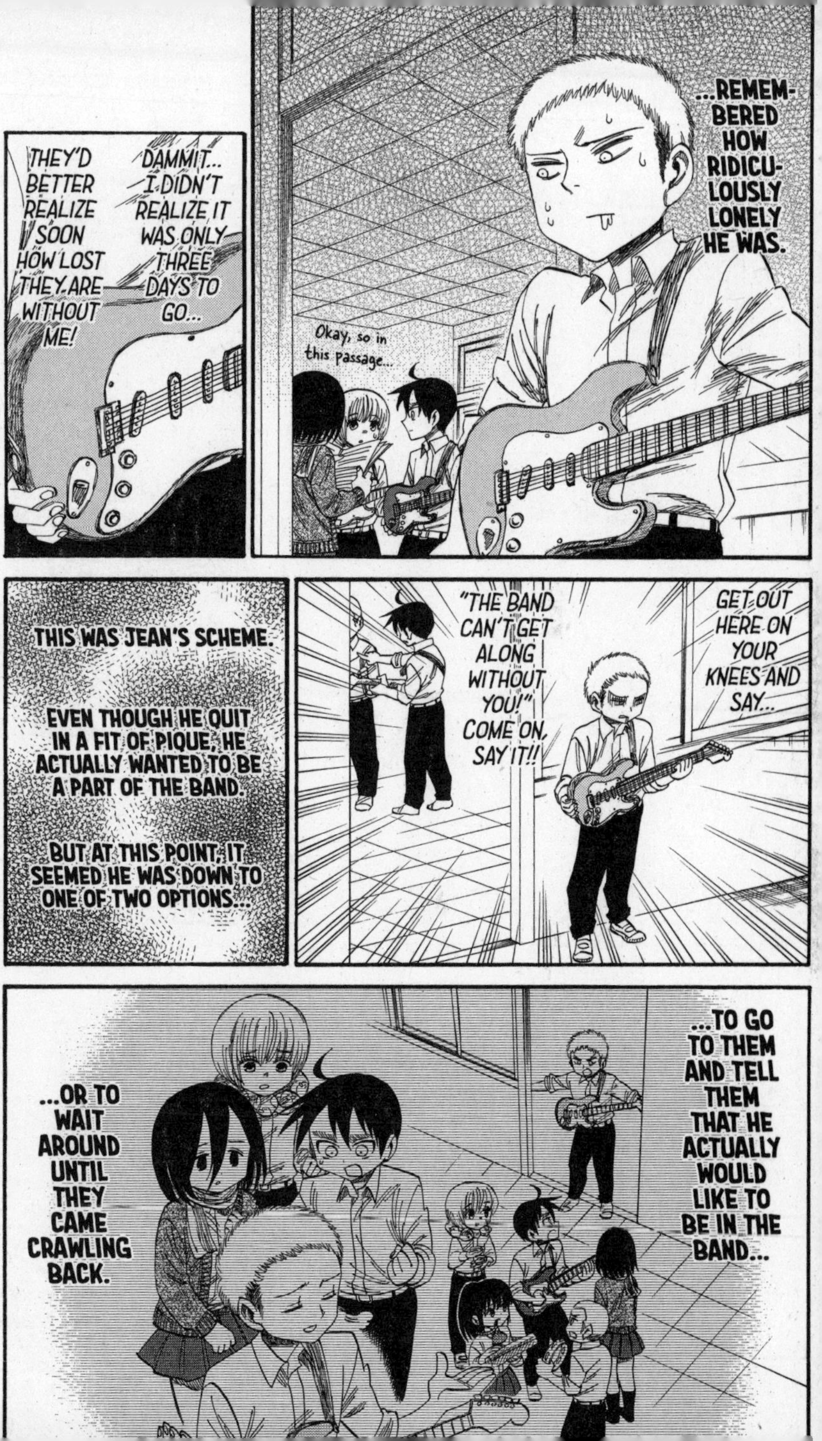
...REMEMBERED HOW RIDICULOUSLY LONELY HE WAS.
Okay, so in this passage...
DAMMIT... I DIDN'T REALIZE IT WAS ONLY THREE DAYS TO GO...
THEY'D BETTER REALIZE SOON HOW LOST THEY ARE WITHOUT ME!
GET OUT HERE ON YOUR KNEES AND SAY...
"THE BAND CAN'T GET ALONG WITHOUT YOU!" COME ON, SAY IT!!
THIS WAS JEAN'S SCHEME.
EVEN THOUGH HE QUIT IN A FIT OF PIQUE, HE ACTUALLY WANTED TO BE A PART OF THE BAND.
BUT AT THIS POINT, IT SEEMED HE WAS DOWN TO ONE OF TWO OPTIONS...
...TO GO TO THEM AND TELL THEM THAT HE ACTUALLY WOULD LIKE TO BE IN THE BAND...
...OR TO WAIT AROUND UNTIL THEY CAME CRAWLING BACK.

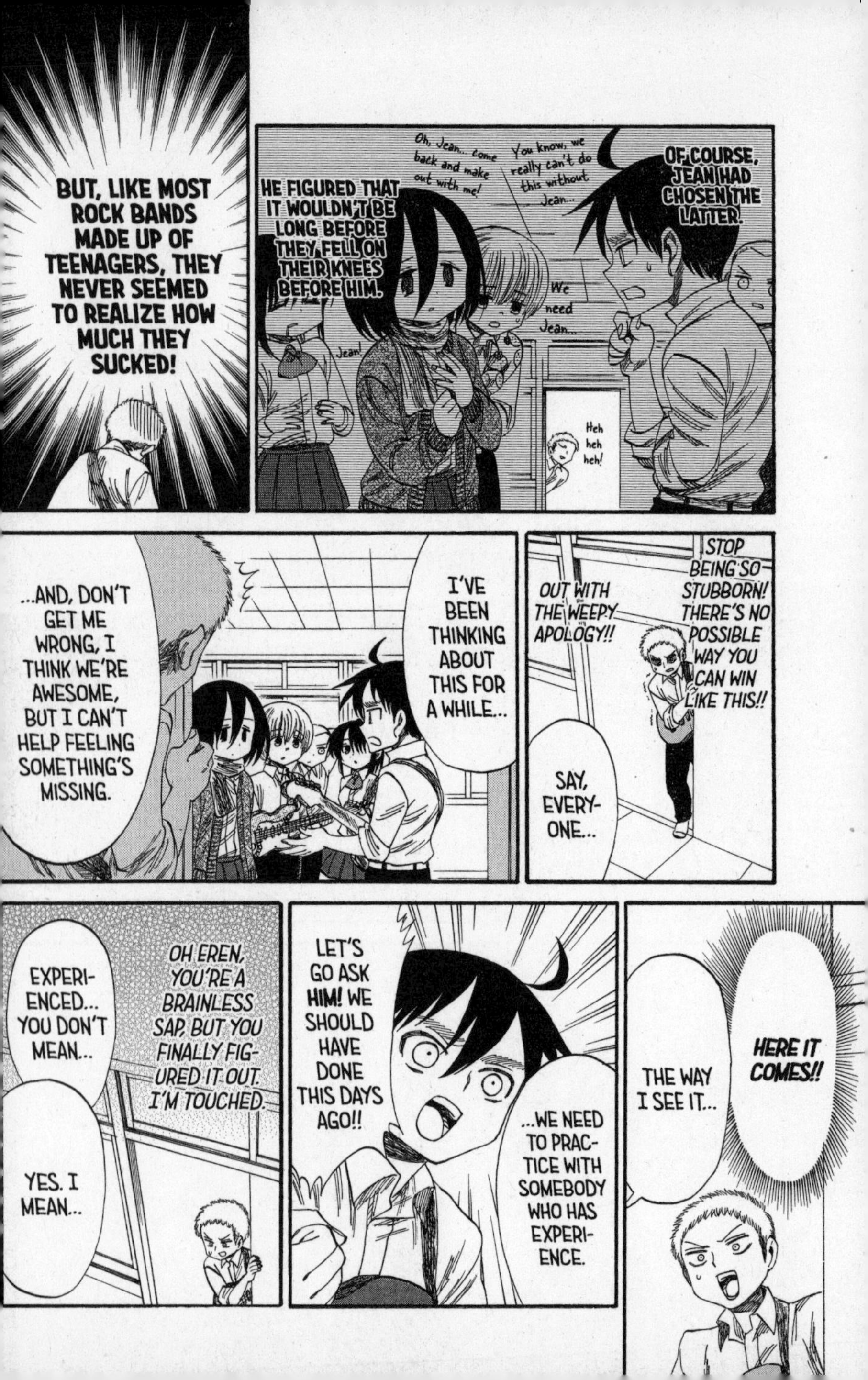

OF COURSE, JEAN HAD CHOSEN THE LATTER.
You know, we really can't do this without Jean...
Oh, Jean... come back and make out with me!
HE FIGURED THAT IT WOULDN'T BE LONG BEFORE THEY FELL ON THEIR KNEES BEFORE HIM.
We need Jean...
Jean!
Heh heh heh!
BUT, LIKE MOST ROCK BANDS MADE UP OF TEENAGERS, THEY NEVER SEEMED TO REALIZE HOW MUCH THEY SUCKED!
STOP BEING SO STUBBORN! THERE'S NO POSSIBLE WAY YOU CAN WIN LIKE THIS!!
OUT WITH THE WEEPY APOLOGY!!
SAY, EVERYONE...
I'VE BEEN THINKING ABOUT THIS FOR A WHILE...
...AND, DON'T GET ME WRONG, I THINK WE'RE AWESOME, BUT I CAN'T HELP FEELING SOMETHING'S MISSING.
HERE IT COMES!!
THE WAY I SEE IT...
...WE NEED TO PRACTICE WITH SOMEBODY WHO HAS EXPERIENCE.
LET'S GO ASK HIM! WE SHOULD HAVE DONE THIS DAYS AGO!!
OH EREN, YOU'RE A BRAINLESS SAP, BUT YOU FINALLY FIGURED IT OUT. I'M TOUCHED.
EXPERIENCED... YOU DON'T MEAN...
YES. I MEAN...

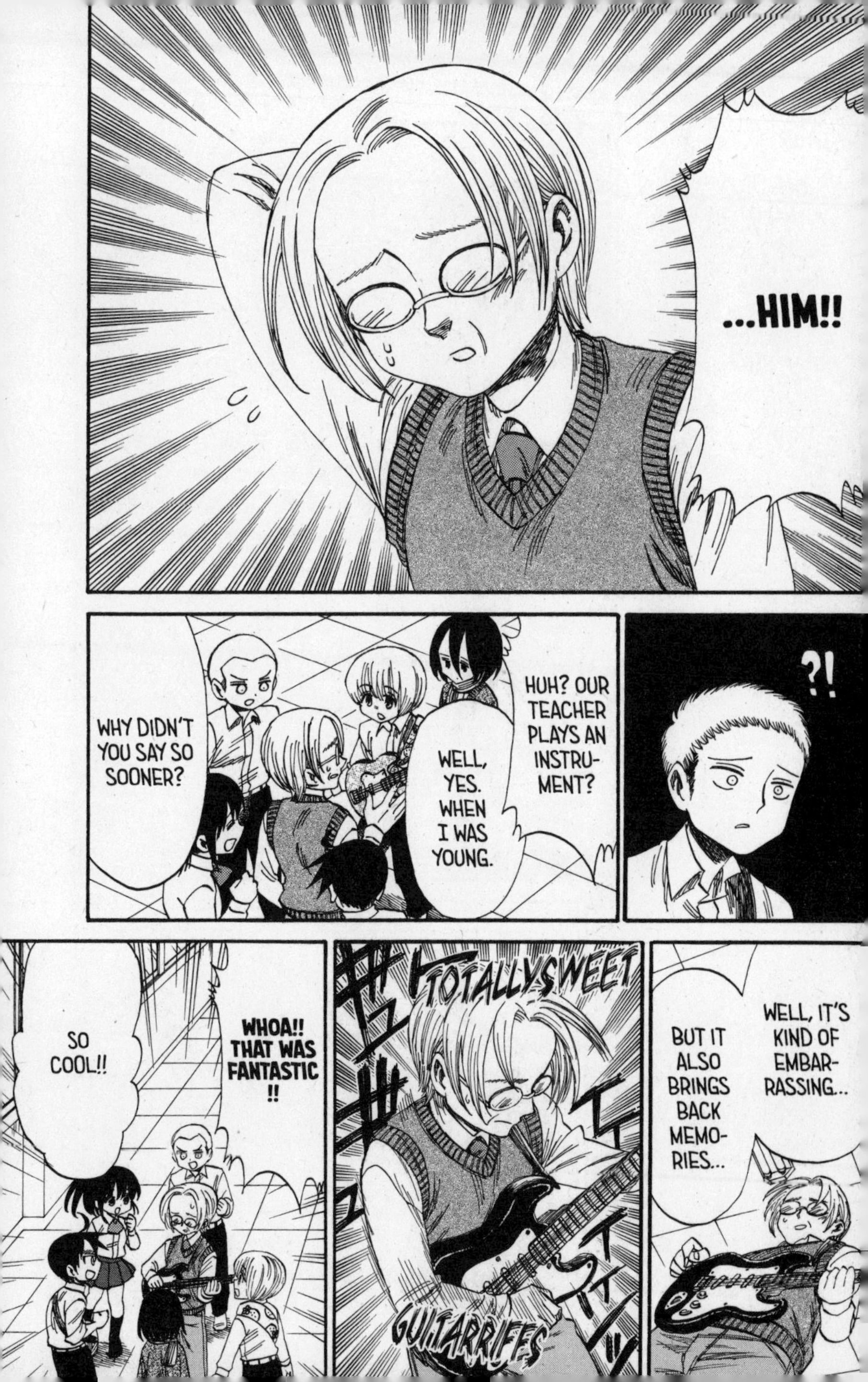

...HIM!!
?!
HUH? OUR TEACHER PLAYS AN INSTRUMENT?
WELL, YES. WHEN I WAS YOUNG.
WHY DIDN'T YOU SAY SO SOONER?
WELL, IT'S KIND OF EMBARRASSING...
BUT IT ALSO BRINGS BACK MEMORIES...
TOTALLYSWEET
GUITARRIFFS
WHOA!! THAT WAS FANTASTIC!!
SO COOL!!

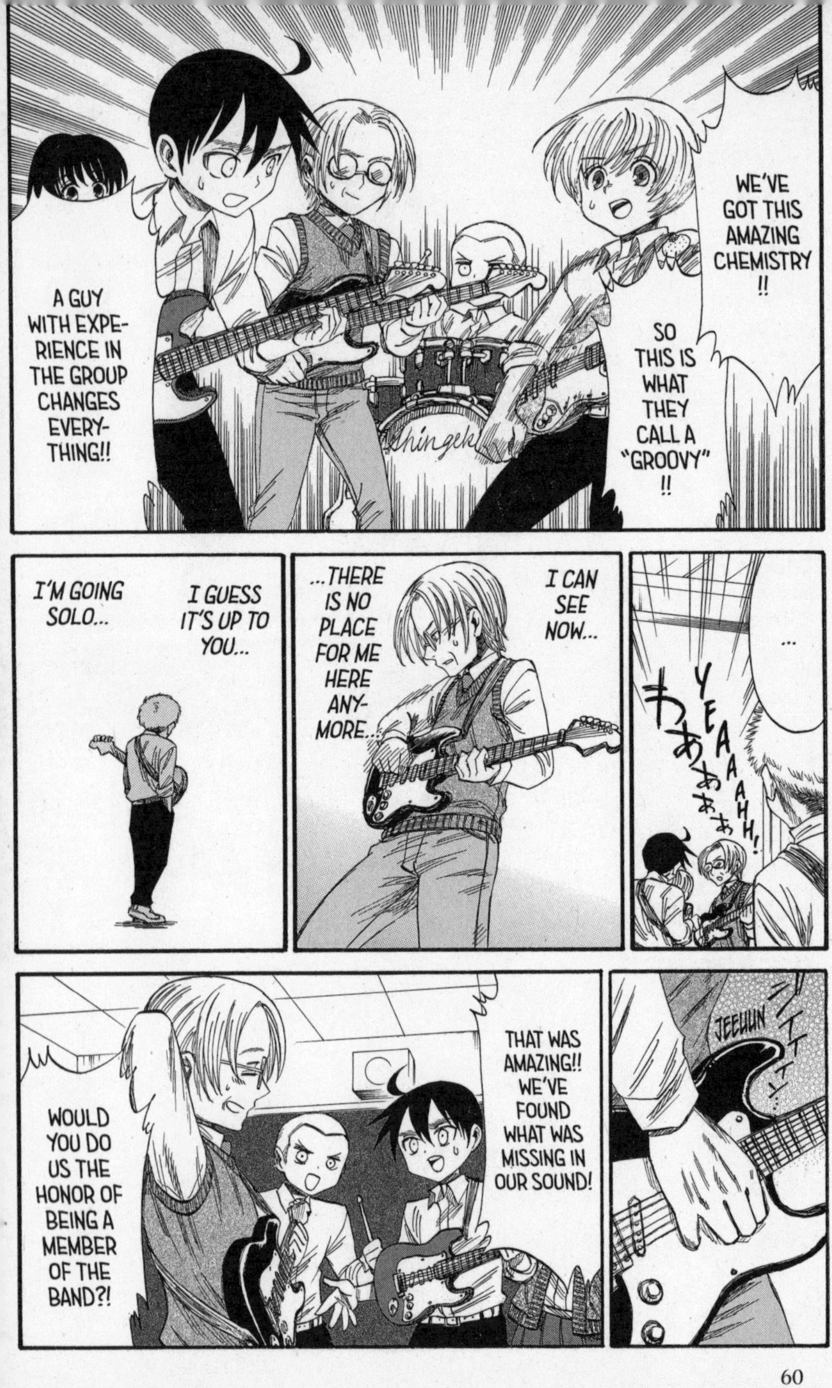
WE'VE GOT THIS AMAZING CHEMISTRY!!
SO THIS IS WHAT THEY CALL A "GROOVY"!!
A GUY WITH EXPERIENCE IN THE GROUP CHANGES EVERYTHING!!
...
わあああ
YEAAAAHH!
I CAN SEE NOW...
...THERE IS NO PLACE FOR ME HERE ANYMORE...
I GUESS IT'S UP TO YOU...
I'M GOING SOLO...
ジイイイン...
JEEUUN
THAT WAS AMAZING!! WE'VE FOUND WHAT WAS MISSING IN OUR SOUND!
WOULD YOU DO US THE HONOR OF BEING A MEMBER OF THE BAND?!

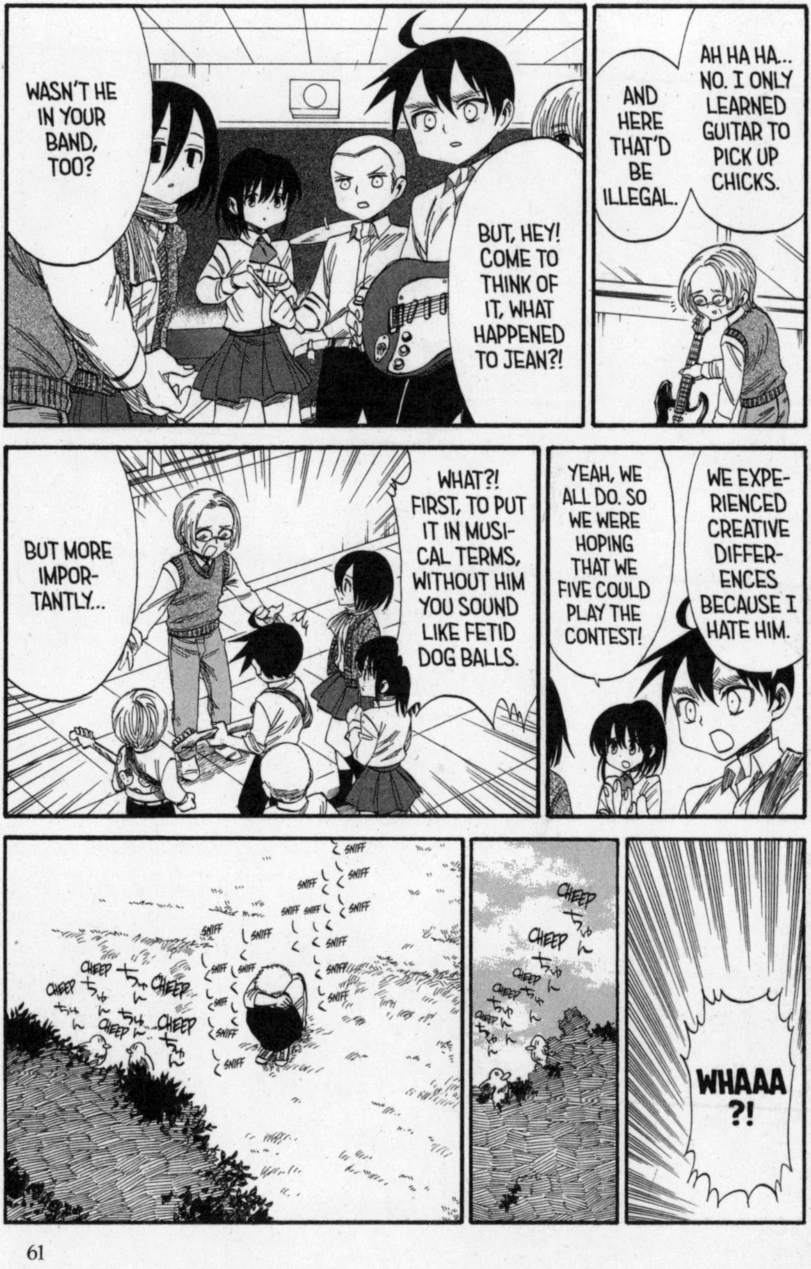
AH HA HA... NO. I ONLY LEARNED GUITAR TO PICK UP CHICKS.
AND HERE THAT'D BE ILLEGAL.
BUT, HEY! COME TO THINK OF IT, WHAT HAPPENED TO JEAN?!
WASN'T HE IN YOUR BAND, TOO?
WE EXPERIENCED CREATIVE DIFFERENCES BECAUSE I HATE HIM.
YEAH, WE ALL DO. SO WE WERE HOPING THAT WE FIVE COULD PLAY THE CONTEST!
WHAT?! FIRST, TO PUT IT IN MUSICAL TERMS, WITHOUT HIM YOU SOUND LIKE FETID DOG BALLS.
BUT MORE IMPORTANTLY...
WHAAA ?!
CHEEP ちゅん
CHEEP ちゅん
CHEEP ちゅん
CHEEP ちゅん
CHEEP ちゅん
SNIFF
SNIFF
SNIFF
SNIFF
CHEEP ちゅん
CHEEP ちゅん
CHEEP ちゅん
CHEEP ちゅん
CHEEP ちゅん

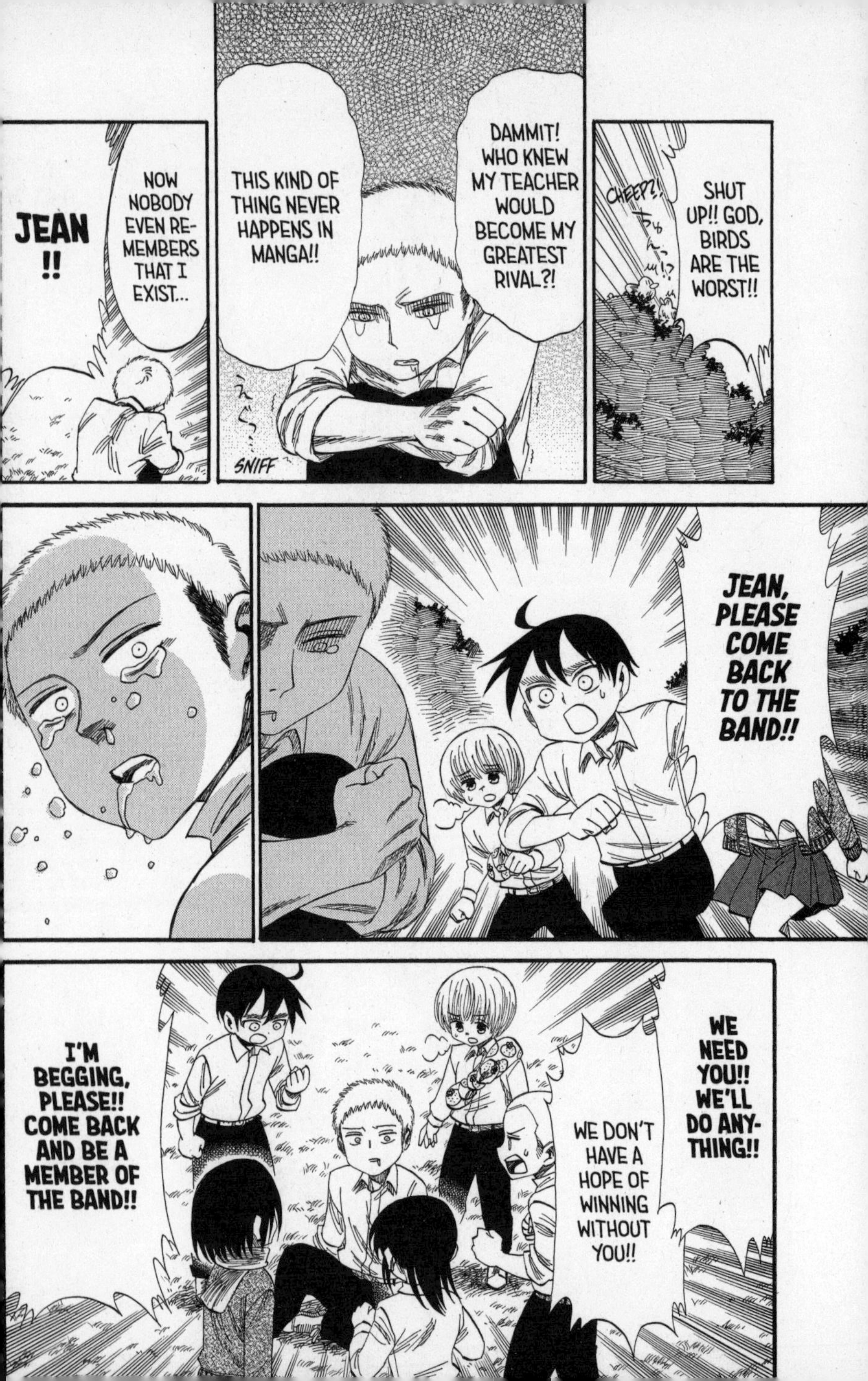
CHEEP?!
SHUT UP!! GOD, BIRDS ARE THE WORST!!
DAMMIT! WHO KNEW MY TEACHER WOULD BECOME MY GREATEST RIVAL?!
THIS KIND OF THING NEVER HAPPENS IN MANGA!!
SNIFF
NOW NOBODY EVEN RE-MEMBERS THAT I EXIST...
JEAN !!
JEAN, PLEASE COME BACK TO THE BAND!!
WE NEED YOU!! WE'LL DO ANY-THING!!
WE DON'T HAVE A HOPE OF WINNING WITHOUT YOU!!
I'M BEGGING, PLEASE!! COME BACK AND BE A MEMBER OF THE BAND!!

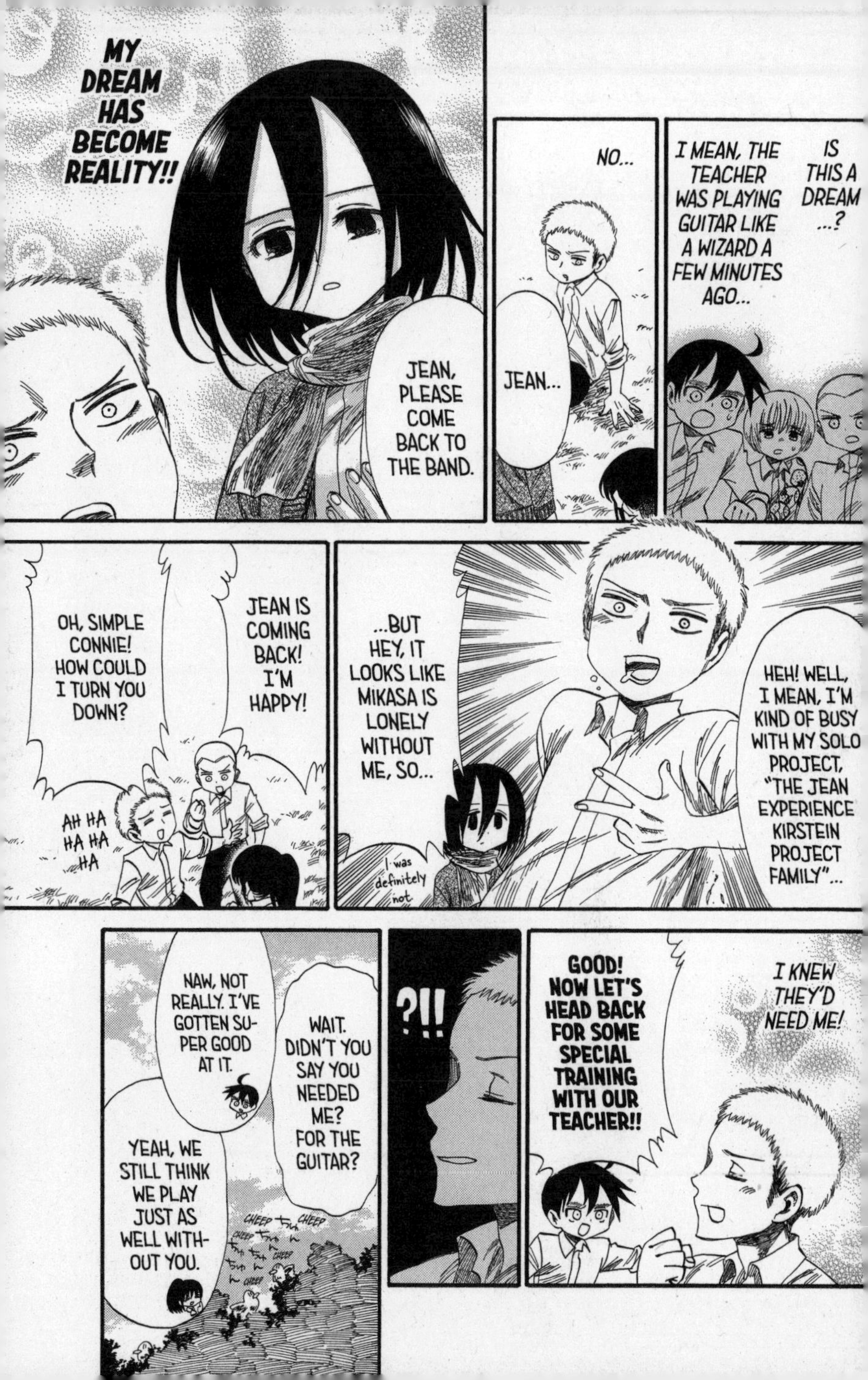
IS THIS A DREAM ...?
I MEAN, THE TEACHER WAS PLAYING GUITAR LIKE A WIZARD A FEW MINUTES AGO...
NO...
JEAN...
JEAN, PLEASE COME BACK TO THE BAND.
MY DREAM HAS BECOME REALITY!!
HEH! WELL, I MEAN, I'M KIND OF BUSY WITH MY SOLO PROJECT, "THE JEAN EXPERIENCE KIRSTEIN PROJECT FAMILY"...
...BUT HEY, IT LOOKS LIKE MIKASA IS LONELY WITHOUT ME, SO...
I was definitely not
JEAN IS COMING BACK! I'M HAPPY!
OH, SIMPLE CONNIE! HOW COULD I TURN YOU DOWN?
AH HA HA HA HA
I KNEW THEY'D NEED ME!
GOOD! NOW LET'S HEAD BACK FOR SOME SPECIAL TRAINING WITH OUR TEACHER!!
?!!
WAIT. DIDN'T YOU SAY YOU NEEDED ME? FOR THE GUITAR?
NAW, NOT REALLY. I'VE GOTTEN SUPER GOOD AT IT.
YEAH, WE STILL THINK WE PLAY JUST AS WELL WITHOUT YOU.
CHEEP CHEEP CHEEP CHEEP CHEEP

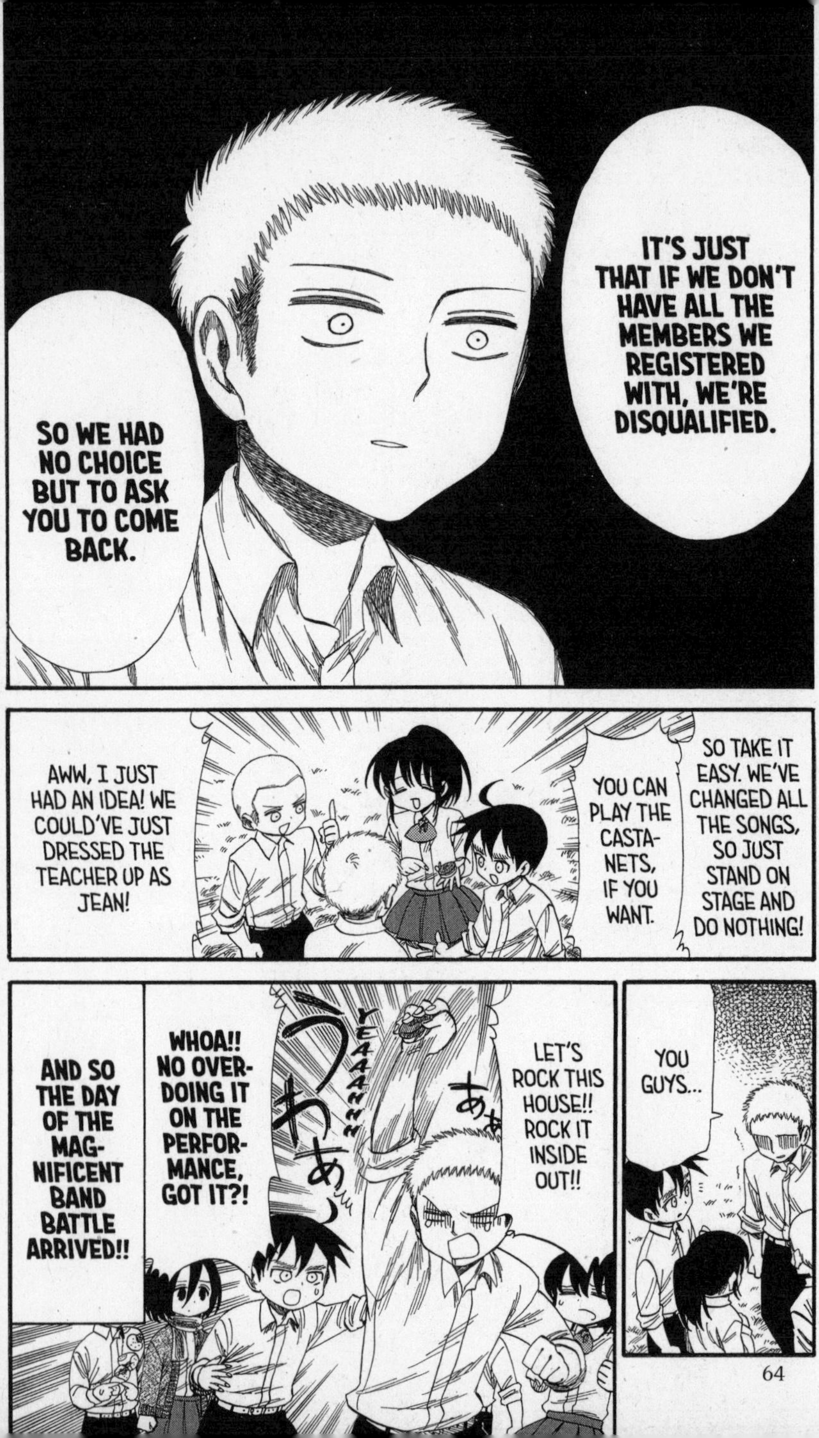
IT'S JUST THAT IF WE DON'T HAVE ALL THE MEMBERS WE REGISTERED WITH, WE'RE DISQUALIFIED.
SO WE HAD NO CHOICE BUT TO ASK YOU TO COME BACK.
SO TAKE IT EASY. WE'VE CHANGED ALL THE SONGS, SO JUST STAND ON STAGE AND DO NOTHING!
YOU CAN PLAY THE CASTANETS, IF YOU WANT.
AWW, I JUST HAD AN IDEA! WE COULD'VE JUST DRESSED THE TEACHER UP AS JEAN!
YOU GUYS...
LET'S ROCK THIS HOUSE!! ROCK IT INSIDE OUT!!
ああ
うわあ
YEAAAAHHH
WHOA!! NO OVERDOING IT ON THE PERFORMANCE, GOT IT?!
AND SO THE DAY OF THE MAGNIFICENT BAND BATTLE ARRIVED!!

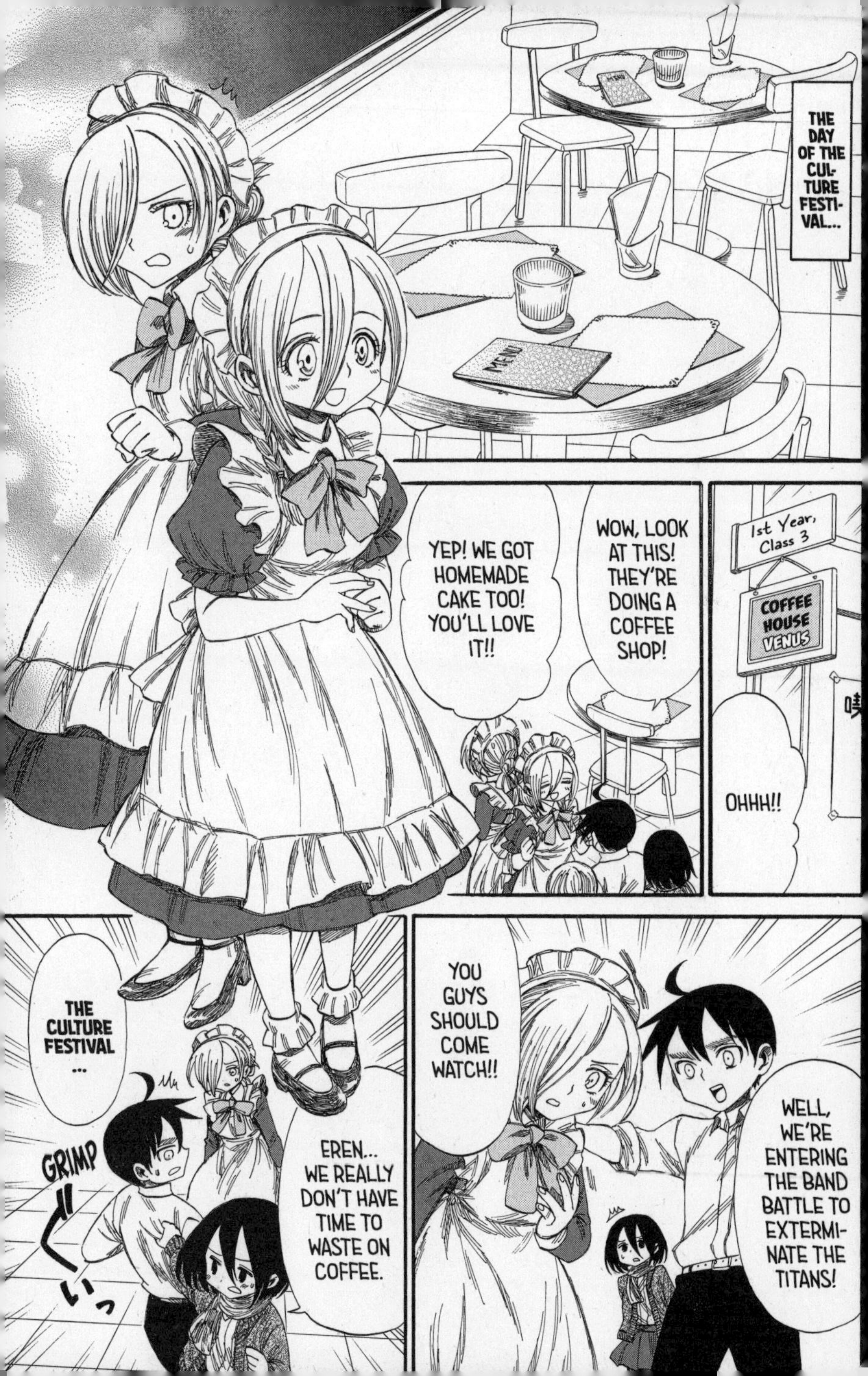
THE DAY OF THE CULTURE FESTIVAL...
1st Year, Class 3
COFFEE HOUSE VENUS
OHHH!!
WOW, LOOK AT THIS! THEY'RE DOING A COFFEE SHOP!
YEP! WE GOT HOMEMADE CAKE TOO! YOU'LL LOVE IT!!
WELL, WE'RE ENTERING THE BAND BATTLE TO EXTERMINATE THE TITANS!
YOU GUYS SHOULD COME WATCH!!
EREN... WE REALLY DON'T HAVE TIME TO WASTE ON COFFEE.
GRIMP
THE CULTURE FESTIVAL ...

THIRTY-FIFTH PERIOD: HOW TO TAKE THE CULTURE FROM A CULTURE FAIR

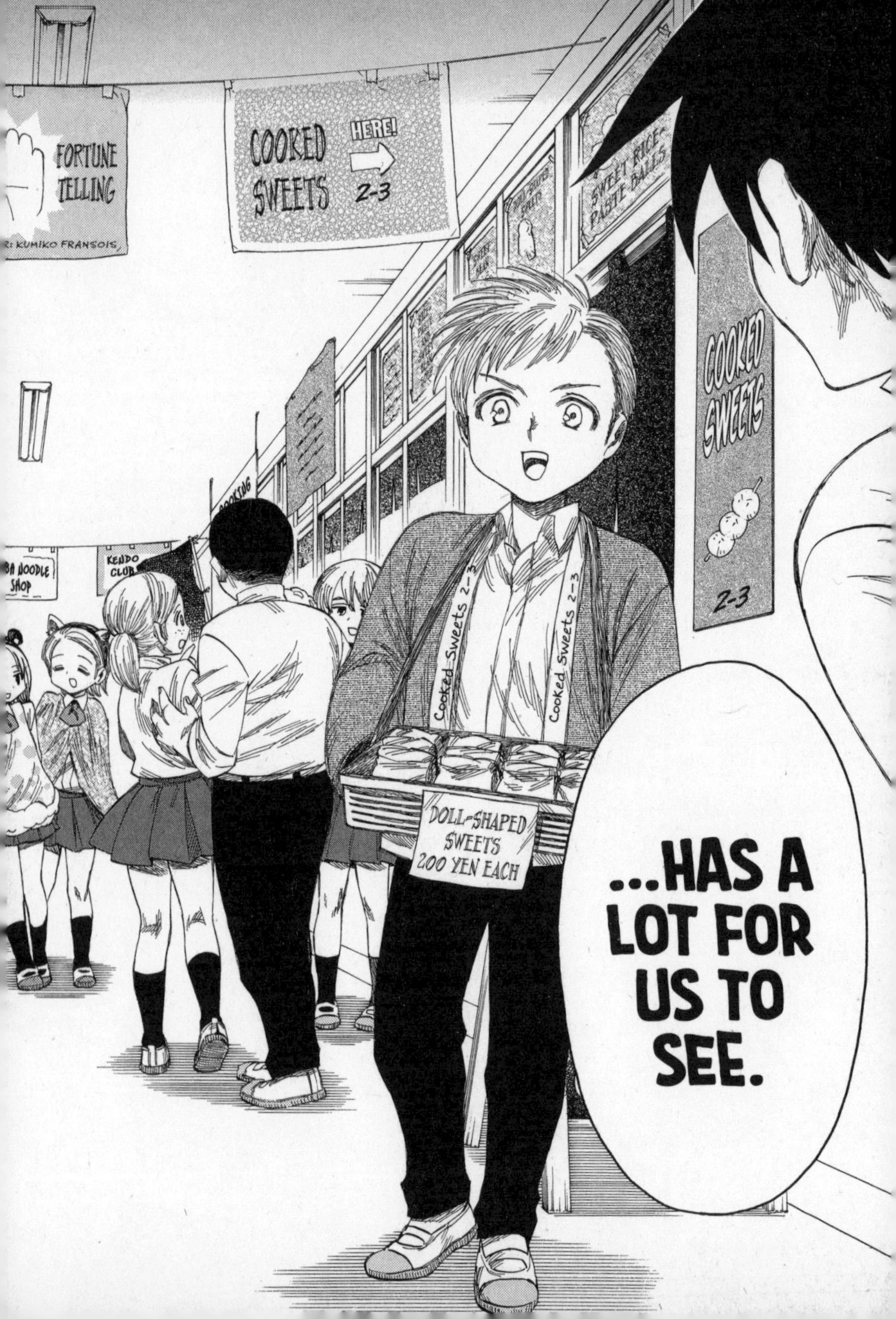
...HAS A LOT FOR US TO SEE.
COOKED SWEETS
2-3
SWEET RICE-PASTE BALLS
COOKED SWEETS
HERE!
2-3
FORTUNE TELLING
KUMIKO FRANSOIS
KENDO CLUB
Cooked Sweets 2-3
Cooked Sweets 2-3
DOLL-SHAPED SWEETS
200 YEN EACH

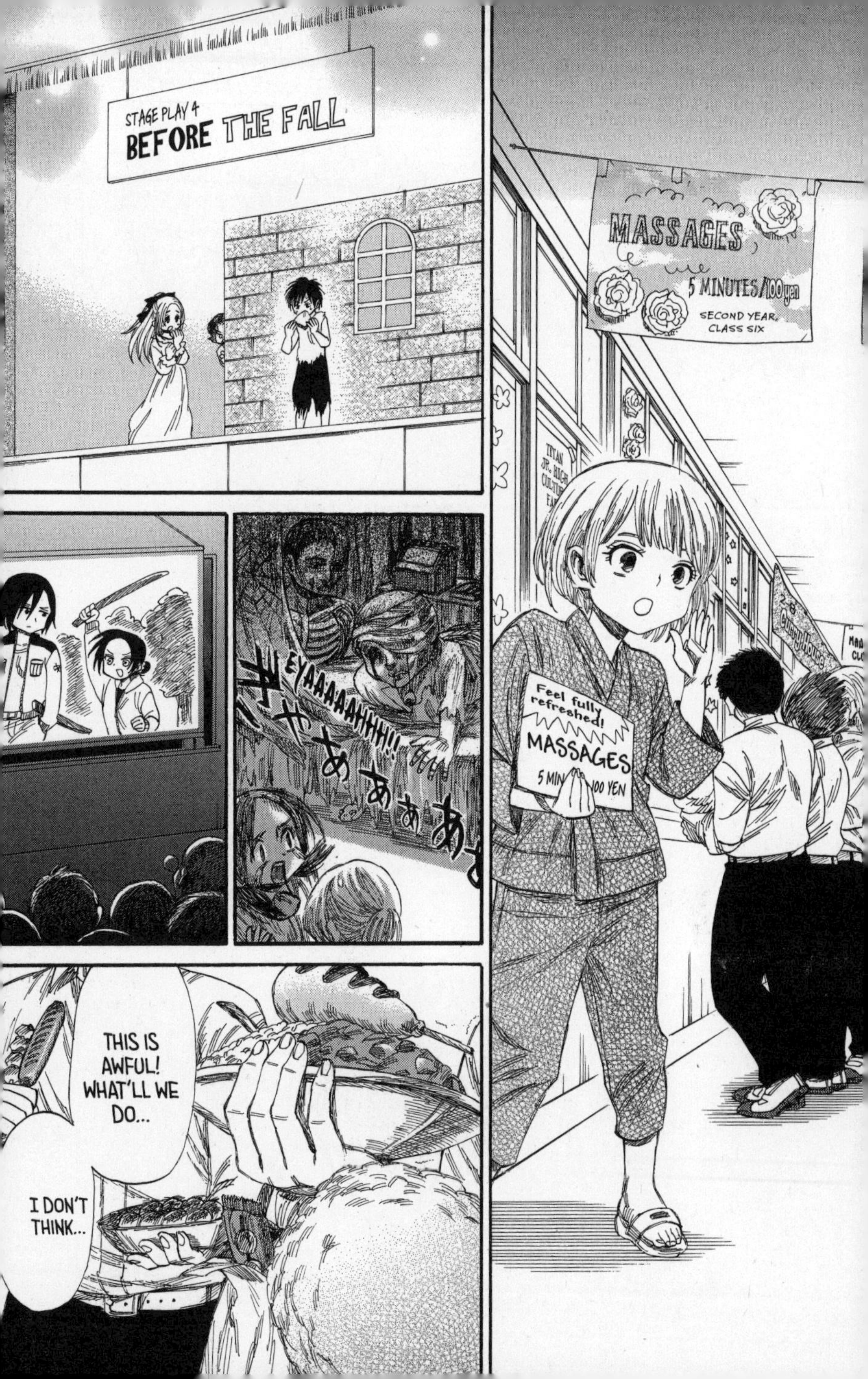
MASSAGES
5 MINUTES/100 yen
SECOND YEAR, CLASS SIX
Feel fully refreshed!
MASSAGES
5 MIN
100 YEN
STAGE PLAY 4
BEFORE THE FALL
EYAAAAAHHH!!
THIS IS AWFUL! WHAT'LL WE DO...
I DON'T THINK...

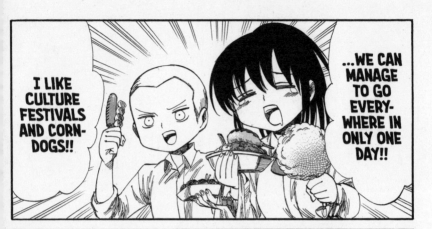

...WE CAN MANAGE TO GO EVERY-WHERE IN ONLY ONE DAY!!
I LIKE CULTURE FESTIVALS AND CORN-DOGS!!
EREN, DID YOU KNOW THERE WERE CORN-DOGS AT CULTURE FESTIVALS?
TEA CEREMONY CLUB ← TEA ROOM
I SURE DID, CONNIE! ISN'T IT GREAT?
IT'S LIKE WE'RE IN SCHOOL BUT NOT IN SCHOOL!
BUT AREN'T YOU GUYS EATING TOO MUCH?
WE'RE ABOUT TO GO ON STAGE...
NNG
DONNG
DINNG
DONNG
All students please gather in the gym-nasium.
HEY! SEE?
It's almost time for Attack Junior High's world-famous...
CHATTER
CHATTER
TWITCH
...BATTLE OF THE BANDS!!

*250 yen is about $2.50.

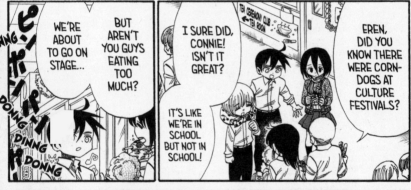

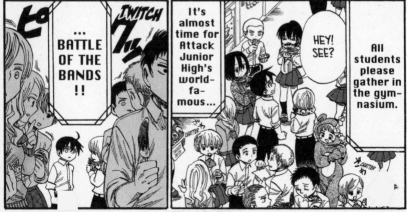

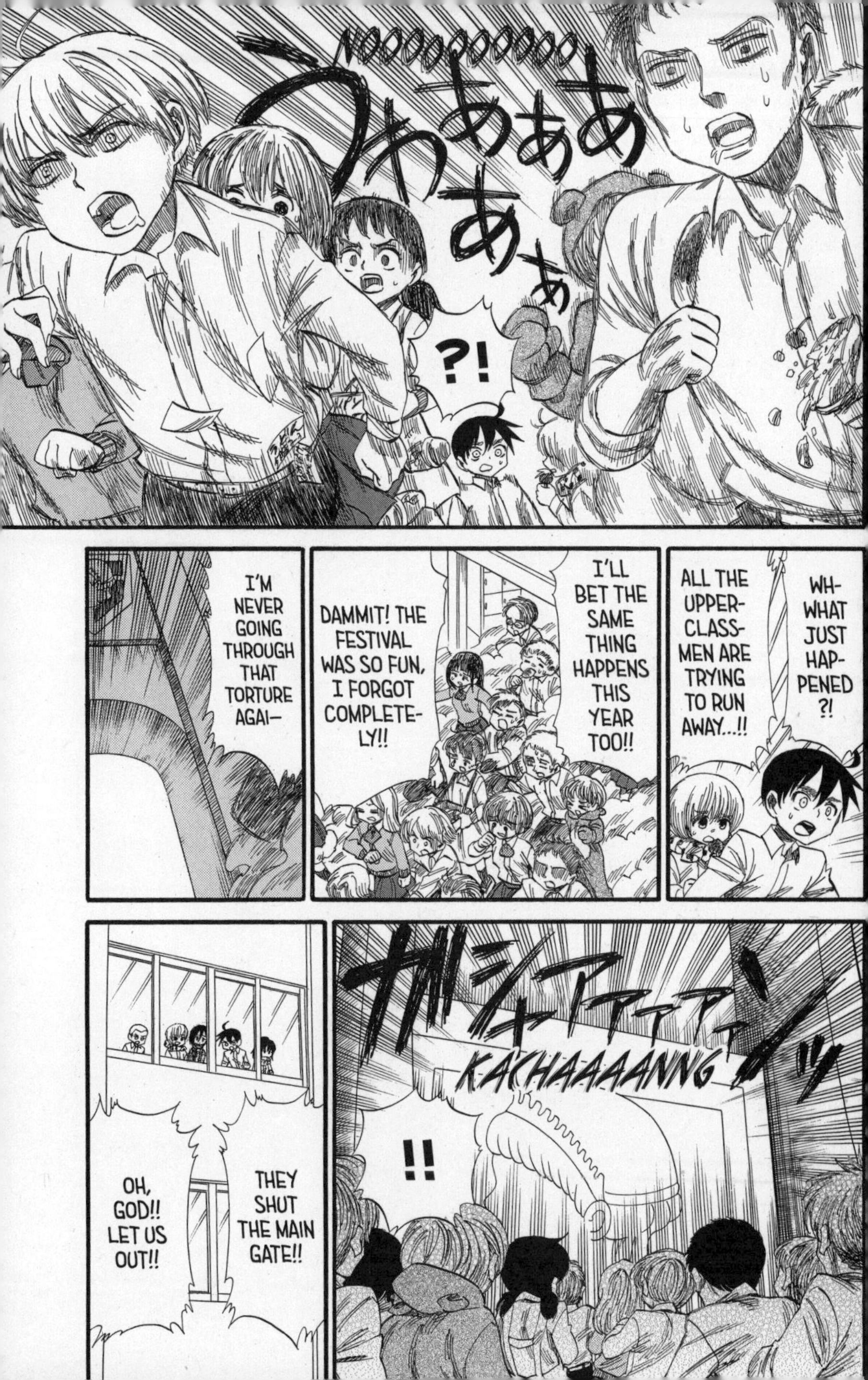

NOOOOOOOOOOO
うわああああぁぁ
?!
WH-WHAT JUST HAP-PENED?!
ALL THE UPPER-CLASS-MEN ARE TRYING TO RUN AWAY...!!
I'LL BET THE SAME THING HAPPENS THIS YEAR TOO!!
DAMMIT! THE FESTIVAL WAS SO FUN, I FORGOT COMPLETE-LY!!
I'M NEVER GOING THROUGH THAT TORTURE AGAI–
KACHAAAAANNG
!!
THEY SHUT THE MAIN GATE!!
OH, GOD!! LET US OUT!!

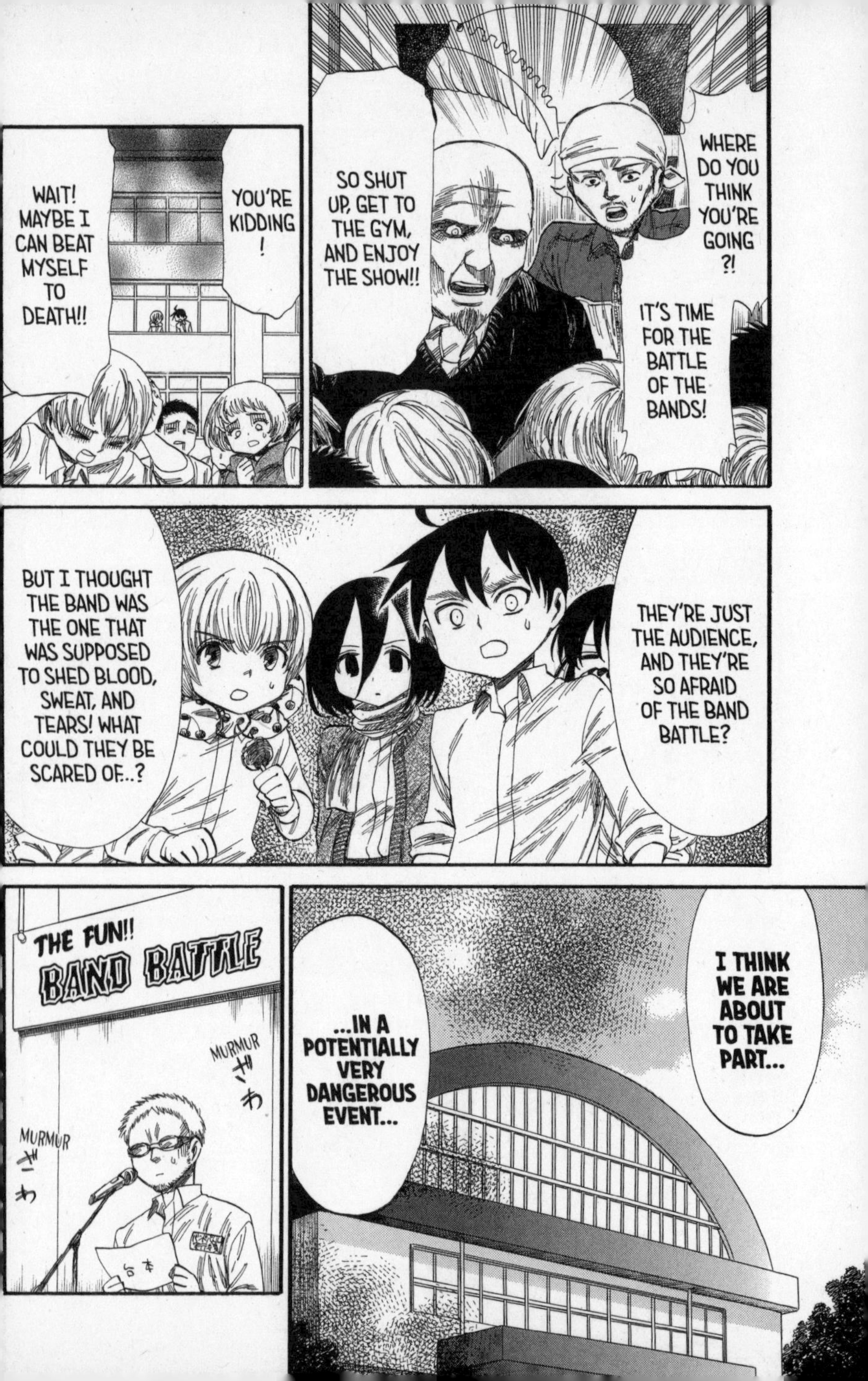
WHERE DO YOU THINK YOU'RE GOING ?!
IT'S TIME FOR THE BATTLE OF THE BANDS!
SO SHUT UP, GET TO THE GYM, AND ENJOY THE SHOW!!
YOU'RE KIDDING !
WAIT! MAYBE I CAN BEAT MYSELF TO DEATH!!
THEY'RE JUST THE AUDIENCE, AND THEY'RE SO AFRAID OF THE BAND BATTLE?
BUT I THOUGHT THE BAND WAS THE ONE THAT WAS SUPPOSED TO SHED BLOOD, SWEAT, AND TEARS! WHAT COULD THEY BE SCARED OF...?
I THINK WE ARE ABOUT TO TAKE PART...
...IN A POTENTIALLY VERY DANGEROUS EVENT...
THE FUN!!
BAND BATTLE
MURMUR ざわ
MURMUR ざわ
台本

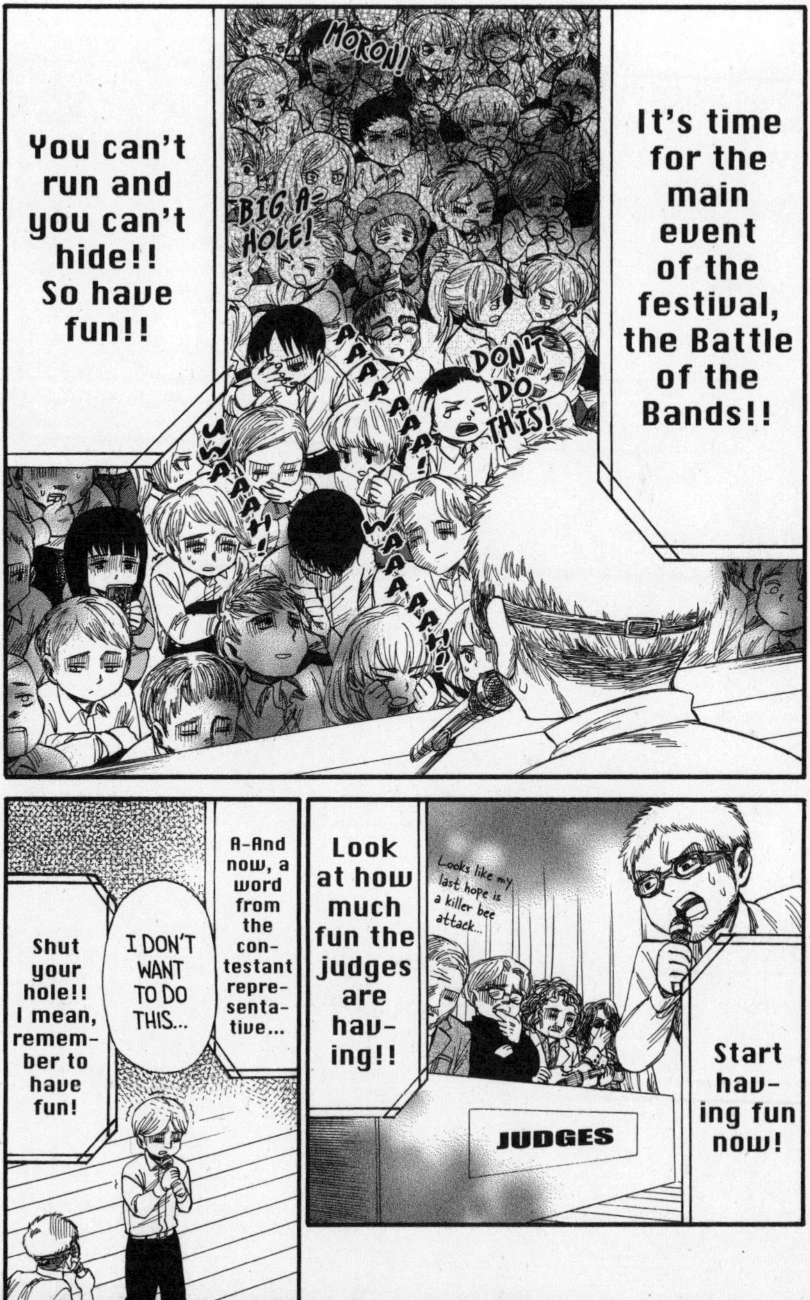
It's time for the main event of the festival, the Battle of the Bands!!
MORON!
DON'T DO THIS!
AAAAAA!
WAAAAAAH!
BIG A-HOLE!
UWAAAAH!
You can't run and you can't hide!! So have fun!!
Start hav-ing fun now!
Looks like my last hope is a killer bee attack...
JUDGES
Look at how much fun the judges are hav-ing!!
A-And now, a word from the con-testant repre-senta-tive...
I DON'T WANT TO DO THIS...
Shut your hole!! I mean, remem-ber to have fun!

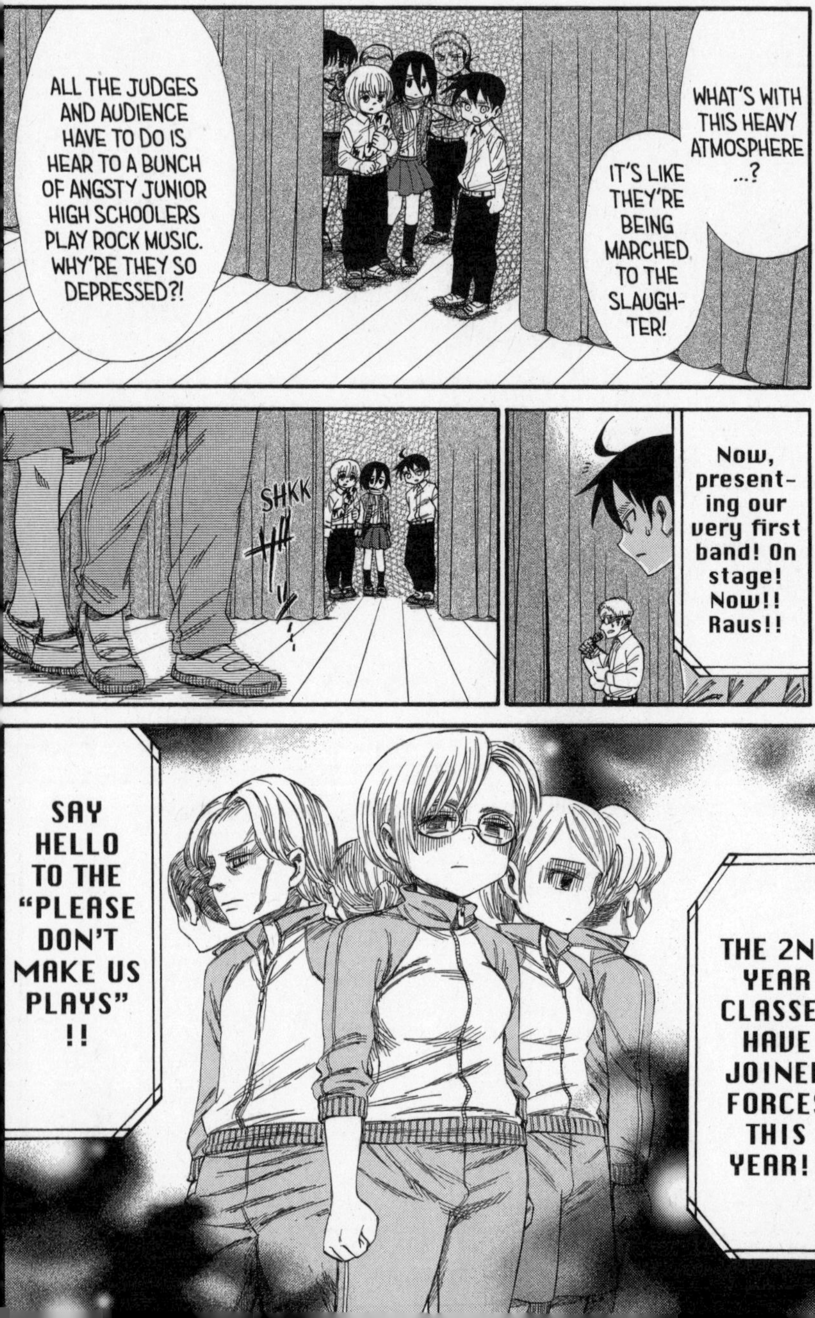
WHAT'S WITH THIS HEAVY ATMOSPHERE ...?
IT'S LIKE THEY'RE BEING MARCHED TO THE SLAUGH-TER!
ALL THE JUDGES AND AUDIENCE HAVE TO DO IS HEAR TO A BUNCH OF ANGSTY JUNIOR HIGH SCHOOLERS PLAY ROCK MUSIC. WHY'RE THEY SO DEPRESSED?!
Now, present-ing our very first band! On stage! Now!! Raus!!
SHKK
THE 2ND YEAR CLASSES HAVE JOINED FORCES THIS YEAR!!
SAY HELLO TO THE "PLEASE DON'T MAKE US PLAYS" !!

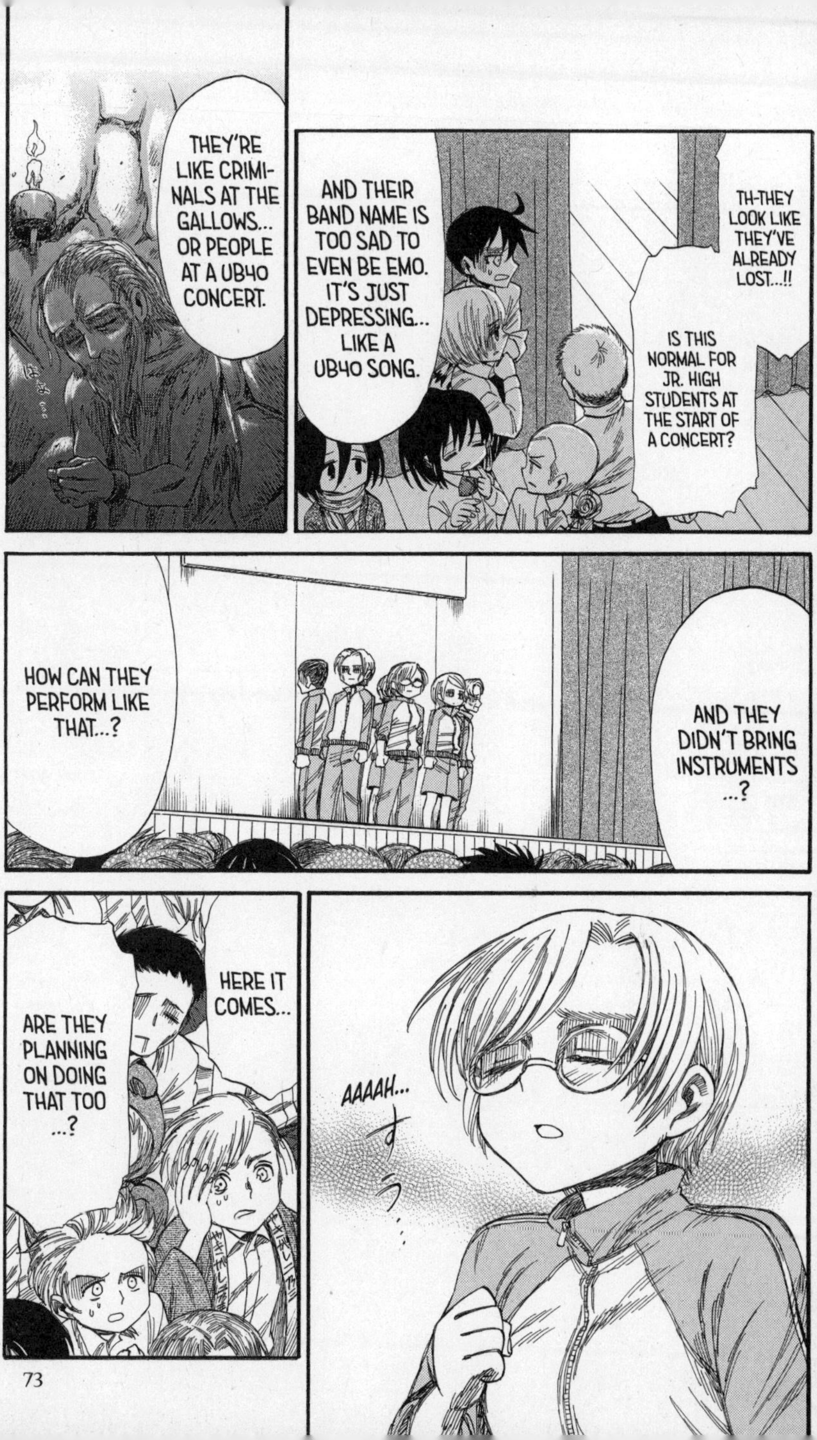
TH-THEY LOOK LIKE THEY'VE ALREADY LOST...!!
IS THIS NORMAL FOR JR. HIGH STUDENTS AT THE START OF A CONCERT?
AND THEIR BAND NAME IS TOO SAD TO EVEN BE EMO. IT'S JUST DEPRESSING... LIKE A UB40 SONG.
THEY'RE LIKE CRIMINALS AT THE GALLOWS... OR PEOPLE AT A UB40 CONCERT.
AND THEY DIDN'T BRING INSTRUMENTS ...?
HOW CAN THEY PERFORM LIKE THAT...?
AAAAH...
HERE IT COMES...
ARE THEY PLANNING ON DOING THAT TOO ...?

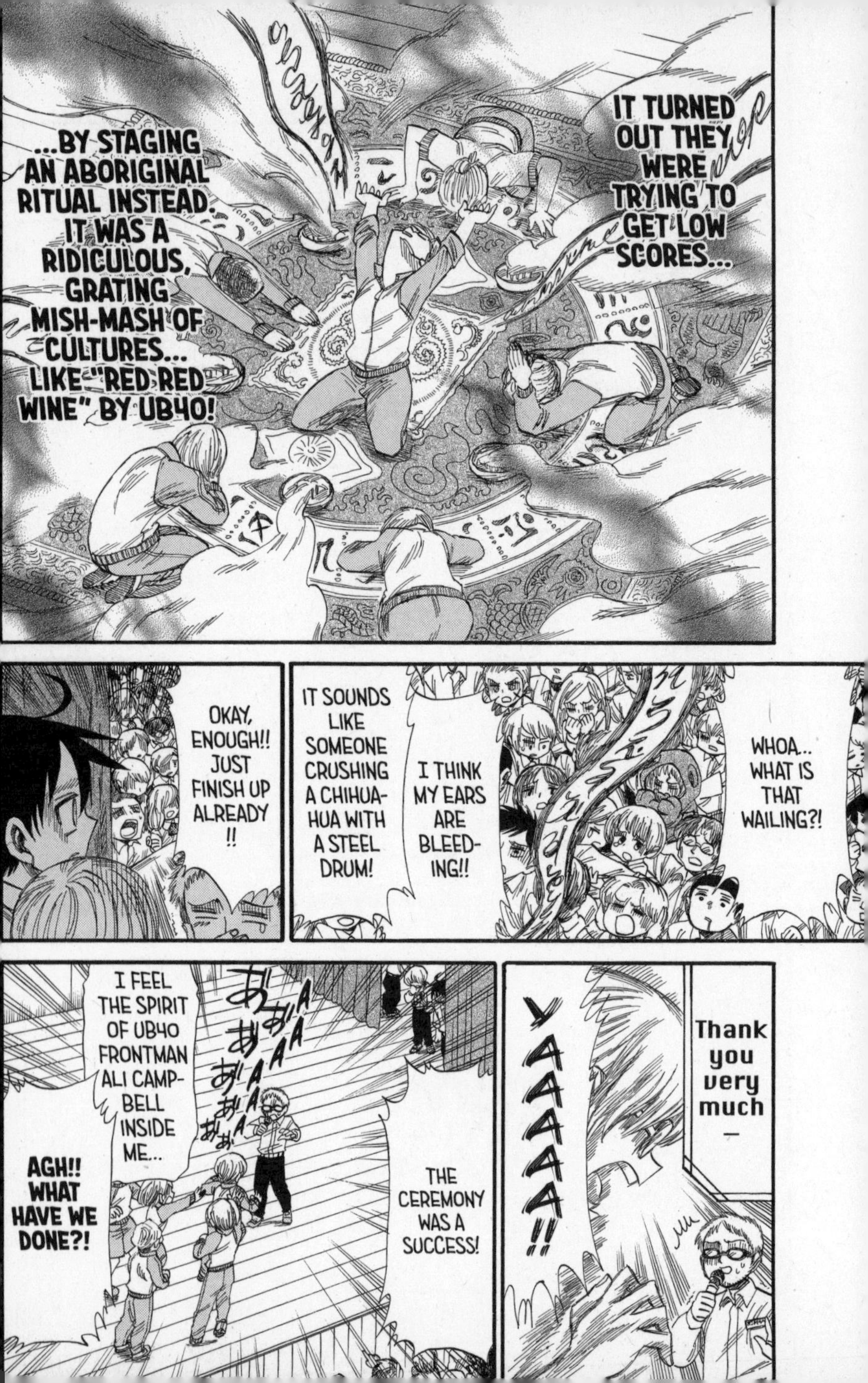
IT TURNED OUT THEY WERE TRYING TO GET LOW SCORES...
...BY STAGING AN ABORIGINAL RITUAL INSTEAD. IT WAS A RIDICULOUS, GRATING MISH-MASH OF CULTURES... LIKE "RED RED WINE" BY UB40!
WHOA... WHAT IS THAT WAILING?!
I THINK MY EARS ARE BLEED-ING!!
IT SOUNDS LIKE SOMEONE CRUSHING A CHIHUA-HUA WITH A STEEL DRUM!
OKAY, ENOUGH!! JUST FINISH UP ALREADY!!
Thank you very much —
YAAAAA!!
あAあAあAあAあAあA
I FEEL THE SPIRIT OF UB40 FRONTMAN ALI CAMP-BELL INSIDE ME...
THE CEREMONY WAS A SUCCESS!
AGH!! WHAT HAVE WE DONE?!

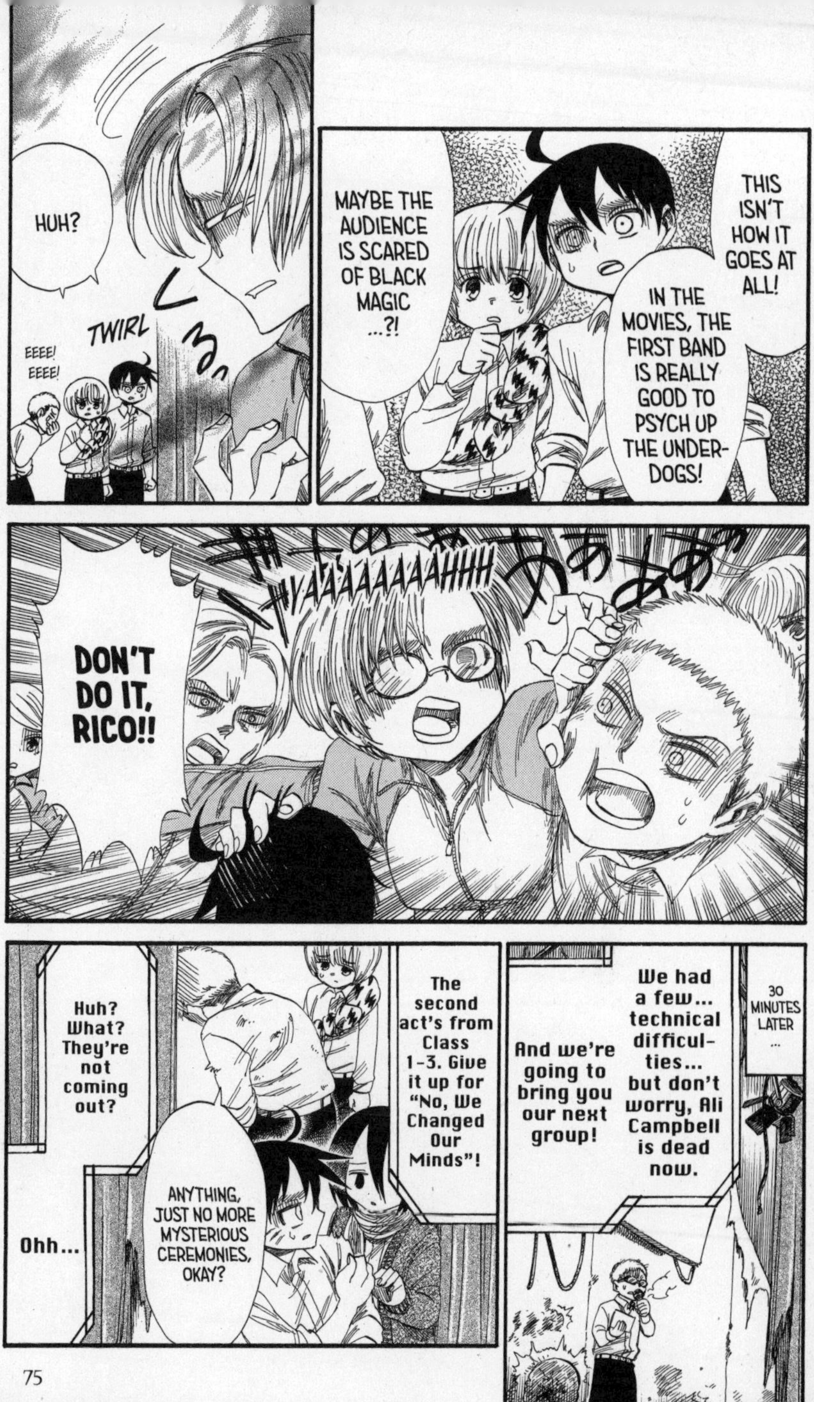
THIS ISN'T HOW IT GOES AT ALL!
IN THE MOVIES, THE FIRST BAND IS REALLY GOOD TO PSYCH UP THE UNDER-DOGS!
MAYBE THE AUDIENCE IS SCARED OF BLACK MAGIC ...?!
HUH?
TWIRL
EEEE! EEEE!
HYAAAAAAAHHH
DON'T DO IT, RICO!!
30 MINUTES LATER ...
We had a few... technical difficul-ties... but don't worry, Ali Campbell is dead now.
And we're going to bring you our next group!
The second act's from Class 1-3. Give it up for "No, We Changed Our Minds"!
Huh? What? They're not coming out?
ANYTHING, JUST NO MORE MYSTERIOUS CEREMONIES, OKAY?
Ohh...

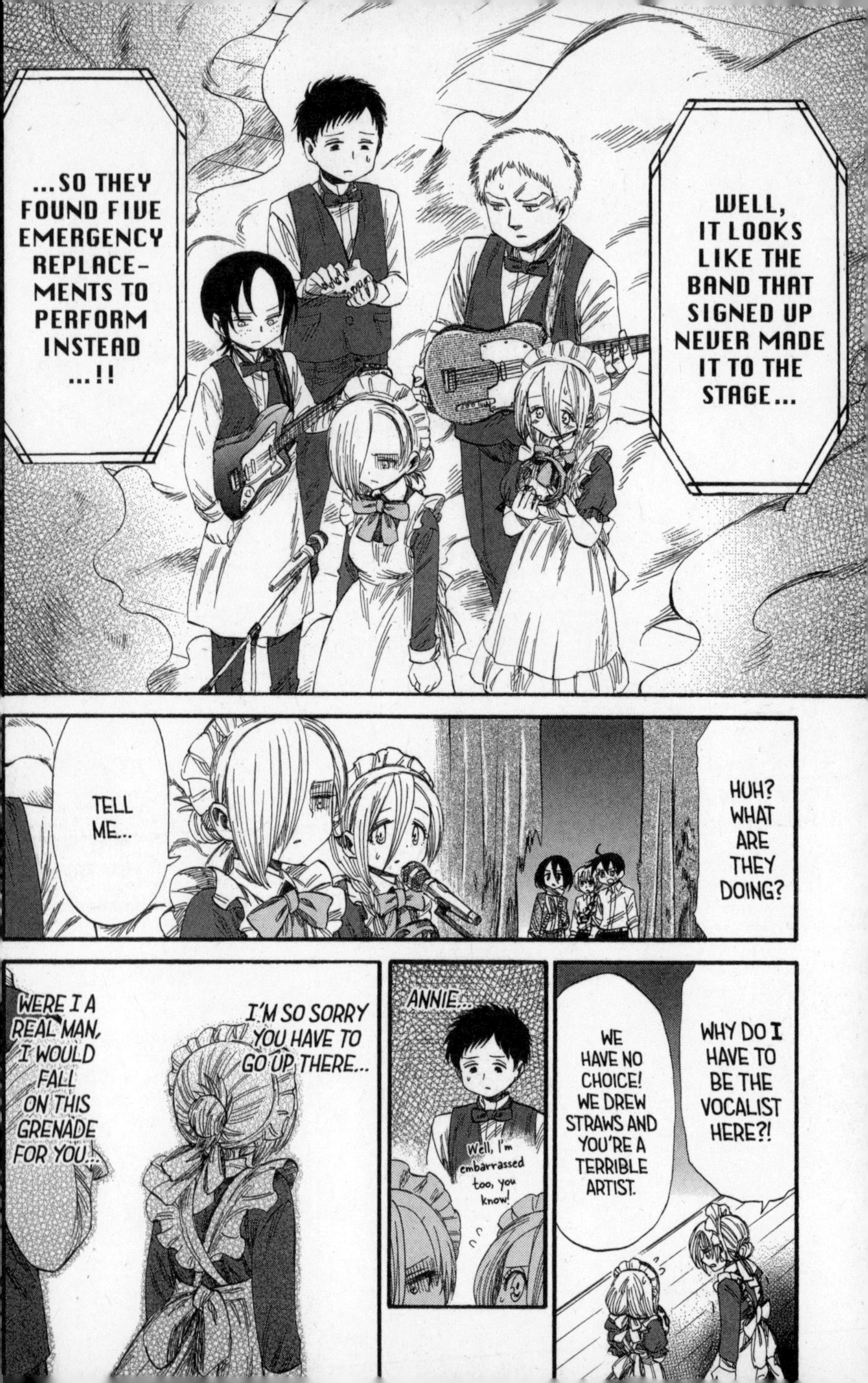
WELL, IT LOOKS LIKE THE BAND THAT SIGNED UP NEVER MADE IT TO THE STAGE...
...SO THEY FOUND FIVE EMERGENCY REPLACE-MENTS TO PERFORM INSTEAD...!!
HUH? WHAT ARE THEY DOING?
TELL ME...
WHY DO I HAVE TO BE THE VOCALIST HERE?!
WE HAVE NO CHOICE! WE DREW STRAWS AND YOU'RE A TERRIBLE ARTIST.
ANNIE...
Well, I'm embarrassed too, you know!
I'M SO SORRY YOU HAVE TO GO UP THERE...
WERE I A REAL MAN, I WOULD FALL ON THIS GRENADE FOR YOU...

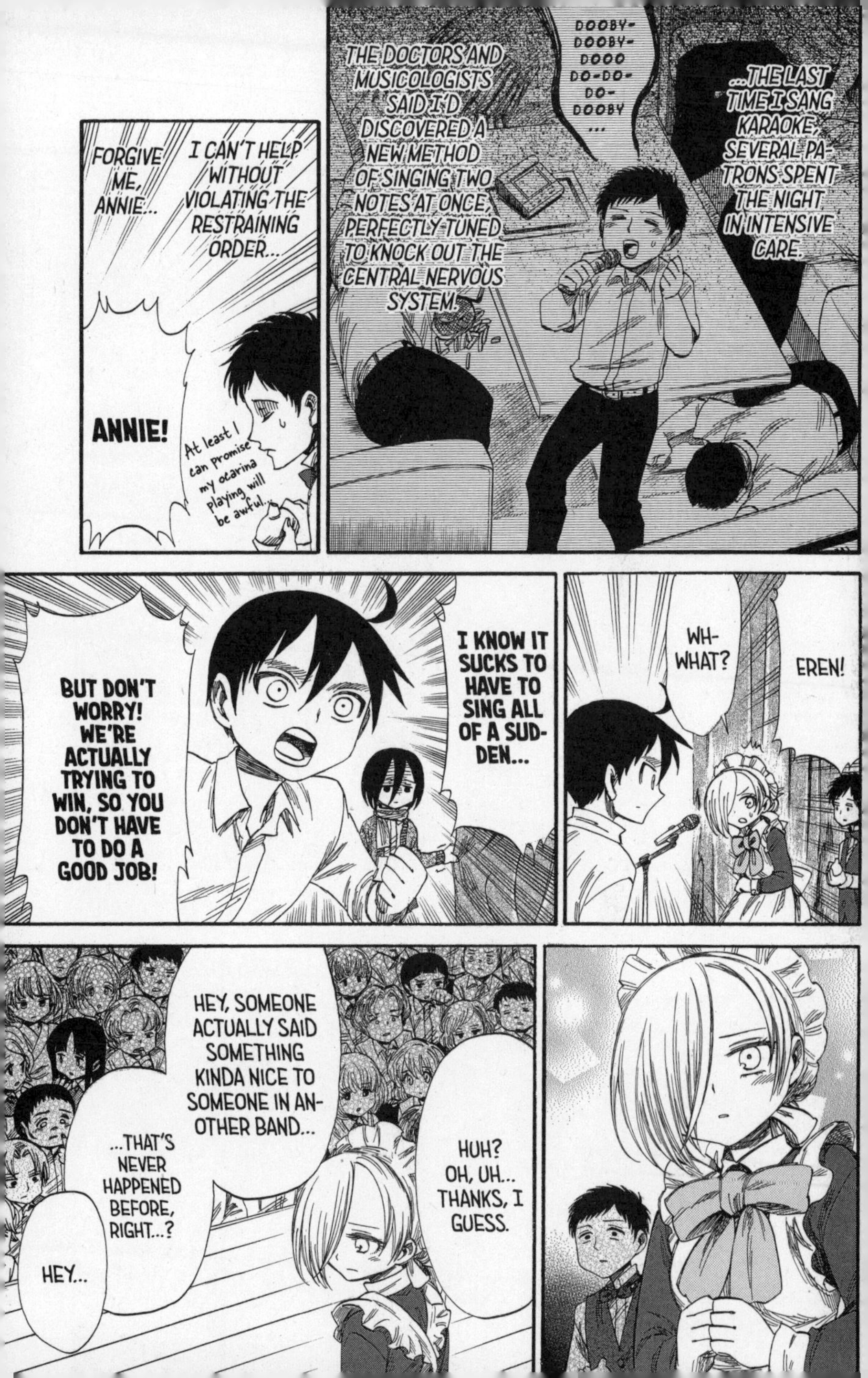
...THE LAST TIME I SANG KARAOKE, SEVERAL PATRONS SPENT THE NIGHT IN INTENSIVE CARE.
DOOBY-DOOBY-DOOO DO-DO-DO-DOOBY...
THE DOCTORS AND MUSICOLOGISTS SAID I'D DISCOVERED A NEW METHOD OF SINGING TWO NOTES AT ONCE, PERFECTLY TUNED TO KNOCK OUT THE CENTRAL NERVOUS SYSTEM.
I CAN'T HELP WITHOUT VIOLATING THE RESTRAINING ORDER...
FORGIVE ME, ANNIE...
ANNIE!
At least I can promise my ocarina playing will be awful...
EREN!
WH-WHAT?
I KNOW IT SUCKS TO HAVE TO SING ALL OF A SUDDEN...
BUT DON'T WORRY! WE'RE ACTUALLY TRYING TO WIN, SO YOU DON'T HAVE TO DO A GOOD JOB!
HUH? OH, UH... THANKS, I GUESS.
HEY, SOMEONE ACTUALLY SAID SOMETHING KINDA NICE TO SOMEONE IN ANOTHER BAND...
...THAT'S NEVER HAPPENED BEFORE, RIGHT...?
HEY...

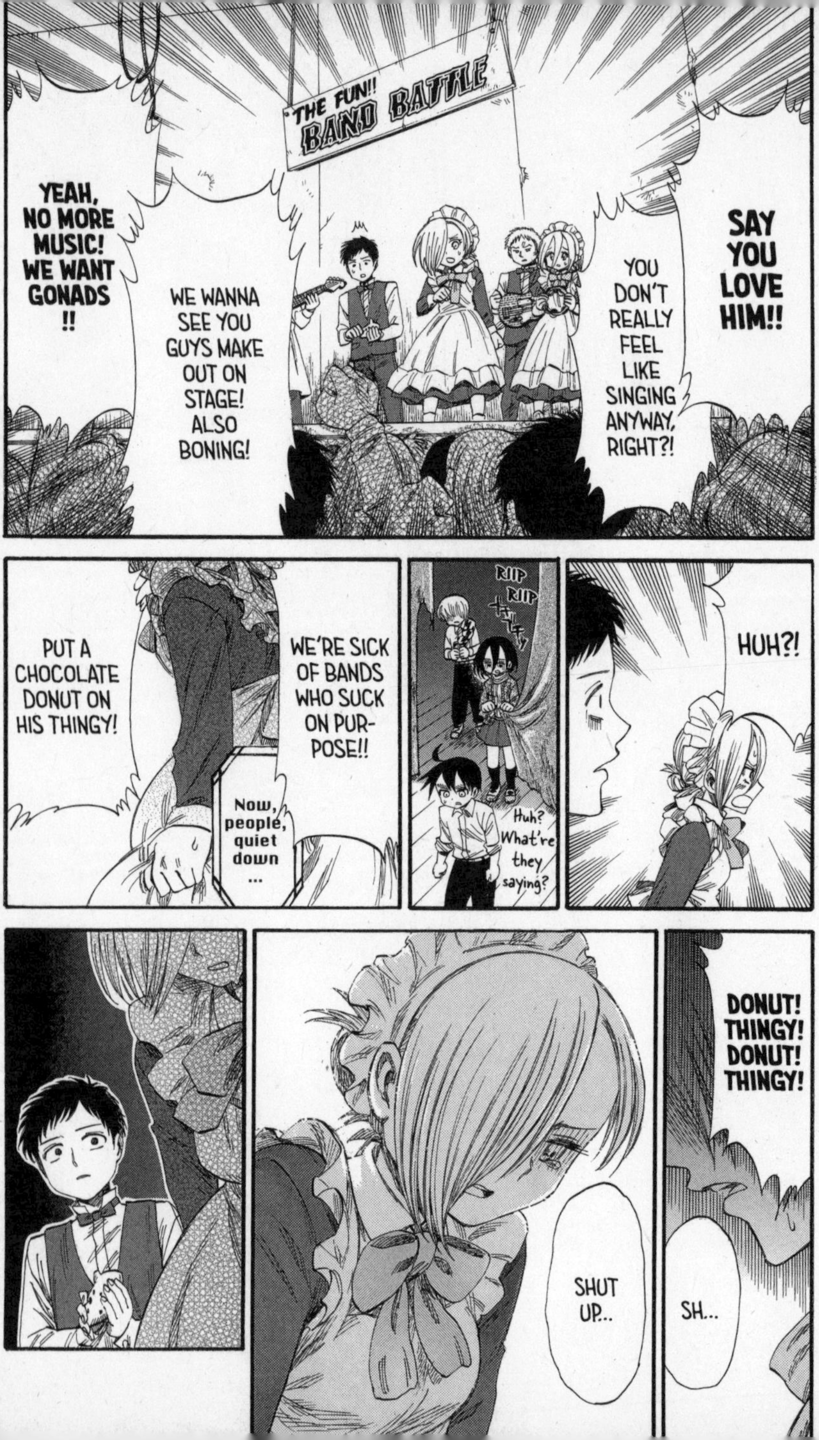
THE FUN!! BAND BATTLE
SAY YOU LOVE HIM!!
YOU DON'T REALLY FEEL LIKE SINGING ANYWAY, RIGHT?!
WE WANNA SEE YOU GUYS MAKE OUT ON STAGE! ALSO BONING!
YEAH, NO MORE MUSIC! WE WANT GONADS !!
HUH?!
RIIP RIIP
Huh? What're they saying?
WE'RE SICK OF BANDS WHO SUCK ON PURPOSE!!
PUT A CHOCOLATE DONUT ON HIS THINGY!
Now, people, quiet down ...
DONUT! THINGY! DONUT! THINGY!
SH...
SHUT UP...

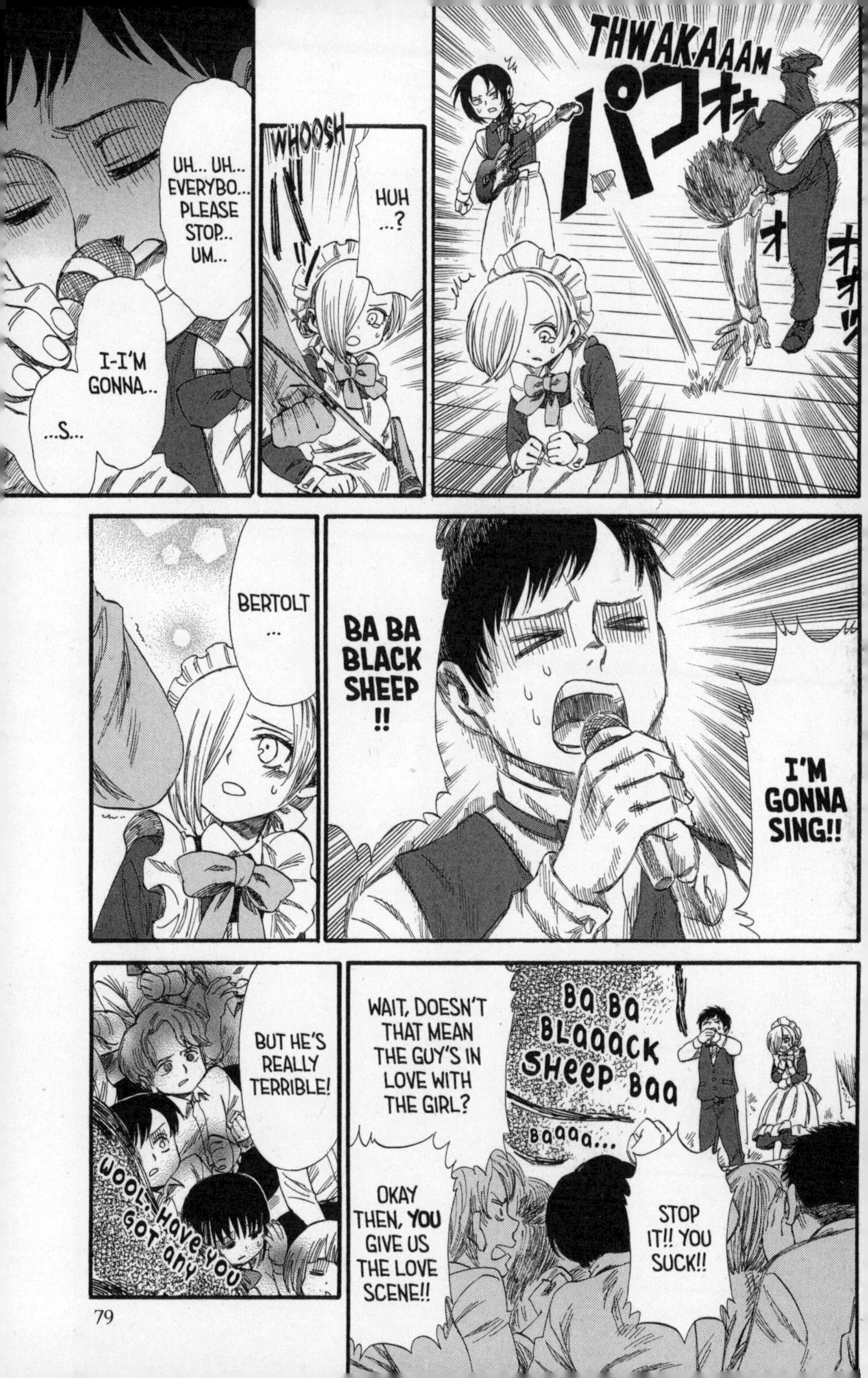

THWAKAAAM
パコォォ
オ
オオッ
WHOOSH
HUH ...?
UH... UH... EVERYBO... PLEASE STOP... UM...
I-I'M GONNA...
...S...
I'M GONNA SING!!
BA BA BLACK SHEEP !!
BERTOLT ...
Ba Ba Blaaack Sheep Baa
Baaaa...
STOP IT!! YOU SUCK!!
WAIT, DOESN'T THAT MEAN THE GUY'S IN LOVE WITH THE GIRL?
OKAY THEN, YOU GIVE US THE LOVE SCENE!!
BUT HE'S REALLY TERRIBLE!
WOOL, Have you GOT any

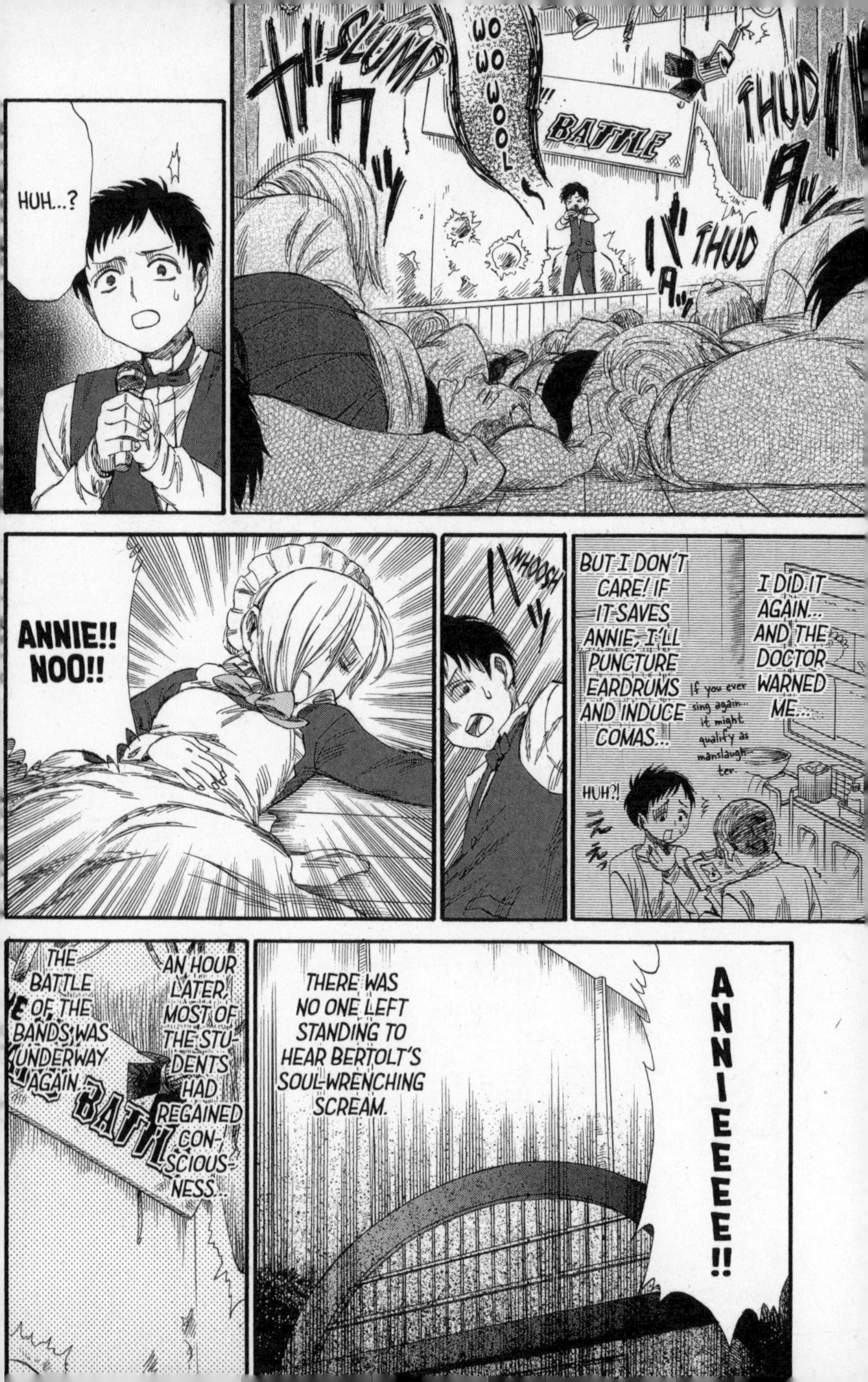
WO WO WO WOOL
SLUMP
BATTLE
THUD
THUD
HUH...?
I DID IT AGAIN... AND THE DOCTOR WARNED ME...
If you ever sing again... it might qualify as manslaughter.
HUH?!
BUT I DON'T CARE! IF IT SAVES ANNIE, I'LL PUNCTURE EARDRUMS AND INDUCE COMAS...
WHOOSH
ANNIE!! NOO!!
ANNIEEEE!!
THERE WAS NO ONE LEFT STANDING TO HEAR BERTOLT'S SOUL-WRENCHING SCREAM.
AN HOUR LATER, MOST OF THE STUDENTS HAD REGAINED CONSCIOUSNESS...
THE BATTLE OF THE BANDS WAS UNDERWAY AGAIN...

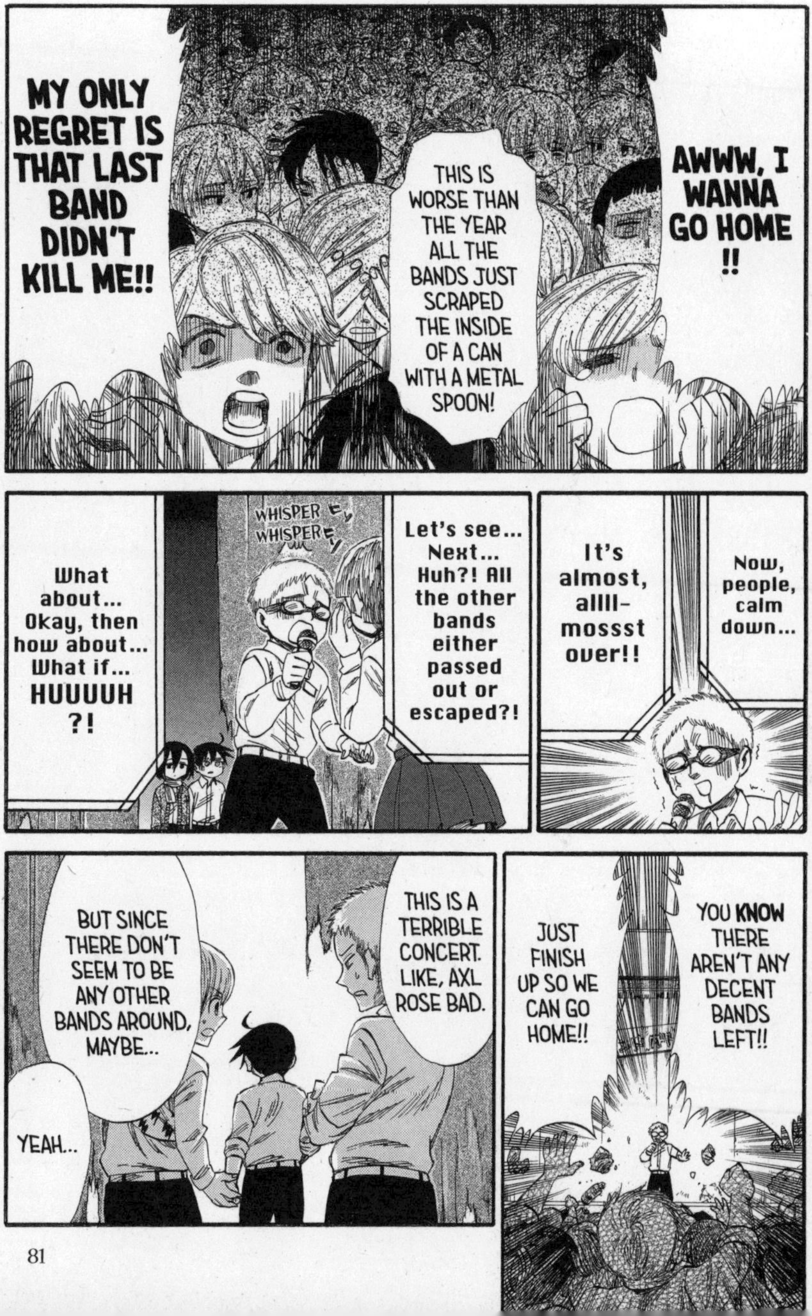
AWWW, I WANNA GO HOME!!
THIS IS WORSE THAN THE YEAR ALL THE BANDS JUST SCRAPED THE INSIDE OF A CAN WITH A METAL SPOON!
MY ONLY REGRET IS THAT LAST BAND DIDN'T KILL ME!!
Now, people, calm down...
It's almost, allll-mossst over!!
Let's see... Next... Huh?! All the other bands either passed out or escaped?!
WHISPER
WHISPER
What about... Okay, then how about... What if... HUUUUH ?!
YOU KNOW THERE AREN'T ANY DECENT BANDS LEFT!!
JUST FINISH UP SO WE CAN GO HOME!!
THIS IS A TERRIBLE CONCERT. LIKE, AXL ROSE BAD.
BUT SINCE THERE DON'T SEEM TO BE ANY OTHER BANDS AROUND, MAYBE...
YEAH...

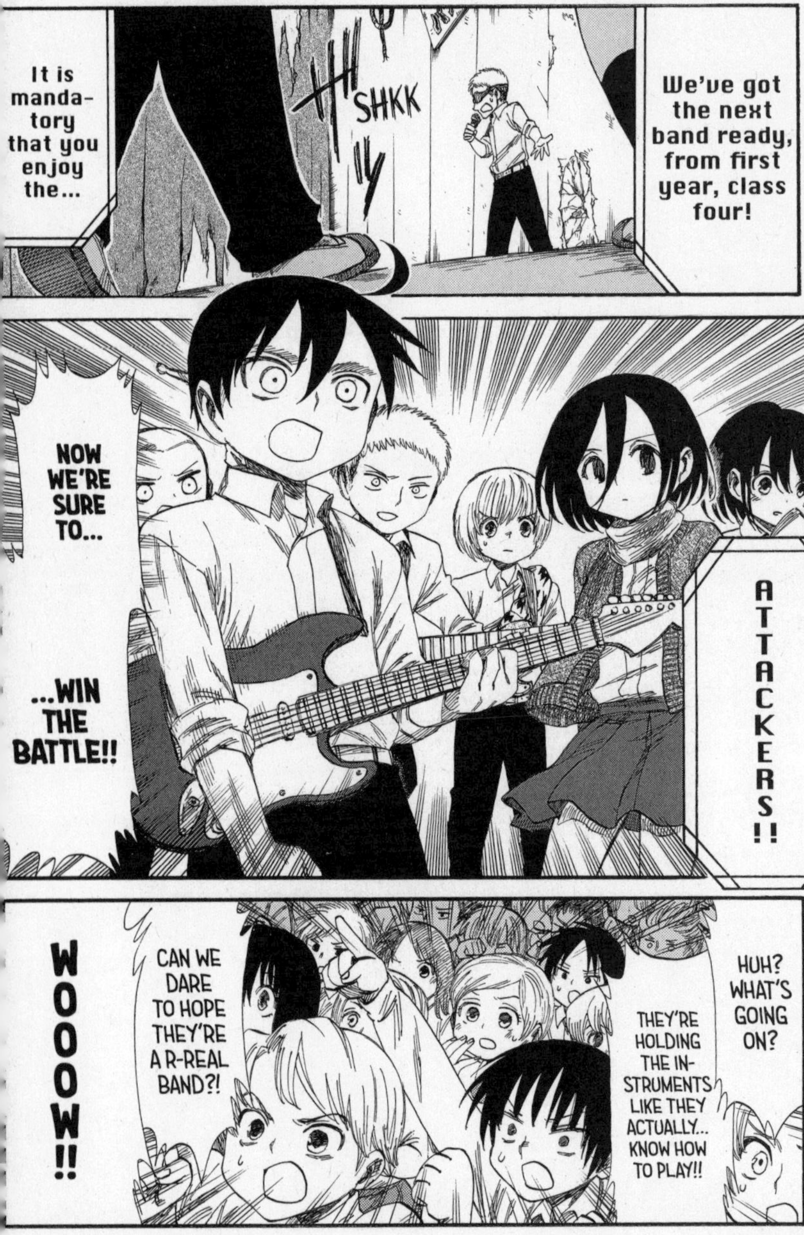
We've got the next band ready, from first year, class four!
SHKK
It is mandatory that you enjoy the...
ATTACKERS!!
NOW WE'RE SURE TO...
...WIN THE BATTLE!!
HUH? WHAT'S GOING ON?
THEY'RE HOLDING THE INSTRUMENTS LIKE THEY ACTUALLY... KNOW HOW TO PLAY!!
CAN WE DARE TO HOPE THEY'RE A R-REAL BAND?!
WOOOOW!!

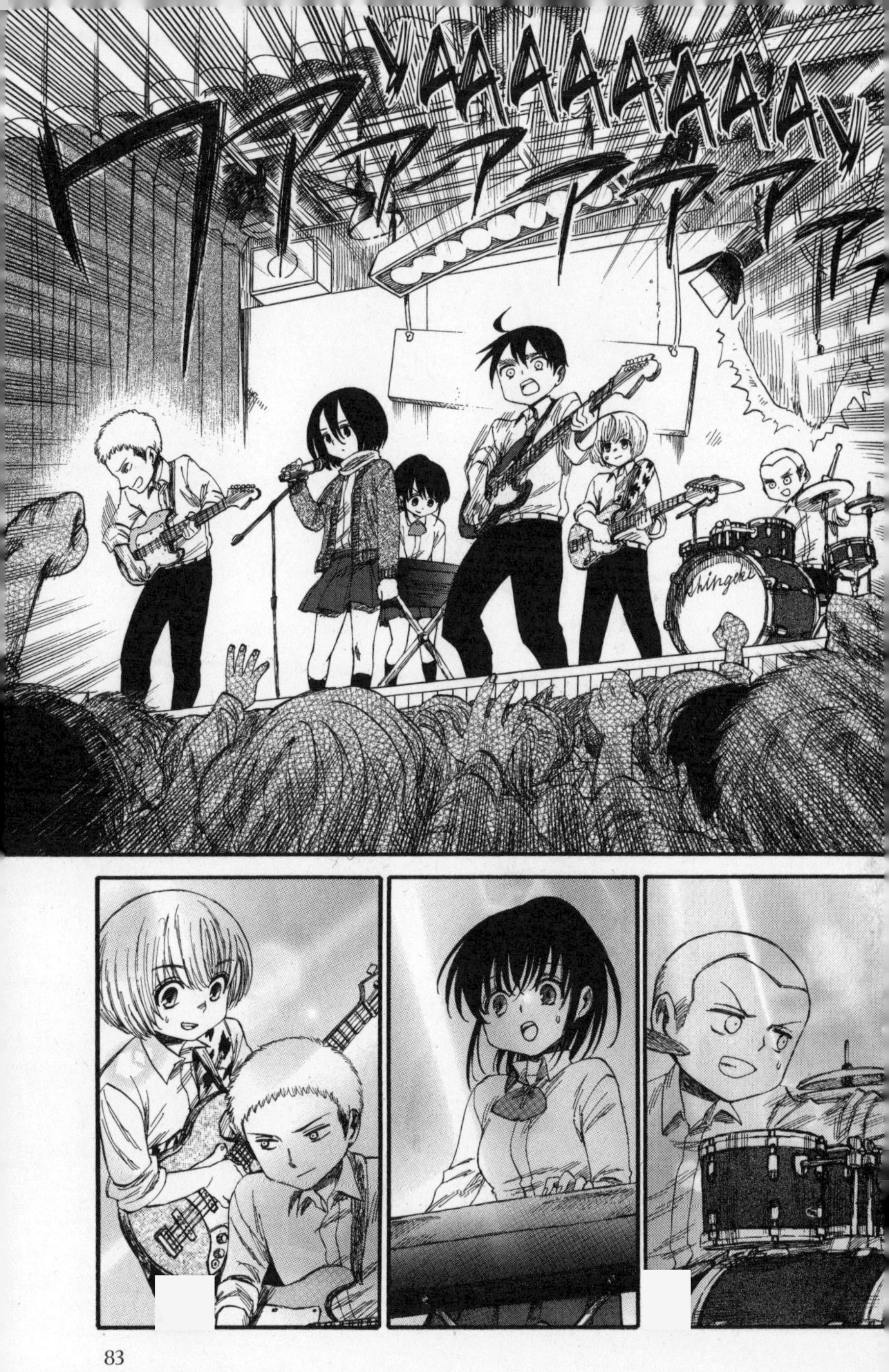
YAAAAAAAAY
Shingeki

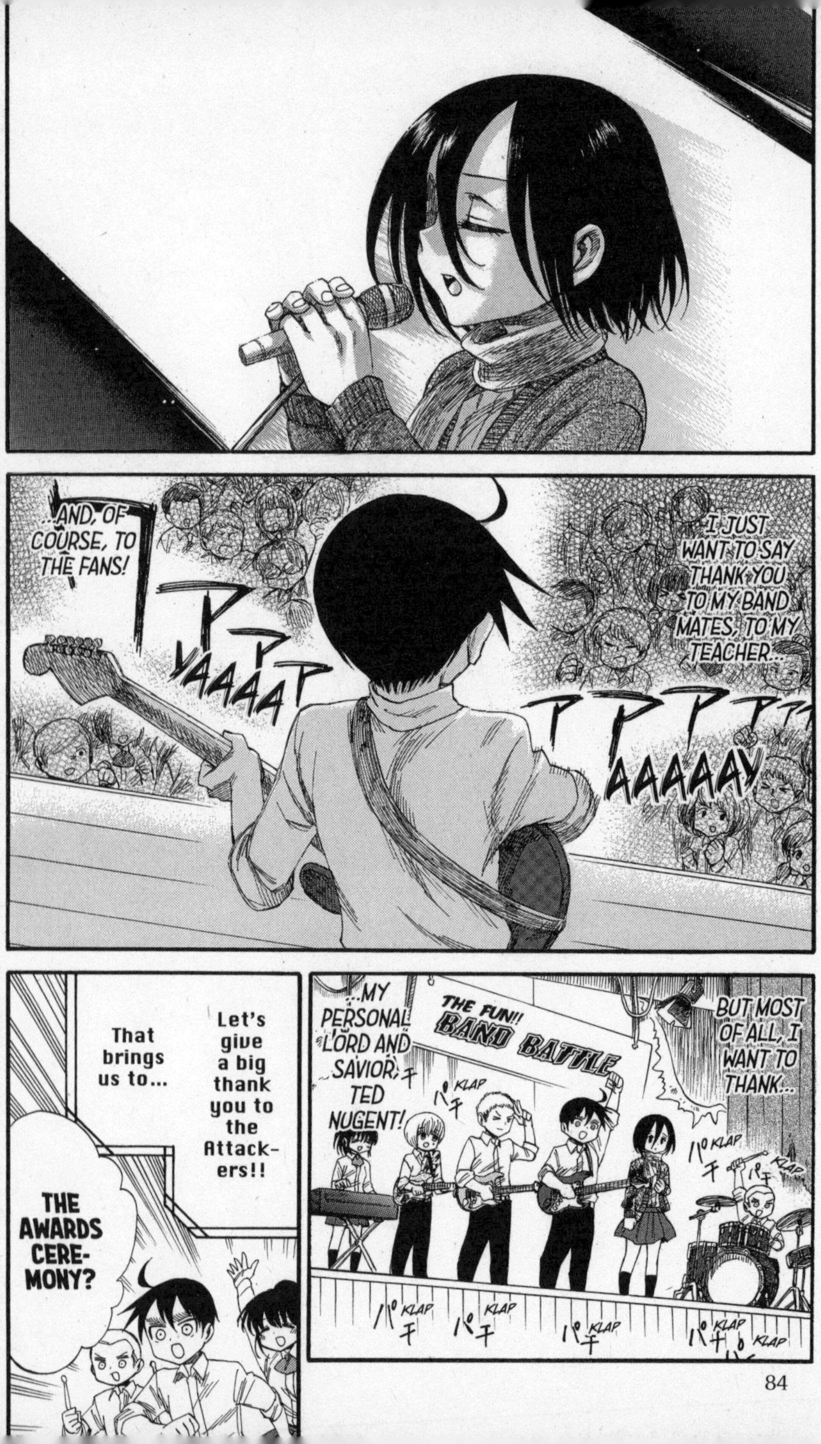
I JUST WANT TO SAY THANK YOU TO MY BAND MATES, TO MY TEACHER...
AAAAAY
YAAAAP
...AND, OF COURSE, TO THE FANS!
BUT MOST OF ALL, I WANT TO THANK...
...MY PERSONAL LORD AND SAVIOR, TED NUGENT!
THE FUN!! BAND BATTLE
KLAP
Let's give a big thank you to the Attackers!!
That brings us to...
THE AWARDS CEREMONY?

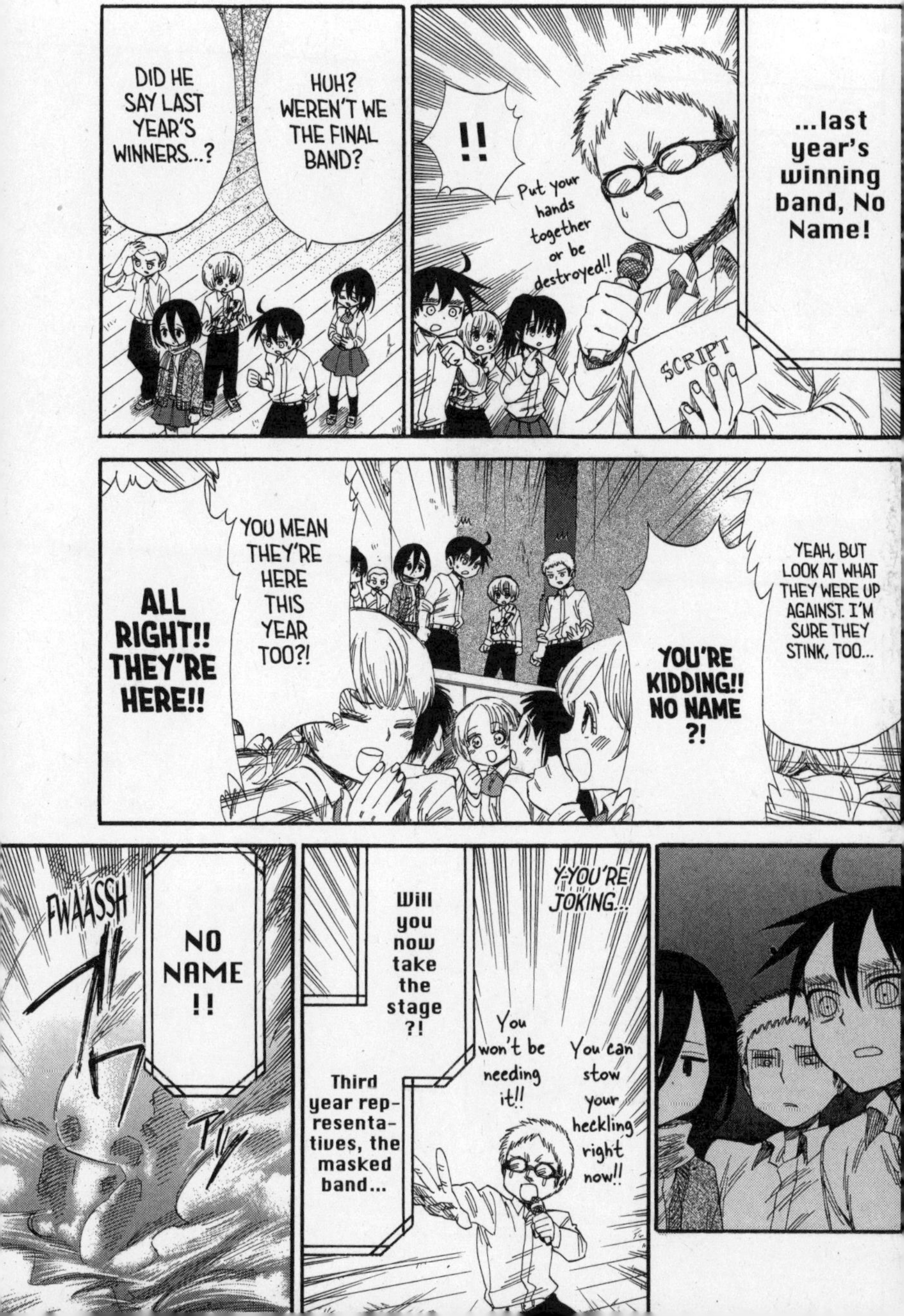
...last year's winning band, No Name!
!!
Put your hands together or be destroyed!!
HUH? WEREN'T WE THE FINAL BAND?
DID HE SAY LAST YEAR'S WINNERS...?
YEAH, BUT LOOK AT WHAT THEY WERE UP AGAINST. I'M SURE THEY STINK, TOO...
YOU'RE KIDDING!! NO NAME ?!
YOU MEAN THEY'RE HERE THIS YEAR TOO?!
ALL RIGHT!! THEY'RE HERE!!
Y-YOU'RE JOKING...
You can stow your heckling right now!!
You won't be needing it!!
Will you now take the stage ?!
Third year representatives, the masked band...
NO NAME !!
FWAASSH

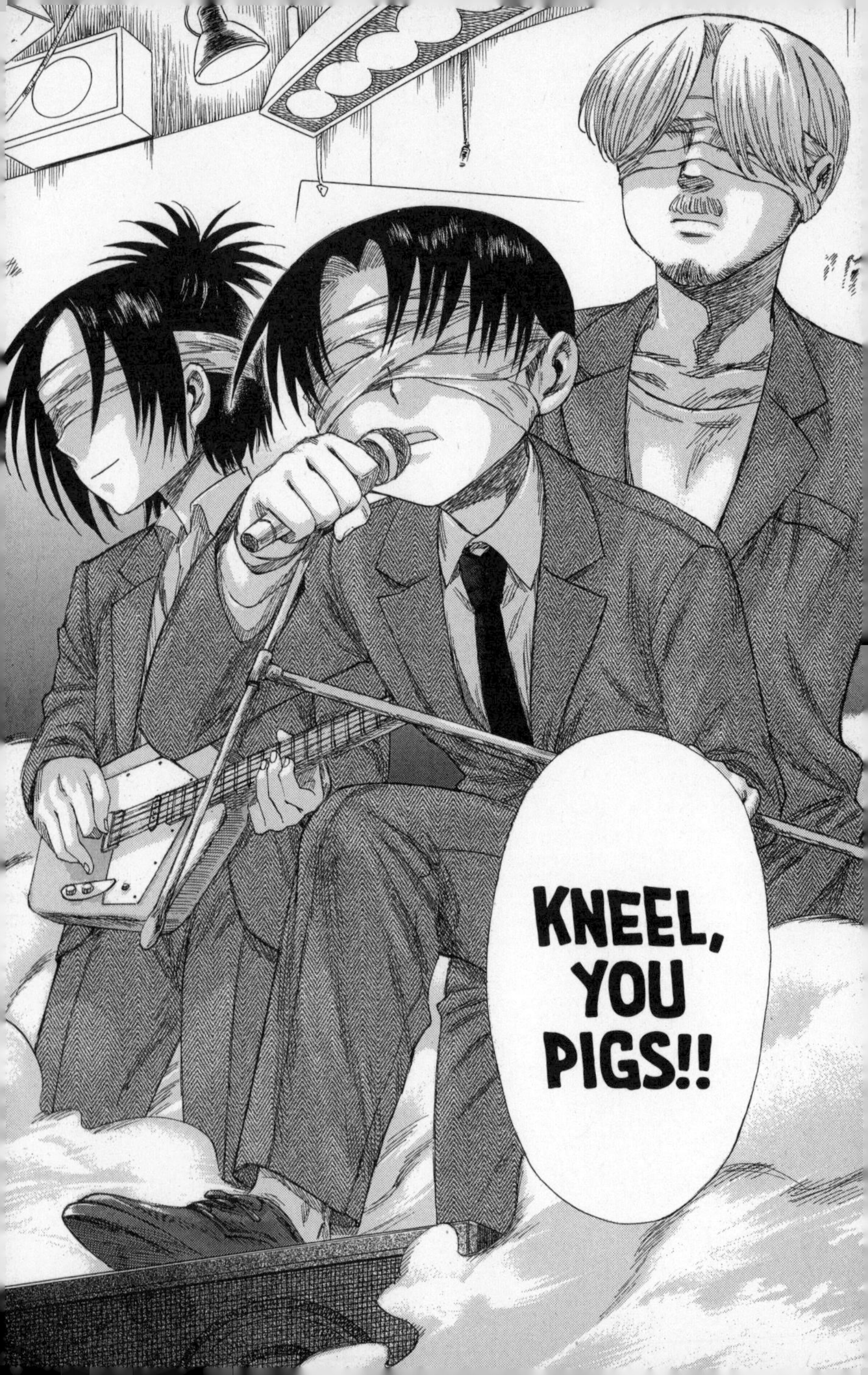
KNEEL, YOU PIGS!!

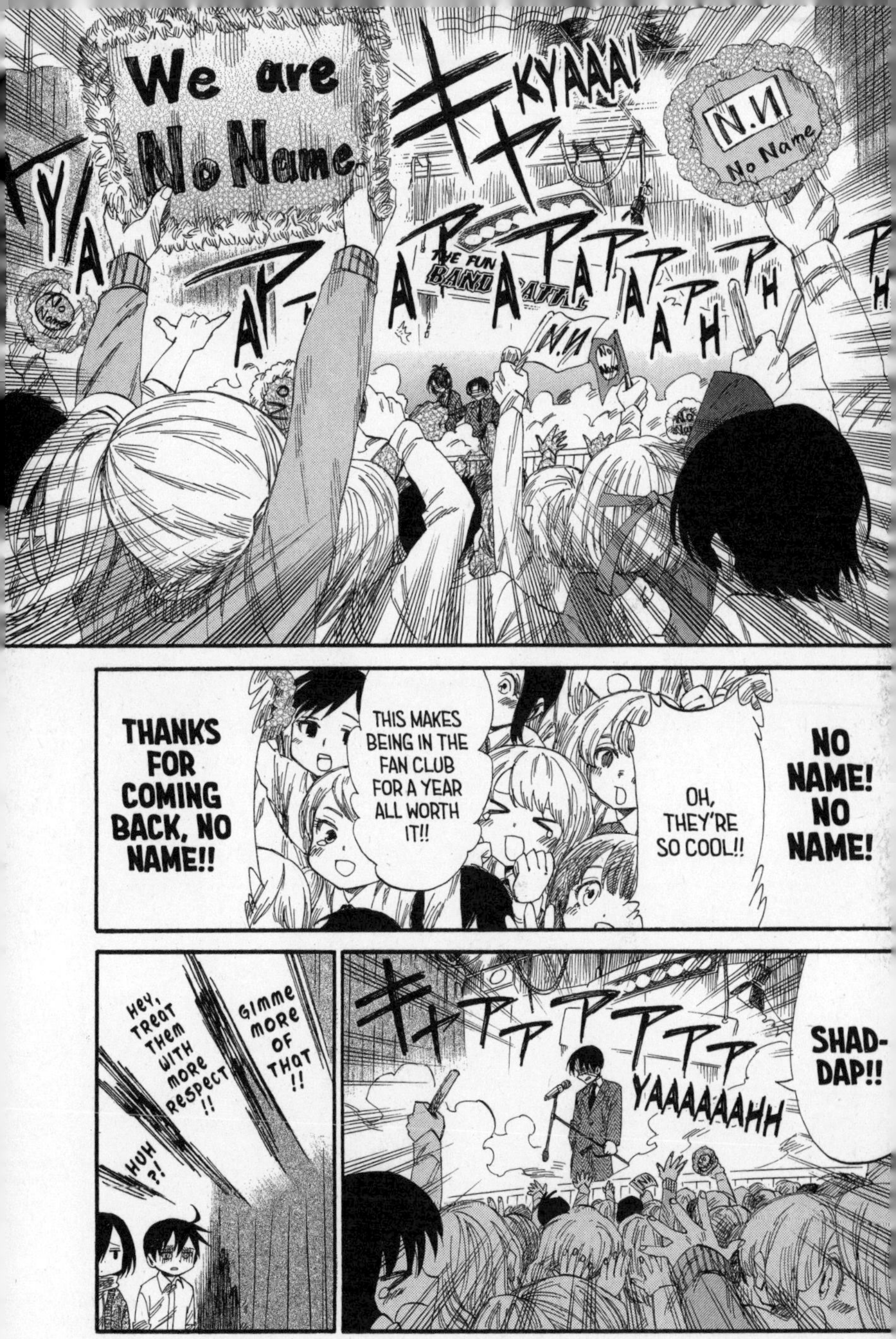
We are No Name
KYAAA!
N.N
No Name
THE FUN
BAND
NO NAME! NO NAME!
OH, THEY'RE SO COOL!!
THIS MAKES BEING IN THE FAN CLUB FOR A YEAR ALL WORTH IT!!
THANKS FOR COMING BACK, NO NAME!!
SHAD-DAP!!
YAAAAAAHH
Gimme more of that!!
Hey, treat them with more respect!!
HUH?!

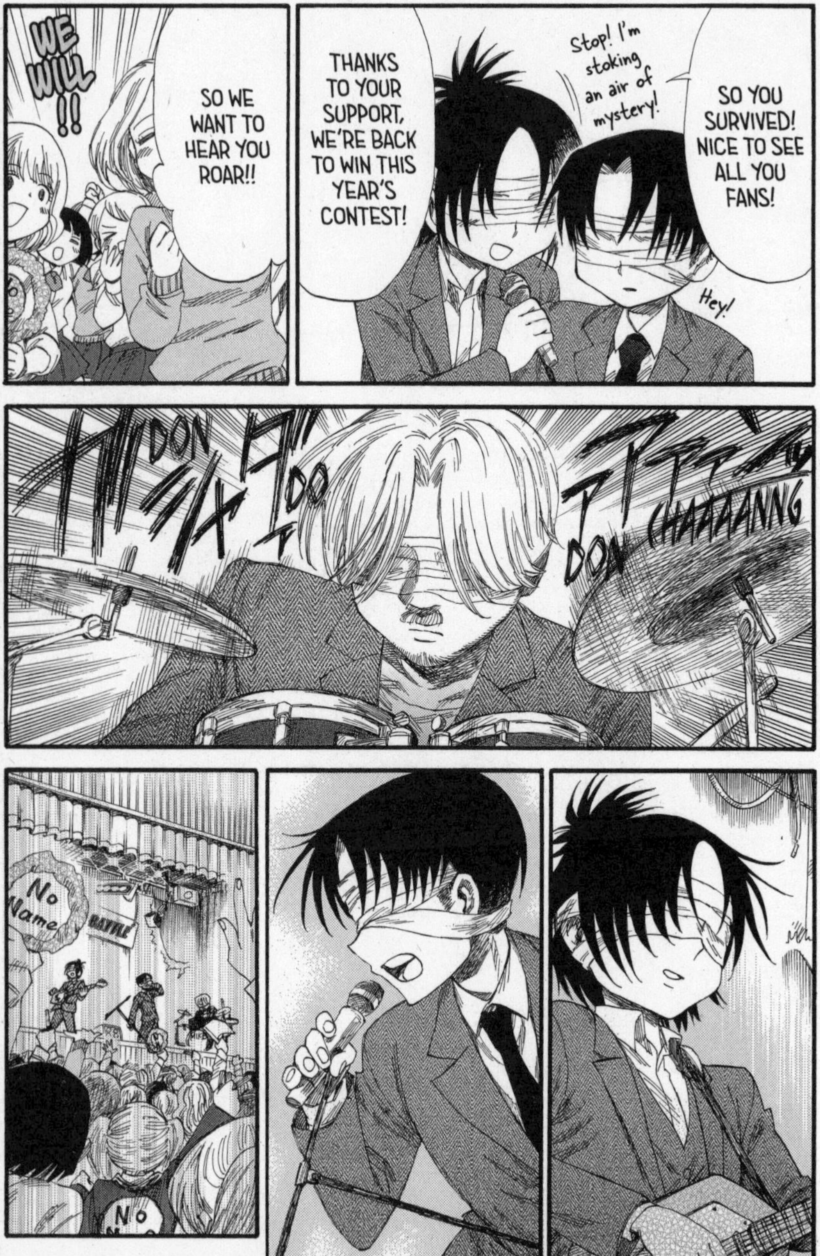
SO YOU SURVIVED! NICE TO SEE ALL YOU FANS!
Stop! I'm stoking an air of mystery!
Hey!
THANKS TO YOUR SUPPORT, WE'RE BACK TO WIN THIS YEAR'S CONTEST!
SO WE WANT TO HEAR YOU ROAR!!
WE WILL !!
CHAAAANNG
DON
DOO
DON
No Name
No

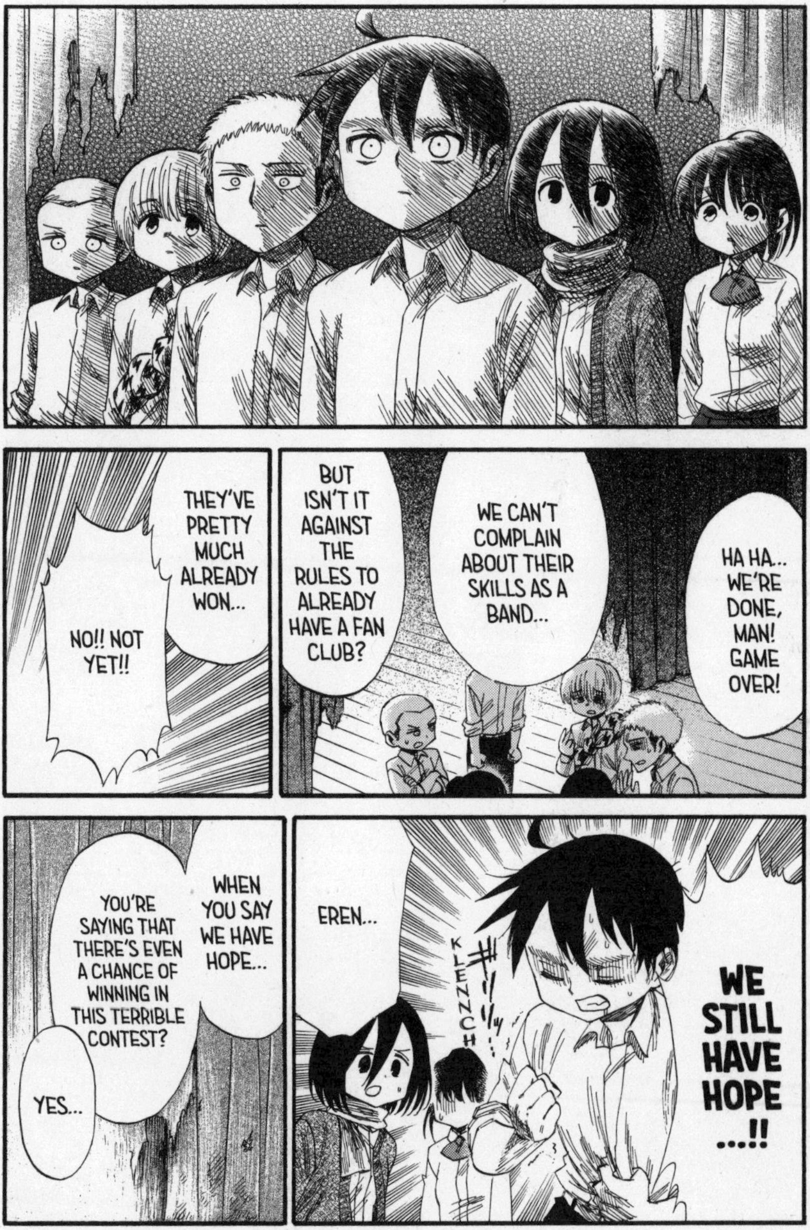
HA HA... WE'RE DONE, MAN! GAME OVER!
WE CAN'T COMPLAIN ABOUT THEIR SKILLS AS A BAND...
BUT ISN'T IT AGAINST THE RULES TO ALREADY HAVE A FAN CLUB?
THEY'VE PRETTY MUCH ALREADY WON...
NO!! NOT YET!!
WE STILL HAVE HOPE ...!!
KLENNCH
EREN...
WHEN YOU SAY WE HAVE HOPE...
YOU'RE SAYING THAT THERE'S EVEN A CHANCE OF WINNING IN THIS TERRIBLE CONTEST?
YES...

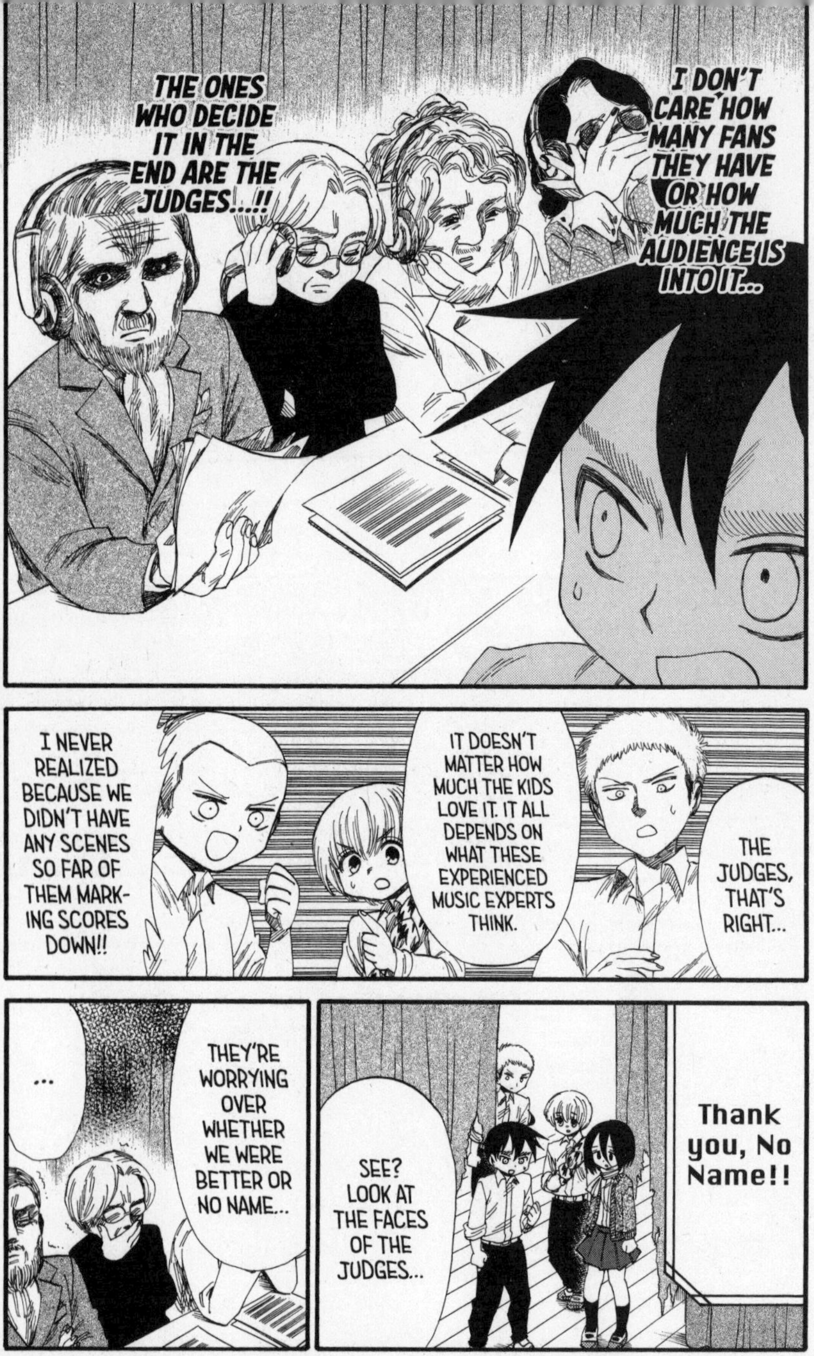
I DON'T CARE HOW MANY FANS THEY HAVE OR HOW MUCH THE AUDIENCE IS INTO IT...
THE ONES WHO DECIDE IT IN THE END ARE THE JUDGES...!!
THE JUDGES, THAT'S RIGHT...
IT DOESN'T MATTER HOW MUCH THE KIDS LOVE IT. IT ALL DEPENDS ON WHAT THESE EXPERIENCED MUSIC EXPERTS THINK.
I NEVER REALIZED BECAUSE WE DIDN'T HAVE ANY SCENES SO FAR OF THEM MARK-ING SCORES DOWN!!
Thank you, No Name!!
SEE? LOOK AT THE FACES OF THE JUDGES...
THEY'RE WORRYING OVER WHETHER WE WERE BETTER OR NO NAME...
...

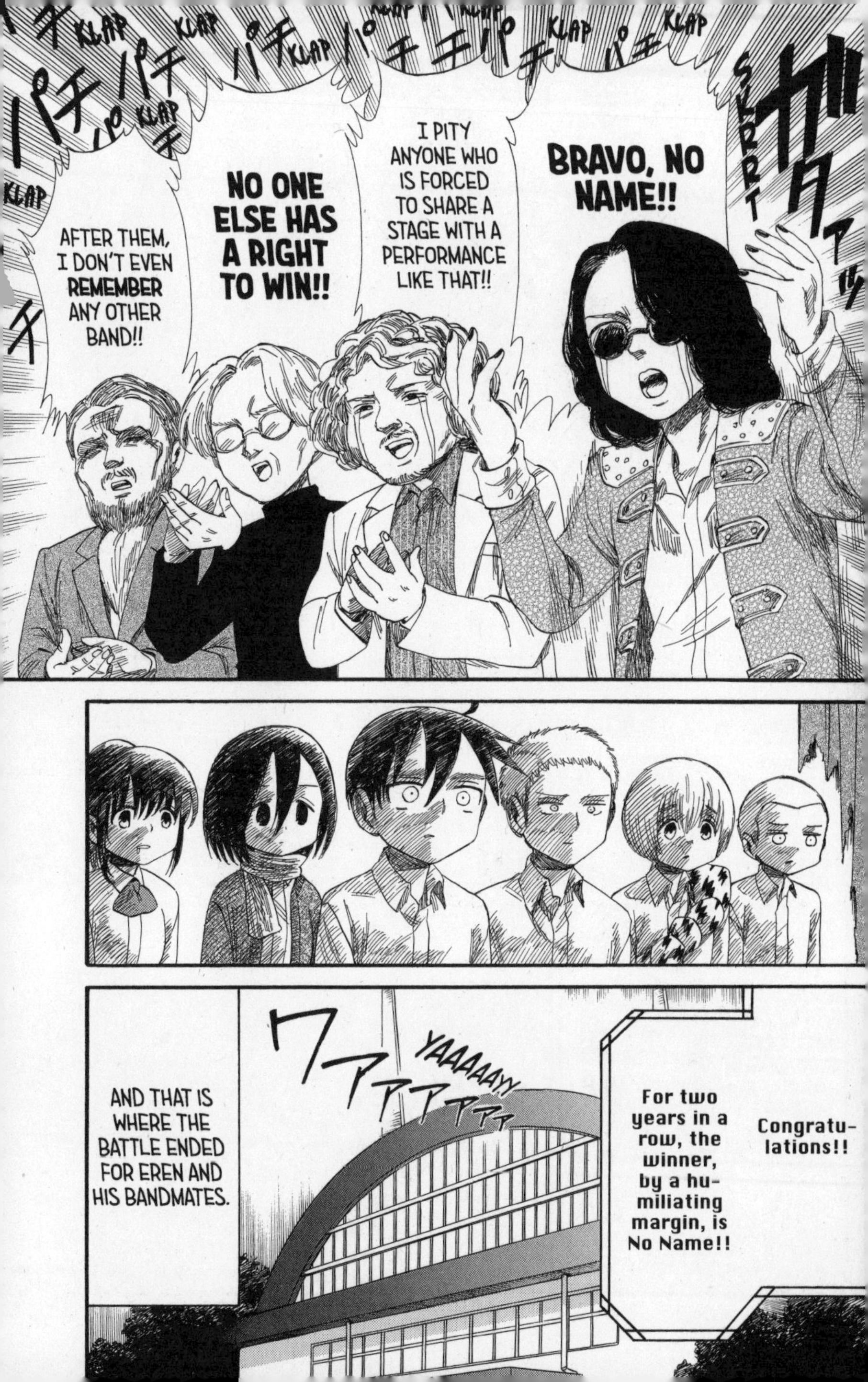
SLRRT
KLAP KLAP KLAP KLAP KLAP KLAP KLAP
BRAVO, NO NAME!!
I PITY ANYONE WHO IS FORCED TO SHARE A STAGE WITH A PERFORMANCE LIKE THAT!!
NO ONE ELSE HAS A RIGHT TO WIN!!
AFTER THEM, I DON'T EVEN REMEMBER ANY OTHER BAND!!
Congratulations!!
For two years in a row, the winner, by a humiliating margin, is No Name!!
YAAAAAYY
AND THAT IS WHERE THE BATTLE ENDED FOR EREN AND HIS BANDMATES.

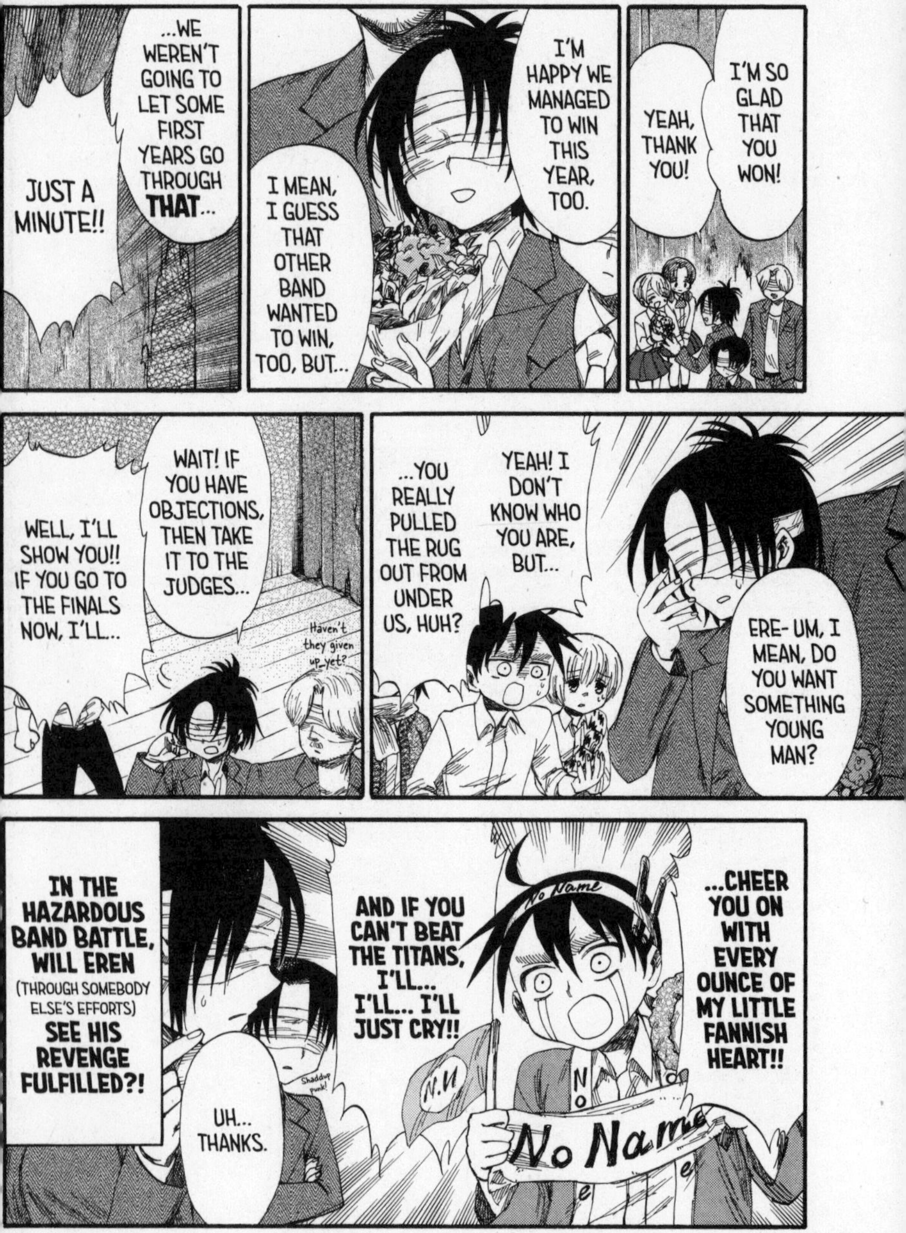
I'M SO GLAD THAT YOU WON!
YEAH, THANK YOU!
I'M HAPPY WE MANAGED TO WIN THIS YEAR, TOO.
I MEAN, I GUESS THAT OTHER BAND WANTED TO WIN, TOO, BUT...
...WE WEREN'T GOING TO LET SOME FIRST YEARS GO THROUGH **THAT**...
JUST A MINUTE!!
ERE- UM, I MEAN, DO YOU WANT SOMETHING YOUNG MAN?
YEAH! I DON'T KNOW WHO YOU ARE, BUT...
...YOU REALLY PULLED THE RUG OUT FROM UNDER US, HUH?
WAIT! IF YOU HAVE OBJECTIONS, THEN TAKE IT TO THE JUDGES...
Haven't they given up yet?
WELL, I'LL SHOW YOU!! IF YOU GO TO THE FINALS NOW, I'LL...
...CHEER YOU ON WITH EVERY OUNCE OF MY LITTLE FANNISH HEART!!
No Name
No Name
AND IF YOU CAN'T BEAT THE TITANS, I'LL... I'LL... I'LL JUST CRY!!
Shaddup punk!
UH... THANKS.
IN THE HAZARDOUS BAND BATTLE, WILL EREN (THROUGH SOMEBODY ELSE'S EFFORTS) SEE HIS REVENGE FULFILLED?!

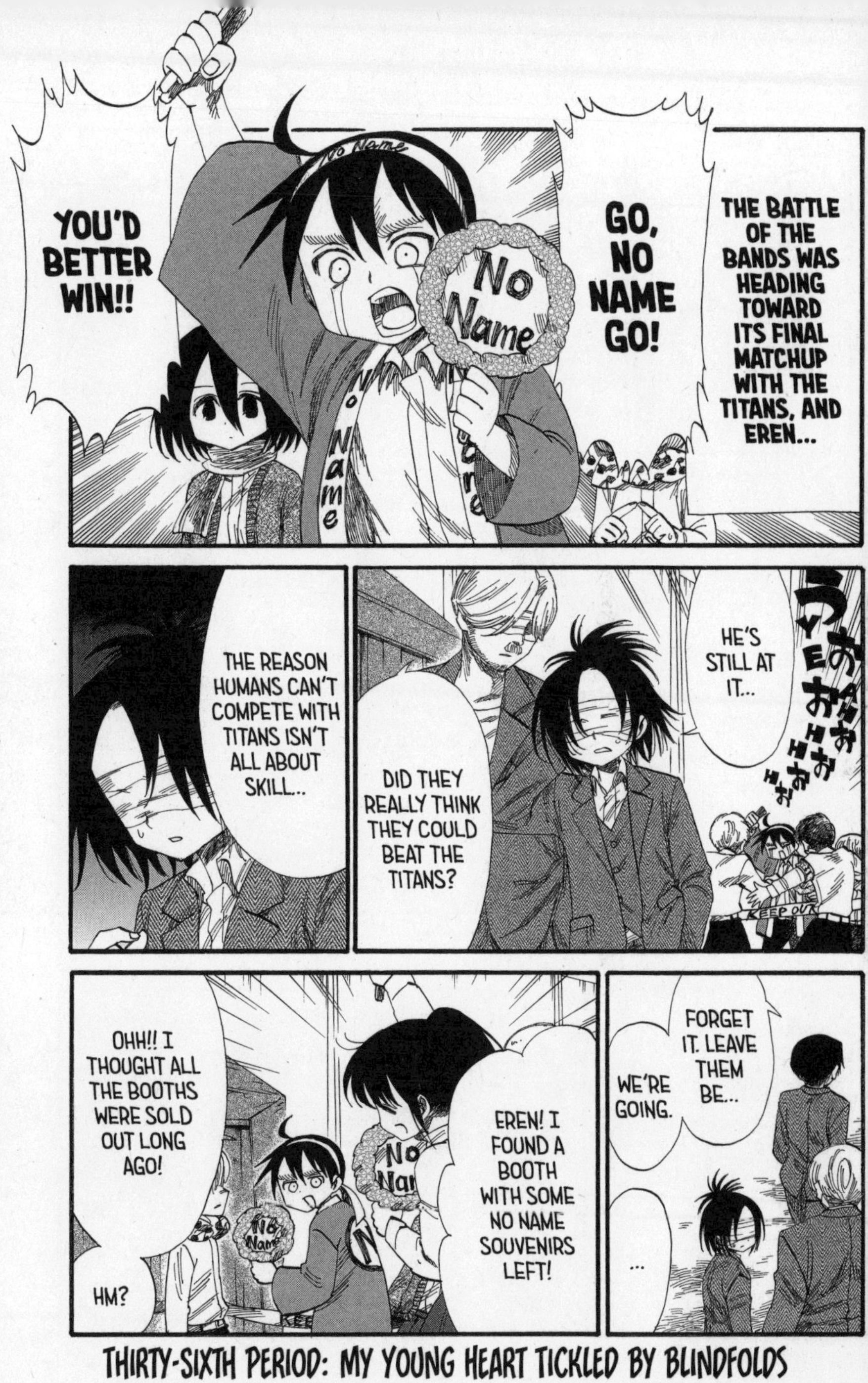
THE BATTLE OF THE BANDS WAS HEADING TOWARD ITS FINAL MATCHUP WITH THE TITANS, AND EREN...
GO, NO NAME GO!
YOU'D BETTER WIN!!
No Name
HE'S STILL AT IT...
DID THEY REALLY THINK THEY COULD BEAT THE TITANS?
KEEP OUT
THE REASON HUMANS CAN'T COMPETE WITH TITANS ISN'T ALL ABOUT SKILL...
FORGET IT. LEAVE THEM BE...
WE'RE GOING.
...
EREN! I FOUND A BOOTH WITH SOME NO NAME SOUVENIRS LEFT!
OHH!! I THOUGHT ALL THE BOOTHS WERE SOLD OUT LONG AGO!
HM?

THIRTY-SIXTH PERIOD: MY YOUNG HEART TICKLED BY BLINDFOLDS

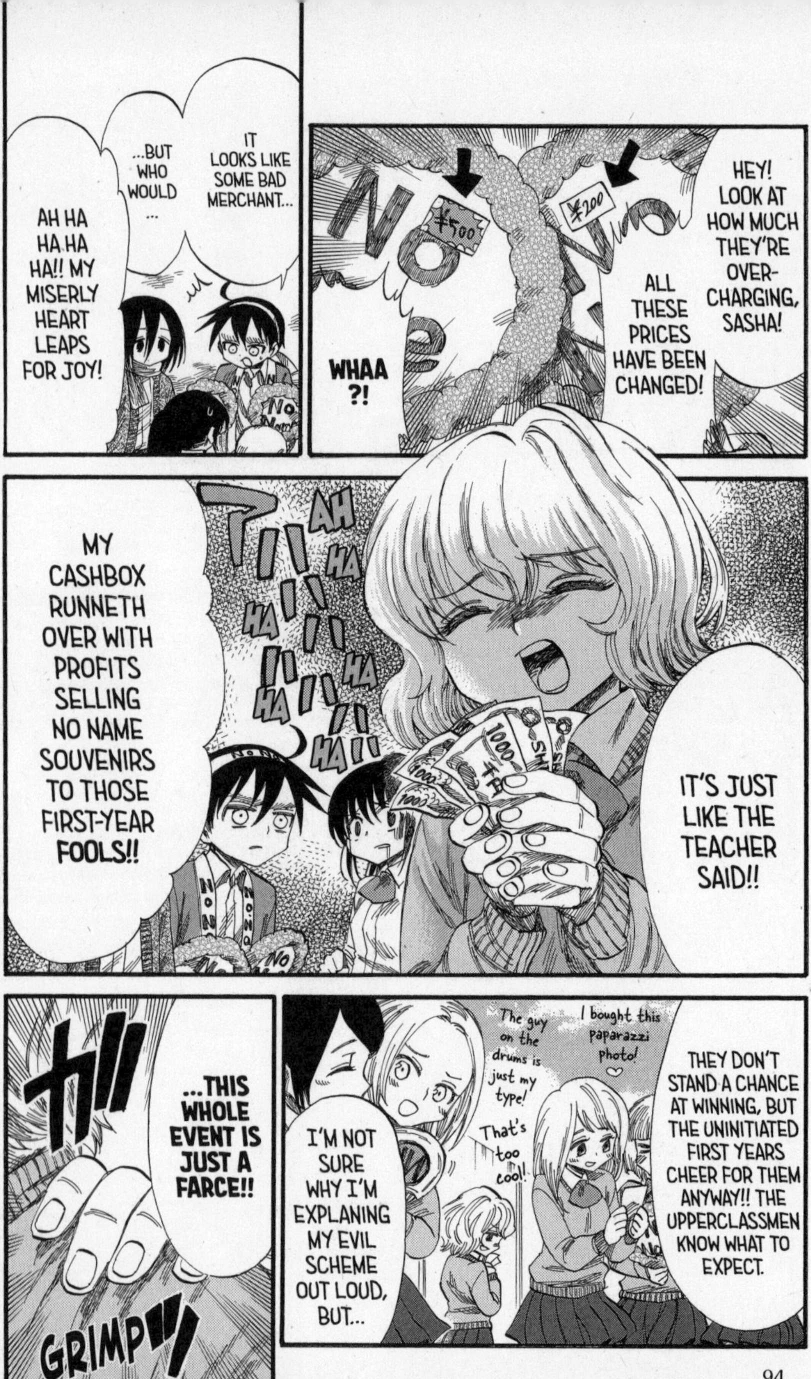

HEY! LOOK AT HOW MUCH THEY'RE OVER-CHARGING, SASHA!
¥200
¥500
ALL THESE PRICES HAVE BEEN CHANGED!
WHAA ?!
IT LOOKS LIKE SOME BAD MERCHANT...
...BUT WHO WOULD ...
AH HA HA HA HA!! MY MISERLY HEART LEAPS FOR JOY!
IT'S JUST LIKE THE TEACHER SAID!!
AH HA HA HA HA HA!!
MY CASHBOX RUNNETH OVER WITH PROFITS SELLING NO NAME SOUVENIRS TO THOSE FIRST-YEAR FOOLS!!
THEY DON'T STAND A CHANCE AT WINNING, BUT THE UNINITIATED FIRST YEARS CHEER FOR THEM ANYWAY!! THE UPPERCLASSMEN KNOW WHAT TO EXPECT.
I bought this paparazzi photo!
The guy on the drums is just my type!
That's too cool!
I'M NOT SURE WHY I'M EXPLAINING MY EVIL SCHEME OUT LOUD, BUT...
...THIS WHOLE EVENT IS JUST A FARCE!!
GRIMP

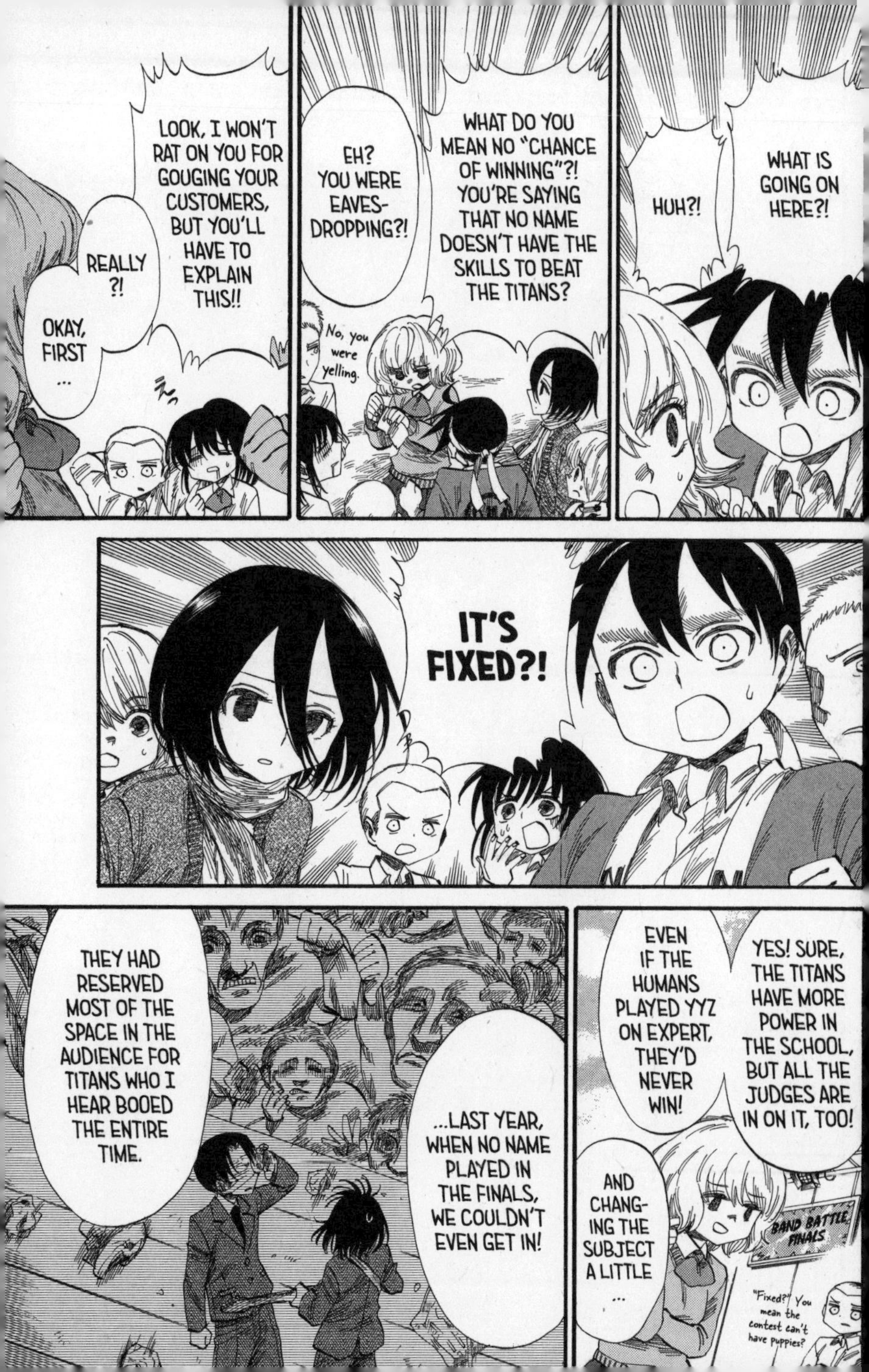
WHAT IS GOING ON HERE?!
HUH?!
WHAT DO YOU MEAN NO "CHANCE OF WINNING"?! YOU'RE SAYING THAT NO NAME DOESN'T HAVE THE SKILLS TO BEAT THE TITANS?
EH? YOU WERE EAVES-DROPPING?!
No, you were yelling.
LOOK, I WON'T RAT ON YOU FOR GOUGING YOUR CUSTOMERS, BUT YOU'LL HAVE TO EXPLAIN THIS!!
REALLY ?!
OKAY, FIRST ...
IT'S FIXED?!
YES! SURE, THE TITANS HAVE MORE POWER IN THE SCHOOL, BUT ALL THE JUDGES ARE IN ON IT, TOO!
EVEN IF THE HUMANS PLAYED YYZ ON EXPERT, THEY'D NEVER WIN!
BAND BATTLE FINALS
AND CHANG-ING THE SUBJECT A LITTLE ...
"Fixed?" You mean the contest can't have puppies?
...LAST YEAR, WHEN NO NAME PLAYED IN THE FINALS, WE COULDN'T EVEN GET IN!
THEY HAD RESERVED MOST OF THE SPACE IN THE AUDIENCE FOR TITANS WHO I HEAR BOOED THE ENTIRE TIME.

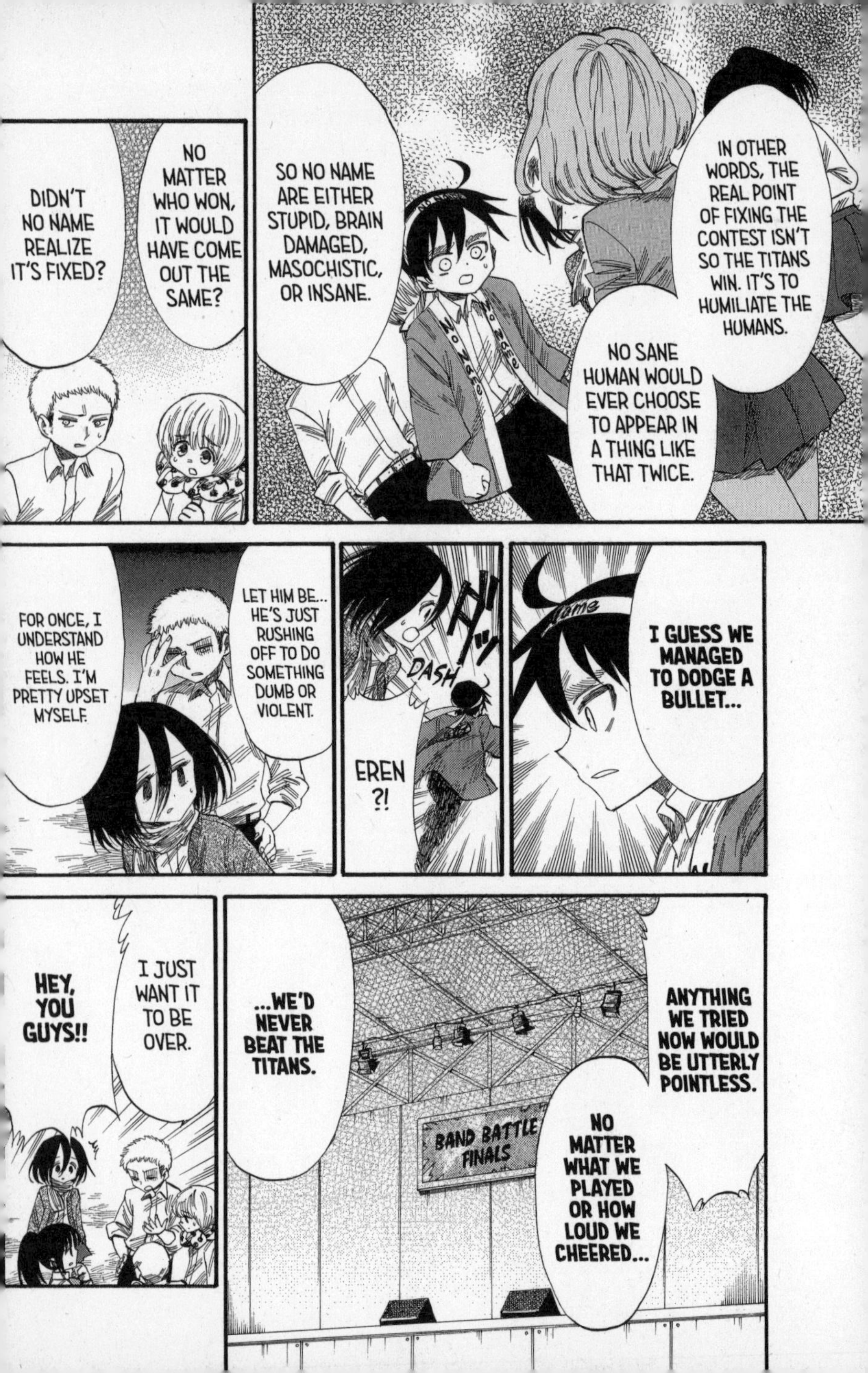
IN OTHER WORDS, THE REAL POINT OF FIXING THE CONTEST ISN'T SO THE TITANS WIN. IT'S TO HUMILIATE THE HUMANS.
NO SANE HUMAN WOULD EVER CHOOSE TO APPEAR IN A THING LIKE THAT TWICE.
SO NO NAME ARE EITHER STUPID, BRAIN DAMAGED, MASOCHISTIC, OR INSANE.
NO MATTER WHO WON, IT WOULD HAVE COME OUT THE SAME?
DIDN'T NO NAME REALIZE IT'S FIXED?
I GUESS WE MANAGED TO DODGE A BULLET...
DASH
EREN ?!
LET HIM BE... HE'S JUST RUSHING OFF TO DO SOMETHING DUMB OR VIOLENT.
FOR ONCE, I UNDERSTAND HOW HE FEELS. I'M PRETTY UPSET MYSELF.
ANYTHING WE TRIED NOW WOULD BE UTTERLY POINTLESS.
NO MATTER WHAT WE PLAYED OR HOW LOUD WE CHEERED...
BAND BATTLE FINALS
...WE'D NEVER BEAT THE TITANS.
I JUST WANT IT TO BE OVER.
HEY, YOU GUYS!!

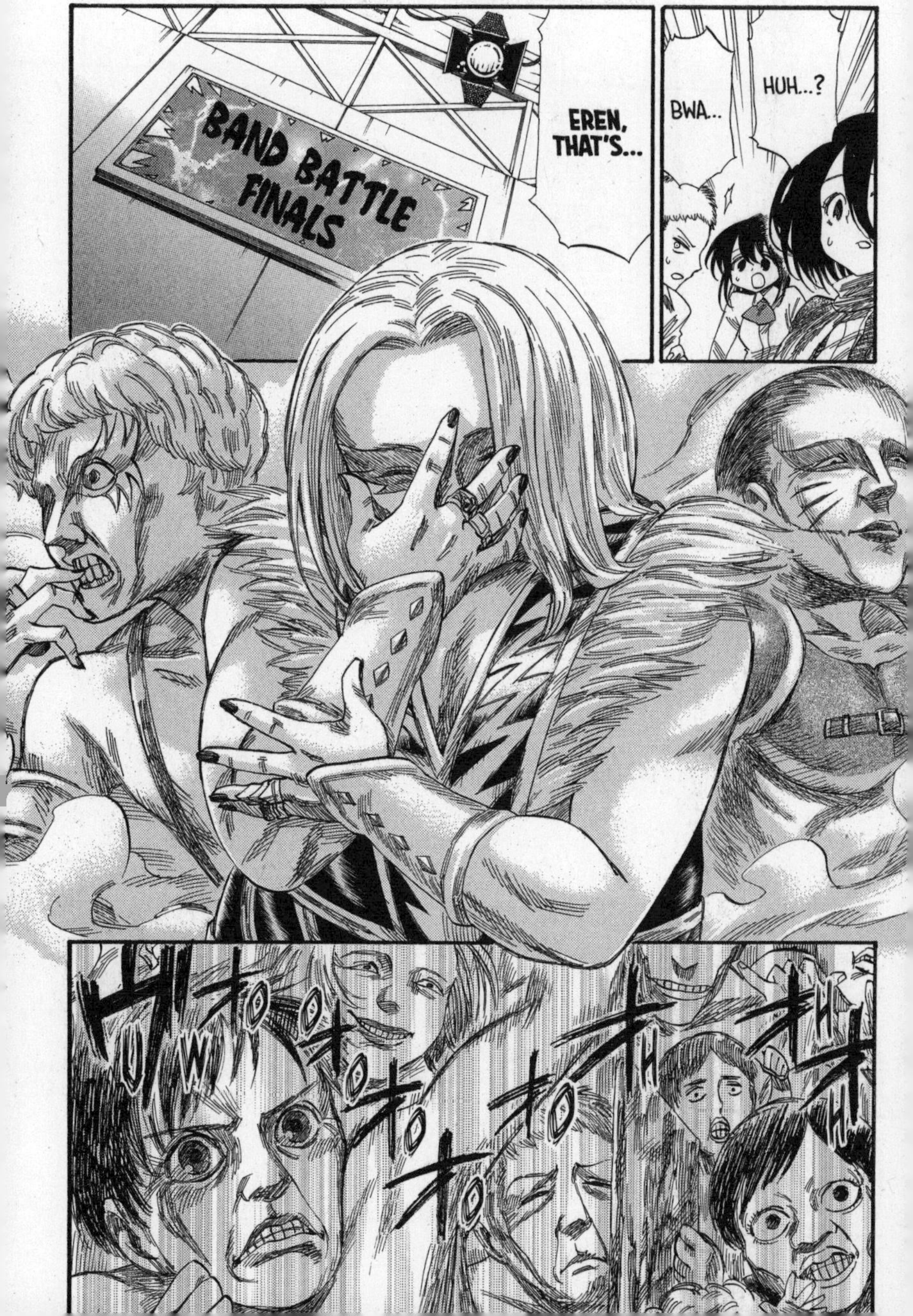
HUH...?
BWA...
EREN, THAT'S...
BAND BATTLE FINALS

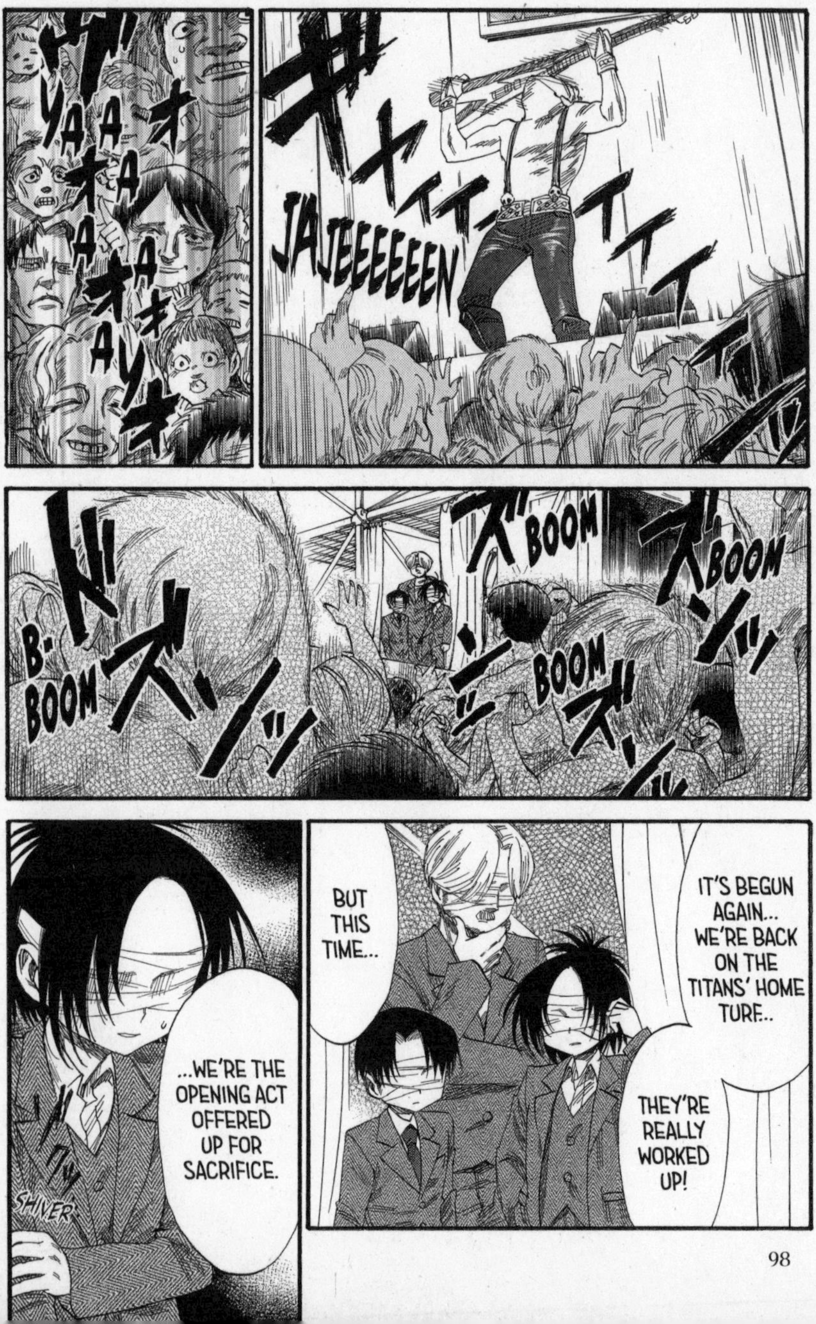
JAJEEEEEEN
YAAAAAAAY
BOOM
BOOM
BOOM
B-BOOM
IT'S BEGUN AGAIN... WE'RE BACK ON THE TITANS' HOME TURF...
THEY'RE REALLY WORKED UP!
BUT THIS TIME...
...WE'RE THE OPENING ACT OFFERED UP FOR SACRIFICE.
SHIVER

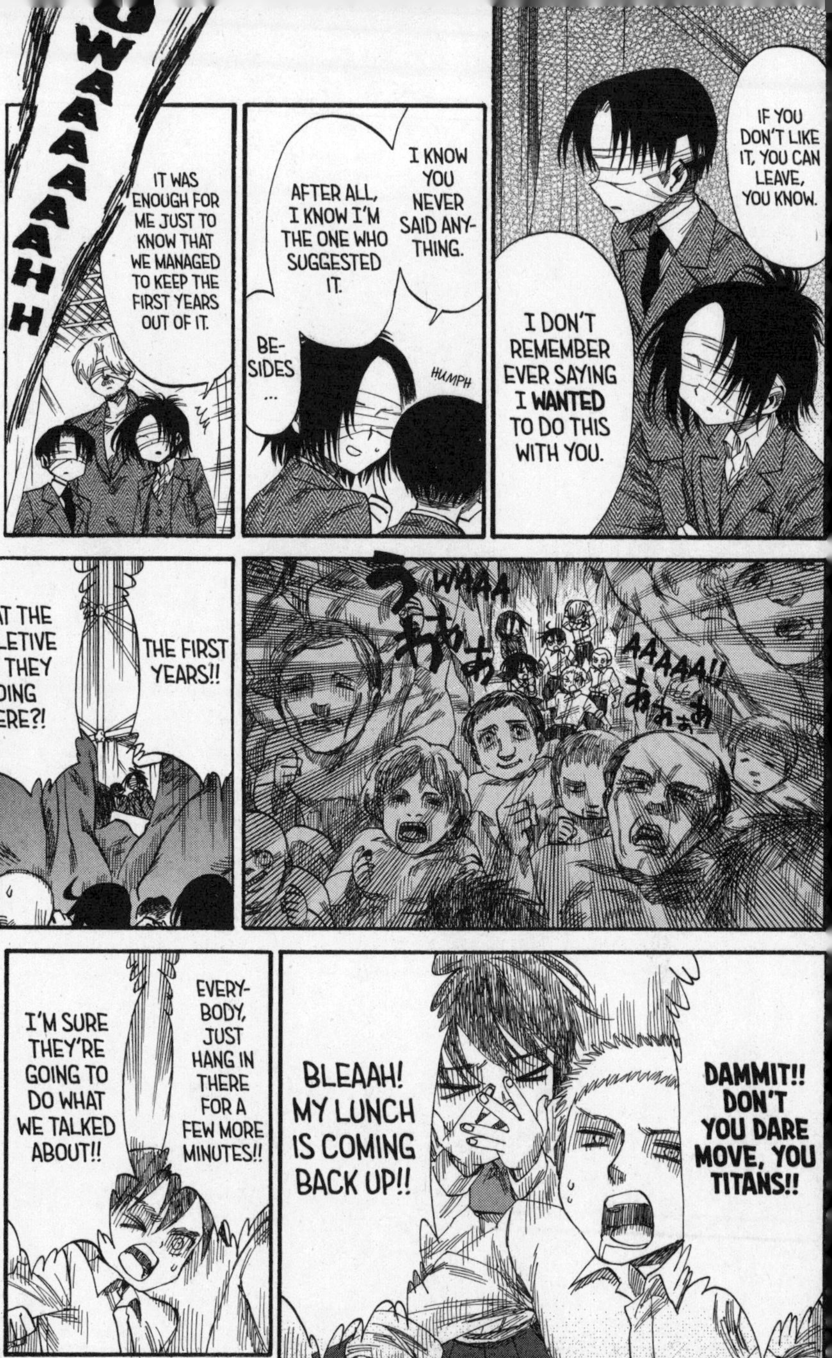
IF YOU DON'T LIKE IT, YOU CAN LEAVE, YOU KNOW.
I DON'T REMEMBER EVER SAYING I **WANTED** TO DO THIS WITH YOU.
I KNOW YOU NEVER SAID ANYTHING.
AFTER ALL, I KNOW I'M THE ONE WHO SUGGESTED IT.
BESIDES...
HUMPH
WAAAAAAAHH
IT WAS ENOUGH FOR ME JUST TO KNOW THAT WE MANAGED TO KEEP THE FIRST YEARS OUT OF IT.
WAAAA
AAAAA!!
THE FIRST YEARS!!
WHAT THE EXPLETIVE ARE THEY DOING THERE?!
DAMMIT!! DON'T YOU DARE MOVE, YOU TITANS!!
BLEAAH! MY LUNCH IS COMING BACK UP!!
EVERYBODY, JUST HANG IN THERE FOR A FEW MORE MINUTES!!
I'M SURE THEY'RE GOING TO DO WHAT WE TALKED ABOUT!!

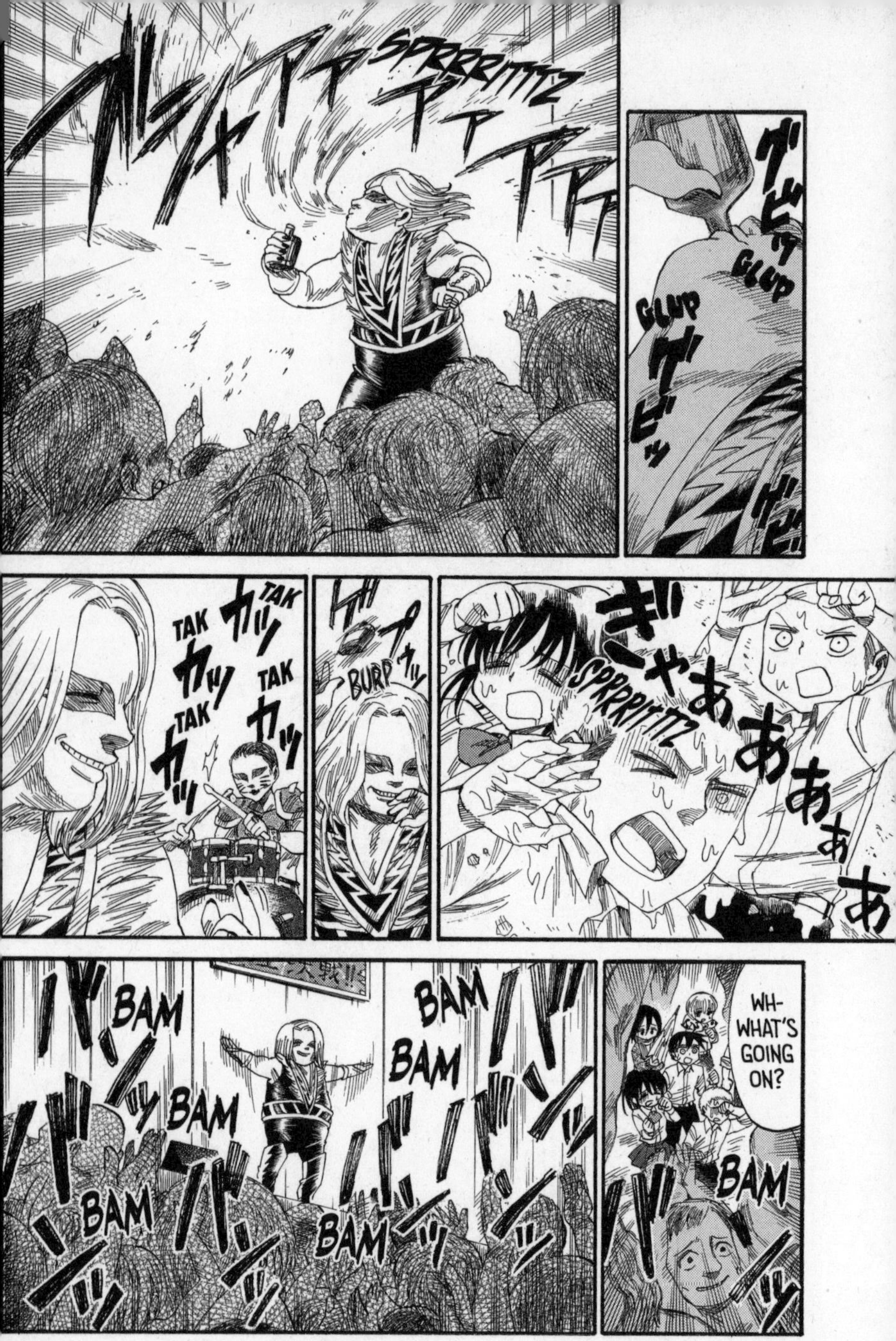
GLUP
GLUP
SPRRRITTTZ
ぎゃああああ
SPRRRITTTZ
BURP
TAK
TAK
TAK
TAK
WH- WHAT'S GOING ON?
BAM
BAM
BAM
BAM
BAM
BAM
BAM

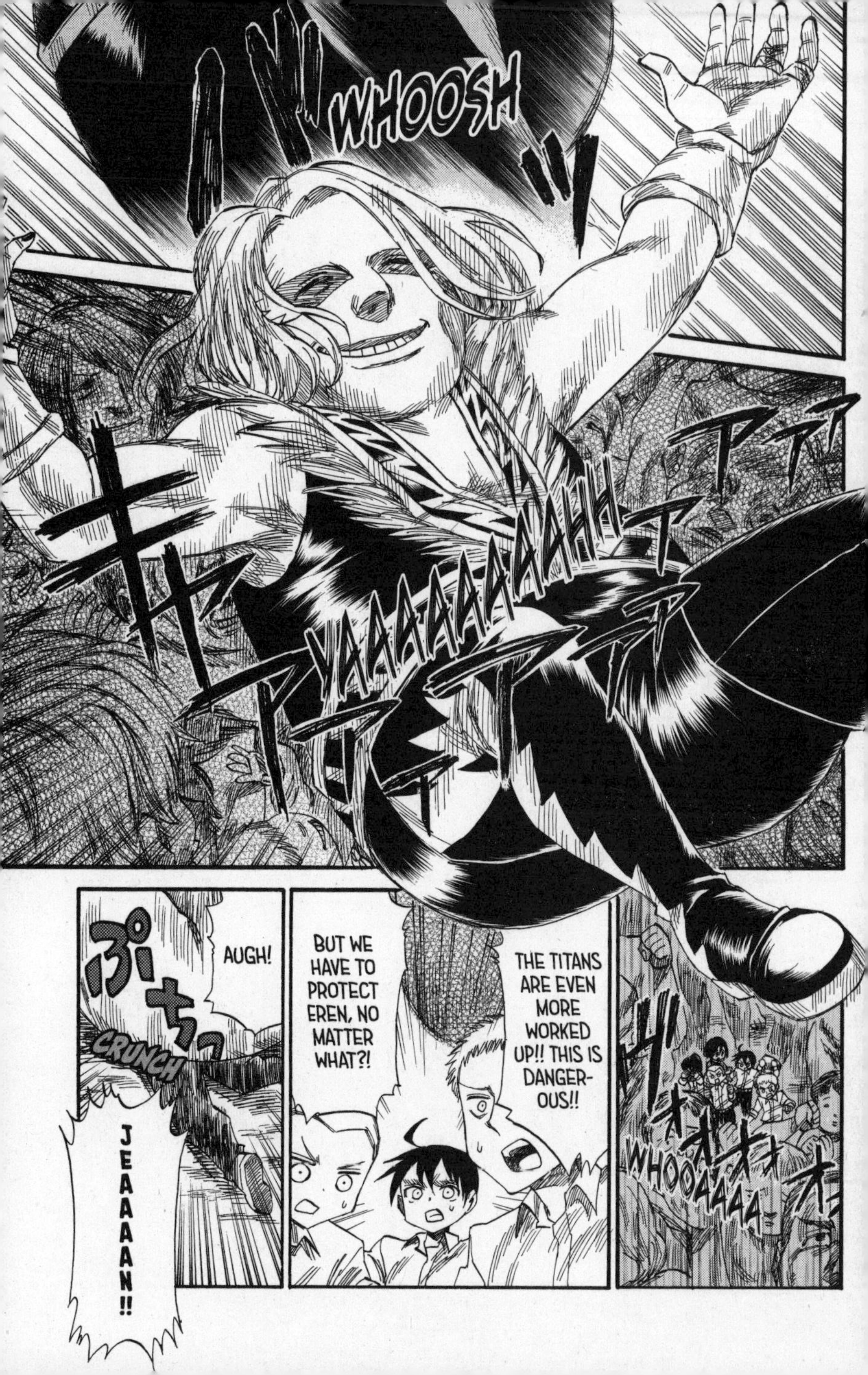
WHOOSH
YAAAAAAAAHH
THE TITANS ARE EVEN MORE WORKED UP!! THIS IS DANGER-OUS!!
WHOOAAAA
BUT WE HAVE TO PROTECT EREN, NO MATTER WHAT?!
AUGH!
CRUNCH
JEAAAAAN!!

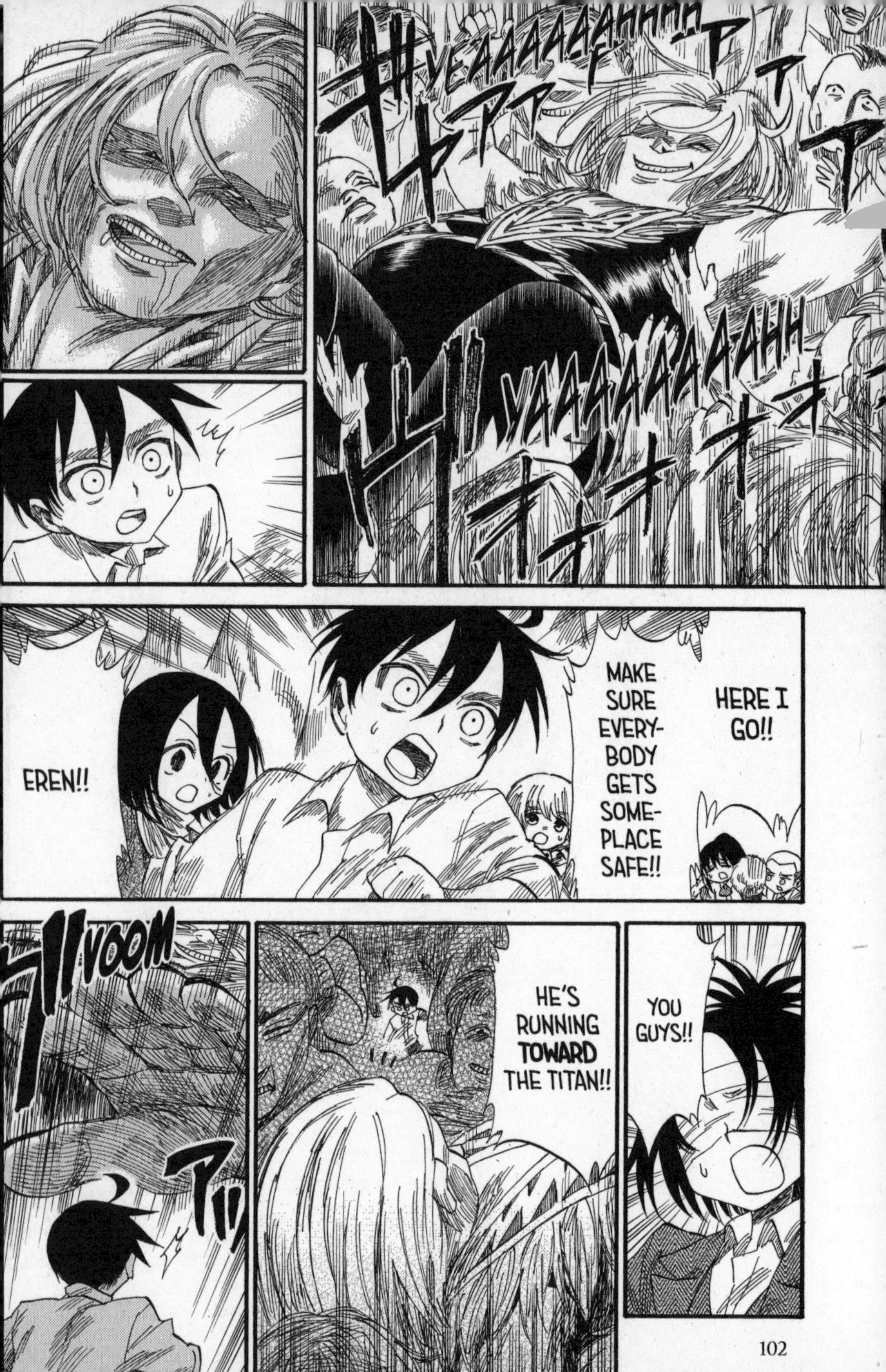
YEAAAAAAhhhh
YAAAAAAAAAAHH
HERE I GO!!
MAKE SURE EVERYBODY GETS SOMEPLACE SAFE!!
EREN!!
YOU GUYS!!
HE'S RUNNING **TOWARD** THE TITAN!!
VOOM

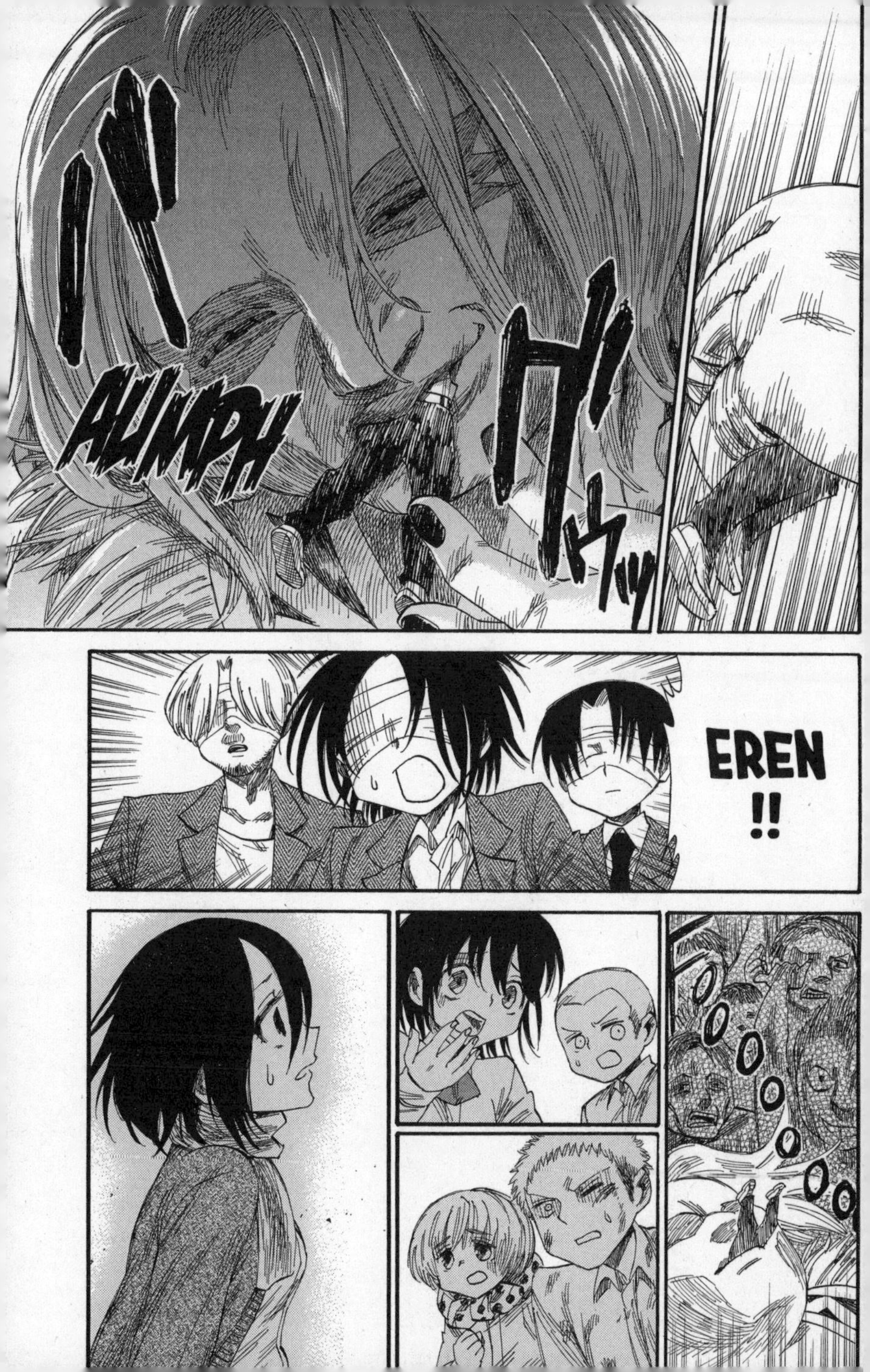
AUMPH
EREN !!

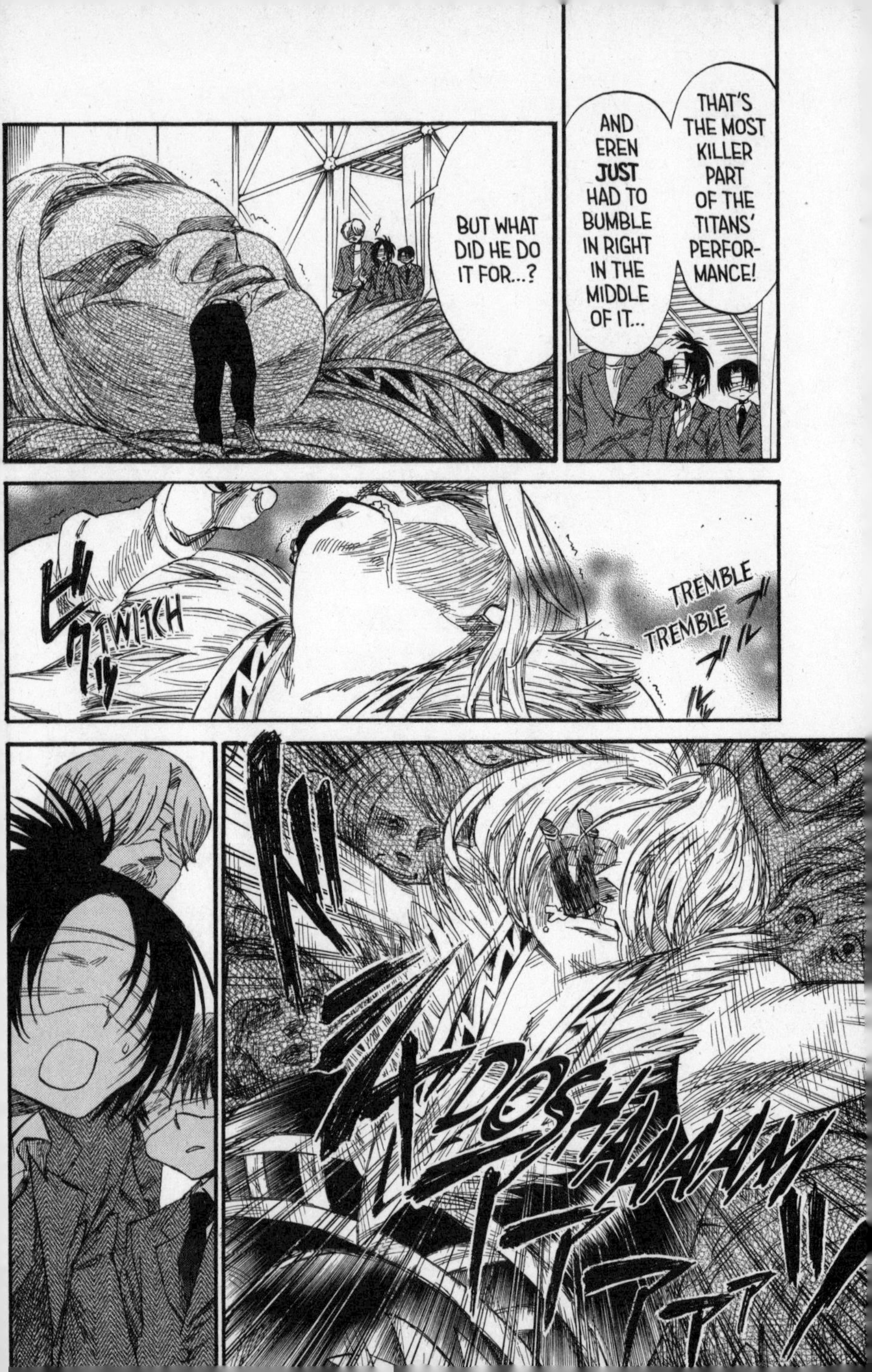
THAT'S THE MOST KILLER PART OF THE TITANS' PERFOR-MANCE!
AND EREN JUST HAD TO BUMBLE IN RIGHT IN THE MIDDLE OF IT...
BUT WHAT DID HE DO IT FOR...?
TREMBLE TREMBLE
TWITCH
DOSHAAAAM

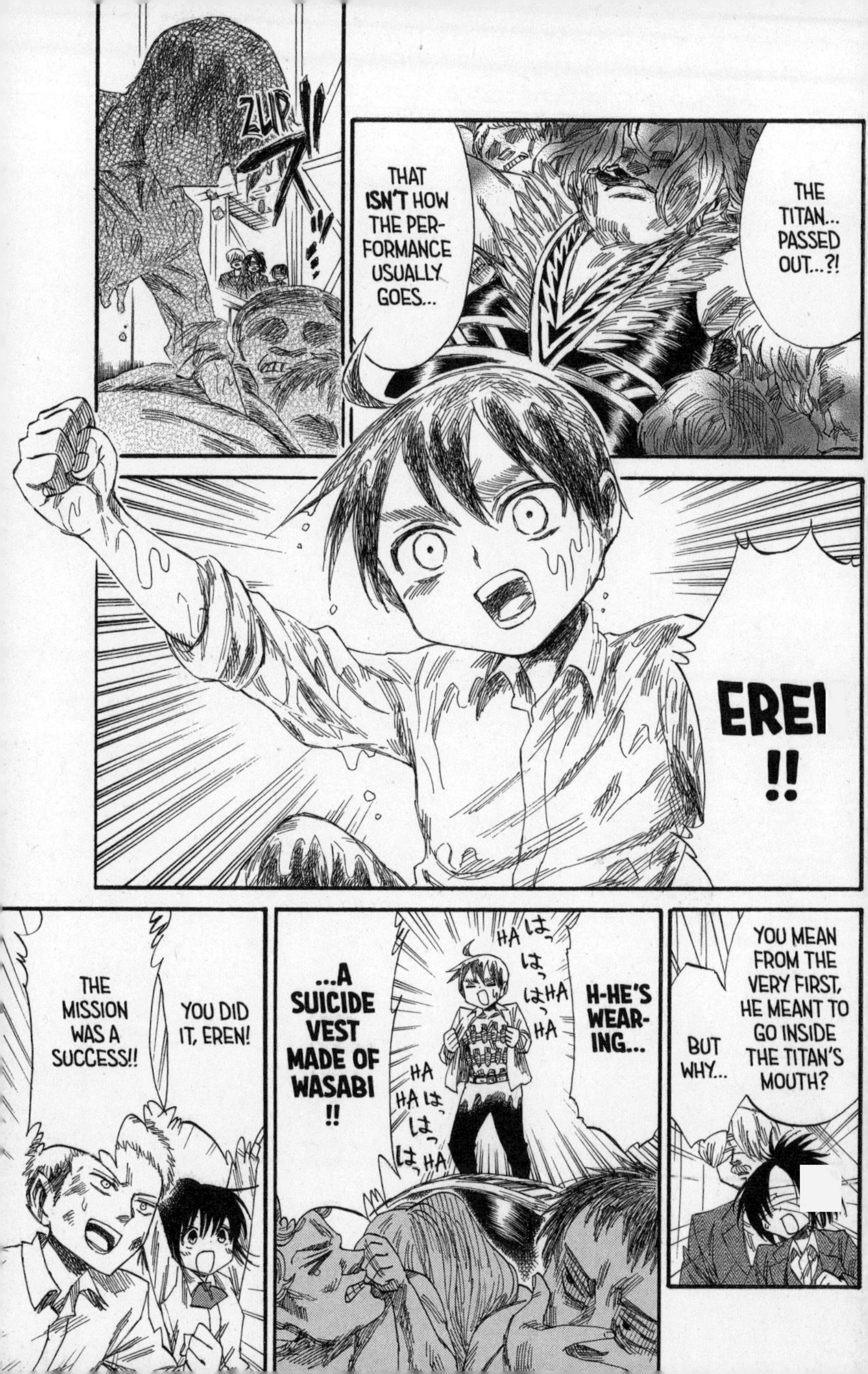
THE TITAN... PASSED OUT...?!
THAT ISN'T HOW THE PER-FORMANCE USUALLY GOES...
ZUIP
EREI !!
YOU MEAN FROM THE VERY FIRST, HE MEANT TO GO INSIDE THE TITAN'S MOUTH?
BUT WHY...
H-HE'S WEAR-ING...
HA はっ はっ はっ HA HA
HA HA はっ はっ はっ HA
...A SUICIDE VEST MADE OF WASABI !!
YOU DID IT, EREN!
THE MISSION WAS A SUCCESS!!

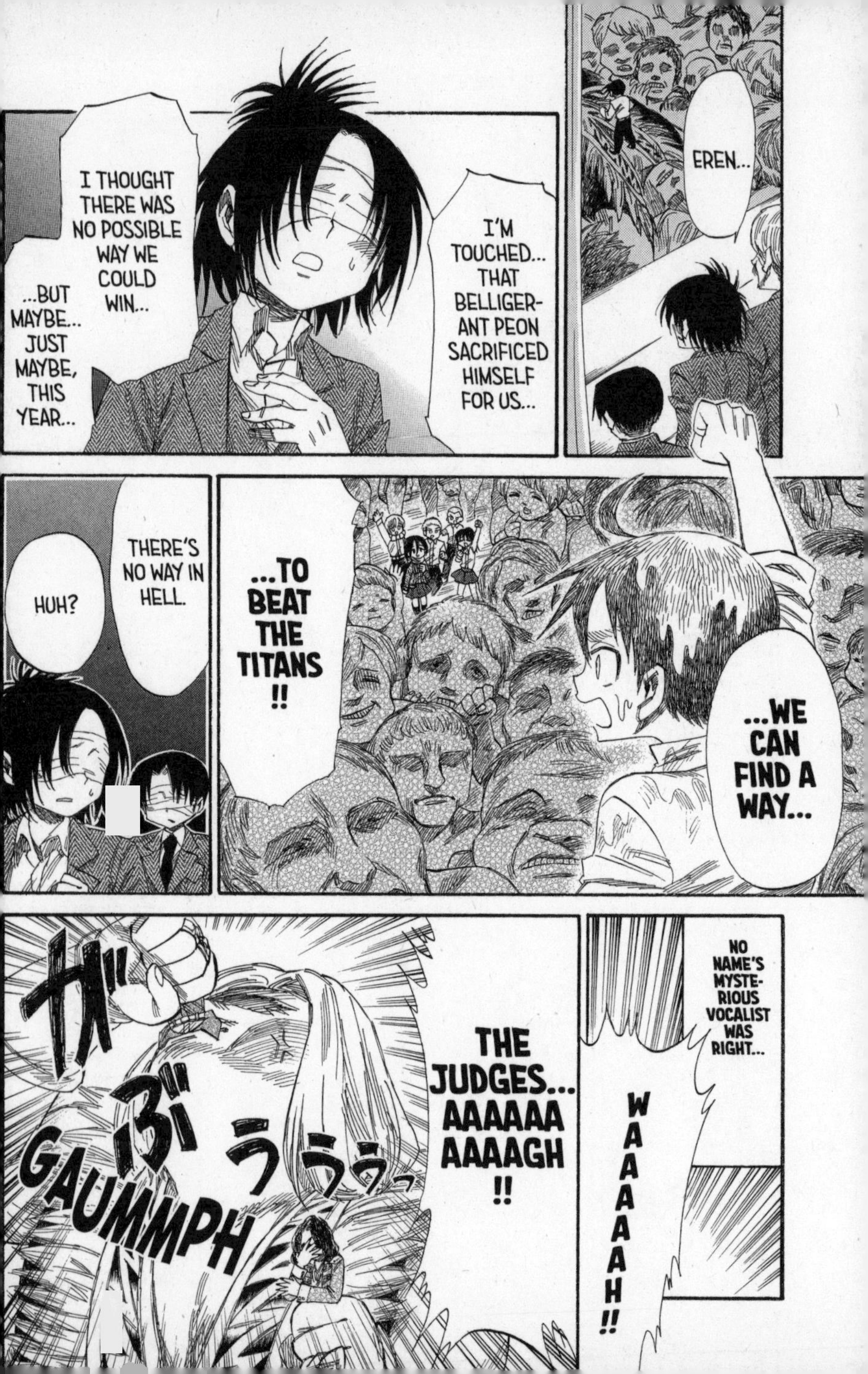
EREN...
I'M TOUCHED... THAT BELLIGER-ANT PEON SACRIFICED HIMSELF FOR US...
I THOUGHT THERE WAS NO POSSIBLE WAY WE COULD WIN...
...BUT MAYBE... JUST MAYBE, THIS YEAR...
...WE CAN FIND A WAY...
...TO BEAT THE TITANS!!
THERE'S NO WAY IN HELL.
HUH?
NO NAME'S MYSTE-RIOUS VOCALIST WAS RIGHT...
WAAAAAAAH!!
THE JUDGES... AAAAAAAAAAGH!!
GAUMMPH

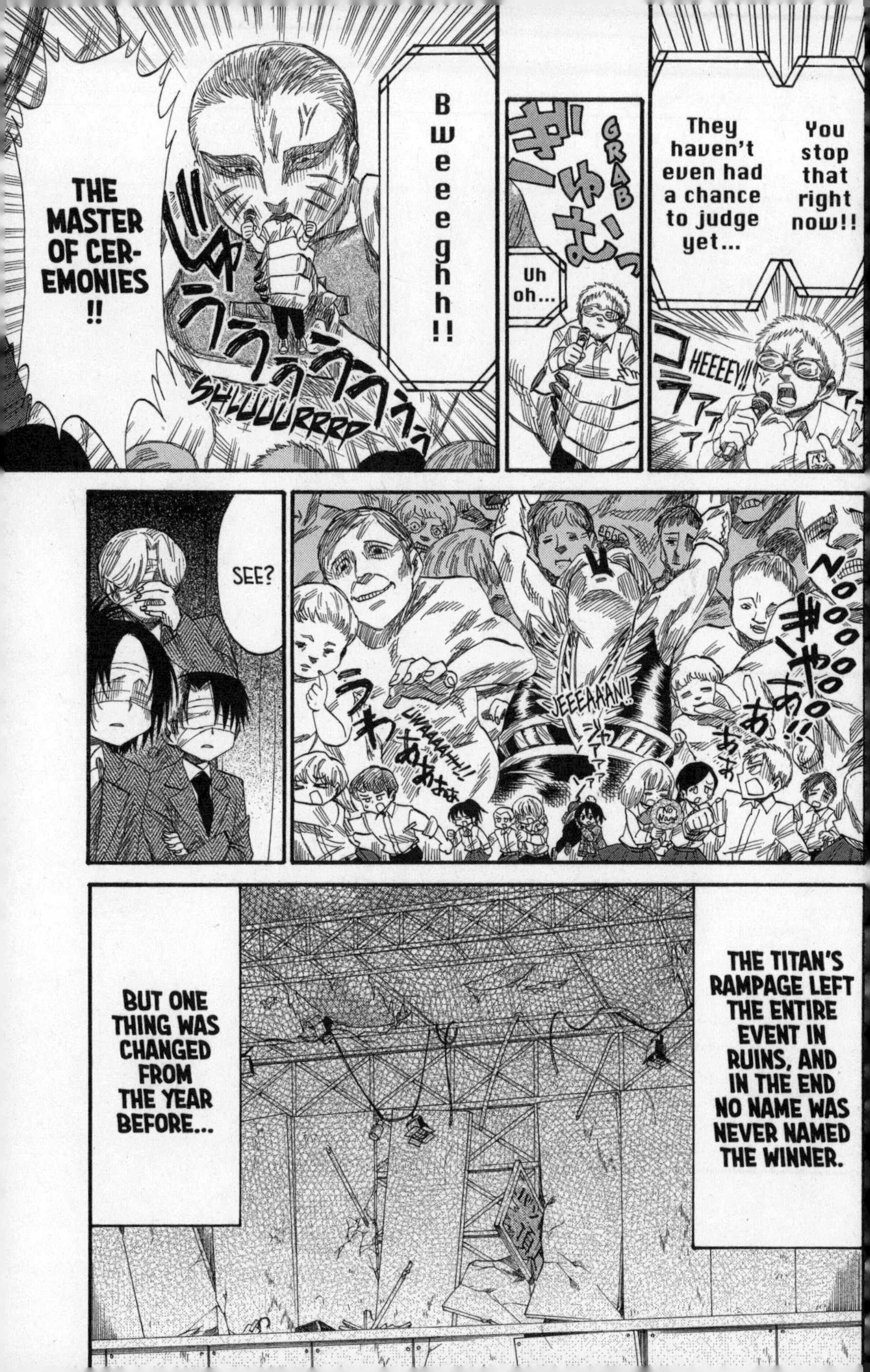
You stop that right now!!
They haven't even had a chance to judge yet...
HEEEEY!!
GRAB
Uh oh...
Bweeeghh!!
THE MASTER OF CEREMONIES!!
SHLUUURRRP
NOOOOO!!
JEEEAAAN!!
UWAAAAH!!
SEE?
THE TITAN'S RAMPAGE LEFT THE ENTIRE EVENT IN RUINS, AND IN THE END NO NAME WAS NEVER NAMED THE WINNER.
BUT ONE THING WAS CHANGED FROM THE YEAR BEFORE...

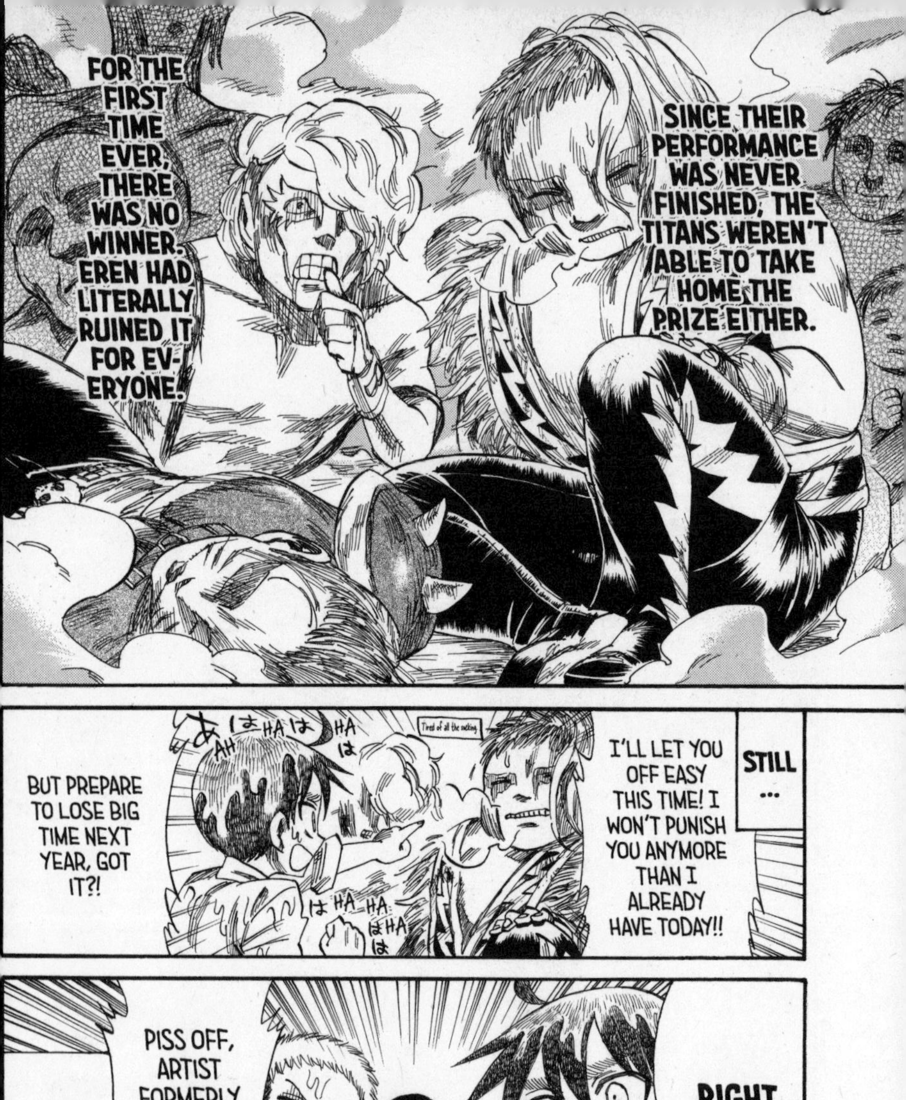
SINCE THEIR PERFORMANCE WAS NEVER FINISHED, THE TITANS WEREN'T ABLE TO TAKE HOME THE PRIZE EITHER.
FOR THE FIRST TIME EVER, THERE WAS NO WINNER. EREN HAD LITERALLY RUINED IT FOR EV-ERYONE.
STILL ...
I'LL LET YOU OFF EASY THIS TIME! I WON'T PUNISH YOU ANYMORE THAN I ALREADY HAVE TODAY!!
Tired of all the sucking
あ AH は HA は HA は
は HA HA は HA は
BUT PREPARE TO LOSE BIG TIME NEXT YEAR, GOT IT?!
RIGHT, EVERY-BODY?!
PISS OFF, ARTIST FORMERLY KNOWN AS PUTZ! I'M GIVING UP THE GUITAR FOREVER!!
...THE PRICE THEY PAID WAS TOO HIGH.

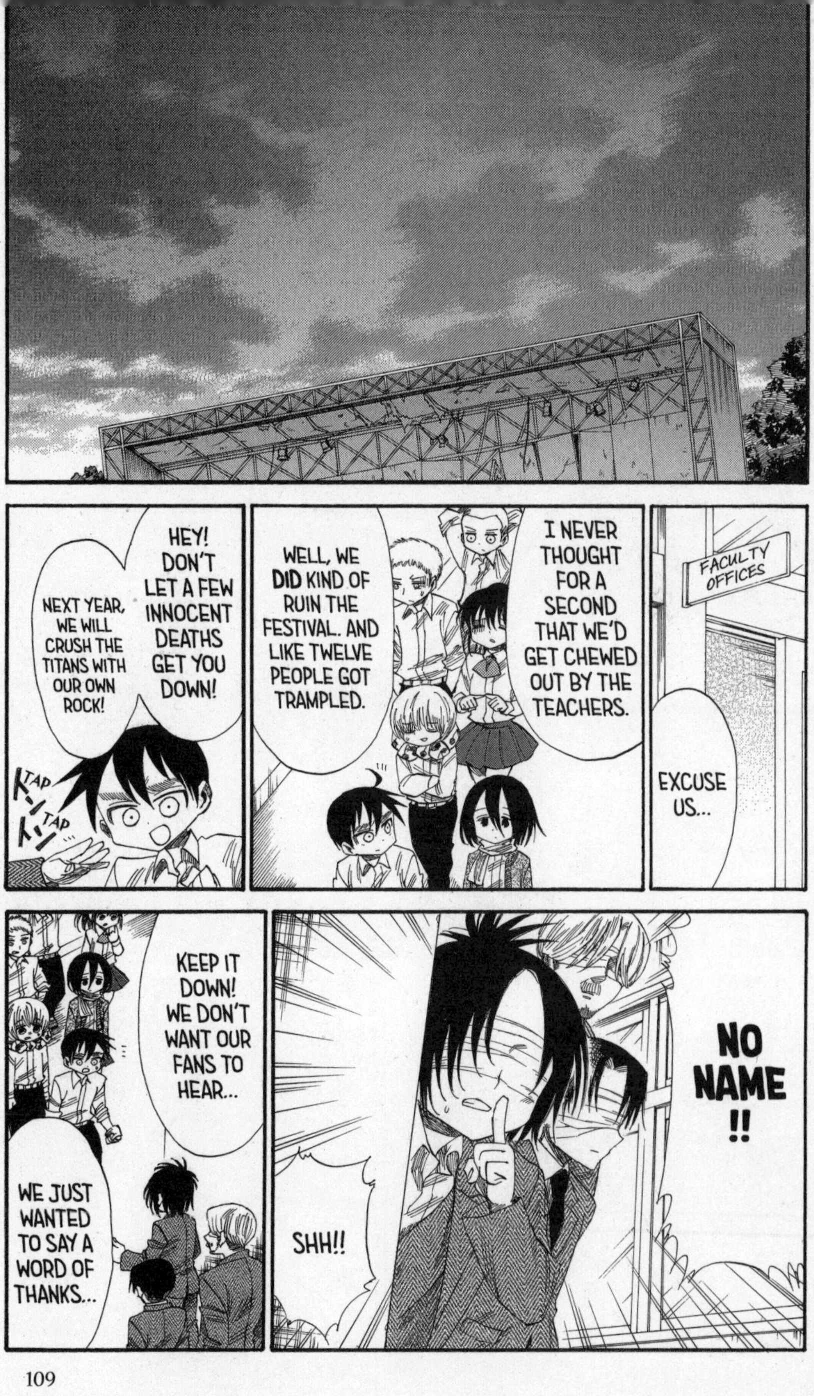
FACULTY OFFICES
EXCUSE US...
I NEVER THOUGHT FOR A SECOND THAT WE'D GET CHEWED OUT BY THE TEACHERS.
WELL, WE DID KIND OF RUIN THE FESTIVAL. AND LIKE TWELVE PEOPLE GOT TRAMPLED.
HEY! DON'T LET A FEW INNOCENT DEATHS GET YOU DOWN!
NEXT YEAR, WE WILL CRUSH THE TITANS WITH OUR OWN ROCK!
TAP TAP
NO NAME!!
SHH!!
KEEP IT DOWN! WE DON'T WANT OUR FANS TO HEAR...
WE JUST WANTED TO SAY A WORD OF THANKS...

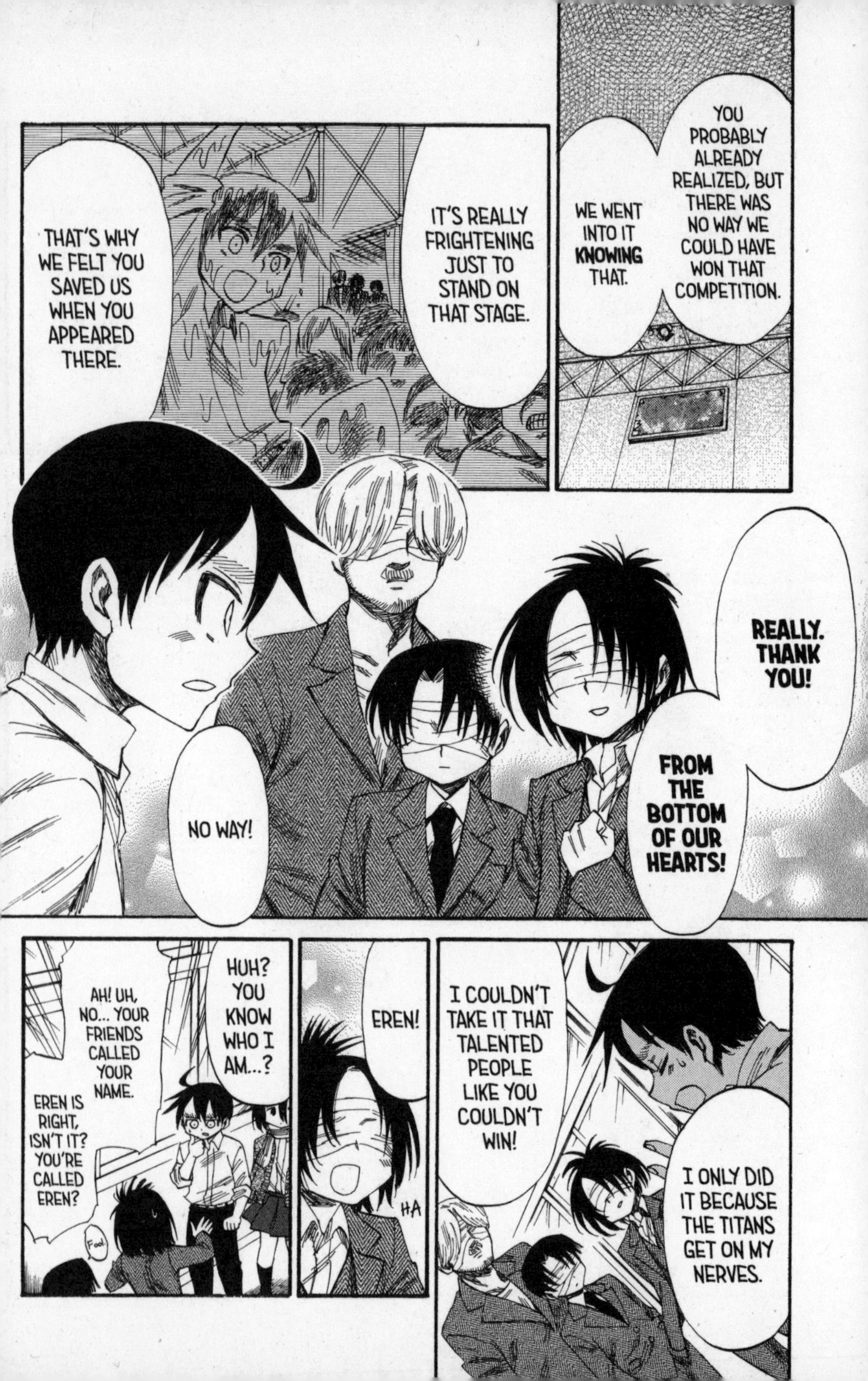
YOU PROBABLY ALREADY REALIZED, BUT THERE WAS NO WAY WE COULD HAVE WON THAT COMPETITION.
WE WENT INTO IT **KNOWING** THAT.
IT'S REALLY FRIGHTENING JUST TO STAND ON THAT STAGE.
THAT'S WHY WE FELT YOU SAVED US WHEN YOU APPEARED THERE.
REALLY. THANK YOU!
FROM THE BOTTOM OF OUR HEARTS!
NO WAY!
I COULDN'T TAKE IT THAT TALENTED PEOPLE LIKE YOU COULDN'T WIN!
I ONLY DID IT BECAUSE THE TITANS GET ON MY NERVES.
EREN!
HA
HUH? YOU KNOW WHO I AM...?
AH! UH, NO... YOUR FRIENDS CALLED YOUR NAME.
EREN IS RIGHT, ISN'T IT? YOU'RE CALLED EREN?
Fool.

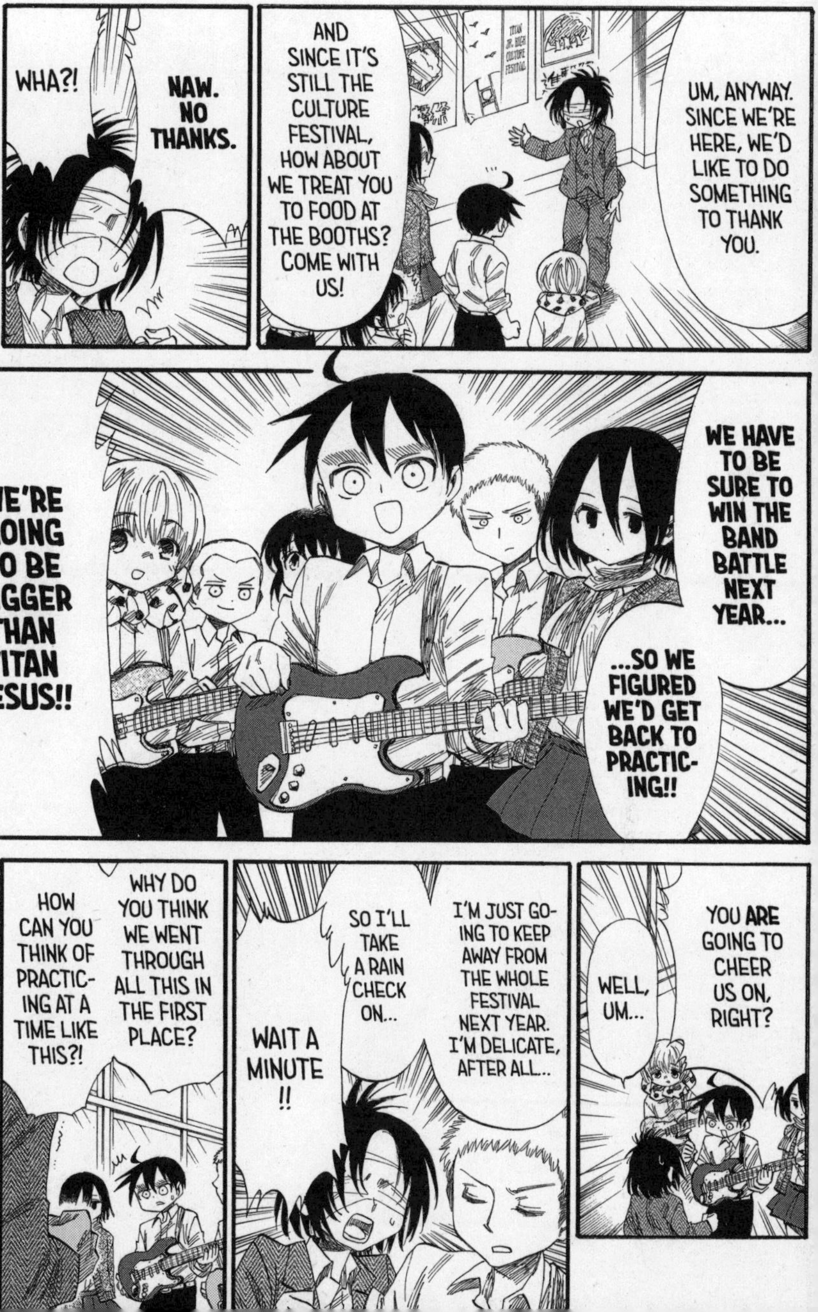
UM, ANYWAY. SINCE WE'RE HERE, WE'D LIKE TO DO SOMETHING TO THANK YOU.
TITAN JR. HIGH CULTURE FESTIVAL
AND SINCE IT'S STILL THE CULTURE FESTIVAL, HOW ABOUT WE TREAT YOU TO FOOD AT THE BOOTHS? COME WITH US!
NAW. NO THANKS.
WHA?!
WE HAVE TO BE SURE TO WIN THE BAND BATTLE NEXT YEAR...
...SO WE FIGURED WE'D GET BACK TO PRACTIC-ING!!
WE'RE GOING TO BE BIGGER THAN TITAN JESUS!!
YOU ARE GOING TO CHEER US ON, RIGHT?
WELL, UM...
I'M JUST GO-ING TO KEEP AWAY FROM THE WHOLE FESTIVAL NEXT YEAR. I'M DELICATE, AFTER ALL...
SO I'LL TAKE A RAIN CHECK ON...
WAIT A MINUTE!!
WHY DO YOU THINK WE WENT THROUGH ALL THIS IN THE FIRST PLACE?
HOW CAN YOU THINK OF PRACTIC-ING AT A TIME LIKE THIS?!

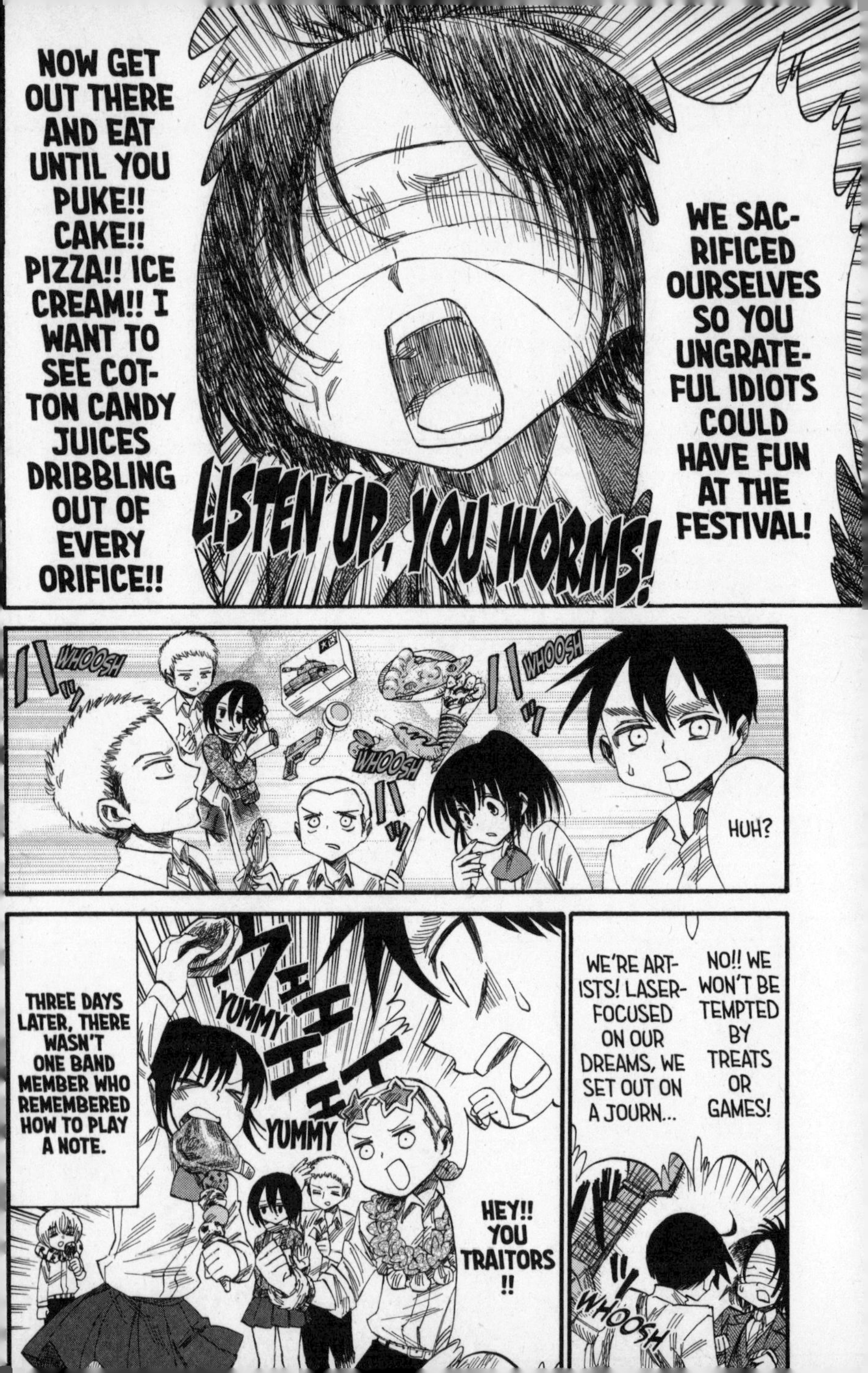

WE SACRIFICED OURSELVES SO YOU UNGRATEFUL IDIOTS COULD HAVE FUN AT THE FESTIVAL!
LISTEN UP, YOU WORMS!
NOW GET OUT THERE AND EAT UNTIL YOU PUKE!! CAKE!! PIZZA!! ICE CREAM!! I WANT TO SEE COTTON CANDY JUICES DRIBBLING OUT OF EVERY ORIFICE!!
WHOOSH
HUH?
WHOOSH
WHOOSH
NO!! WE WON'T BE TEMPTED BY TREATS OR GAMES!
WE'RE ARTISTS! LASER-FOCUSED ON OUR DREAMS, WE SET OUT ON A JOURN...
WHOOSH
HEY!! YOU TRAITORS!!
YUMMY
YUMMY
THREE DAYS LATER, THERE WASN'T ONE BAND MEMBER WHO REMEMBERED HOW TO PLAY A NOTE.

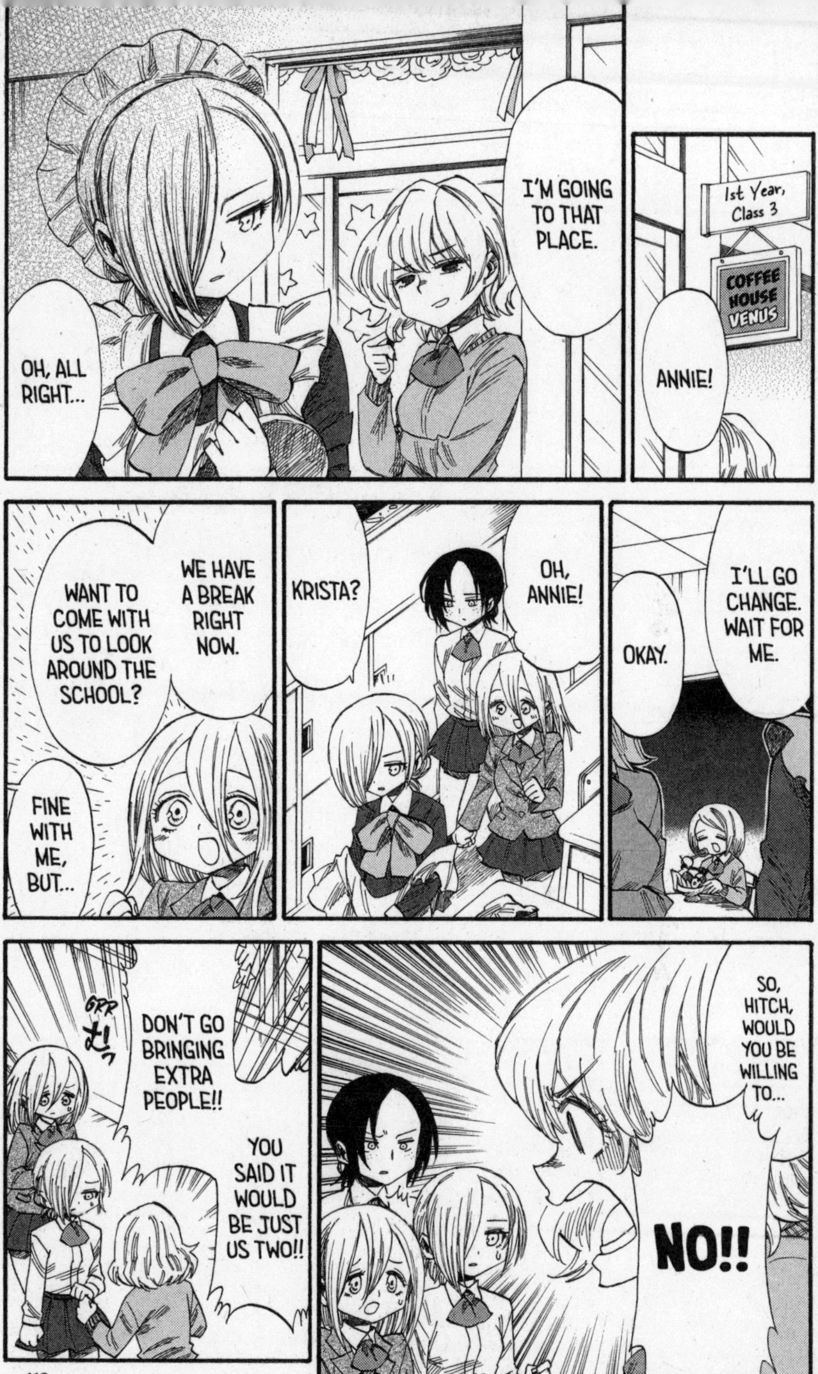
1st Year, Class 3
COFFEE HOUSE VENUS
ANNIE!
I'M GOING TO THAT PLACE.
OH, ALL RIGHT...
I'LL GO CHANGE. WAIT FOR ME.
OKAY.
OH, ANNIE!
KRISTA?
WE HAVE A BREAK RIGHT NOW.
WANT TO COME WITH US TO LOOK AROUND THE SCHOOL?
FINE WITH ME, BUT...
SO, HITCH, WOULD YOU BE WILLING TO...
NO!!
GRR
DON'T GO BRINGING EXTRA PEOPLE!!
YOU SAID IT WOULD BE JUST US TWO!!

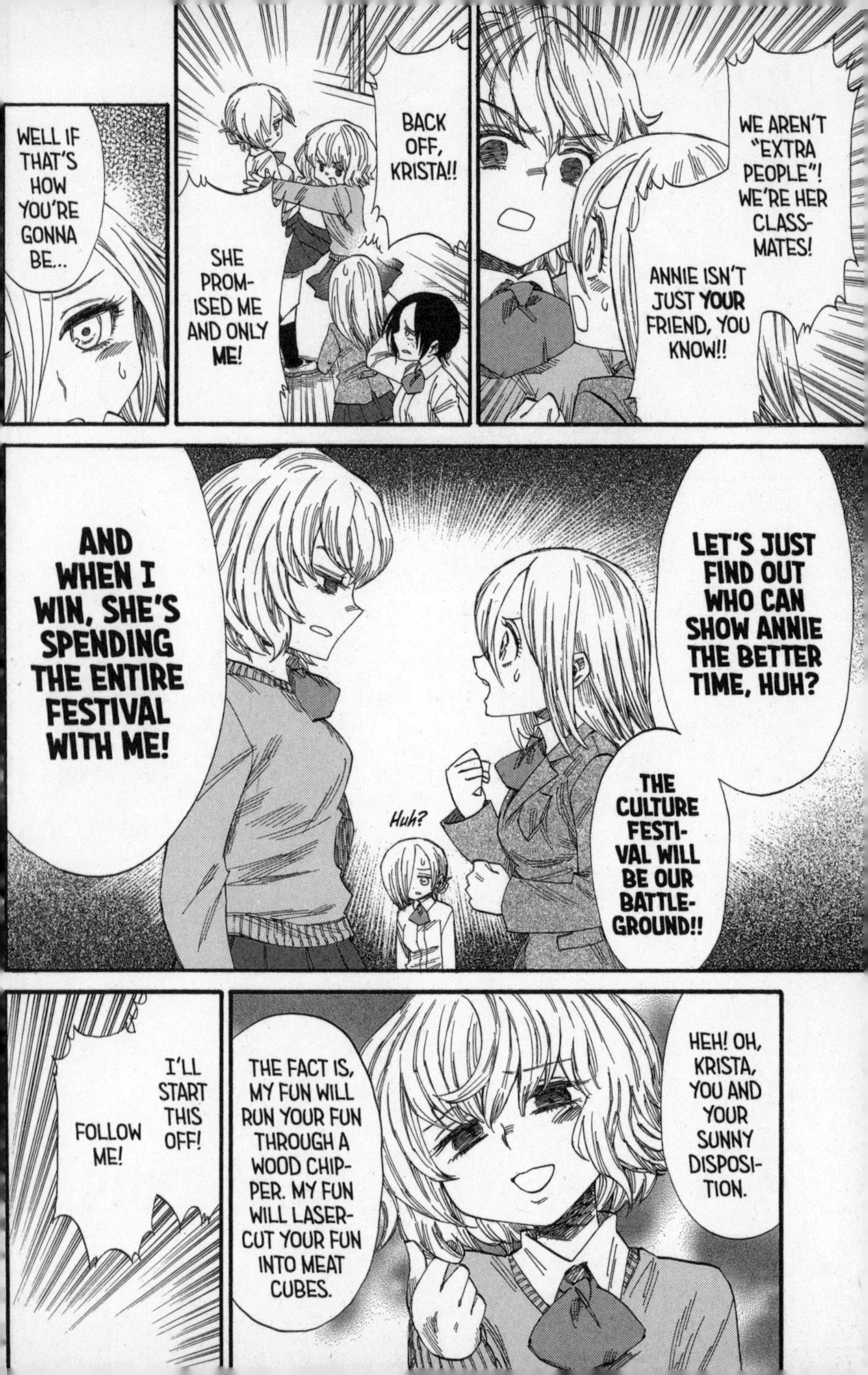
WE AREN'T "EXTRA PEOPLE"! WE'RE HER CLASSMATES!
ANNIE ISN'T JUST **YOUR** FRIEND, YOU KNOW!!
BACK OFF, KRISTA!!
SHE PROMISED ME AND ONLY **ME**!
WELL IF THAT'S HOW YOU'RE GONNA BE...
LET'S JUST FIND OUT WHO CAN SHOW ANNIE THE BETTER TIME, HUH?
THE CULTURE FESTIVAL WILL BE OUR BATTLEGROUND!!
Huh?
AND WHEN I WIN, SHE'S SPENDING THE ENTIRE FESTIVAL WITH ME!
HEH! OH, KRISTA, YOU AND YOUR SUNNY DISPOSITION.
THE FACT IS, MY FUN WILL RUN YOUR FUN THROUGH A WOOD CHIPPER. MY FUN WILL LASER-CUT YOUR FUN INTO MEAT CUBES.
I'LL START THIS OFF!
FOLLOW ME!

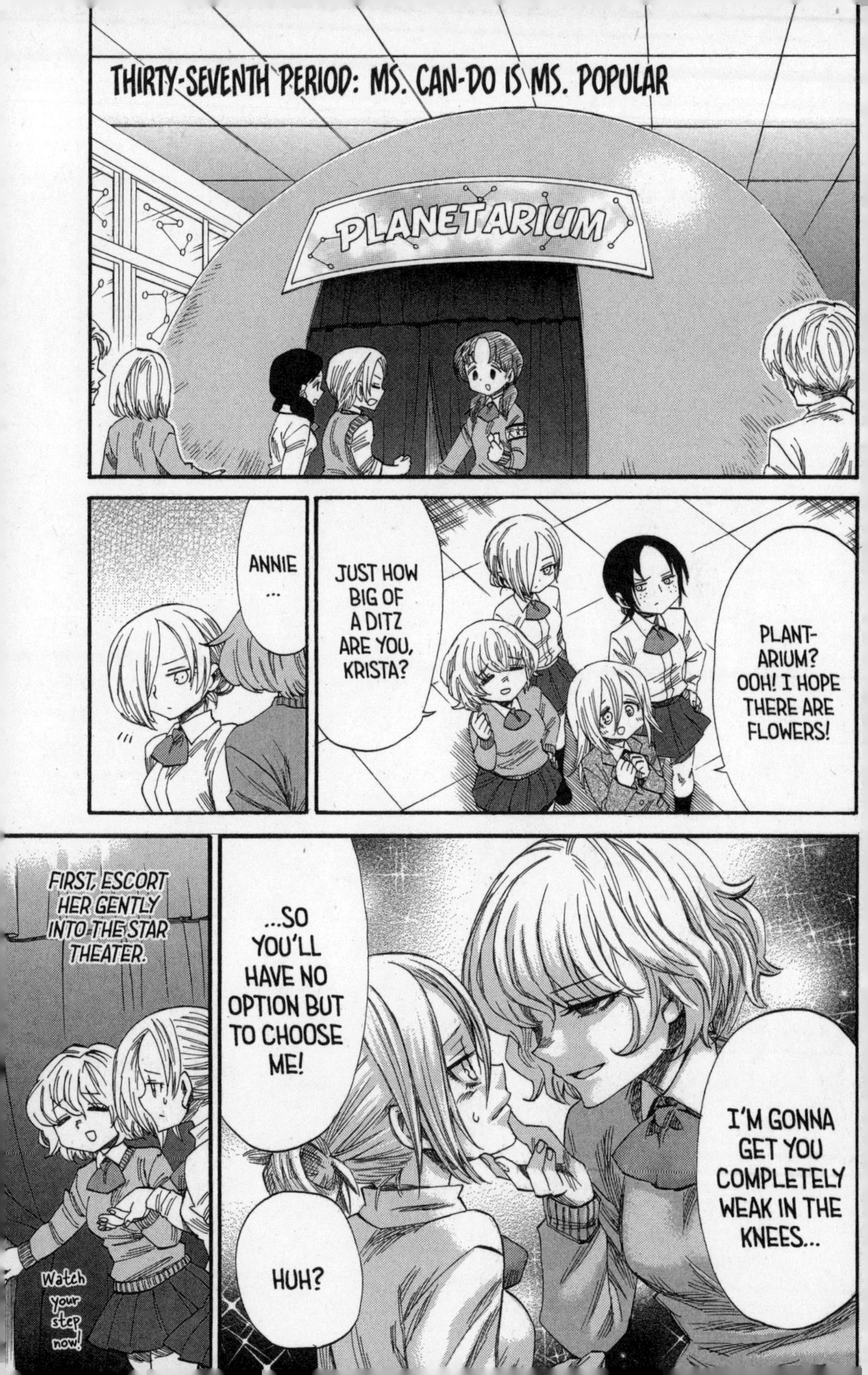
THIRTY-SEVENTH PERIOD: MS. CAN-DO IS MS. POPULAR
PLANETARIUM
PLANT-ARIUM? OOH! I HOPE THERE ARE FLOWERS!
JUST HOW BIG OF A DITZ ARE YOU, KRISTA?
ANNIE ...
I'M GONNA GET YOU COMPLETELY WEAK IN THE KNEES...
...SO YOU'LL HAVE NO OPTION BUT TO CHOOSE ME!
HUH?
FIRST, ESCORT HER GENTLY INTO THE STAR THEATER.
Watch your step now!

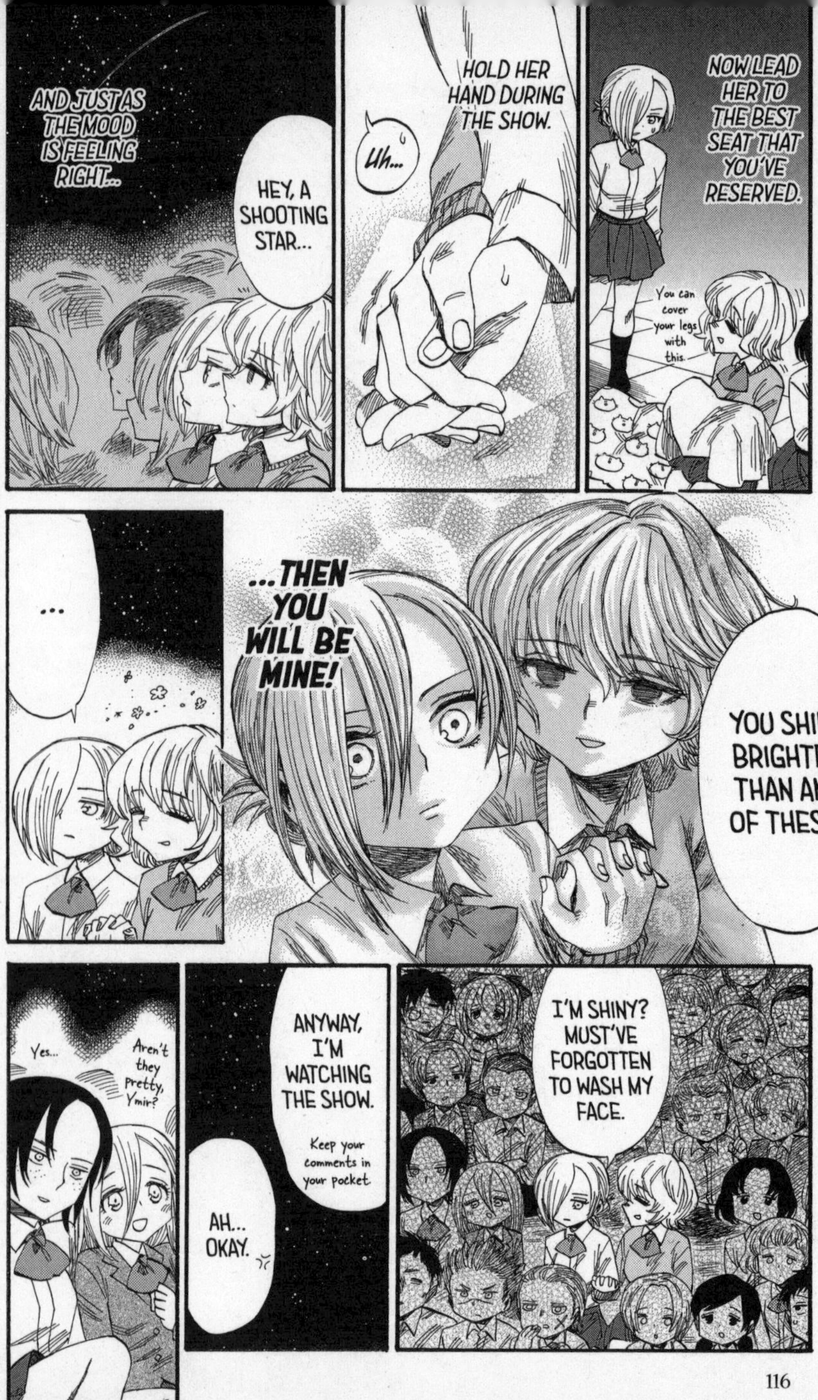
NOW LEAD HER TO THE BEST SEAT THAT YOU'VE RESERVED.
You can cover your legs with this.
HOLD HER HAND DURING THE SHOW.
Uh...
AND JUST AS THE MOOD IS FEELING RIGHT...
HEY, A SHOOTING STAR...
YOU SHINE BRIGHTER THAN ANY OF THESE!
...THEN YOU WILL BE MINE!
...
I'M SHINY? MUST'VE FORGOTTEN TO WASH MY FACE.
ANYWAY, I'M WATCHING THE SHOW.
Keep your comments in your pocket.
AH... OKAY.
Aren't they pretty, Ymir?
Yes...

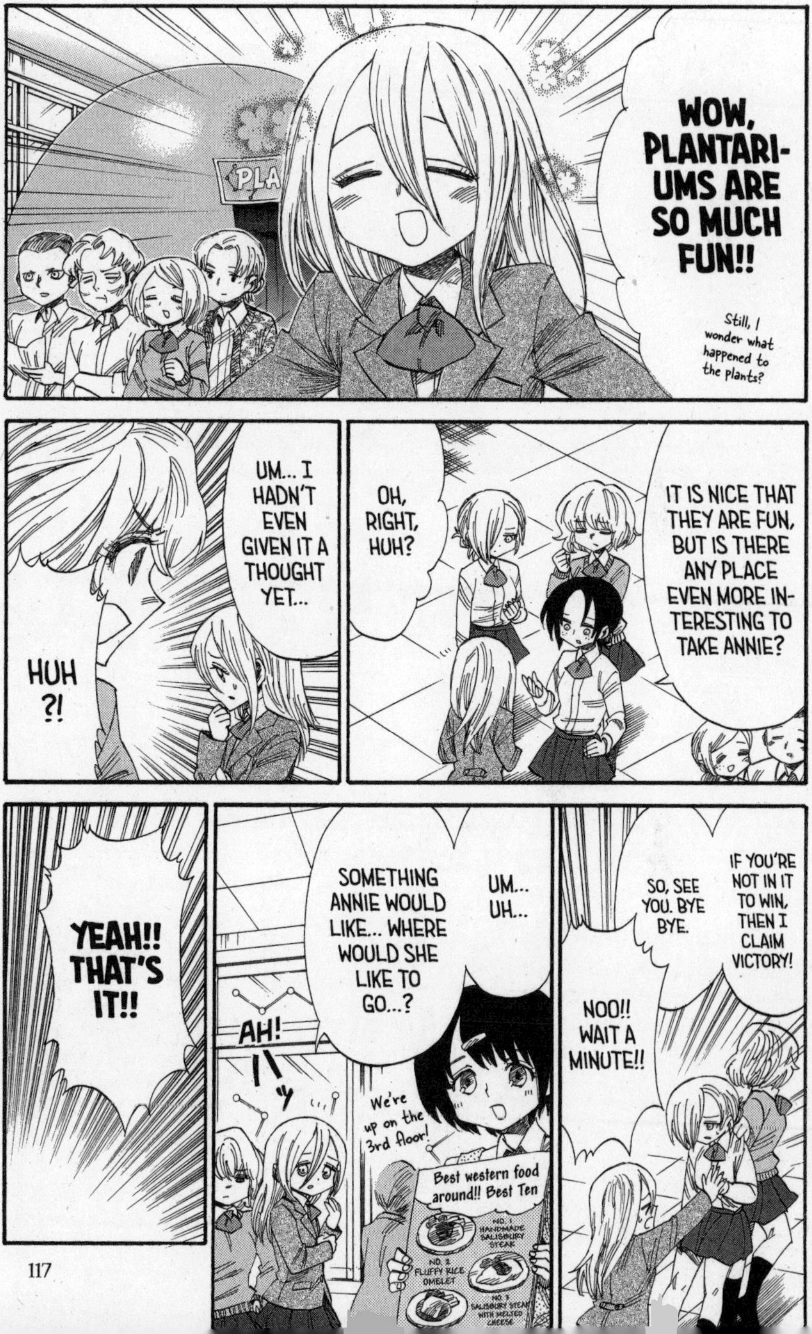
WOW, PLANTARI-UMS ARE SO MUCH FUN!!
Still, I wonder what happened to the plants?
PLA
IT IS NICE THAT THEY ARE FUN, BUT IS THERE ANY PLACE EVEN MORE IN-TERESTING TO TAKE ANNIE?
OH, RIGHT, HUH?
UM... I HADN'T EVEN GIVEN IT A THOUGHT YET...
HUH ?!
IF YOU'RE NOT IN IT TO WIN, THEN I CLAIM VICTORY!
SO, SEE YOU. BYE BYE.
NOO!! WAIT A MINUTE!!
UM... UH...
SOMETHING ANNIE WOULD LIKE... WHERE WOULD SHE LIKE TO GO...?
AH!
ハッ
We're up on the 3rd floor!
Best western food around!! Best Ten
NO. 1 HANDMADE SALISBURY STEAK
NO. 2 FLUFFY RICE OMELET
NO. 3 SALISBURY STEAK WITH MELTED CHEESE
YEAH!! THAT'S IT!!

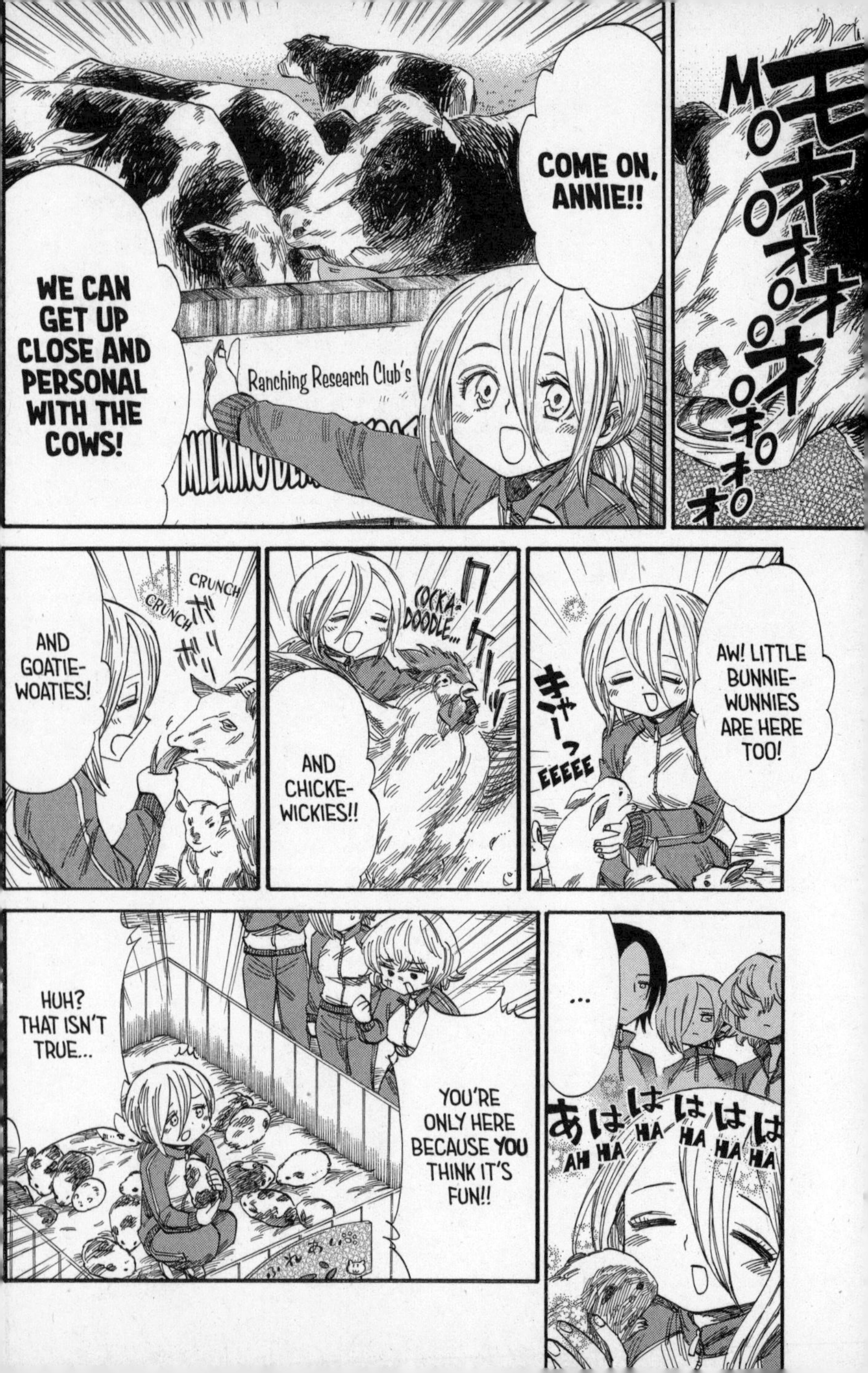
MOOOOOO
COME ON, ANNIE!!
Ranching Research Club's
MILKING DE
WE CAN GET UP CLOSE AND PERSONAL WITH THE COWS!
AW! LITTLE BUNNIE-WUNNIES ARE HERE TOO!
EEEEE
COCKA-DOODLE...
AND CHICKE-WICKIES!!
CRUNCH
CRUNCH
AND GOATIE-WOATIES!
...
あははははは
AH HA HA HA HA HA
YOU'RE ONLY HERE BECAUSE YOU THINK IT'S FUN!!
HUH? THAT ISN'T TRUE...

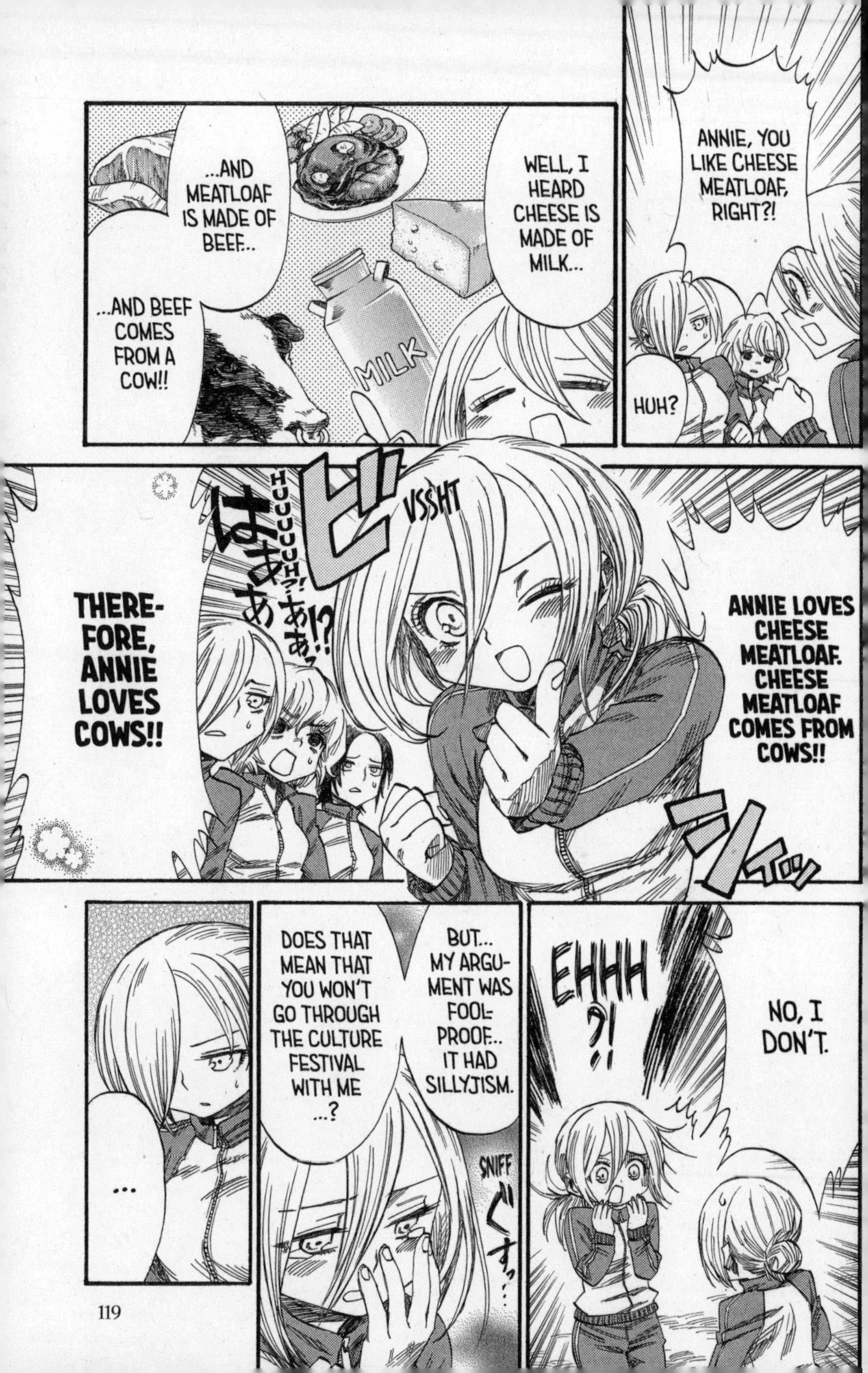
ANNIE, YOU LIKE CHEESE MEATLOAF, RIGHT?!
HUH?
WELL, I HEARD CHEESE IS MADE OF MILK...
...AND MEATLOAF IS MADE OF BEEF...
...AND BEEF COMES FROM A COW!!
MILK
ANNIE LOVES CHEESE MEATLOAF. CHEESE MEATLOAF COMES FROM COWS!!
VSSHT
HUUUUUUH?!
THEREFORE, ANNIE LOVES COWS!!
NO, I DON'T.
EHHH?!!
BUT... MY ARGUMENT WAS FOOLPROOF... IT HAD SILLYJISM.
DOES THAT MEAN THAT YOU WON'T GO THROUGH THE CULTURE FESTIVAL WITH ME...?
SNIFF
...

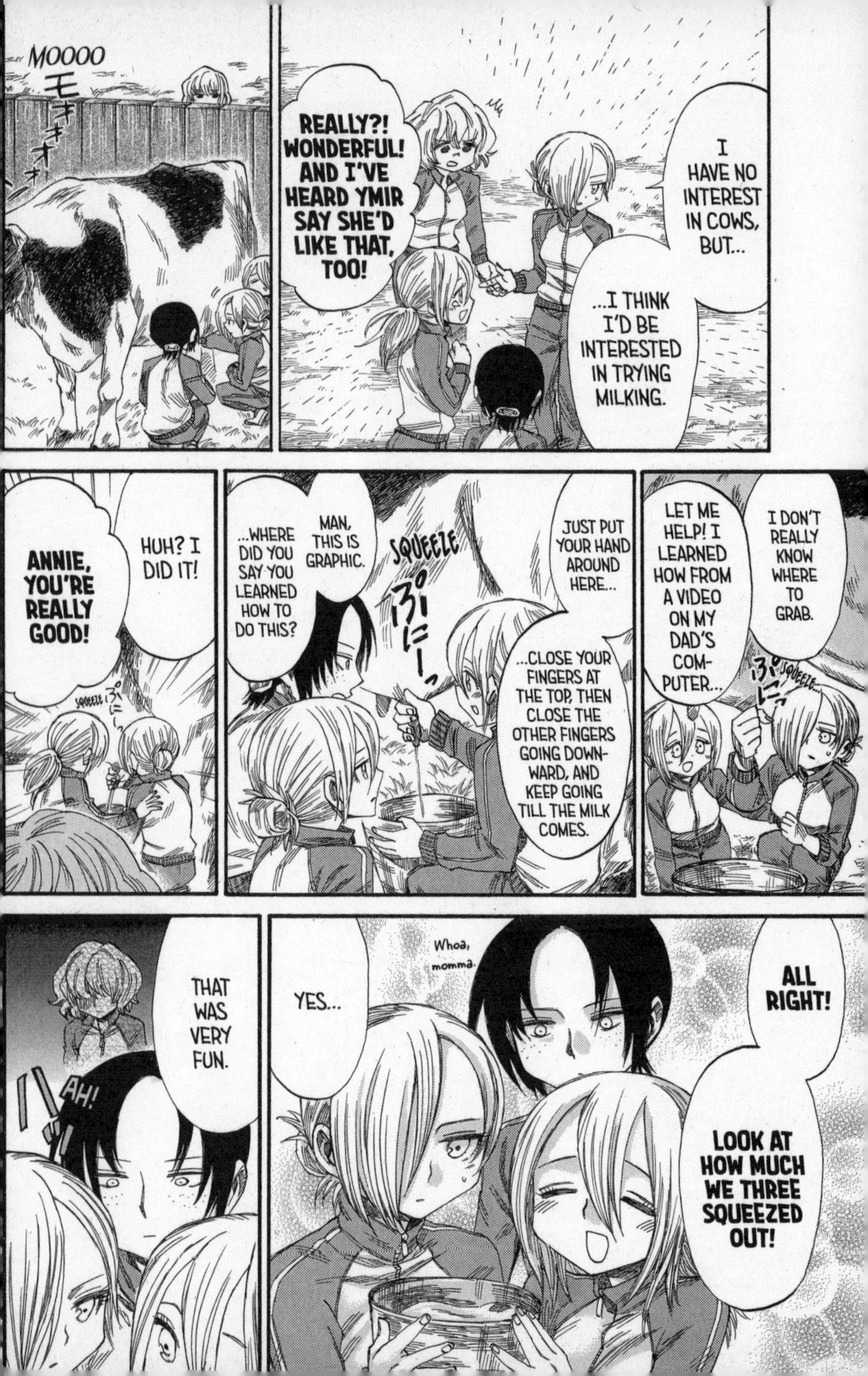
I HAVE NO INTEREST IN COWS, BUT...
...I THINK I'D BE INTERESTED IN TRYING MILKING.
REALLY?! WONDERFUL! AND I'VE HEARD YMIR SAY SHE'D LIKE THAT, TOO!
MOOOO
I DON'T REALLY KNOW WHERE TO GRAB.
LET ME HELP! I LEARNED HOW FROM A VIDEO ON MY DAD'S COM-PUTER...
SQUEEZE
JUST PUT YOUR HAND AROUND HERE...
...CLOSE YOUR FINGERS AT THE TOP, THEN CLOSE THE OTHER FINGERS GOING DOWN-WARD, AND KEEP GOING TILL THE MILK COMES.
SQUEEZE
MAN, THIS IS GRAPHIC.
...WHERE DID YOU SAY YOU LEARNED HOW TO DO THIS?
HUH? I DID IT!
ANNIE, YOU'RE REALLY GOOD!
SQUEEZE
ALL RIGHT!
LOOK AT HOW MUCH WE THREE SQUEEZED OUT!
Whoa, momma.
YES...
THAT WAS VERY FUN.
AH!

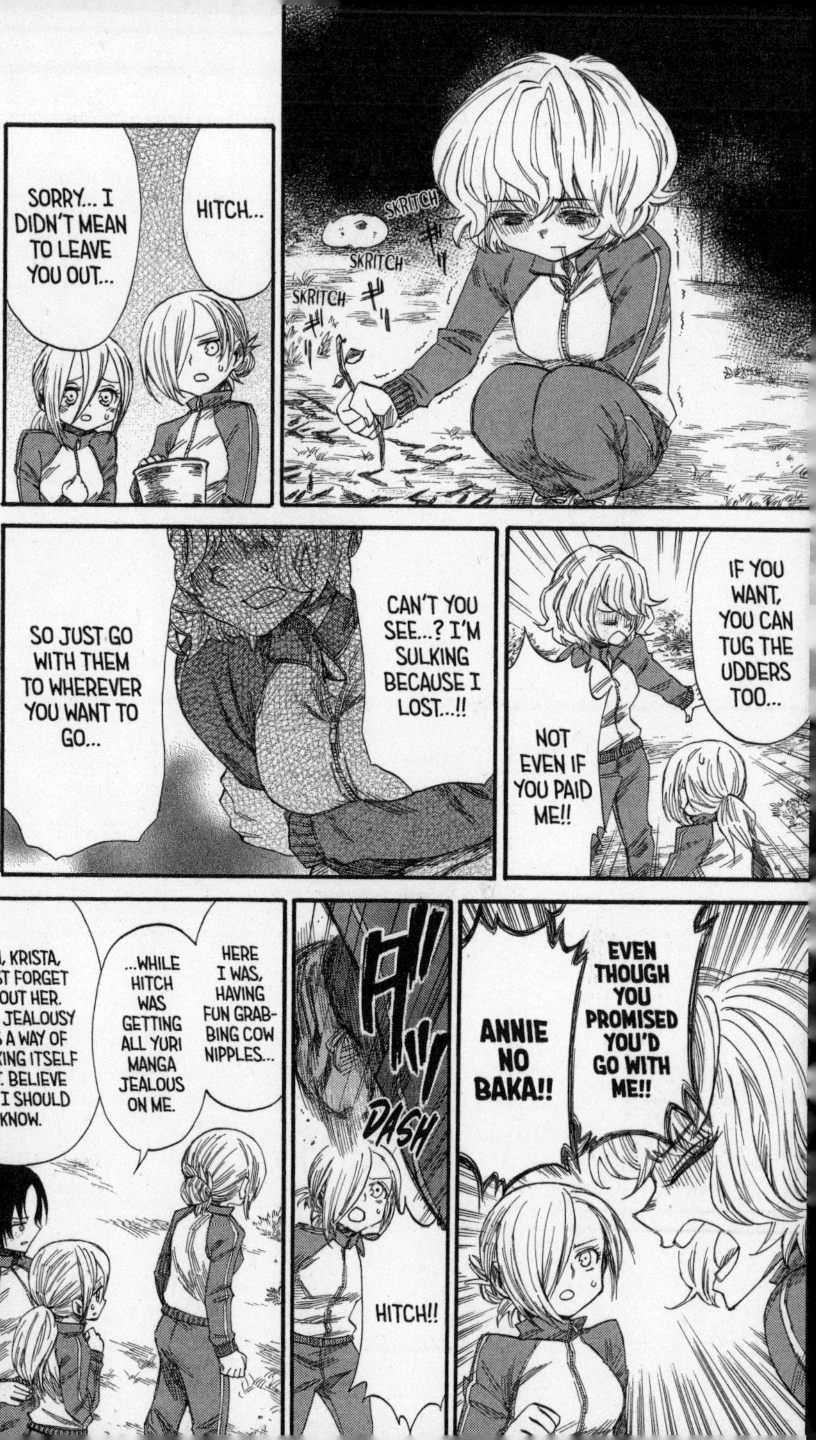
SKRITCH
SKRITCH
SKRITCH
HITCH...
SORRY... I DIDN'T MEAN TO LEAVE YOU OUT...
IF YOU WANT, YOU CAN TUG THE UDDERS TOO...
NOT EVEN IF YOU PAID ME!!
CAN'T YOU SEE...? I'M SULKING BECAUSE I LOST...!!
SO JUST GO WITH THEM TO WHEREVER YOU WANT TO GO...
EVEN THOUGH YOU PROMISED YOU'D GO WITH ME!!
ANNIE NO BAKA!!
DASH
HITCH!!
HERE I WAS, HAVING FUN GRAB-BING COW NIPPLES...
...WHILE HITCH WAS GETTING ALL YURI MANGA JEALOUS ON ME.
OH, KRISTA, JUST FORGET ABOUT HER. YURI JEALOUSY HAS A WAY OF WORKING ITSELF OUT. BELIEVE ME, I SHOULD KNOW.

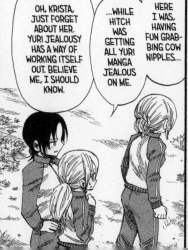

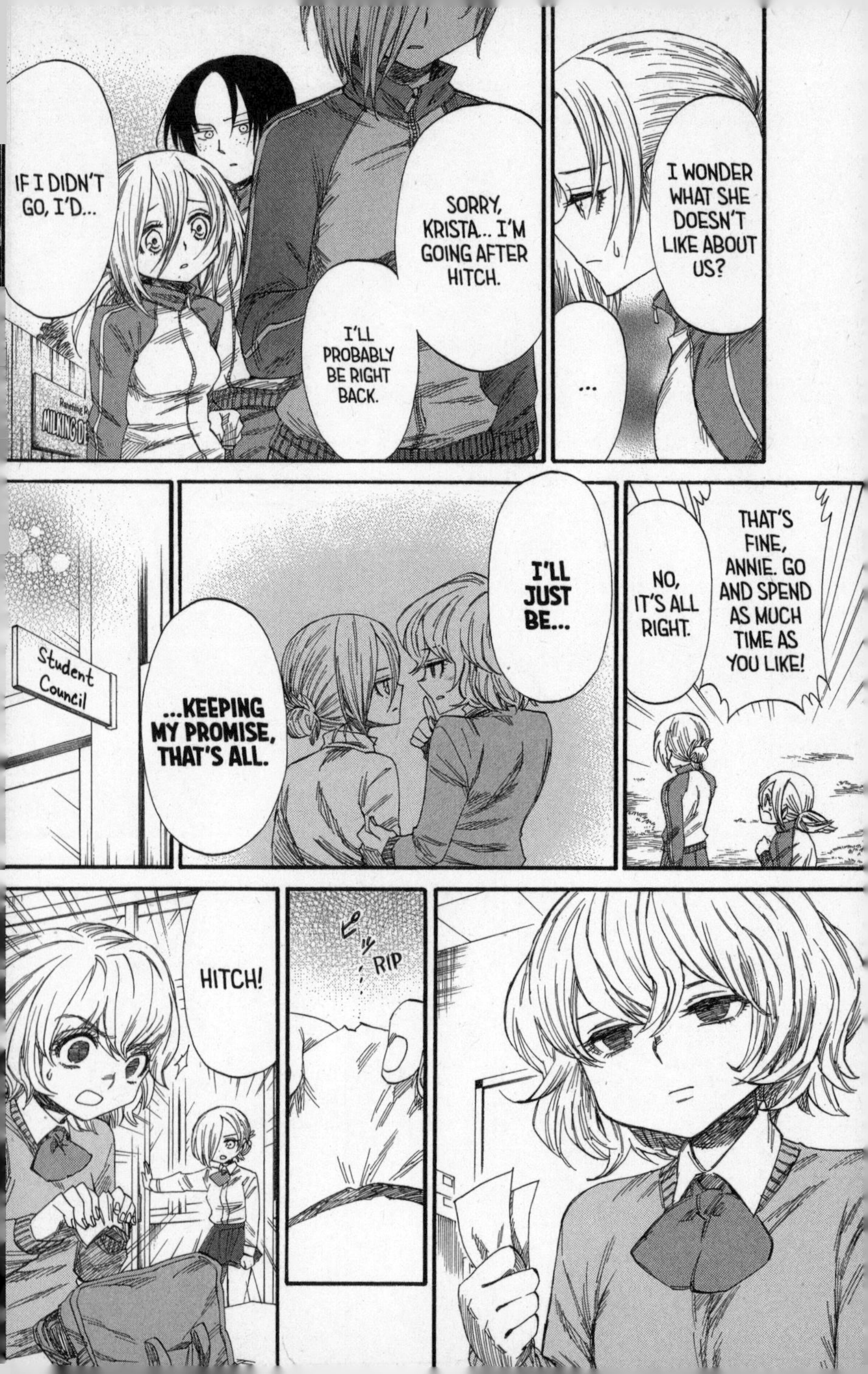
I WONDER WHAT SHE DOESN'T LIKE ABOUT US?
...
SORRY, KRISTA... I'M GOING AFTER HITCH.
I'LL PROBABLY BE RIGHT BACK.
IF I DIDN'T GO, I'D...
THAT'S FINE, ANNIE. GO AND SPEND AS MUCH TIME AS YOU LIKE!
NO, IT'S ALL RIGHT.
I'LL JUST BE...
...KEEPING MY PROMISE, THAT'S ALL.
Student Council
RIP
HITCH!

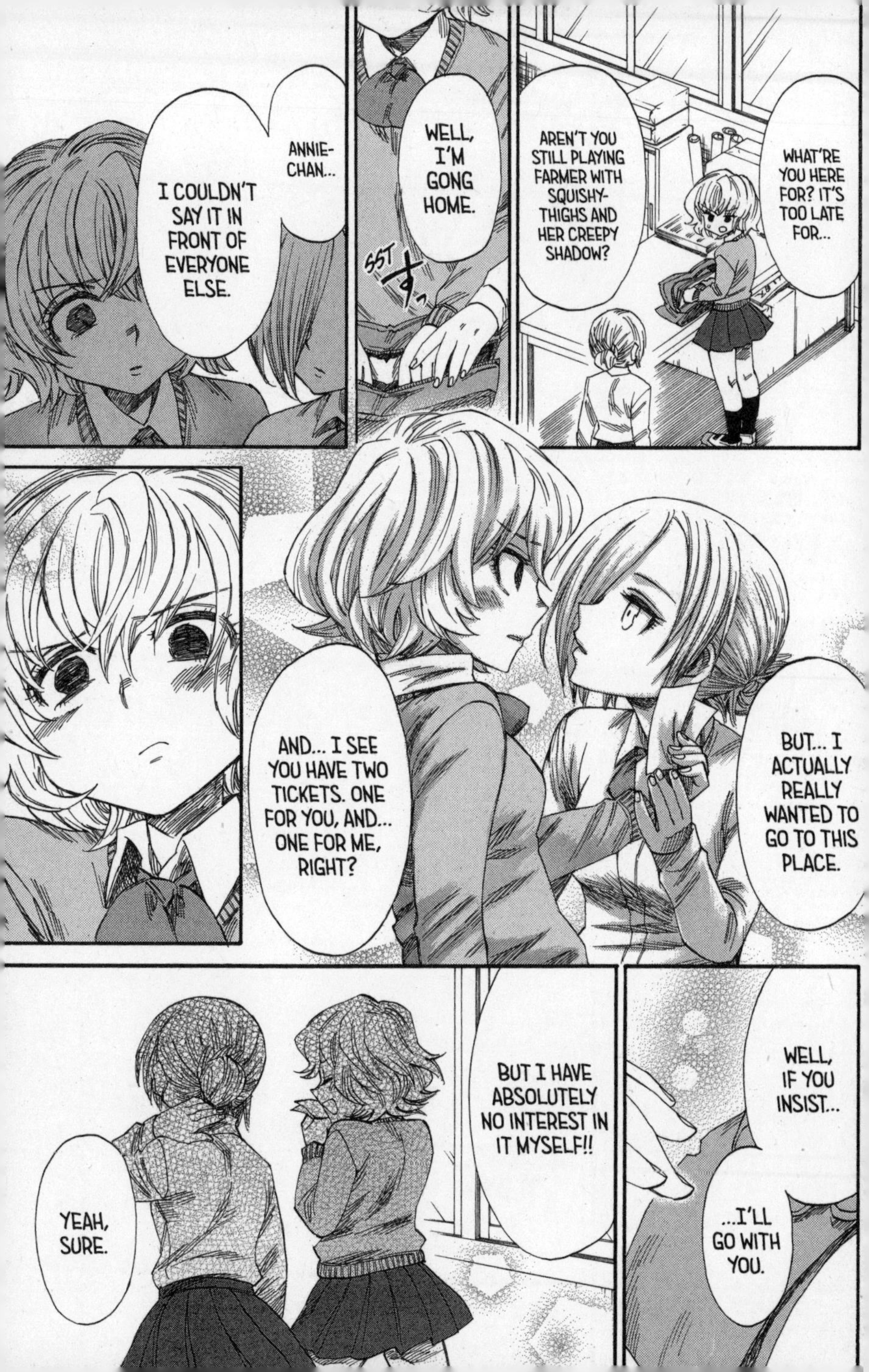
WHAT'RE YOU HERE FOR? IT'S TOO LATE FOR...
AREN'T YOU STILL PLAYING FARMER WITH SQUISHY-THIGHS AND HER CREEPY SHADOW?
WELL, I'M GONG HOME.
SST
ANNIE-CHAN...
I COULDN'T SAY IT IN FRONT OF EVERYONE ELSE.
BUT... I ACTUALLY REALLY WANTED TO GO TO THIS PLACE.
AND... I SEE YOU HAVE TWO TICKETS. ONE FOR YOU, AND... ONE FOR ME, RIGHT?
WELL, IF YOU INSIST...
...I'LL GO WITH YOU.
BUT I HAVE ABSOLUTELY NO INTEREST IN IT MYSELF!!
YEAH, SURE.

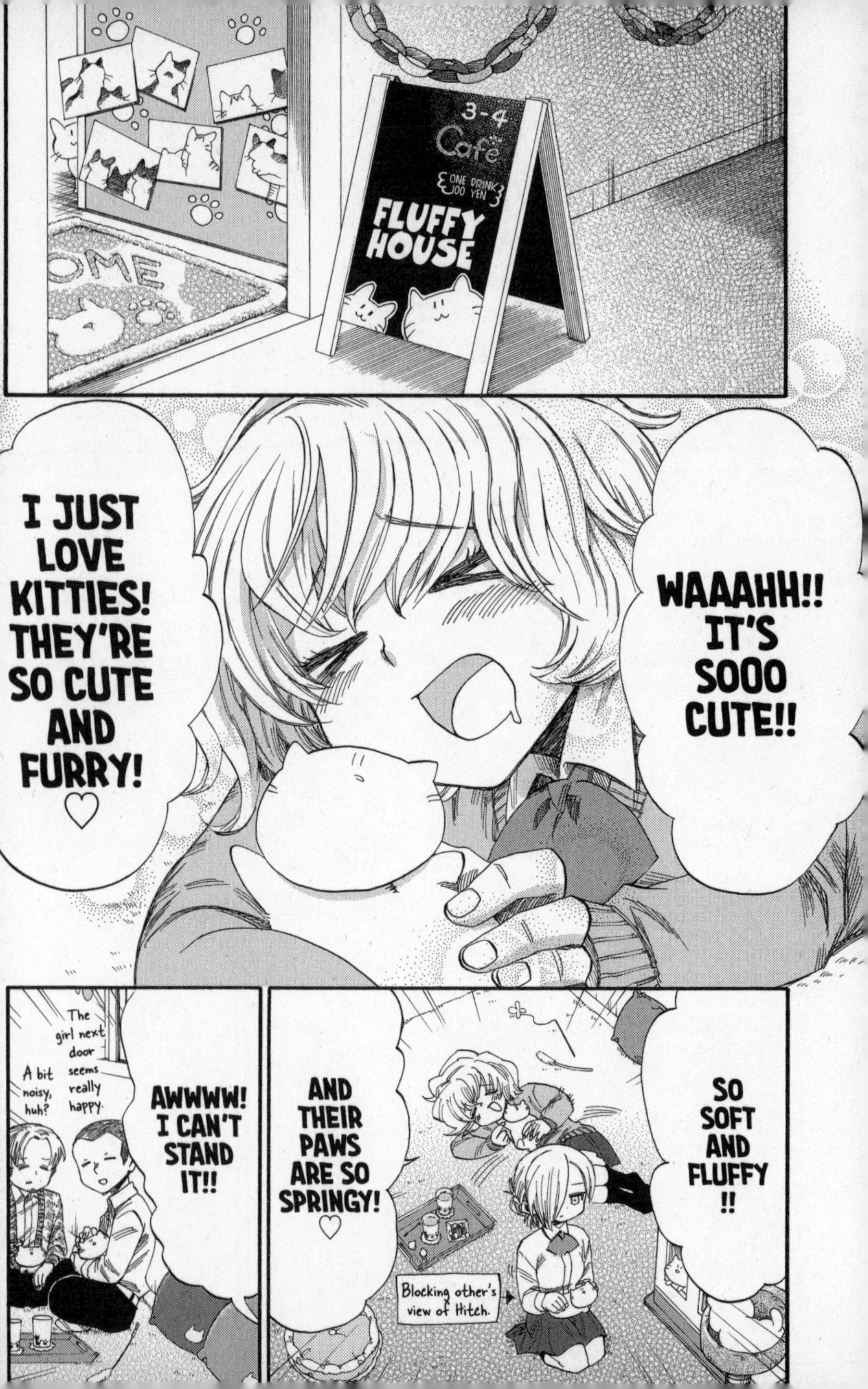
3-4
Café
ONE DRINK 100 YEN
FLUFFY HOUSE
WAAAHH!! IT'S SOOO CUTE!!
I JUST LOVE KITTIES! THEY'RE SO CUTE AND FURRY! ♡
SO SOFT AND FLUFFY!!
AND THEIR PAWS ARE SO SPRINGY! ♡
Blocking other's view of Hitch.
AWWWW! I CAN'T STAND IT!!
The girl next door seems really happy.
A bit noisy, huh?

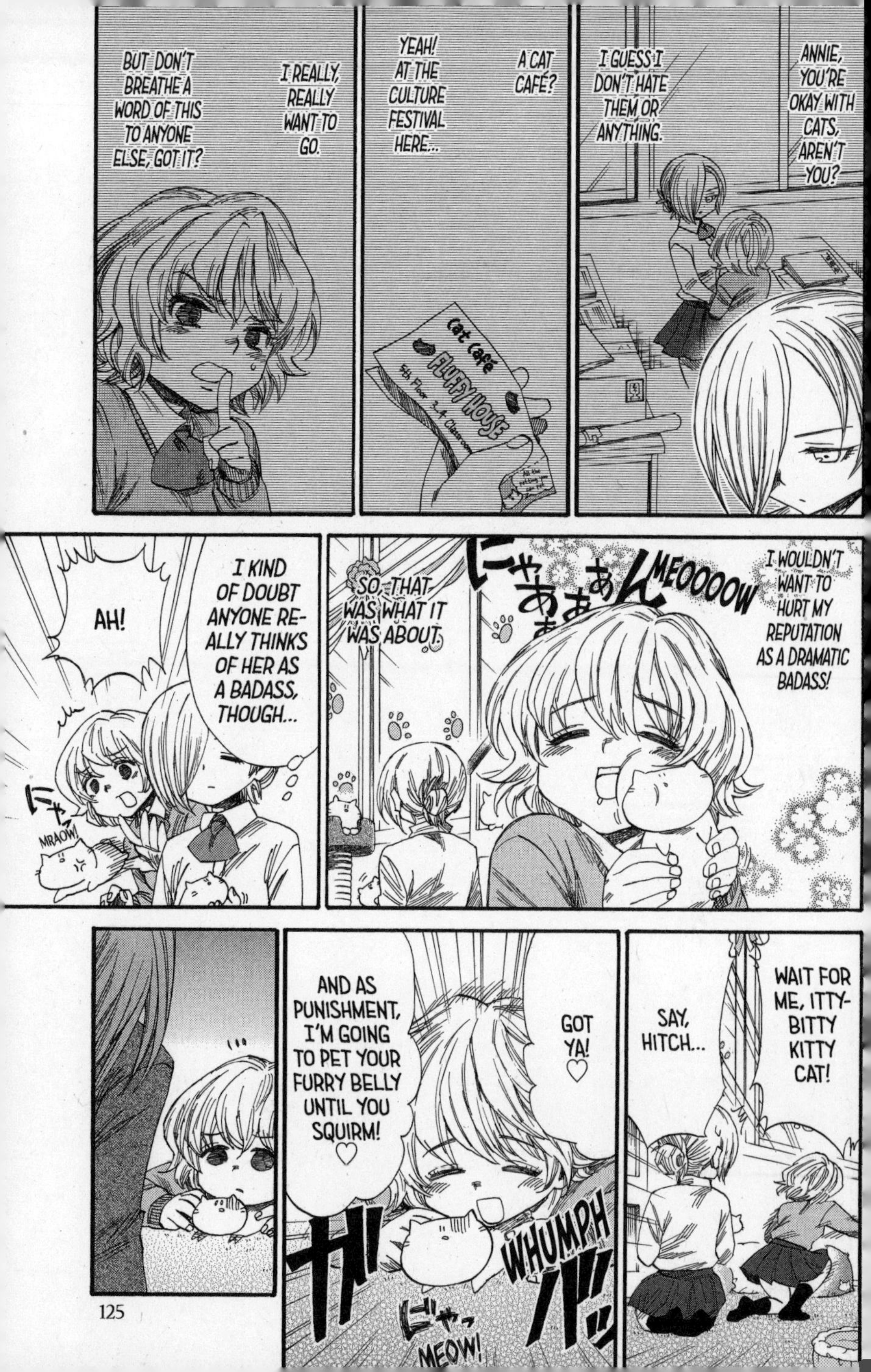
ANNIE, YOU'RE OKAY WITH CATS, AREN'T YOU?
I GUESS I DON'T HATE THEM OR ANYTHING.
A CAT CAFÉ?
YEAH! AT THE CULTURE FESTIVAL HERE...
Cat Café
FLUFFY HOUSE
5th Floor 2-A Classroom
I REALLY, REALLY WANT TO GO.
BUT DON'T BREATHE A WORD OF THIS TO ANYONE ELSE, GOT IT?
I WOULDN'T WANT TO HURT MY REPUTATION AS A DRAMATIC BADASS!
MEOOOOW
SO THAT WAS WHAT IT WAS ABOUT.
I KIND OF DOUBT ANYONE REALLY THINKS OF HER AS A BADASS, THOUGH...
AH!
MRAOW!
WAIT FOR ME, ITTY-BITTY KITTY CAT!
SAY, HITCH...
GOT YA! ♡
AND AS PUNISHMENT, I'M GOING TO PET YOUR FURRY BELLY UNTIL YOU SQUIRM! ♡
WHUMPH
MEOW!

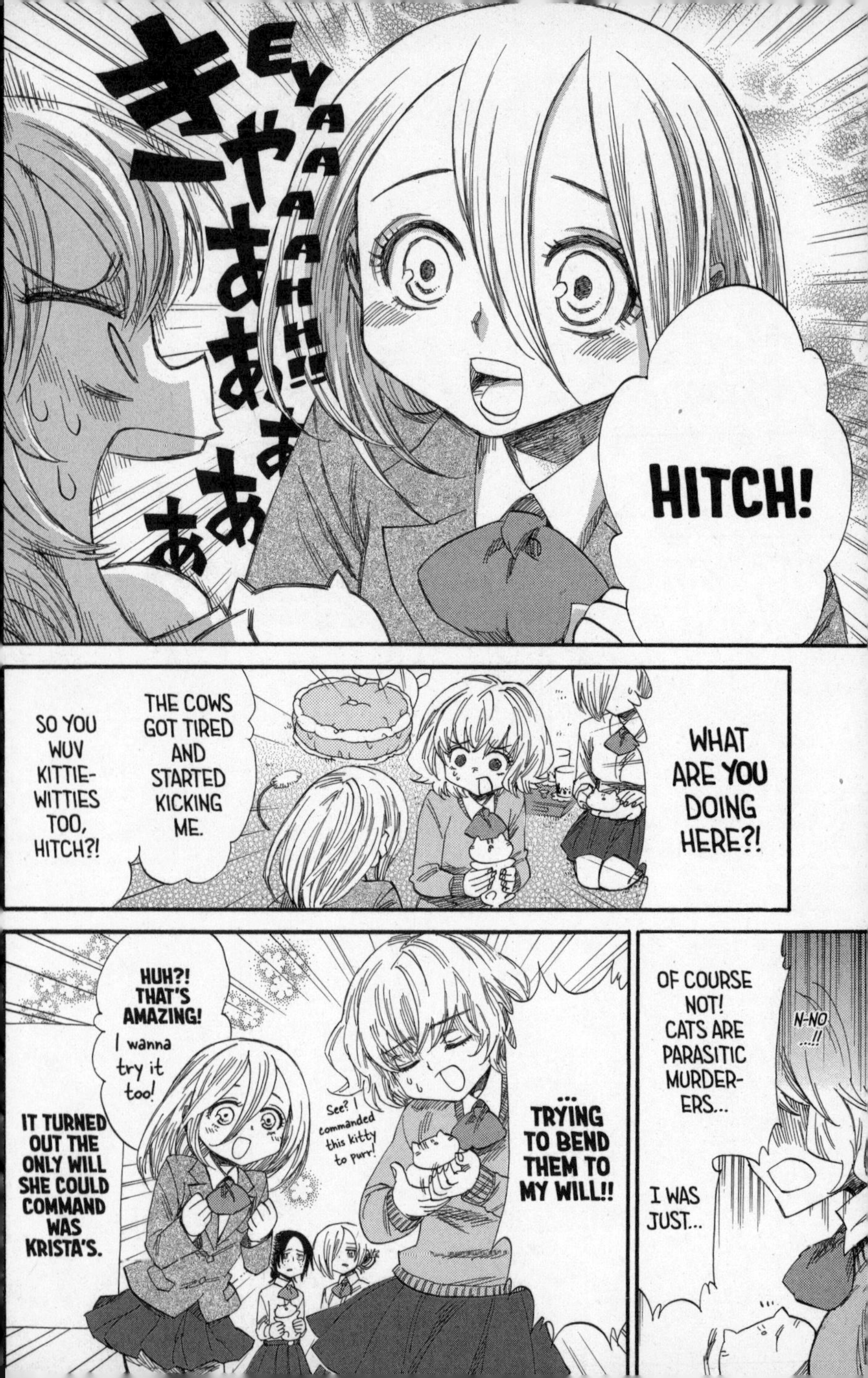
HITCH!
EYAAAAHH!!
WHAT ARE YOU DOING HERE?!
THE COWS GOT TIRED AND STARTED KICKING ME.
SO YOU WUV KITTIE-WITTIES TOO, HITCH?!
N-NO ...!!
OF COURSE NOT! CATS ARE PARASITIC MURDERERS...
I WAS JUST...
...TRYING TO BEND THEM TO MY WILL!!
See? I commanded this kitty to purr!
HUH?! THAT'S AMAZING!
I wanna try it too!
IT TURNED OUT THE ONLY WILL SHE COULD COMMAND WAS KRISTA'S.

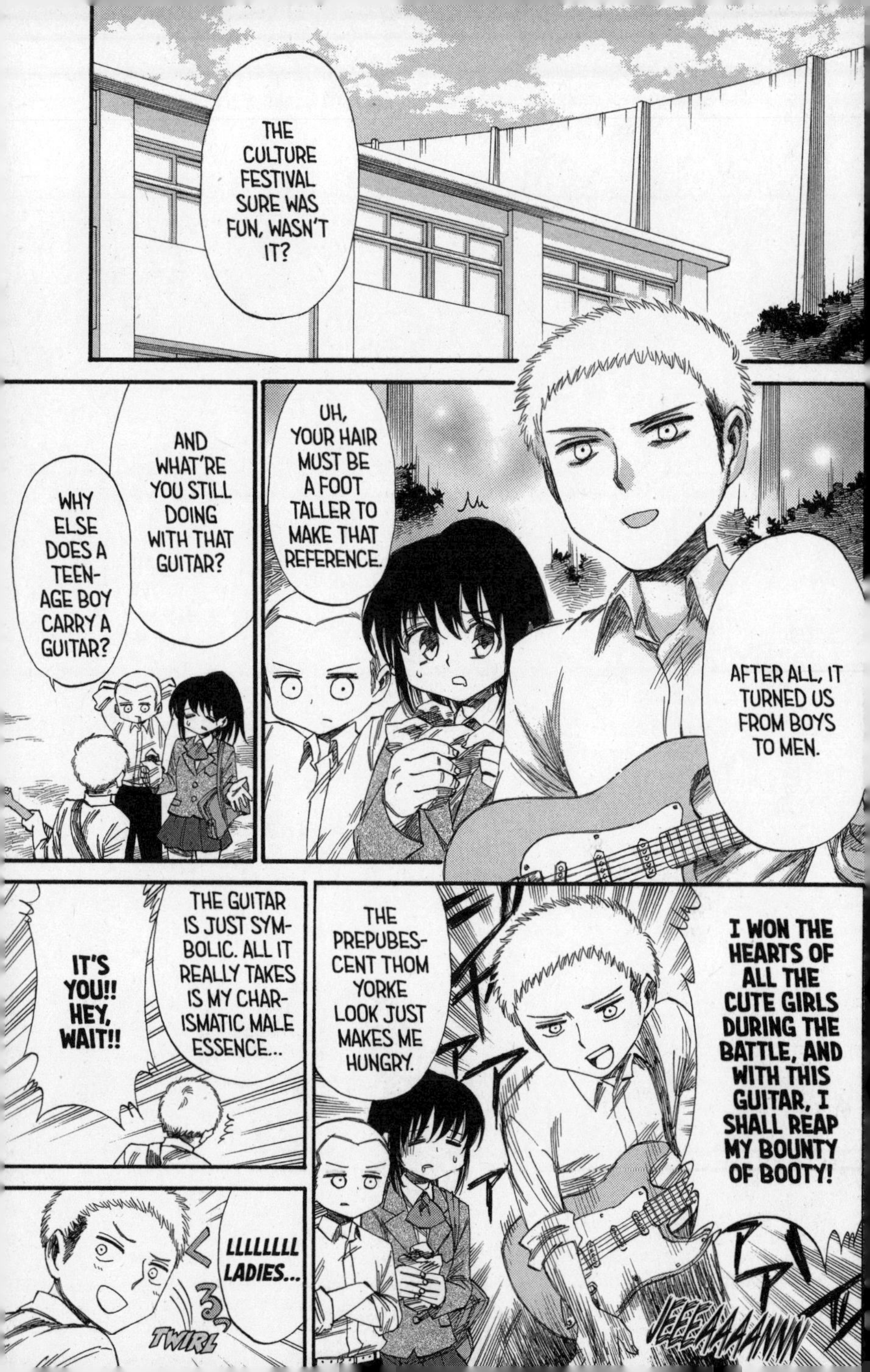
THE CULTURE FESTIVAL SURE WAS FUN, WASN'T IT?
AFTER ALL, IT TURNED US FROM BOYS TO MEN.
UH, YOUR HAIR MUST BE A FOOT TALLER TO MAKE THAT REFERENCE.
AND WHAT'RE YOU STILL DOING WITH THAT GUITAR?
WHY ELSE DOES A TEEN-AGE BOY CARRY A GUITAR?
I WON THE HEARTS OF ALL THE CUTE GIRLS DURING THE BATTLE, AND WITH THIS GUITAR, I SHALL REAP MY BOUNTY OF BOOTY!
THE PREPUBES-CENT THOM YORKE LOOK JUST MAKES ME HUNGRY.
JEEEAAAANN
THE GUITAR IS JUST SYM-BOLIC. ALL IT REALLY TAKES IS MY CHAR-ISMATIC MALE ESSENCE...
IT'S YOU!! HEY, WAIT!!
LLLLLLLL LADIES...
TWIRL

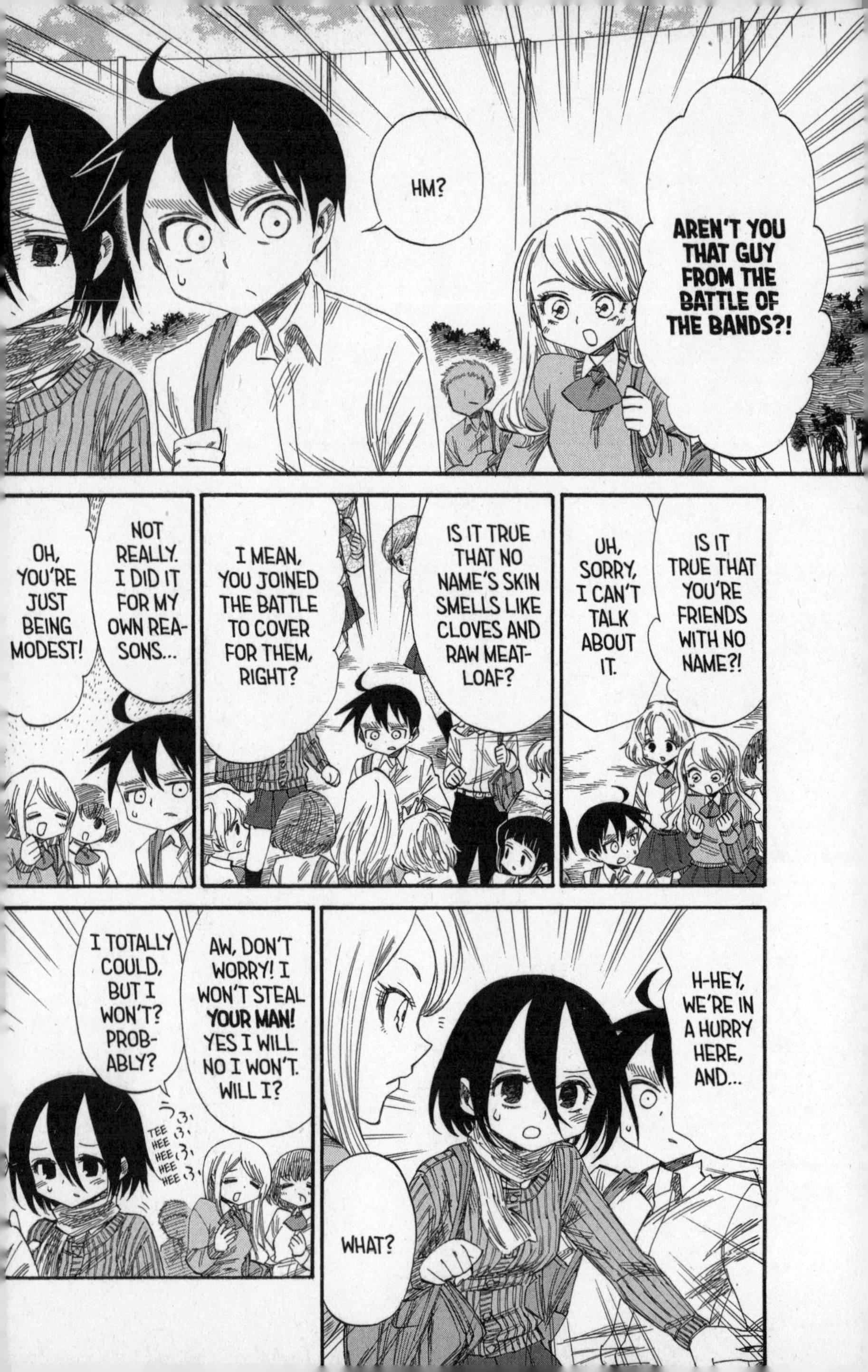
AREN'T YOU THAT GUY FROM THE BATTLE OF THE BANDS?!
HM?
IS IT TRUE THAT YOU'RE FRIENDS WITH NO NAME?!
UH, SORRY, I CAN'T TALK ABOUT IT.
IS IT TRUE THAT NO NAME'S SKIN SMELLS LIKE CLOVES AND RAW MEAT-LOAF?
I MEAN, YOU JOINED THE BATTLE TO COVER FOR THEM, RIGHT?
NOT REALLY. I DID IT FOR MY OWN REA-SONS...
OH, YOU'RE JUST BEING MODEST!
H-HEY, WE'RE IN A HURRY HERE, AND...
WHAT?
AW, DON'T WORRY! I WON'T STEAL **YOUR MAN!** YES I WILL. NO I WON'T. WILL I?
I TOTALLY COULD, BUT I WON'T? PROB-ABLY?
うふふふふ
TEE HEE HEE HEE HEE

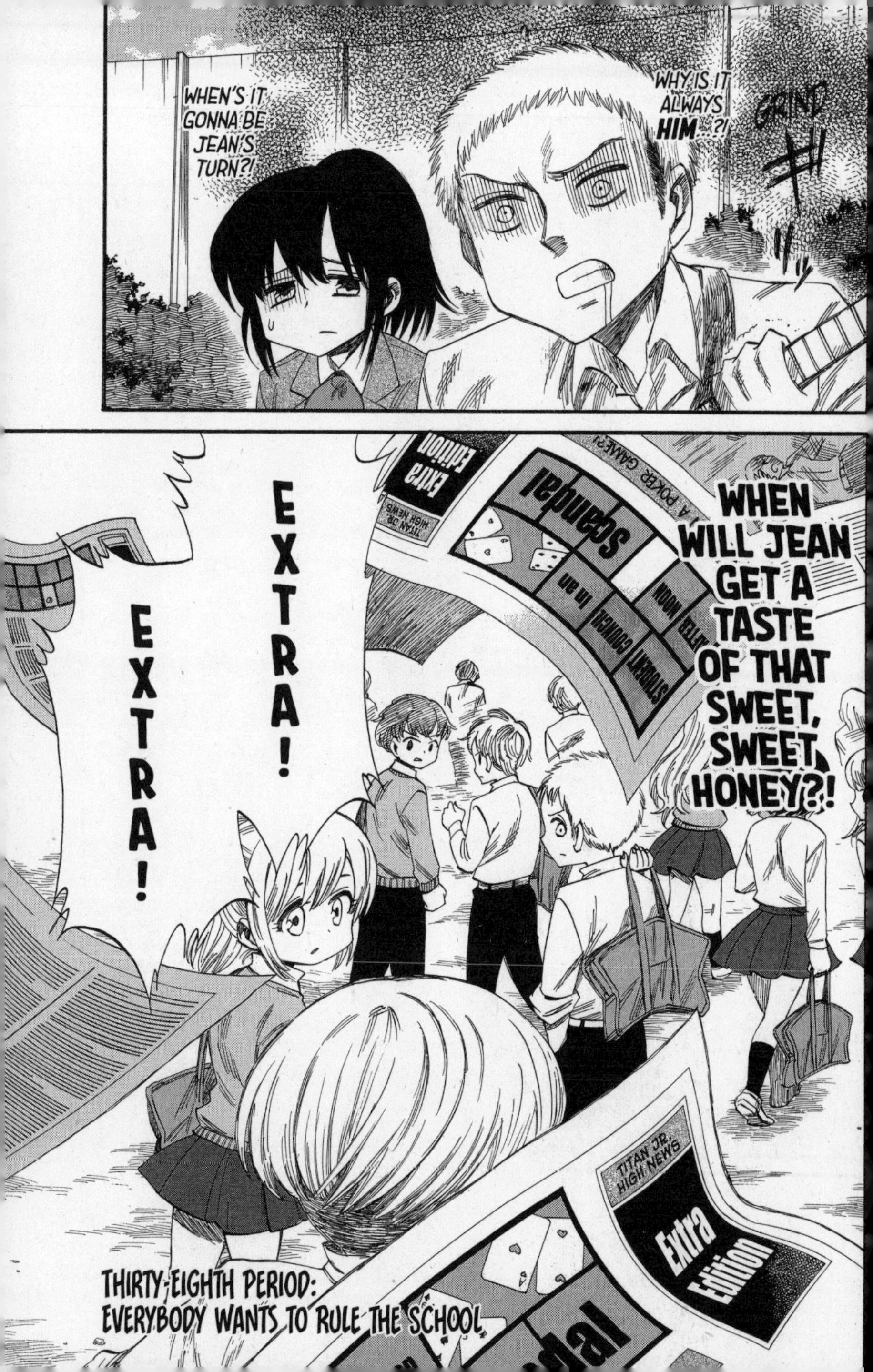
WHY IS IT ALWAYS HIM...?!
GRIND
WHEN'S IT GONNA BE JEAN'S TURN?!
WHEN WILL JEAN GET A TASTE OF THAT SWEET, SWEET HONEY?!
TITAN JR. HIGH NEWS
Extra Edition
Scandal
EXTRA!
EXTRA!
TITAN JR. HIGH NEWS
Extra Edition
THIRTY-EIGHTH PERIOD:
EVERYBODY WANTS TO RULE THE SCHOOL

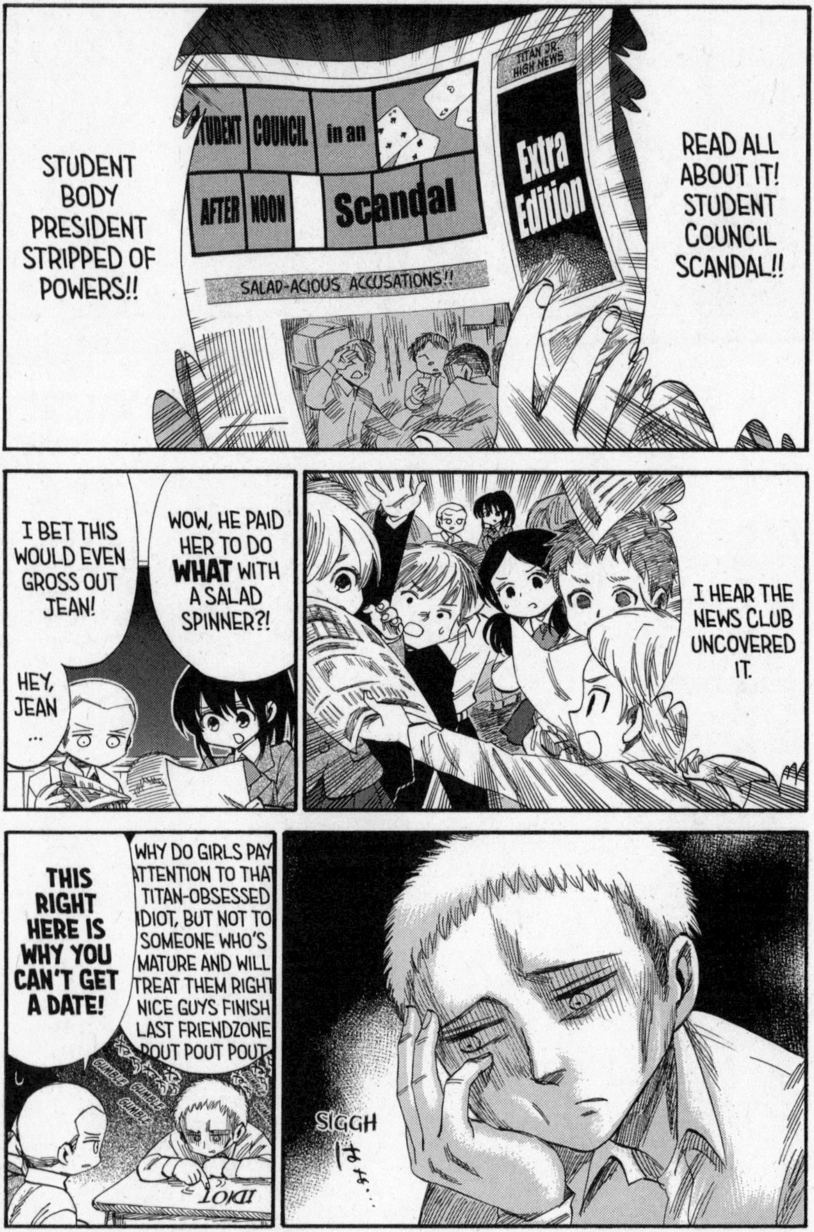
READ ALL ABOUT IT! STUDENT COUNCIL SCANDAL!!
TITAN JR. HIGH NEWS
Extra Edition
TUDENT COUNCIL in an AFTER NOON Scandal
SALAD-ACIOUS ACCUSATIONS!!
STUDENT BODY PRESIDENT STRIPPED OF POWERS!!
I HEAR THE NEWS CLUB UNCOVERED IT.
WOW, HE PAID HER TO DO **WHAT** WITH A SALAD SPINNER?!
I BET THIS WOULD EVEN GROSS OUT JEAN!
HEY, JEAN ...
SIGGH
はぁ…
WHY DO GIRLS PAY ATTENTION TO THAT TITAN-OBSESSED IDIOT, BUT NOT TO SOMEONE WHO'S MATURE AND WILL TREAT THEM RIGHT NICE GUYS FINISH LAST FRIENDZONE POUT POUT POUT
THIS RIGHT HERE IS WHY YOU CAN'T GET A DATE!
GUMBLE GUMBLE GUMBLE GUMBLE
IDIOT

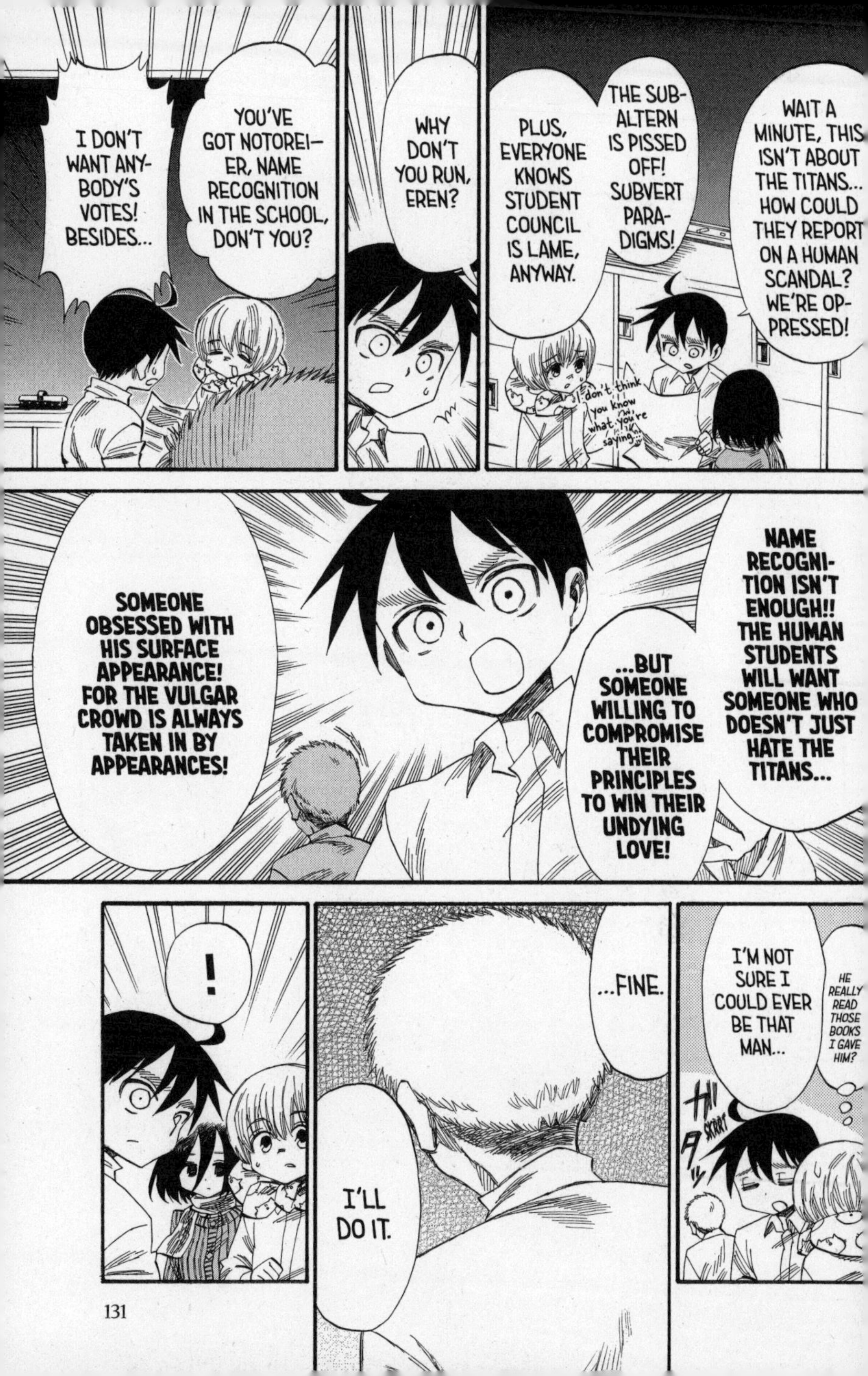
WAIT A MINUTE, THIS ISN'T ABOUT THE TITANS... HOW COULD THEY REPORT ON A HUMAN SCANDAL? WE'RE OPPRESSED!
THE SUBALTERN IS PISSED OFF! SUBVERT PARADIGMS!
PLUS, EVERYONE KNOWS STUDENT COUNCIL IS LAME, ANYWAY.
I don't think you know what you're saying...
WHY DON'T YOU RUN, EREN?
YOU'VE GOT NOTOREIER, NAME RECOGNITION IN THE SCHOOL, DON'T YOU?
I DON'T WANT ANYBODY'S VOTES! BESIDES...
NAME RECOGNITION ISN'T ENOUGH!! THE HUMAN STUDENTS WILL WANT SOMEONE WHO DOESN'T JUST HATE THE TITANS...
...BUT SOMEONE WILLING TO COMPROMISE THEIR PRINCIPLES TO WIN THEIR UNDYING LOVE!
SOMEONE OBSESSED WITH HIS SURFACE APPEARANCE! FOR THE VULGAR CROWD IS ALWAYS TAKEN IN BY APPEARANCES!
HE REALLY READ THOSE BOOKS I GAVE HIM?
I'M NOT SURE I COULD EVER BE THAT MAN...
ガタッ
SKRRT
...FINE.
I'LL DO IT.
!

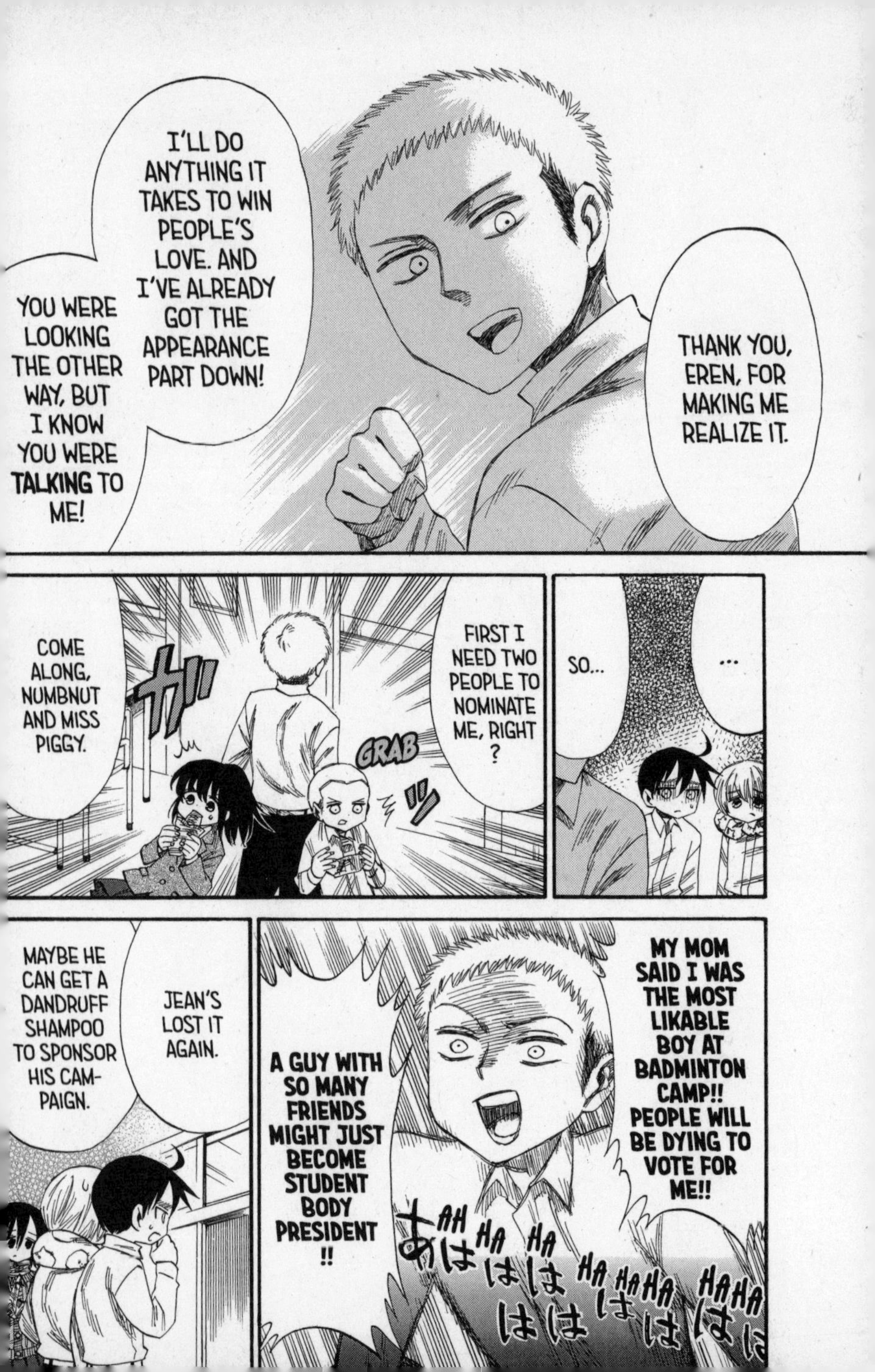
THANK YOU, EREN, FOR MAKING ME REALIZE IT.
I'LL DO ANYTHING IT TAKES TO WIN PEOPLE'S LOVE. AND I'VE ALREADY GOT THE APPEARANCE PART DOWN!
YOU WERE LOOKING THE OTHER WAY, BUT I KNOW YOU WERE **TALKING** TO ME!
...
SO...
FIRST I NEED TWO PEOPLE TO NOMINATE ME, RIGHT?
GRAB
ガッ
COME ALONG, NUMBNUT AND MISS PIGGY.
MY MOM SAID I WAS THE MOST LIKABLE BOY AT BADMINTON CAMP!! PEOPLE WILL BE DYING TO VOTE FOR ME!!
A GUY WITH SO MANY FRIENDS MIGHT JUST BECOME STUDENT BODY PRESIDENT!!
AH HA HA HA HA HA HA HA
あはははははははは
JEAN'S LOST IT AGAIN.
MAYBE HE CAN GET A DANDRUFF SHAMPOO TO SPONSOR HIS CAM-PAIGN.

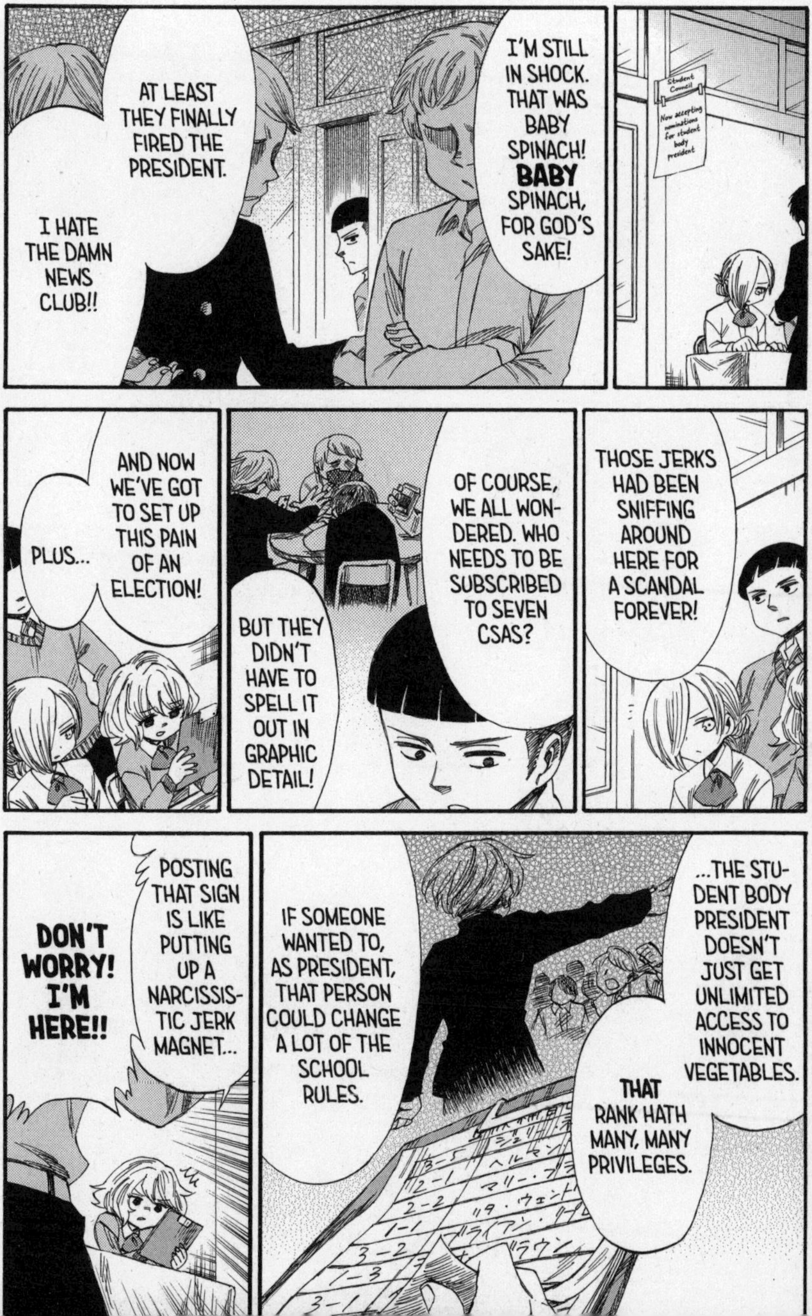
Student Council
Now accepting nominations for student body president
I'M STILL IN SHOCK. THAT WAS BABY SPINACH! **BABY** SPINACH, FOR GOD'S SAKE!
AT LEAST THEY FINALLY FIRED THE PRESIDENT.
I HATE THE DAMN NEWS CLUB!!
THOSE JERKS HAD BEEN SNIFFING AROUND HERE FOR A SCANDAL FOREVER!
OF COURSE, WE ALL WONDERED. WHO NEEDS TO BE SUBSCRIBED TO SEVEN CSAS?
BUT THEY DIDN'T HAVE TO SPELL IT OUT IN GRAPHIC DETAIL!
AND NOW WE'VE GOT TO SET UP THIS PAIN OF AN ELECTION!
PLUS...
...THE STUDENT BODY PRESIDENT DOESN'T JUST GET UNLIMITED ACCESS TO INNOCENT VEGETABLES.
THAT RANK HATH MANY, MANY PRIVILEGES.
IF SOMEONE WANTED TO, AS PRESIDENT, THAT PERSON COULD CHANGE A LOT OF THE SCHOOL RULES.
POSTING THAT SIGN IS LIKE PUTTING UP A NARCISSISTIC JERK MAGNET...
DON'T WORRY! I'M HERE!!

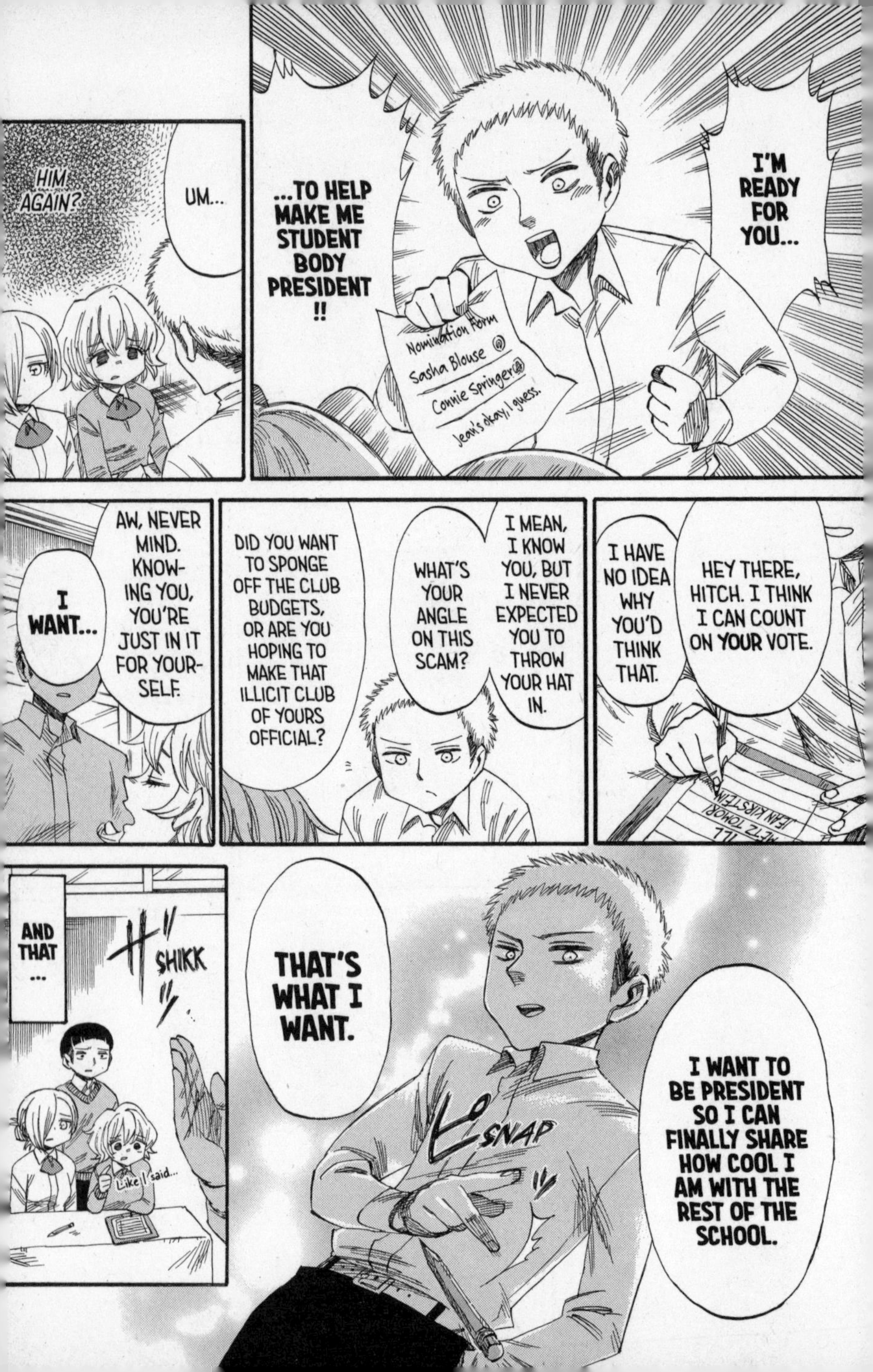
I'M READY FOR YOU...
...TO HELP MAKE ME STUDENT BODY PRESIDENT!!
Nomination Form
Sasha Blouse @
Connie Springer @
Jean's okay, I guess.
UM...
HIM AGAIN?
HEY THERE, HITCH. I THINK I CAN COUNT ON YOUR VOTE.
I HAVE NO IDEA WHY YOU'D THINK THAT.
JEAN KIRSTEIN
I MEAN, I KNOW YOU, BUT I NEVER EXPECTED YOU TO THROW YOUR HAT IN.
WHAT'S YOUR ANGLE ON THIS SCAM?
DID YOU WANT TO SPONGE OFF THE CLUB BUDGETS, OR ARE YOU HOPING TO MAKE THAT ILLICIT CLUB OF YOURS OFFICIAL?
AW, NEVER MIND. KNOWING YOU, YOU'RE JUST IN IT FOR YOURSELF.
I WANT...
I WANT TO BE PRESIDENT SO I CAN FINALLY SHARE HOW COOL I AM WITH THE REST OF THE SCHOOL.
SNAP
THAT'S WHAT I WANT.
SHIKK
AND THAT...
Like I said...

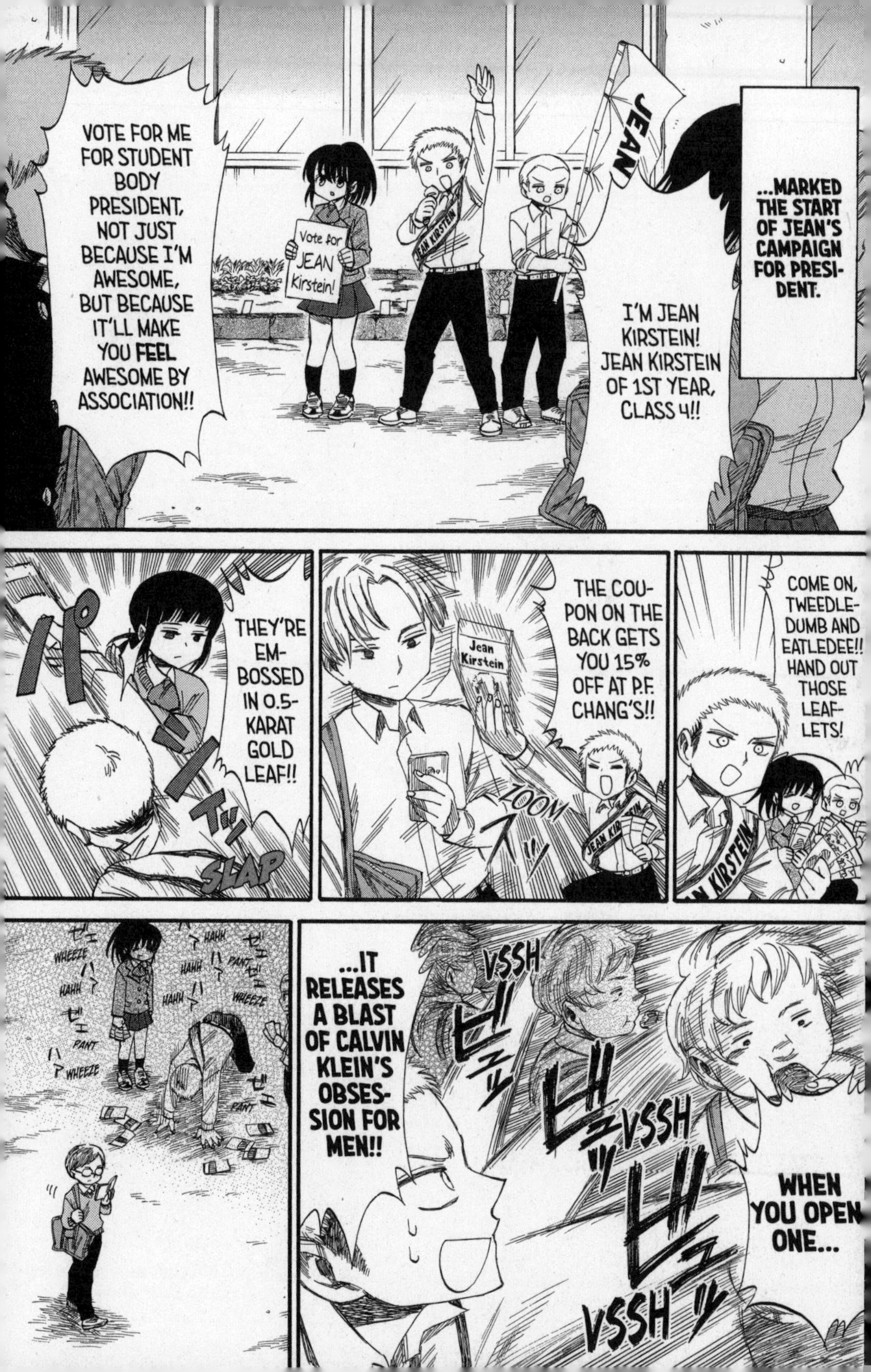
...MARKED THE START OF JEAN'S CAMPAIGN FOR PRESIDENT.
JEAN
I'M JEAN KIRSTEIN! JEAN KIRSTEIN OF 1ST YEAR, CLASS 4!!
JEAN KIRSTEIN
Vote for JEAN Kirstein!
VOTE FOR ME FOR STUDENT BODY PRESIDENT, NOT JUST BECAUSE I'M AWESOME, BUT BECAUSE IT'LL MAKE YOU **FEEL** AWESOME BY ASSOCIATION!!
COME ON, TWEEDLEDUMB AND EATLEDEE!! HAND OUT THOSE LEAFLETS!
THE COUPON ON THE BACK GETS YOU 15% OFF AT P.F. CHANG'S!!
Jean Kirstein
ZOOM
JEAN KIRSTEIN
THEY'RE EMBOSSED IN 0.5-KARAT GOLD LEAF!!
SLAP
WHEN YOU OPEN ONE...
VSSH
...IT RELEASES A BLAST OF CALVIN KLEIN'S OBSESSION FOR MEN!!
VSSH
VSSH
WHEEZE
HAHH
HAHH
PANT
HAHH
HAHH
WHEEZE
PANT
WHEEZE
PANT

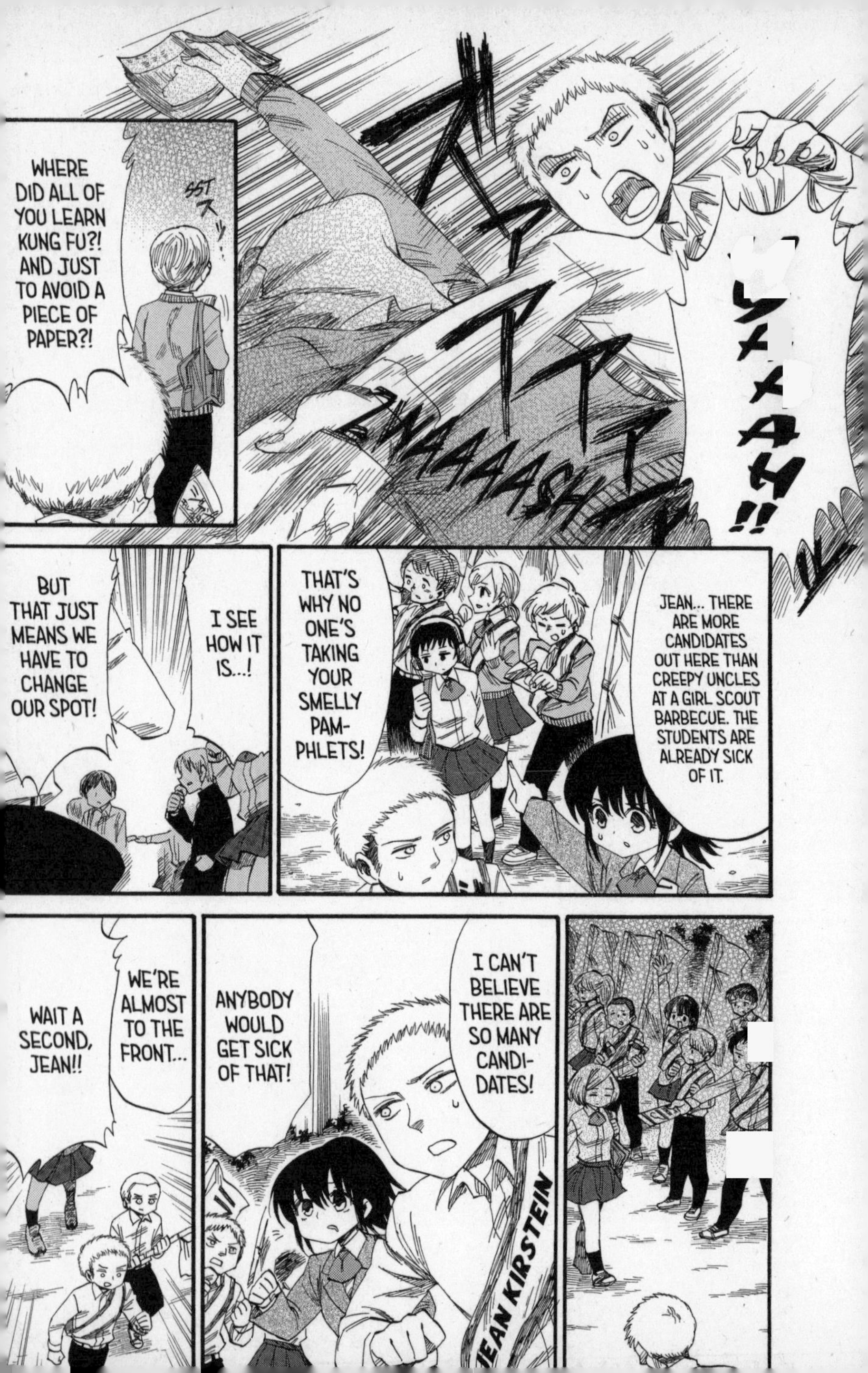
ZWAAAASH
SST
WHERE DID ALL OF YOU LEARN KUNG FU?! AND JUST TO AVOID A PIECE OF PAPER?!
JEAN... THERE ARE MORE CANDIDATES OUT HERE THAN CREEPY UNCLES AT A GIRL SCOUT BARBECUE. THE STUDENTS ARE ALREADY SICK OF IT.
THAT'S WHY NO ONE'S TAKING YOUR SMELLY PAMPHLETS!
I SEE HOW IT IS...!
BUT THAT JUST MEANS WE HAVE TO CHANGE OUR SPOT!
I CAN'T BELIEVE THERE ARE SO MANY CANDIDATES!
ANYBODY WOULD GET SICK OF THAT!
JEAN KIRSTEIN
WE'RE ALMOST TO THE FRONT...
WAIT A SECOND, JEAN!!

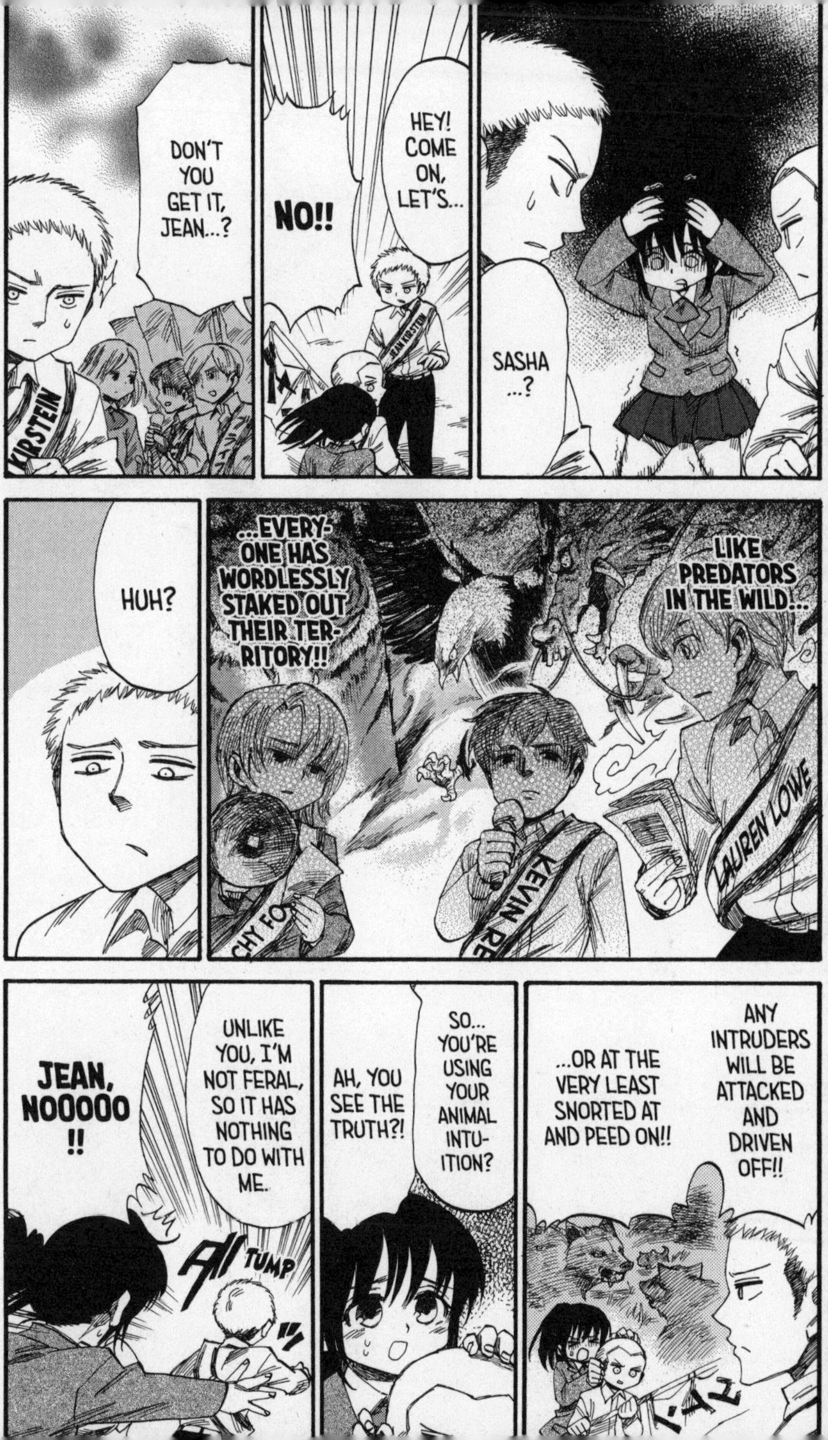
SASHA ...?
HEY! COME ON, LET'S...
NO!!
JEAN KIRSTEIN
DON'T YOU GET IT, JEAN...?
KIRSTEIN
LIKE PREDATORS IN THE WILD...
...EVERY-ONE HAS WORDLESSLY STAKED OUT THEIR TER-RITORY!!
LAUREN LOWE
HUH?
ANY INTRUDERS WILL BE ATTACKED AND DRIVEN OFF!!
...OR AT THE VERY LEAST SNORTED AT AND PEED ON!!
SO... YOU'RE USING YOUR ANIMAL INTU-ITION?
AH, YOU SEE THE TRUTH?!
UNLIKE YOU, I'M NOT FERAL, SO IT HAS NOTHING TO DO WITH ME.
JEAN, NOOOOO!!
TUMP

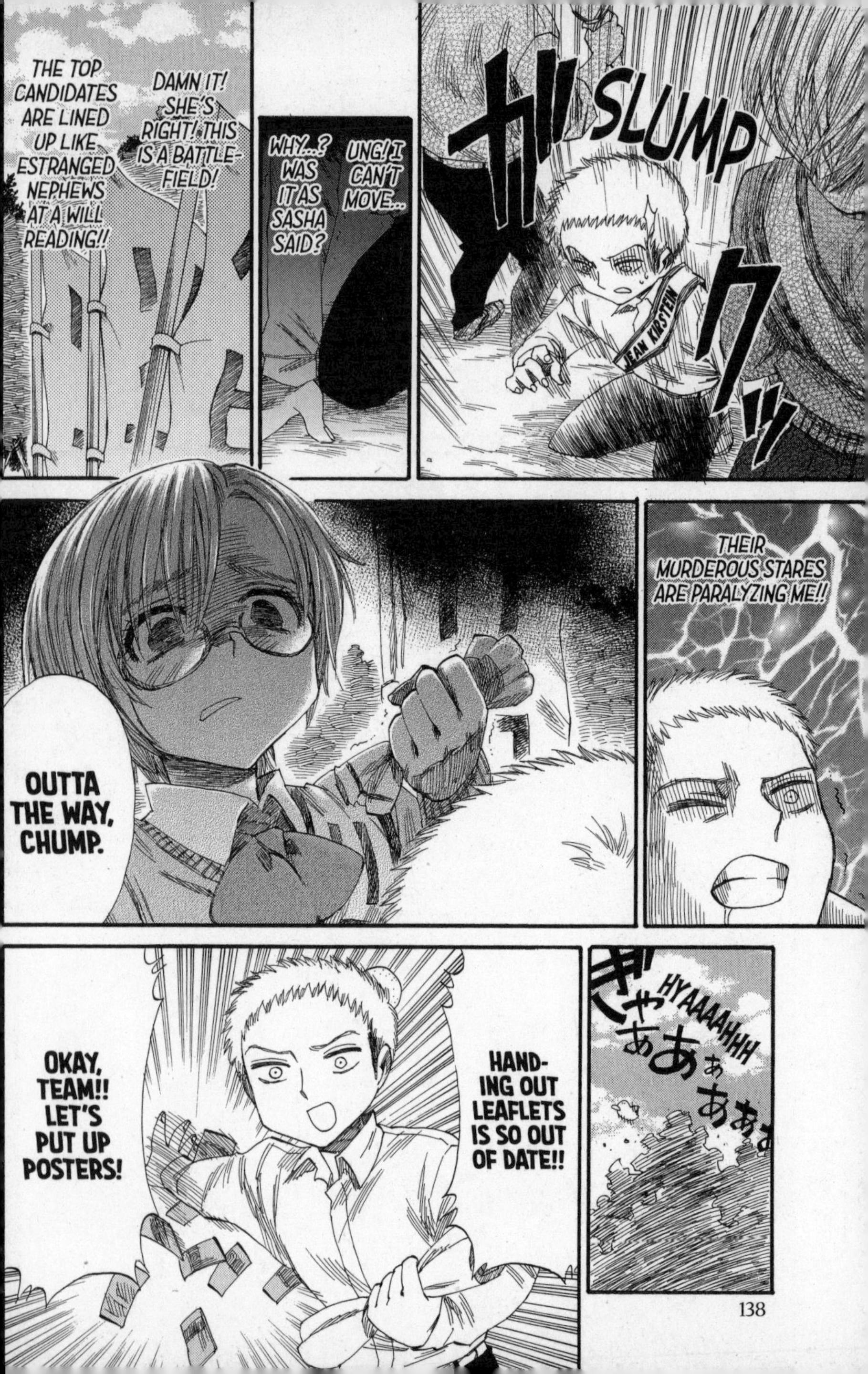
SLUMP
ガクッ
UNG! I CAN'T MOVE...
WHY...? WAS IT AS SASHA SAID?
DAMN IT! SHE'S RIGHT! THIS IS A BATTLE-FIELD!
THE TOP CANDIDATES ARE LINED UP LIKE ESTRANGED NEPHEWS AT A WILL READING!!
JEAN KIRSTEIN
THEIR MURDEROUS STARES ARE PARALYZING ME!!
OUTTA THE WAY, CHUMP.
HYAAAAHHH
ぎゃああぁあああ
HAND-ING OUT LEAFLETS IS SO OUT OF DATE!!
OKAY, TEAM!! LET'S PUT UP POSTERS!

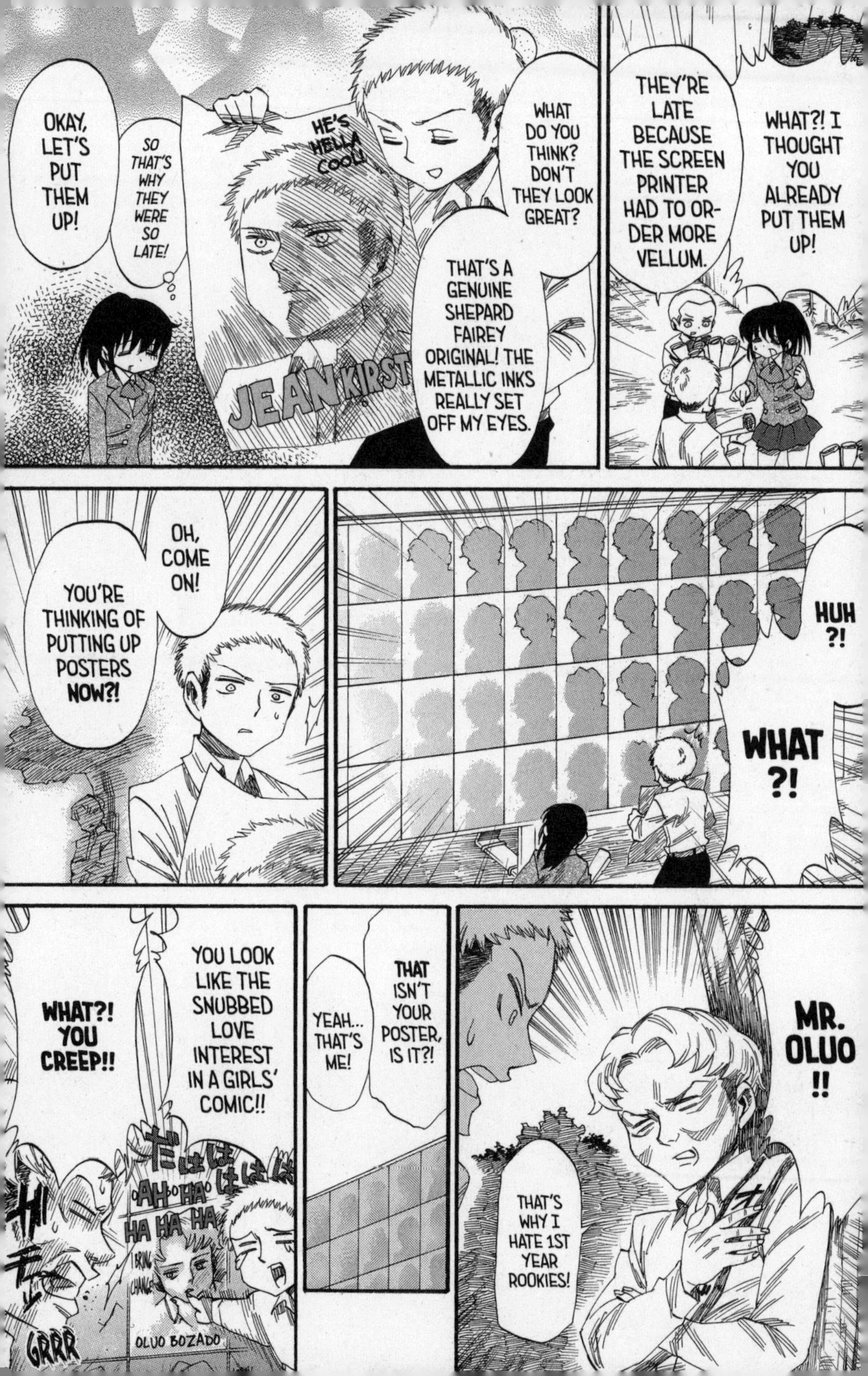
WHAT?! I THOUGHT YOU ALREADY PUT THEM UP!
THEY'RE LATE BECAUSE THE SCREEN PRINTER HAD TO OR-DER MORE VELLUM.
WHAT DO YOU THINK? DON'T THEY LOOK GREAT?
HE'S HELLA COOL!
THAT'S A GENUINE SHEPARD FAIREY ORIGINAL! THE METALLIC INKS REALLY SET OFF MY EYES.
JEAN KIRST
SO THAT'S WHY THEY WERE SO LATE!
OKAY, LET'S PUT THEM UP!
HUH?!
WHAT?!
OH, COME ON!
YOU'RE THINKING OF PUTTING UP POSTERS NOW?!
MR. OLUO!!
THAT'S WHY I HATE 1ST YEAR ROOKIES!
THAT ISN'T YOUR POSTER, IS IT?!
YEAH... THAT'S ME!
YOU LOOK LIKE THE SNUBBED LOVE INTEREST IN A GIRLS' COMIC!!
WHAT?! YOU CREEP!!
だはははははは
AH HA HA HA HA HA
I BRING CHANGE
OLUO BOZADO
GRRR

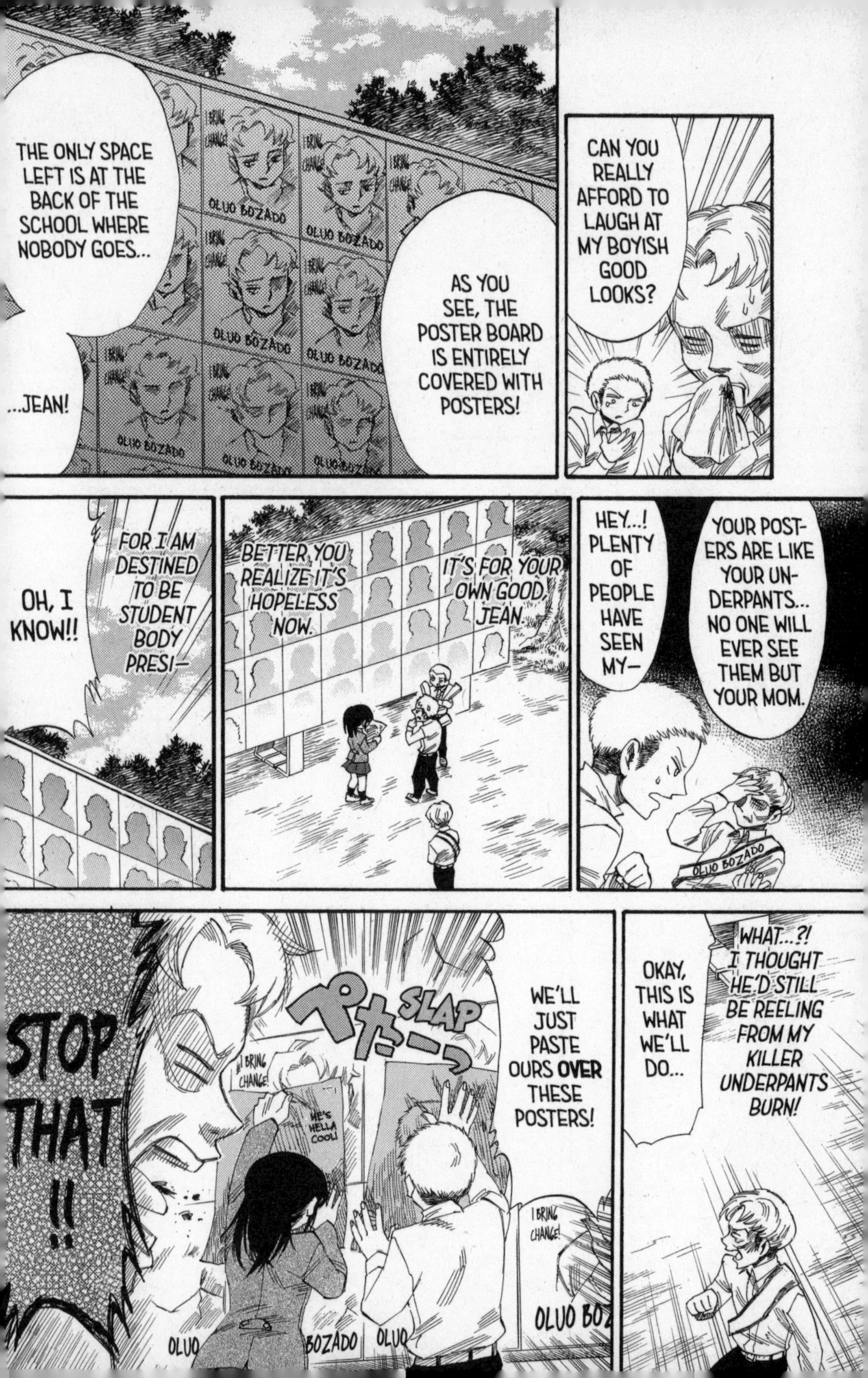
CAN YOU REALLY AFFORD TO LAUGH AT MY BOYISH GOOD LOOKS?
AS YOU SEE, THE POSTER BOARD IS ENTIRELY COVERED WITH POSTERS!
THE ONLY SPACE LEFT IS AT THE BACK OF THE SCHOOL WHERE NOBODY GOES...
...JEAN!
I BRING CHANGE!
OLUO BOZADO
YOUR POSTERS ARE LIKE YOUR UNDERPANTS... NO ONE WILL EVER SEE THEM BUT YOUR MOM.
HEY...! PLENTY OF PEOPLE HAVE SEEN MY—
OLUO BOZADO
IT'S FOR YOUR OWN GOOD, JEAN.
BETTER YOU REALIZE IT'S HOPELESS NOW.
FOR I AM DESTINED TO BE STUDENT BODY PRESI—
OH, I KNOW!!
WHAT...?! I THOUGHT HE'D STILL BE REELING FROM MY KILLER UNDERPANTS BURN!
OKAY, THIS IS WHAT WE'LL DO...
WE'LL JUST PASTE OURS OVER THESE POSTERS!
ペターッ
SLAP
I BRING CHANGE!
HE'S HELLA COOL!
I BRING CHANGE!
OLUO BOZ
OLUO BOZADO OLUO
STOP THAT!!

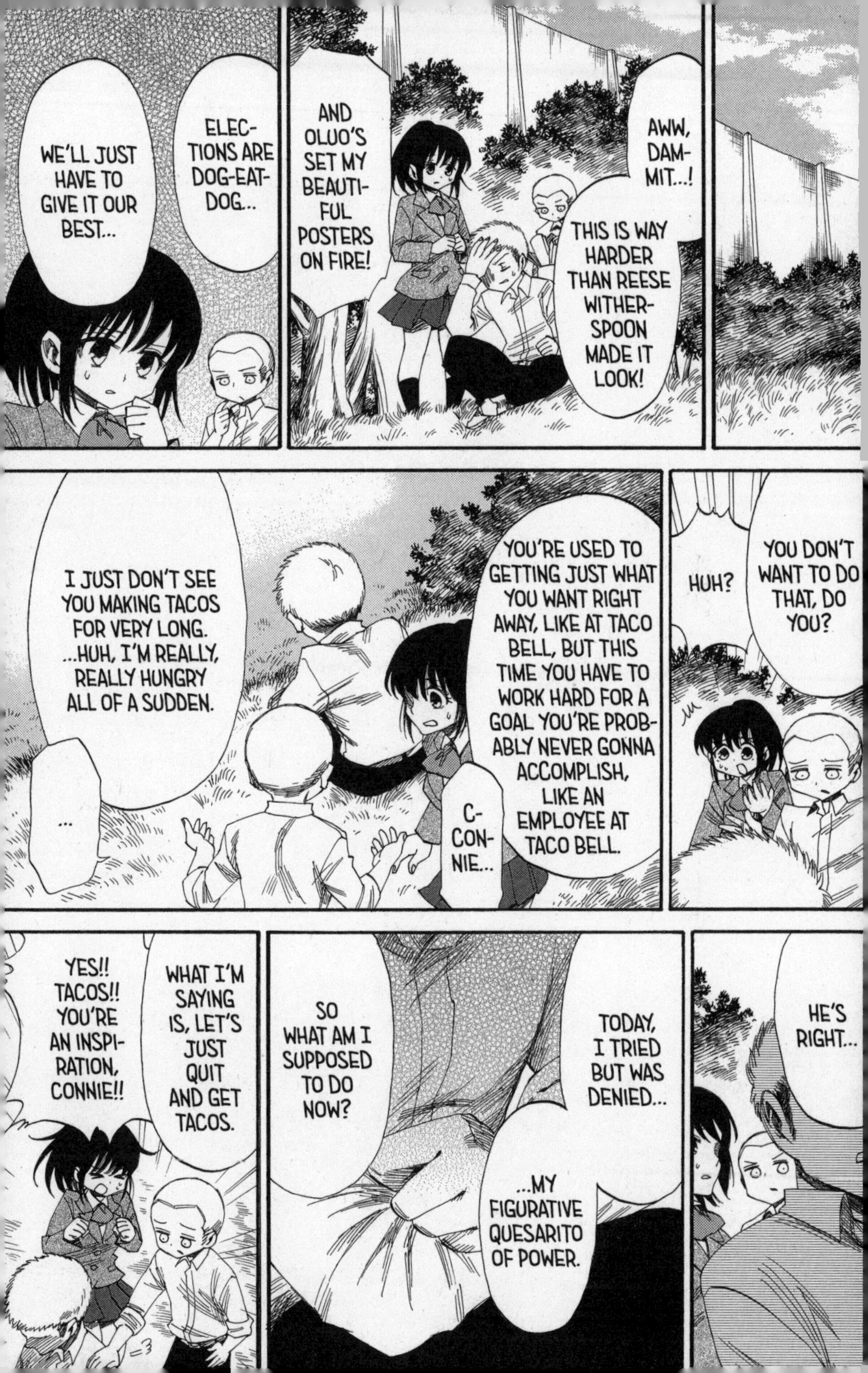
AWW, DAMMIT...!
THIS IS WAY HARDER THAN REESE WITHERSPOON MADE IT LOOK!
AND OLUO'S SET MY BEAUTIFUL POSTERS ON FIRE!
ELECTIONS ARE DOG-EAT-DOG...
WE'LL JUST HAVE TO GIVE IT OUR BEST...
YOU DON'T WANT TO DO THAT, DO YOU?
HUH?
YOU'RE USED TO GETTING JUST WHAT YOU WANT RIGHT AWAY, LIKE AT TACO BELL, BUT THIS TIME YOU HAVE TO WORK HARD FOR A GOAL YOU'RE PROBABLY NEVER GONNA ACCOMPLISH, LIKE AN EMPLOYEE AT TACO BELL.
C-CONNIE...
I JUST DON'T SEE YOU MAKING TACOS FOR VERY LONG. ...HUH, I'M REALLY, REALLY HUNGRY ALL OF A SUDDEN.
...
HE'S RIGHT...
TODAY, I TRIED BUT WAS DENIED...
...MY FIGURATIVE QUESARITO OF POWER.
SO WHAT AM I SUPPOSED TO DO NOW?
WHAT I'M SAYING IS, LET'S JUST QUIT AND GET TACOS.
YES!! TACOS!! YOU'RE AN INSPIRATION, CONNIE!!

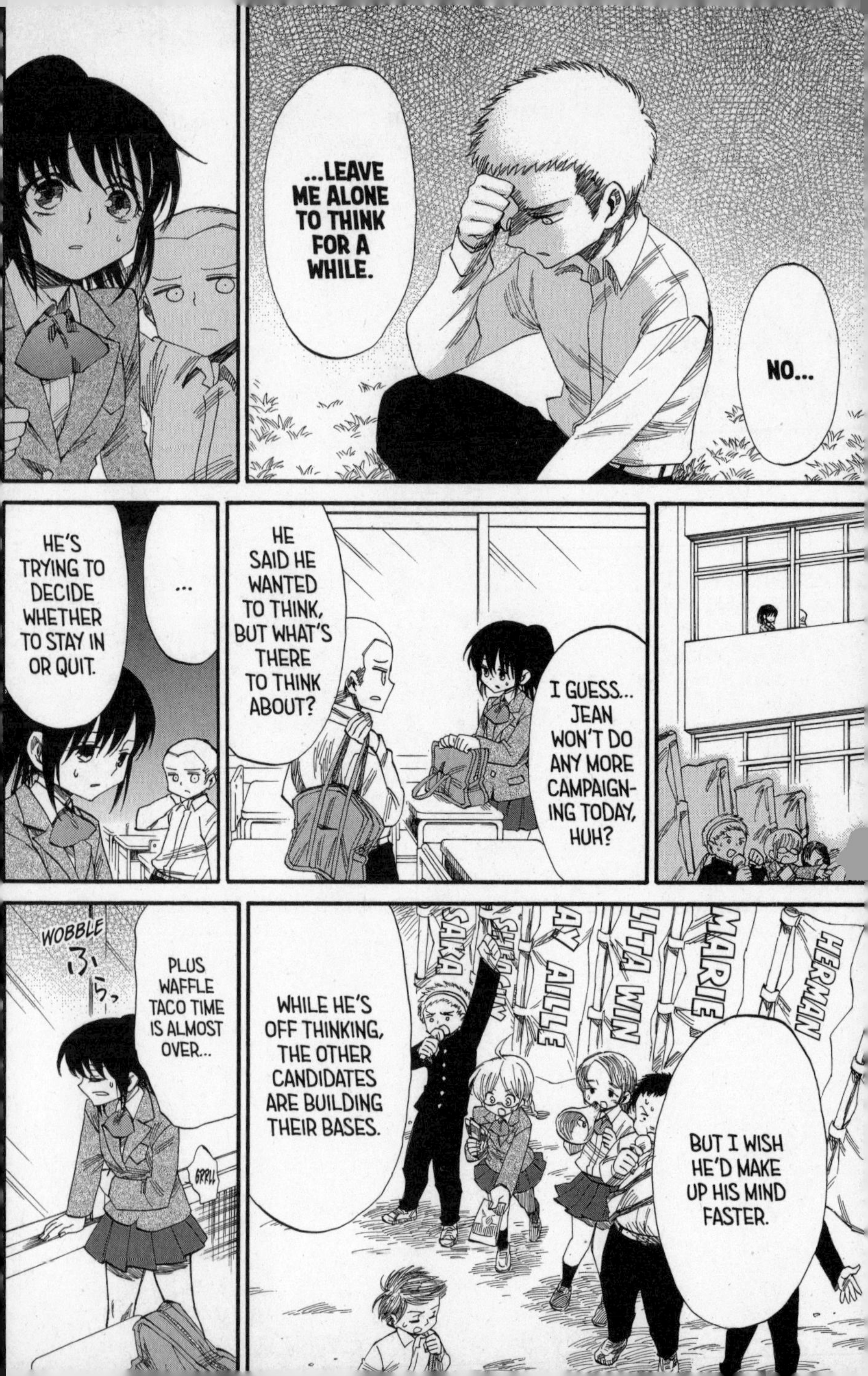
NO...
...LEAVE ME ALONE TO THINK FOR A WHILE.
I GUESS... JEAN WON'T DO ANY MORE CAMPAIGNING TODAY, HUH?
HE SAID HE WANTED TO THINK, BUT WHAT'S THERE TO THINK ABOUT?
...
HE'S TRYING TO DECIDE WHETHER TO STAY IN OR QUIT.
HERMAN
MARIE
LITA WIN
WHILE HE'S OFF THINKING, THE OTHER CANDIDATES ARE BUILDING THEIR BASES.
BUT I WISH HE'D MAKE UP HIS MIND FASTER.
WOBBLE
ふらっ
PLUS WAFFLE TACO TIME IS ALMOST OVER...
GRRLL

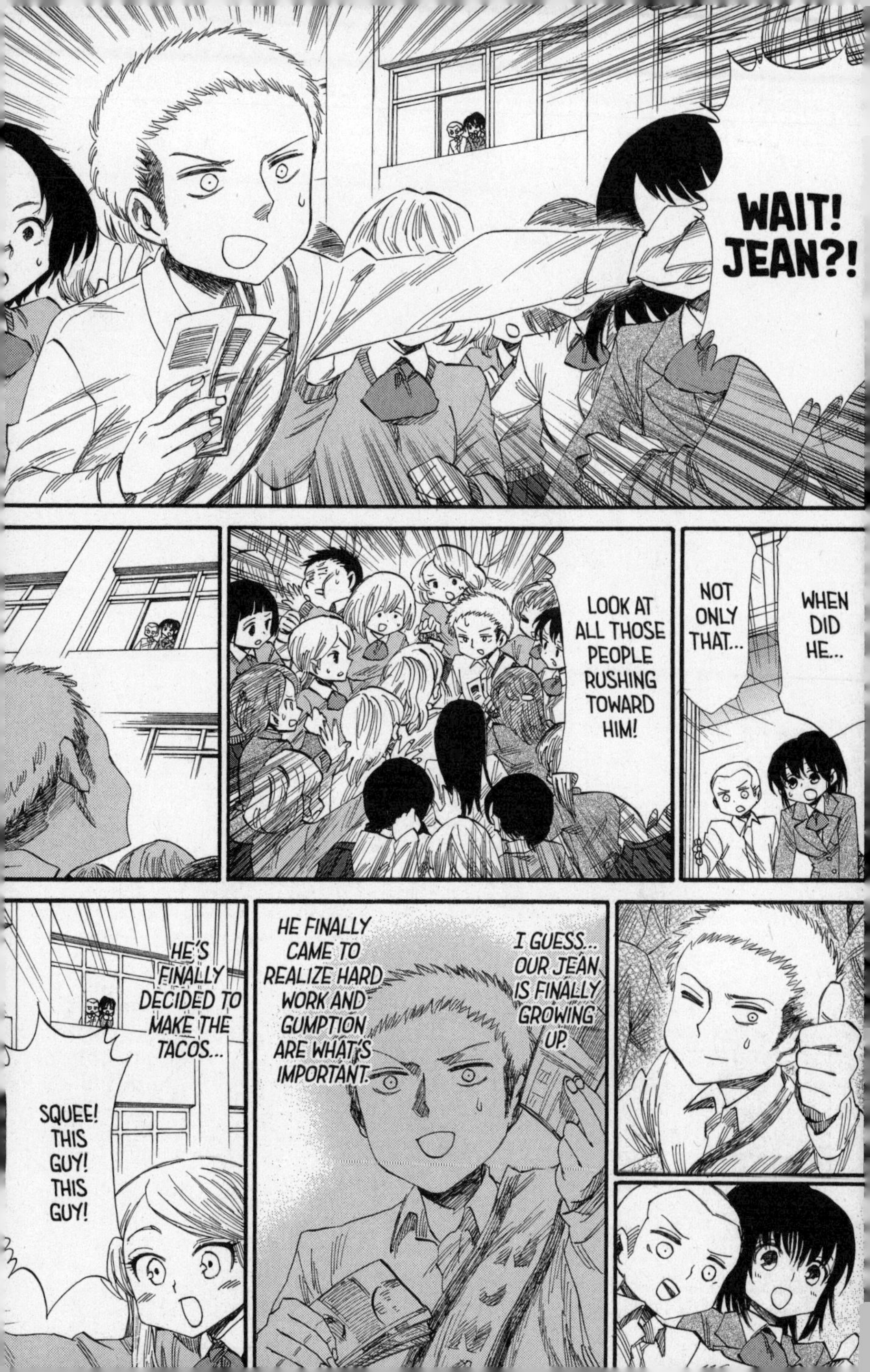
WAIT! JEAN?!
WHEN DID HE...
NOT ONLY THAT...
LOOK AT ALL THOSE PEOPLE RUSHING TOWARD HIM!
I GUESS... OUR JEAN IS FINALLY GROWING UP.
HE FINALLY CAME TO REALIZE HARD WORK AND GUMPTION ARE WHAT'S IMPORTANT.
HE'S FINALLY DECIDED TO MAKE THE TACOS...
SQUEE! THIS GUY! THIS GUY!

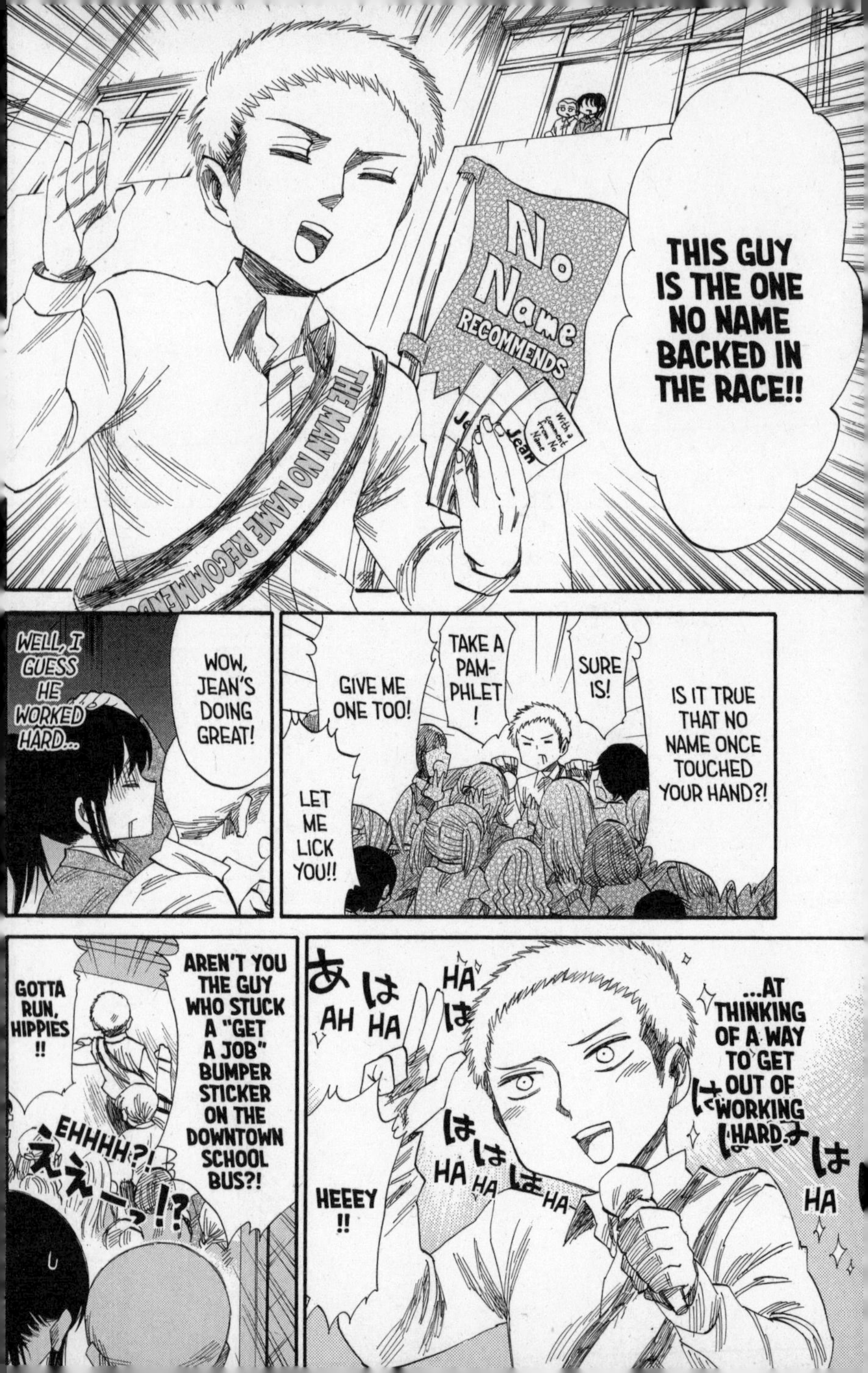
THIS GUY IS THE ONE NO NAME BACKED IN THE RACE!!
No Name RECOMMENDS
With a comment from No Name
Jean
THE MAN NO NAME RECOMMENDS
IS IT TRUE THAT NO NAME ONCE TOUCHED YOUR HAND?!
SURE IS!
TAKE A PAMPHLET!
GIVE ME ONE TOO!
LET ME LICK YOU!!
WOW, JEAN'S DOING GREAT!
WELL, I GUESS HE WORKED HARD...
...AT THINKING OF A WAY TO GET OUT OF WORKING HARD
は HA
はは HA
あはは AH HA HA
ははは HA HA HA
HEEEY!!
AREN'T YOU THE GUY WHO STUCK A "GET A JOB" BUMPER STICKER ON THE DOWNTOWN SCHOOL BUS?!
GOTTA RUN, HIPPIES!!
ええーっ!? EHHHH?!

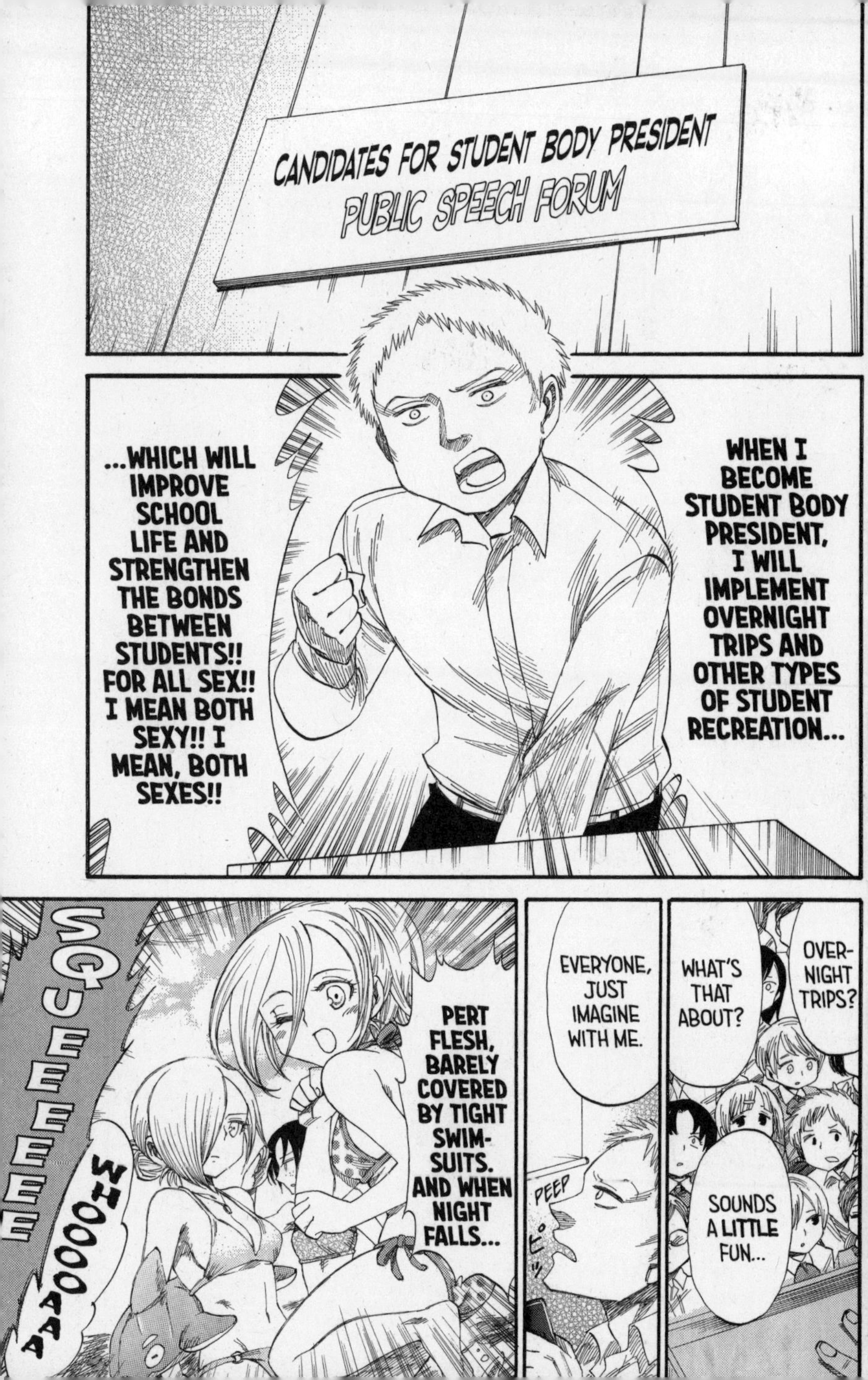
CANDIDATES FOR STUDENT BODY PRESIDENT
PUBLIC SPEECH FORUM
WHEN I BECOME STUDENT BODY PRESIDENT, I WILL IMPLEMENT OVERNIGHT TRIPS AND OTHER TYPES OF STUDENT RECREATION...
...WHICH WILL IMPROVE SCHOOL LIFE AND STRENGTHEN THE BONDS BETWEEN STUDENTS!! FOR ALL SEX!! I MEAN BOTH SEXY!! I MEAN, BOTH SEXES!!
OVER-NIGHT TRIPS?
WHAT'S THAT ABOUT?
SOUNDS A LITTLE FUN...
EVERYONE, JUST IMAGINE WITH ME.
PEEP
PERT FLESH, BARELY COVERED BY TIGHT SWIM-SUITS. AND WHEN NIGHT FALLS...
WHOOOOOAAA
SQUEEEEEEEE

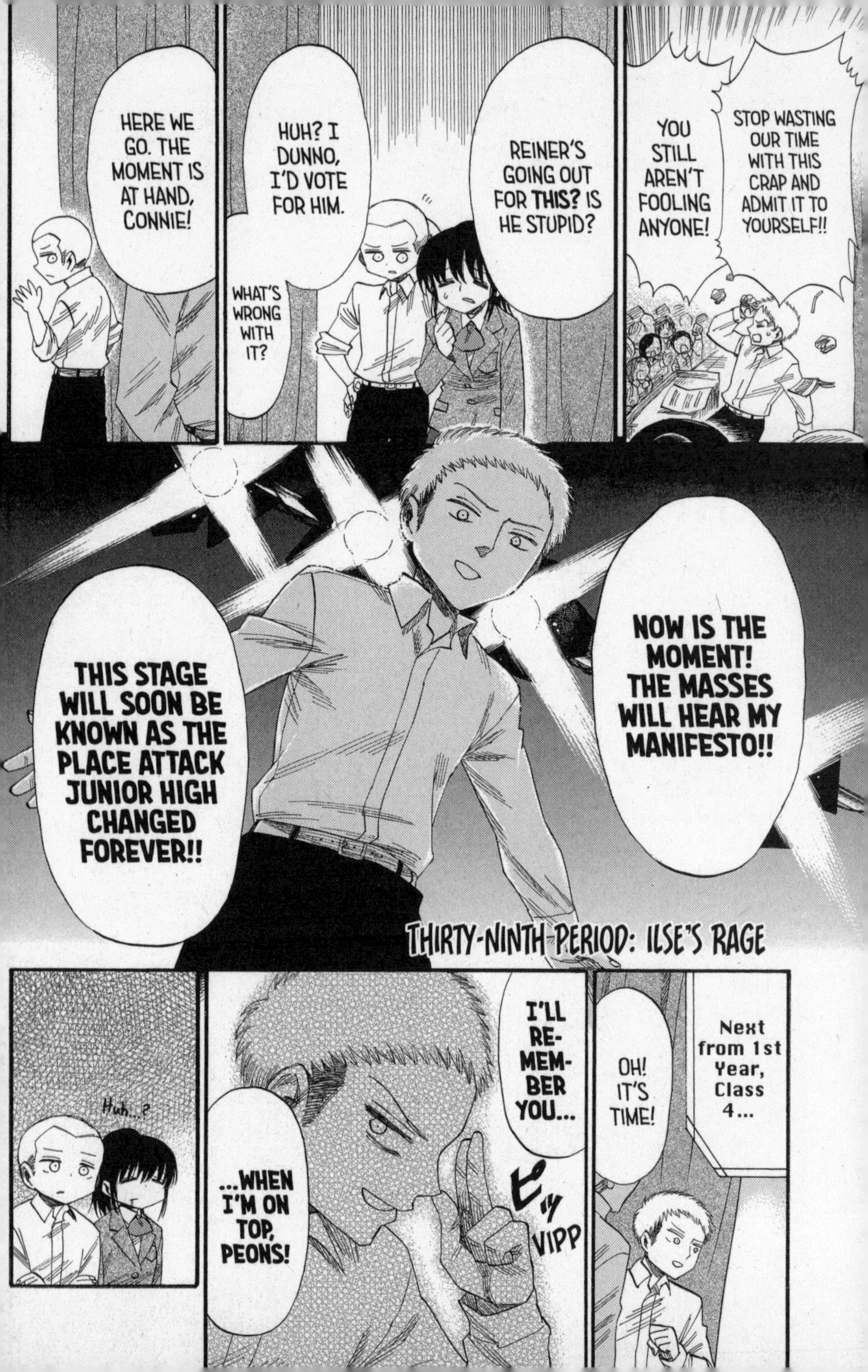

STOP WASTING OUR TIME WITH THIS CRAP AND ADMIT IT TO YOURSELF!!
YOU STILL AREN'T FOOLING ANYONE!
REINER'S GOING OUT FOR THIS? IS HE STUPID?
HUH? I DUNNO, I'D VOTE FOR HIM.
WHAT'S WRONG WITH IT?
HERE WE GO. THE MOMENT IS AT HAND, CONNIE!
NOW IS THE MOMENT! THE MASSES WILL HEAR MY MANIFESTO!!
THIS STAGE WILL SOON BE KNOWN AS THE PLACE ATTACK JUNIOR HIGH CHANGED FOREVER!!
THIRTY-NINTH PERIOD: ILSE'S RAGE
Next from 1st Year, Class 4...
OH! IT'S TIME!
I'LL RE-MEM-BER YOU...
...WHEN I'M ON TOP, PEONS!
VIPP
Huh...?

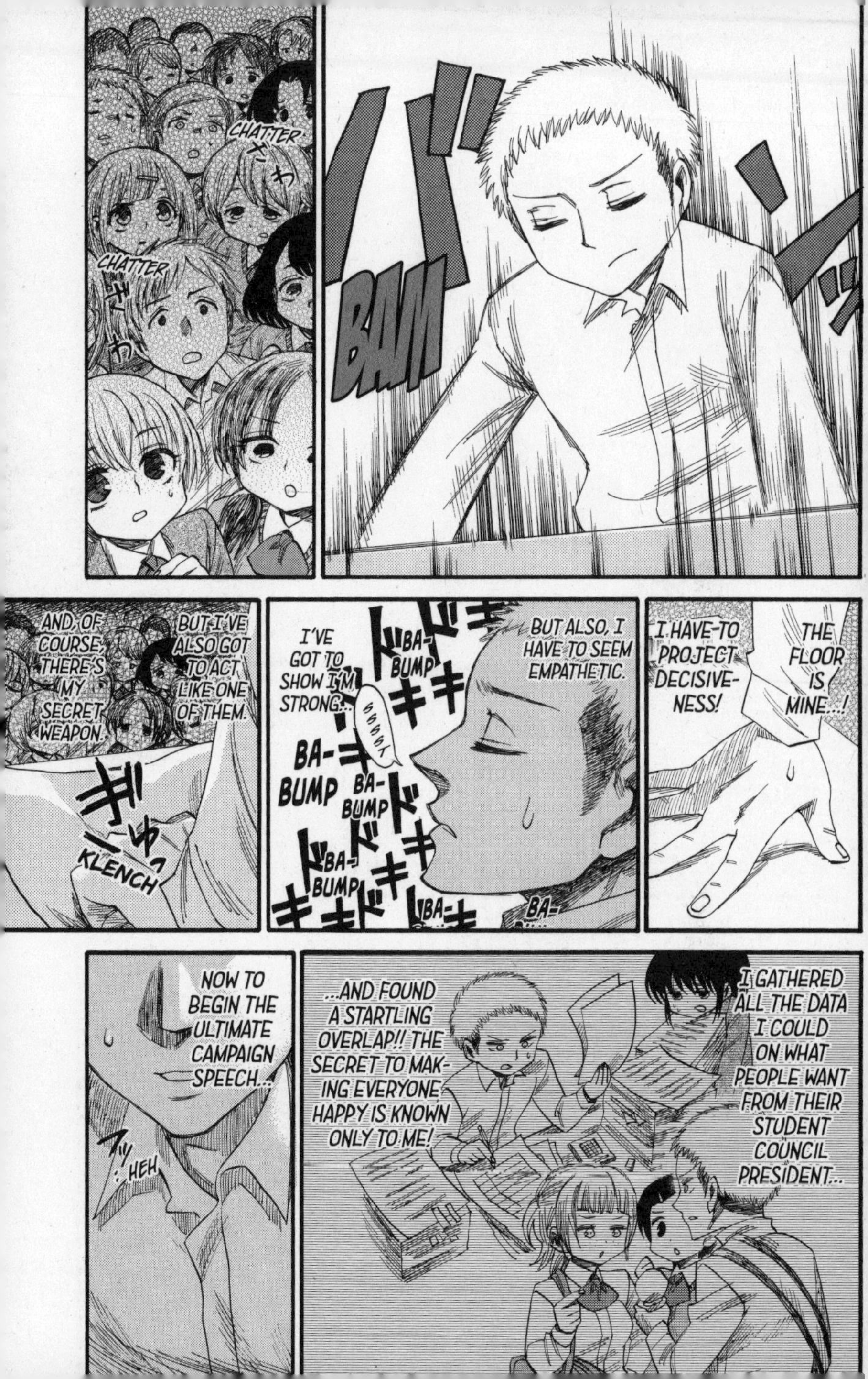
BAM
CHATTER
CHATTER
THE FLOOR IS MINE...!
I HAVE TO PROJECT DECISIVENESS!
BUT ALSO, I HAVE TO SEEM EMPATHETIC.
I'VE GOT TO SHOW I'M STRONG...
BA-BUMP
BA-BUMP
BA-BUMP
BA-BUMP
BA-BUMP
BA-
BA-
BUT I'VE ALSO GOT TO ACT LIKE ONE OF THEM.
AND, OF COURSE, THERE'S MY SECRET WEAPON.
KLENCH
I GATHERED ALL THE DATA I COULD ON WHAT PEOPLE WANT FROM THEIR STUDENT COUNCIL PRESIDENT...
...AND FOUND A STARTLING OVERLAP!! THE SECRET TO MAKING EVERYONE HAPPY IS KNOWN ONLY TO ME!
NOW TO BEGIN THE ULTIMATE CAMPAIGN SPEECH...
HEH

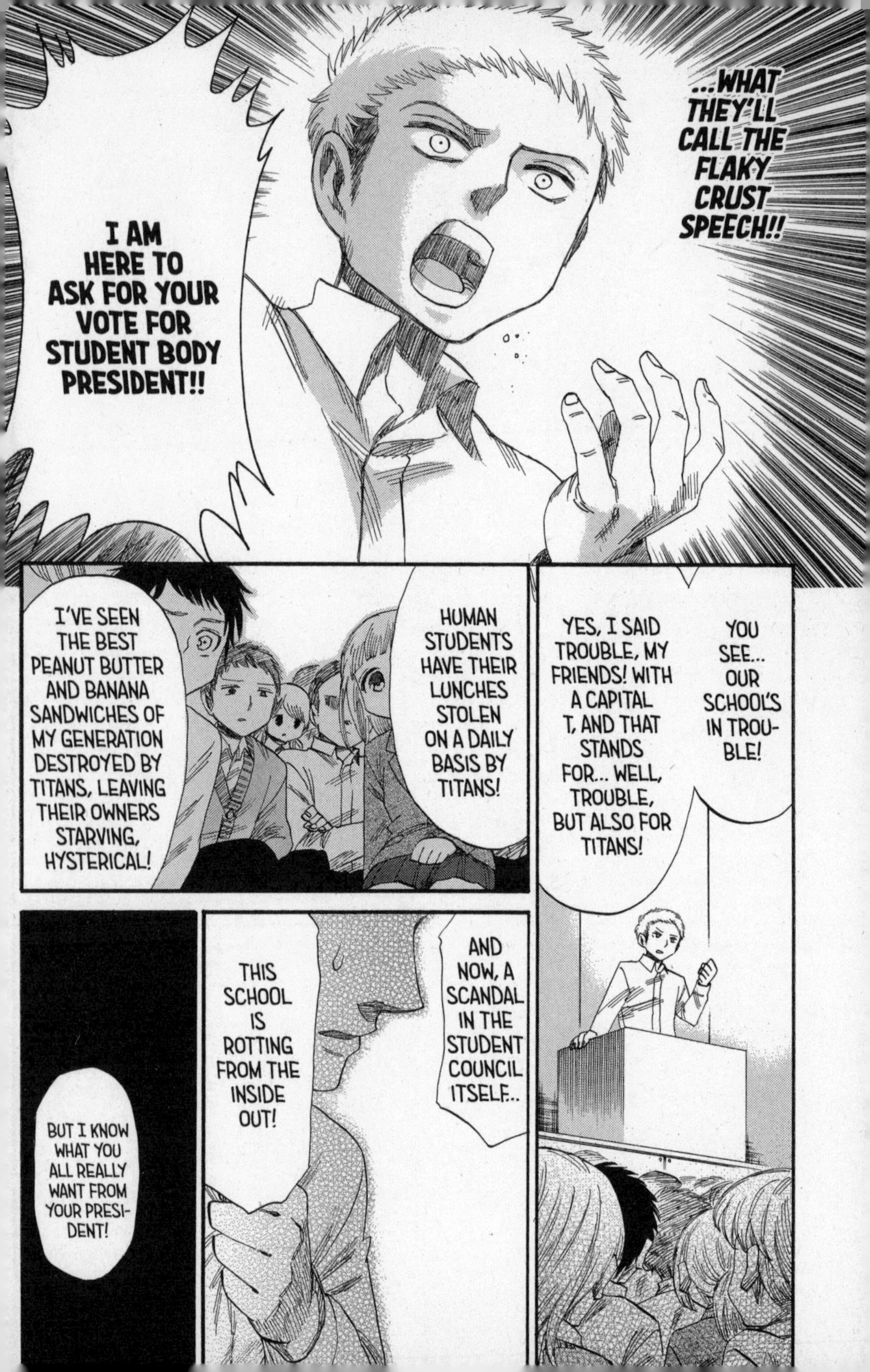
...WHAT THEY'LL CALL THE FLAKY CRUST SPEECH!!
I AM HERE TO ASK FOR YOUR VOTE FOR STUDENT BODY PRESIDENT!!
YOU SEE... OUR SCHOOL'S IN TROU-BLE!
YES, I SAID TROUBLE, MY FRIENDS! WITH A CAPITAL T, AND THAT STANDS FOR... WELL, TROUBLE, BUT ALSO FOR TITANS!
HUMAN STUDENTS HAVE THEIR LUNCHES STOLEN ON A DAILY BASIS BY TITANS!
I'VE SEEN THE BEST PEANUT BUTTER AND BANANA SANDWICHES OF MY GENERATION DESTROYED BY TITANS, LEAVING THEIR OWNERS STARVING, HYSTERICAL!
AND NOW, A SCANDAL IN THE STUDENT COUNCIL ITSELF...
THIS SCHOOL IS ROTTING FROM THE INSIDE OUT!
BUT I KNOW WHAT YOU ALL REALLY WANT FROM YOUR PRESI-DENT!

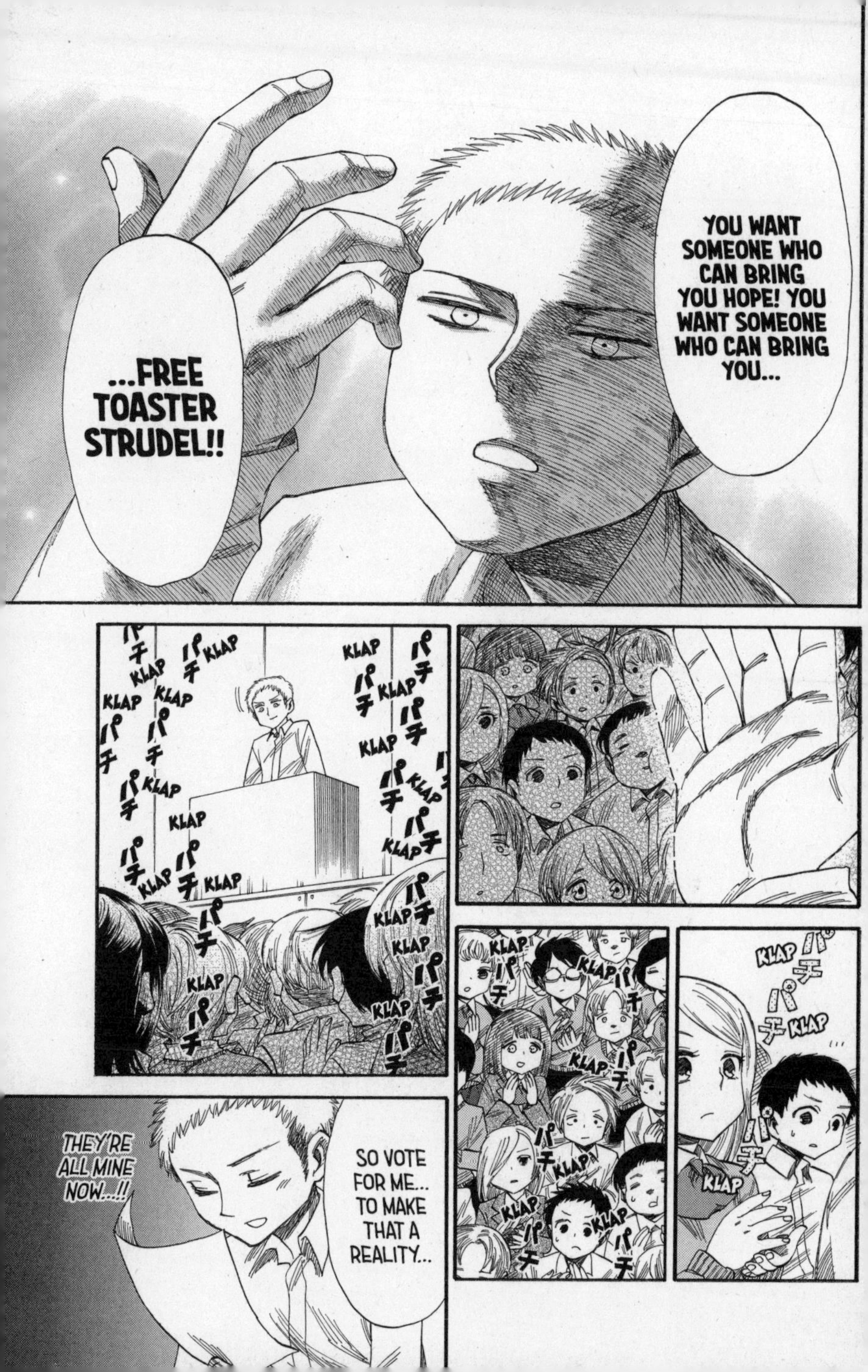
YOU WANT SOMEONE WHO CAN BRING YOU HOPE! YOU WANT SOMEONE WHO CAN BRING YOU...
...FREE TOASTER STRUDEL!!
KLAP
パチ
KLAP
パチ
SO VOTE FOR ME... TO MAKE THAT A REALITY...
THEY'RE ALL MINE NOW...!!

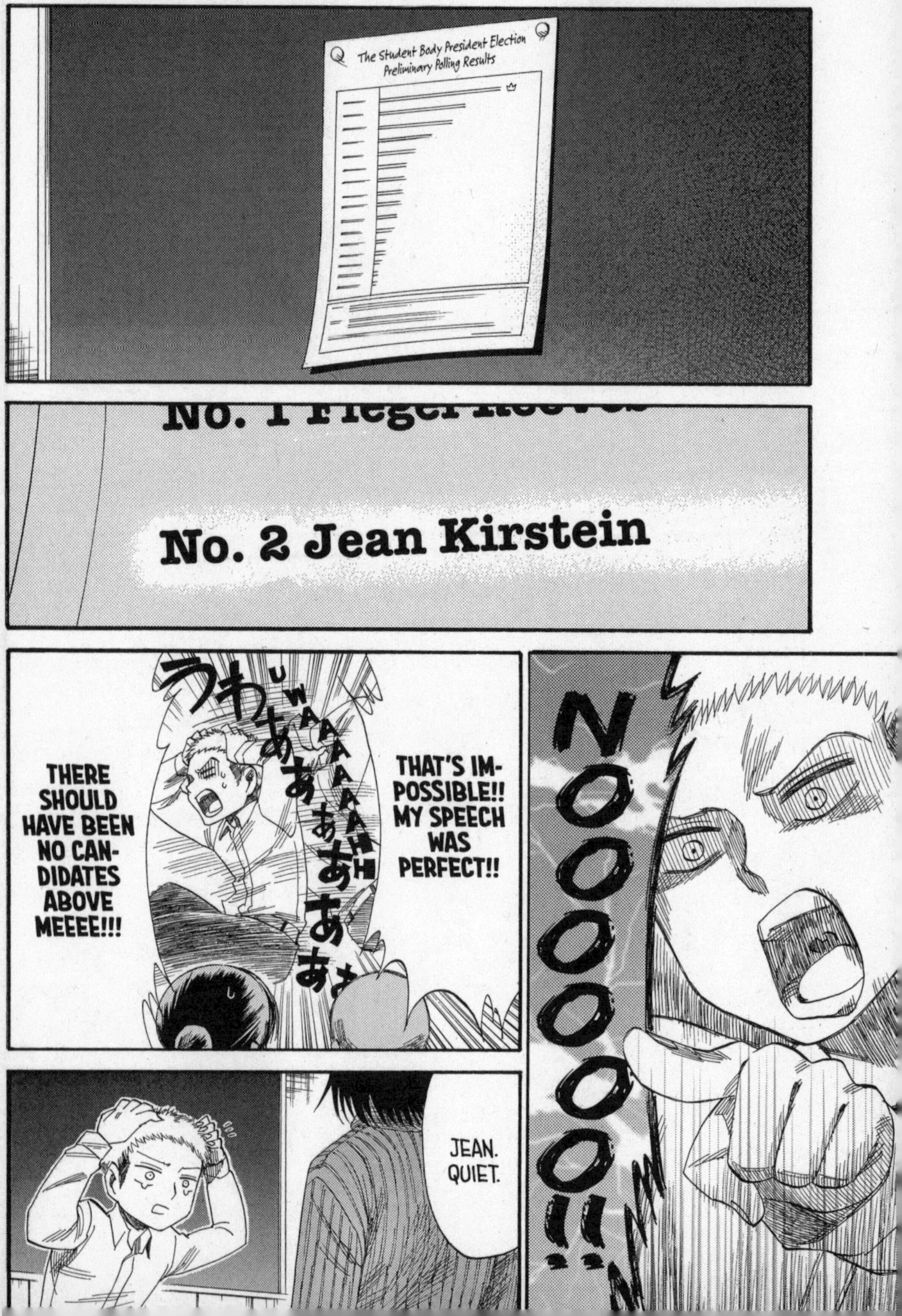
The Student Body President Election
Preliminary Polling Results
No. 2 Jean Kirstein
NOOOOOOOO!!
THAT'S IM-POSSIBLE!! MY SPEECH WAS PERFECT!!
うわあああああ
UWAAAAAAAHH
THERE SHOULD HAVE BEEN NO CAN-DIDATES ABOVE MEEEE!!!
JEAN. QUIET.

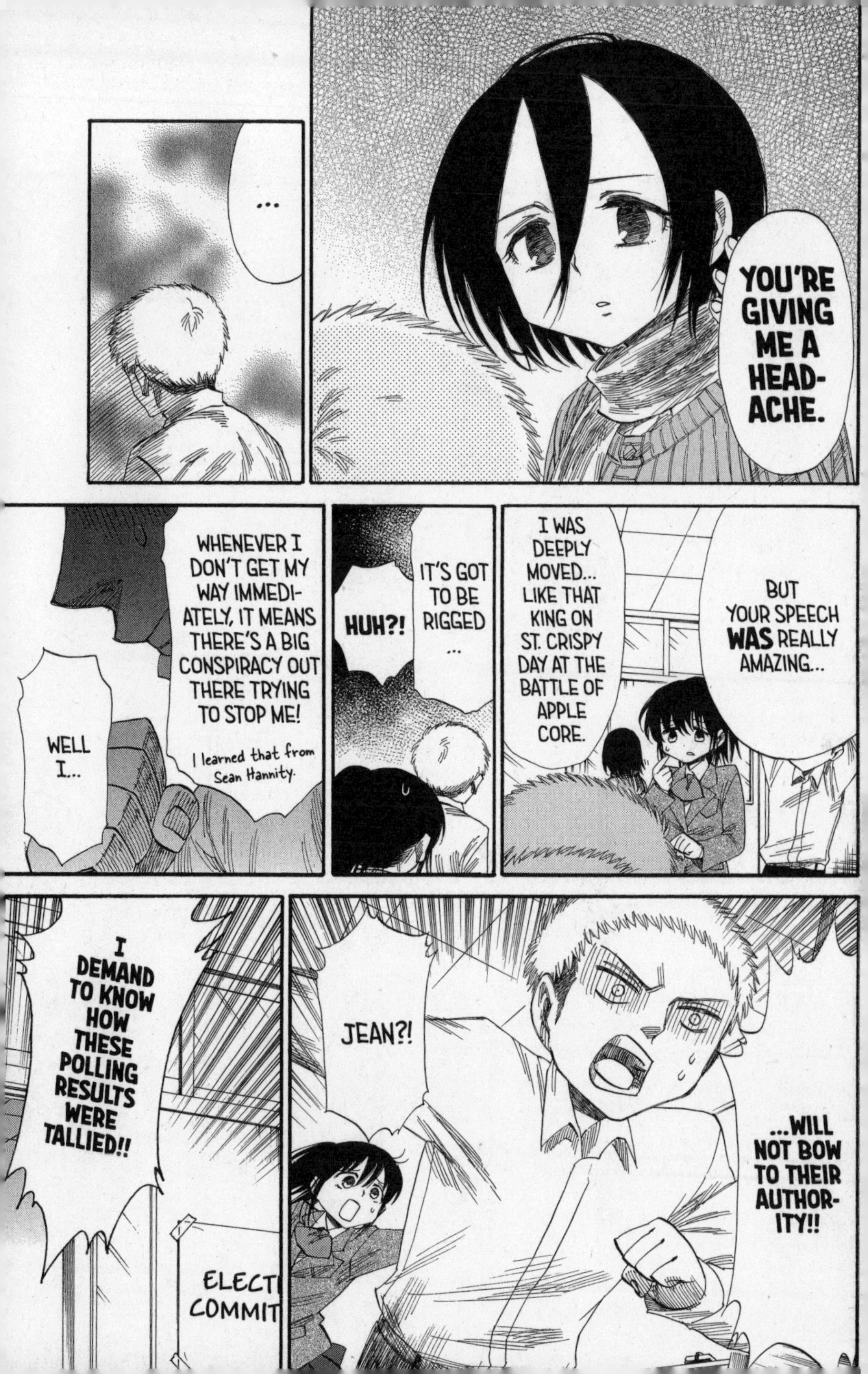
YOU'RE GIVING ME A HEAD-ACHE.
...
BUT YOUR SPEECH WAS REALLY AMAZING...
I WAS DEEPLY MOVED... LIKE THAT KING ON ST. CRISPY DAY AT THE BATTLE OF APPLE CORE.
IT'S GOT TO BE RIGGED ...
HUH?!
WHENEVER I DON'T GET MY WAY IMMEDI-ATELY, IT MEANS THERE'S A BIG CONSPIRACY OUT THERE TRYING TO STOP ME!
I learned that from Sean Hannity.
WELL I...
JEAN?!
...WILL NOT BOW TO THEIR AUTHOR-ITY!!
I DEMAND TO KNOW HOW THESE POLLING RESULTS WERE TALLIED!!
ELECT
COMMIT

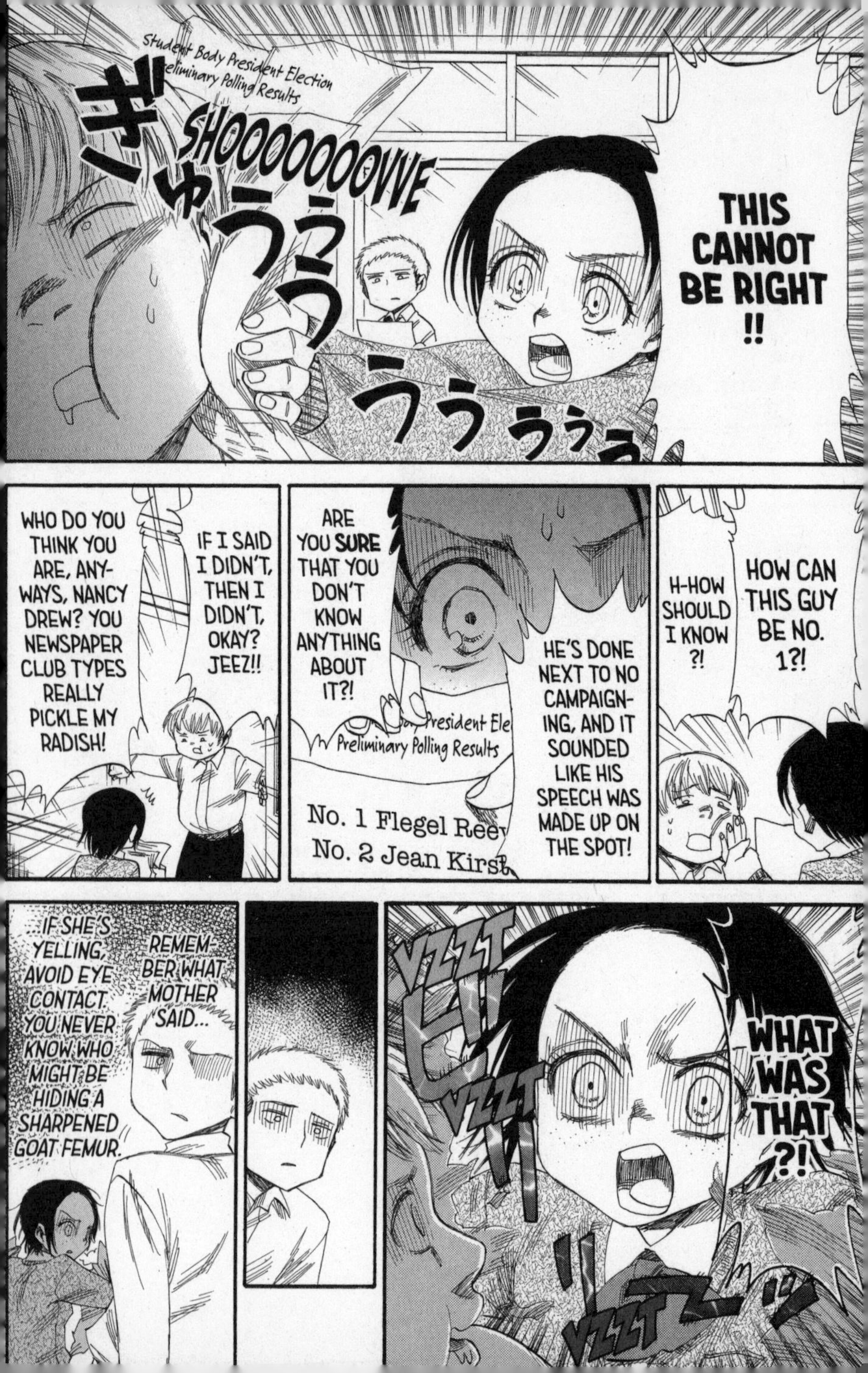
THIS CANNOT BE RIGHT!!
SHOOOOOOOVVE
ぎゅううううううう
Student Body President Election Preliminary Polling Results
HOW CAN THIS GUY BE NO. 1?!
H-HOW SHOULD I KNOW?!
HE'S DONE NEXT TO NO CAMPAIGNING, AND IT SOUNDED LIKE HIS SPEECH WAS MADE UP ON THE SPOT!
ARE YOU SURE THAT YOU DON'T KNOW ANYTHING ABOUT IT?!
President Ele
Preliminary Polling Results
No. 1 Flegel Ree
No. 2 Jean Kirst
IF I SAID I DIDN'T, THEN I DIDN'T, OKAY? JEEZ!!
WHO DO YOU THINK YOU ARE, ANYWAYS, NANCY DREW? YOU NEWSPAPER CLUB TYPES REALLY PICKLE MY RADISH!
WHAT WAS THAT?!
VZZZT
VZZZT
VZZZT
REMEMBER WHAT MOTHER SAID...
...IF SHE'S YELLING, AVOID EYE CONTACT. YOU NEVER KNOW WHO MIGHT BE HIDING A SHARPENED GOAT FEMUR.

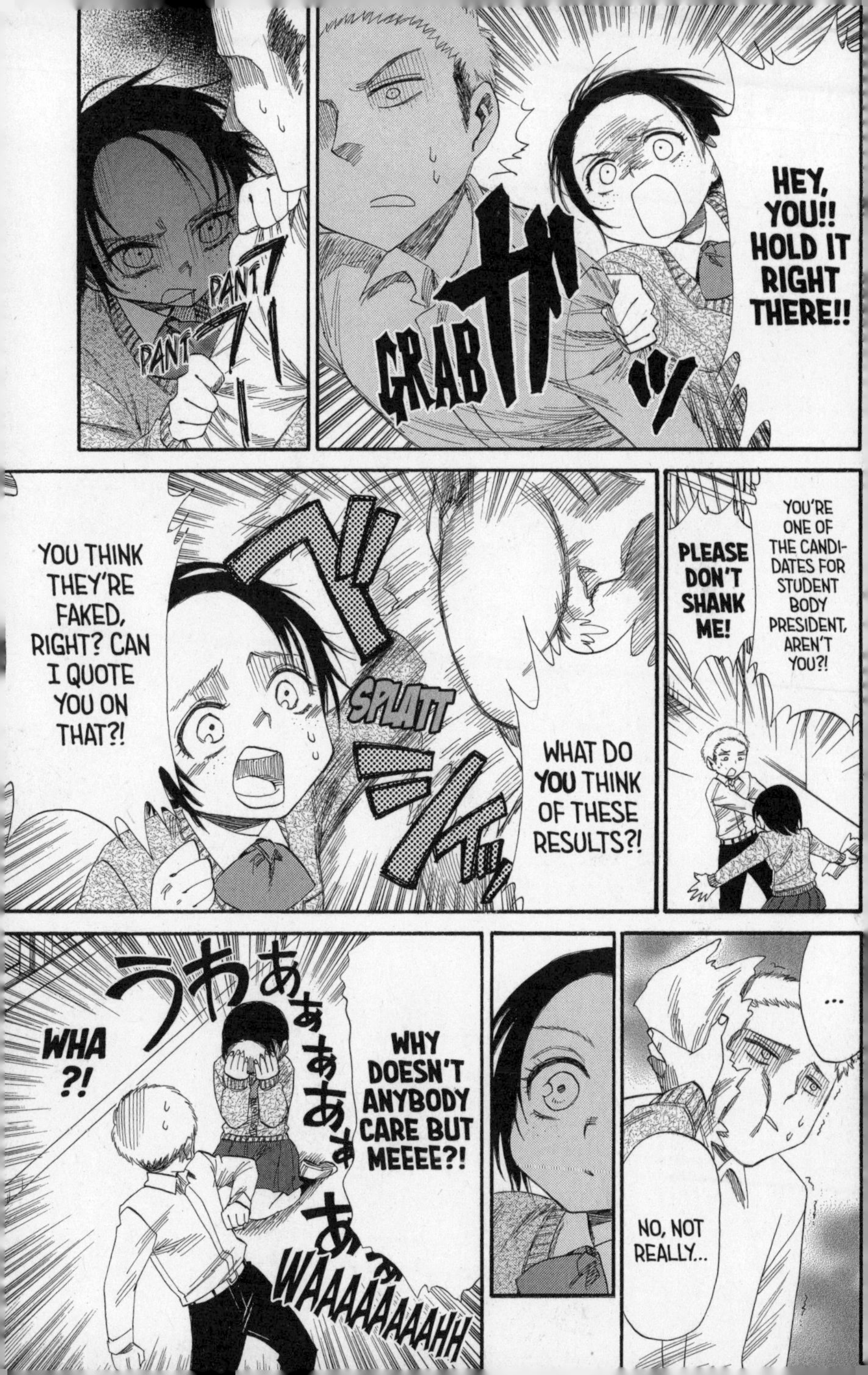
HEY, YOU!! HOLD IT RIGHT THERE!!
GRAB
PANT
PANT
YOU'RE ONE OF THE CANDI-DATES FOR STUDENT BODY PRESIDENT, AREN'T YOU?!
PLEASE DON'T SHANK ME!
WHAT DO YOU THINK OF THESE RESULTS?!
SPLATT
YOU THINK THEY'RE FAKED, RIGHT? CAN I QUOTE YOU ON THAT?!
...
NO, NOT REALLY...
WHY DOESN'T ANYBODY CARE BUT MEEEE?!
WHA ?!
WAAAAAAAAAHH

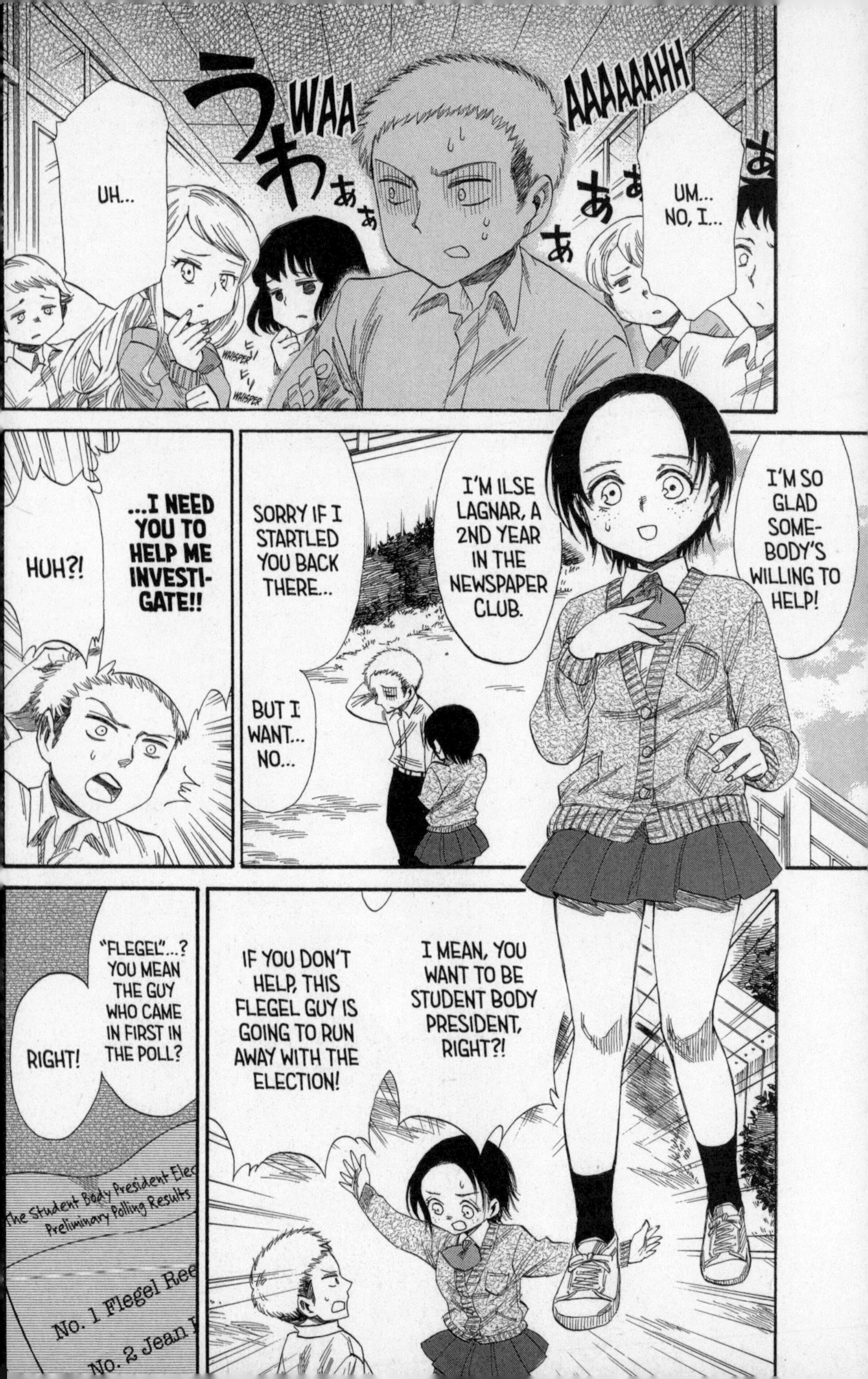
うわあああ
WAA AAAAAAH
あああ
UM... NO, I...
UH...
WHISPER
WHISPER
I'M SO GLAD SOMEBODY'S WILLING TO HELP!
I'M ILSE LAGNAR, A 2ND YEAR IN THE NEWSPAPER CLUB.
SORRY IF I STARTLED YOU BACK THERE...
BUT I WANT... NO...
...I NEED YOU TO HELP ME INVESTIGATE!!
HUH?!
I MEAN, YOU WANT TO BE STUDENT BODY PRESIDENT, RIGHT?!
IF YOU DON'T HELP, THIS FLEGEL GUY IS GOING TO RUN AWAY WITH THE ELECTION!
"FLEGEL"...? YOU MEAN THE GUY WHO CAME IN FIRST IN THE POLL?
RIGHT!
The Student Body President
Preliminary Polling Results
No. 1 Flegel
No. 2 Jean

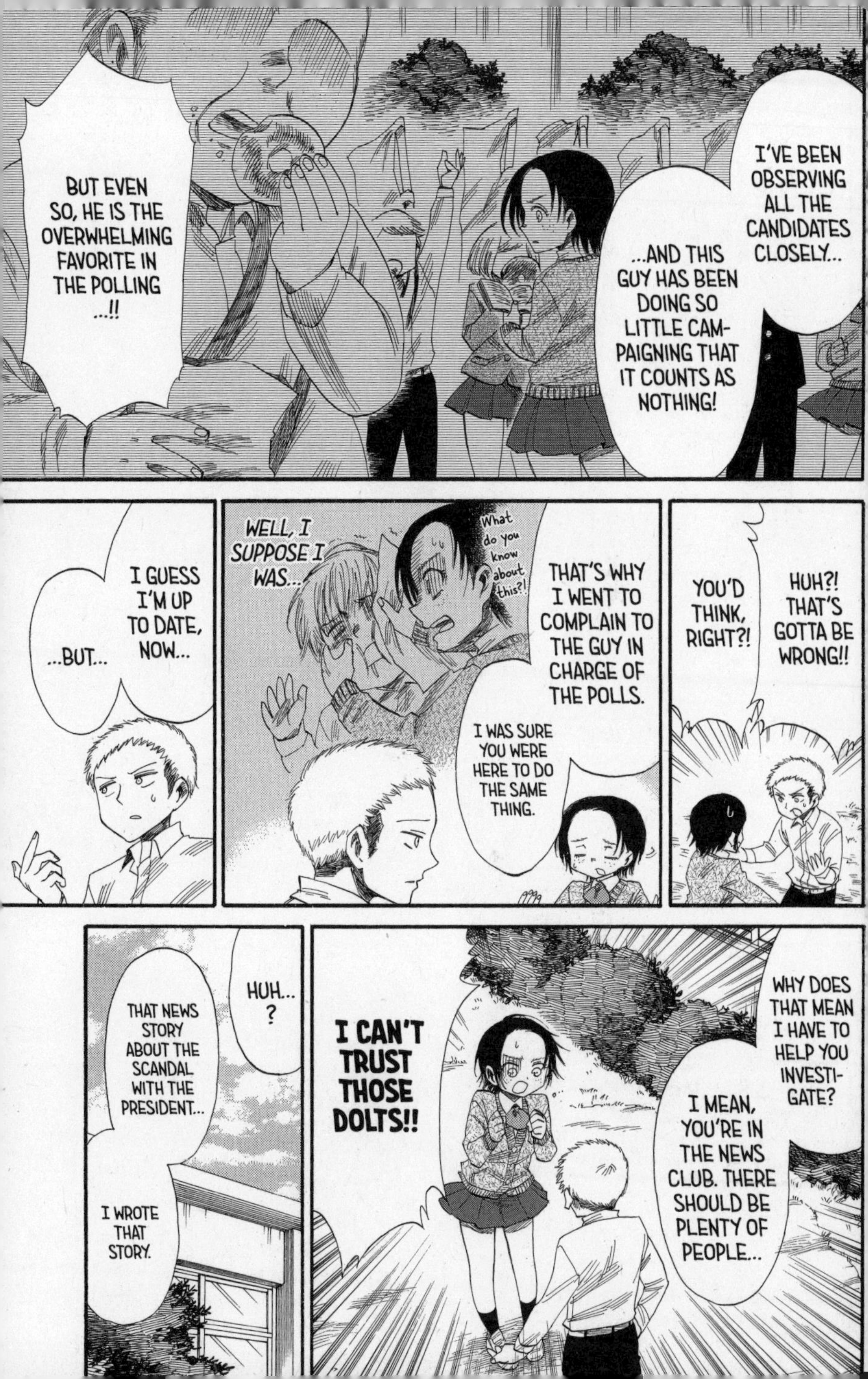
I'VE BEEN OBSERVING ALL THE CANDIDATES CLOSELY...
...AND THIS GUY HAS BEEN DOING SO LITTLE CAM-PAIGNING THAT IT COUNTS AS NOTHING!
BUT EVEN SO, HE IS THE OVERWHELMING FAVORITE IN THE POLLING ...!!
HUH?! THAT'S GOTTA BE WRONG!!
YOU'D THINK, RIGHT?!
THAT'S WHY I WENT TO COMPLAIN TO THE GUY IN CHARGE OF THE POLLS.
I WAS SURE YOU WERE HERE TO DO THE SAME THING.
What do you know about this?!
WELL, I SUPPOSE I WAS...
I GUESS I'M UP TO DATE, NOW...
...BUT...
WHY DOES THAT MEAN I HAVE TO HELP YOU INVESTI-GATE?
I MEAN, YOU'RE IN THE NEWS CLUB. THERE SHOULD BE PLENTY OF PEOPLE...
I CAN'T TRUST THOSE DOLTS!!
HUH... ?
THAT NEWS STORY ABOUT THE SCANDAL WITH THE PRESIDENT...
I WROTE THAT STORY.

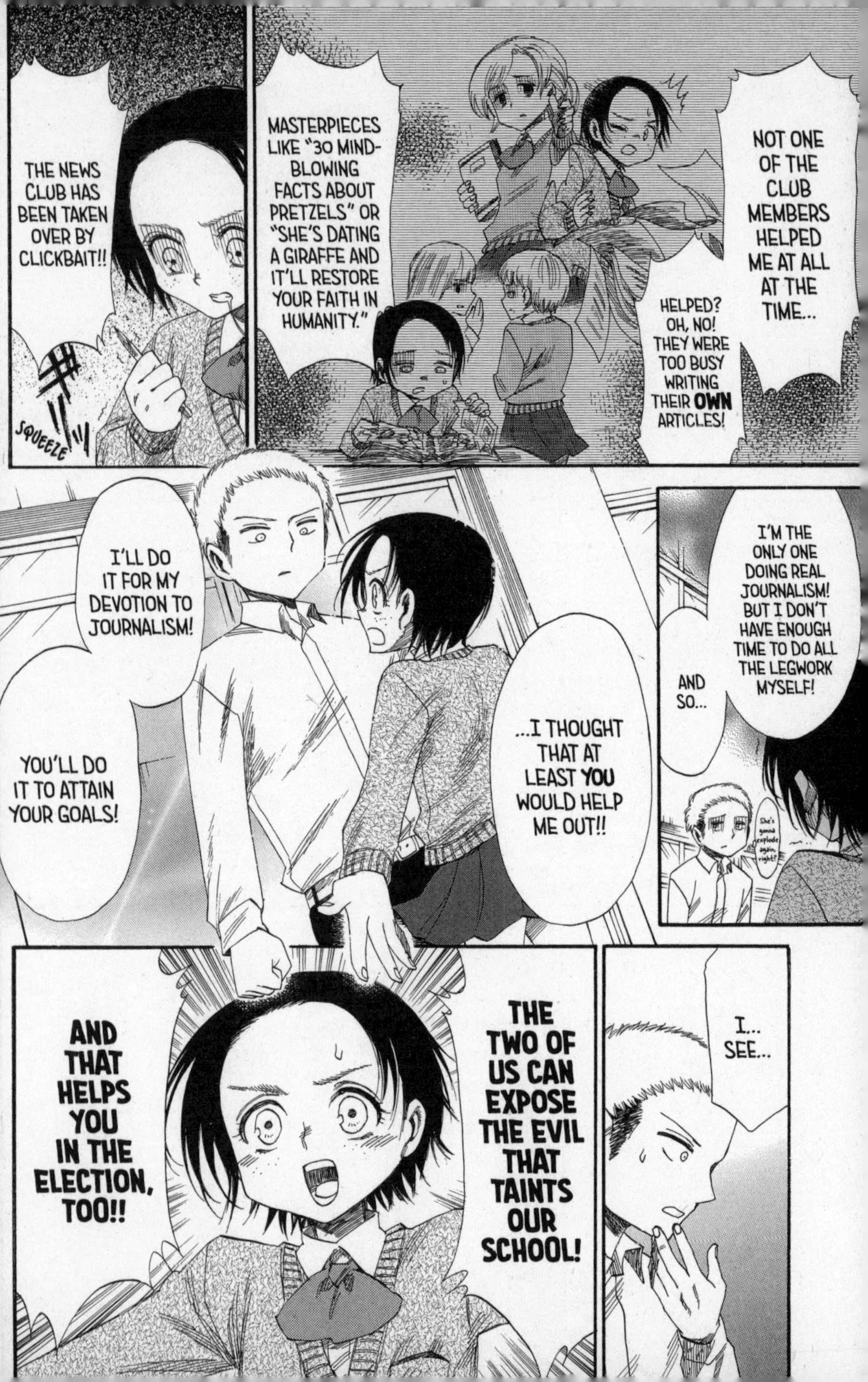
NOT ONE OF THE CLUB MEMBERS HELPED ME AT ALL AT THE TIME...
HELPED? OH, NO! THEY WERE TOO BUSY WRITING THEIR **OWN** ARTICLES!
MASTERPIECES LIKE "30 MIND-BLOWING FACTS ABOUT PRETZELS" OR "SHE'S DATING A GIRAFFE AND IT'LL RESTORE YOUR FAITH IN HUMANITY."
THE NEWS CLUB HAS BEEN TAKEN OVER BY CLICKBAIT!!
SQUEEZE
I'M THE ONLY ONE DOING REAL JOURNALISM! BUT I DON'T HAVE ENOUGH TIME TO DO ALL THE LEGWORK MYSELF!
AND SO...
She's gonna explode again, right?
...I THOUGHT THAT AT LEAST **YOU** WOULD HELP ME OUT!!
I'LL DO IT FOR MY DEVOTION TO JOURNALISM!
YOU'LL DO IT TO ATTAIN YOUR GOALS!
I... SEE...
THE TWO OF US CAN EXPOSE THE EVIL THAT TAINTS OUR SCHOOL!
AND THAT HELPS YOU IN THE ELECTION, TOO!!

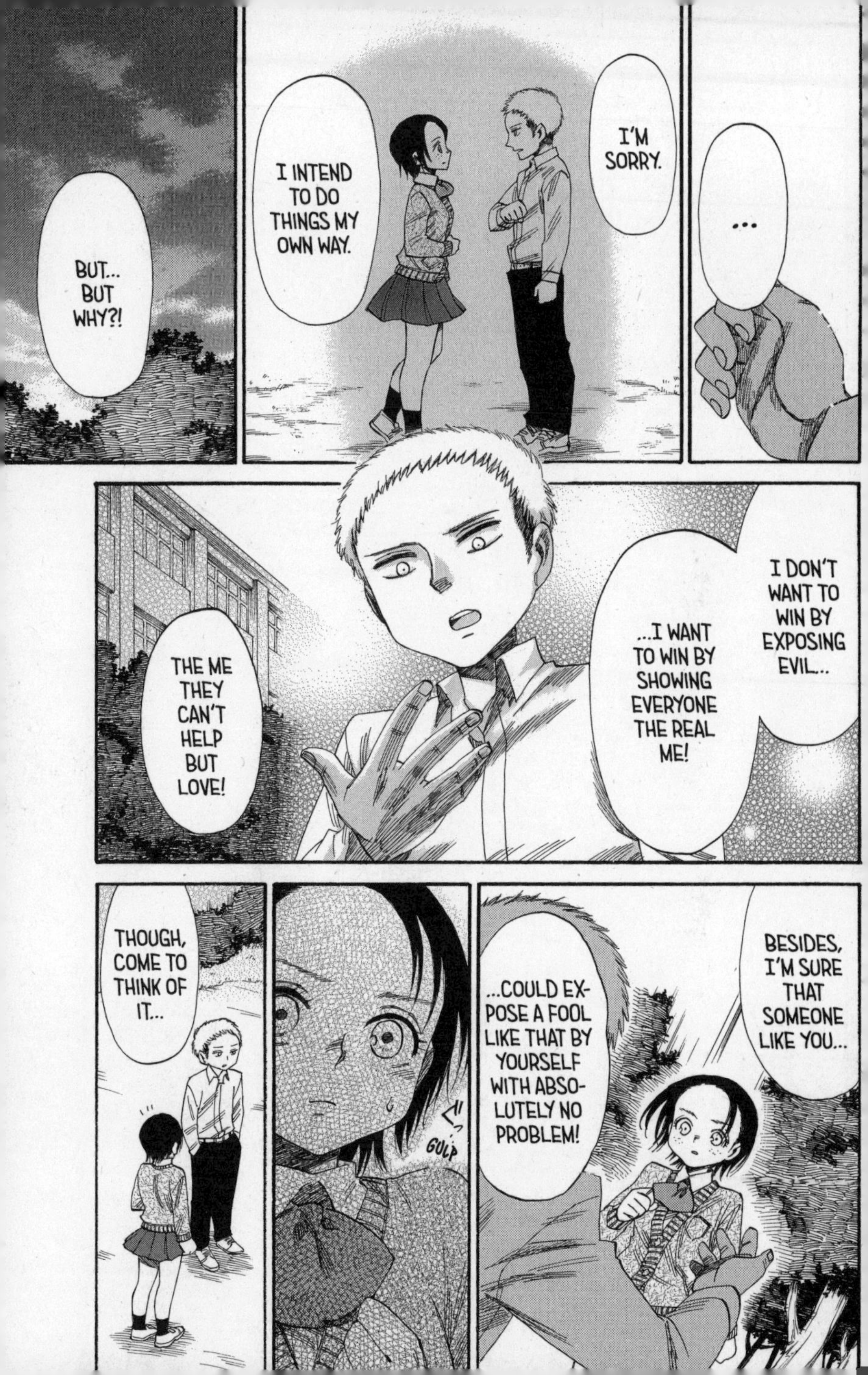
...
I'M SORRY.
I INTEND TO DO THINGS MY OWN WAY.
BUT... BUT WHY?!
I DON'T WANT TO WIN BY EXPOSING EVIL...
...I WANT TO WIN BY SHOWING EVERYONE THE REAL ME!
THE ME THEY CAN'T HELP BUT LOVE!
BESIDES, I'M SURE THAT SOMEONE LIKE YOU...
...COULD EXPOSE A FOOL LIKE THAT BY YOURSELF WITH ABSOLUTELY NO PROBLEM!
GULP
THOUGH, COME TO THINK OF IT...

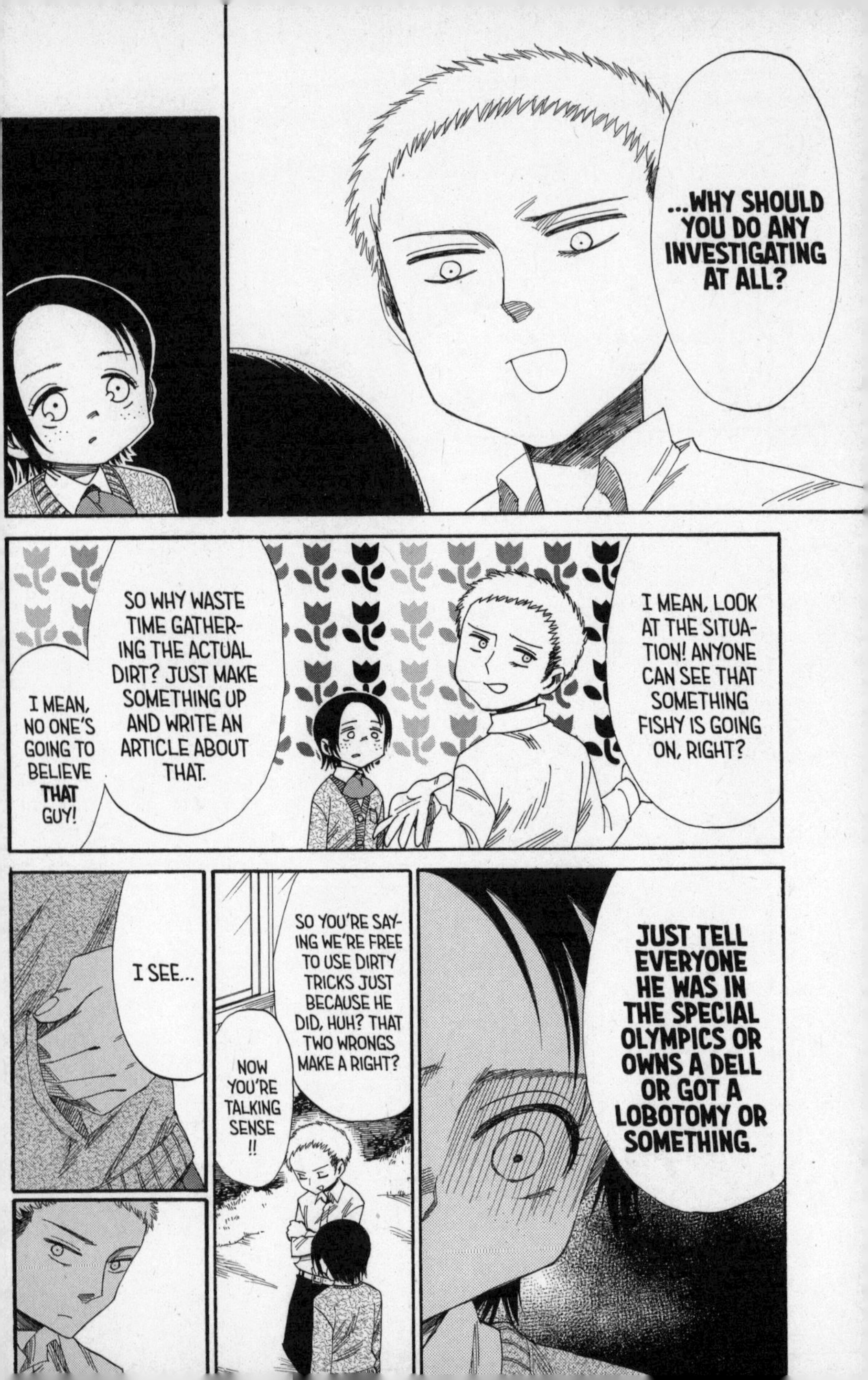
...WHY SHOULD YOU DO ANY INVESTIGATING AT ALL?
I MEAN, LOOK AT THE SITUATION! ANYONE CAN SEE THAT SOMETHING FISHY IS GOING ON, RIGHT?
SO WHY WASTE TIME GATHERING THE ACTUAL DIRT? JUST MAKE SOMETHING UP AND WRITE AN ARTICLE ABOUT THAT.
I MEAN, NO ONE'S GOING TO BELIEVE **THAT** GUY!
JUST TELL EVERYONE HE WAS IN THE SPECIAL OLYMPICS OR OWNS A DELL OR GOT A LOBOTOMY OR SOMETHING.
SO YOU'RE SAYING WE'RE FREE TO USE DIRTY TRICKS JUST BECAUSE HE DID, HUH? THAT TWO WRONGS MAKE A RIGHT?
NOW YOU'RE TALKING SENSE !!
I SEE...

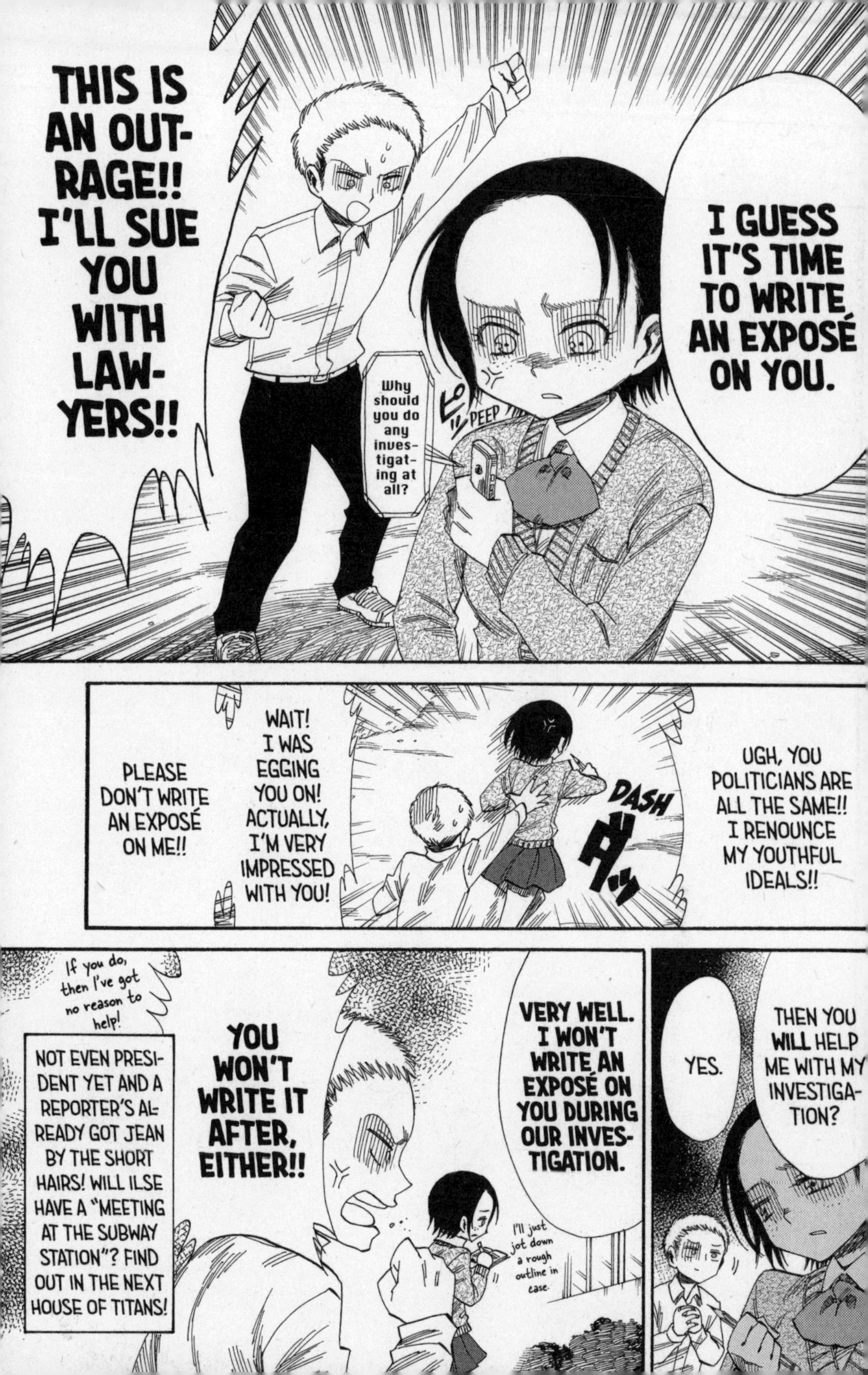
I GUESS IT'S TIME TO WRITE AN EXPOSÉ ON YOU.
Why should you do any inves-tigat-ing at all?
PEEP
THIS IS AN OUT-RAGE!! I'LL SUE YOU WITH LAW-YERS!!
UGH, YOU POLITICIANS ARE ALL THE SAME!! I RENOUNCE MY YOUTHFUL IDEALS!!
DASH
WAIT! I WAS EGGING YOU ON! ACTUALLY, I'M VERY IMPRESSED WITH YOU!
PLEASE DON'T WRITE AN EXPOSÉ ON ME!!
THEN YOU WILL HELP ME WITH MY INVESTIGA-TION?
YES.
VERY WELL. I WON'T WRITE AN EXPOSÉ ON YOU DURING OUR INVES-TIGATION.
YOU WON'T WRITE IT AFTER, EITHER!!
I'll just jot down a rough outline in case.
If you do, then I've got no reason to help!
NOT EVEN PRESI-DENT YET AND A REPORTER'S AL-READY GOT JEAN BY THE SHORT HAIRS! WILL ILSE HAVE A "MEETING AT THE SUBWAY STATION"? FIND OUT IN THE NEXT HOUSE OF TITANS!

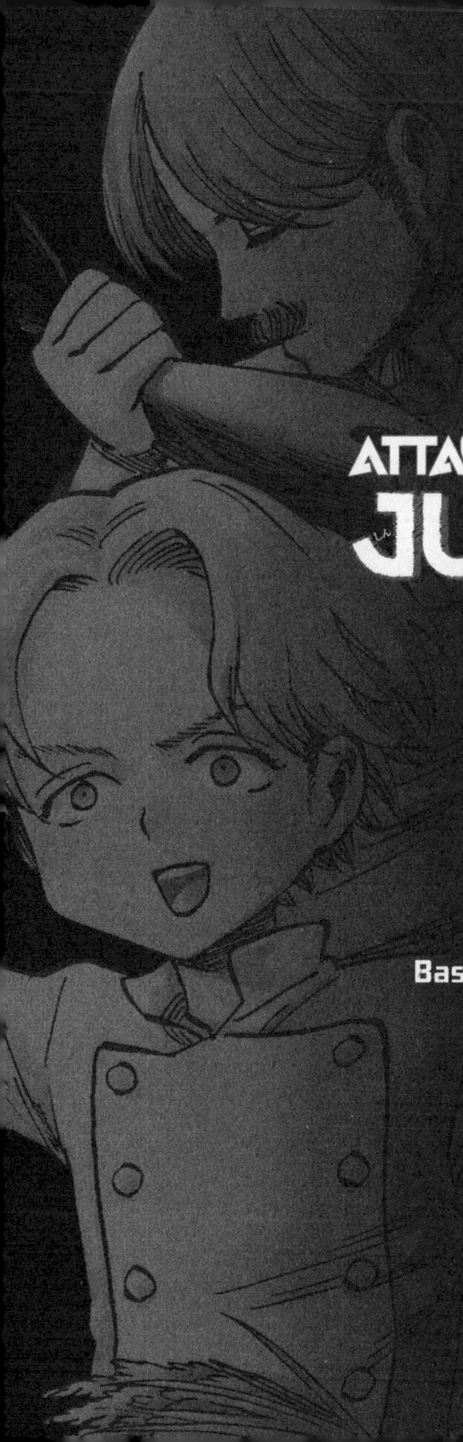

ATTACK on TITAN JUNIOR HIGH

SAKI NAKAGAWA

Based on "Attack on Titan" by
HAJIME ISAYAMA

Contents

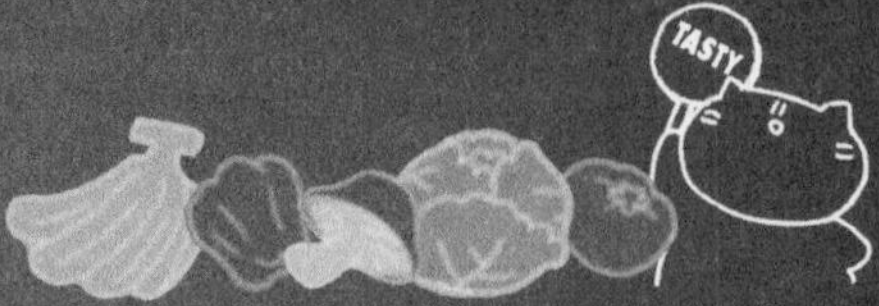
TASTY

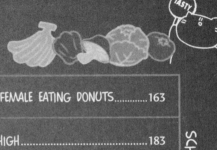

SCHEDULE FOR TUESDAY, DECEMBER 9

ERWIN

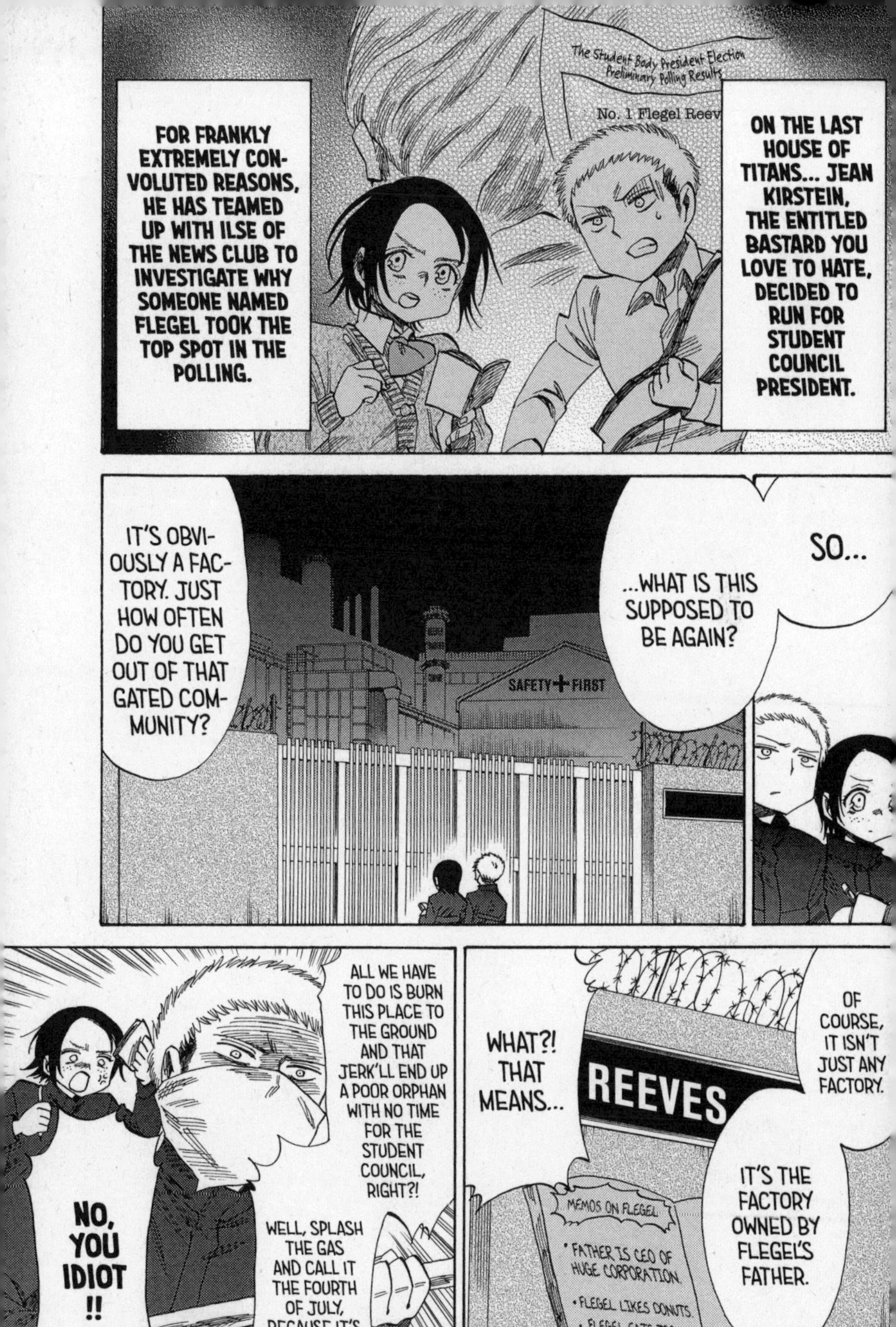
The Student Body President Election Preliminary Polling Results
No. 1 Flegel Reev
ON THE LAST HOUSE OF TITANS... JEAN KIRSTEIN, THE ENTITLED BASTARD YOU LOVE TO HATE, DECIDED TO RUN FOR STUDENT COUNCIL PRESIDENT.
FOR FRANKLY EXTREMELY CONVOLUTED REASONS, HE HAS TEAMED UP WITH ILSE OF THE NEWS CLUB TO INVESTIGATE WHY SOMEONE NAMED FLEGEL TOOK THE TOP SPOT IN THE POLLING.
SO...
...WHAT IS THIS SUPPOSED TO BE AGAIN?
SAFETY + FIRST
IT'S OBVIOUSLY A FACTORY. JUST HOW OFTEN DO YOU GET OUT OF THAT GATED COMMUNITY?
OF COURSE, IT ISN'T JUST ANY FACTORY.
IT'S THE FACTORY OWNED BY FLEGEL'S FATHER.
REEVES
WHAT?! THAT MEANS...
MEMOS ON FLEGEL
• FATHER IS CEO OF HUGE CORPORATION.
• FLEGEL LIKES DONUTS.
• FLEGEL EATS TOO
ALL WE HAVE TO DO IS BURN THIS PLACE TO THE GROUND AND THAT JERK'LL END UP A POOR ORPHAN WITH NO TIME FOR THE STUDENT COUNCIL, RIGHT?!
WELL, SPLASH THE GAS AND CALL IT THE FOURTH OF JULY, BECAUSE IT'S ARSON TIME!
NO, YOU IDIOT!!

FORTIETH PERIOD: DO, A DONUT, A FEMALE EATING DONUTS

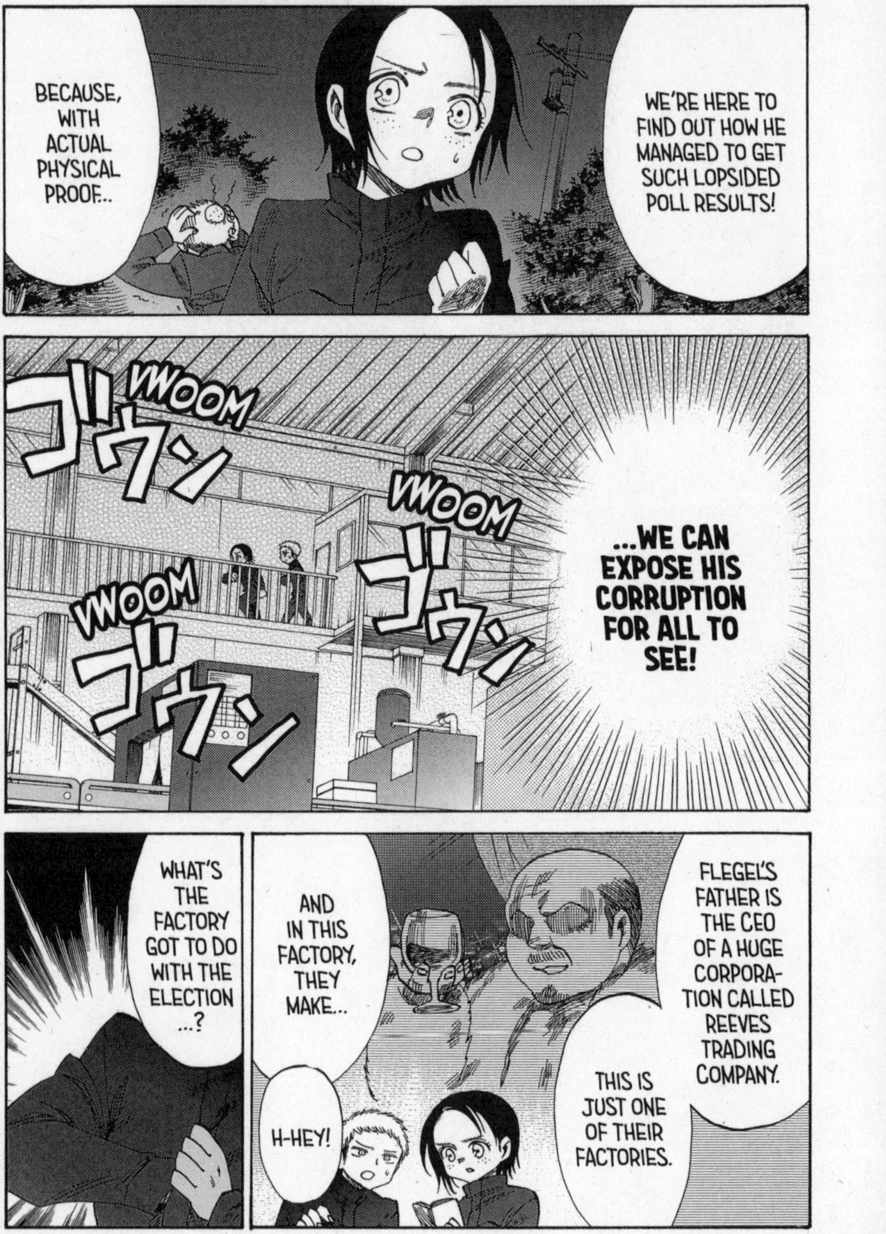
WE'RE HERE TO FIND OUT HOW HE MANAGED TO GET SUCH LOPSIDED POLL RESULTS!
BECAUSE, WITH ACTUAL PHYSICAL PROOF...
...WE CAN EXPOSE HIS CORRUPTION FOR ALL TO SEE!
VWOOM
ゴウン
VWOOM
ゴウン
VWOOM
ゴウン
FLEGEL'S FATHER IS THE CEO OF A HUGE CORPORA-TION CALLED REEVES TRADING COMPANY.
THIS IS JUST ONE OF THEIR FACTORIES.
AND IN THIS FACTORY, THEY MAKE...
H-HEY!
WHAT'S THE FACTORY GOT TO DO WITH THE ELECTION ...?

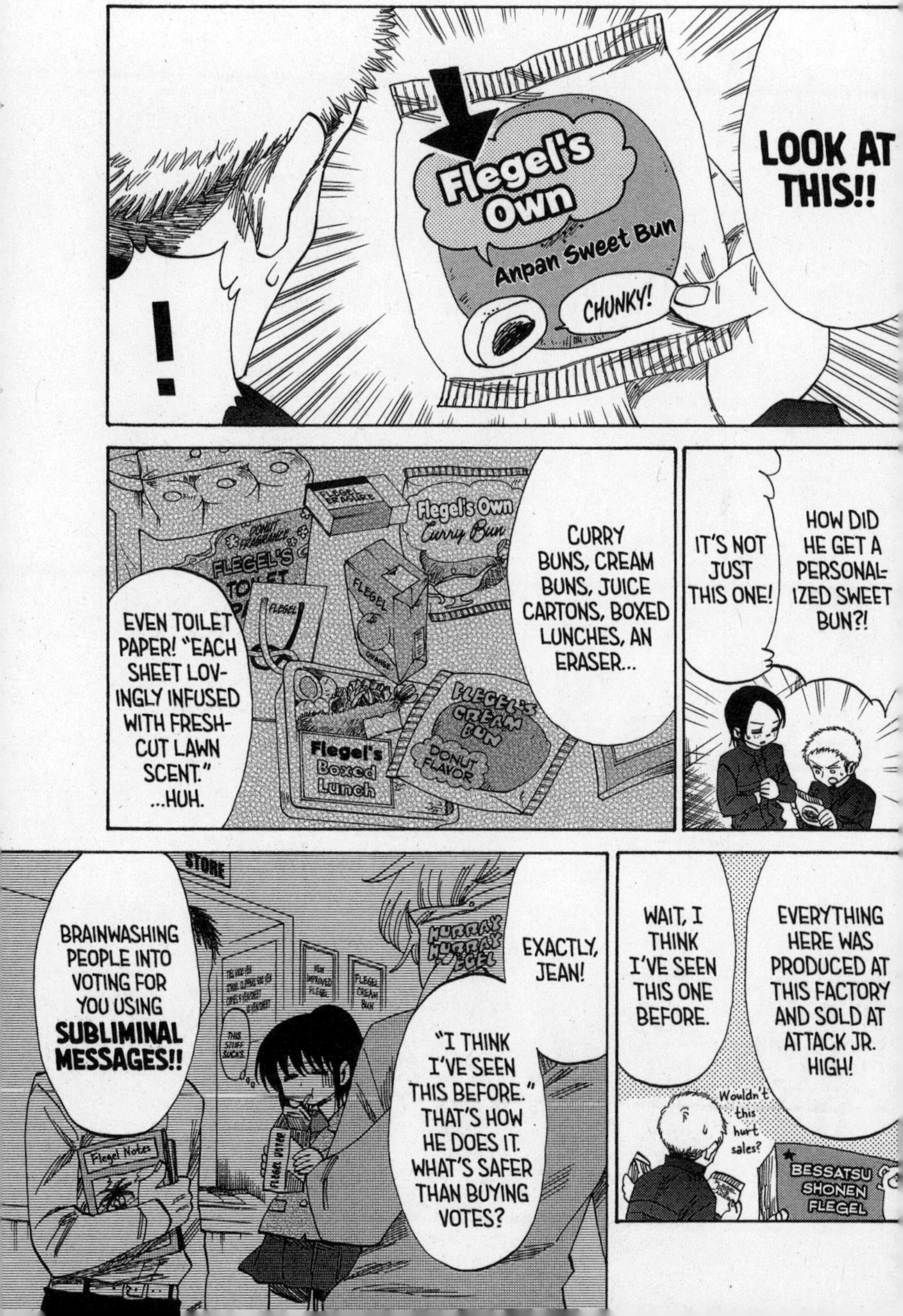
LOOK AT THIS!!
Flegel's Own
Anpan Sweet Bun
CHUNKY!
!
HOW DID HE GET A PERSONALIZED SWEET BUN?!
IT'S NOT JUST THIS ONE!
CURRY BUNS, CREAM BUNS, JUICE CARTONS, BOXED LUNCHES, AN ERASER...
Flegel's Own Curry Bun
FLEGEL
FLEGEL'S CREAM BUN
DONUT FLAVOR
Flegel's Boxed Lunch
DONUT FRAGRANCE
EVEN TOILET PAPER! "EACH SHEET LOVINGLY INFUSED WITH FRESH-CUT LAWN SCENT." ...HUH.
EVERYTHING HERE WAS PRODUCED AT THIS FACTORY AND SOLD AT ATTACK JR. HIGH!
WAIT, I THINK I'VE SEEN THIS ONE BEFORE.
Wouldn't this hurt sales?
BESSATSU SHONEN FLEGEL
EXACTLY, JEAN!
HURRAY HURRAY FLEGEL
"I THINK I'VE SEEN THIS BEFORE." THAT'S HOW HE DOES IT. WHAT'S SAFER THAN BUYING VOTES?
STORE
NEW IMPROVED FLEGEL
FLEGEL CREAM BUN
THIS STUFF SUCKS.
BRAINWASHING PEOPLE INTO VOTING FOR YOU USING **SUBLIMINAL MESSAGES!!**
Flegel Notes

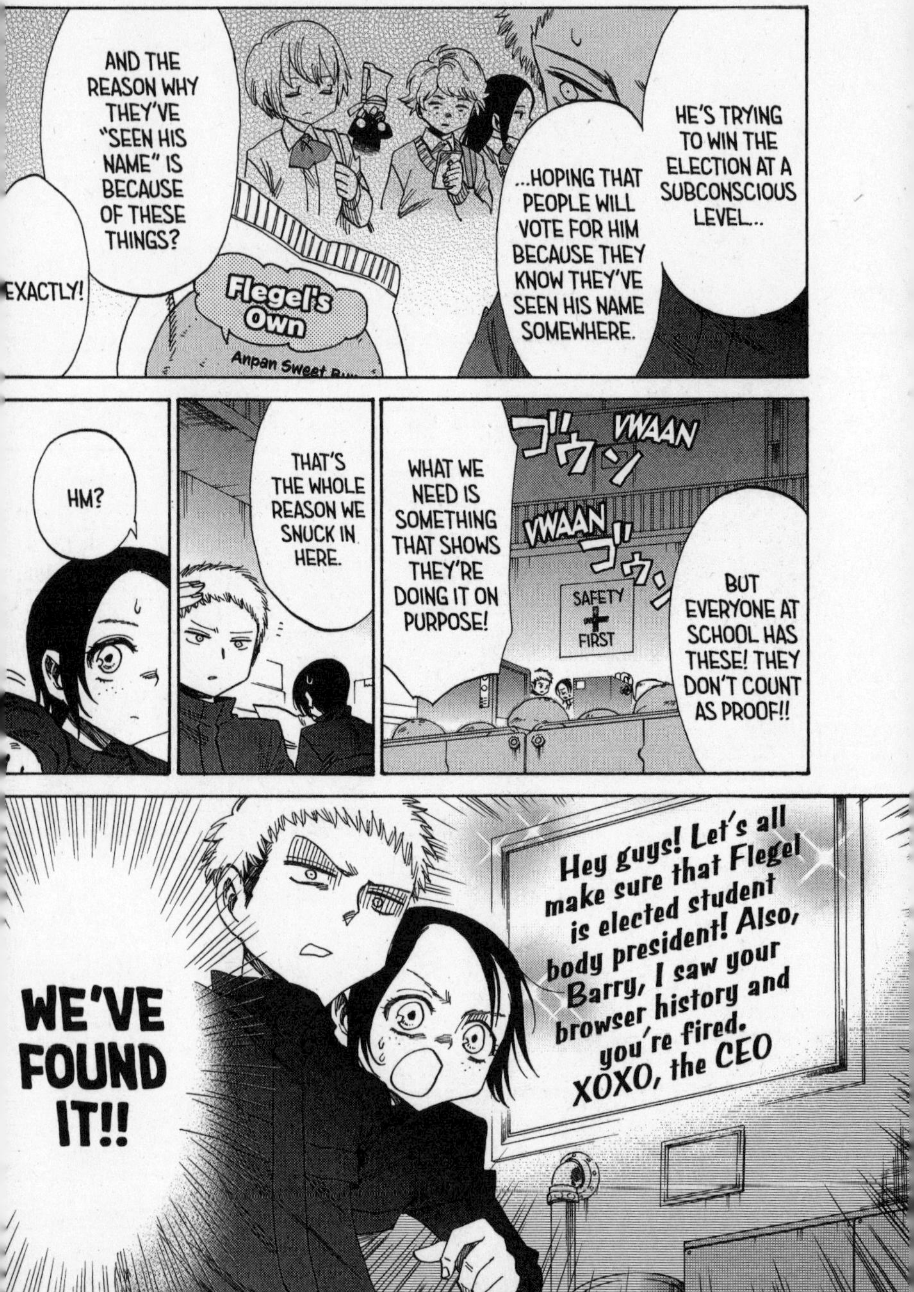
HE'S TRYING TO WIN THE ELECTION AT A SUBCONSCIOUS LEVEL...
...HOPING THAT PEOPLE WILL VOTE FOR HIM BECAUSE THEY KNOW THEY'VE SEEN HIS NAME SOMEWHERE.
AND THE REASON WHY THEY'VE "SEEN HIS NAME" IS BECAUSE OF THESE THINGS?
Flegel's Own
Anpan Sweet
EXACTLY!
VWAAN
VWAAN
BUT EVERYONE AT SCHOOL HAS THESE! THEY DON'T COUNT AS PROOF!!
SAFETY FIRST
WHAT WE NEED IS SOMETHING THAT SHOWS THEY'RE DOING IT ON PURPOSE!
THAT'S THE WHOLE REASON WE SNUCK IN HERE.
HM?
Hey guys! Let's all make sure that Flegel is elected student body president! Also, Barry, I saw your browser history and you're fired. XOXO, the CEO
WE'VE FOUND IT!!

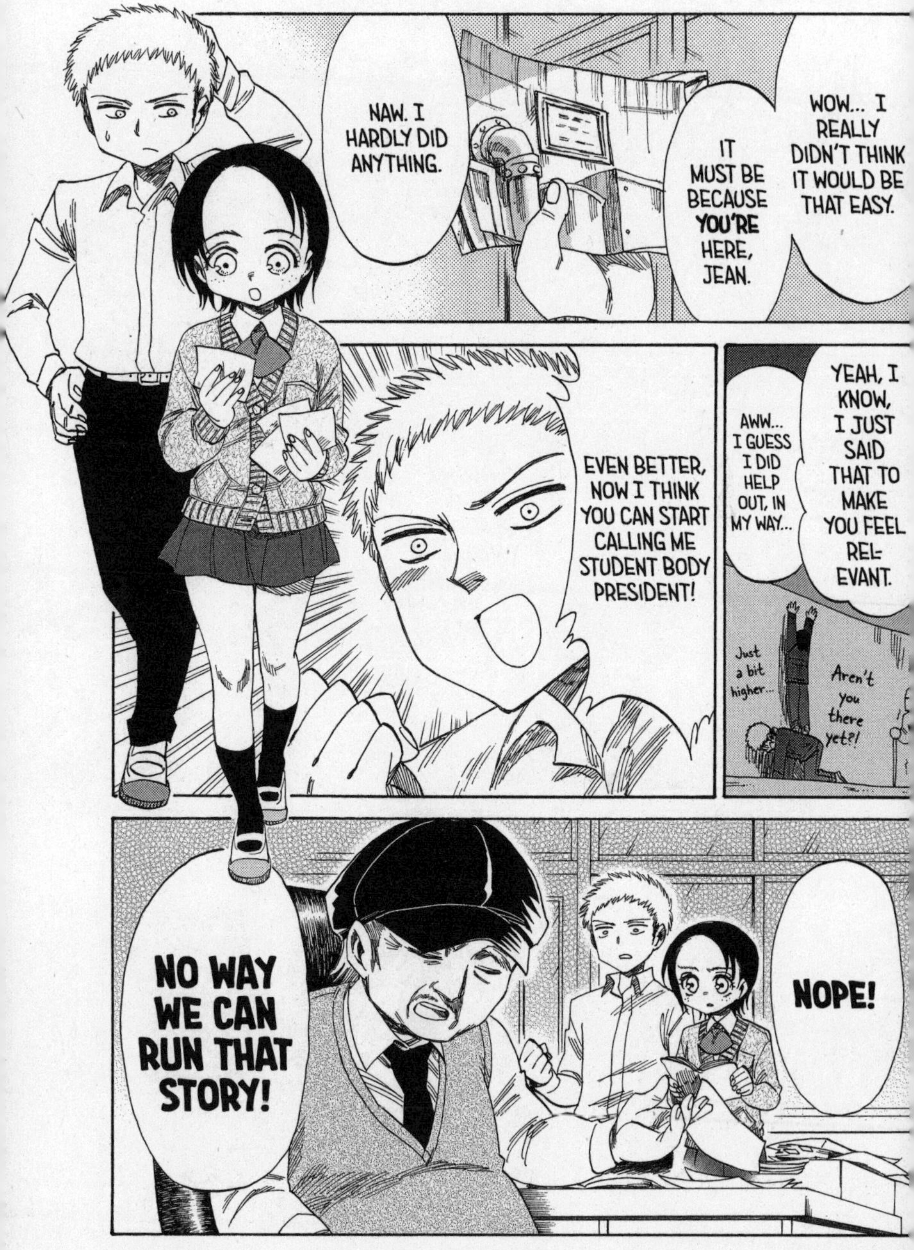
WOW... I REALLY DIDN'T THINK IT WOULD BE THAT EASY.
IT MUST BE BECAUSE YOU'RE HERE, JEAN.
NAW. I HARDLY DID ANYTHING.
YEAH, I KNOW, I JUST SAID THAT TO MAKE YOU FEEL REL-EVANT.
AWW... I GUESS I DID HELP OUT, IN MY WAY...
Aren't you there yet?!
Just a bit higher...
EVEN BETTER, NOW I THINK YOU CAN START CALLING ME STUDENT BODY PRESIDENT!
NOPE!
NO WAY WE CAN RUN THAT STORY!

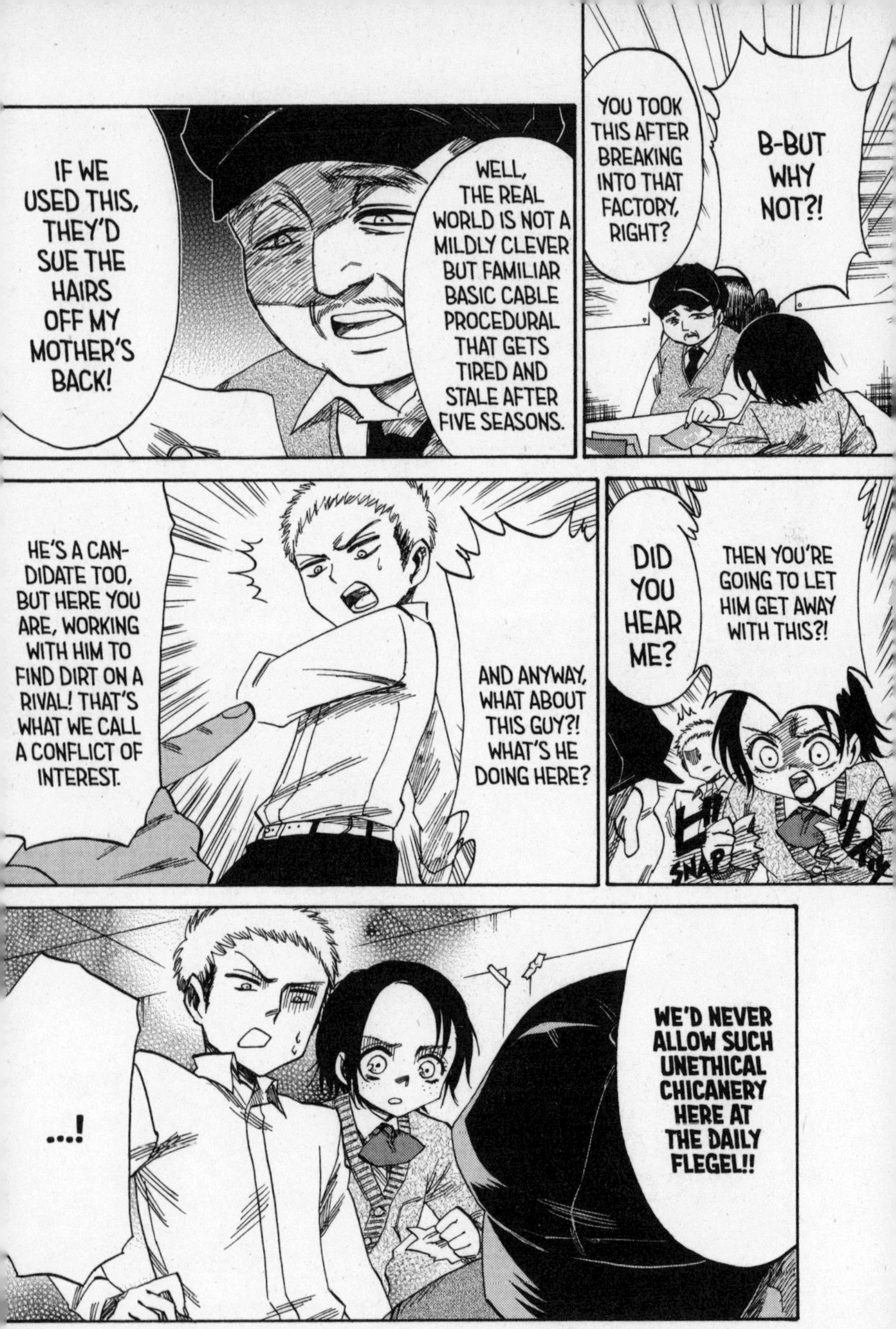
B-BUT WHY NOT?!
YOU TOOK THIS AFTER BREAKING INTO THAT FACTORY, RIGHT?
WELL, THE REAL WORLD IS NOT A MILDLY CLEVER BUT FAMILIAR BASIC CABLE PROCEDURAL THAT GETS TIRED AND STALE AFTER FIVE SEASONS.
IF WE USED THIS, THEY'D SUE THE HAIRS OFF MY MOTHER'S BACK!
THEN YOU'RE GOING TO LET HIM GET AWAY WITH THIS?!
DID YOU HEAR ME?
SNAP
AND ANYWAY, WHAT ABOUT THIS GUY?! WHAT'S HE DOING HERE?
HE'S A CAN-DIDATE TOO, BUT HERE YOU ARE, WORKING WITH HIM TO FIND DIRT ON A RIVAL! THAT'S WHAT WE CALL A CONFLICT OF INTEREST.
WE'D NEVER ALLOW SUCH UNETHICAL CHICANERY HERE AT THE DAILY FLEGEL!!
...!

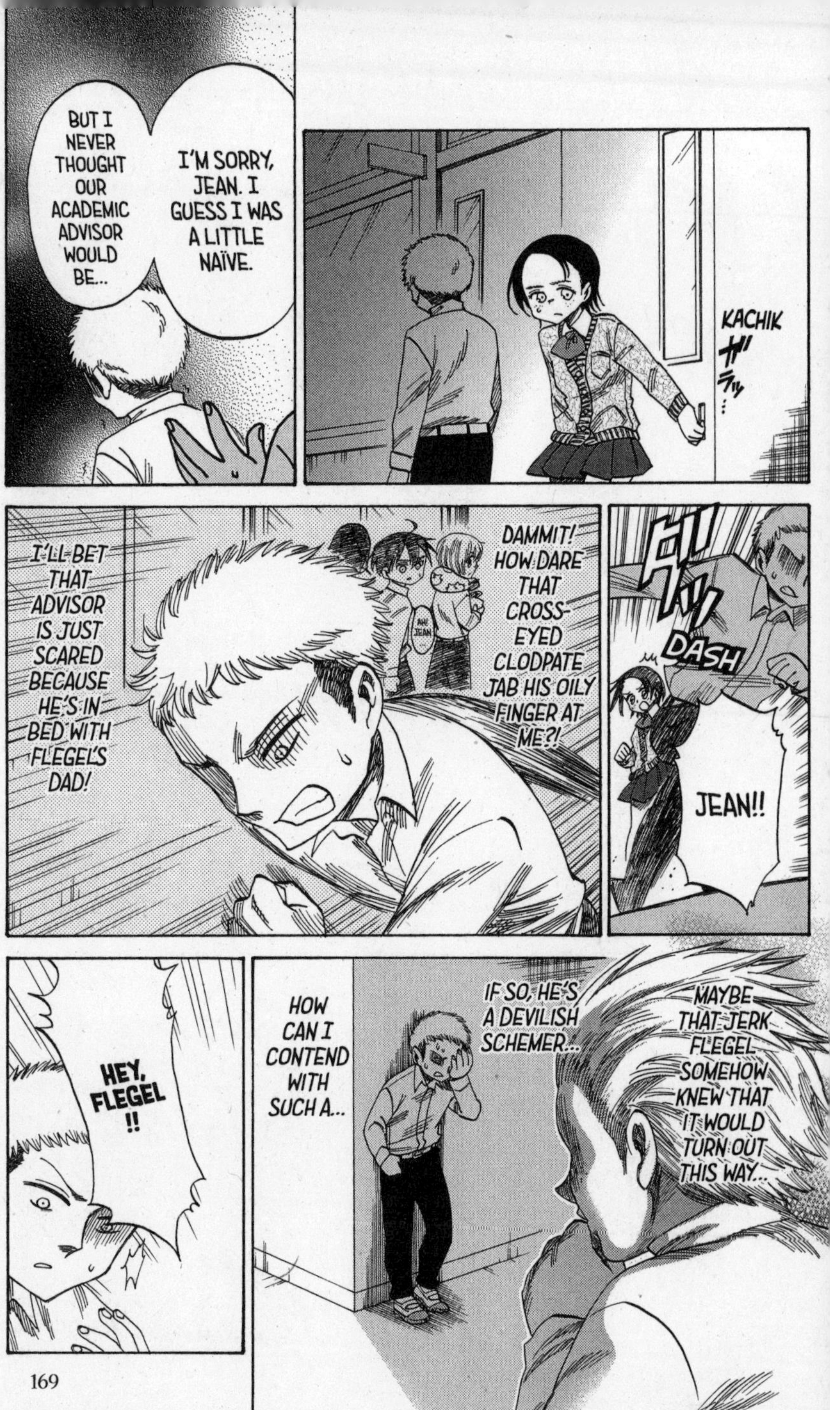
KACHIK
ガラッ…
I'M SORRY, JEAN. I GUESS I WAS A LITTLE NAÏVE.
BUT I NEVER THOUGHT OUR ACADEMIC ADVISOR WOULD BE...
DASH
JEAN!!
DAMMIT! HOW DARE THAT CROSS-EYED CLODPATE JAB HIS OILY FINGER AT ME?!
AH! JEAN
I'LL BET THAT ADVISOR IS JUST SCARED BECAUSE HE'S IN BED WITH FLEGEL'S DAD!
MAYBE THAT JERK FLEGEL SOMEHOW KNEW THAT IT WOULD TURN OUT THIS WAY...
IF SO, HE'S A DEVILISH SCHEMER...
HOW CAN I CONTEND WITH SUCH A...
HEY, FLEGEL!!

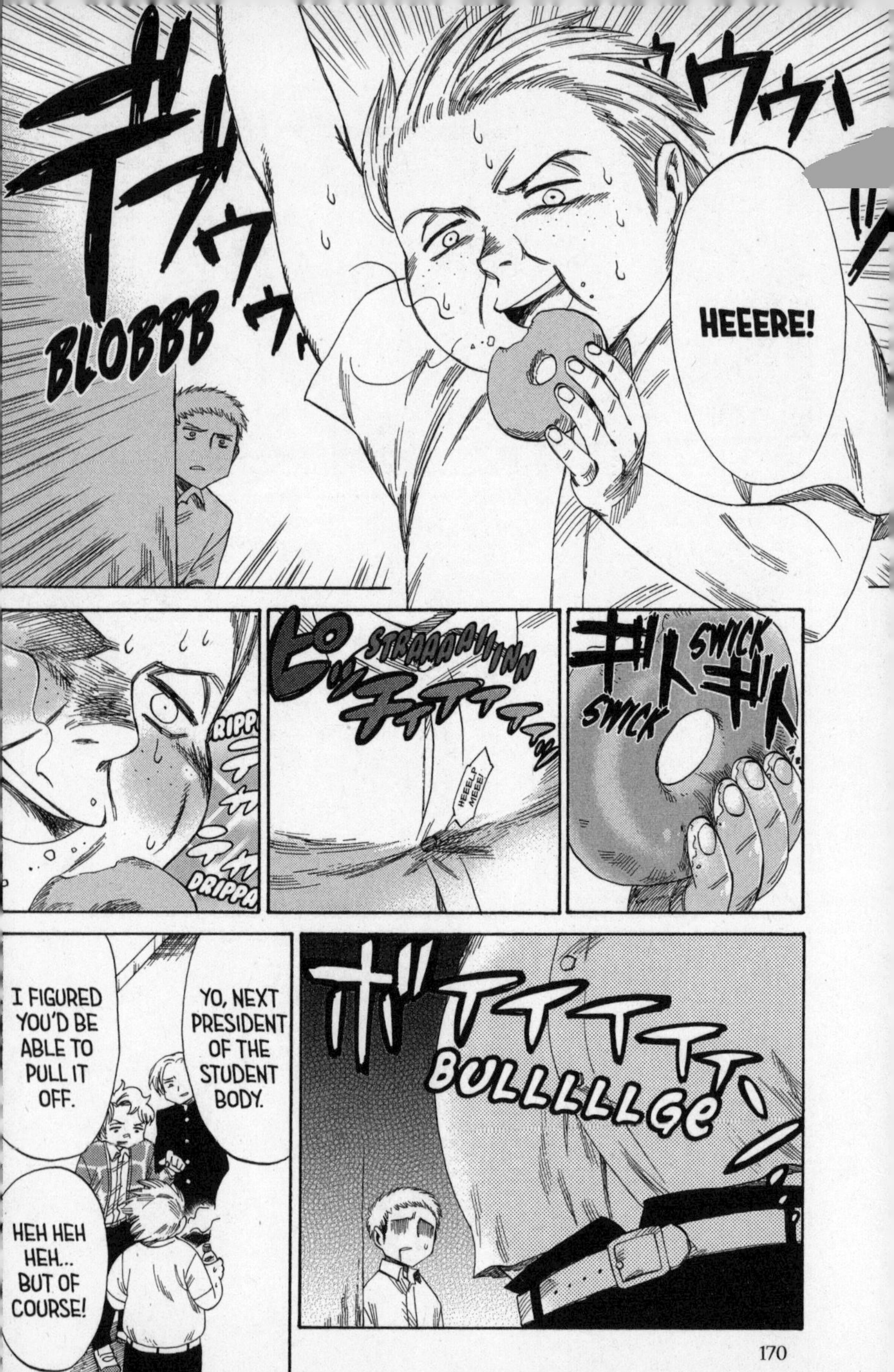
HEEERE!
BLOBBB
SWICK
SWICK
STRAAAAIIINN
HEEELP MEEE!
RIPP
DRIPPA
BULLLLLGE
YO, NEXT PRESIDENT OF THE STUDENT BODY.
I FIGURED YOU'D BE ABLE TO PULL IT OFF.
HEH HEH HEH... BUT OF COURSE!

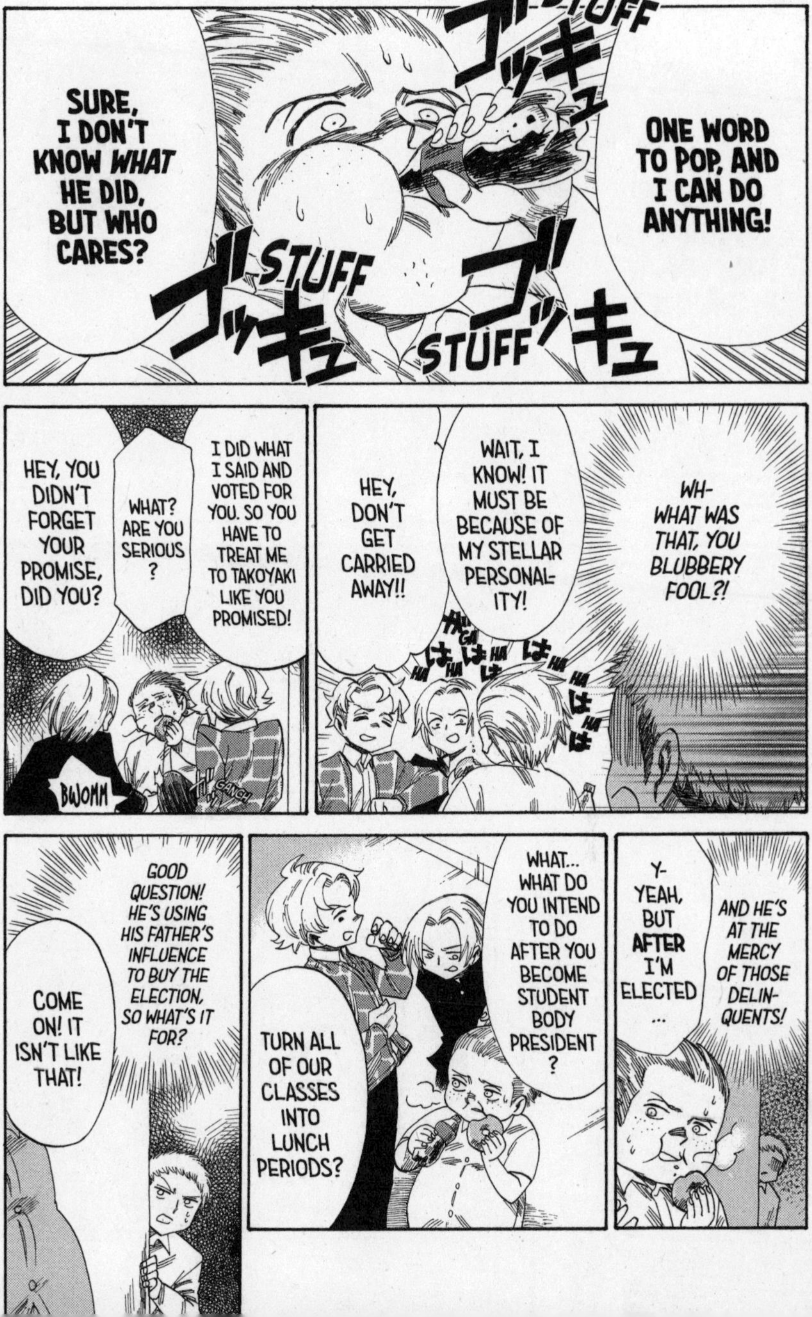
ONE WORD TO POP, AND I CAN DO ANYTHING!
ゴッキュ STUFF
ゴッキュ STUFF
ゴッキュ STUFF
SURE, I DON'T KNOW *WHAT* HE DID, BUT WHO CARES?
WH- WHAT WAS THAT, YOU BLUBBERY FOOL?!
WAIT, I KNOW! IT MUST BE BECAUSE OF MY STELLAR PERSONAL- ITY!
HEY, DON'T GET CARRIED AWAY!!
がはははは GA HA HA HA HA HA HA
I DID WHAT I SAID AND VOTED FOR YOU. SO YOU HAVE TO TREAT ME TO TAKOYAKI LIKE YOU PROMISED!
WHAT? ARE YOU SERIOUS?
HEY, YOU DIDN'T FORGET YOUR PROMISE, DID YOU?
GANCH
BWOMM
AND HE'S AT THE MERCY OF THOSE DELIN- QUENTS!
Y- YEAH, BUT **AFTER** I'M ELECTED ...
WHAT... WHAT DO YOU INTEND TO DO AFTER YOU BECOME STUDENT BODY PRESIDENT?
TURN ALL OF OUR CLASSES INTO LUNCH PERIODS?
GOOD QUESTION! HE'S USING HIS FATHER'S INFLUENCE TO BUY THE ELECTION, SO WHAT'S IT FOR?
COME ON! IT ISN'T LIKE THAT!

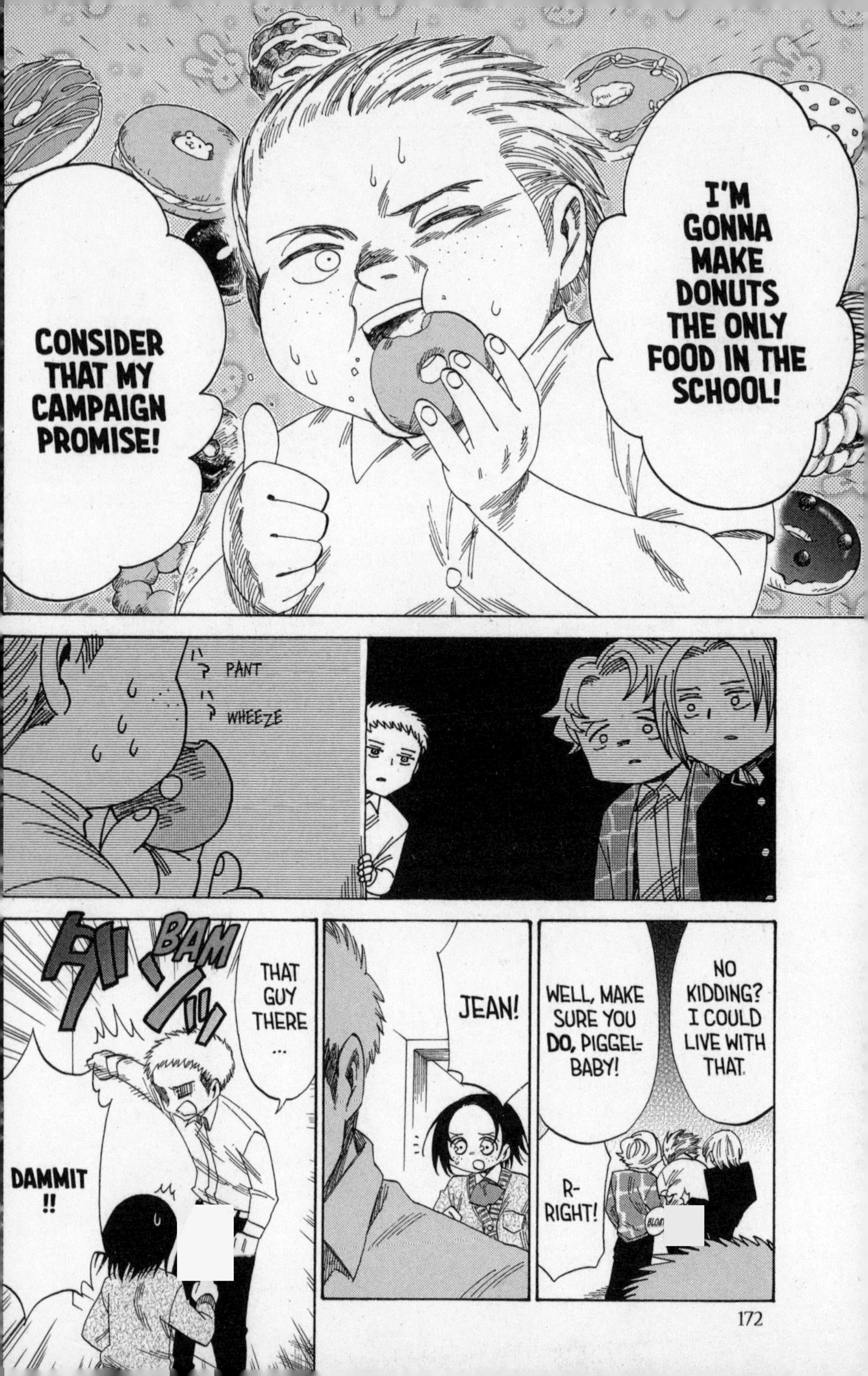
I'M GONNA MAKE DONUTS THE ONLY FOOD IN THE SCHOOL!
CONSIDER THAT MY CAMPAIGN PROMISE!
PANT
WHEEZE
NO KIDDING? I COULD LIVE WITH THAT.
WELL, MAKE SURE YOU DO, PIGGEL-BABY!
R-RIGHT!
JEAN!
BAM
THAT GUY THERE ...
DAMMIT !!

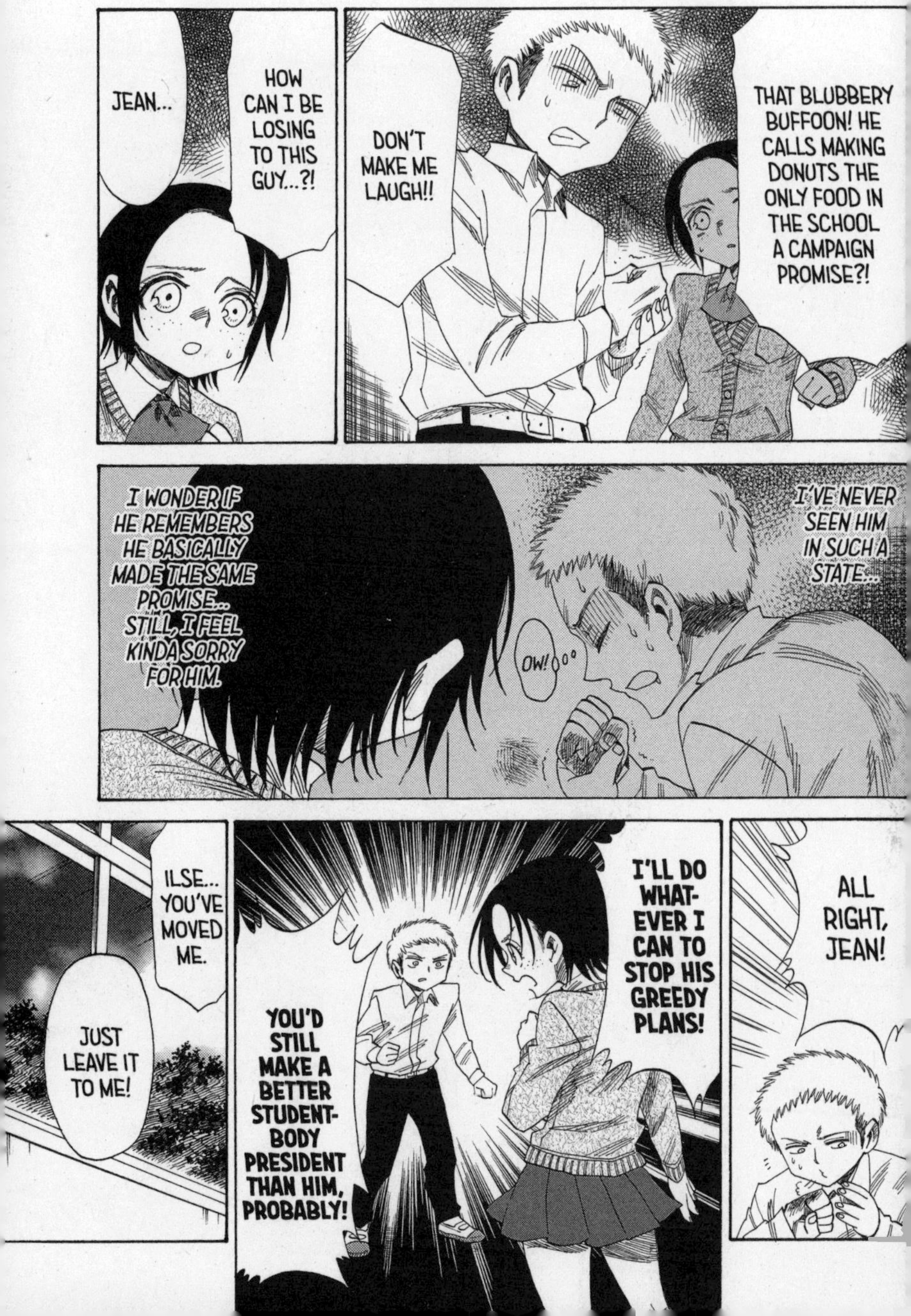
THAT BLUBBERY BUFFOON! HE CALLS MAKING DONUTS THE ONLY FOOD IN THE SCHOOL A CAMPAIGN PROMISE?!
DON'T MAKE ME LAUGH!!
HOW CAN I BE LOSING TO THIS GUY...?!
JEAN...
I'VE NEVER SEEN HIM IN SUCH A STATE...
OW!
I WONDER IF HE REMEMBERS HE BASICALLY MADE THE SAME PROMISE... STILL, I FEEL KINDA SORRY FOR HIM.
ALL RIGHT, JEAN!
I'LL DO WHAT-EVER I CAN TO STOP HIS GREEDY PLANS!
YOU'D STILL MAKE A BETTER STUDENT-BODY PRESIDENT THAN HIM, PROBABLY!
ILSE... YOU'VE MOVED ME.
JUST LEAVE IT TO ME!

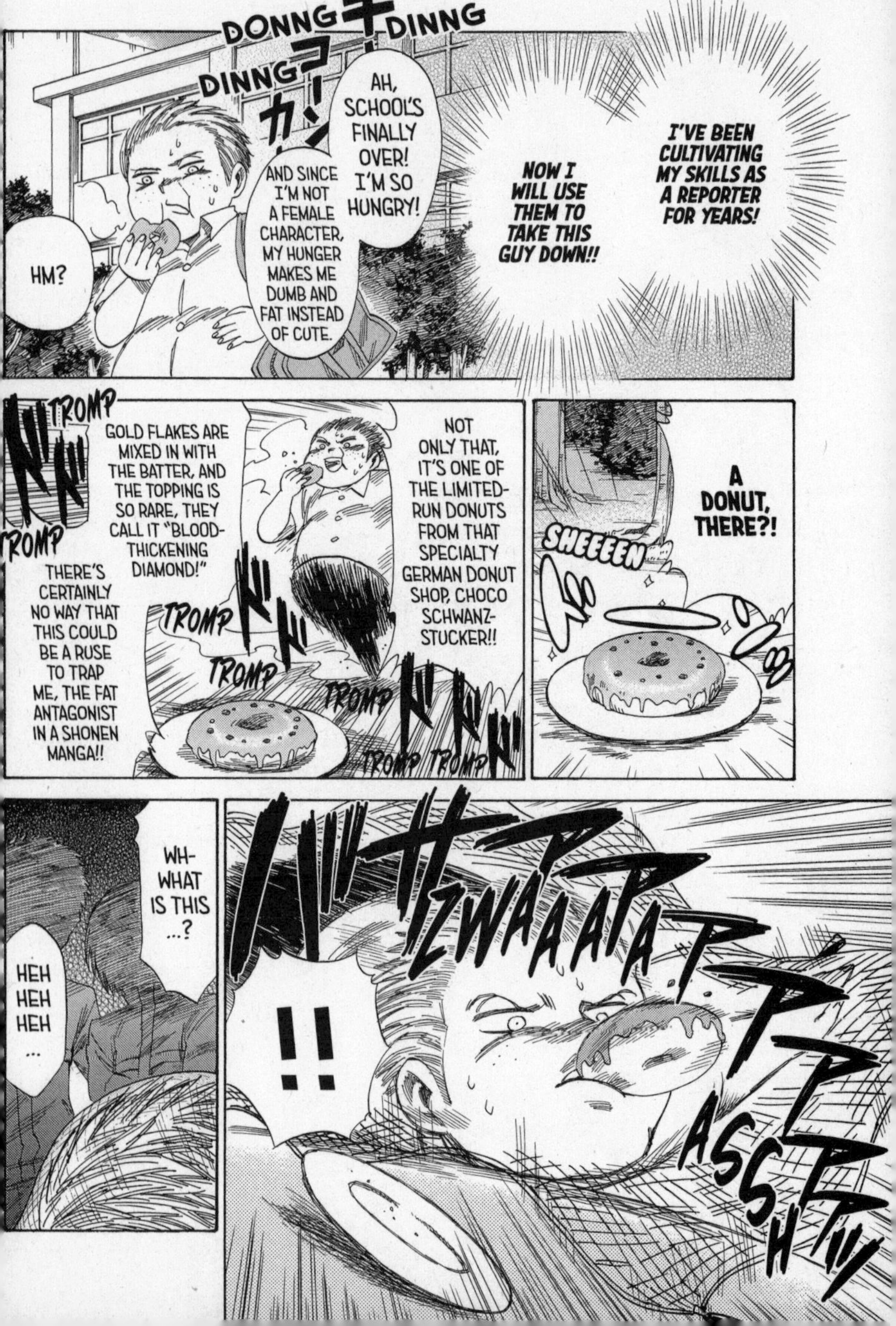
I'VE BEEN CULTIVATING MY SKILLS AS A REPORTER FOR YEARS!
NOW I WILL USE THEM TO TAKE THIS GUY DOWN!!
DONNG DINNG
DINNG
AH, SCHOOL'S FINALLY OVER! I'M SO HUNGRY!
AND SINCE I'M NOT A FEMALE CHARACTER, MY HUNGER MAKES ME DUMB AND FAT INSTEAD OF CUTE.
HM?
A DONUT, THERE?!
SHEEEEN
NOT ONLY THAT, IT'S ONE OF THE LIMITED-RUN DONUTS FROM THAT SPECIALTY GERMAN DONUT SHOP, CHOCO SCHWANZ-STUCKER!!
GOLD FLAKES ARE MIXED IN WITH THE BATTER, AND THE TOPPING IS SO RARE, THEY CALL IT "BLOOD-THICKENING DIAMOND!"
TROMP
TROMP
THERE'S CERTAINLY NO WAY THAT THIS COULD BE A RUSE TO TRAP ME, THE FAT ANTAGONIST IN A SHONEN MANGA!!
TROMP
TROMP
TROMP
TROMP TROMP
ZWAAAAP
ASSH
!!
WH-WHAT IS THIS ...?
HEH HEH HEH ...

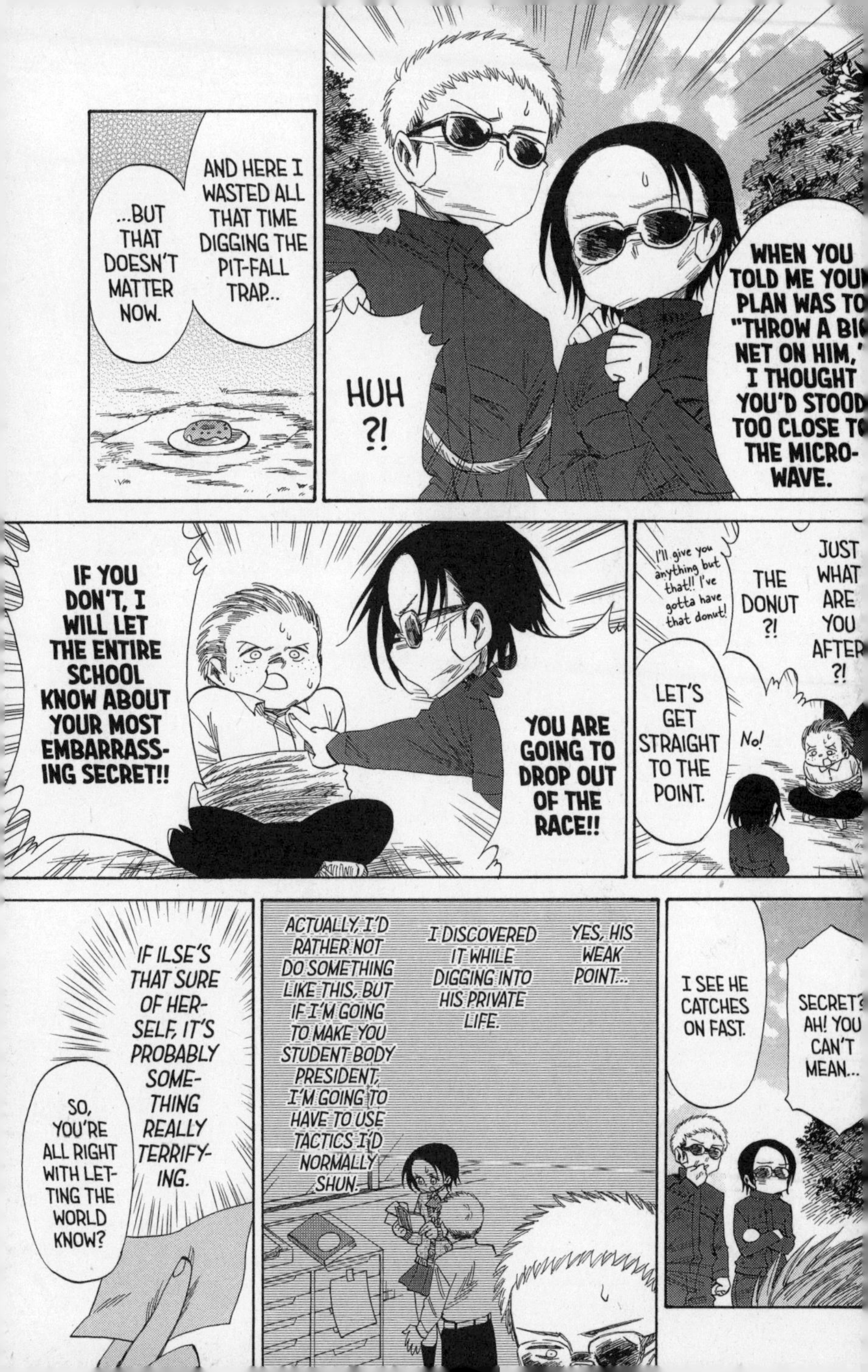
WHEN YOU TOLD ME YOUR PLAN WAS TO "THROW A BIG NET ON HIM," I THOUGHT YOU'D STOOD TOO CLOSE TO THE MICRO-WAVE.
HUH ?!
AND HERE I WASTED ALL THAT TIME DIGGING THE PIT-FALL TRAP...
...BUT THAT DOESN'T MATTER NOW.
JUST WHAT ARE YOU AFTER ?!
THE DONUT ?!
I'll give you anything but that!! I've gotta have that donut!
LET'S GET STRAIGHT TO THE POINT.
No!
YOU ARE GOING TO DROP OUT OF THE RACE!!
IF YOU DON'T, I WILL LET THE ENTIRE SCHOOL KNOW ABOUT YOUR MOST EMBARRASS-ING SECRET!!
SECRET? AH! YOU CAN'T MEAN...
I SEE HE CATCHES ON FAST.
YES, HIS WEAK POINT...
I DISCOVERED IT WHILE DIGGING INTO HIS PRIVATE LIFE.
ACTUALLY, I'D RATHER NOT DO SOMETHING LIKE THIS, BUT IF I'M GOING TO MAKE YOU STUDENT BODY PRESIDENT, I'M GOING TO HAVE TO USE TACTICS I'D NORMALLY SHUN.
IF ILSE'S THAT SURE OF HER-SELF, IT'S PROBABLY SOME-THING REALLY TERRIFY-ING.
SO, YOU'RE ALL RIGHT WITH LET-TING THE WORLD KNOW?

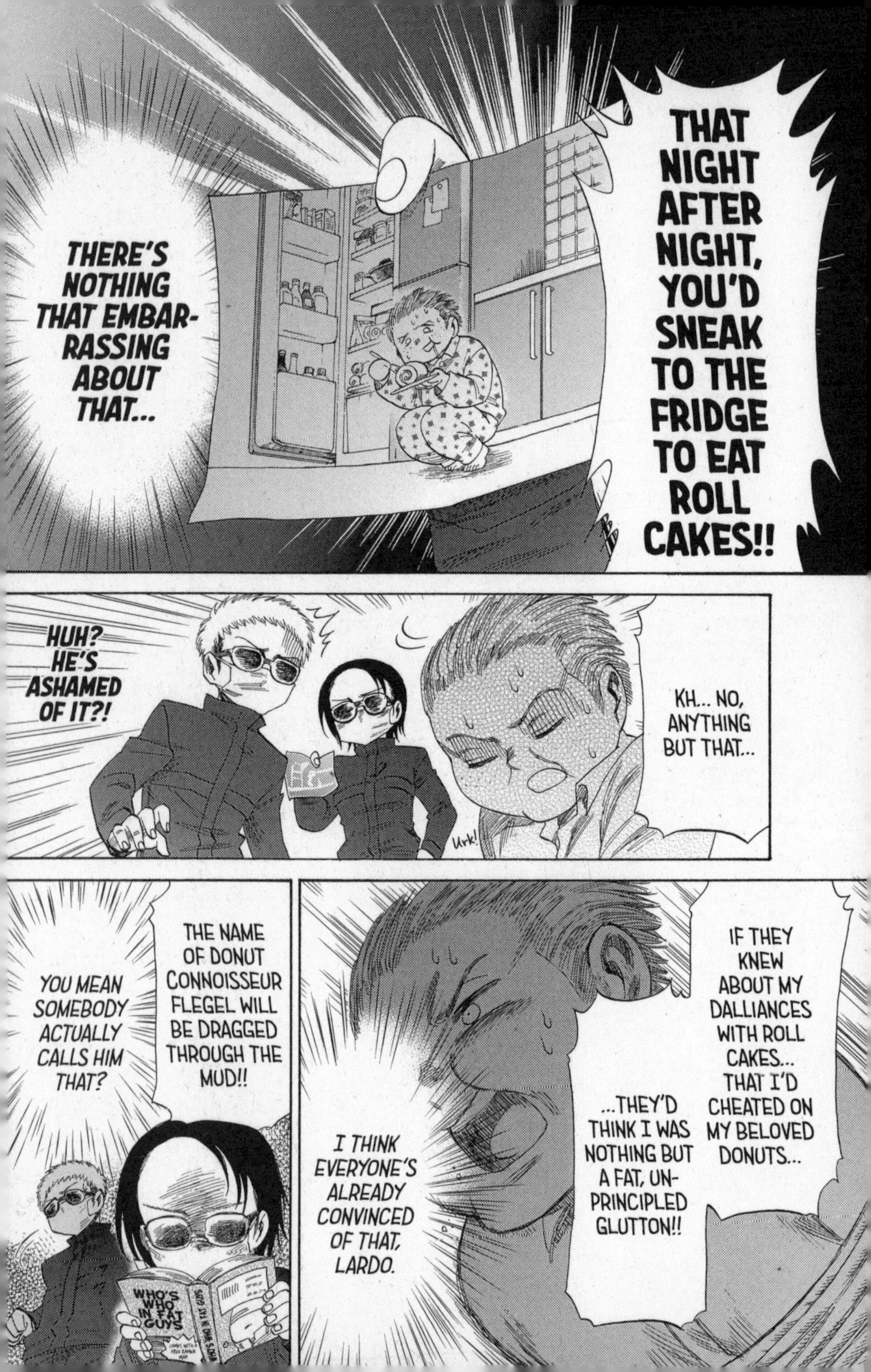
THAT NIGHT AFTER NIGHT, YOU'D SNEAK TO THE FRIDGE TO EAT ROLL CAKES!!
THERE'S NOTHING THAT EMBARRASSING ABOUT THAT...
KH... NO, ANYTHING BUT THAT...
Urk!
HUH? HE'S ASHAMED OF IT?!
IF THEY KNEW ABOUT MY DALLIANCES WITH ROLL CAKES... THAT I'D CHEATED ON MY BELOVED DONUTS...
...THEY'D THINK I WAS NOTHING BUT A FAT, UN-PRINCIPLED GLUTTON!!
I THINK EVERYONE'S ALREADY CONVINCED OF THAT, LARDO.
THE NAME OF DONUT CONNOISSEUR FLEGEL WILL BE DRAGGED THROUGH THE MUD!!
YOU MEAN SOMEBODY ACTUALLY CALLS HIM THAT?
WHO'S WHO IN FAT GUYS

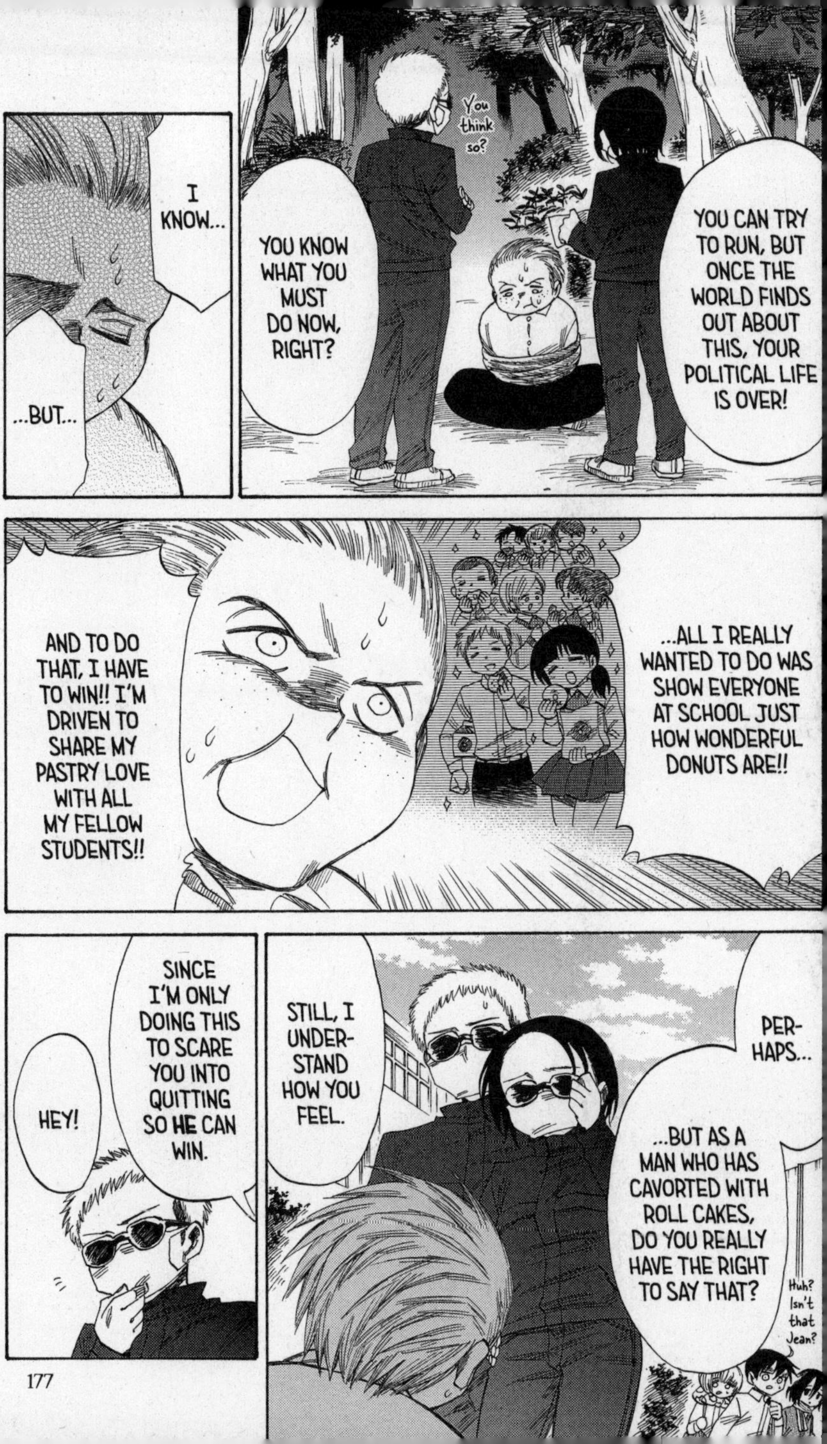
YOU CAN TRY TO RUN, BUT ONCE THE WORLD FINDS OUT ABOUT THIS, YOUR POLITICAL LIFE IS OVER!
You think so?
YOU KNOW WHAT YOU MUST DO NOW, RIGHT?
I KNOW...
...BUT...
...ALL I REALLY WANTED TO DO WAS SHOW EVERYONE AT SCHOOL JUST HOW WONDERFUL DONUTS ARE!!
AND TO DO THAT, I HAVE TO WIN!! I'M DRIVEN TO SHARE MY PASTRY LOVE WITH ALL MY FELLOW STUDENTS!!
PER-HAPS...
STILL, I UNDER-STAND HOW YOU FEEL.
...BUT AS A MAN WHO HAS CAVORTED WITH ROLL CAKES, DO YOU REALLY HAVE THE RIGHT TO SAY THAT?
Huh? Isn't that Jean?
SINCE I'M ONLY DOING THIS TO SCARE YOU INTO QUITTING SO HE CAN WIN.
HEY!

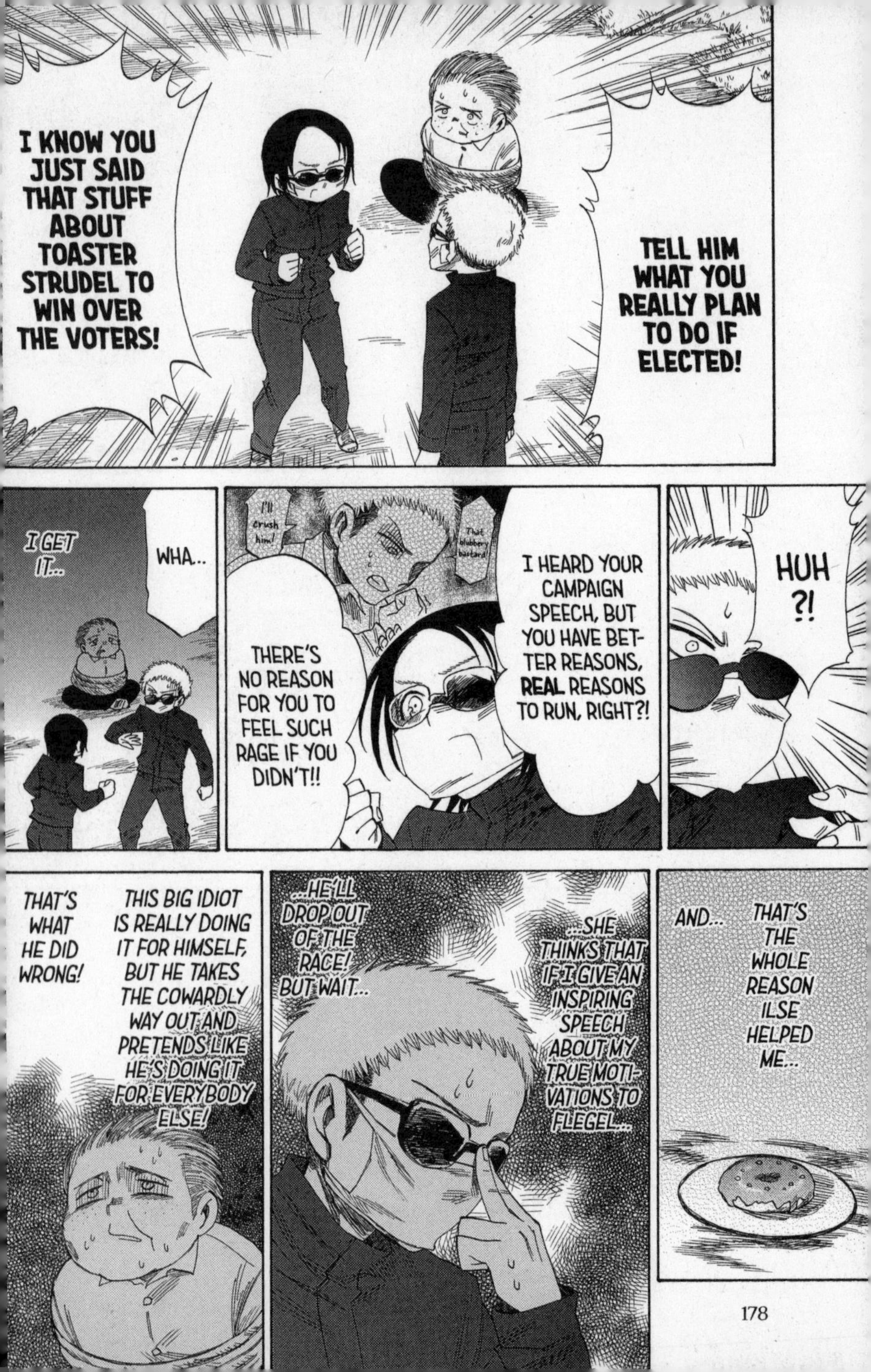
I KNOW YOU JUST SAID THAT STUFF ABOUT TOASTER STRUDEL TO WIN OVER THE VOTERS!
TELL HIM WHAT YOU REALLY PLAN TO DO IF ELECTED!
HUH ?!
I HEARD YOUR CAMPAIGN SPEECH, BUT YOU HAVE BETTER REASONS, REAL REASONS TO RUN, RIGHT?!
That blubbery bastard!
I'll crush him!
THERE'S NO REASON FOR YOU TO FEEL SUCH RAGE IF YOU DIDN'T!!
WHA...
I GET IT...
THAT'S THE WHOLE REASON ILSE HELPED ME...
AND...
...SHE THINKS THAT IF I GIVE AN INSPIRING SPEECH ABOUT MY TRUE MOTIVATIONS TO FLEGEL...
...HE'LL DROP OUT OF THE RACE! BUT WAIT...
THIS BIG IDIOT IS REALLY DOING IT FOR HIMSELF, BUT HE TAKES THE COWARDLY WAY OUT AND PRETENDS LIKE HE'S DOING IT FOR EVERYBODY ELSE!
THAT'S WHAT HE DID WRONG!

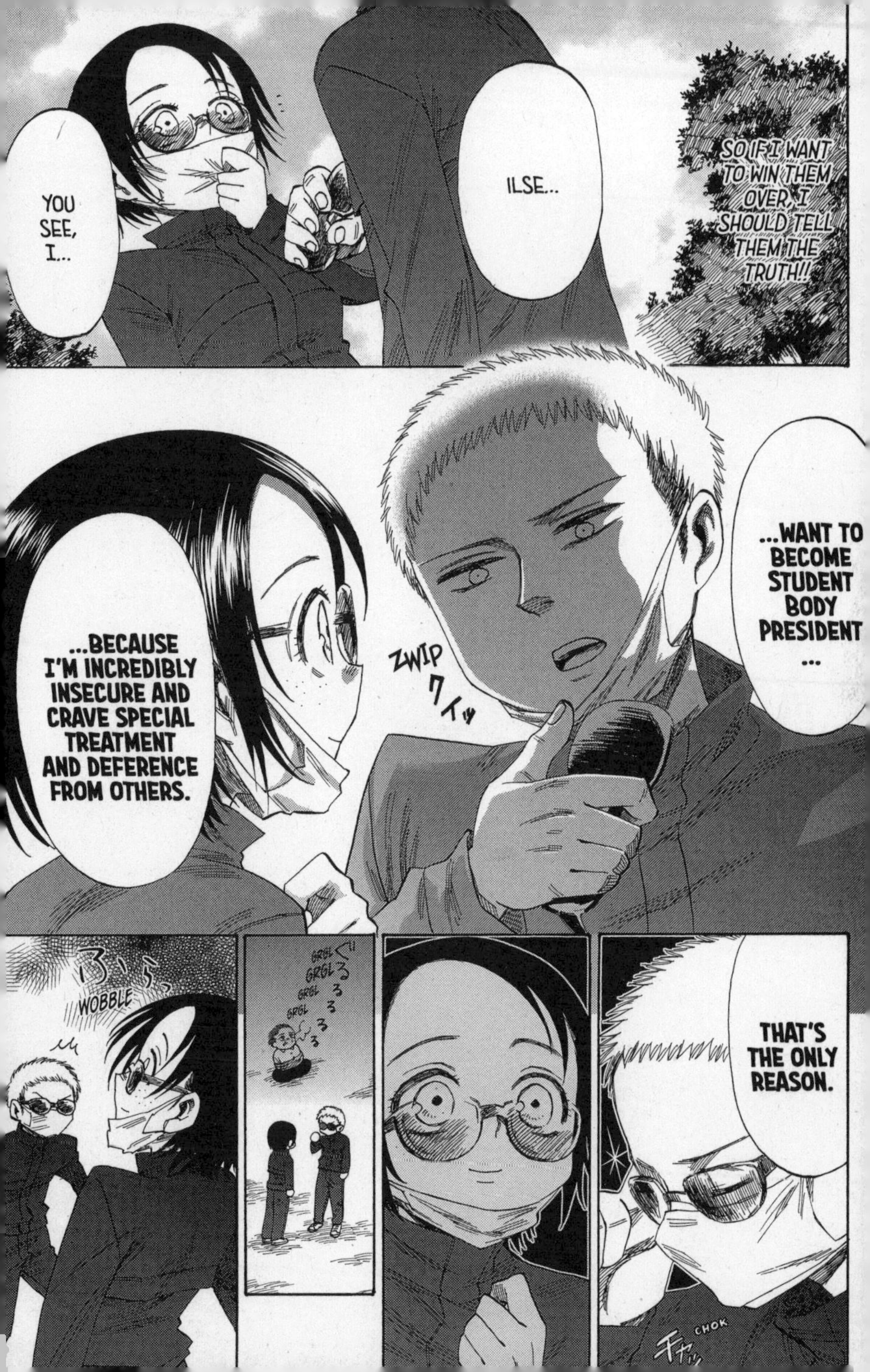
SO IF I WANT TO WIN THEM OVER, I SHOULD TELL THEM THE TRUTH!!
ILSE...
YOU SEE, I...
...WANT TO BECOME STUDENT BODY PRESIDENT ...
ZWIP
...BECAUSE I'M INCREDIBLY INSECURE AND CRAVE SPECIAL TREATMENT AND DEFERENCE FROM OTHERS.
THAT'S THE ONLY REASON.
CHOK
GRGL
GRGL
GRGL
GRGL
WOBBLE

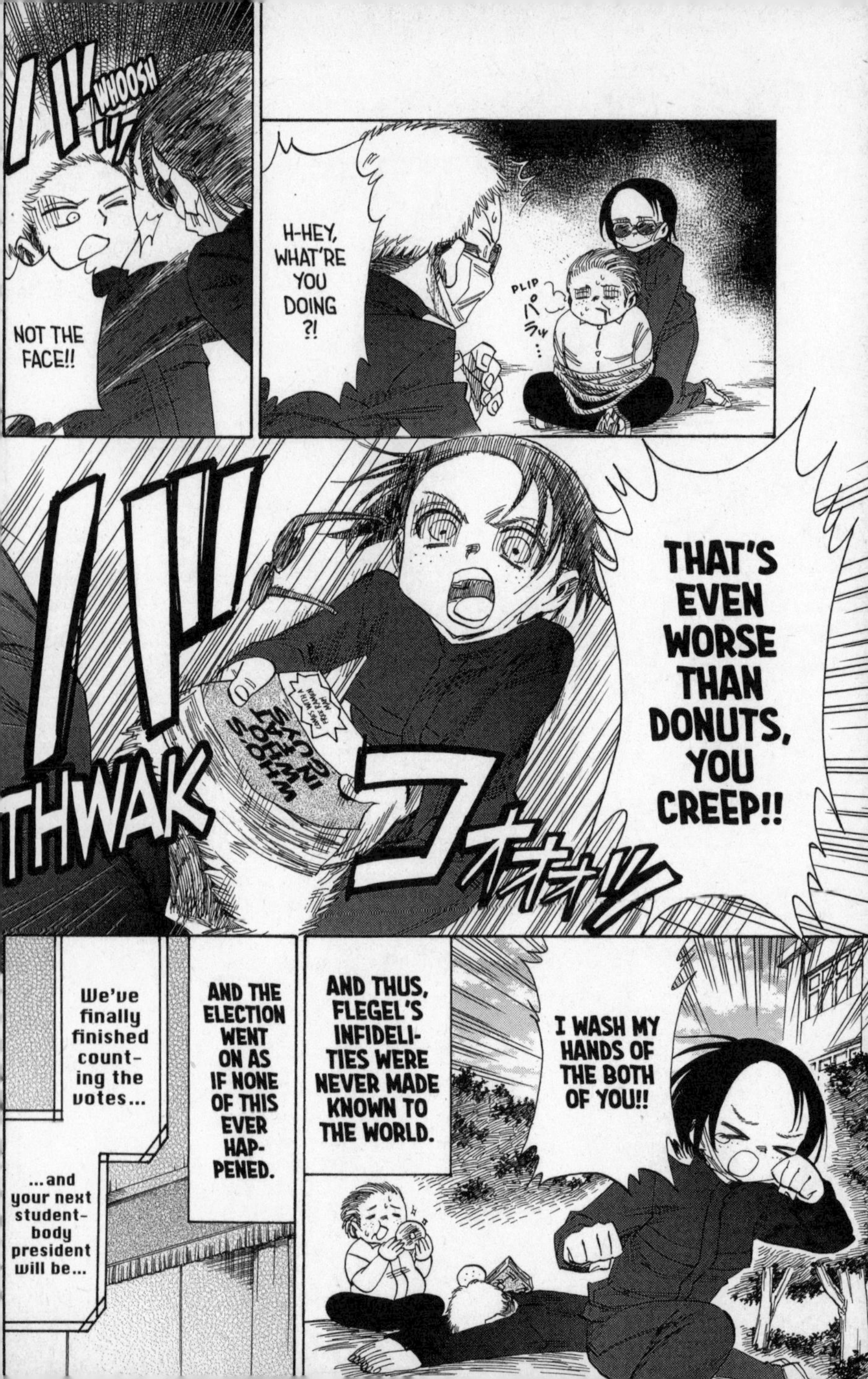
H-HEY, WHAT'RE YOU DOING?!
PLIP
WHOOSH
NOT THE FACE!!
THAT'S EVEN WORSE THAN DONUTS, YOU CREEP!!
THWAK
I WASH MY HANDS OF THE BOTH OF YOU!!
AND THUS, FLEGEL'S INFIDELITIES WERE NEVER MADE KNOWN TO THE WORLD.
AND THE ELECTION WENT ON AS IF NONE OF THIS EVER HAPPENED.
We've finally finished counting the votes...
...and your next student-body president will be...

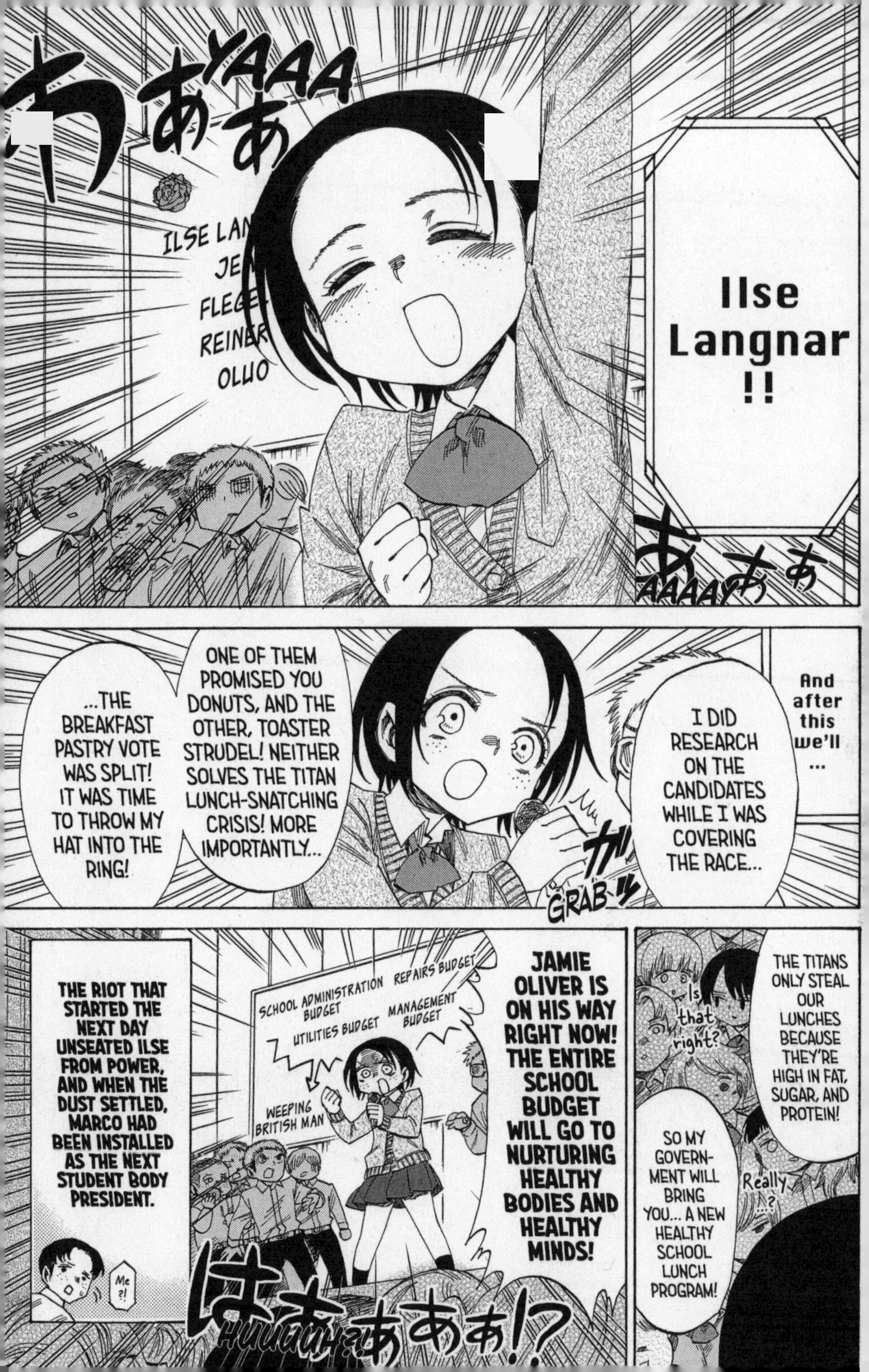

Ilse Langnar !!
わあああ YAAAA
ILSE LAN
JE
FLEGE
REINER
OLUO
ああ AAAAY
And after this we'll ...
I DID RESEARCH ON THE CANDIDATES WHILE I WAS COVERING THE RACE...
GRAB
ONE OF THEM PROMISED YOU DONUTS, AND THE OTHER, TOASTER STRUDEL! NEITHER SOLVES THE TITAN LUNCH-SNATCHING CRISIS! MORE IMPORTANTLY...
...THE BREAKFAST PASTRY VOTE WAS SPLIT! IT WAS TIME TO THROW MY HAT INTO THE RING!
THE TITANS ONLY STEAL OUR LUNCHES BECAUSE THEY'RE HIGH IN FAT, SUGAR, AND PROTEIN!
Is that right?
SO MY GOVERNMENT WILL BRING YOU... A NEW HEALTHY SCHOOL LUNCH PROGRAM!
Really ...?
JAMIE OLIVER IS ON HIS WAY RIGHT NOW! THE ENTIRE SCHOOL BUDGET WILL GO TO NURTURING HEALTHY BODIES AND HEALTHY MINDS!
REPAIRS BUDGET
SCHOOL ADMINISTRATION BUDGET
MANAGEMENT BUDGET
UTILITIES BUDGET
WEEPING BRITISH MAN
はあああ!? HUUUUH?!
THE RIOT THAT STARTED THE NEXT DAY UNSEATED ILSE FROM POWER, AND WHEN THE DUST SETTLED, MARCO HAD BEEN INSTALLED AS THE NEXT STUDENT BODY PRESIDENT.
Me ?!

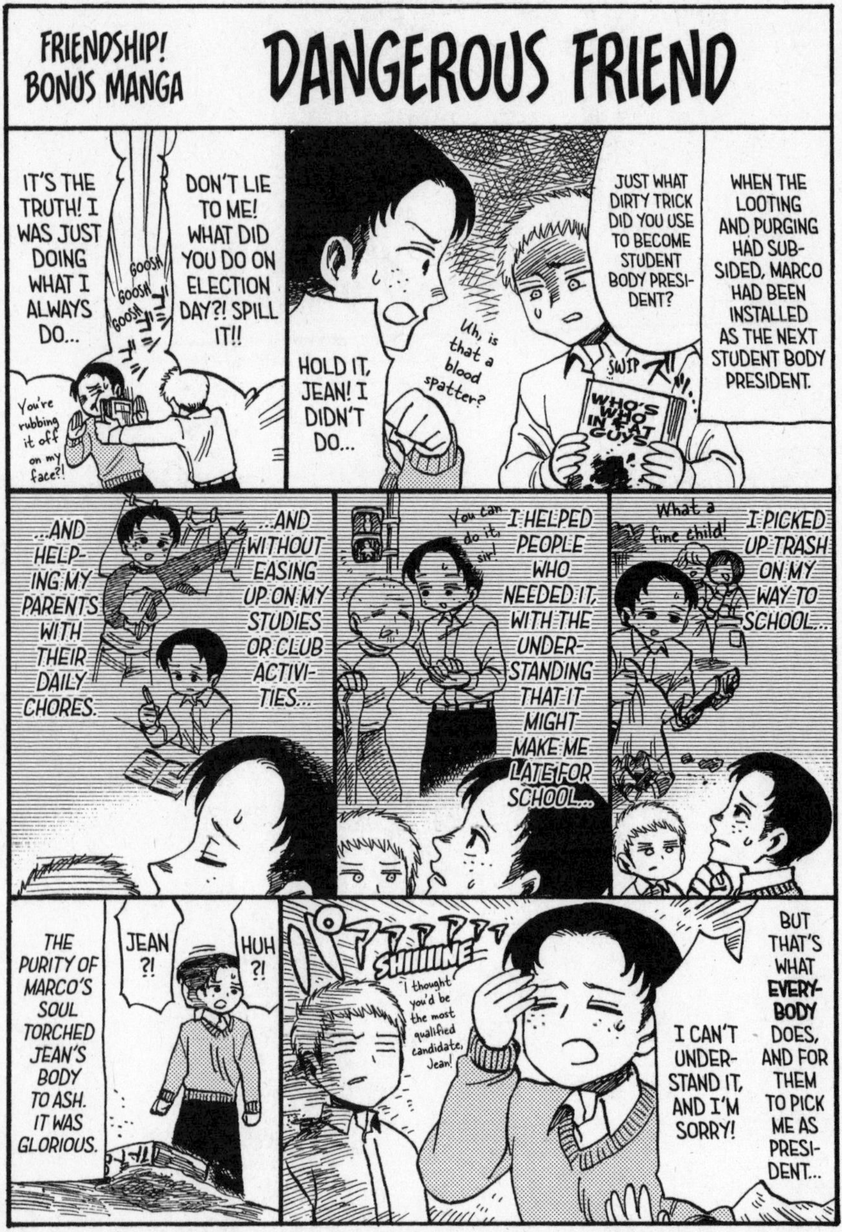
FRIENDSHIP! BONUS MANGA
DANGEROUS FRIEND
WHEN THE LOOTING AND PURGING HAD SUBSIDED, MARCO HAD BEEN INSTALLED AS THE NEXT STUDENT BODY PRESIDENT.
JUST WHAT DIRTY TRICK DID YOU USE TO BECOME STUDENT BODY PRESIDENT?
SWIP
Uh, is that a blood spatter?
HOLD IT, JEAN! I DIDN'T DO...
DON'T LIE TO ME! WHAT DID YOU DO ON ELECTION DAY?! SPILL IT!!
IT'S THE TRUTH! I WAS JUST DOING WHAT I ALWAYS DO...
GOOSH
GOOSH
GOOSH
You're rubbing it off on my face?!
I PICKED UP TRASH ON MY WAY TO SCHOOL...
What a fine child!
I HELPED PEOPLE WHO NEEDED IT, WITH THE UNDERSTANDING THAT IT MIGHT MAKE ME LATE FOR SCHOOL...
You can do it, sir!
...AND WITHOUT EASING UP ON MY STUDIES OR CLUB ACTIVITIES...
...AND HELPING MY PARENTS WITH THEIR DAILY CHORES.
BUT THAT'S WHAT EVERYBODY DOES, AND FOR THEM TO PICK ME AS PRESIDENT...
I CAN'T UNDERSTAND IT, AND I'M SORRY!
SHIIIIINE
I thought you'd be the most qualified candidate, Jean!
HUH?!
JEAN?!
THE PURITY OF MARCO'S SOUL TORCHED JEAN'S BODY TO ASH. IT WAS GLORIOUS.

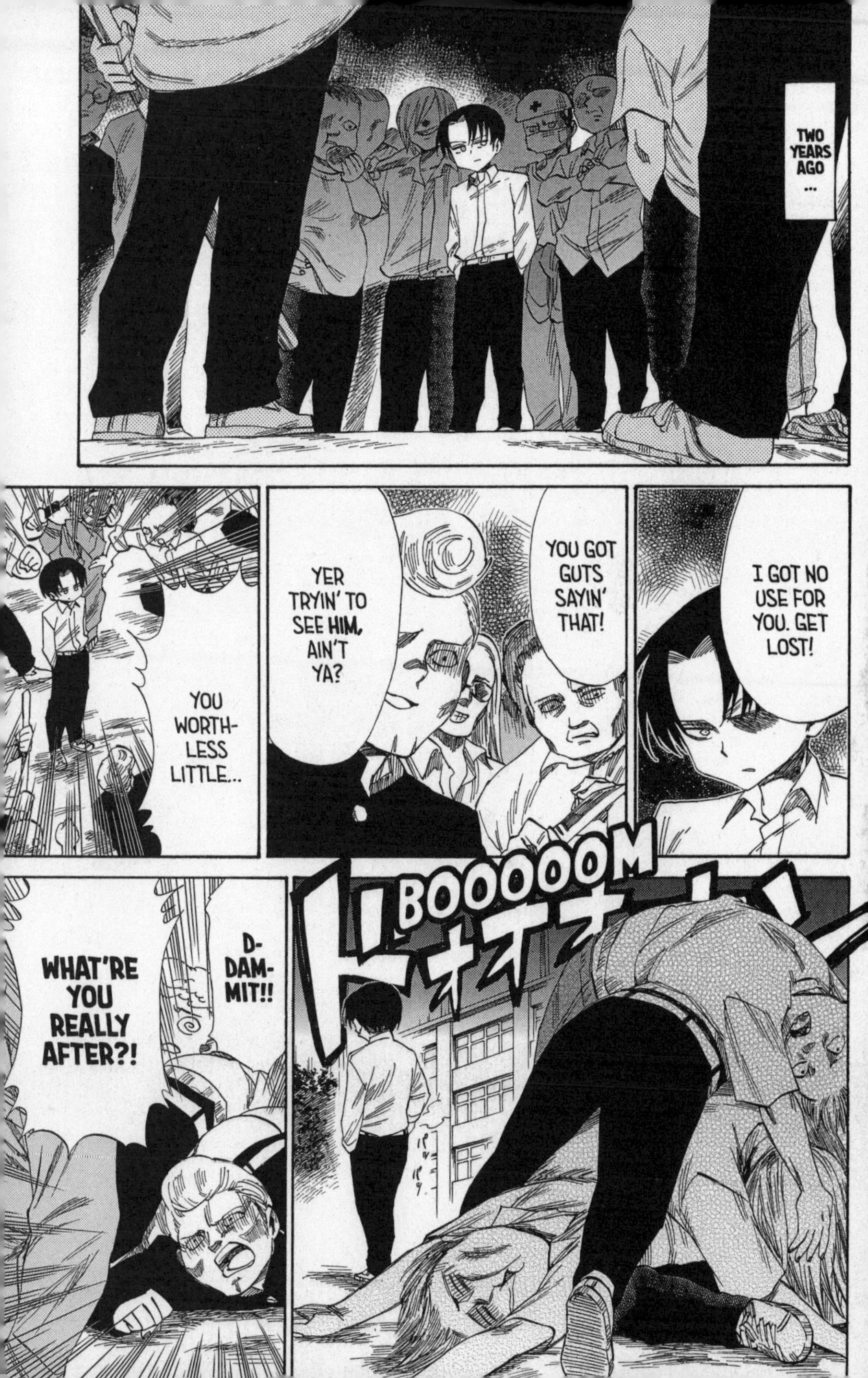
TWO YEARS AGO ...
I GOT NO USE FOR YOU. GET LOST!
YOU GOT GUTS SAYIN' THAT!
YER TRYIN' TO SEE HIM, AIN'T YA?
YOU WORTH-LESS LITTLE...
BOOOOOM
D-DAM-MIT!!
WHAT'RE YOU REALLY AFTER?!

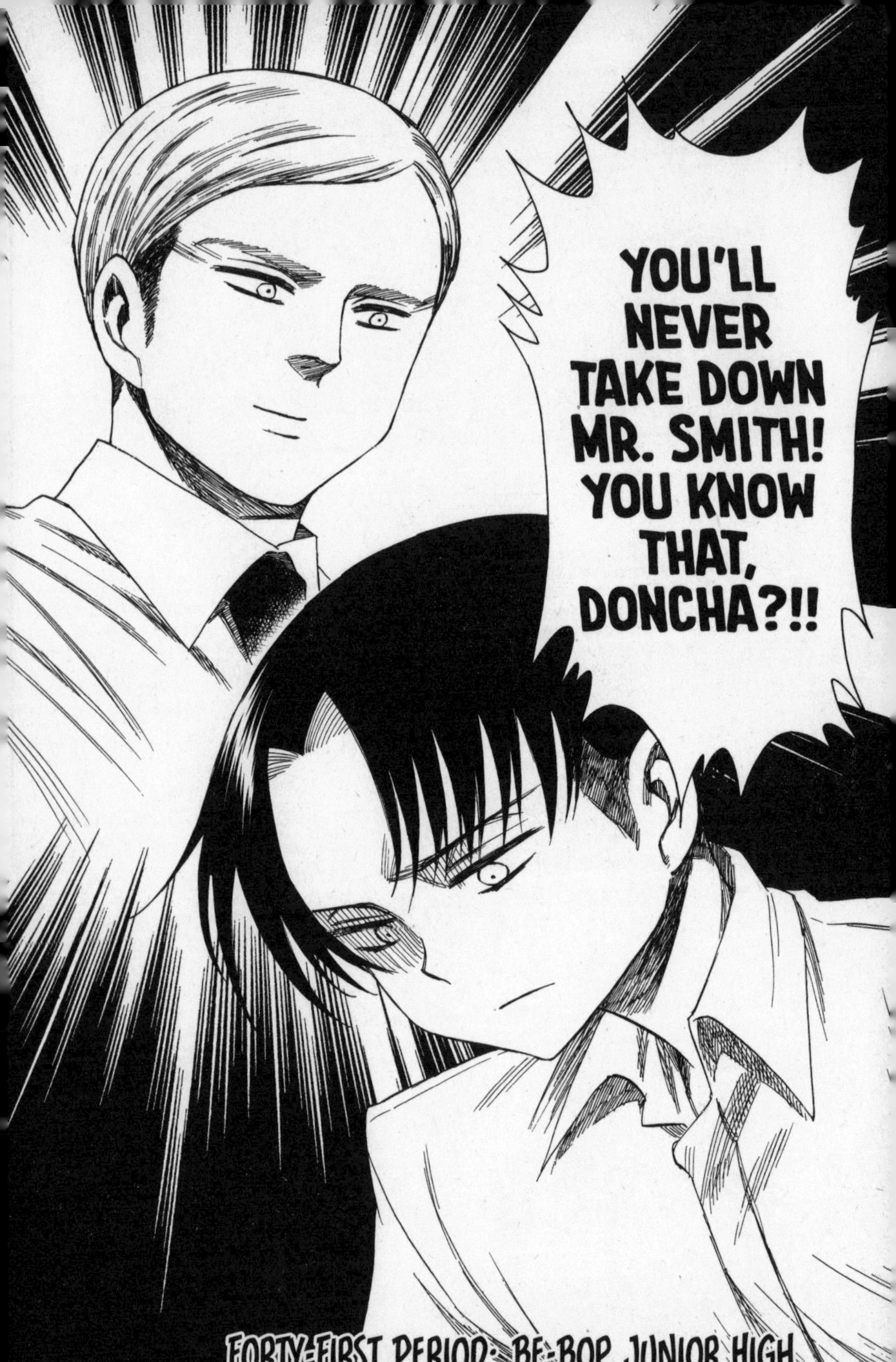
YOU'LL NEVER TAKE DOWN MR. SMITH! YOU KNOW THAT, DONCHA?!!

FORTY-FIRST PERIOD: BE-BOP JUNIOR HIGH

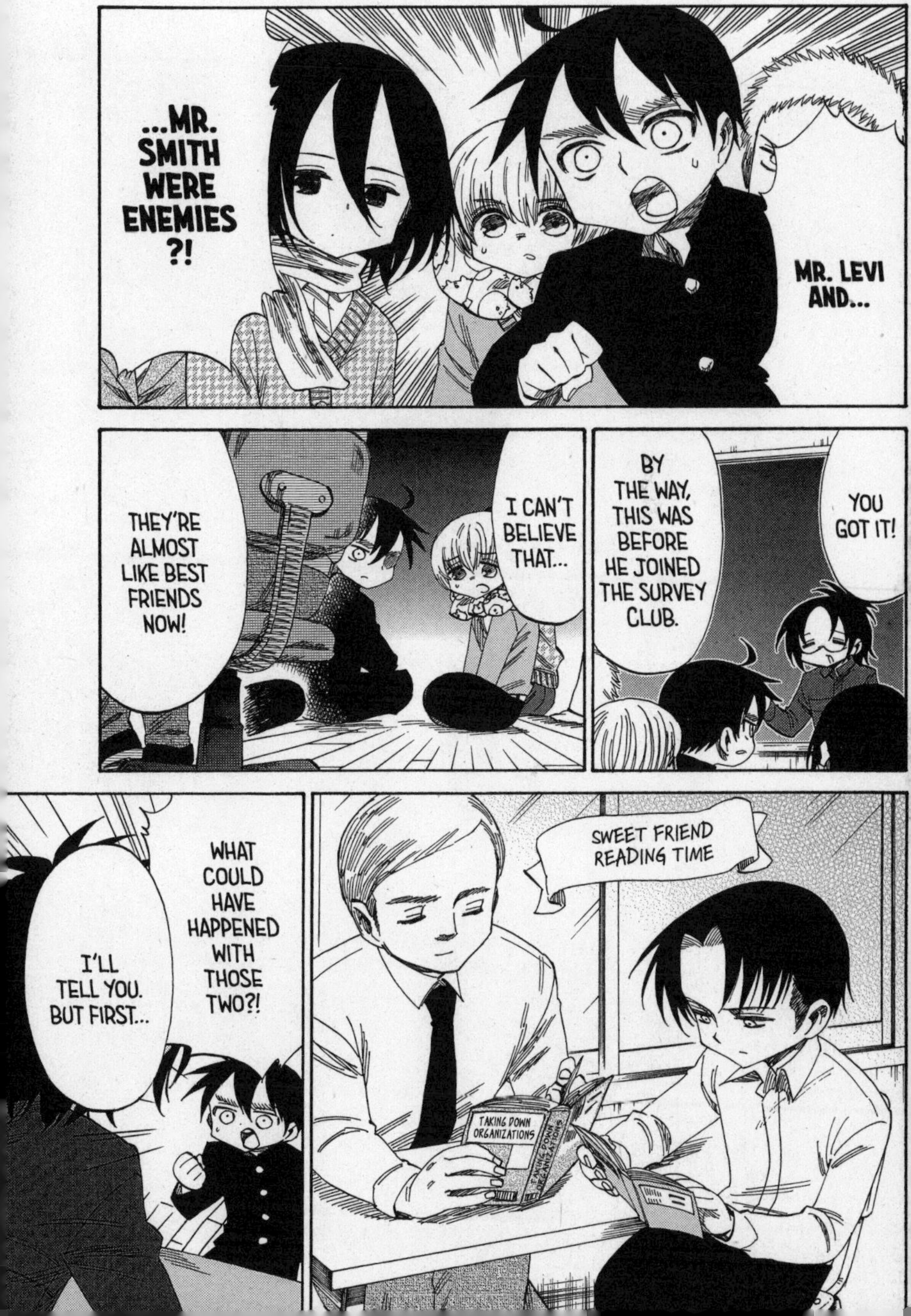
MR. LEVI AND...
...MR. SMITH WERE ENEMIES?!
YOU GOT IT!
BY THE WAY, THIS WAS BEFORE HE JOINED THE SURVEY CLUB.
I CAN'T BELIEVE THAT...
THEY'RE ALMOST LIKE BEST FRIENDS NOW!
SWEET FRIEND READING TIME
TAKING DOWN ORGANIZATIONS
WHAT COULD HAVE HAPPENED WITH THOSE TWO?!
I'LL TELL YOU. BUT FIRST...

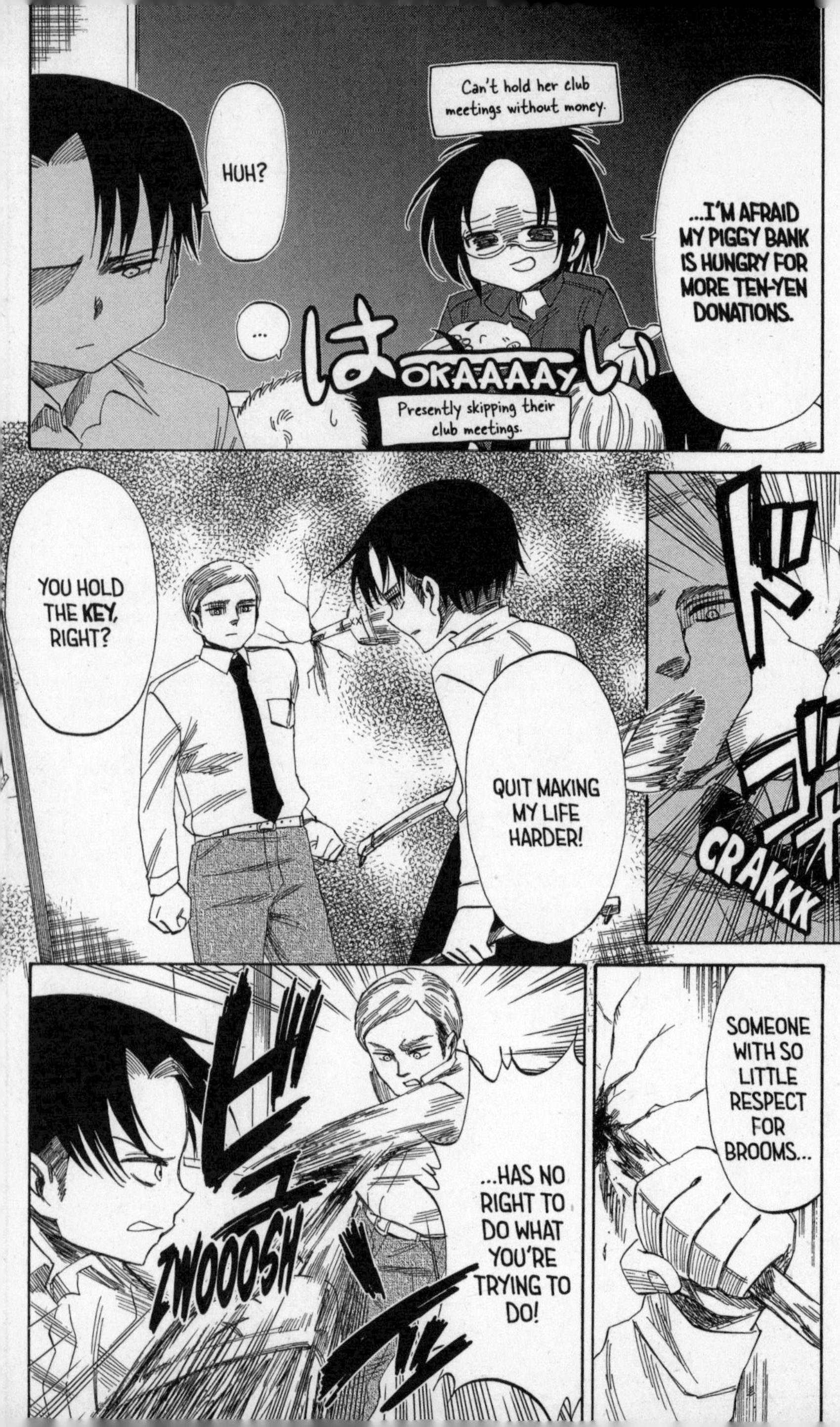
...I'M AFRAID MY PIGGY BANK IS HUNGRY FOR MORE TEN-YEN DONATIONS.
Can't hold her club meetings without money.
HUH?
OKAAAAY
Presently skipping their club meetings.
...
CRAKKK
QUIT MAKING MY LIFE HARDER!
YOU HOLD THE KEY, RIGHT?
SOMEONE WITH SO LITTLE RESPECT FOR BROOMS...
...HAS NO RIGHT TO DO WHAT YOU'RE TRYING TO DO!
ZWOOOSH

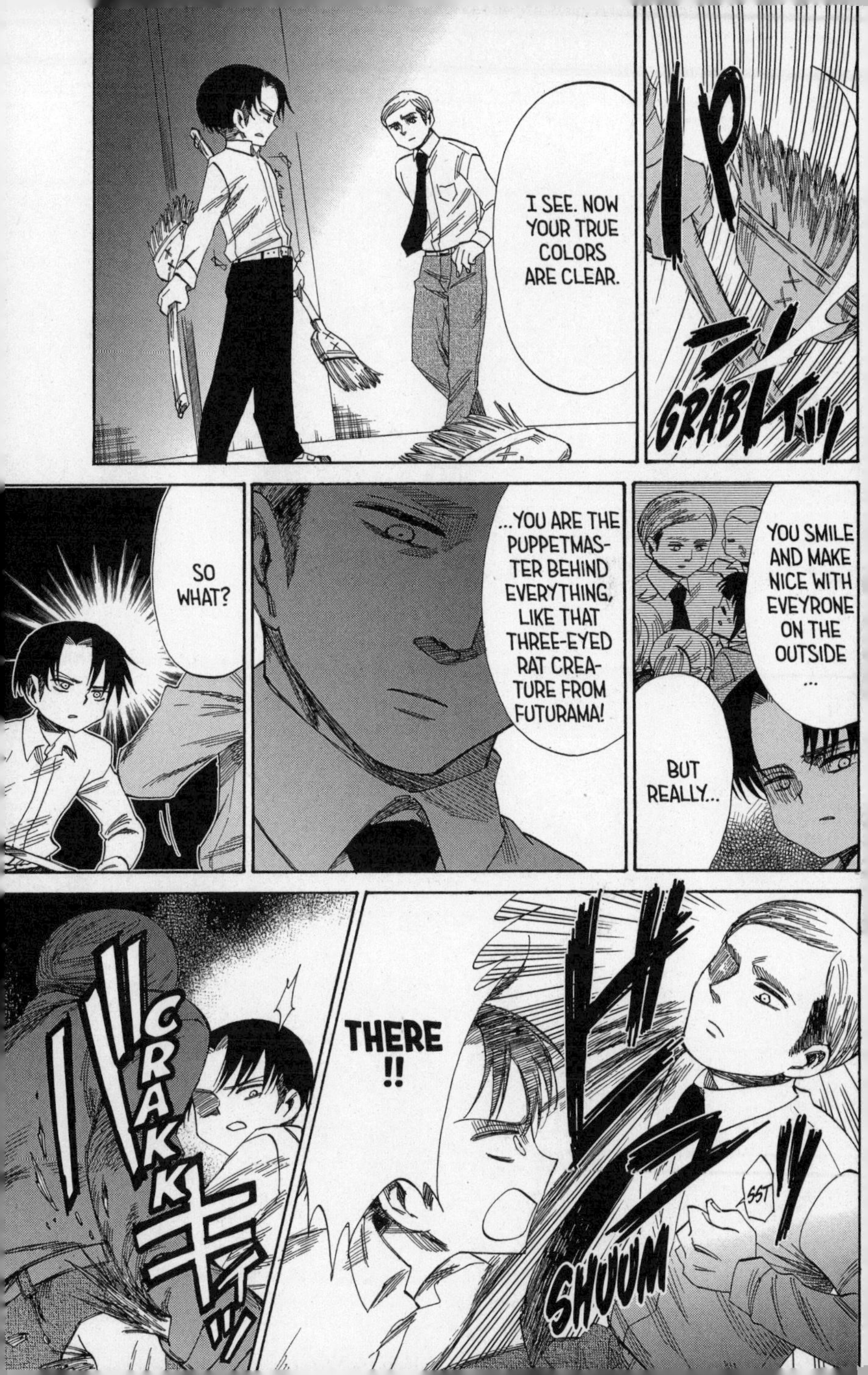
GRAB
I SEE. NOW YOUR TRUE COLORS ARE CLEAR.
YOU SMILE AND MAKE NICE WITH EVEYRONE ON THE OUTSIDE ...
BUT REALLY...
...YOU ARE THE PUPPETMAS-TER BEHIND EVERYTHING, LIKE THAT THREE-EYED RAT CREA-TURE FROM FUTURAMA!
SO WHAT?
THERE !!
SST
SHUUM
CRAKK

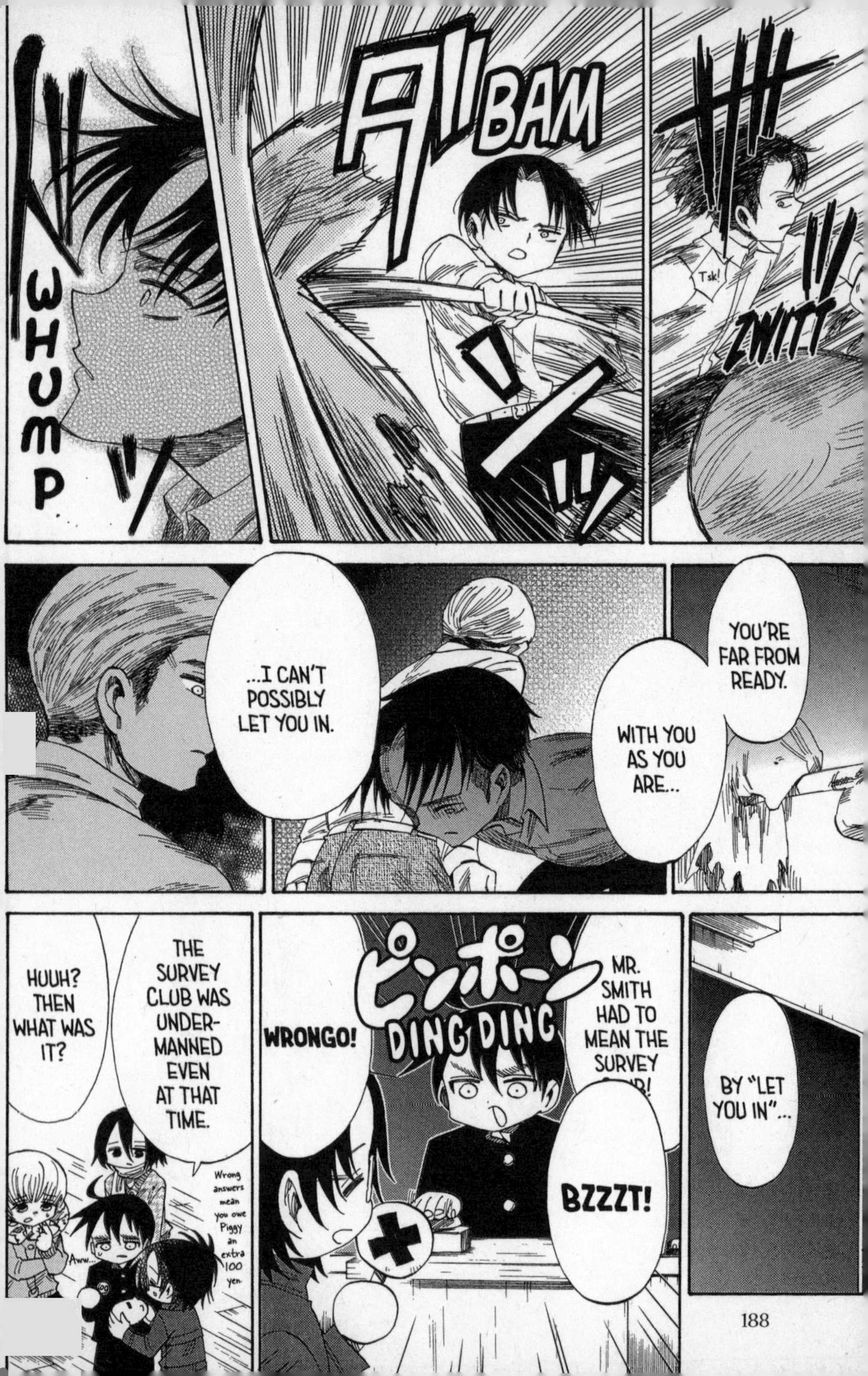
Tsk!
ZWITT
BAM
WHUMP
YOU'RE FAR FROM READY.
WITH YOU AS YOU ARE...
...I CAN'T POSSIBLY LET YOU IN.
BY "LET YOU IN"...
MR. SMITH HAD TO MEAN THE SURVEY
ピンポーン
DING DING
BZZZT!
WRONGO!
THE SURVEY CLUB WAS UNDER-MANNED EVEN AT THAT TIME.
HUUH? THEN WHAT WAS IT?
Wrong answers mean you owe Piggy an extra 100 yen.
Aww...

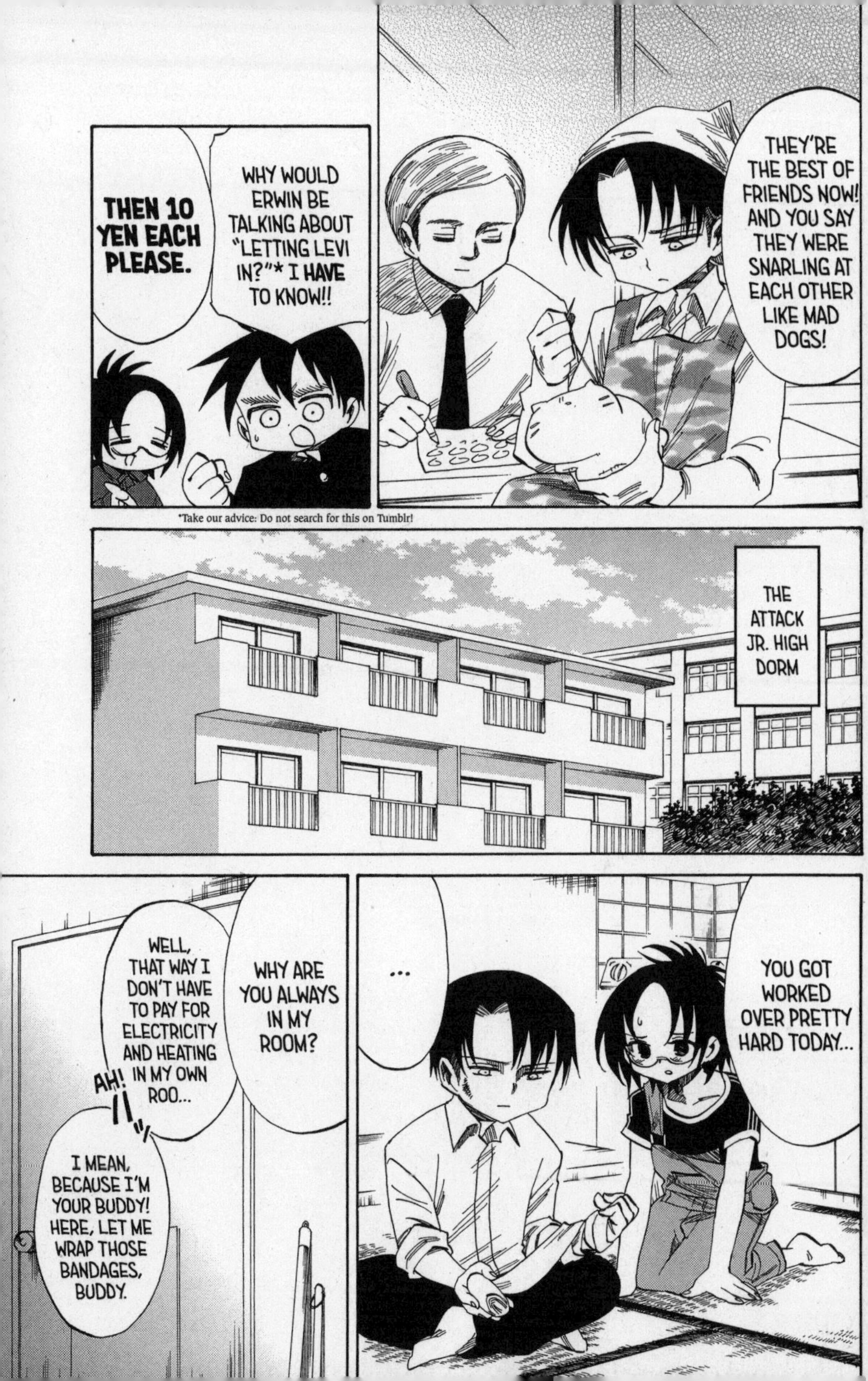
THEY'RE THE BEST OF FRIENDS NOW! AND YOU SAY THEY WERE SNARLING AT EACH OTHER LIKE MAD DOGS!
WHY WOULD ERWIN BE TALKING ABOUT "LETTING LEVI IN?"* I HAVE TO KNOW!!
THEN 10 YEN EACH PLEASE.
THE ATTACK JR. HIGH DORM
YOU GOT WORKED OVER PRETTY HARD TODAY...
...
WHY ARE YOU ALWAYS IN MY ROOM?
WELL, THAT WAY I DON'T HAVE TO PAY FOR ELECTRICITY AND HEATING IN MY OWN ROO...
AH!
I MEAN, BECAUSE I'M YOUR BUDDY! HERE, LET ME WRAP THOSE BANDAGES, BUDDY.

*Take our advice: Do not search for this on Tumblr!

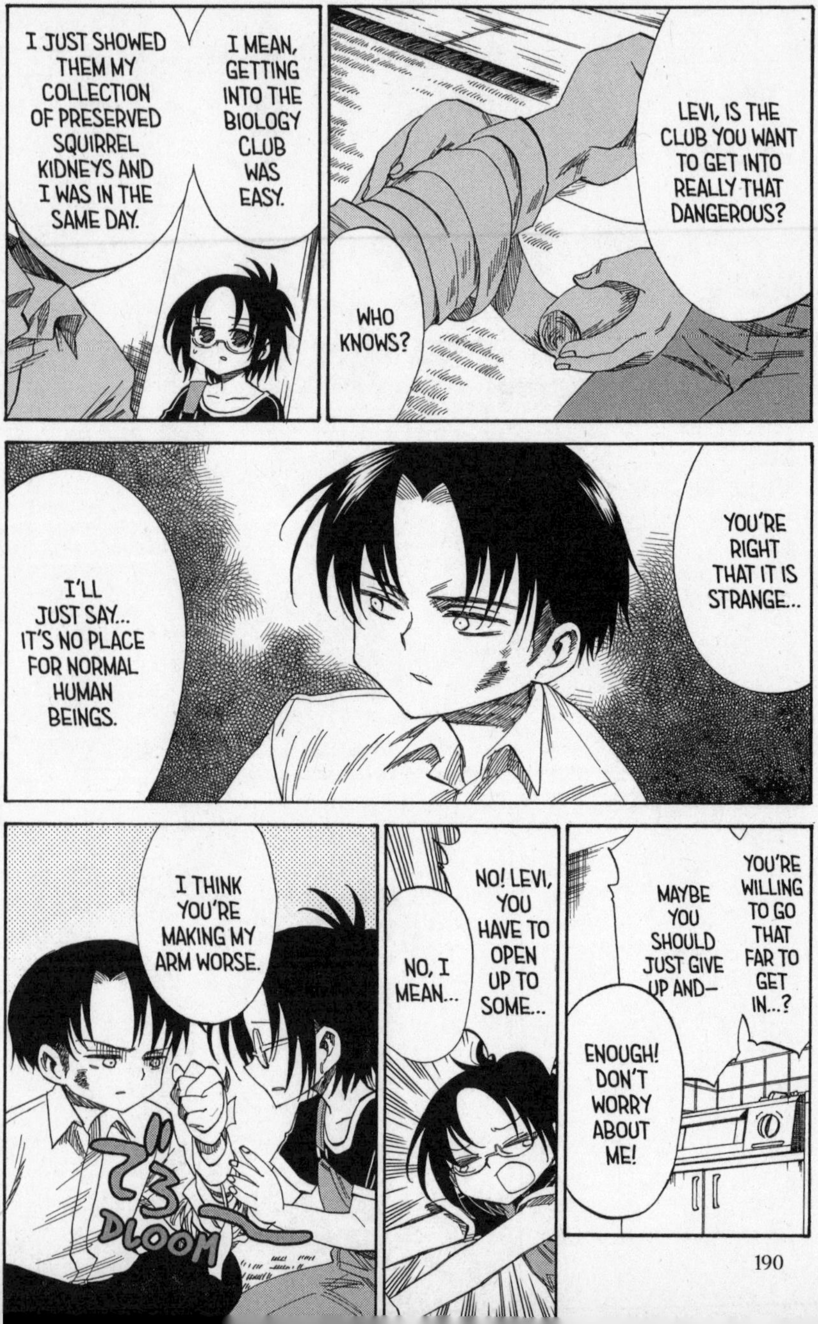

LEVI, IS THE CLUB YOU WANT TO GET INTO REALLY THAT DANGEROUS?
WHO KNOWS?
I MEAN, GETTING INTO THE BIOLOGY CLUB WAS EASY.
I JUST SHOWED THEM MY COLLECTION OF PRESERVED SQUIRREL KIDNEYS AND I WAS IN THE SAME DAY.
YOU'RE RIGHT THAT IT IS STRANGE...
I'LL JUST SAY... IT'S NO PLACE FOR NORMAL HUMAN BEINGS.
YOU'RE WILLING TO GO THAT FAR TO GET IN...?
MAYBE YOU SHOULD JUST GIVE UP AND—
ENOUGH! DON'T WORRY ABOUT ME!
NO! LEVI, YOU HAVE TO OPEN UP TO SOME...
NO, I MEAN...
I THINK YOU'RE MAKING MY ARM WORSE.
DLOOM

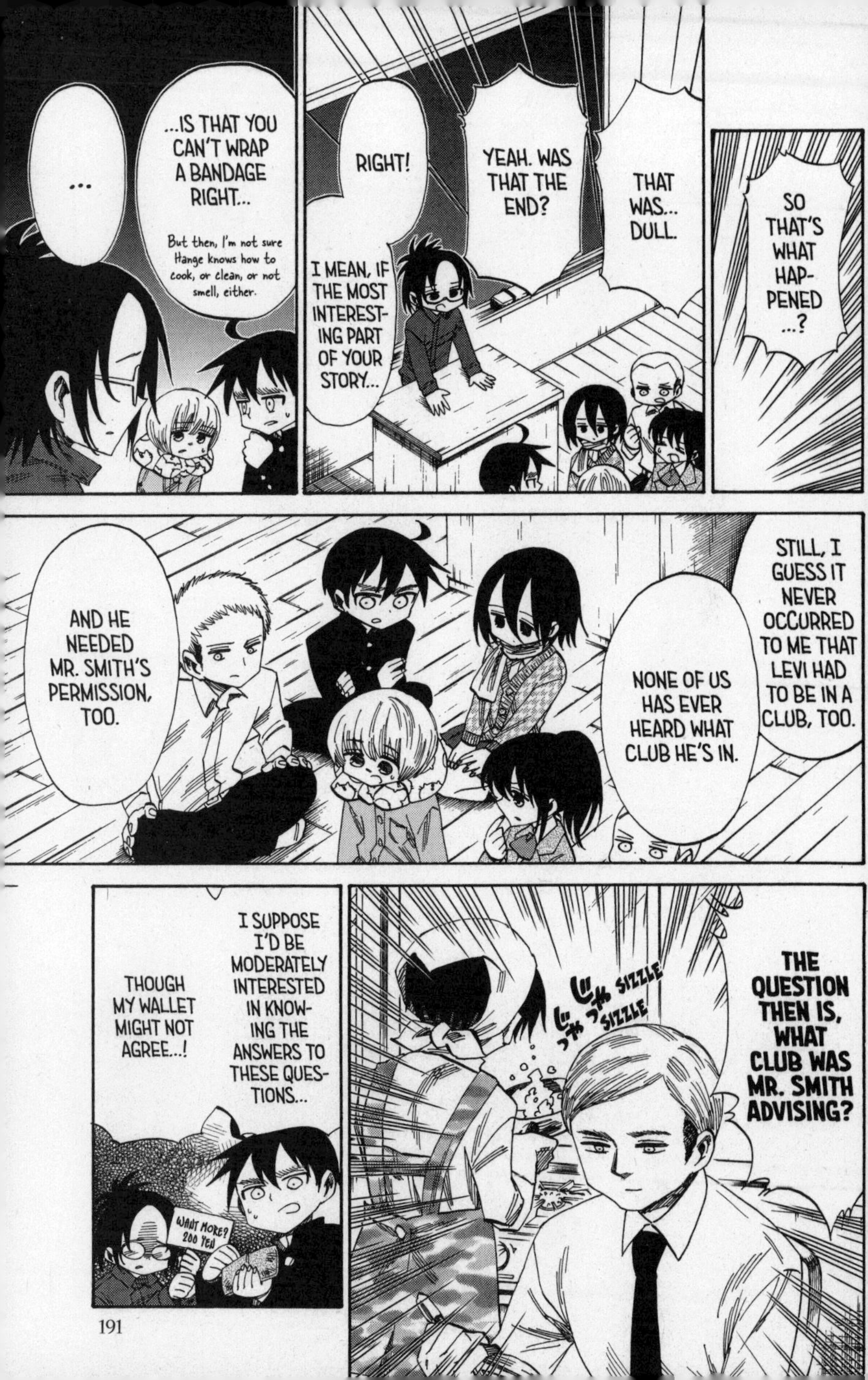
SO THAT'S WHAT HAP-PENED ...?
THAT WAS... DULL.
YEAH. WAS THAT THE END?
RIGHT!
I MEAN, IF THE MOST INTEREST-ING PART OF YOUR STORY...
...IS THAT YOU CAN'T WRAP A BANDAGE RIGHT...
But then, I'm not sure Hange knows how to cook, or clean, or not smell, either.
...
STILL, I GUESS IT NEVER OCCURRED TO ME THAT LEVI HAD TO BE IN A CLUB, TOO.
NONE OF US HAS EVER HEARD WHAT CLUB HE'S IN.
AND HE NEEDED MR. SMITH'S PERMISSION, TOO.
THE QUESTION THEN IS, WHAT CLUB WAS MR. SMITH ADVISING?
SIZZLE
SIZZLE
I SUPPOSE I'D BE MODERATELY INTERESTED IN KNOW-ING THE ANSWERS TO THESE QUES-TIONS...
THOUGH MY WALLET MIGHT NOT AGREE...!
WANT MORE? 200 YEN

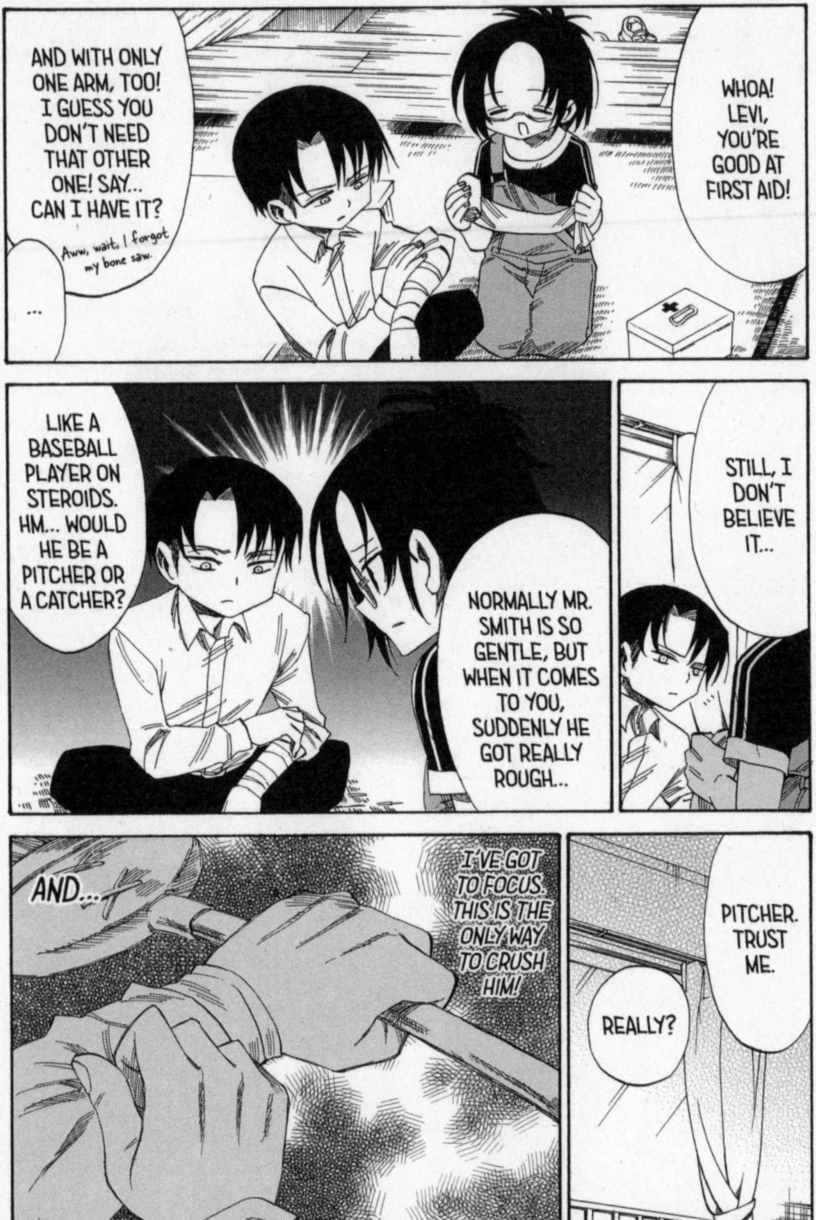
WHOA! LEVI, YOU'RE GOOD AT FIRST AID!
AND WITH ONLY ONE ARM, TOO! I GUESS YOU DON'T NEED THAT OTHER ONE! SAY... CAN I HAVE IT?
Aww, wait, I forgot my bone saw.
...
STILL, I DON'T BELIEVE IT...
NORMALLY MR. SMITH IS SO GENTLE, BUT WHEN IT COMES TO YOU, SUDDENLY HE GOT REALLY ROUGH...
LIKE A BASEBALL PLAYER ON STEROIDS. HM... WOULD HE BE A PITCHER OR A CATCHER?
PITCHER. TRUST ME.
REALLY?
I'VE GOT TO FOCUS. THIS IS THE ONLY WAY TO CRUSH HIM!
AND...

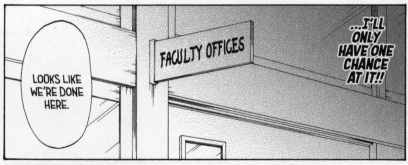

...I'LL ONLY HAVE ONE CHANCE AT IT!!
LOOKS LIKE WE'RE DONE HERE.
FACULTY OFFICES
NOT FOR ME. I'VE GOT LOTS MORE TO DO TODAY.
AFTER ALL, IT'S THE FINAL DAY FOR STUDENT CLUB APPLI-CATIONS.
OH. WELL, I JUST DO IT ON A FIRST-COME, FIRST-SERVED BASIS, SO I'M DONE.
OH, THAT'S VERY... UM... LAZY.
WHAT ABOUT YOUR CLUB, MR. SMITH?
GASP
OH, IT'S JUST LIKE ALWAYS.
NOT EVEN ONE PERSON WANTED TO ENTER.
A-AH. IT WAS ALWAYS THAT WAY, HUH? CHIN UP...
SHUMP

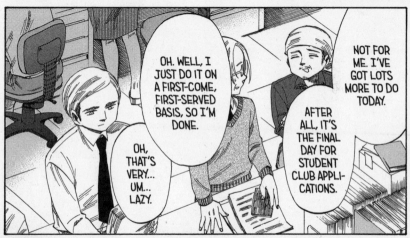

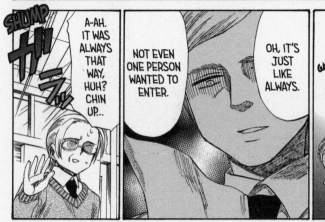

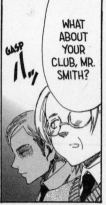

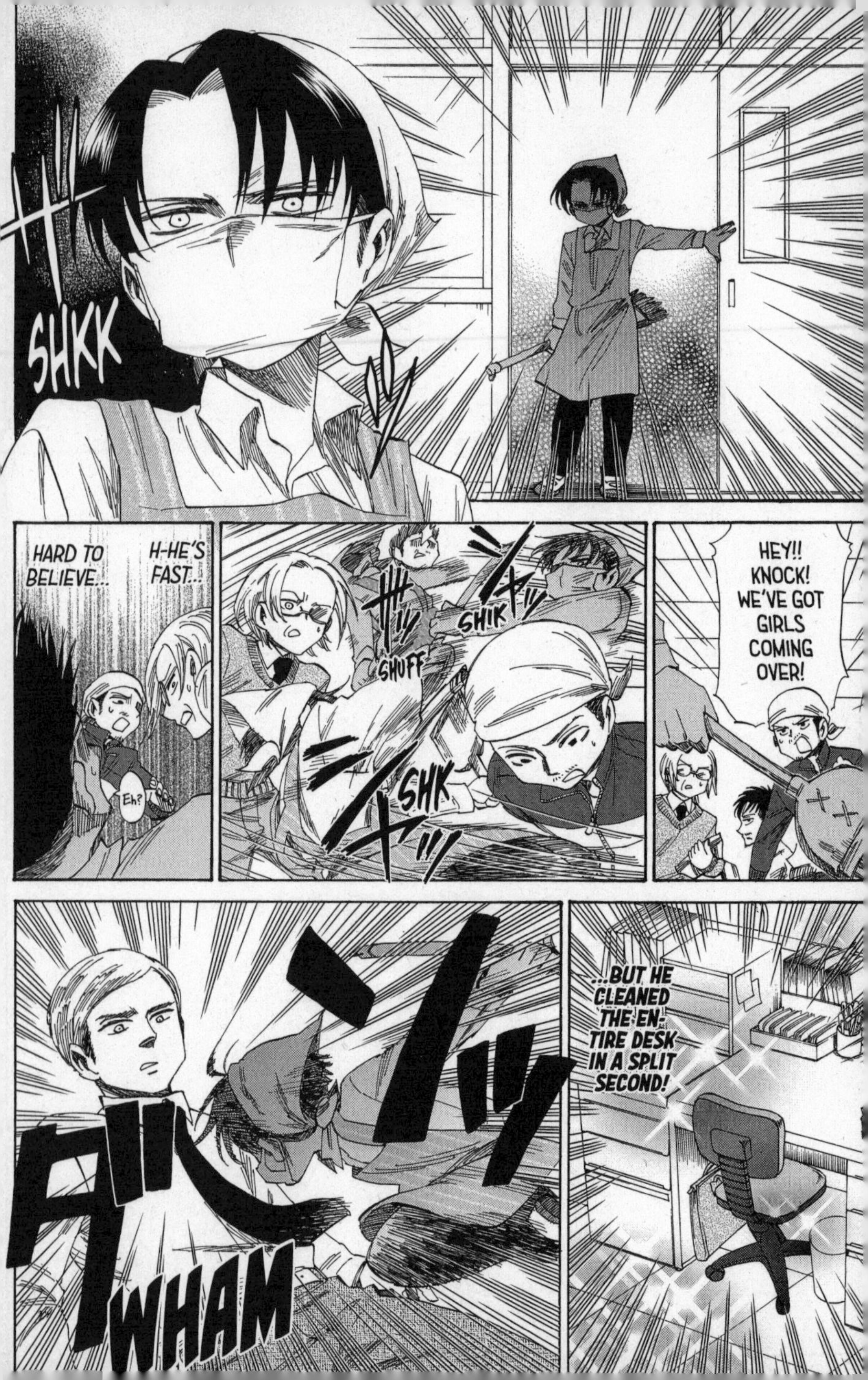
SHKK
HEY!! KNOCK! WE'VE GOT GIRLS COMING OVER!
SHIK
SHUFF
SHK
H-HE'S FAST...
HARD TO BELIEVE...
Eh?
...BUT HE CLEANED THE EN- TIRE DESK IN A SPLIT SECOND!
WHAM

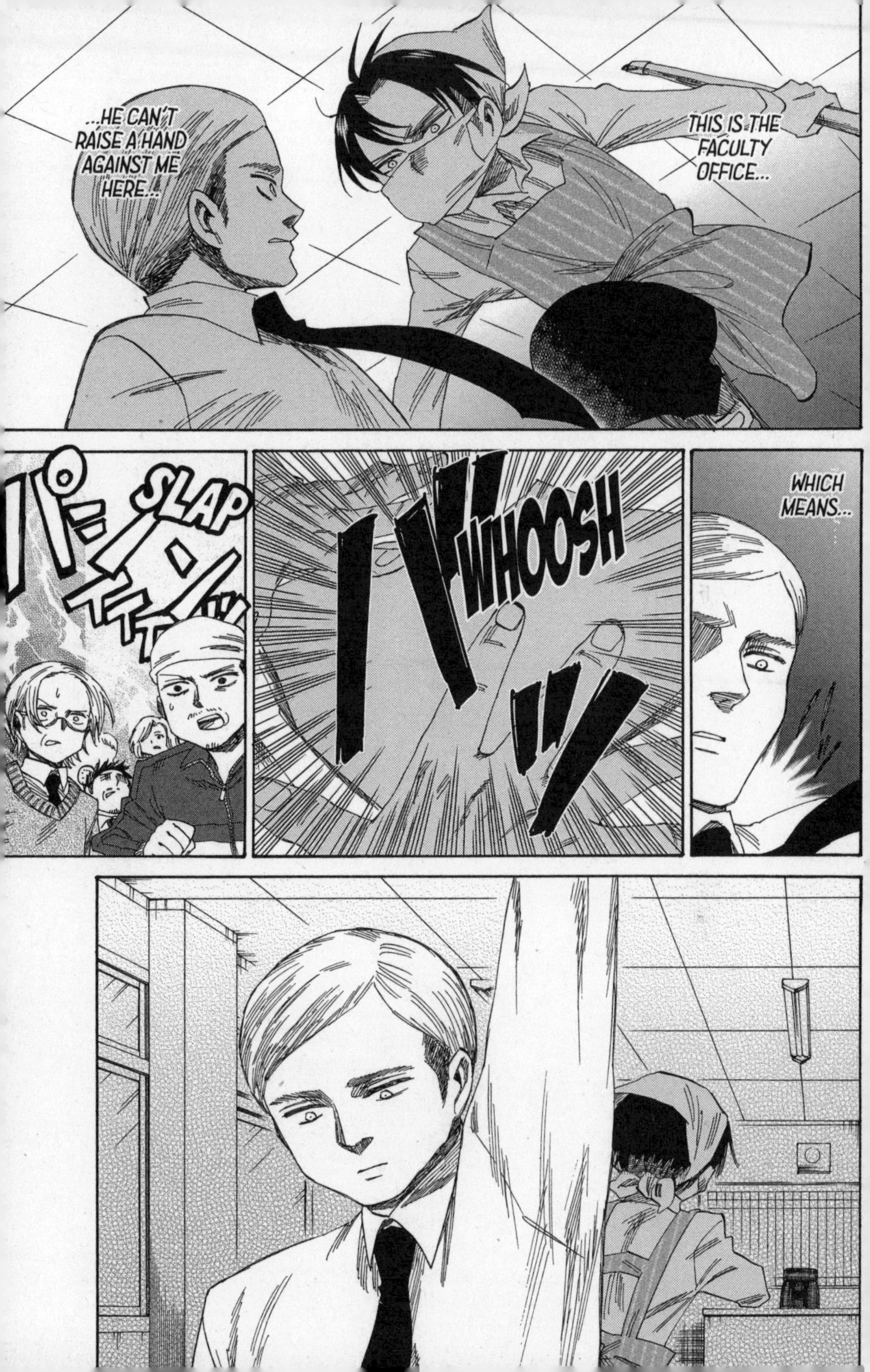
THIS IS THE FACULTY OFFICE...
...HE CAN'T RAISE A HAND AGAINST ME HERE...
WHICH MEANS...
WHOOSH
SLAP

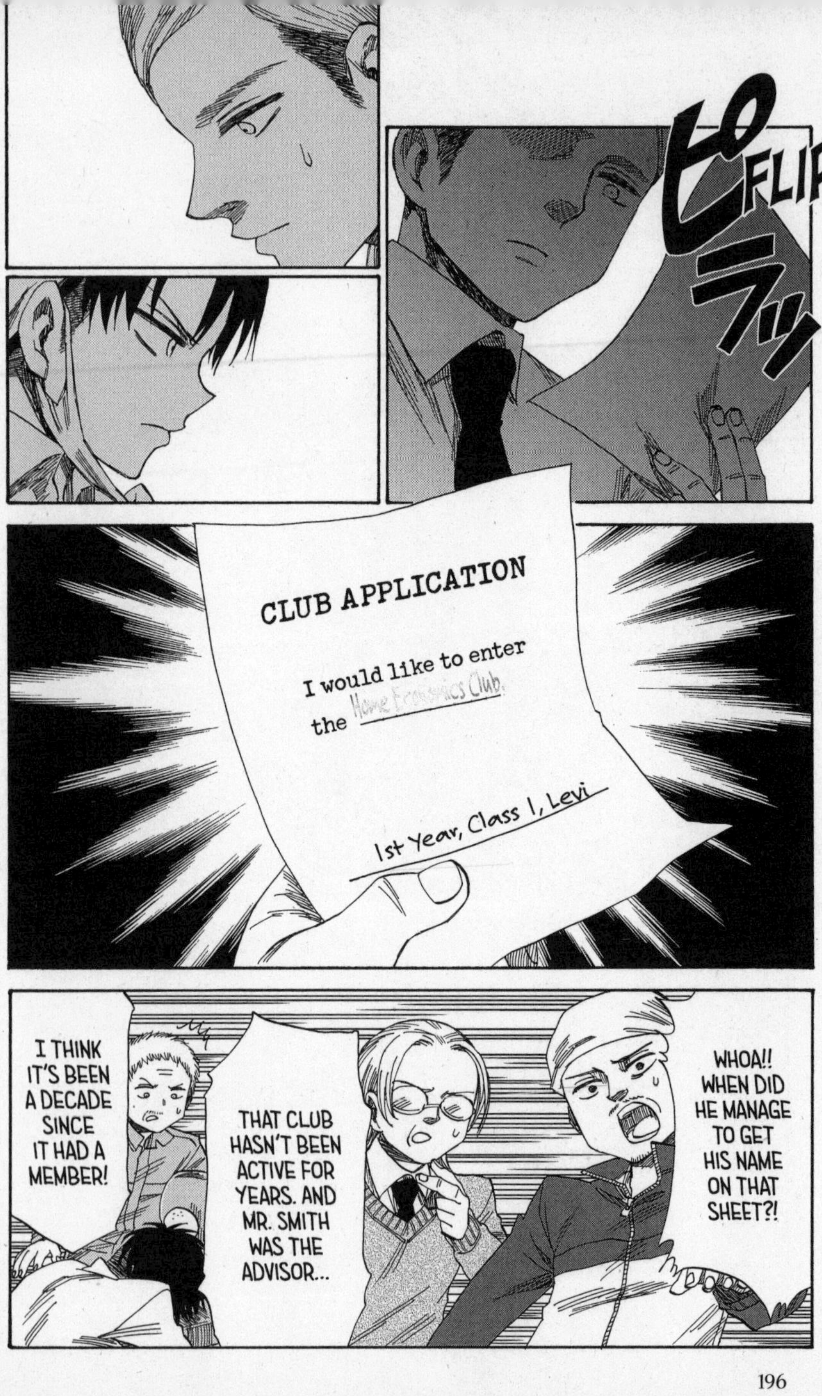
ピラッ FLIP
CLUB APPLICATION
I would like to enter the Home Economics Club.
1st Year, Class 1, Levi
WHOA!! WHEN DID HE MANAGE TO GET HIS NAME ON THAT SHEET?!
THAT CLUB HASN'T BEEN ACTIVE FOR YEARS. AND MR. SMITH WAS THE ADVISOR...
I THINK IT'S BEEN A DECADE SINCE IT HAD A MEMBER!

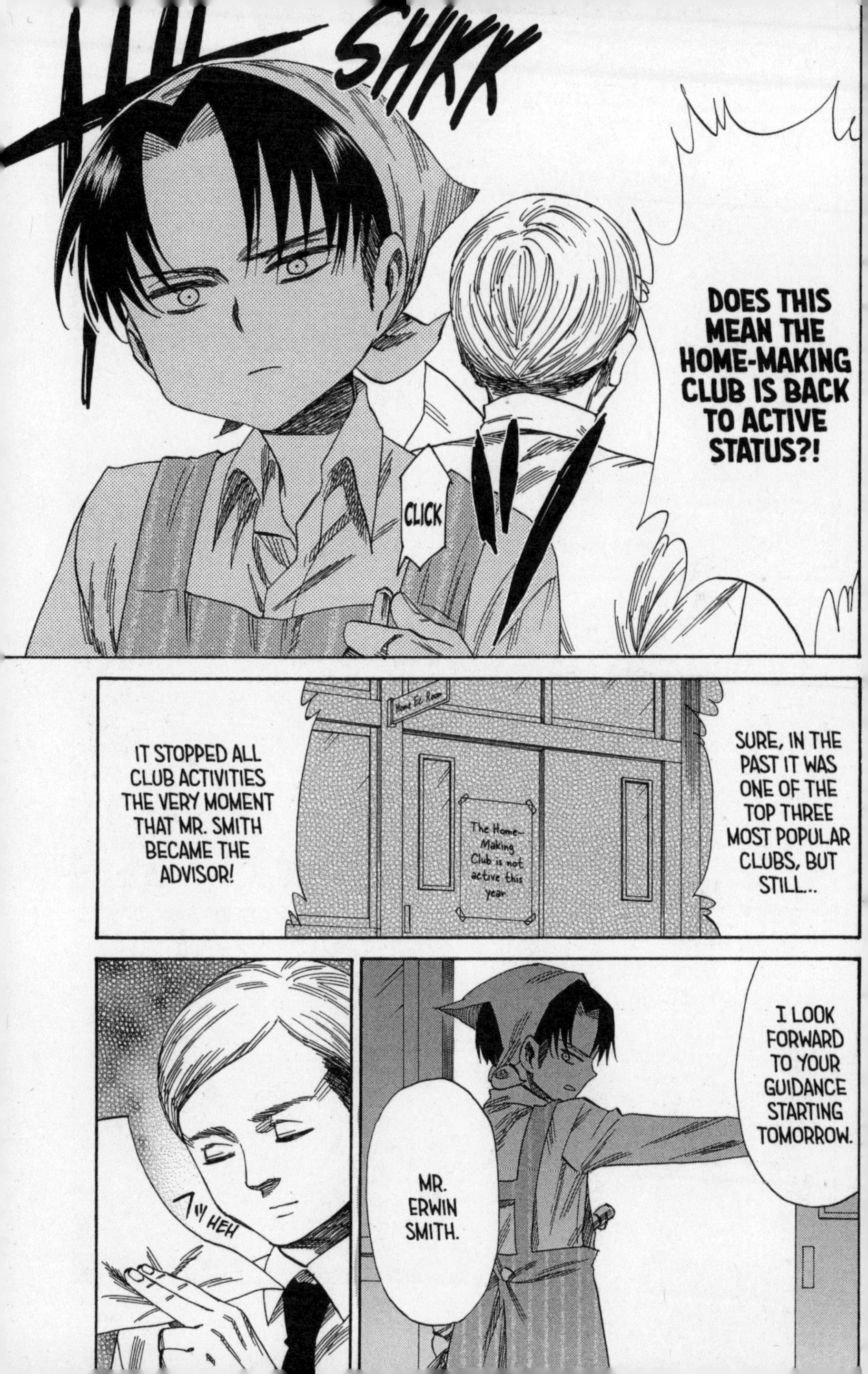
SHRK
DOES THIS MEAN THE HOME-MAKING CLUB IS BACK TO ACTIVE STATUS?!
CLICK
SURE, IN THE PAST IT WAS ONE OF THE TOP THREE MOST POPULAR CLUBS, BUT STILL...
Home Ec Room
The Home-Making Club is not active this year
IT STOPPED ALL CLUB ACTIVITIES THE VERY MOMENT THAT MR. SMITH BECAME THE ADVISOR!
I LOOK FORWARD TO YOUR GUIDANCE STARTING TOMORROW.
MR. ERWIN SMITH.
ヘッ HEH

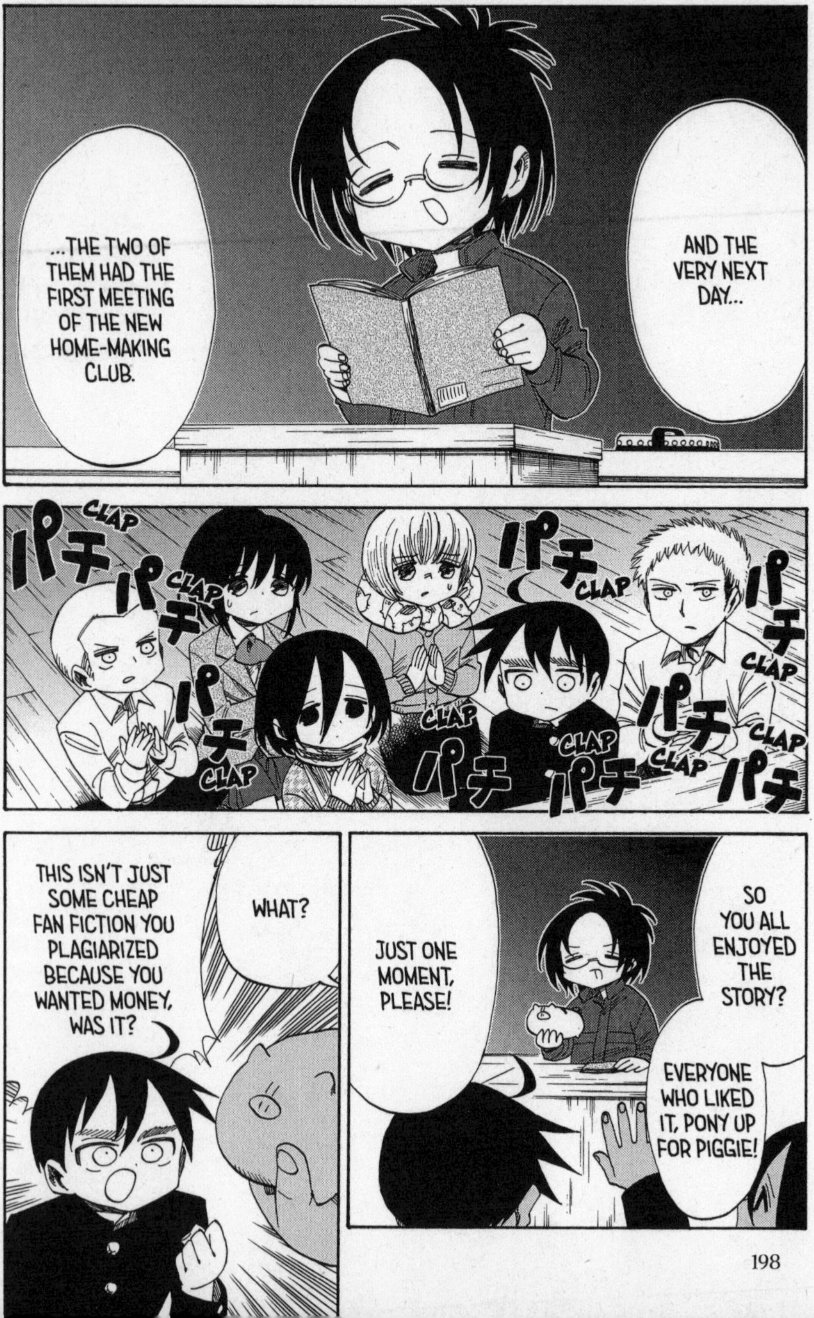
AND THE VERY NEXT DAY...
...THE TWO OF THEM HAD THE FIRST MEETING OF THE NEW HOME-MAKING CLUB.
パチ
CLAP
パチ
CLAP
パチ
CLAP
パチ
CLAP
パチ
CLAP
パチ
CLAP
パチ
CLAP
パチ
CLAP
SO YOU ALL ENJOYED THE STORY?
EVERYONE WHO LIKED IT, PONY UP FOR PIGGIE!
JUST ONE MOMENT, PLEASE!
WHAT?
THIS ISN'T JUST SOME CHEAP FAN FICTION YOU PLAGIARIZED BECAUSE YOU WANTED MONEY, WAS IT?

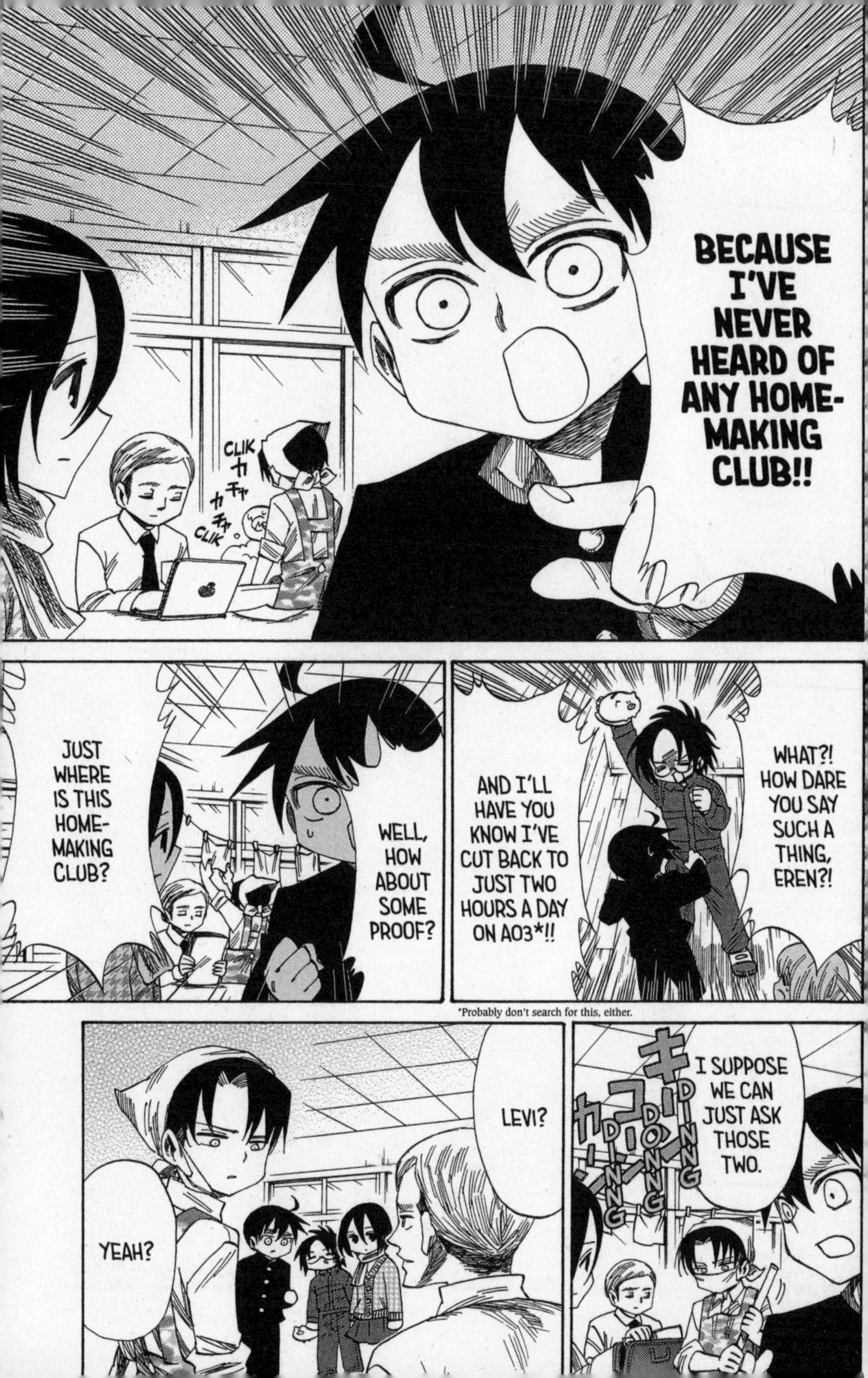
BECAUSE I'VE NEVER HEARD OF ANY HOME-MAKING CLUB!!
CLIK
カチャ
カチャ
CLIK
WHAT?! HOW DARE YOU SAY SUCH A THING, EREN?!
AND I'LL HAVE YOU KNOW I'VE CUT BACK TO JUST TWO HOURS A DAY ON AO3*!!
WELL, HOW ABOUT SOME PROOF?
JUST WHERE IS THIS HOME-MAKING CLUB?
キーンコーン
DING DONG DING
I SUPPOSE WE CAN JUST ASK THOSE TWO.
LEVI?
YEAH?

*Probably don't search for this, either.

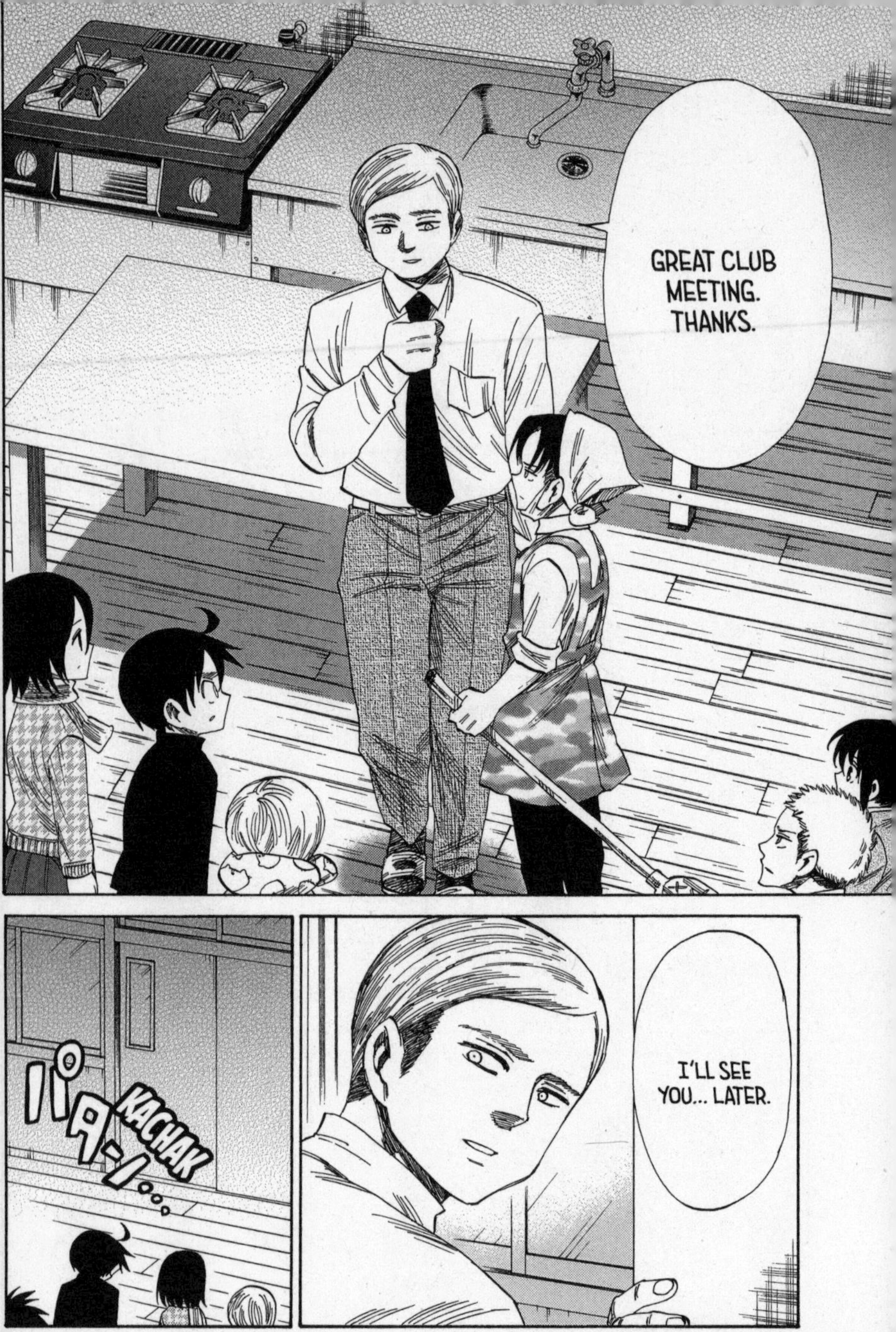
GREAT CLUB MEETING. THANKS.
I'LL SEE YOU... LATER.
パターン
KACHAK

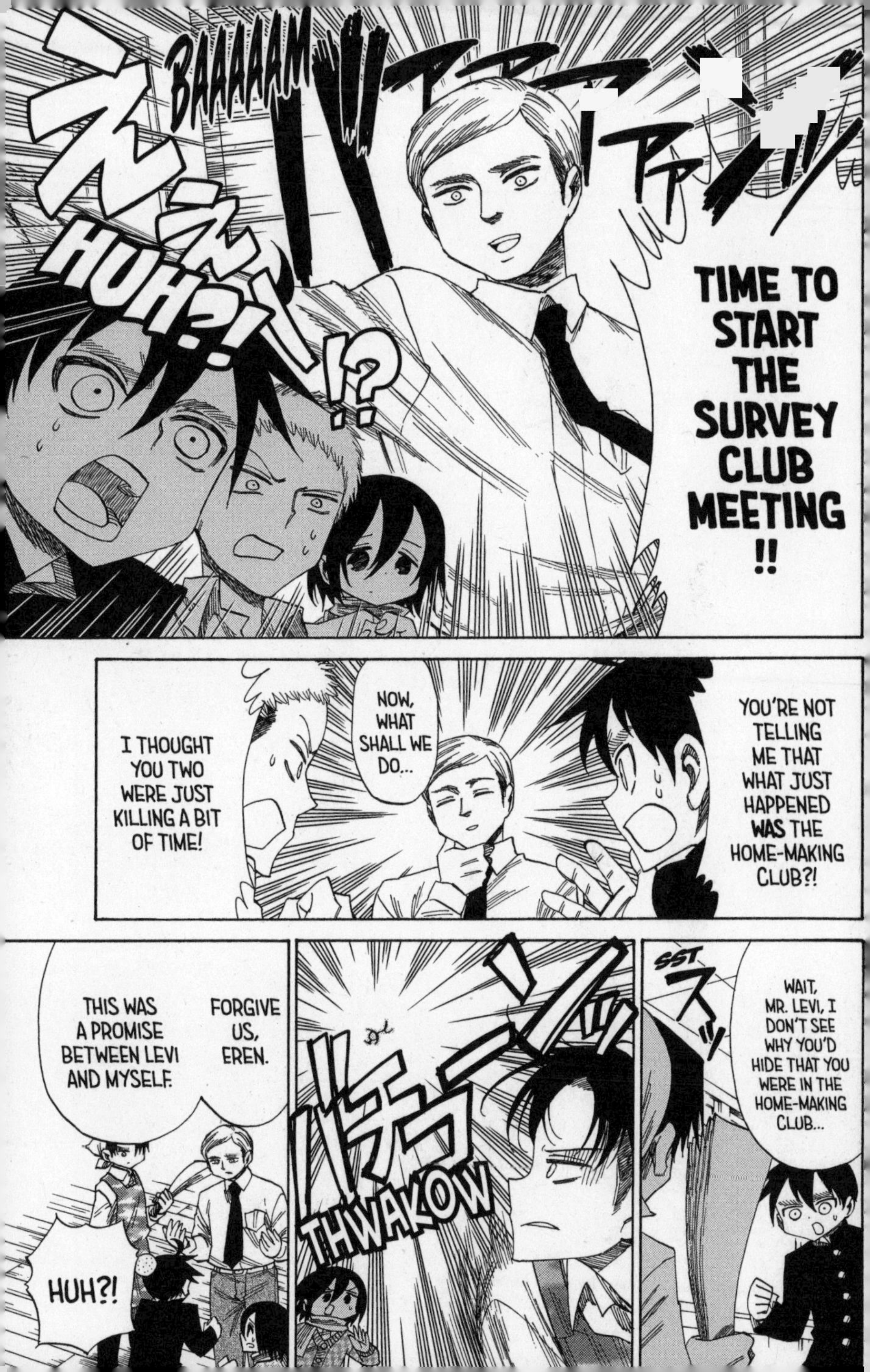
BAAAAAM
TIME TO START THE SURVEY CLUB MEETING!!
HUH?!
!?
YOU'RE NOT TELLING ME THAT WHAT JUST HAPPENED WAS THE HOME-MAKING CLUB?!
NOW, WHAT SHALL WE DO...
I THOUGHT YOU TWO WERE JUST KILLING A BIT OF TIME!
SST
WAIT, MR. LEVI, I DON'T SEE WHY YOU'D HIDE THAT YOU WERE IN THE HOME-MAKING CLUB...
THWAKOW
FORGIVE US, EREN.
THIS WAS A PROMISE BETWEEN LEVI AND MYSELF.
HUH?!

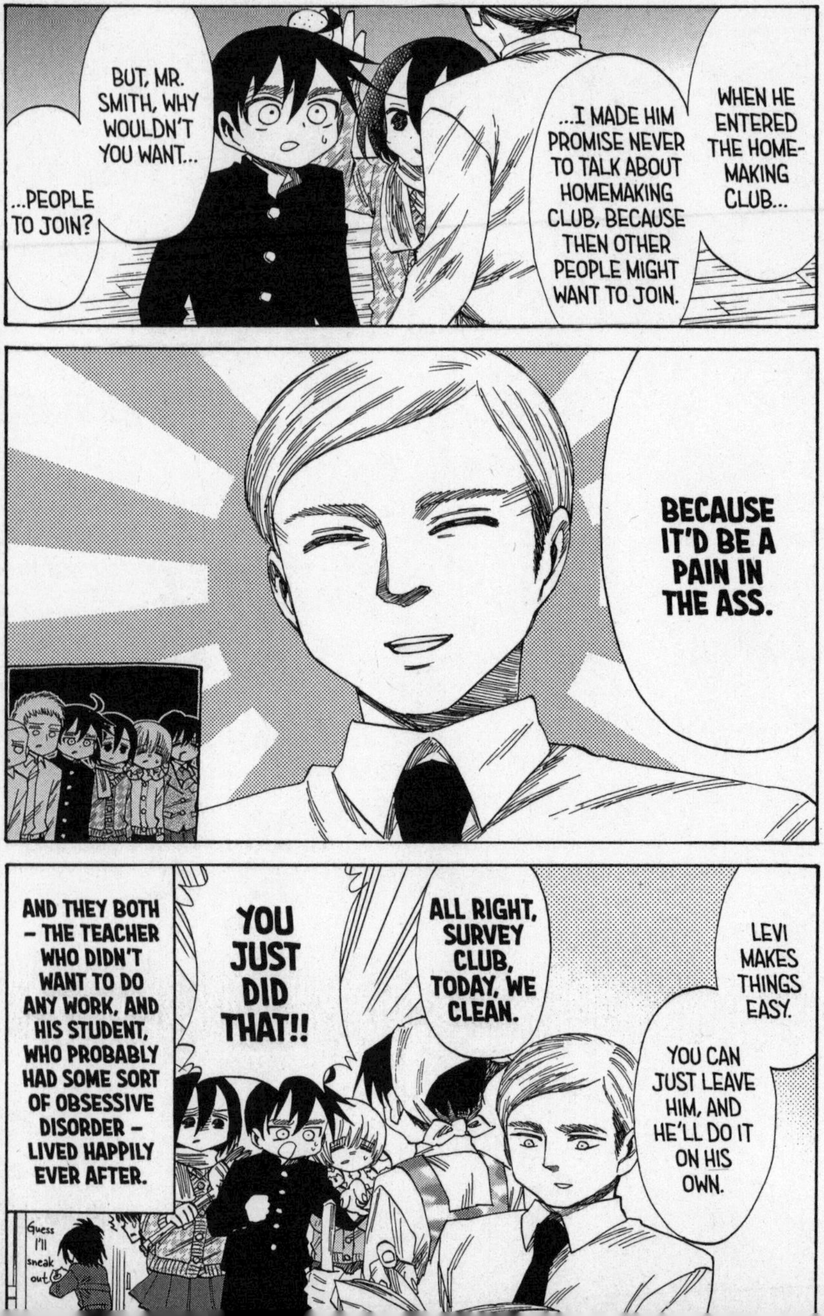
WHEN HE ENTERED THE HOME-MAKING CLUB...
...I MADE HIM PROMISE NEVER TO TALK ABOUT HOMEMAKING CLUB, BECAUSE THEN OTHER PEOPLE MIGHT WANT TO JOIN.
BUT, MR. SMITH, WHY WOULDN'T YOU WANT...
...PEOPLE TO JOIN?
BECAUSE IT'D BE A PAIN IN THE ASS.
LEVI MAKES THINGS EASY.
YOU CAN JUST LEAVE HIM, AND HE'LL DO IT ON HIS OWN.
ALL RIGHT, SURVEY CLUB, TODAY, WE CLEAN.
YOU JUST DID THAT!!
AND THEY BOTH – THE TEACHER WHO DIDN'T WANT TO DO ANY WORK, AND HIS STUDENT, WHO PROBABLY HAD SOME SORT OF OBSESSIVE DISORDER – LIVED HAPPILY EVER AFTER.
Guess I'll sneak out

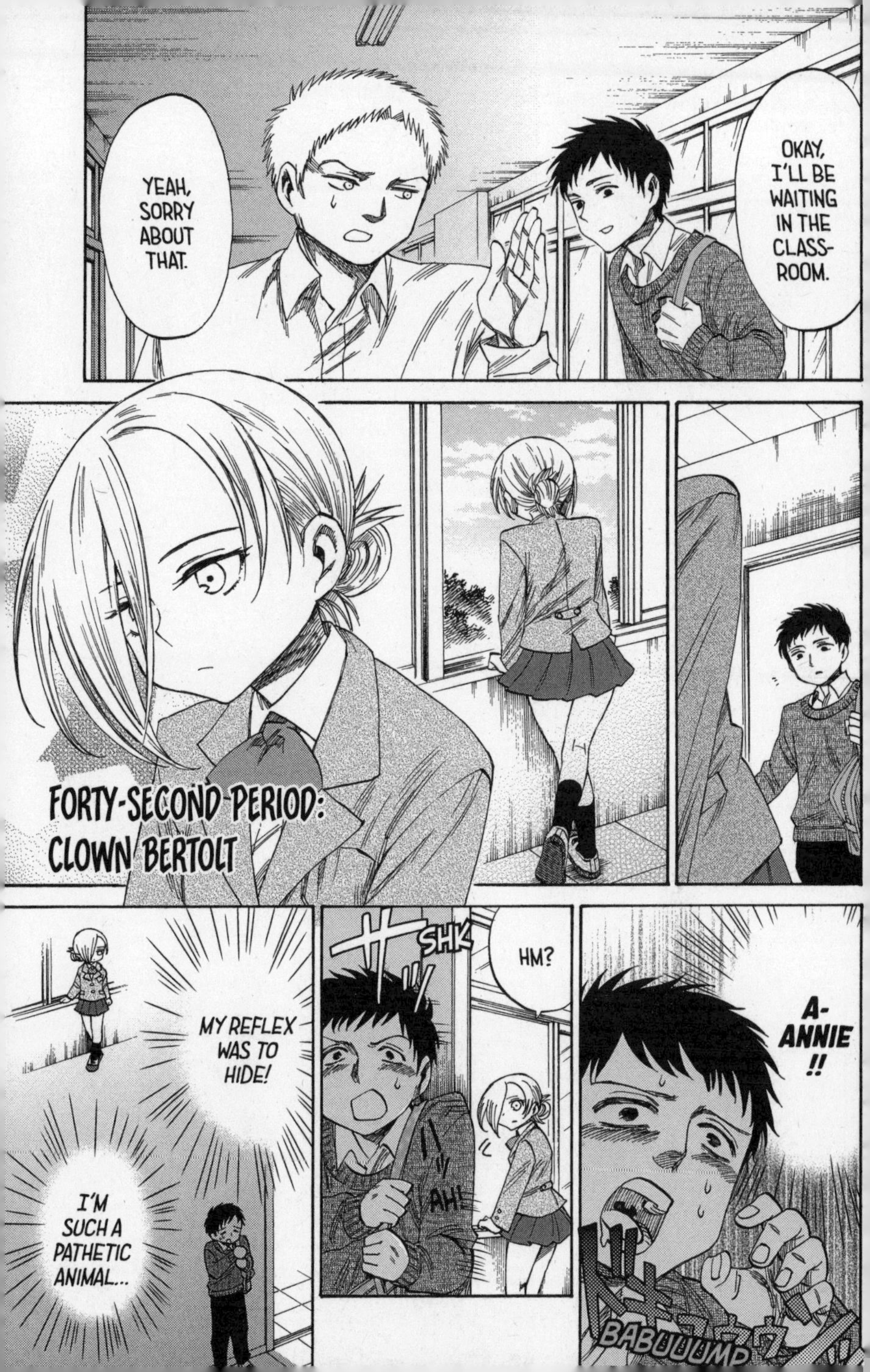
OKAY, I'LL BE WAITING IN THE CLASSROOM.
YEAH, SORRY ABOUT THAT.
FORTY-SECOND PERIOD: CLOWN BERTOLT
A-ANNIE!!
BABUUUMP
HM?
SHK
AH!
MY REFLEX WAS TO HIDE!
I'M SUCH A PATHETIC ANIMAL...

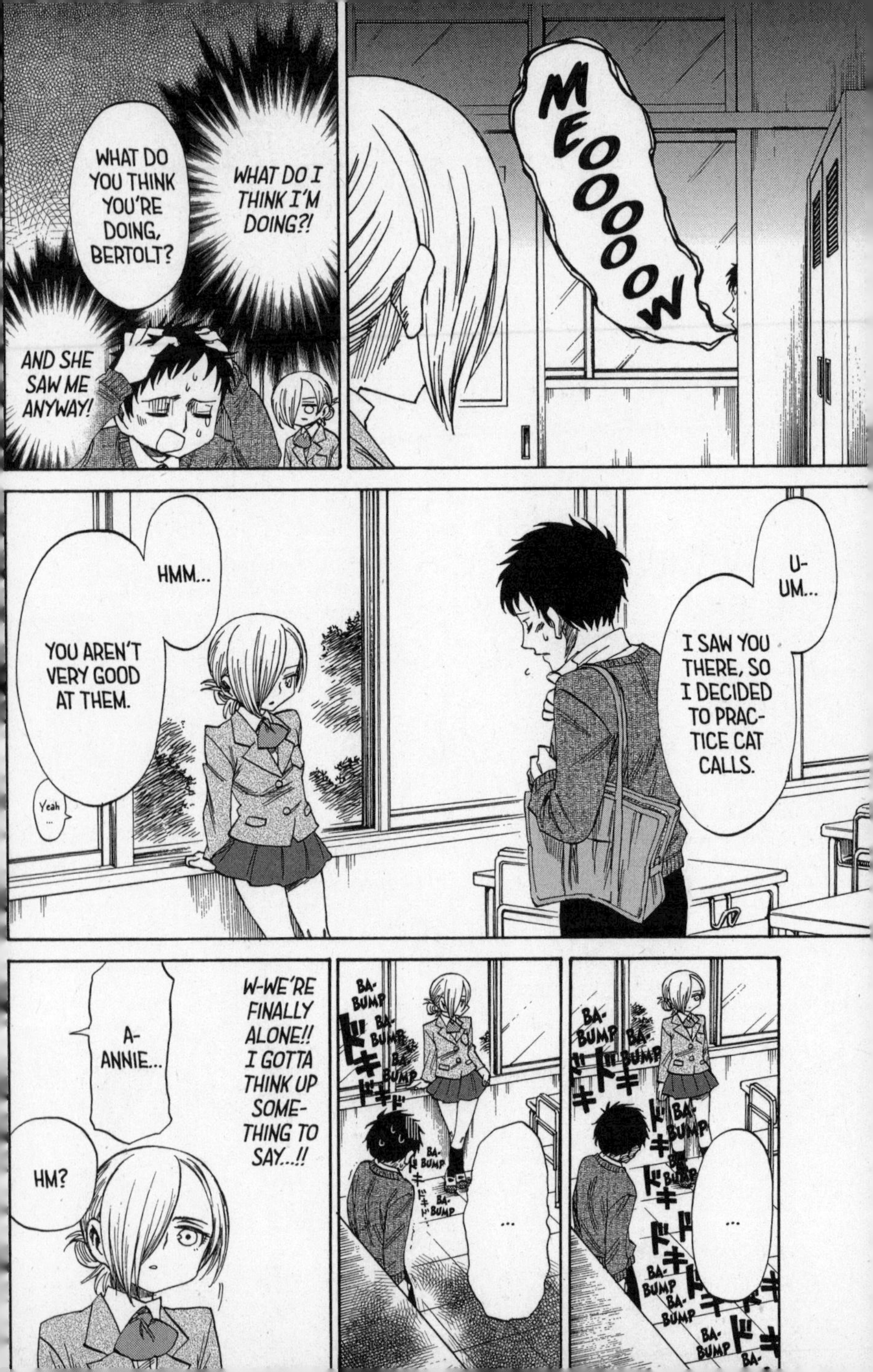
MEOOOOOW
WHAT DO I THINK I'M DOING?!
WHAT DO YOU THINK YOU'RE DOING, BERTOLT?
AND SHE SAW ME ANYWAY!
U-UM...
I SAW YOU THERE, SO I DECIDED TO PRACTICE CAT CALLS.
HMM...
YOU AREN'T VERY GOOD AT THEM.
Yeah...
BA-BUMP BA-BUMP BA-BUMP BA-BUMP BA-BUMP BA-BUMP
...
BA-BUMP BA-BUMP BA-BUMP BA-BUMP
...
W-WE'RE FINALLY ALONE!! I GOTTA THINK UP SOME-THING TO SAY...!!
A-ANNIE...
HM?

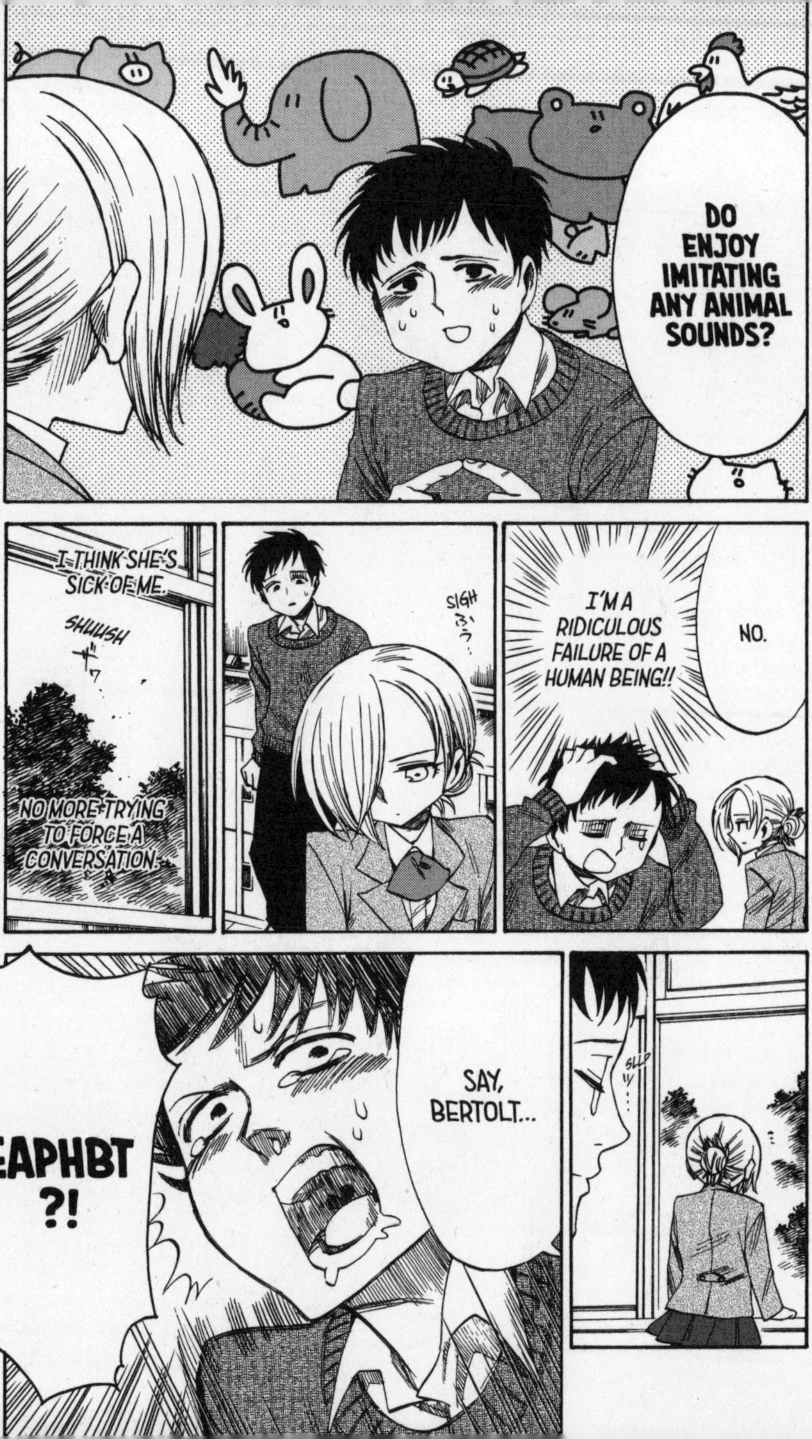
DO ENJOY IMITATING ANY ANIMAL SOUNDS?
NO.
I'M A RIDICULOUS FAILURE OF A HUMAN BEING!!
SIGH
I THINK SHE'S SICK OF ME.
SHUUSH
NO MORE TRYING TO FORCE A CONVERSATION.
SLLP
SAY, BERTOLT...
EAPHBT ?!

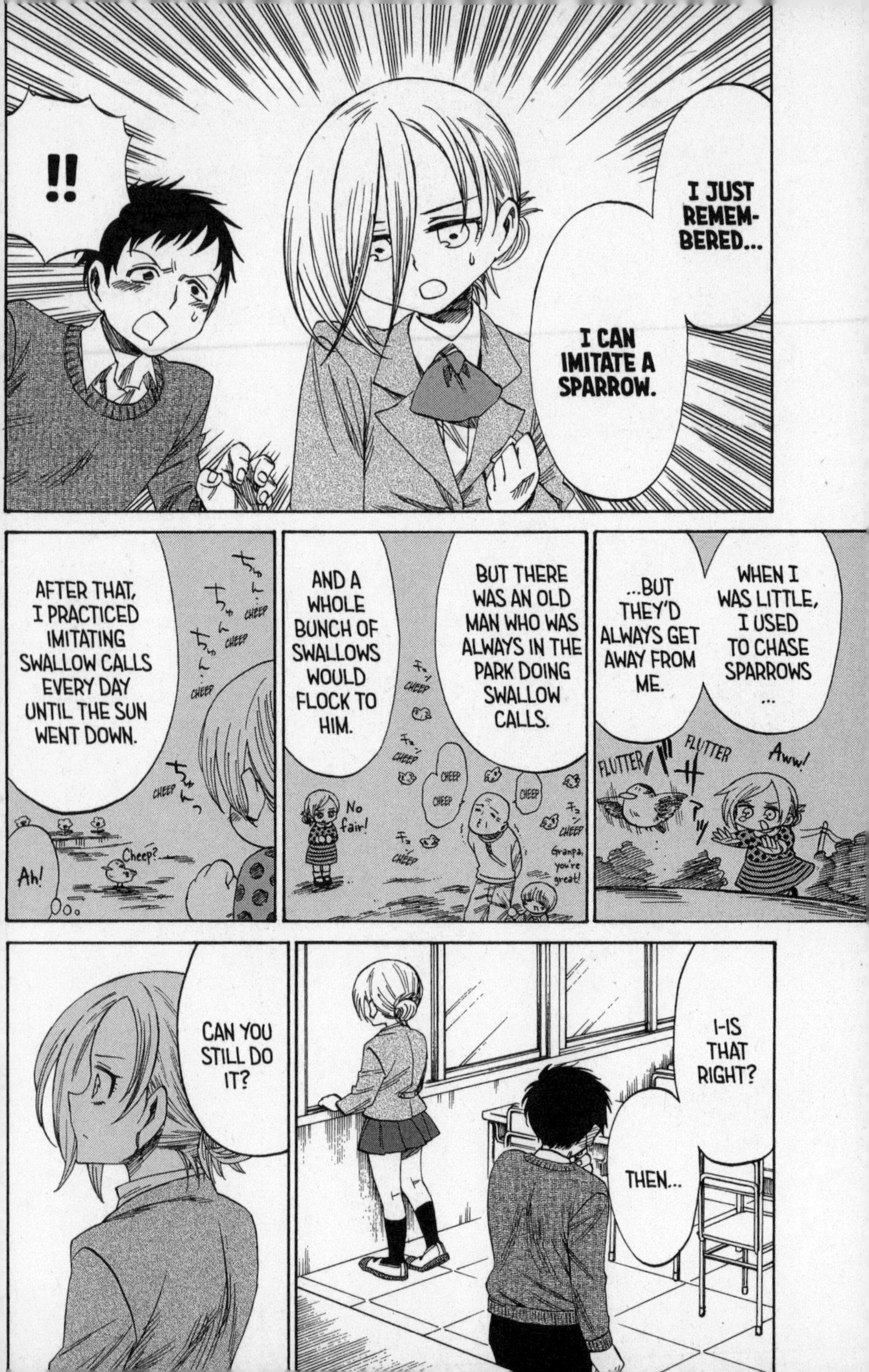
I JUST REMEMBERED...
I CAN IMITATE A SPARROW.
!!
WHEN I WAS LITTLE, I USED TO CHASE SPARROWS ...
...BUT THEY'D ALWAYS GET AWAY FROM ME.
FLUTTER
FLUTTER
Aww!
BUT THERE WAS AN OLD MAN WHO WAS ALWAYS IN THE PARK DOING SWALLOW CALLS.
AND A WHOLE BUNCH OF SWALLOWS WOULD FLOCK TO HIM.
CHEEP
CHEEP
CHEEP
CHEEP
CHEEP
CHEEP
CHEEP
Granpa, you're great!
No fair!
AFTER THAT, I PRACTICED IMITATING SWALLOW CALLS EVERY DAY UNTIL THE SUN WENT DOWN.
CHEEP
CHEEP
CHEEP
CHEEP
Cheep?
Ah!
I-IS THAT RIGHT?
THEN...
CAN YOU STILL DO IT?

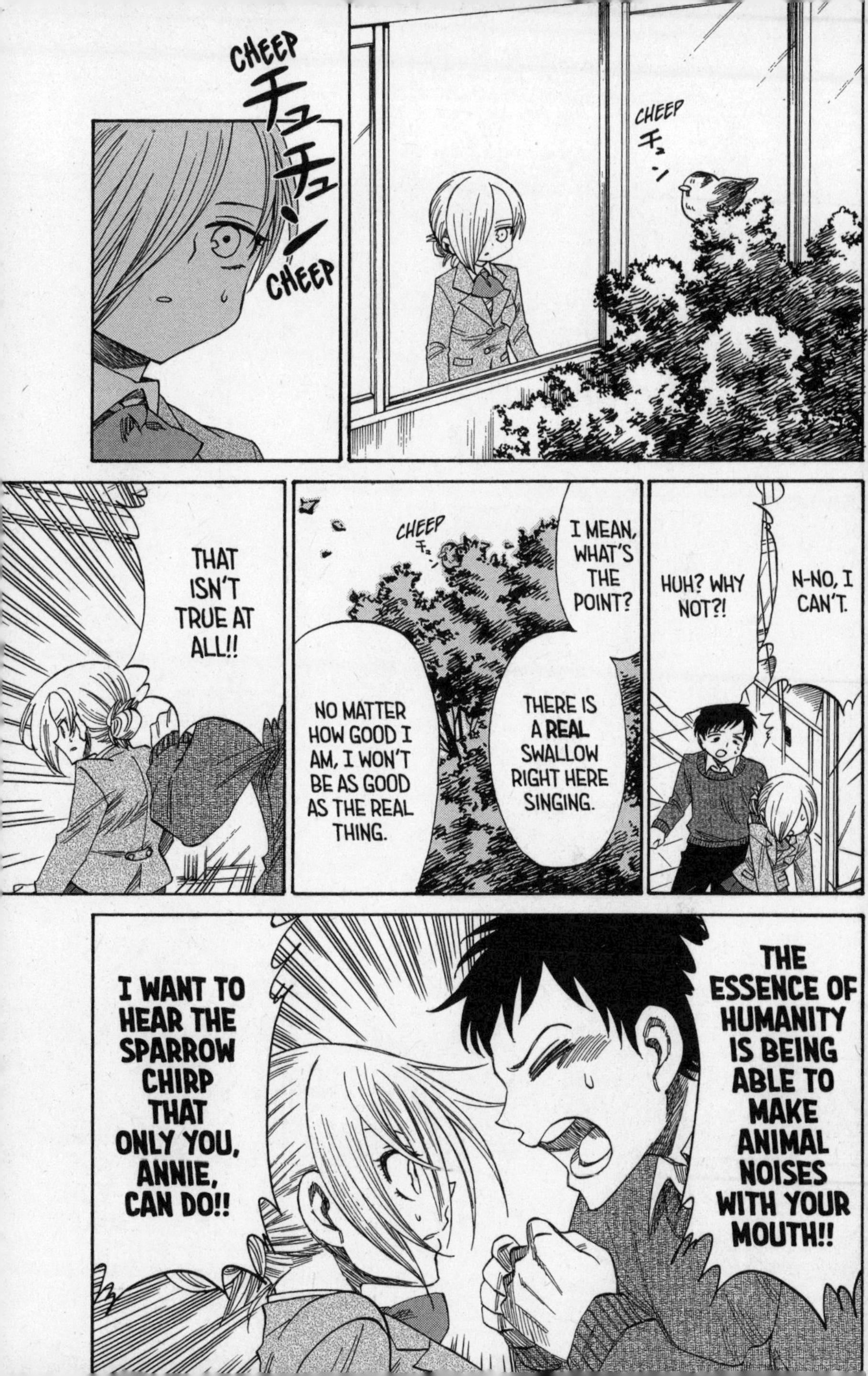
CHEEP
チュン
CHEEP
チュチュン
CHEEP
N-NO, I CAN'T.
HUH? WHY NOT?!
I MEAN, WHAT'S THE POINT?
CHEEP
チュン
THERE IS A REAL SWALLOW RIGHT HERE SINGING.
NO MATTER HOW GOOD I AM, I WON'T BE AS GOOD AS THE REAL THING.
THAT ISN'T TRUE AT ALL!!
THE ESSENCE OF HUMANITY IS BEING ABLE TO MAKE ANIMAL NOISES WITH YOUR MOUTH!!
I WANT TO HEAR THE SPARROW CHIRP THAT ONLY YOU, ANNIE, CAN DO!!

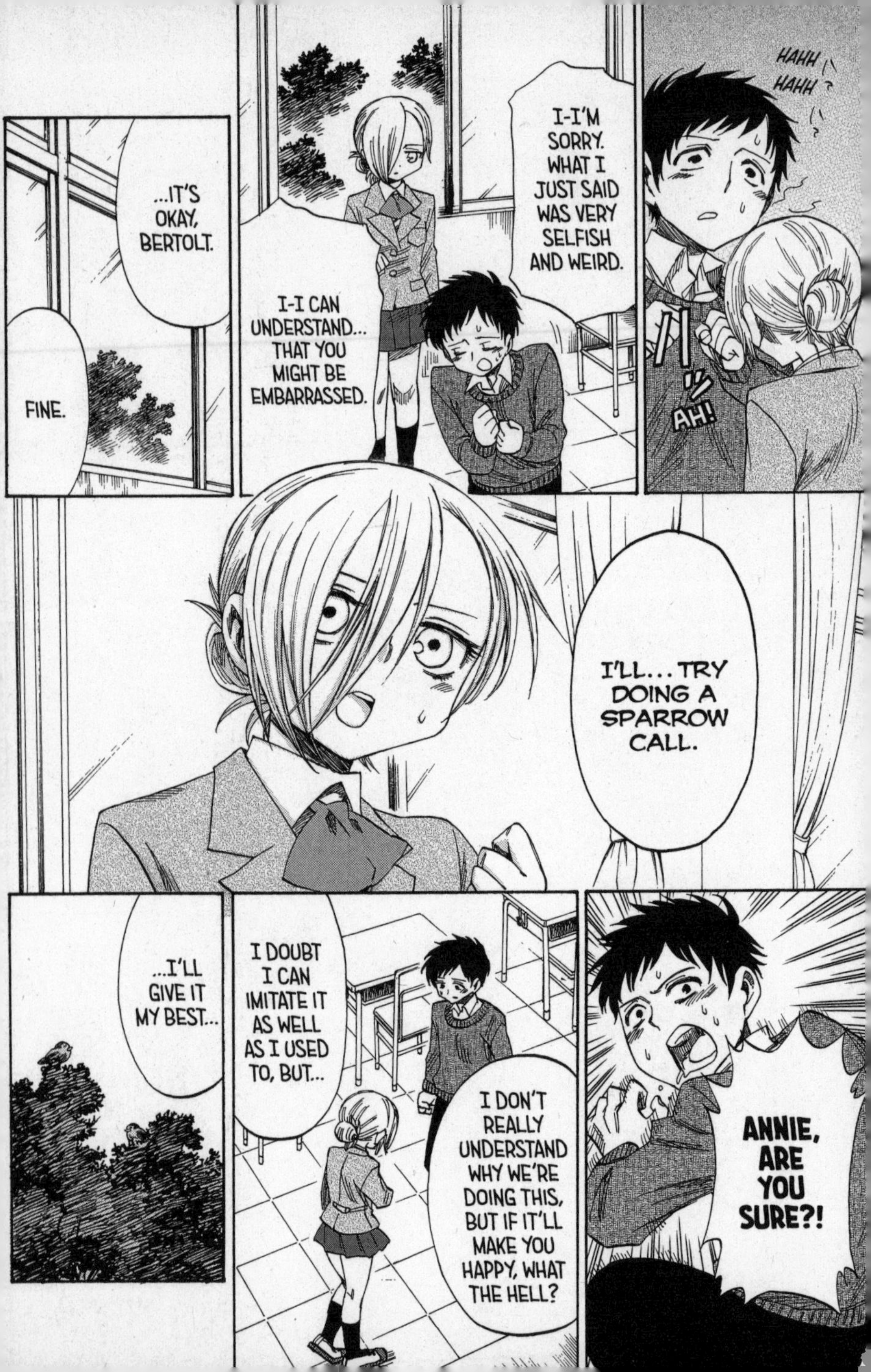
HAHH HAHH
AH!
I-I'M SORRY. WHAT I JUST SAID WAS VERY SELFISH AND WEIRD.
I-I CAN UNDERSTAND... THAT YOU MIGHT BE EMBARRASSED.
...IT'S OKAY, BERTOLT.
FINE.
I'LL... TRY DOING A SPARROW CALL.
ANNIE, ARE YOU SURE?!
I DOUBT I CAN IMITATE IT AS WELL AS I USED TO, BUT...
I DON'T REALLY UNDERSTAND WHY WE'RE DOING THIS, BUT IF IT'LL MAKE YOU HAPPY, WHAT THE HELL?
...I'LL GIVE IT MY BEST...

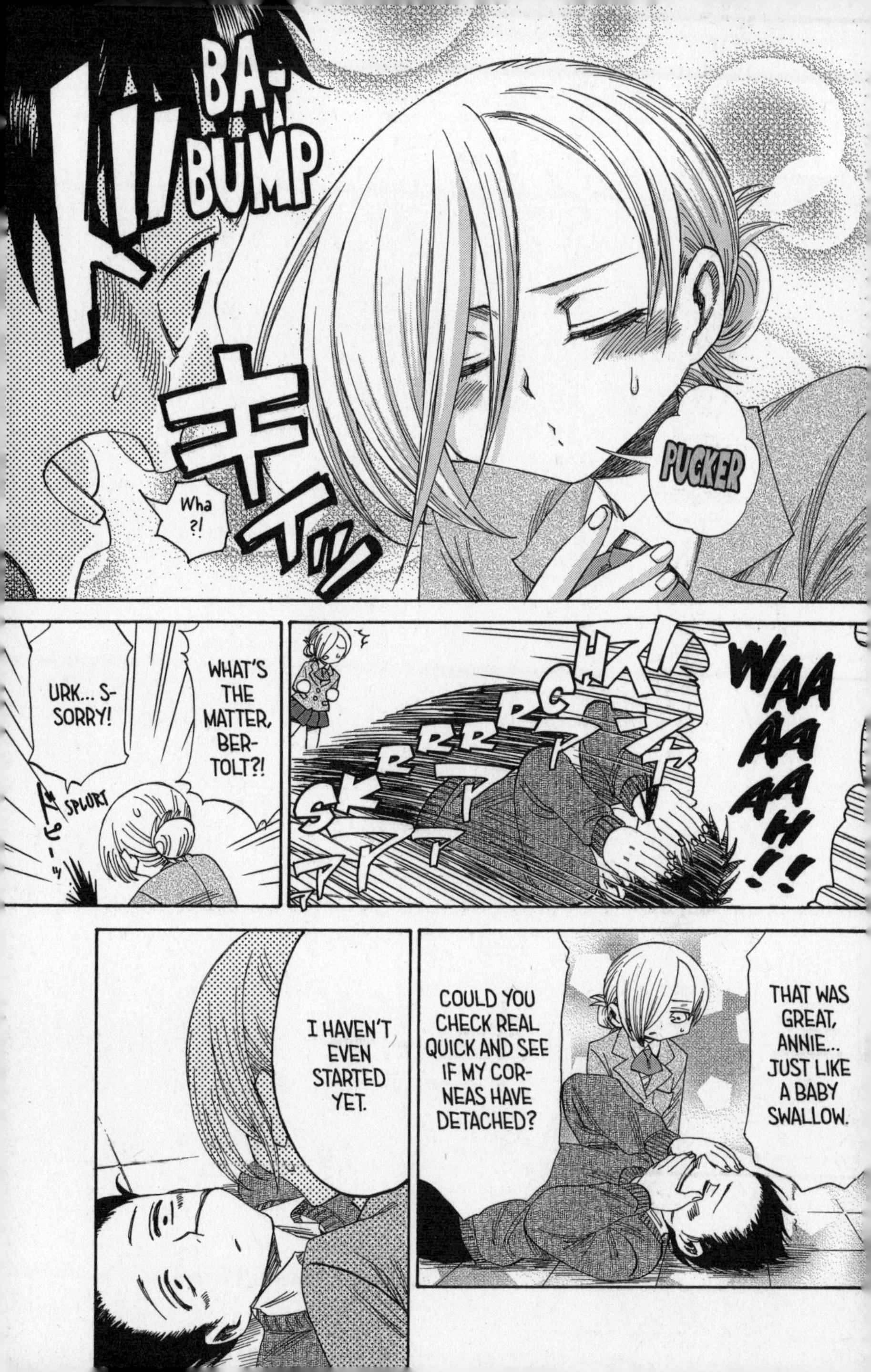
BA-BUMP
PUCKER
Wha ?!
WAAAAAAAH!!
SKRRRRCH!!
WHAT'S THE MATTER, BERTOLT?!
URK... S-SORRY!
SPLURT
THAT WAS GREAT, ANNIE... JUST LIKE A BABY SWALLOW.
COULD YOU CHECK REAL QUICK AND SEE IF MY CORNEAS HAVE DETACHED?
I HAVEN'T EVEN STARTED YET.

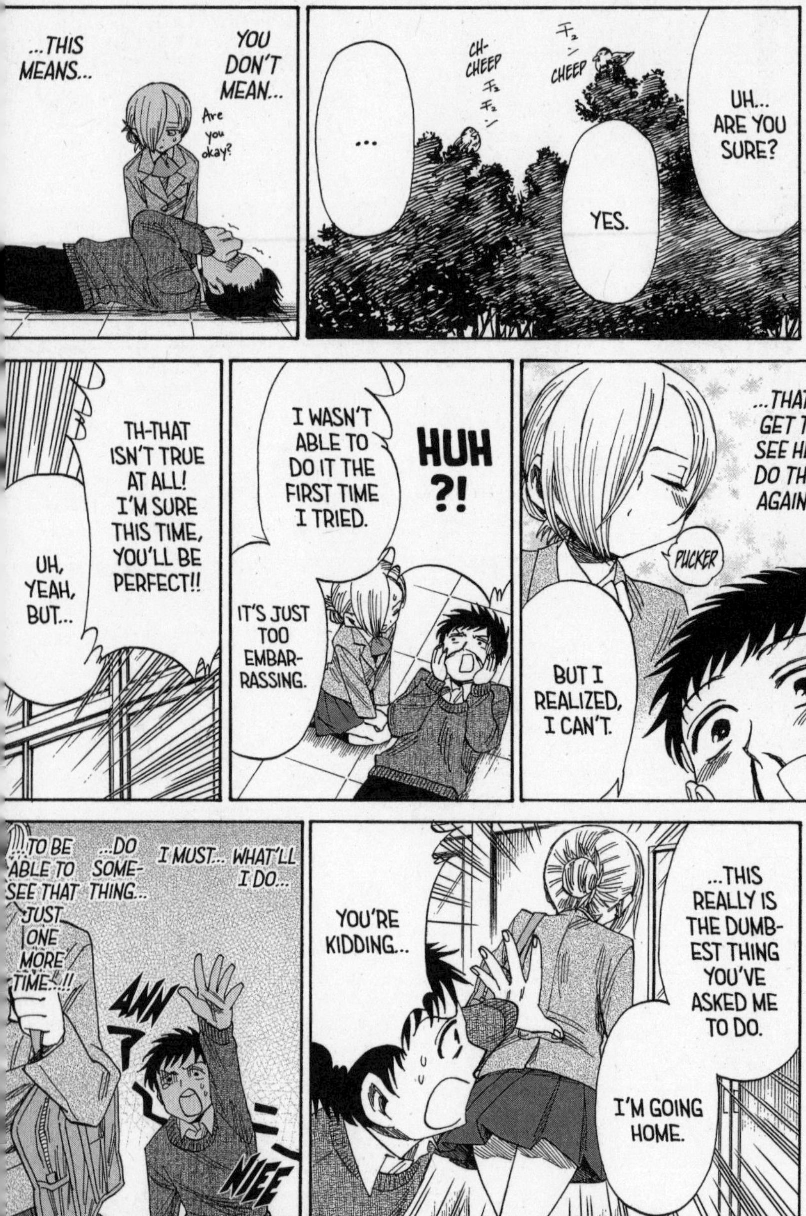
UH... ARE YOU SURE?
YES.
CHEEP
CH-CHEEP
...
YOU DON'T MEAN...
...THIS MEANS...
Are you okay?
...THAT I GET TO SEE HER DO THAT AGAIN?!
PUCKER
BUT I REALIZED, I CAN'T.
HUH ?!
I WASN'T ABLE TO DO IT THE FIRST TIME I TRIED.
IT'S JUST TOO EMBARRASSING.
TH-THAT ISN'T TRUE AT ALL! I'M SURE THIS TIME, YOU'LL BE PERFECT!!
UH, YEAH, BUT...
...THIS REALLY IS THE DUMBEST THING YOU'VE ASKED ME TO DO.
YOU'RE KIDDING...
I'M GOING HOME.
WHAT'LL I DO...
I MUST...
...DO SOMETHING...
...TO BE ABLE TO SEE THAT JUST ONE MORE TIME...!!
ANN
NIEE

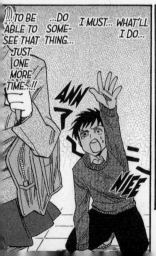

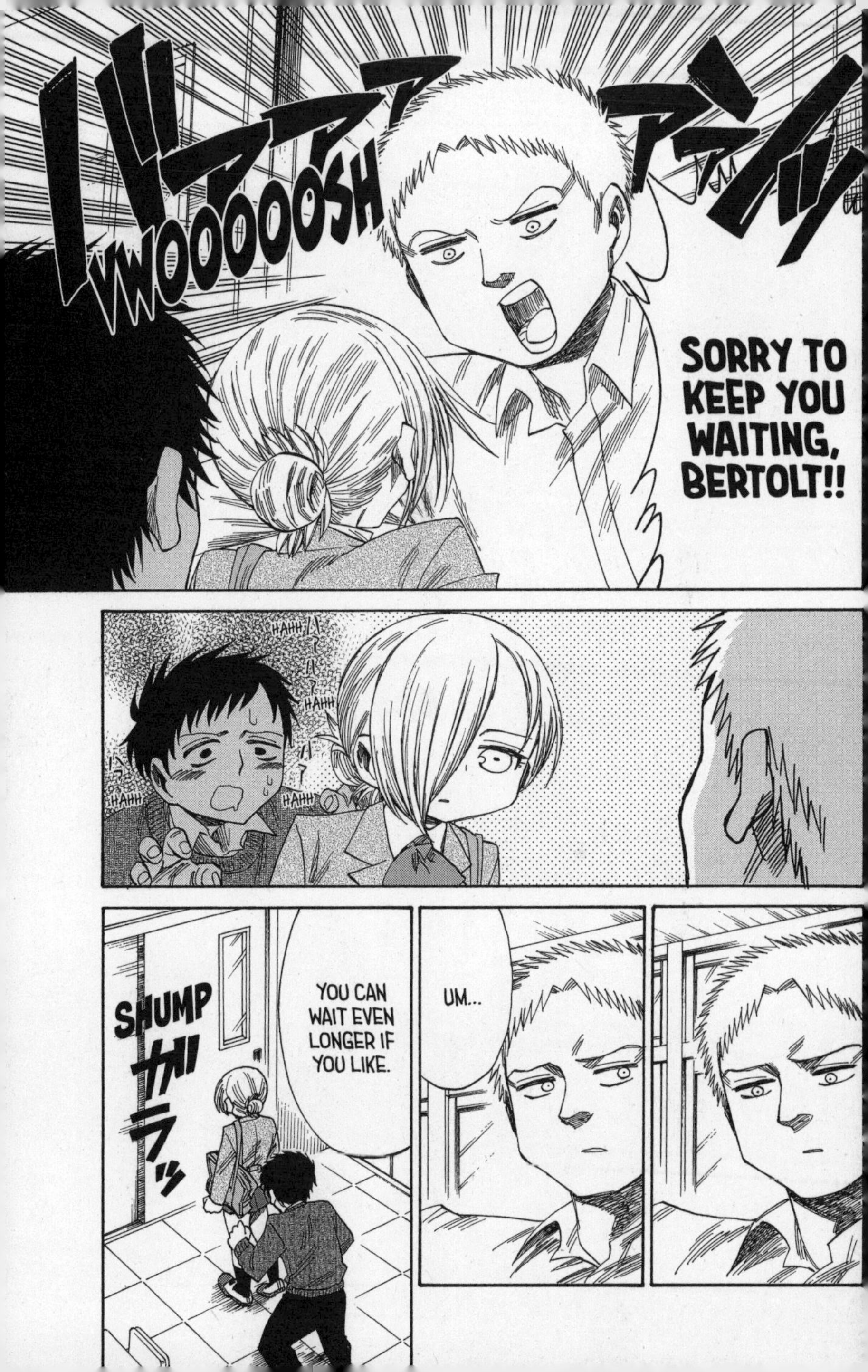
WOOOOOSH
SORRY TO KEEP YOU WAITING, BERTOLT!!
HAHH
HAHH
HAHH
HAHH
UM...
YOU CAN WAIT EVEN LONGER IF YOU LIKE.
SHUMP

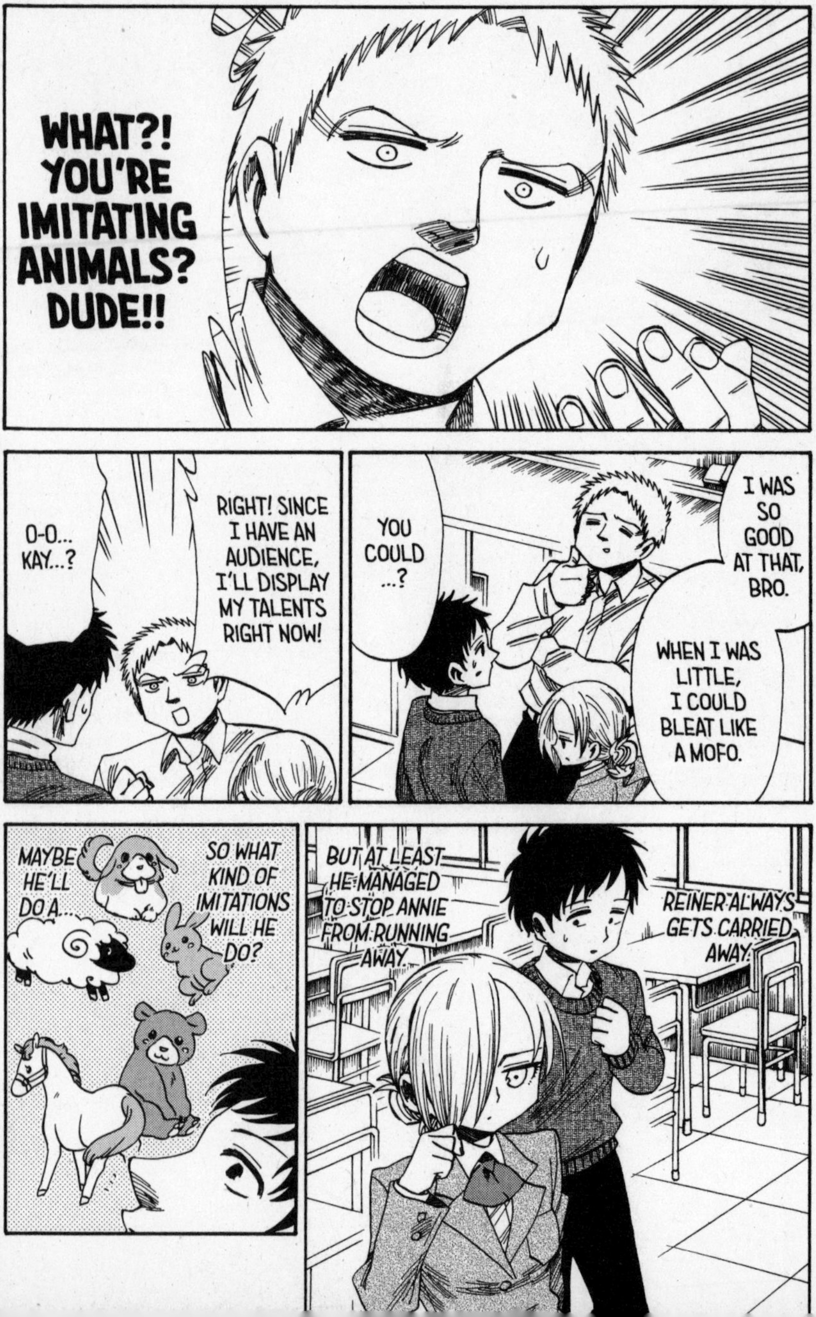
WHAT?! YOU'RE IMITATING ANIMALS? DUDE!!
I WAS SO GOOD AT THAT, BRO.
WHEN I WAS LITTLE, I COULD BLEAT LIKE A MOFO.
YOU COULD ...?
RIGHT! SINCE I HAVE AN AUDIENCE, I'LL DISPLAY MY TALENTS RIGHT NOW!
O-O... KAY...?
REINER ALWAYS GETS CARRIED AWAY.
BUT AT LEAST HE MANAGED TO STOP ANNIE FROM RUNNING AWAY.
SO WHAT KIND OF IMITATIONS WILL HE DO?
MAYBE HE'LL DO A...

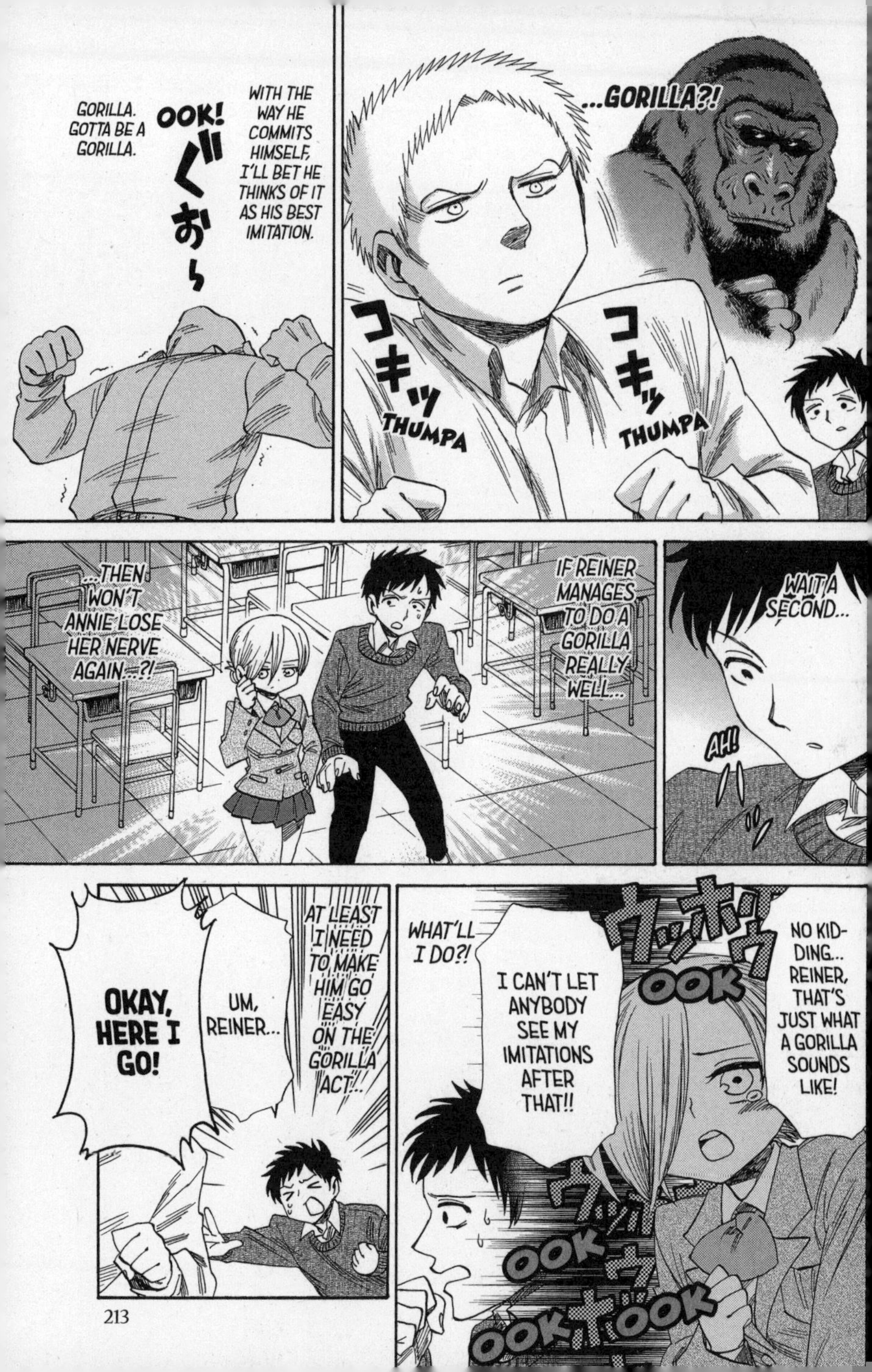
...GORILLA?!
コキッ
THUMPA
コキッ
THUMPA
WITH THE WAY HE COMMITS HIMSELF, I'LL BET HE THINKS OF IT AS HIS BEST IMITATION.
OOK!
ぐぉら
GORILLA. GOTTA BE A GORILLA.
WAIT A SECOND...
AH!
IF REINER MANAGES TO DO A GORILLA REALLY WELL...
...THEN WON'T ANNIE LOSE HER NERVE AGAIN...?!
NO KIDDING... REINER, THAT'S JUST WHAT A GORILLA SOUNDS LIKE!
OOK
WHAT'LL I DO?!
I CAN'T LET ANYBODY SEE MY IMITATIONS AFTER THAT!!
OOK
OOK
OOK
AT LEAST I NEED TO MAKE HIM GO EASY ON THE GORILLA ACT...
UM, REINER...
OKAY, HERE I GO!

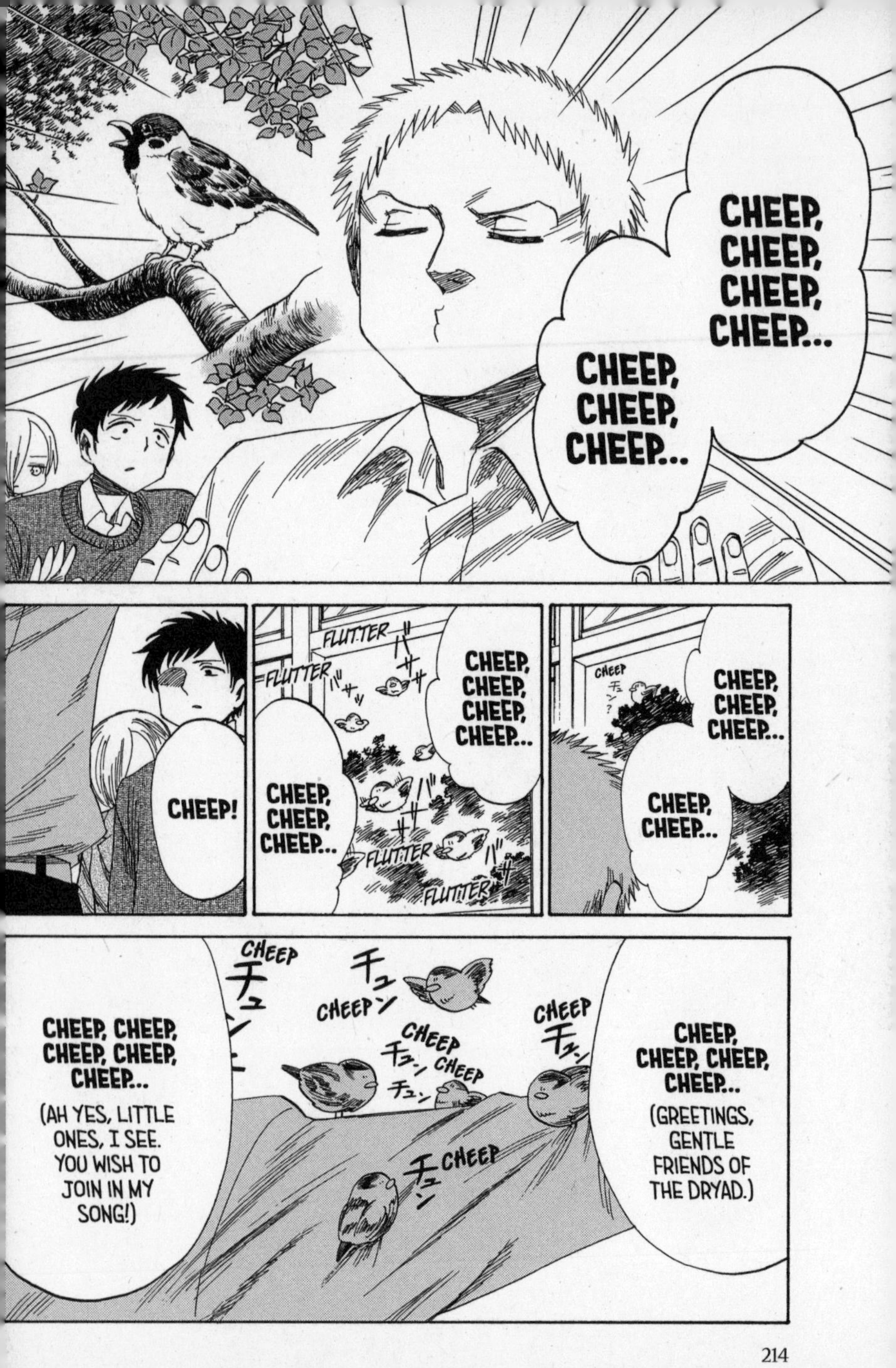
CHEEP, CHEEP, CHEEP, CHEEP...
CHEEP, CHEEP, CHEEP...
CHEEP
CHEEP, CHEEP, CHEEP...
CHEEP, CHEEP...
FLUTTER
FLUTTER
CHEEP, CHEEP, CHEEP, CHEEP...
CHEEP, CHEEP, CHEEP...
FLUTTER
FLUTTER
CHEEP!
CHEEP, CHEEP, CHEEP, CHEEP... (GREETINGS, GENTLE FRIENDS OF THE DRYAD.)
CHEEP
CHEEP
CHEEP
CHEEP
CHEEP
CHEEP
CHEEP, CHEEP, CHEEP, CHEEP, CHEEP... (AH YES, LITTLE ONES, I SEE. YOU WISH TO JOIN IN MY SONG!)

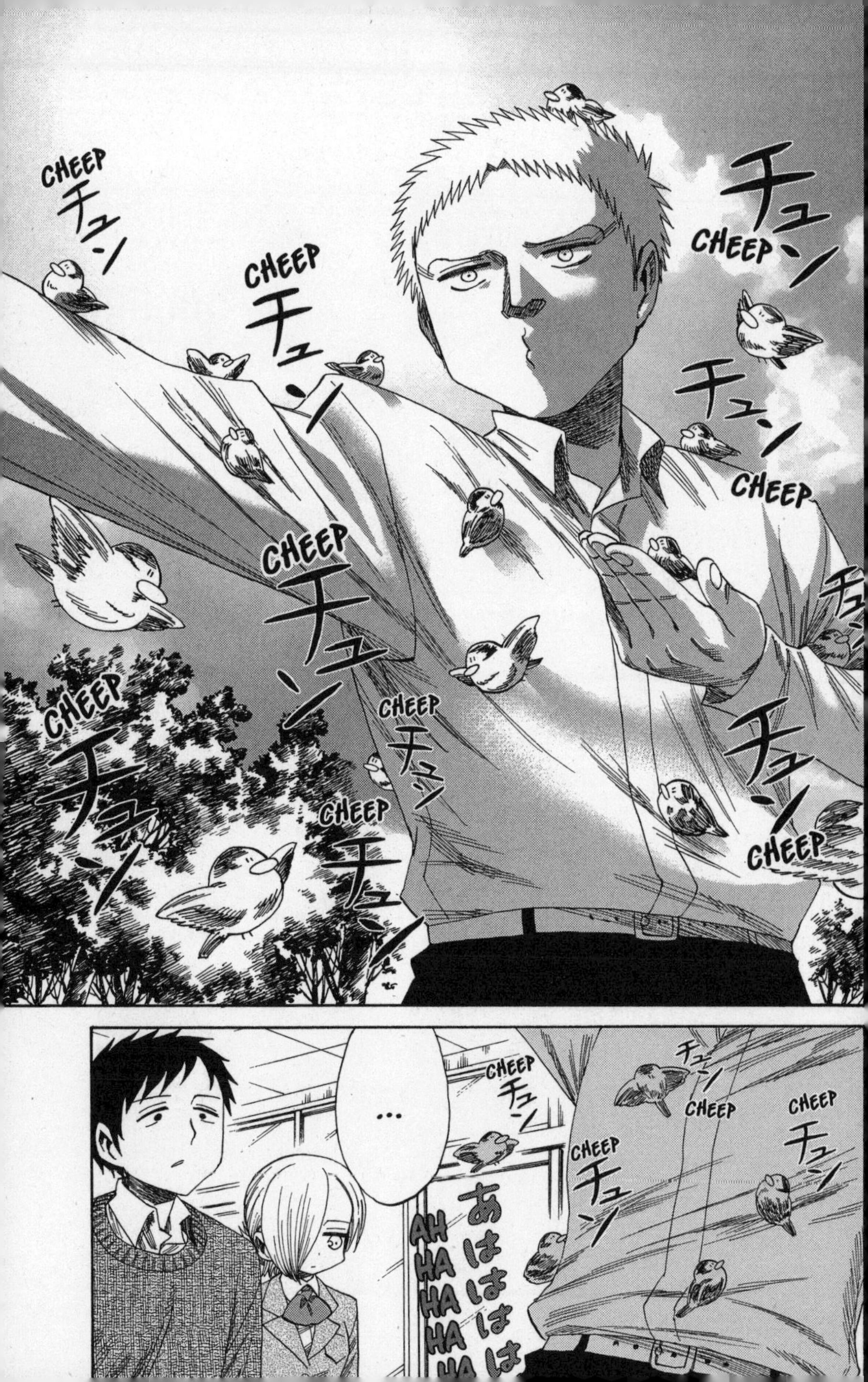
チュン
CHEEP
チュン
CHEEP
チュン
チュン
CHEEP
CHEEP
チュン
CHEEP
チュン
CHEEP
チュン
CHEEP
チュン
CHEEP
チュン
CHEEP
チュン
CHEEP
チュン
CHEEP
チュン
CHEEP
チュン
CHEEP
チュン
CHEEP
チュン
CHEEP
チュン
あはははは
AH HA HA HA HA HA
...

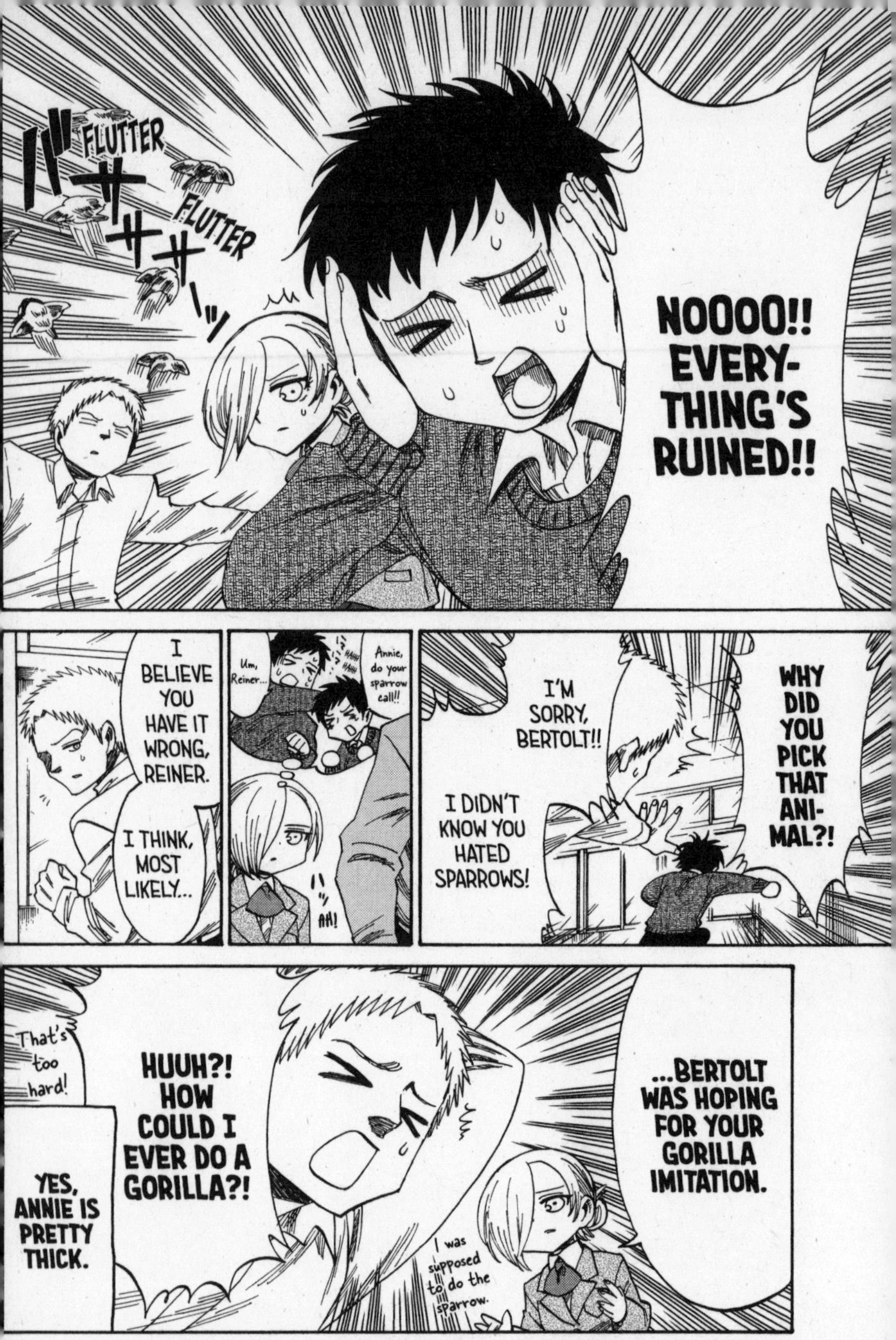
FLUTTER
FLUTTER
NOOOO!! EVERY-THING'S RUINED!!
WHY DID YOU PICK THAT ANI-MAL?!
I'M SORRY, BERTOLT!!
I DIDN'T KNOW YOU HATED SPARROWS!
Annie, do your sparrow call!!
Um, Reiner...
AH!
I BELIEVE YOU HAVE IT WRONG, REINER.
I THINK, MOST LIKELY...
...BERTOLT WAS HOPING FOR YOUR GORILLA IMITATION.
HUUH?! HOW COULD I EVER DO A GORILLA?!
I was supposed to do the sparrow.
That's too hard!
YES, ANNIE IS PRETTY THICK.

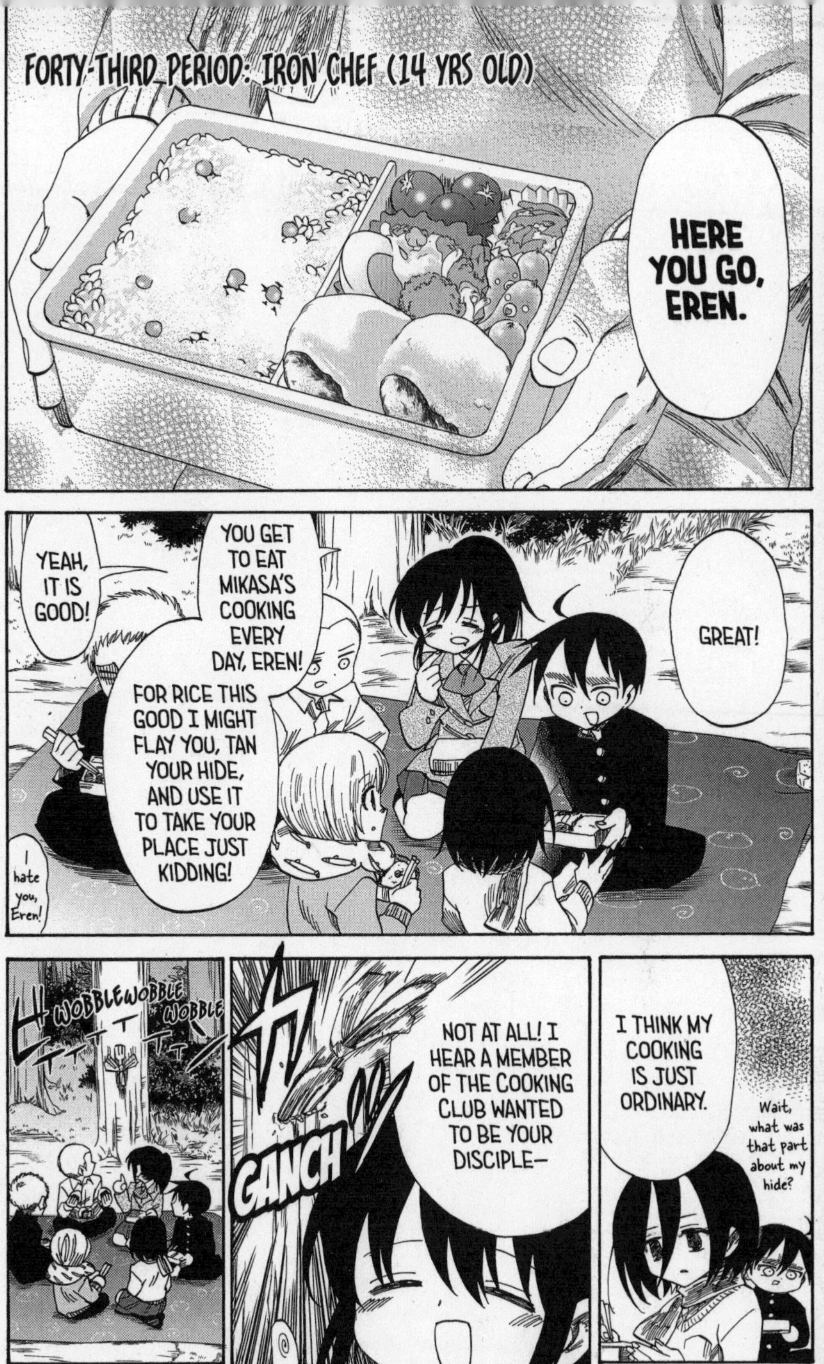
FORTY-THIRD PERIOD: IRON CHEF (14 YRS OLD)
HERE YOU GO, EREN.
GREAT!
YOU GET TO EAT MIKASA'S COOKING EVERY DAY, EREN!
YEAH, IT IS GOOD!
FOR RICE THIS GOOD I MIGHT FLAY YOU, TAN YOUR HIDE, AND USE IT TO TAKE YOUR PLACE JUST KIDDING!
I hate you, Eren!
I THINK MY COOKING IS JUST ORDINARY.
Wait, what was that part about my hide?
NOT AT ALL! I HEAR A MEMBER OF THE COOKING CLUB WANTED TO BE YOUR DISCIPLE–
GANCH
WOBBLEWOBBLE WOBBLE

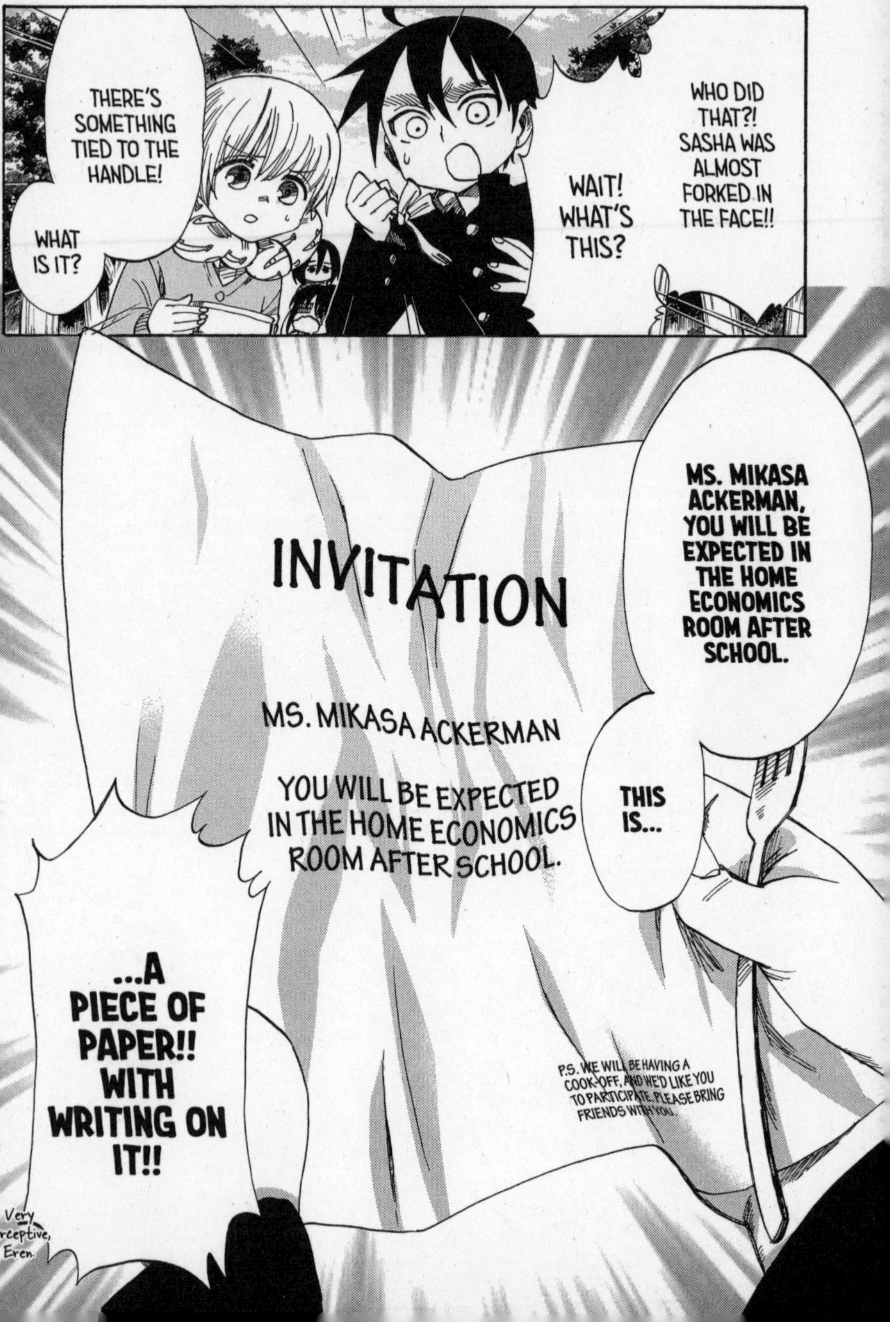
WHO DID THAT?! SASHA WAS ALMOST FORKED IN THE FACE!!
WAIT! WHAT'S THIS?
THERE'S SOMETHING TIED TO THE HANDLE!
WHAT IS IT?
MS. MIKASA ACKERMAN, YOU WILL BE EXPECTED IN THE HOME ECONOMICS ROOM AFTER SCHOOL.
THIS IS...
INVITATION
MS. MIKASA ACKERMAN
YOU WILL BE EXPECTED IN THE HOME ECONOMICS ROOM AFTER SCHOOL.
P.S. WE WILL BE HAVING A COOK-OFF, AND WE'D LIKE YOU TO PARTICIPATE. PLEASE BRING FRIENDS WITH YOU.
...A PIECE OF PAPER!! WITH WRITING ON IT!!
Very perceptive, Eren.

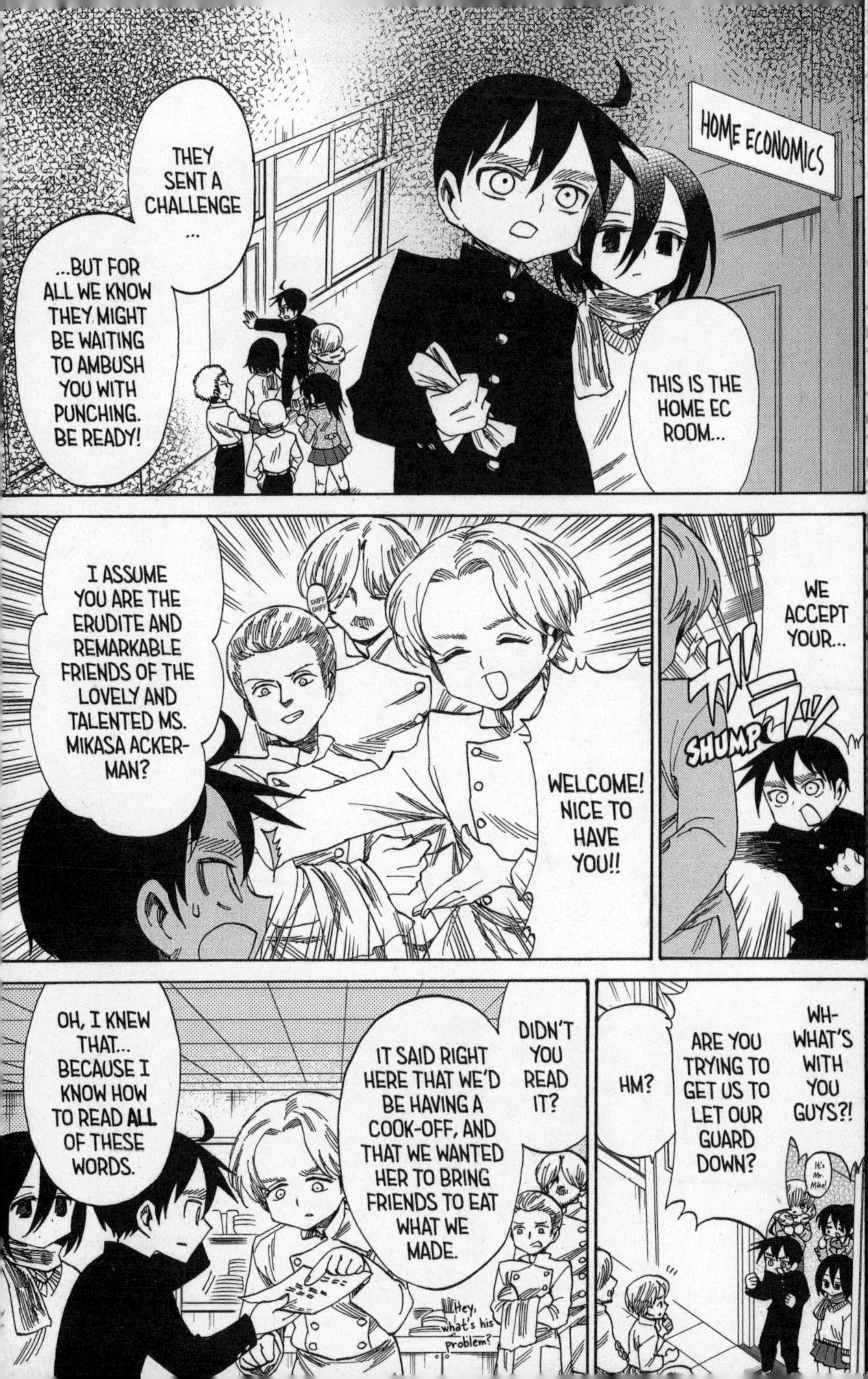
HOME ECONOMICS
THIS IS THE HOME EC ROOM...
THEY SENT A CHALLENGE ...
...BUT FOR ALL WE KNOW THEY MIGHT BE WAITING TO AMBUSH YOU WITH PUNCHING. BE READY!
WE ACCEPT YOUR...
SHUMP
WELCOME! NICE TO HAVE YOU!!
SNIFF SNIFF
I ASSUME YOU ARE THE ERUDITE AND REMARKABLE FRIENDS OF THE LOVELY AND TALENTED MS. MIKASA ACKER-MAN?
WH- WHAT'S WITH YOU GUYS?!
It's Mr. Mike!
ARE YOU TRYING TO GET US TO LET OUR GUARD DOWN?
HM?
DIDN'T YOU READ IT?
IT SAID RIGHT HERE THAT WE'D BE HAVING A COOK-OFF, AND THAT WE WANTED HER TO BRING FRIENDS TO EAT WHAT WE MADE.
Hey, what's his problem?
OH, I KNEW THAT... BECAUSE I KNOW HOW TO READ ALL OF THESE WORDS.

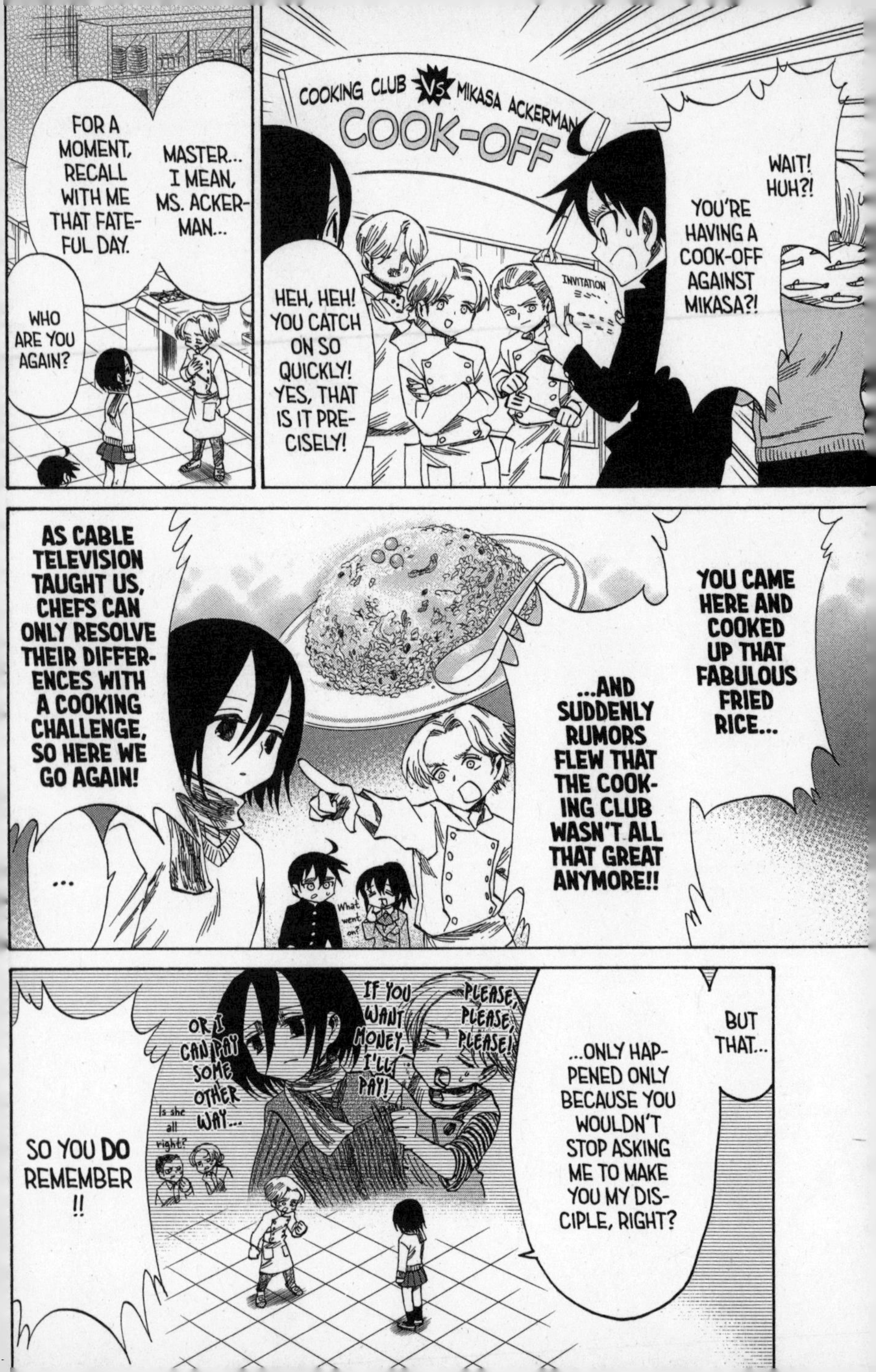
WAIT! HUH?!
YOU'RE HAVING A COOK-OFF AGAINST MIKASA?!
COOKING CLUB VS MIKASA ACKERMAN COOK-OFF
INVITATION
HEH, HEH! YOU CATCH ON SO QUICKLY! YES, THAT IS IT PRECISELY!
MASTER... I MEAN, MS. ACKERMAN...
FOR A MOMENT, RECALL WITH ME THAT FATEFUL DAY.
WHO ARE YOU AGAIN?
YOU CAME HERE AND COOKED UP THAT FABULOUS FRIED RICE...
...AND SUDDENLY RUMORS FLEW THAT THE COOKING CLUB WASN'T ALL THAT GREAT ANYMORE!!
AS CABLE TELEVISION TAUGHT US, CHEFS CAN ONLY RESOLVE THEIR DIFFERENCES WITH A COOKING CHALLENGE, SO HERE WE GO AGAIN!
What went on?
...
BUT THAT...
...ONLY HAPPENED ONLY BECAUSE YOU WOULDN'T STOP ASKING ME TO MAKE YOU MY DISCIPLE, RIGHT?
PLEASE, PLEASE, PLEASE!
IF YOU WANT MONEY, I'LL PAY!
OR I CAN PAY SOME OTHER WAY...
Is she all right?
SO YOU DO REMEMBER!!

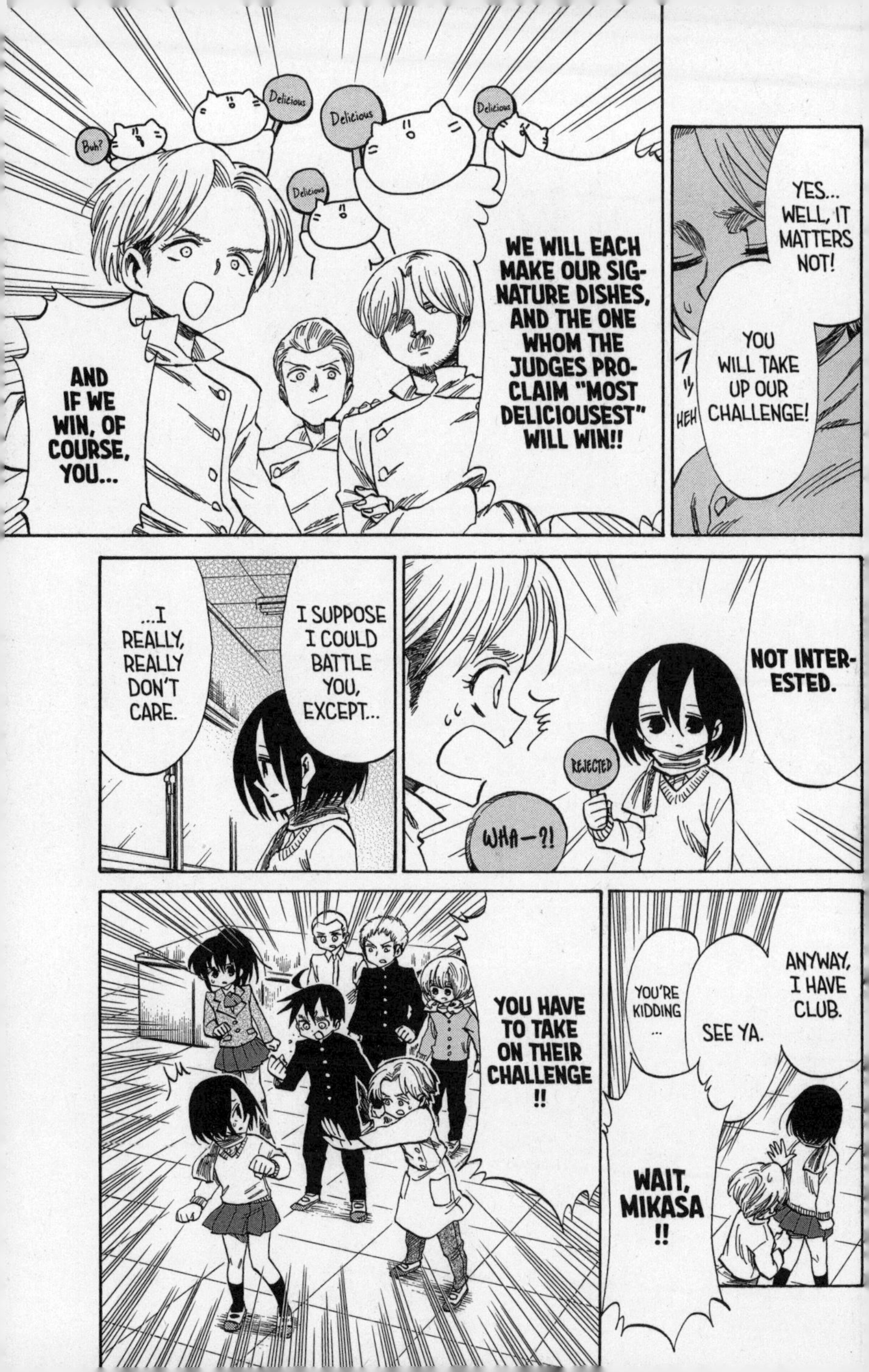
YES... WELL, IT MATTERS NOT!
YOU WILL TAKE UP OUR CHALLENGE!
HEH
Delicious
Delicious
Delicious
Buh?
Delicious
WE WILL EACH MAKE OUR SIGNATURE DISHES, AND THE ONE WHOM THE JUDGES PROCLAIM "MOST DELICIOUSEST" WILL WIN!!
AND IF WE WIN, OF COURSE, YOU...
NOT INTERESTED.
REJECTED
WHA—?!
I SUPPOSE I COULD BATTLE YOU, EXCEPT...
...I REALLY, REALLY DON'T CARE.
ANYWAY, I HAVE CLUB.
SEE YA.
YOU'RE KIDDING ...
WAIT, MIKASA!!
YOU HAVE TO TAKE ON THEIR CHALLENGE!!

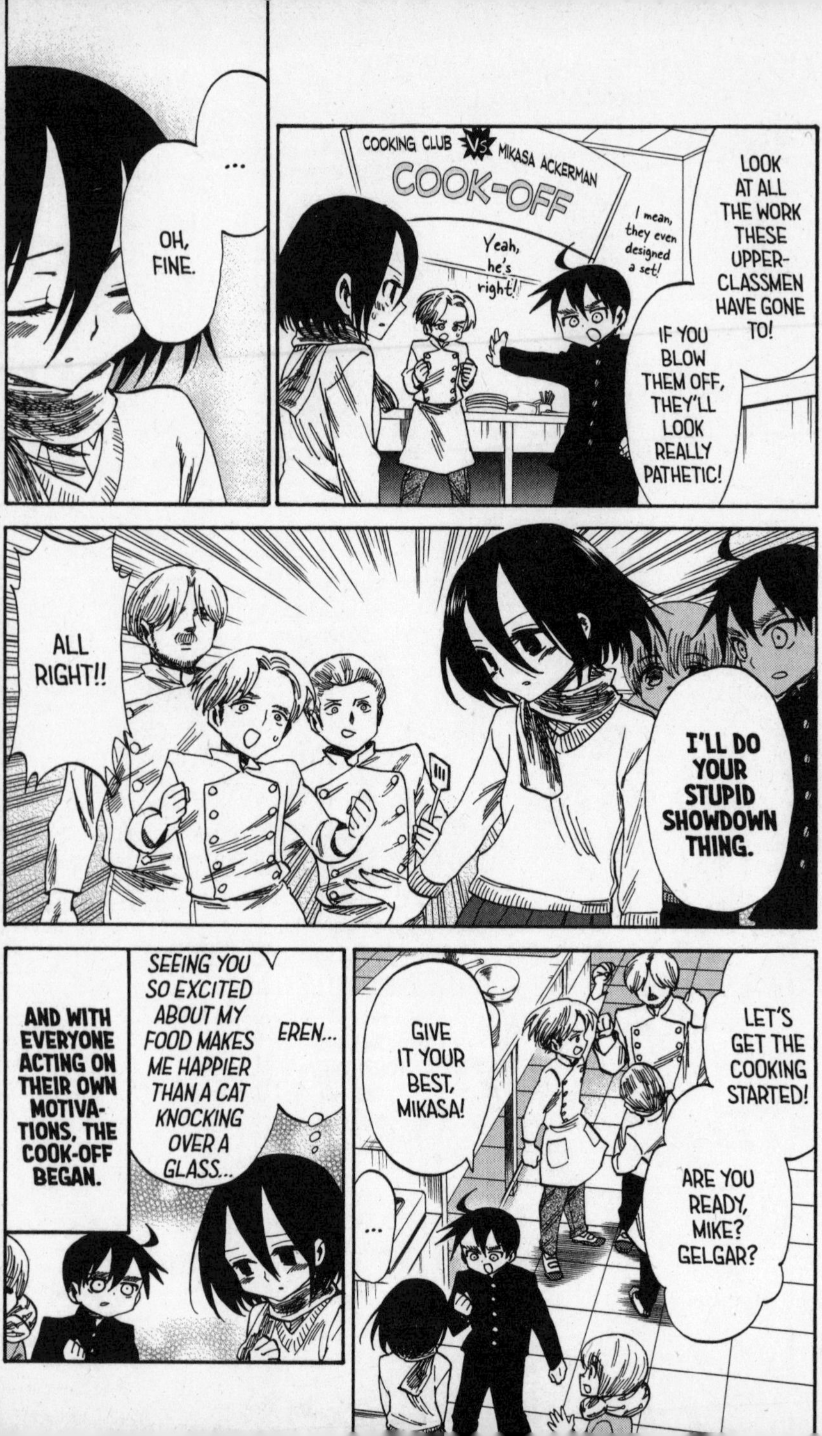
COOKING CLUB VS MIKASA ACKERMAN
COOK-OFF
LOOK AT ALL THE WORK THESE UPPER-CLASSMEN HAVE GONE TO!
IF YOU BLOW THEM OFF, THEY'LL LOOK REALLY PATHETIC!
I mean, they even designed a set!
Yeah, he's right!
...
OH, FINE.
I'LL DO YOUR STUPID SHOWDOWN THING.
ALL RIGHT!!
LET'S GET THE COOKING STARTED!
ARE YOU READY, MIKE? GELGAR?
GIVE IT YOUR BEST, MIKASA!
...
EREN...
SEEING YOU SO EXCITED ABOUT MY FOOD MAKES ME HAPPIER THAN A CAT KNOCKING OVER A GLASS...
AND WITH EVERYONE ACTING ON THEIR OWN MOTIVA-TIONS, THE COOK-OFF BEGAN.

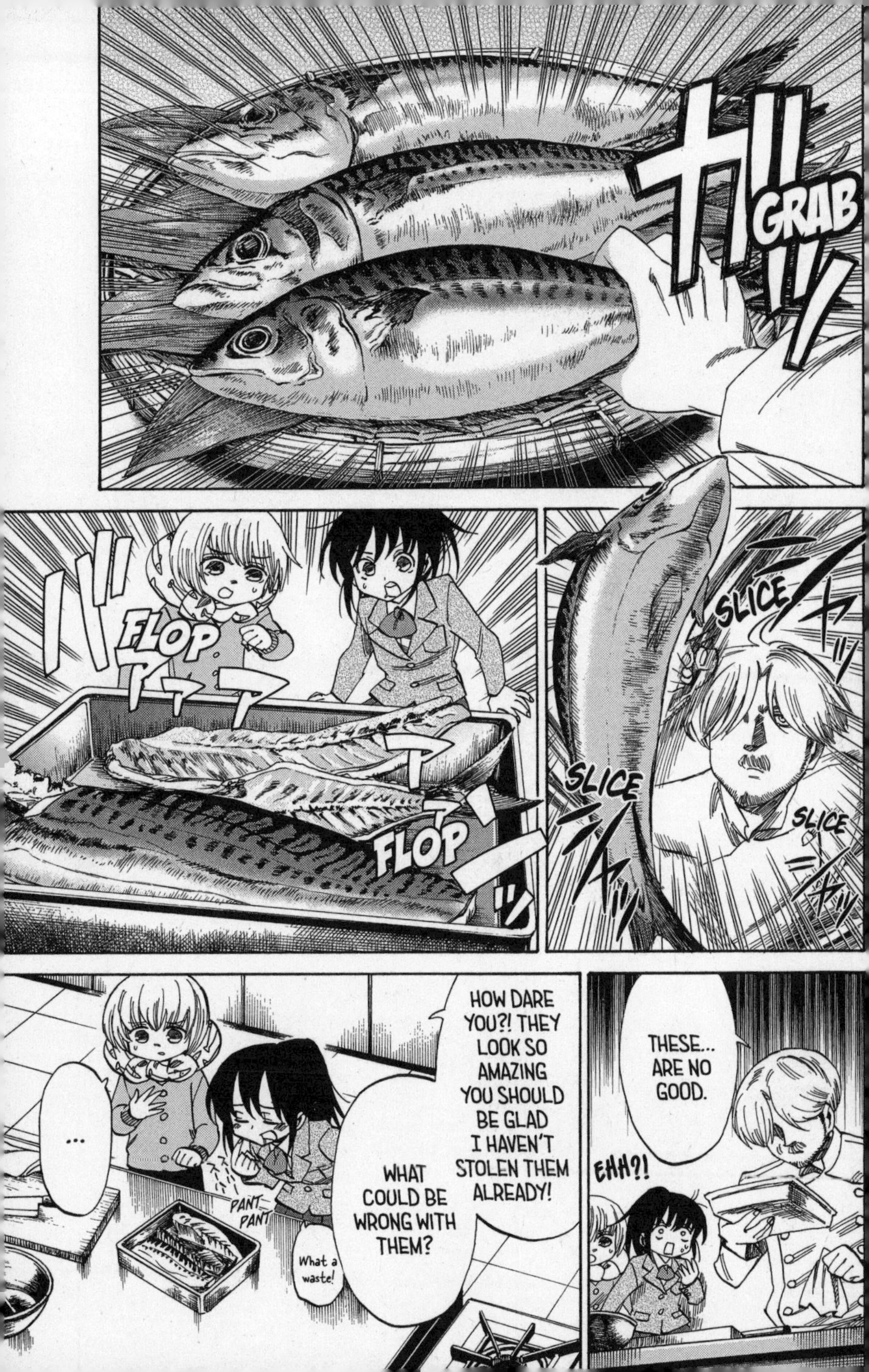
GRAB
SLICE
SLICE
SLICE
FLOP
FLOP
THESE... ARE NO GOOD.
EHH?!
HOW DARE YOU?! THEY LOOK SO AMAZING YOU SHOULD BE GLAD I HAVEN'T STOLEN THEM ALREADY!
WHAT COULD BE WRONG WITH THEM?
What a waste!
PANT PANT
...

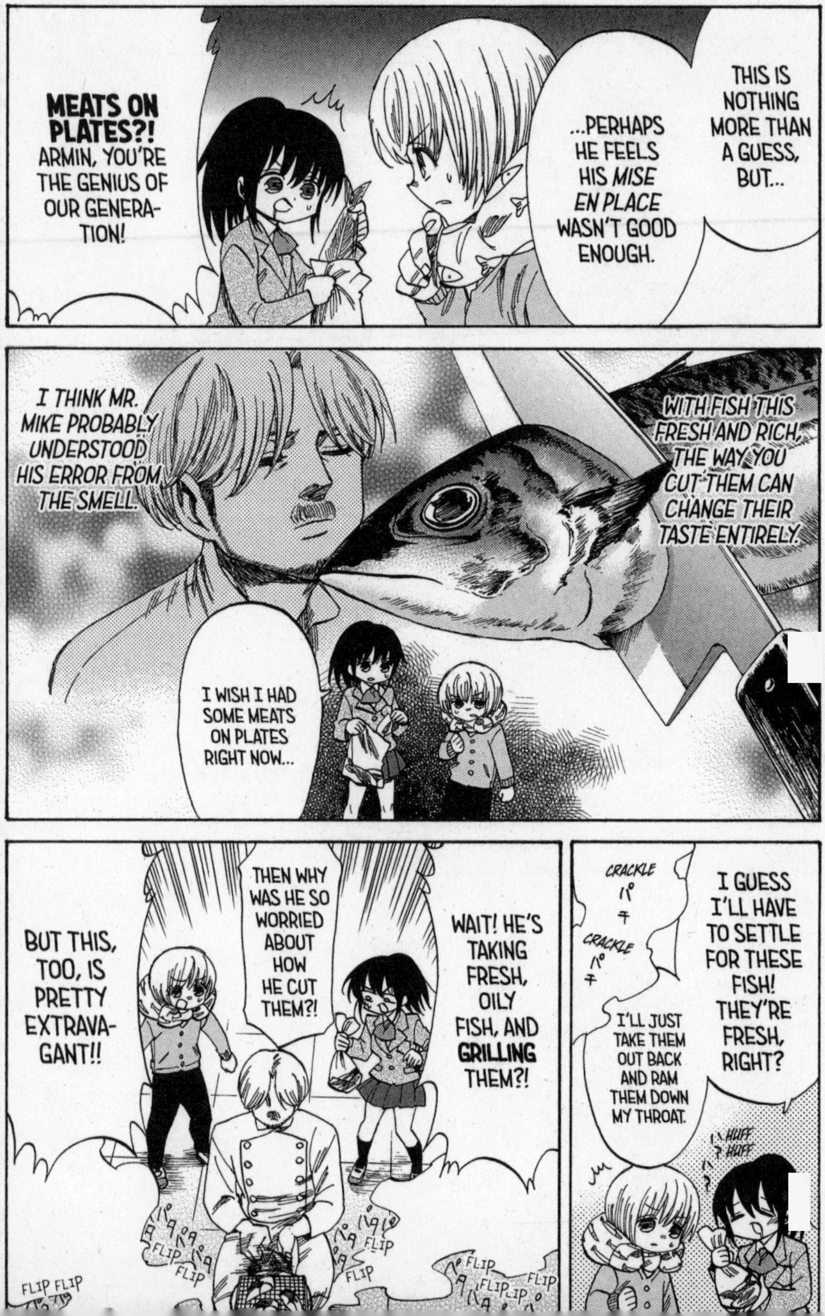
THIS IS NOTHING MORE THAN A GUESS, BUT...
...PERHAPS HE FEELS HIS *MISE EN PLACE* WASN'T GOOD ENOUGH.
MEATS ON PLATES?! ARMIN, YOU'RE THE GENIUS OF OUR GENERATION!
WITH FISH THIS FRESH AND RICH, THE WAY YOU CUT THEM CAN CHANGE THEIR TASTE ENTIRELY.
I THINK MR. MIKE PROBABLY UNDERSTOOD HIS ERROR FROM THE SMELL.
I WISH I HAD SOME MEATS ON PLATES RIGHT NOW...
I GUESS I'LL HAVE TO SETTLE FOR THESE FISH! THEY'RE FRESH, RIGHT?
CRACKLE パチ
CRACKLE パチ
I'LL JUST TAKE THEM OUT BACK AND RAM THEM DOWN MY THROAT.
HUFF HUFF
WAIT! HE'S TAKING FRESH, OILY FISH, AND **GRILLING** THEM?!
THEN WHY WAS HE SO WORRIED ABOUT HOW HE CUT THEM?!
BUT THIS, TOO, IS PRETTY EXTRAVAGANT!!
FLIP FLIP FLIP FLIP FLIP FLIP FLIP FLIP FLIP

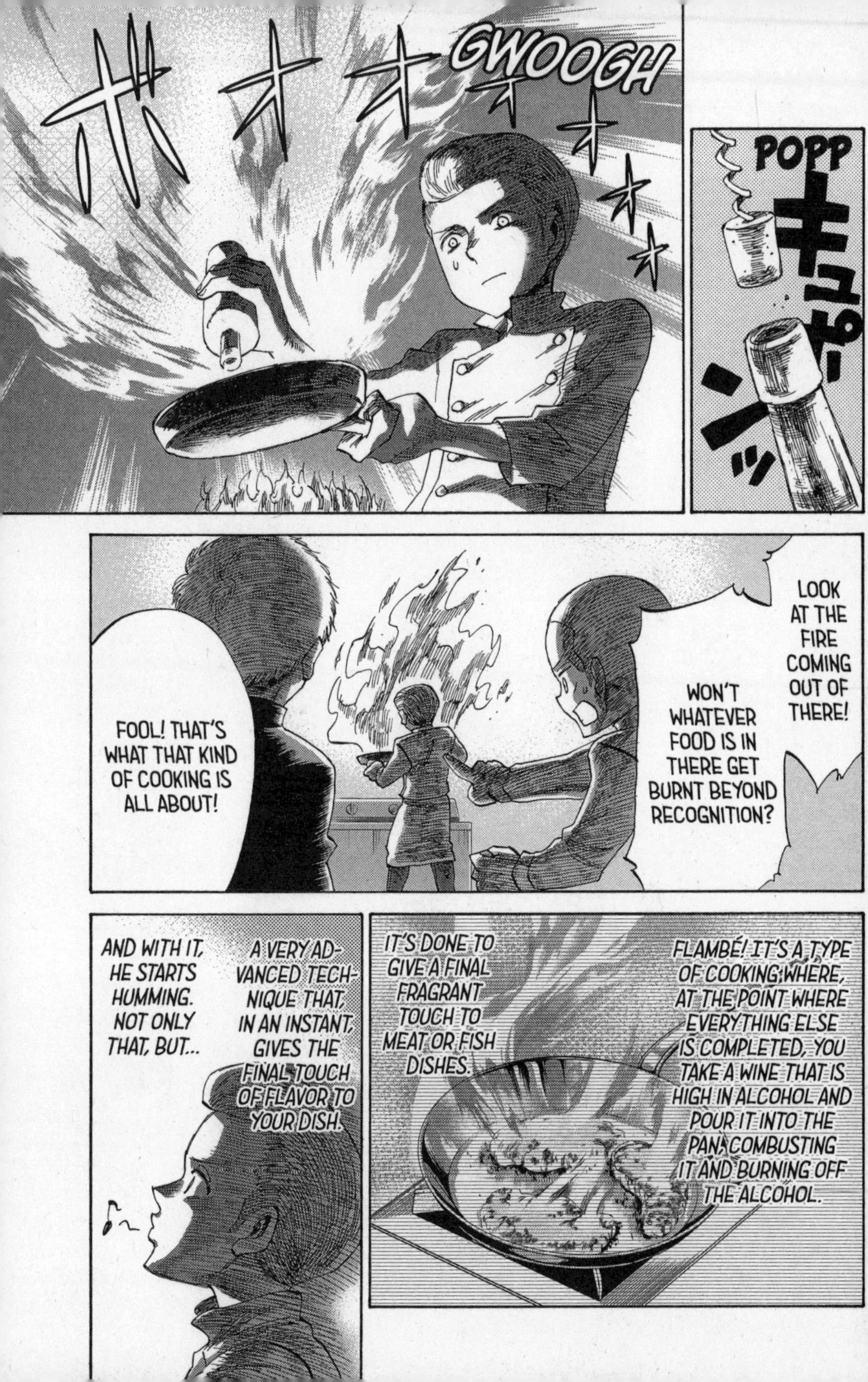
POPP
キュポーンッ
GWOOGH
ボオオオォォォォ
LOOK AT THE FIRE COMING OUT OF THERE!
WON'T WHATEVER FOOD IS IN THERE GET BURNT BEYOND RECOGNITION?
FOOL! THAT'S WHAT THAT KIND OF COOKING IS ALL ABOUT!
FLAMBÉ! IT'S A TYPE OF COOKING WHERE, AT THE POINT WHERE EVERYTHING ELSE IS COMPLETED, YOU TAKE A WINE THAT IS HIGH IN ALCOHOL AND POUR IT INTO THE PAN, COMBUSTING IT AND BURNING OFF THE ALCOHOL.
IT'S DONE TO GIVE A FINAL FRAGRANT TOUCH TO MEAT OR FISH DISHES.
A VERY ADVANCED TECHNIQUE THAT, IN AN INSTANT, GIVES THE FINAL TOUCH OF FLAVOR TO YOUR DISH.
AND WITH IT, HE STARTS HUMMING. NOT ONLY THAT, BUT...

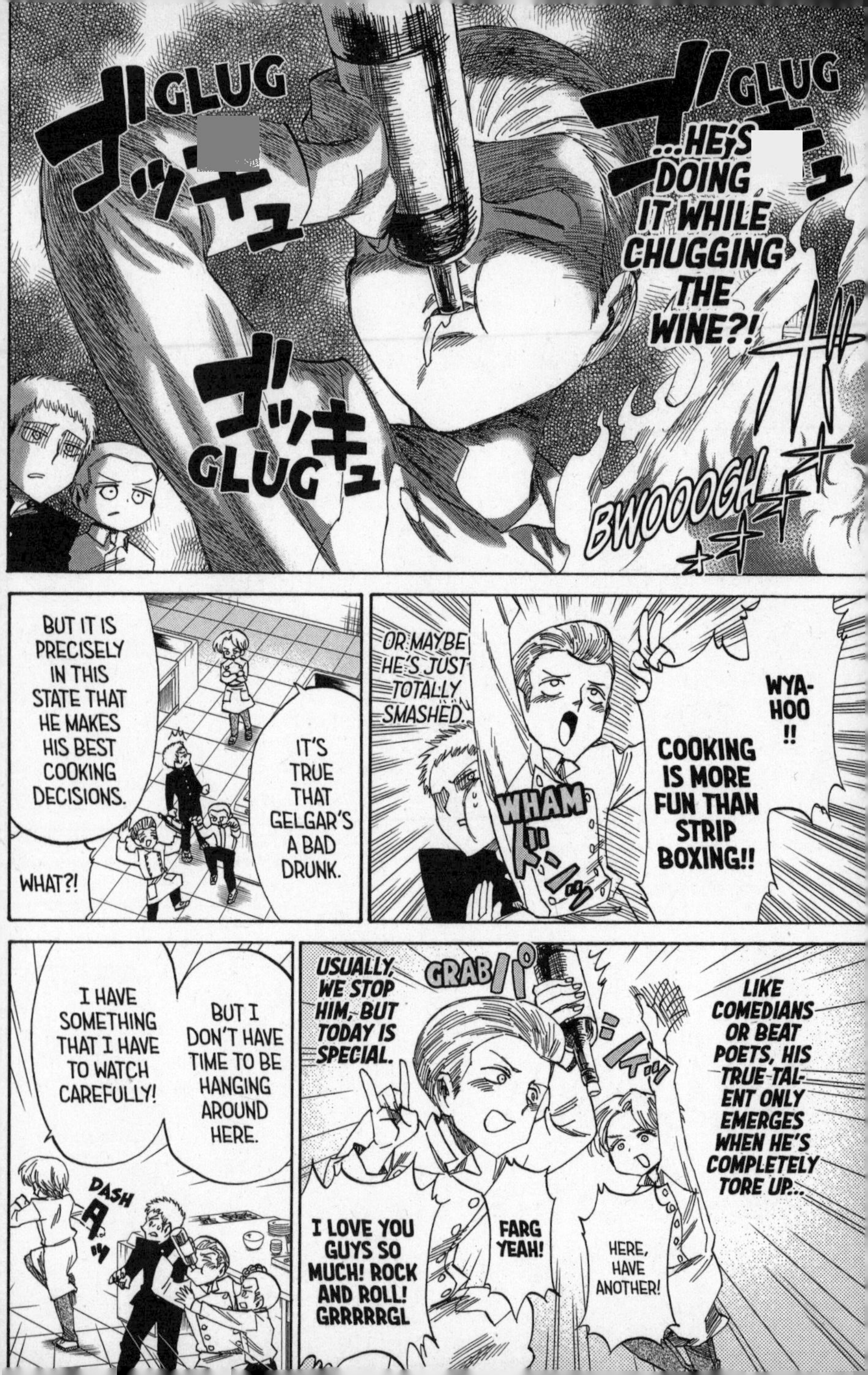
GLUG
ゴッキュ
GLUG
...HE'S DOING IT WHILE CHUGGING THE WINE?!
GLUG
ゴッキュ
BWOOOGH
WYA-HOO!!
COOKING IS MORE FUN THAN STRIP BOXING!!
OR MAYBE HE'S JUST TOTALLY SMASHED.
WHAM
IT'S TRUE THAT GELGAR'S A BAD DRUNK.
BUT IT IS PRECISELY IN THIS STATE THAT HE MAKES HIS BEST COOKING DECISIONS.
WHAT?!
LIKE COMEDIANS OR BEAT POETS, HIS TRUE TAL-ENT ONLY EMERGES WHEN HE'S COMPLETELY TORE UP...
GRAB
USUALLY, WE STOP HIM, BUT TODAY IS SPECIAL.
HERE, HAVE ANOTHER!
FARG YEAH!
I LOVE YOU GUYS SO MUCH! ROCK AND ROLL! GRRRRRGL
BUT I DON'T HAVE TIME TO BE HANGING AROUND HERE.
I HAVE SOMETHING THAT I HAVE TO WATCH CAREFULLY!
DASH

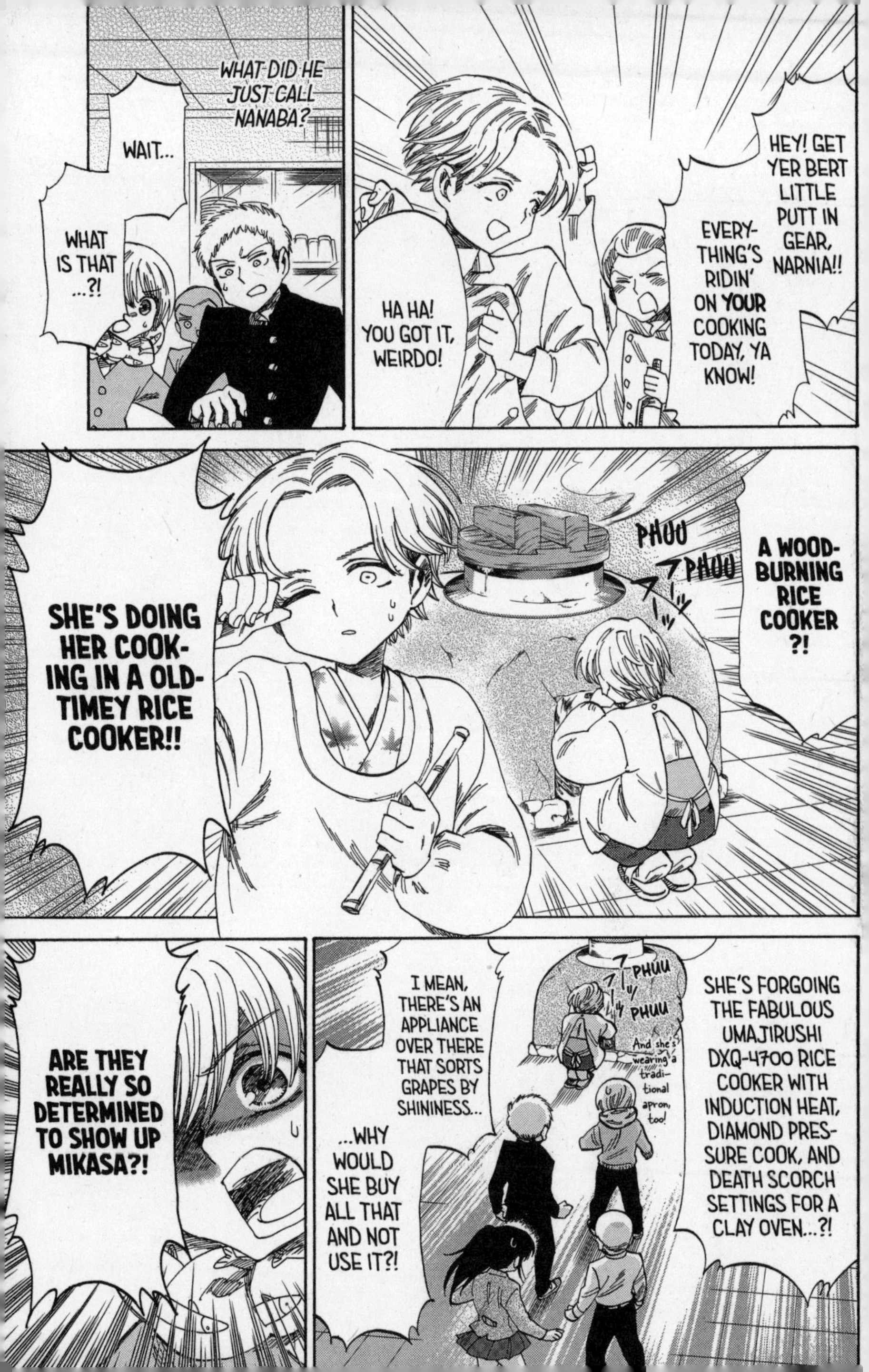
HEY! GET YER BERT LITTLE PUTT IN GEAR, NARNIA!!
EVERY-THING'S RIDIN' ON YOUR COOKING TODAY, YA KNOW!
HA HA! YOU GOT IT, WEIRDO!
WHAT DID HE JUST CALL NANABA?
WAIT...
WHAT IS THAT ...?!
A WOOD-BURNING RICE COOKER?!
PHUU PHUU
SHE'S DOING HER COOK-ING IN A OLD-TIMEY RICE COOKER!!
SHE'S FORGOING THE FABULOUS UMAJIRUSHI DXQ-4700 RICE COOKER WITH INDUCTION HEAT, DIAMOND PRES-SURE COOK, AND DEATH SCORCH SETTINGS FOR A CLAY OVEN...?!
PHUU PHUU
And she's wearing a tradi-tional apron, too!
I MEAN, THERE'S AN APPLIANCE OVER THERE THAT SORTS GRAPES BY SHININESS...
...WHY WOULD SHE BUY ALL THAT AND NOT USE IT?!
ARE THEY REALLY SO DETERMINED TO SHOW UP MIKASA?!

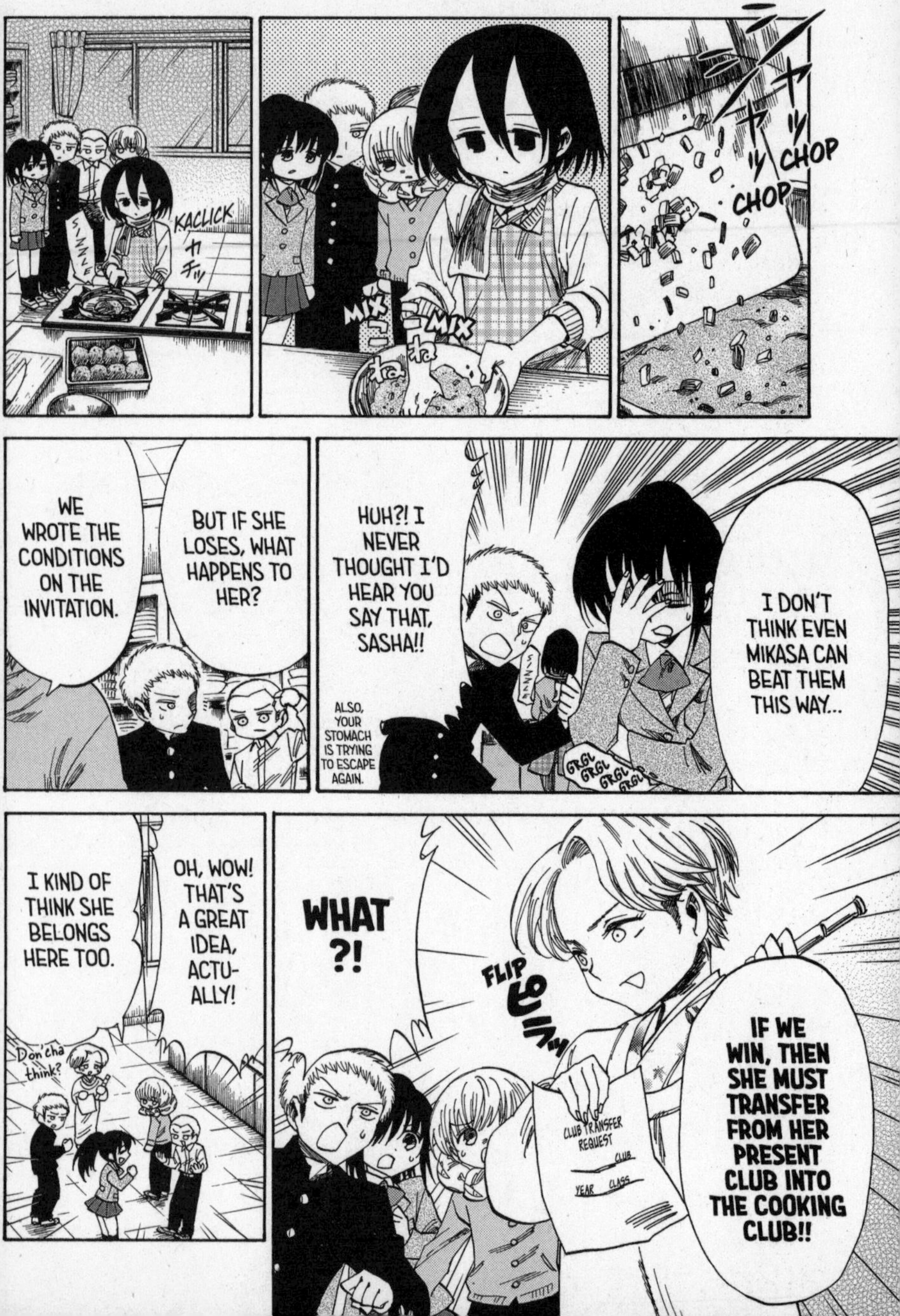
CHOP
CHOP
MIX
MIX
KACLICK
SIZZLE
I DON'T THINK EVEN MIKASA CAN BEAT THEM THIS WAY...
GRGL GRGL GRGL GRGL
HUH?! I NEVER THOUGHT I'D HEAR YOU SAY THAT, SASHA!!
SIZZLE
ALSO, YOUR STOMACH IS TRYING TO ESCAPE AGAIN.
BUT IF SHE LOSES, WHAT HAPPENS TO HER?
WE WROTE THE CONDITIONS ON THE INVITATION.
IF WE WIN, THEN SHE MUST TRANSFER FROM HER PRESENT CLUB INTO THE COOKING CLUB!!
CLUB TRANSFER REQUEST
CLUB
YEAR CLASS
FLIP
WHAT?!
OH, WOW! THAT'S A GREAT IDEA, ACTUALLY!
I KIND OF THINK SHE BELONGS HERE TOO.
Don'cha think?

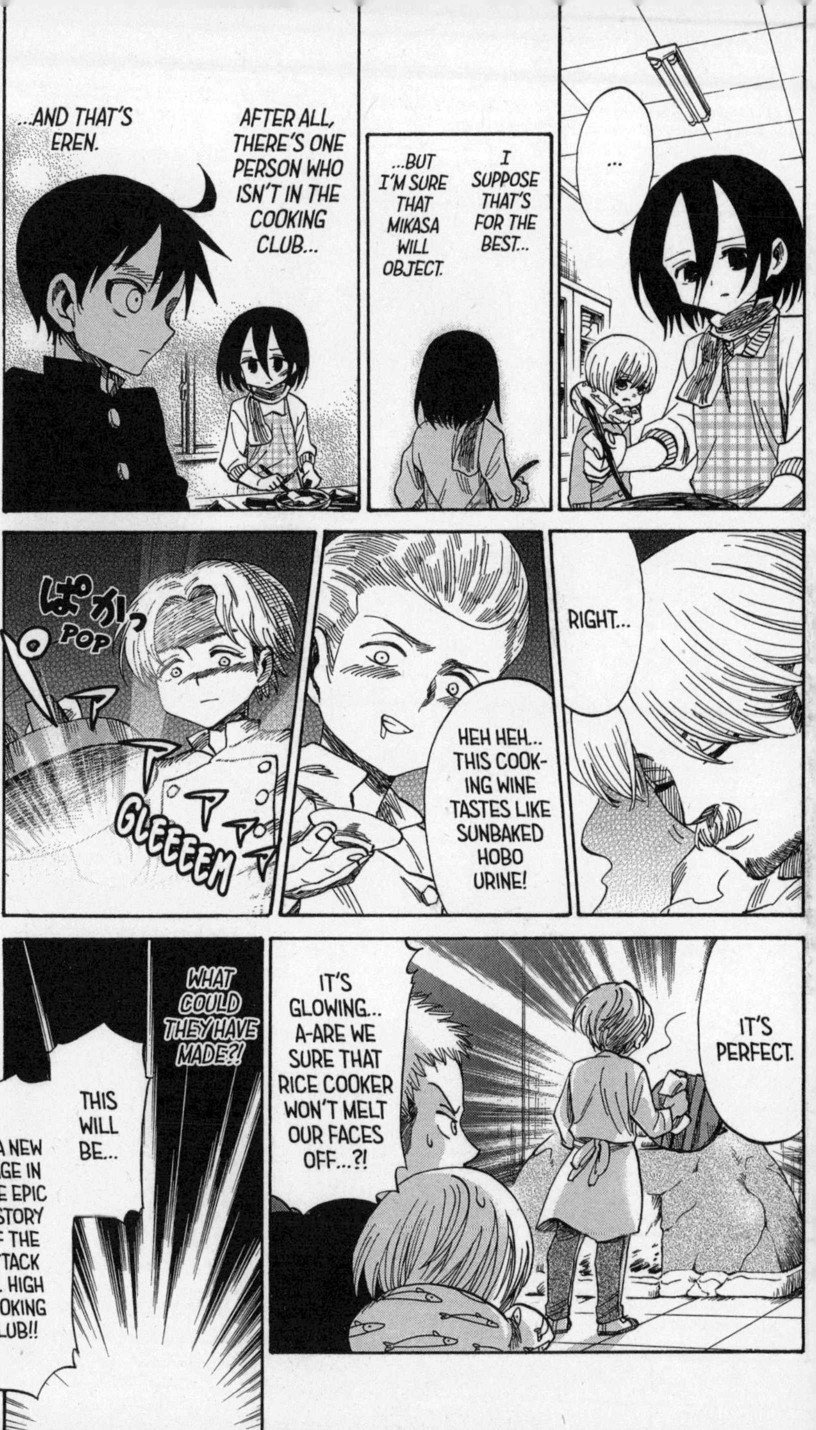
...
I SUPPOSE THAT'S FOR THE BEST...
...BUT I'M SURE THAT MIKASA WILL OBJECT.
AFTER ALL, THERE'S ONE PERSON WHO ISN'T IN THE COOKING CLUB...
...AND THAT'S EREN.
RIGHT...
HEH HEH... THIS COOK-ING WINE TASTES LIKE SUNBAKED HOBO URINE!
ぱかっ
POP
GLEEEEEM
IT'S PERFECT.
IT'S GLOWING... A-ARE WE SURE THAT RICE COOKER WON'T MELT OUR FACES OFF...?!
WHAT COULD THEY HAVE MADE?!
THIS WILL BE...
...A NEW PAGE IN THE EPIC HISTORY OF THE ATTACK JR. HIGH COOKING CLUB!!

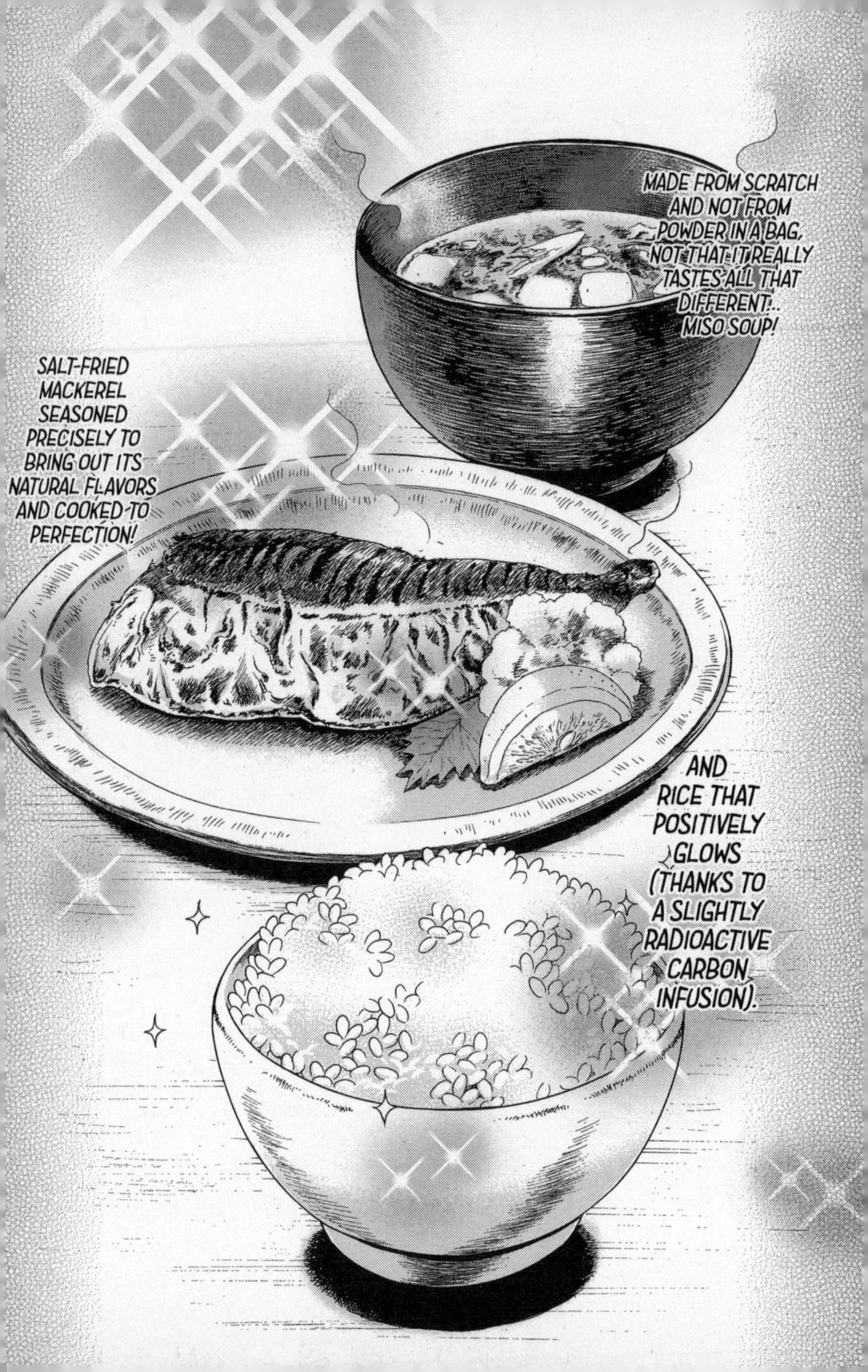
MADE FROM SCRATCH AND NOT FROM POWDER IN A BAG, NOT THAT IT REALLY TASTES ALL THAT DIFFERENT... MISO SOUP!
SALT-FRIED MACKEREL SEASONED PRECISELY TO BRING OUT ITS NATURAL FLAVORS AND COOKED TO PERFECTION!
AND RICE THAT POSITIVELY GLOWS (THANKS TO A SLIGHTLY RADIOACTIVE CARBON INFUSION).

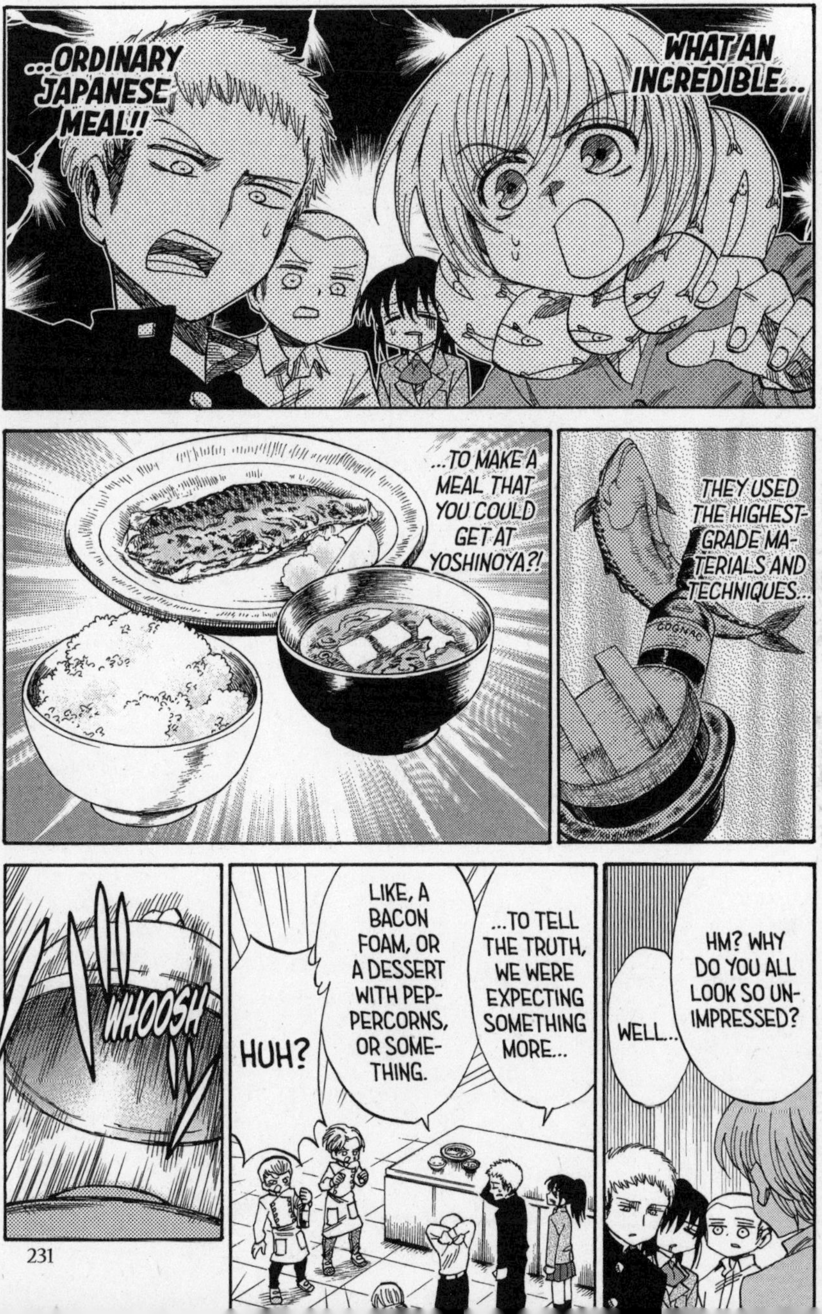
WHAT AN INCREDIBLE...
...ORDINARY JAPANESE MEAL!!
THEY USED THE HIGHEST-GRADE MATERIALS AND TECHNIQUES...
COGNAC
...TO MAKE A MEAL THAT YOU COULD GET AT YOSHINOYA?!
HM? WHY DO YOU ALL LOOK SO UNIMPRESSED?
WELL...
...TO TELL THE TRUTH, WE WERE EXPECTING SOMETHING MORE...
LIKE, A BACON FOAM, OR A DESSERT WITH PEPPERCORNS, OR SOMETHING.
HUH?
WHOOSH

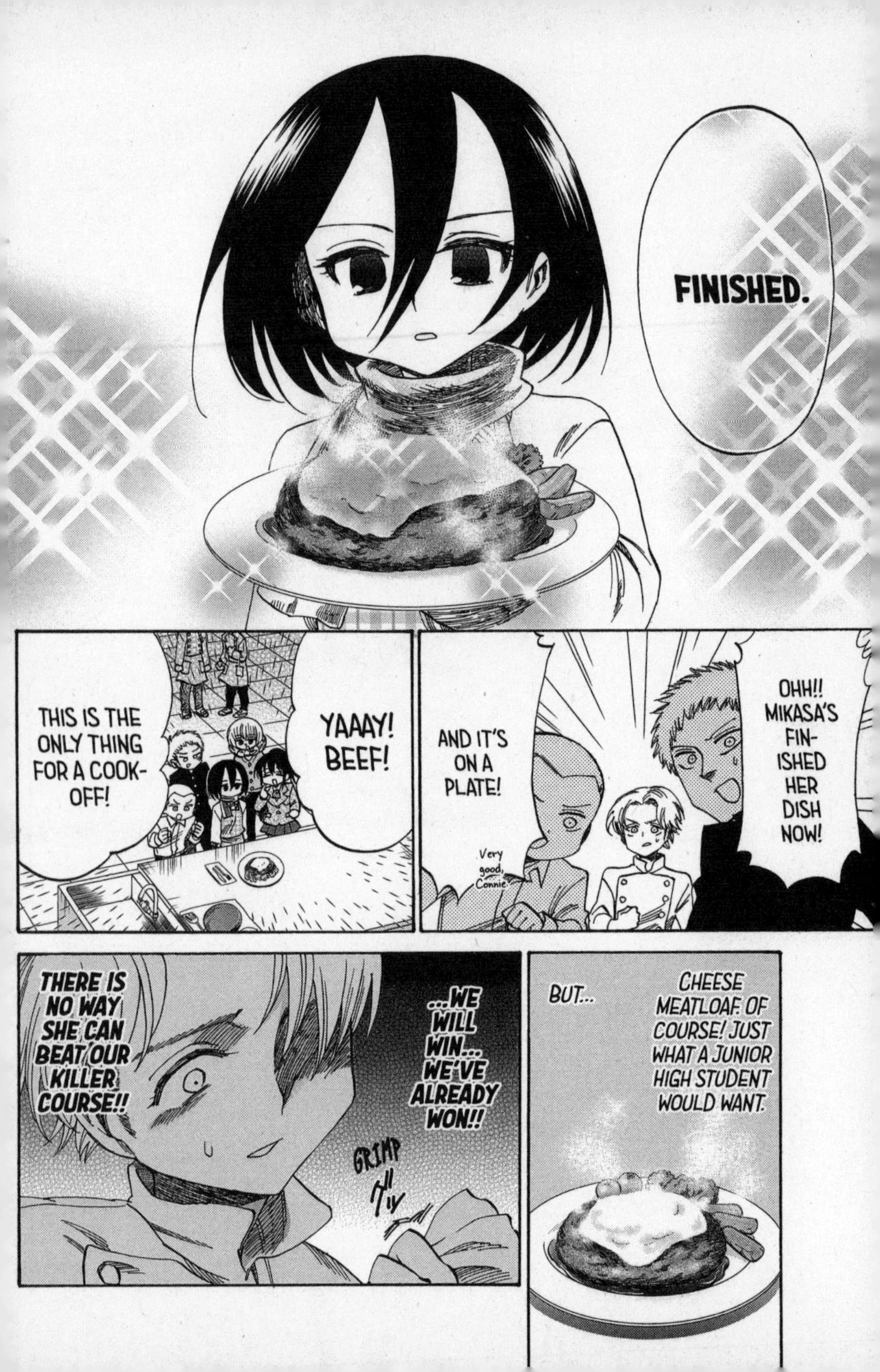
FINISHED.
OHH!! MIKASA'S FIN-ISHED HER DISH NOW!
AND IT'S ON A PLATE!
Very good, Connie.
YAAAY! BEEF!
THIS IS THE ONLY THING FOR A COOK-OFF!
CHEESE MEATLOAF, OF COURSE! JUST WHAT A JUNIOR HIGH STUDENT WOULD WANT.
BUT...
...WE WILL WIN... WE'VE ALREADY WON!!
THERE IS NO WAY SHE CAN BEAT OUR KILLER COURSE!!
GRIMP

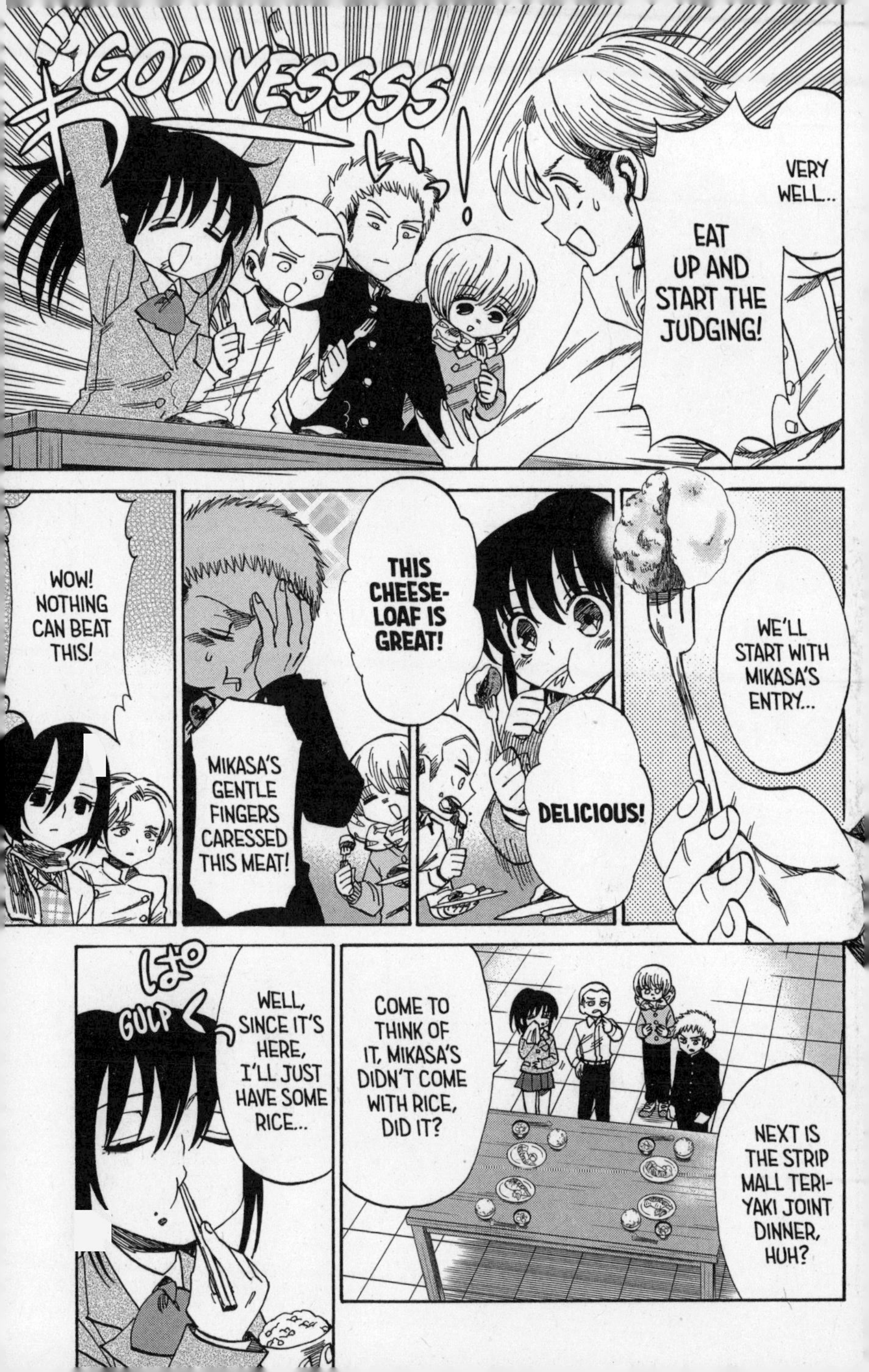
VERY WELL..
EAT UP AND START THE JUDGING!
GOD YESSSS
WE'LL START WITH MIKASA'S ENTRY...
DELICIOUS!
THIS CHEESE-LOAF IS GREAT!
MIKASA'S GENTLE FINGERS CARESSED THIS MEAT!
WOW! NOTHING CAN BEAT THIS!
NEXT IS THE STRIP MALL TERI-YAKI JOINT DINNER, HUH?
COME TO THINK OF IT, MIKASA'S DIDN'T COME WITH RICE, DID IT?
WELL, SINCE IT'S HERE, I'LL JUST HAVE SOME RICE...
GULP

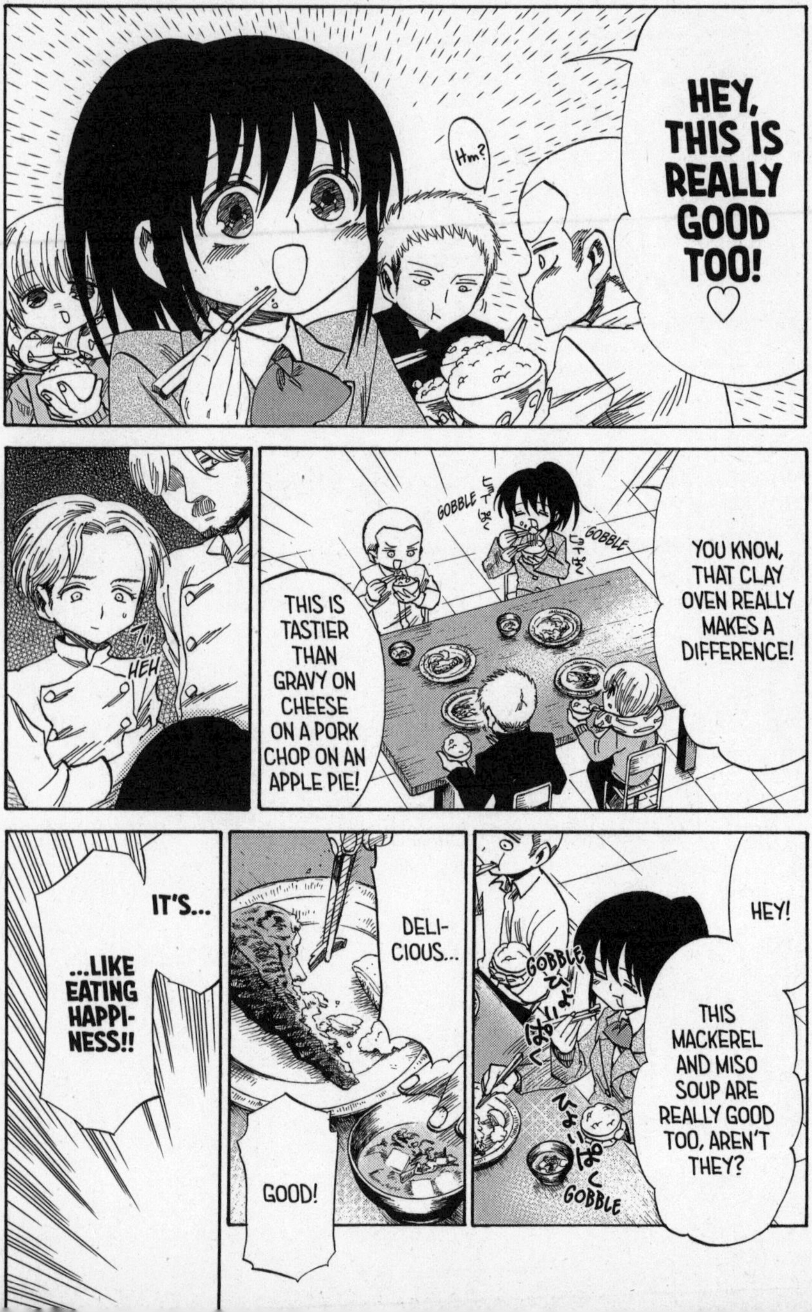
HEY, THIS IS REALLY GOOD TOO! ♡
Hm?
YOU KNOW, THAT CLAY OVEN REALLY MAKES A DIFFERENCE!
GOBBLE
GOBBLE
THIS IS TASTIER THAN GRAVY ON CHEESE ON A PORK CHOP ON AN APPLE PIE!
HEH
HEY!
THIS MACKEREL AND MISO SOUP ARE REALLY GOOD TOO, AREN'T THEY?
GOBBLE
ひょいぱく
ひょいぱく
GOBBLE
DELI-CIOUS...
GOOD!
IT'S...
...LIKE EATING HAPPI-NESS!!

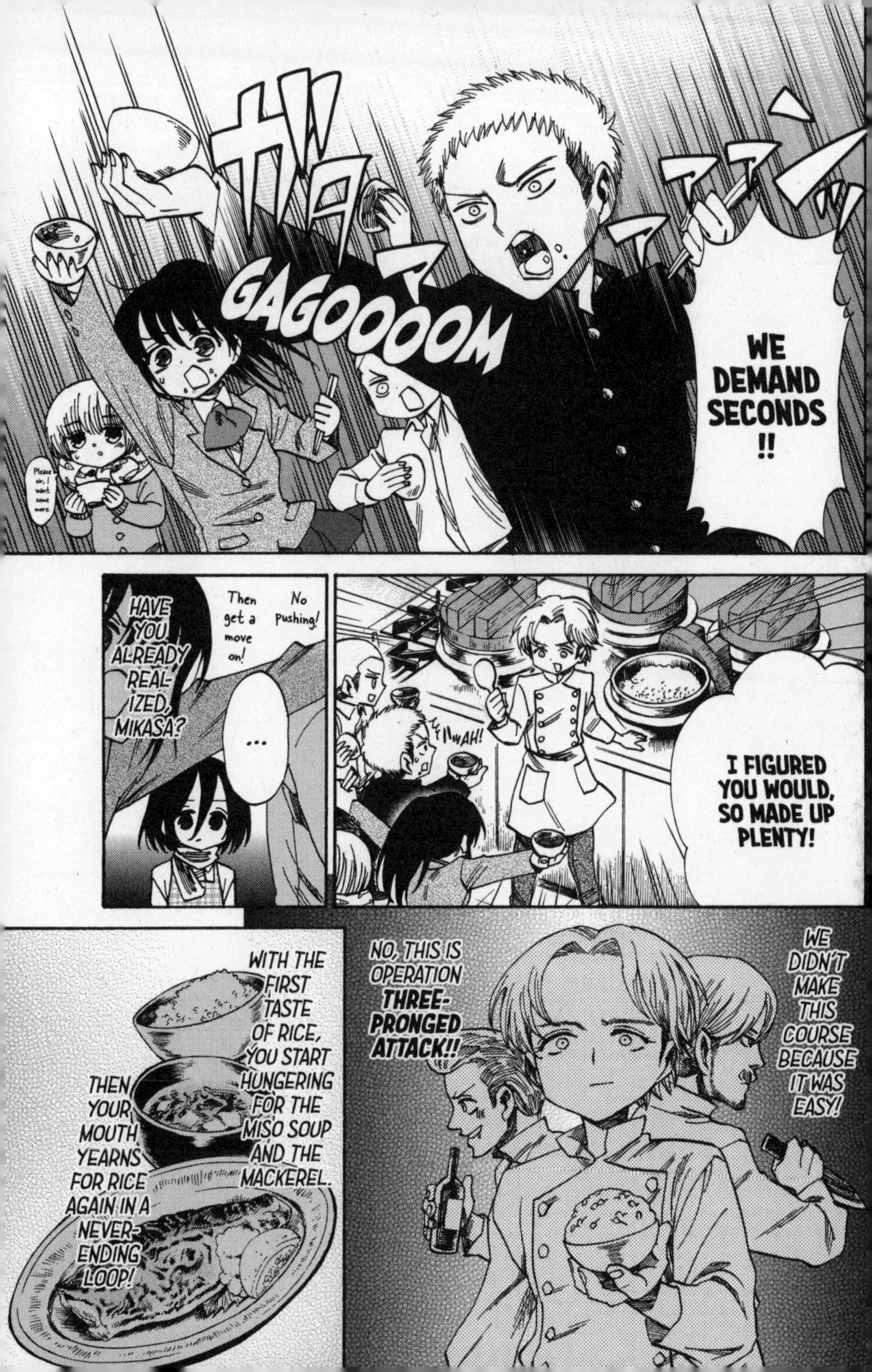
GAGOOOOM
WE DEMAND SECONDS !!
Please sir, I want some more
I FIGURED YOU WOULD, SO MADE UP PLENTY!
WAH!
No pushing!
Then get a move on!
HAVE YOU ALREADY REALIZED, MIKASA?
...
WE DIDN'T MAKE THIS COURSE BECAUSE IT WAS EASY!
NO, THIS IS OPERATION THREE-PRONGED ATTACK!!
WITH THE FIRST TASTE OF RICE, YOU START HUNGERING FOR THE MISO SOUP AND THE MACKEREL.
THEN YOUR MOUTH YEARNS FOR RICE AGAIN IN A NEVER-ENDING LOOP!

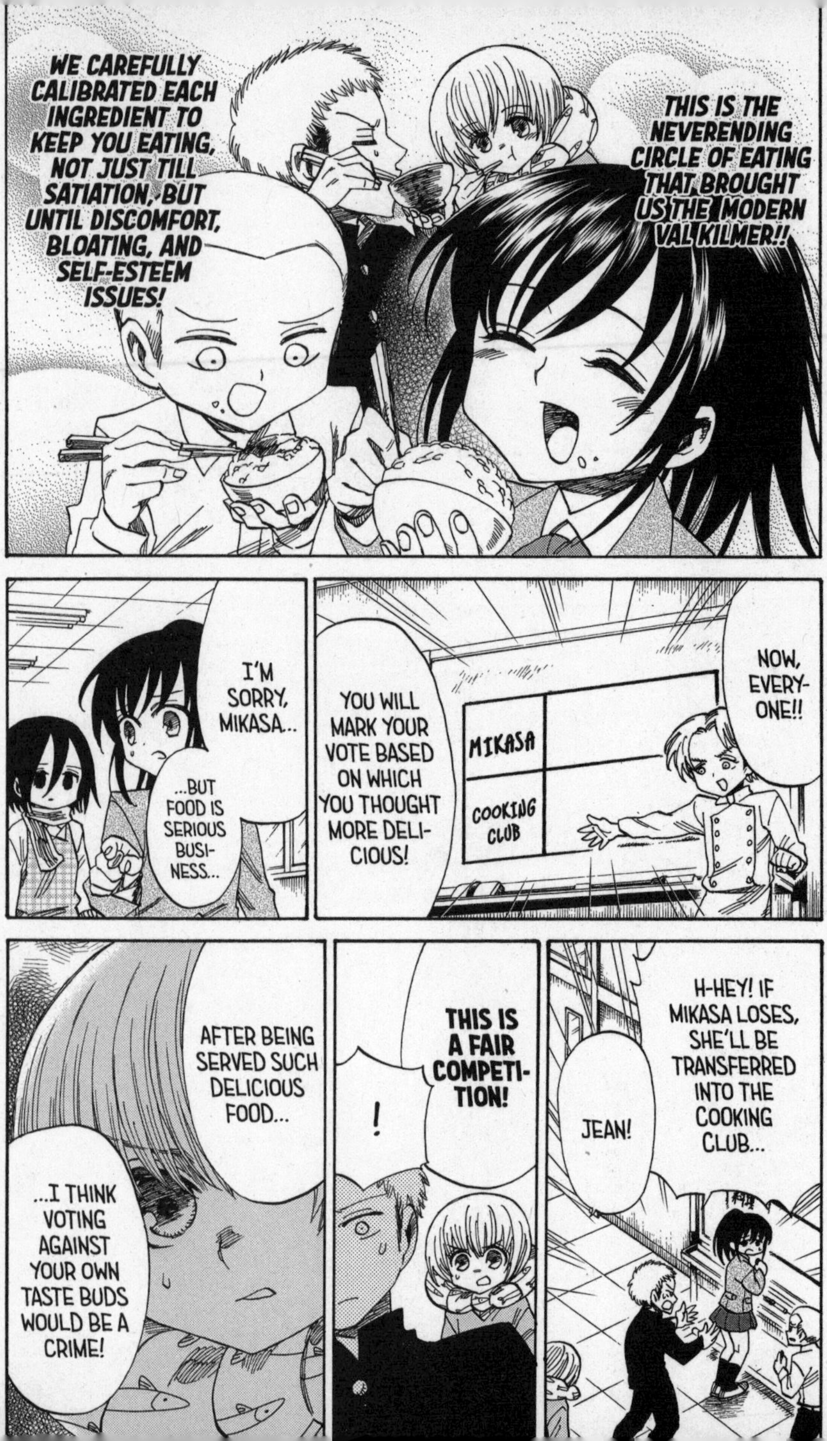
THIS IS THE NEVERENDING CIRCLE OF EATING THAT BROUGHT US THE MODERN VAL KILMER!!
WE CAREFULLY CALIBRATED EACH INGREDIENT TO KEEP YOU EATING, NOT JUST TILL SATIATION, BUT UNTIL DISCOMFORT, BLOATING, AND SELF-ESTEEM ISSUES!
NOW, EVERY-ONE!!
MIKASA
COOKING CLUB
YOU WILL MARK YOUR VOTE BASED ON WHICH YOU THOUGHT MORE DELI-CIOUS!
I'M SORRY, MIKASA...
...BUT FOOD IS SERIOUS BUSI-NESS...
H-HEY! IF MIKASA LOSES, SHE'LL BE TRANSFERRED INTO THE COOKING CLUB...
JEAN!
THIS IS A FAIR COMPETI-TION!
!
AFTER BEING SERVED SUCH DELICIOUS FOOD...
...I THINK VOTING AGAINST YOUR OWN TASTE BUDS WOULD BE A CRIME!

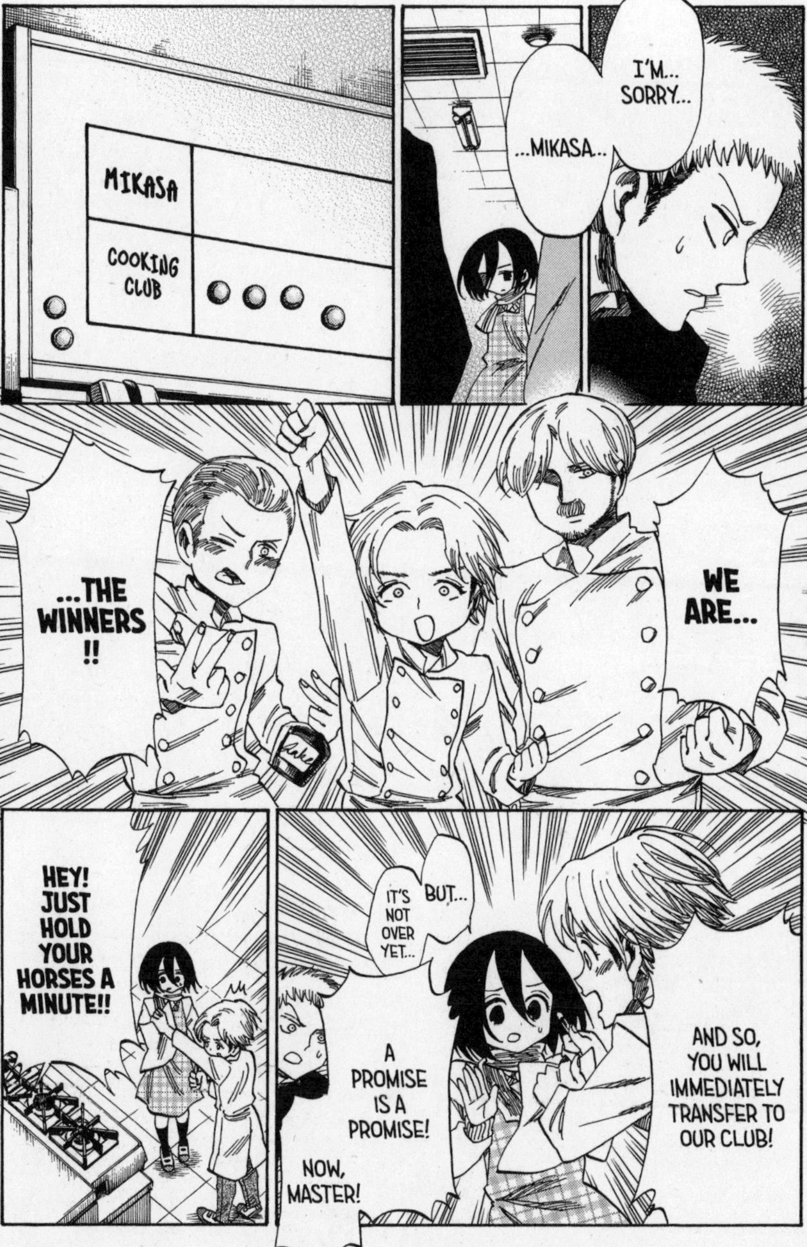

I'M... SORRY...
...MIKASA...
MIKASA
COOKING CLUB
WE ARE...
...THE WINNERS!!
AND SO, YOU WILL IMMEDIATELY TRANSFER TO OUR CLUB!
BUT...
IT'S NOT OVER YET...
A PROMISE IS A PROMISE!
NOW, MASTER!
HEY! JUST HOLD YOUR HORSES A MINUTE!!

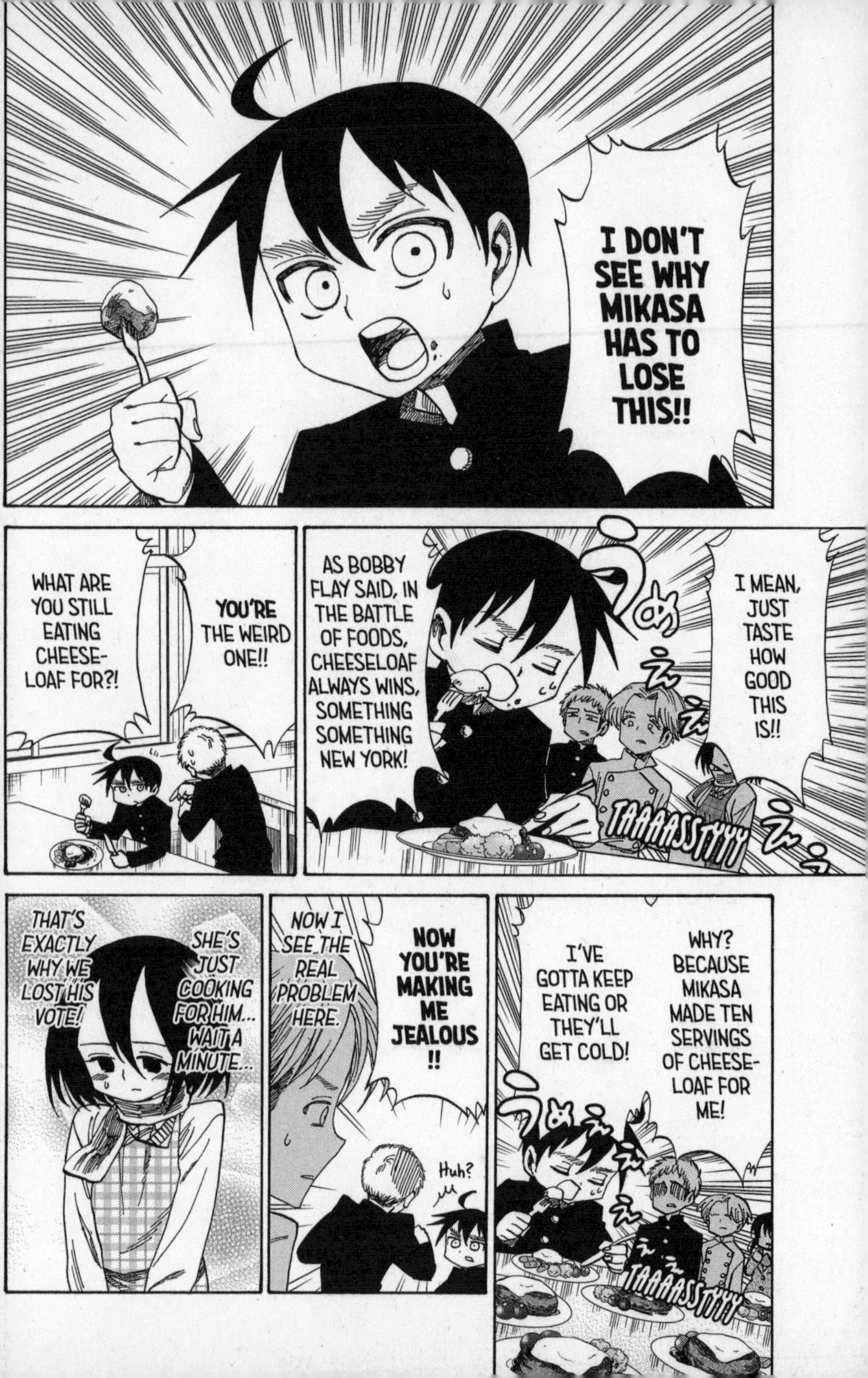
I DON'T SEE WHY MIKASA HAS TO LOSE THIS!!
I MEAN, JUST TASTE HOW GOOD THIS IS!!
AS BOBBY FLAY SAID, IN THE BATTLE OF FOODS, CHEESELOAF ALWAYS WINS, SOMETHING SOMETHING NEW YORK!
TAAAASSTYYY
YOU'RE THE WEIRD ONE!!
WHAT ARE YOU STILL EATING CHEESE-LOAF FOR?!
WHY? BECAUSE MIKASA MADE TEN SERVINGS OF CHEESE-LOAF FOR ME!
I'VE GOTTA KEEP EATING OR THEY'LL GET COLD!
TAAAASSTYYY
NOW YOU'RE MAKING ME JEALOUS!!
NOW I SEE THE REAL PROBLEM HERE.
Huh?
SHE'S JUST COOKING FOR HIM... WAIT A MINUTE...
THAT'S EXACTLY WHY WE LOST HIS VOTE!

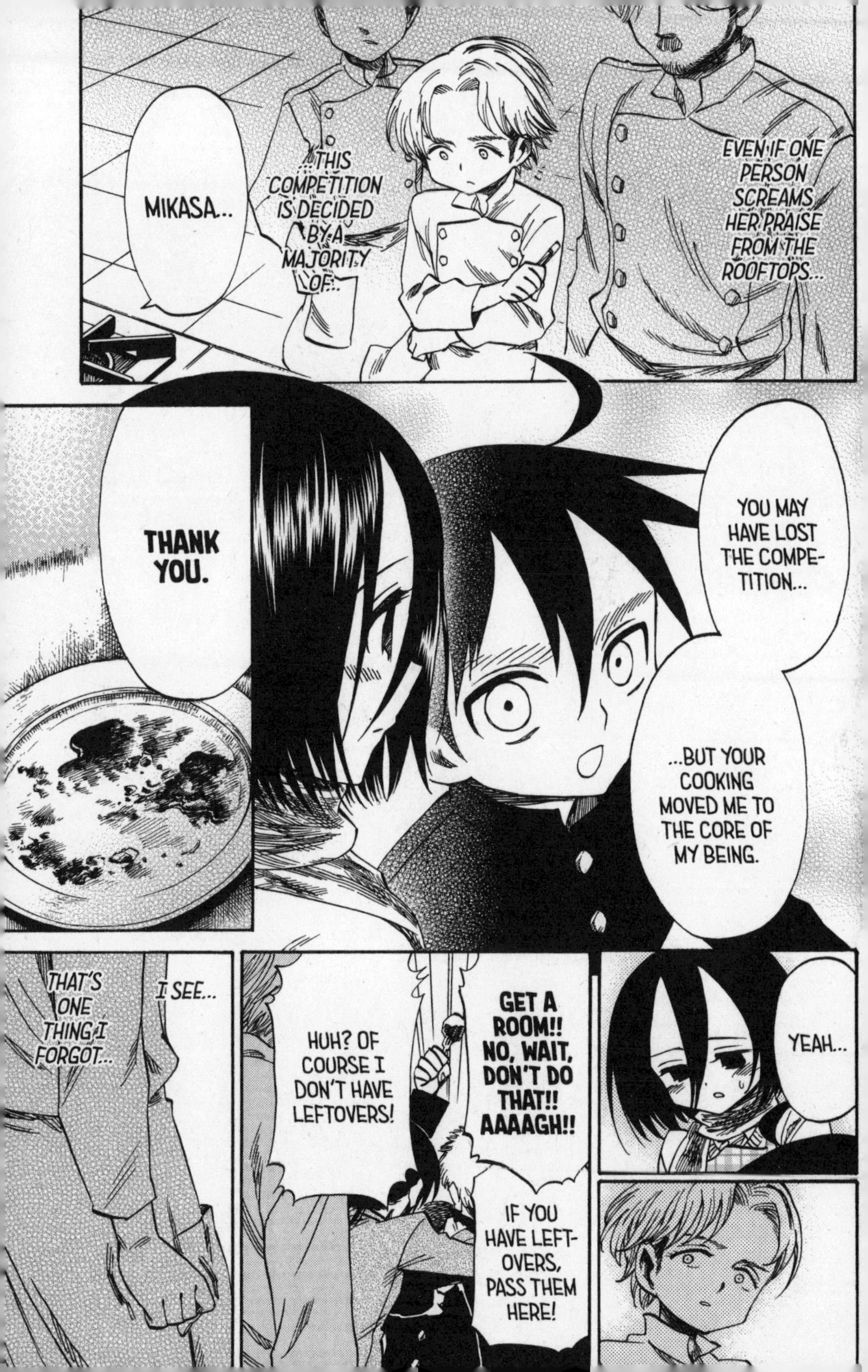
EVEN IF ONE PERSON SCREAMS HER PRAISE FROM THE ROOFTOPS...
...THIS COMPETITION IS DECIDED BY A MAJORITY OF...
MIKASA...
YOU MAY HAVE LOST THE COMPE-TITION...
...BUT YOUR COOKING MOVED ME TO THE CORE OF MY BEING.
THANK YOU.
YEAH...
GET A ROOM!! NO, WAIT, DON'T DO THAT!! AAAAGH!!
IF YOU HAVE LEFT-OVERS, PASS THEM HERE!
HUH? OF COURSE I DON'T HAVE LEFTOVERS!
I SEE...
THAT'S ONE THING I FORGOT...

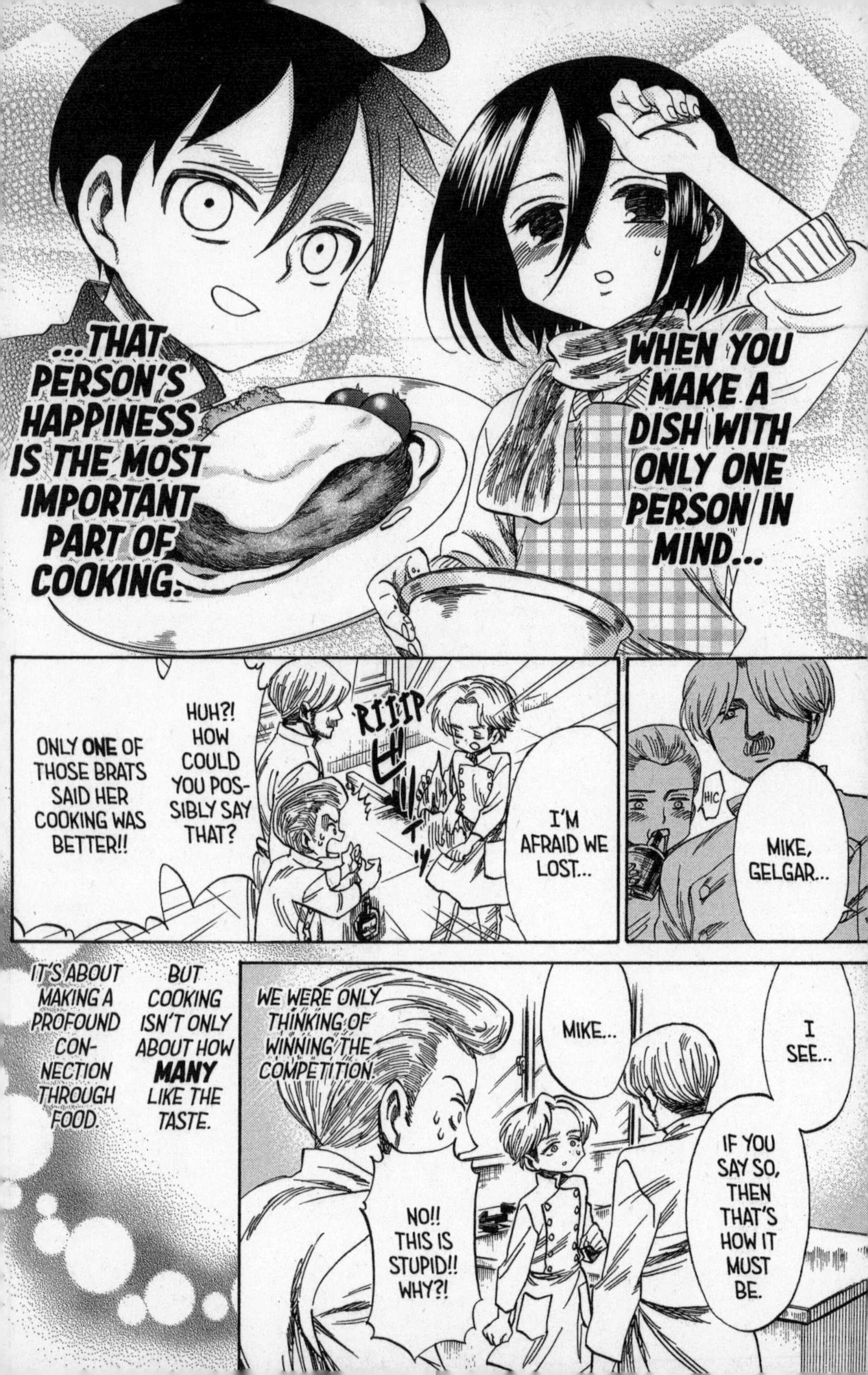
WHEN YOU MAKE A DISH WITH ONLY ONE PERSON IN MIND...
...THAT PERSON'S HAPPINESS IS THE MOST IMPORTANT PART OF COOKING.
HIC
MIKE, GELGAR...
I'M AFRAID WE LOST...
RIIIP
HUH?! HOW COULD YOU POSSIBLY SAY THAT?
ONLY ONE OF THOSE BRATS SAID HER COOKING WAS BETTER!!
I SEE...
MIKE...
IF YOU SAY SO, THEN THAT'S HOW IT MUST BE.
WE WERE ONLY THINKING OF WINNING THE COMPETITION.
NO!! THIS IS STUPID!! WHY?!
BUT COOKING ISN'T ONLY ABOUT HOW MANY LIKE THE TASTE.
IT'S ABOUT MAKING A PROFOUND CONNECTION THROUGH FOOD.

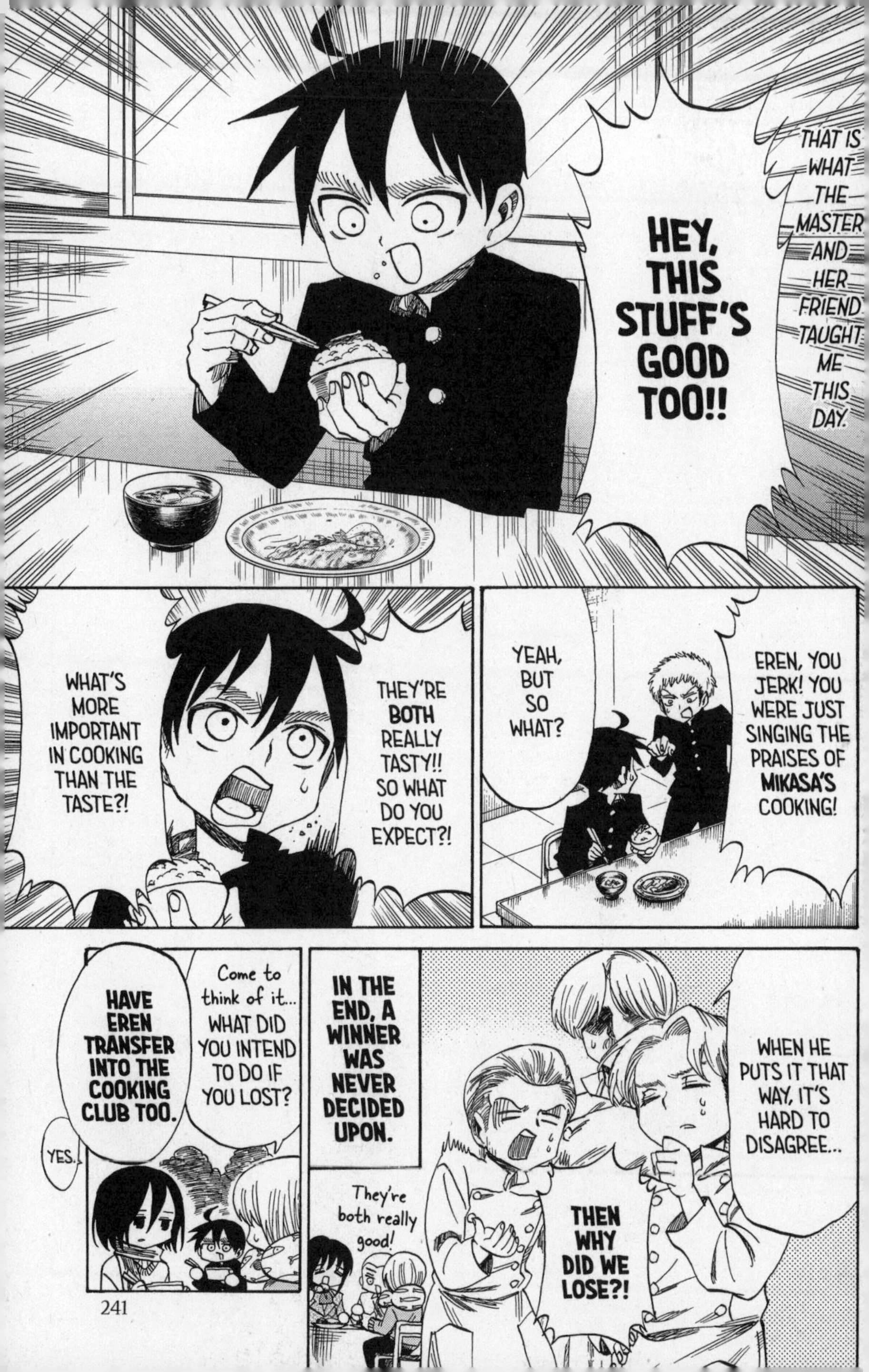
THAT IS WHAT THE MASTER AND HER FRIEND TAUGHT ME THIS DAY.
HEY, THIS STUFF'S GOOD TOO!!
EREN, YOU JERK! YOU WERE JUST SINGING THE PRAISES OF MIKASA'S COOKING!
YEAH, BUT SO WHAT?
THEY'RE BOTH REALLY TASTY!! SO WHAT DO YOU EXPECT?!
WHAT'S MORE IMPORTANT IN COOKING THAN THE TASTE?!
WHEN HE PUTS IT THAT WAY, IT'S HARD TO DISAGREE...
THEN WHY DID WE LOSE?!
They're both really good!
IN THE END, A WINNER WAS NEVER DECIDED UPON.
Come to think of it... WHAT DID YOU INTEND TO DO IF YOU LOST?
HAVE EREN TRANSFER INTO THE COOKING CLUB TOO.
YES.

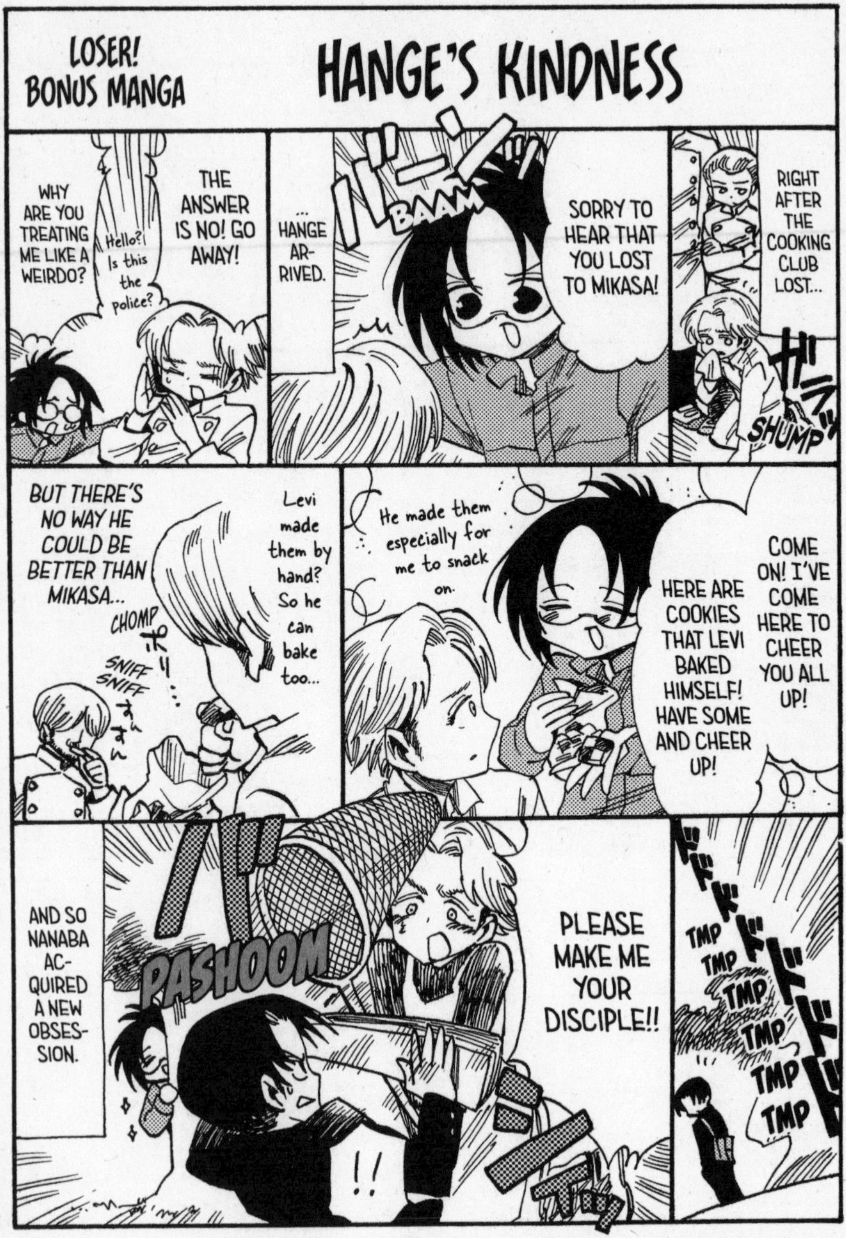

HANGE'S KINDNESS
LOSER! BONUS MANGA
RIGHT AFTER THE COOKING CLUB LOST...
SHUMP
SORRY TO HEAR THAT YOU LOST TO MIKASA!
BAAM
... HANGE ARRIVED.
THE ANSWER IS NO! GO AWAY!
Hello? Is this the police?
WHY ARE YOU TREATING ME LIKE A WEIRDO?
COME ON! I'VE COME HERE TO CHEER YOU ALL UP!
HERE ARE COOKIES THAT LEVI BAKED HIMSELF! HAVE SOME AND CHEER UP!
He made them especially for me to snack on.
Levi made them by hand? So he can bake too...
BUT THERE'S NO WAY HE COULD BE BETTER THAN MIKASA...
CHOMP
SNIFF SNIFF
TMP TMP TMP TMP TMP TMP
PLEASE MAKE ME YOUR DISCIPLE!!
PASHOOM
!!
AND SO NANABA ACQUIRED A NEW OBSESSION.

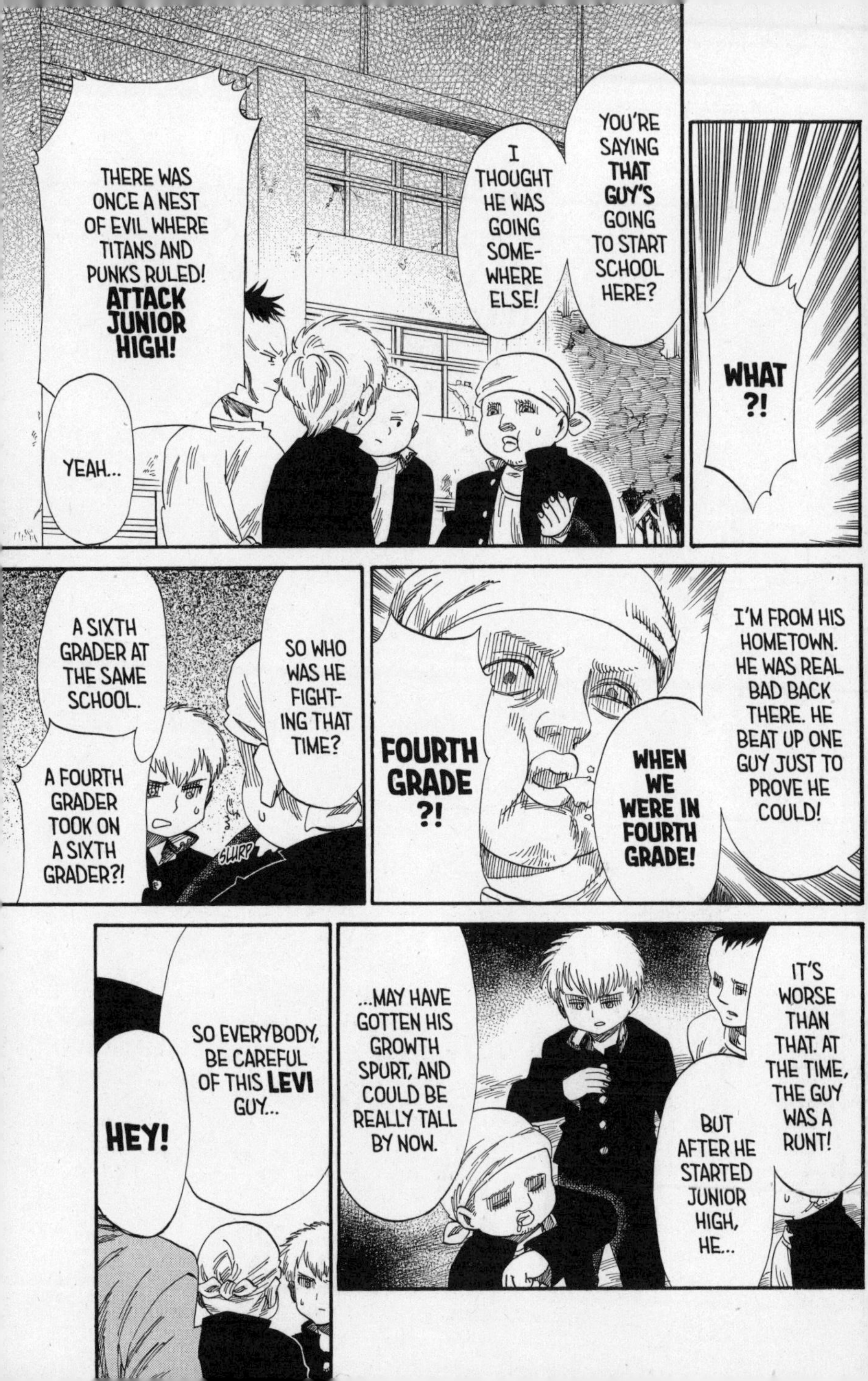
WHAT?!
YOU'RE SAYING THAT GUY'S GOING TO START SCHOOL HERE?
I THOUGHT HE WAS GOING SOME-WHERE ELSE!
THERE WAS ONCE A NEST OF EVIL WHERE TITANS AND PUNKS RULED! ATTACK JUNIOR HIGH!
YEAH...
I'M FROM HIS HOMETOWN. HE WAS REAL BAD BACK THERE. HE BEAT UP ONE GUY JUST TO PROVE HE COULD!
WHEN WE WERE IN FOURTH GRADE!
FOURTH GRADE?!
SO WHO WAS HE FIGHT-ING THAT TIME?
A SIXTH GRADER AT THE SAME SCHOOL.
A FOURTH GRADER TOOK ON A SIXTH GRADER?!
SLURP
IT'S WORSE THAN THAT. AT THE TIME, THE GUY WAS A RUNT!
BUT AFTER HE STARTED JUNIOR HIGH, HE...
...MAY HAVE GOTTEN HIS GROWTH SPURT, AND COULD BE REALLY TALL BY NOW.
SO EVERYBODY, BE CAREFUL OF THIS LEVI GUY...
HEY!

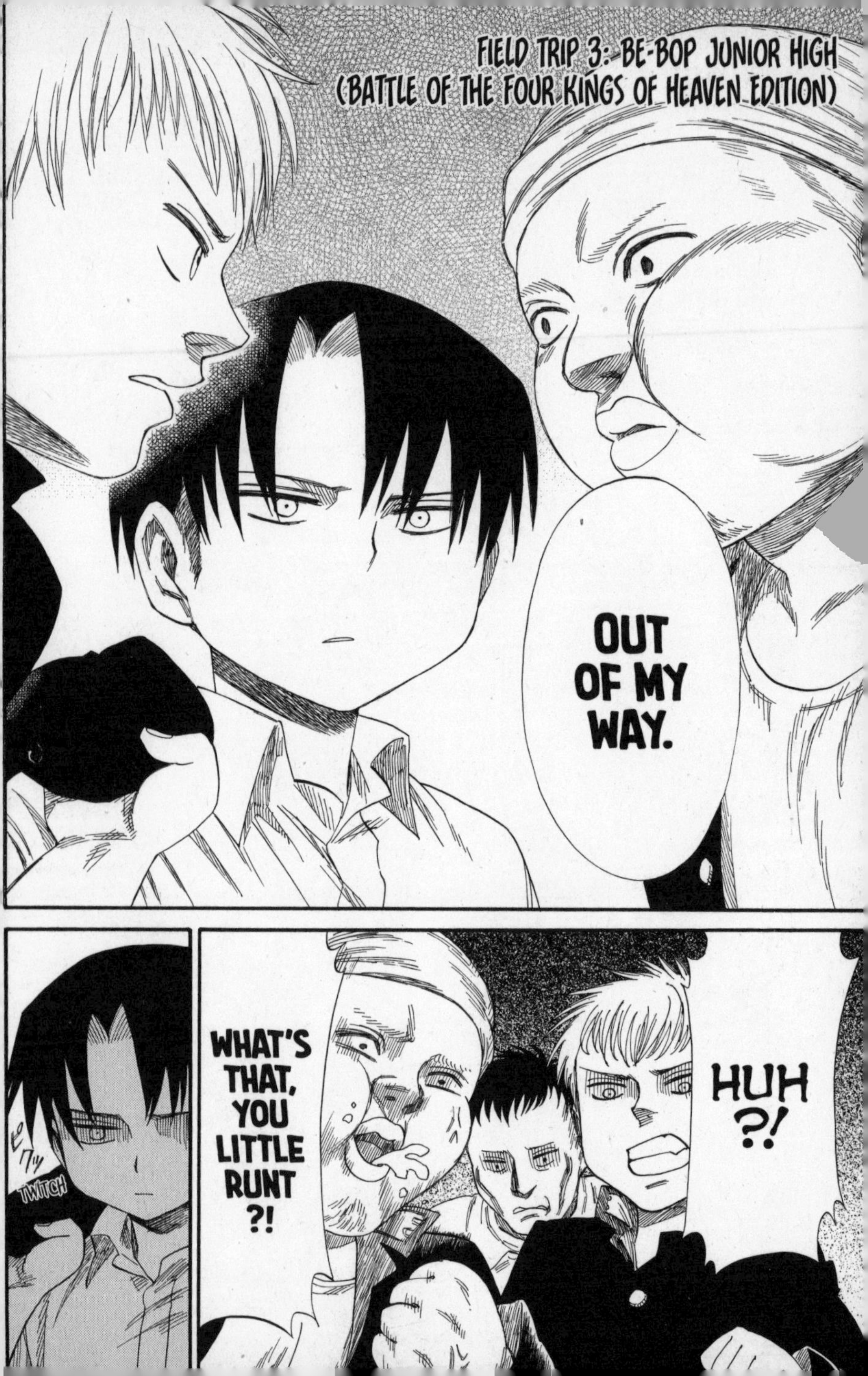
FIELD TRIP 3: BE-BOP JUNIOR HIGH (BATTLE OF THE FOUR KINGS OF HEAVEN EDITION)
OUT OF MY WAY.
HUH ?!
WHAT'S THAT, YOU LITTLE RUNT ?!
ピクッ
TWITCH

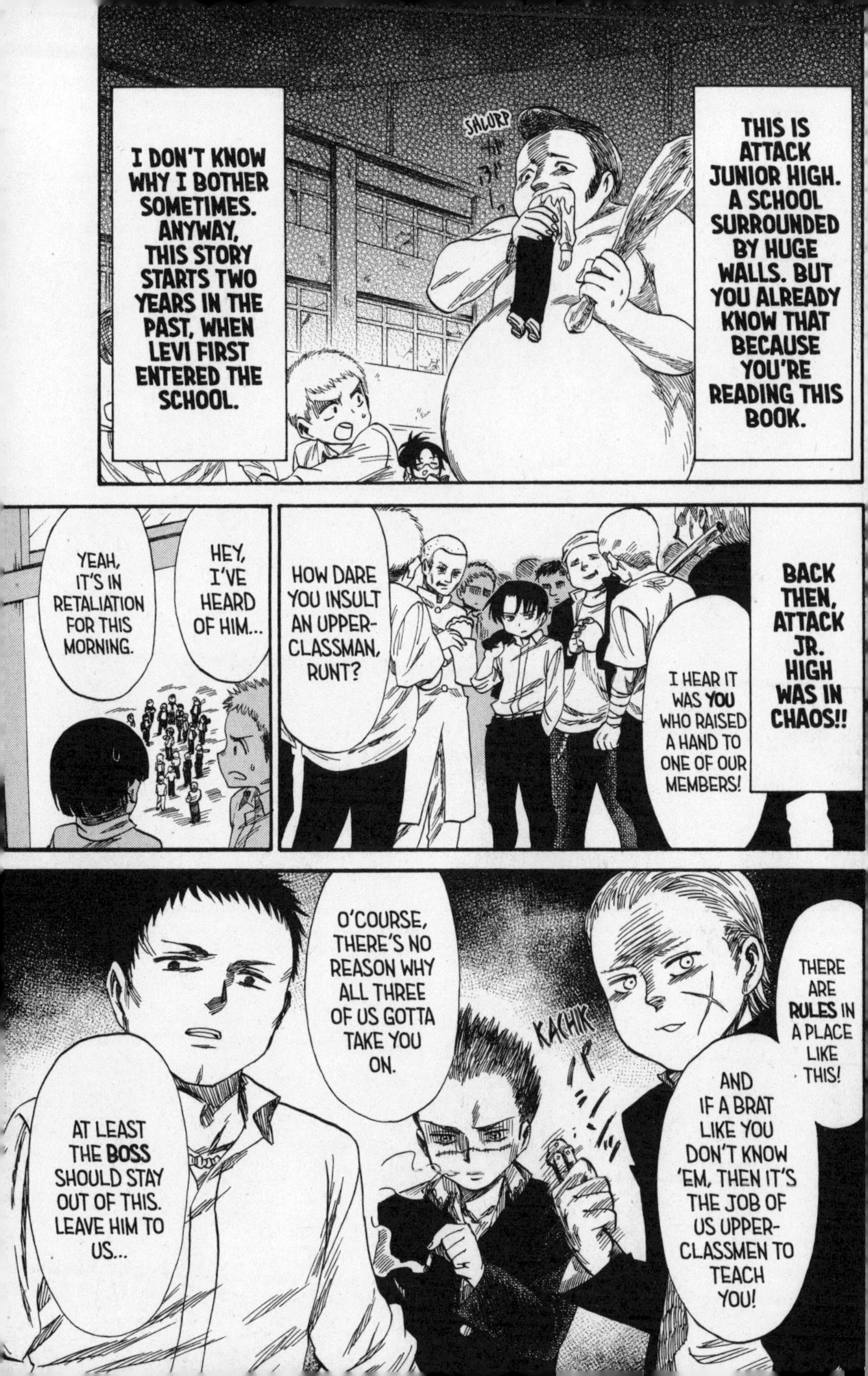
THIS IS ATTACK JUNIOR HIGH. A SCHOOL SURROUNDED BY HUGE WALLS. BUT YOU ALREADY KNOW THAT BECAUSE YOU'RE READING THIS BOOK.
SHLURP
I DON'T KNOW WHY I BOTHER SOMETIMES. ANYWAY, THIS STORY STARTS TWO YEARS IN THE PAST, WHEN LEVI FIRST ENTERED THE SCHOOL.
BACK THEN, ATTACK JR. HIGH WAS IN CHAOS!!
I HEAR IT WAS YOU WHO RAISED A HAND TO ONE OF OUR MEMBERS!
HOW DARE YOU INSULT AN UPPER-CLASSMAN, RUNT?
HEY, I'VE HEARD OF HIM...
YEAH, IT'S IN RETALIATION FOR THIS MORNING.
THERE ARE RULES IN A PLACE LIKE THIS!
AND IF A BRAT LIKE YOU DON'T KNOW 'EM, THEN IT'S THE JOB OF US UPPER-CLASSMEN TO TEACH YOU!
KACHIK
O'COURSE, THERE'S NO REASON WHY ALL THREE OF US GOTTA TAKE YOU ON.
AT LEAST THE BOSS SHOULD STAY OUT OF THIS. LEAVE HIM TO US...

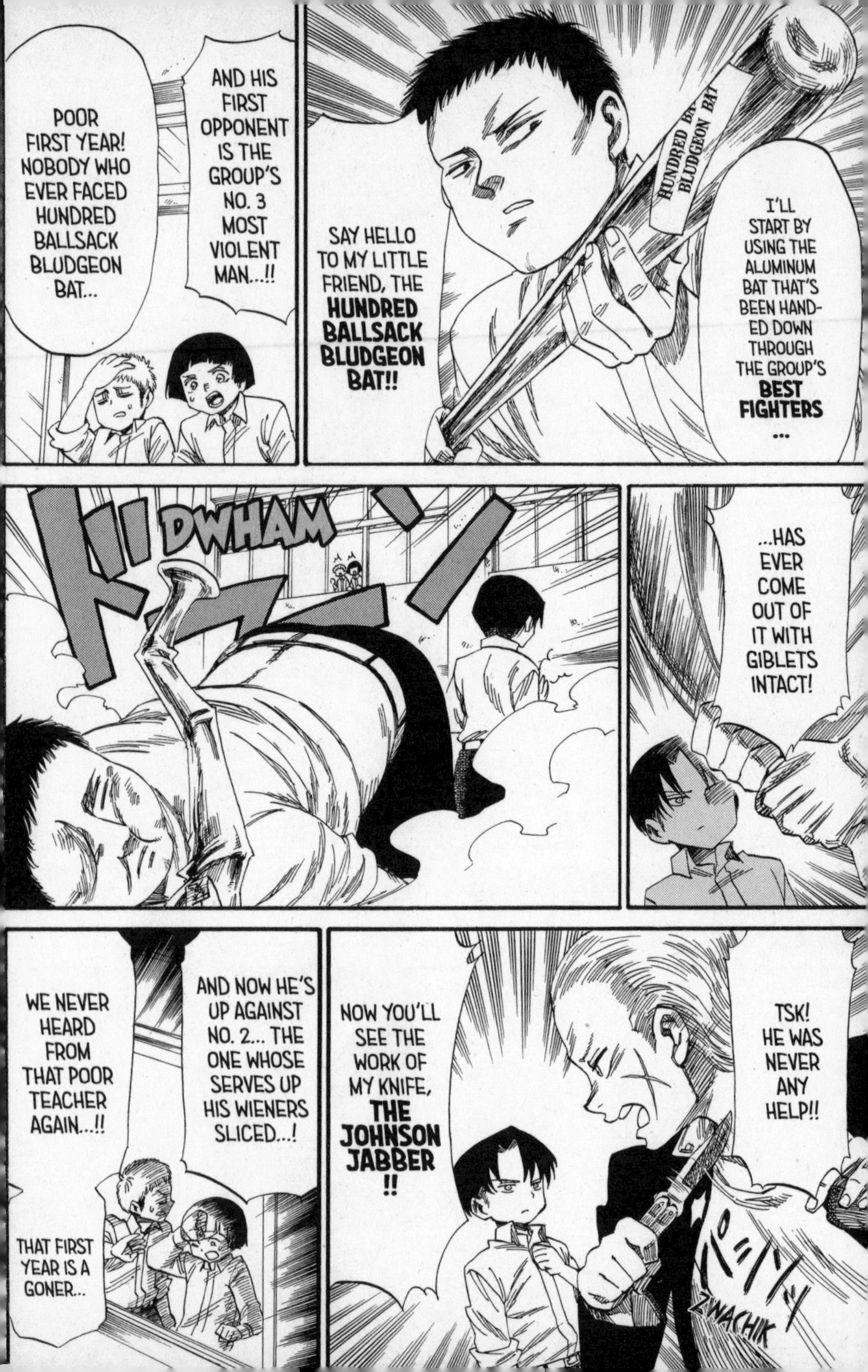

I'LL START BY USING THE ALUMINUM BAT THAT'S BEEN HANDED DOWN THROUGH THE GROUP'S **BEST FIGHTERS**...
SAY HELLO TO MY LITTLE FRIEND, THE **HUNDRED BALLSACK BLUDGEON BAT!!**
AND HIS FIRST OPPONENT IS THE GROUP'S NO. 3 MOST VIOLENT MAN...!!
POOR FIRST YEAR! NOBODY WHO EVER FACED HUNDRED BALLSACK BLUDGEON BAT...
...HAS EVER COME OUT OF IT WITH GIBLETS INTACT!
DWHAM
TSK! HE WAS NEVER ANY HELP!!
NOW YOU'LL SEE THE WORK OF MY KNIFE, **THE JOHNSON JABBER!!**
ZWACHIK
AND NOW HE'S UP AGAINST NO. 2... THE ONE WHOSE SERVES UP HIS WIENERS SLICED...!
WE NEVER HEARD FROM THAT POOR TEACHER AGAIN...!!
THAT FIRST YEAR IS A GONER...

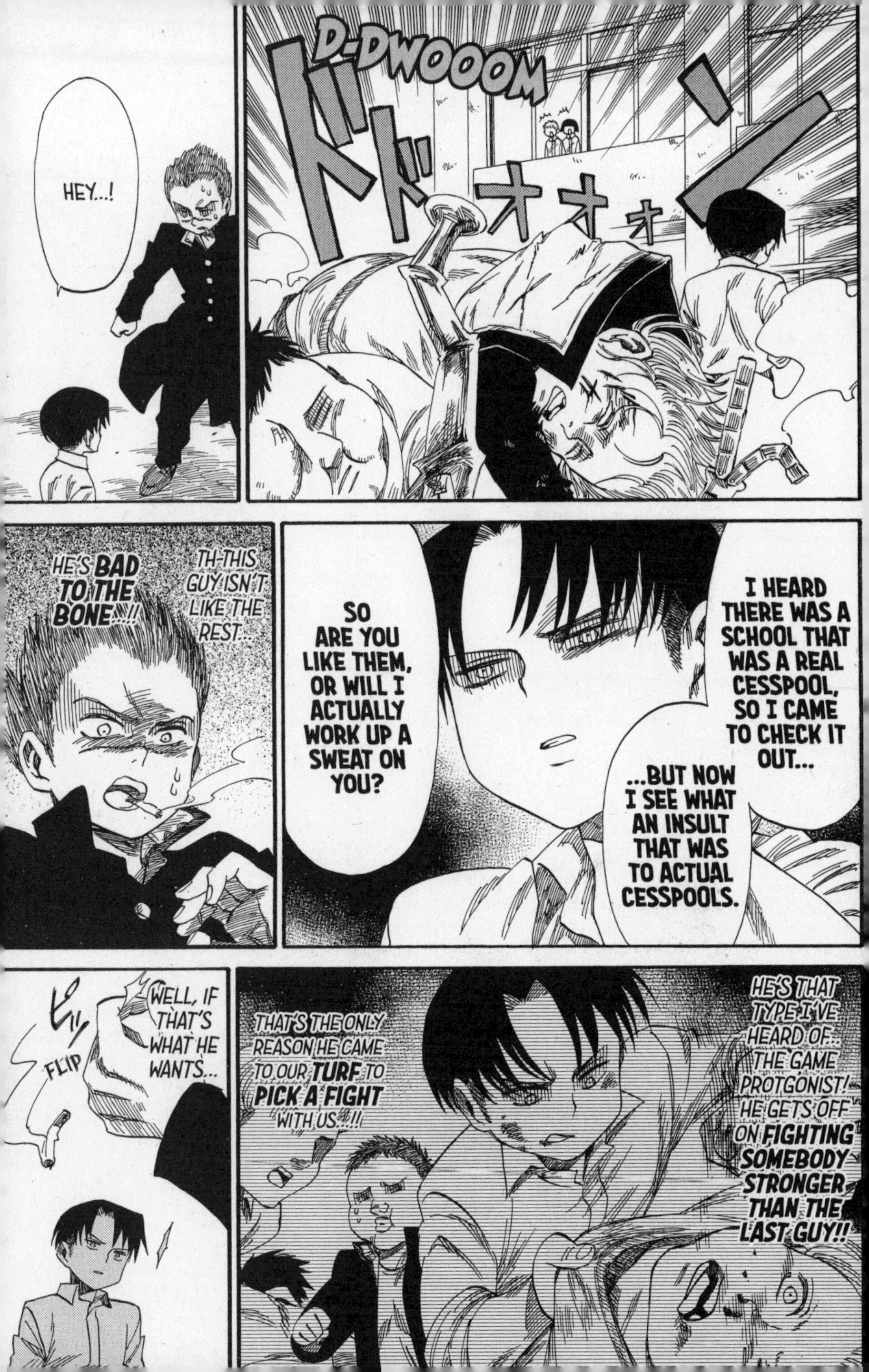

D-DWOOOM
ドドオオォー
HEY...!
I HEARD THERE WAS A SCHOOL THAT WAS A REAL CESSPOOL, SO I CAME TO CHECK IT OUT...
...BUT NOW I SEE WHAT AN INSULT THAT WAS TO ACTUAL CESSPOOLS.
SO ARE YOU LIKE THEM, OR WILL I ACTUALLY WORK UP A SWEAT ON YOU?
TH-THIS GUY ISN'T LIKE THE REST...
HE'S BAD TO THE BONE...!!
HE'S THAT TYPE I'VE HEARD OF... THE GAME PROTGONIST! HE GETS OFF ON FIGHTING SOMEBODY STRONGER THAN THE LAST GUY!!
THAT'S THE ONLY REASON HE CAME TO OUR TURF TO PICK A FIGHT WITH US...!!
WELL, IF THAT'S WHAT HE WANTS...
ピッ
FLIP

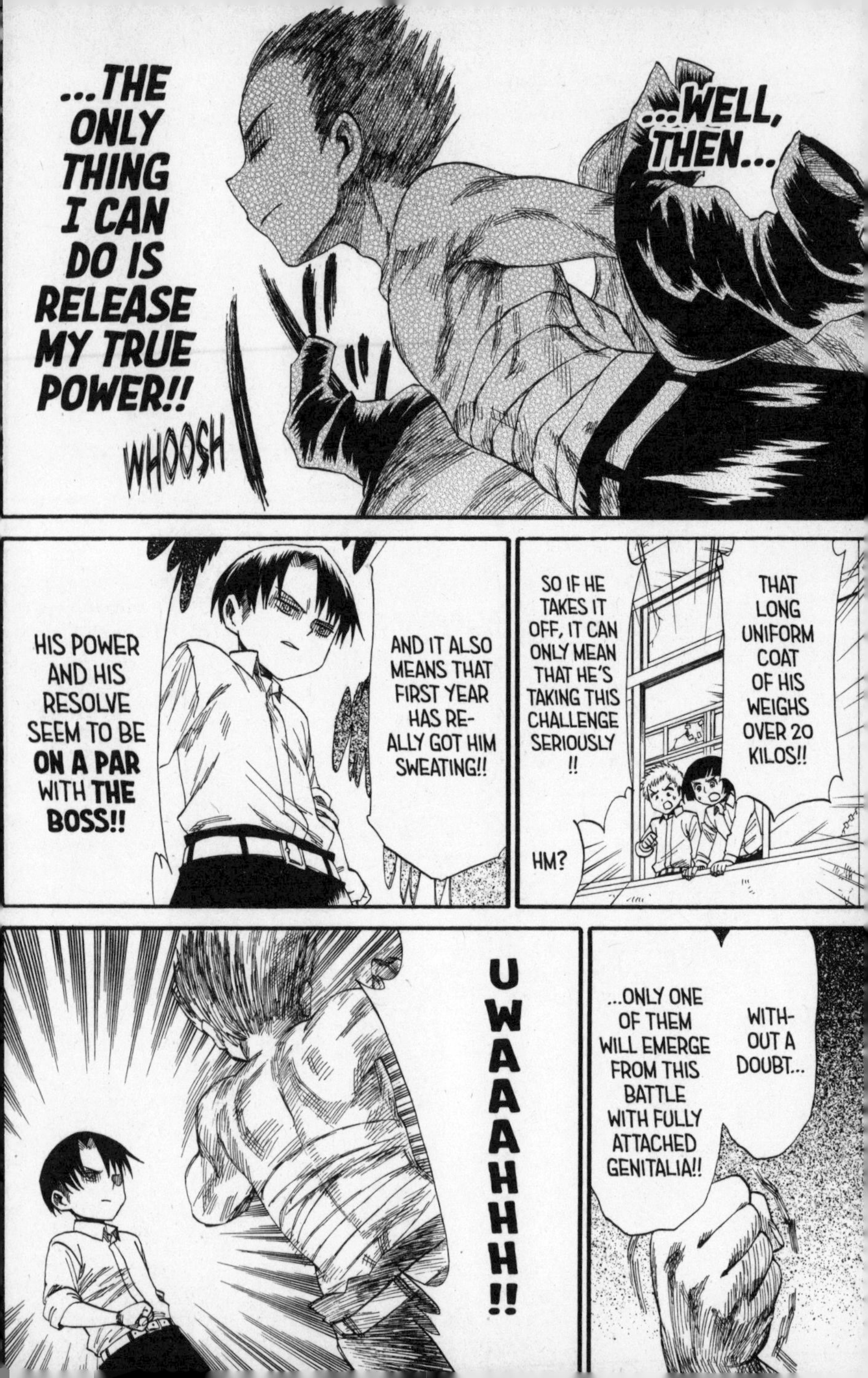
...WELL, THEN...
...THE ONLY THING I CAN DO IS RELEASE MY TRUE POWER!!
WHOOSH
THAT LONG UNIFORM COAT OF HIS WEIGHS OVER 20 KILOS!!
SO IF HE TAKES IT OFF, IT CAN ONLY MEAN THAT HE'S TAKING THIS CHALLENGE SERIOUSLY!!
HM?
AND IT ALSO MEANS THAT FIRST YEAR HAS REALLY GOT HIM SWEATING!!
HIS POWER AND HIS RESOLVE SEEM TO BE ON A PAR WITH THE BOSS!!
WITHOUT A DOUBT...
...ONLY ONE OF THEM WILL EMERGE FROM THIS BATTLE WITH FULLY ATTACHED GENITALIA!!
UWAAAAHHHH!!

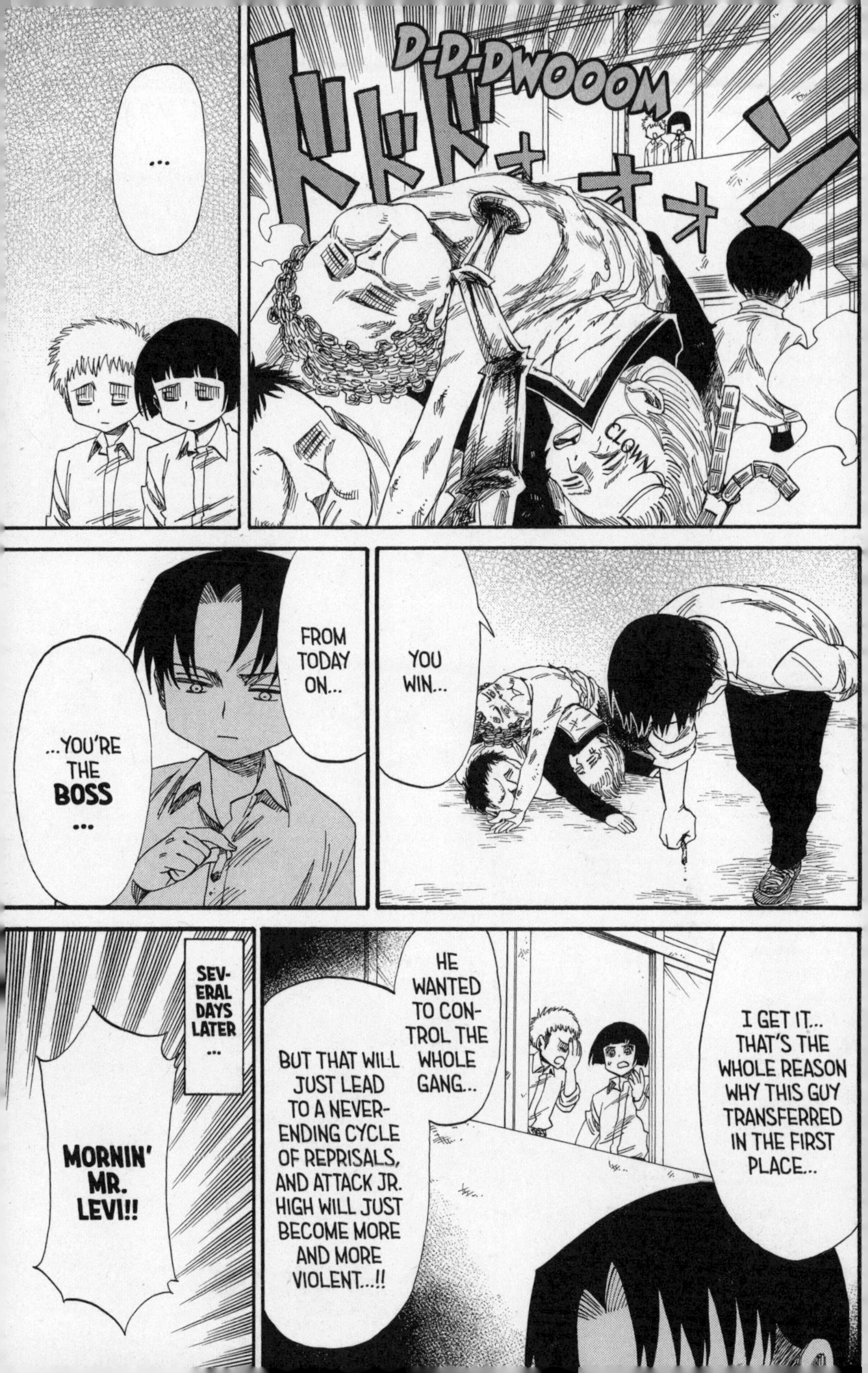
D-D-DWOOOM
CLOWN
...
YOU WIN...
FROM TODAY ON...
...YOU'RE THE **BOSS** ...
I GET IT... THAT'S THE WHOLE REASON WHY THIS GUY TRANSFERRED IN THE FIRST PLACE...
HE WANTED TO CONTROL THE WHOLE GANG...
BUT THAT WILL JUST LEAD TO A NEVER-ENDING CYCLE OF REPRISALS, AND ATTACK JR. HIGH WILL JUST BECOME MORE AND MORE VIOLENT...!!
SEVERAL DAYS LATER ...
MORNIN' MR. LEVI!!

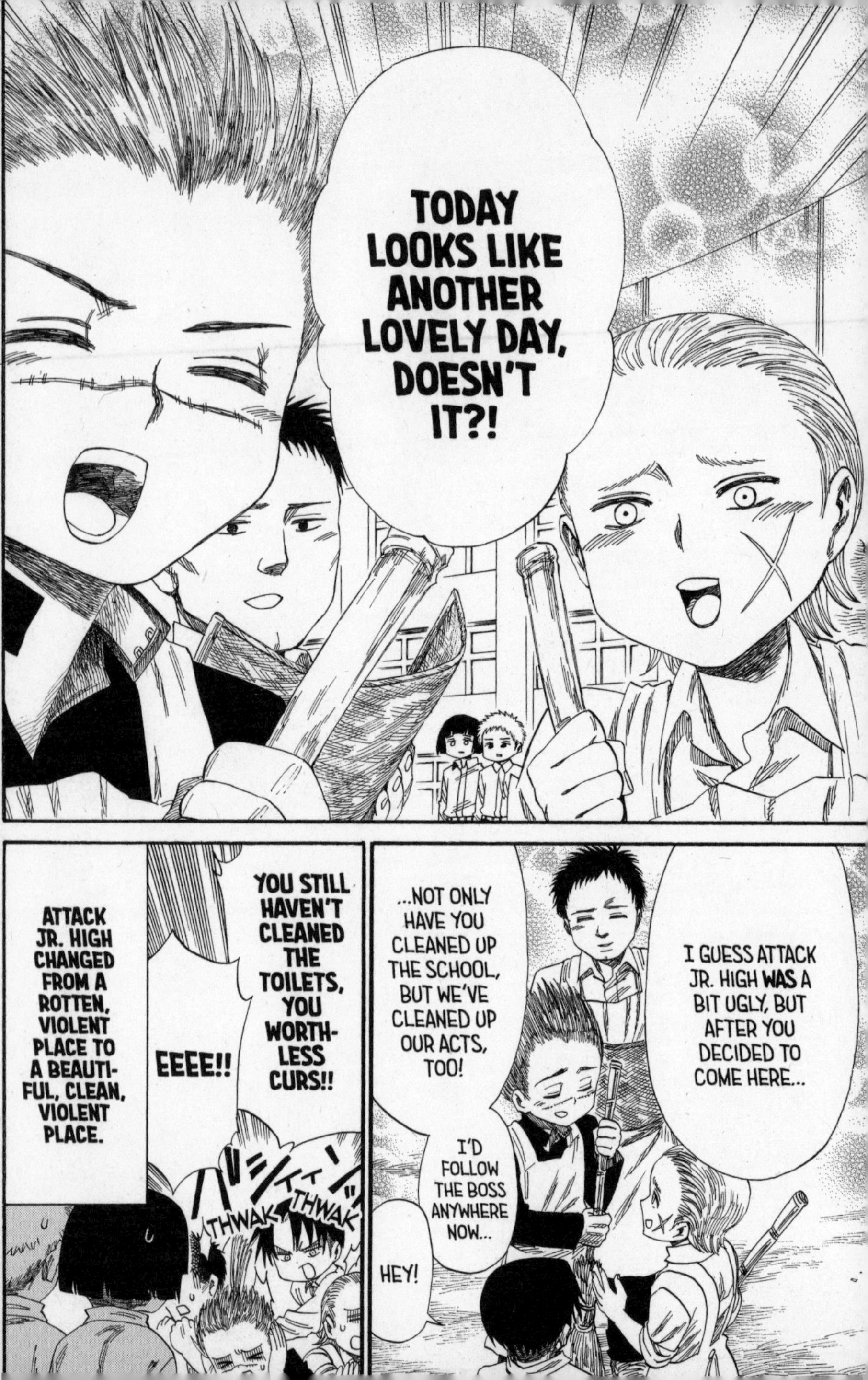
TODAY LOOKS LIKE ANOTHER LOVELY DAY, DOESN'T IT?!
I GUESS ATTACK JR. HIGH WAS A BIT UGLY, BUT AFTER YOU DECIDED TO COME HERE...
...NOT ONLY HAVE YOU CLEANED UP THE SCHOOL, BUT WE'VE CLEANED UP OUR ACTS, TOO!
I'D FOLLOW THE BOSS ANYWHERE NOW...
HEY!
YOU STILL HAVEN'T CLEANED THE TOILETS, YOU WORTH-LESS CURS!!
EEEE!!
THWAK
THWAK
ATTACK JR. HIGH CHANGED FROM A ROTTEN, VIOLENT PLACE TO A BEAUTI-FUL, CLEAN, VIOLENT PLACE.

FIELD TRIP 4: THE BOSS IS NO WEAKLING

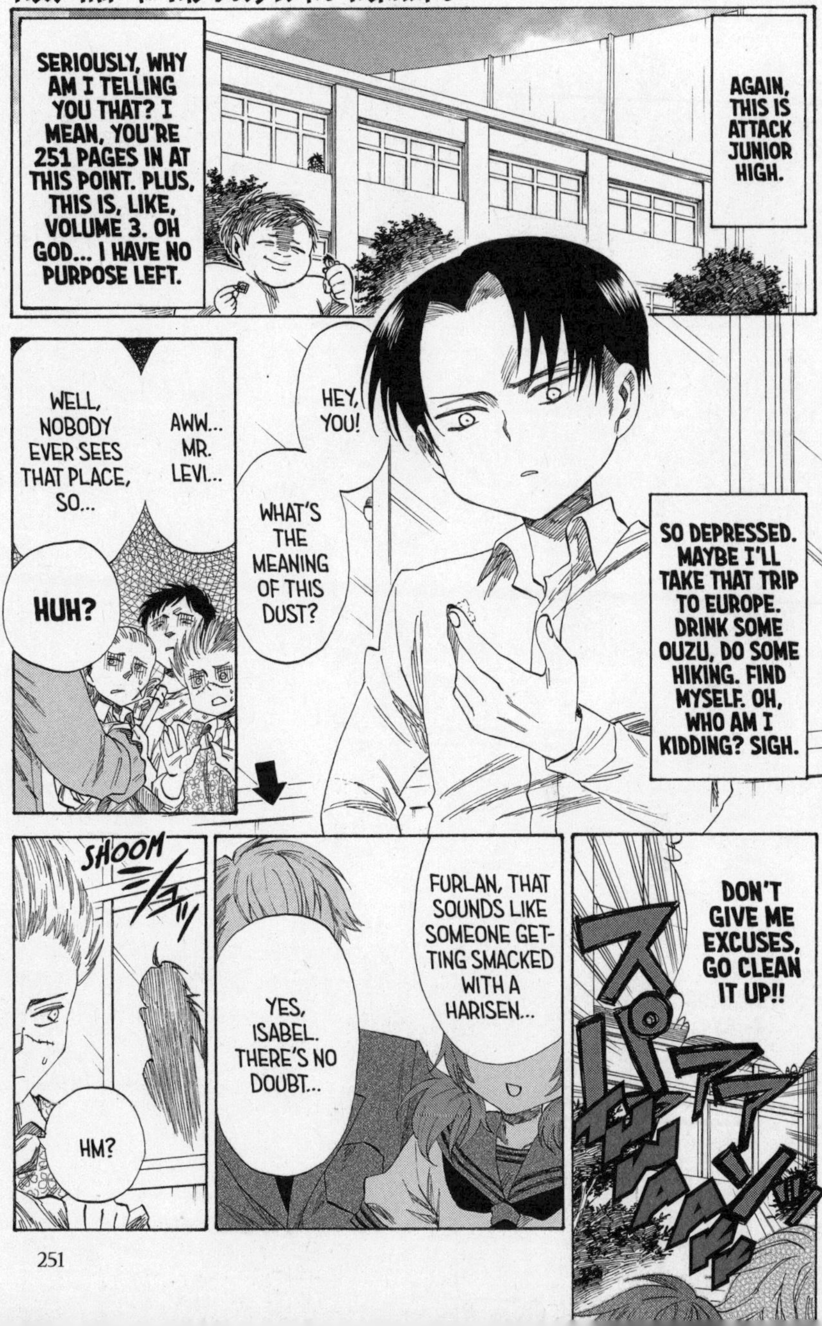
AGAIN, THIS IS ATTACK JUNIOR HIGH.
SERIOUSLY, WHY AM I TELLING YOU THAT? I MEAN, YOU'RE 251 PAGES IN AT THIS POINT. PLUS, THIS IS, LIKE, VOLUME 3. OH GOD... I HAVE NO PURPOSE LEFT.
HEY, YOU!
WHAT'S THE MEANING OF THIS DUST?
SO DEPRESSED. MAYBE I'LL TAKE THAT TRIP TO EUROPE. DRINK SOME OUZU, DO SOME HIKING. FIND MYSELF. OH, WHO AM I KIDDING? SIGH.
AWW... MR. LEVI...
WELL, NOBODY EVER SEES THAT PLACE, SO...
HUH?
DON'T GIVE ME EXCUSES, GO CLEAN IT UP!!
FURLAN, THAT SOUNDS LIKE SOMEONE GETTING SMACKED WITH A HARISEN...
YES, ISABEL. THERE'S NO DOUBT...
SHOOM
HM?

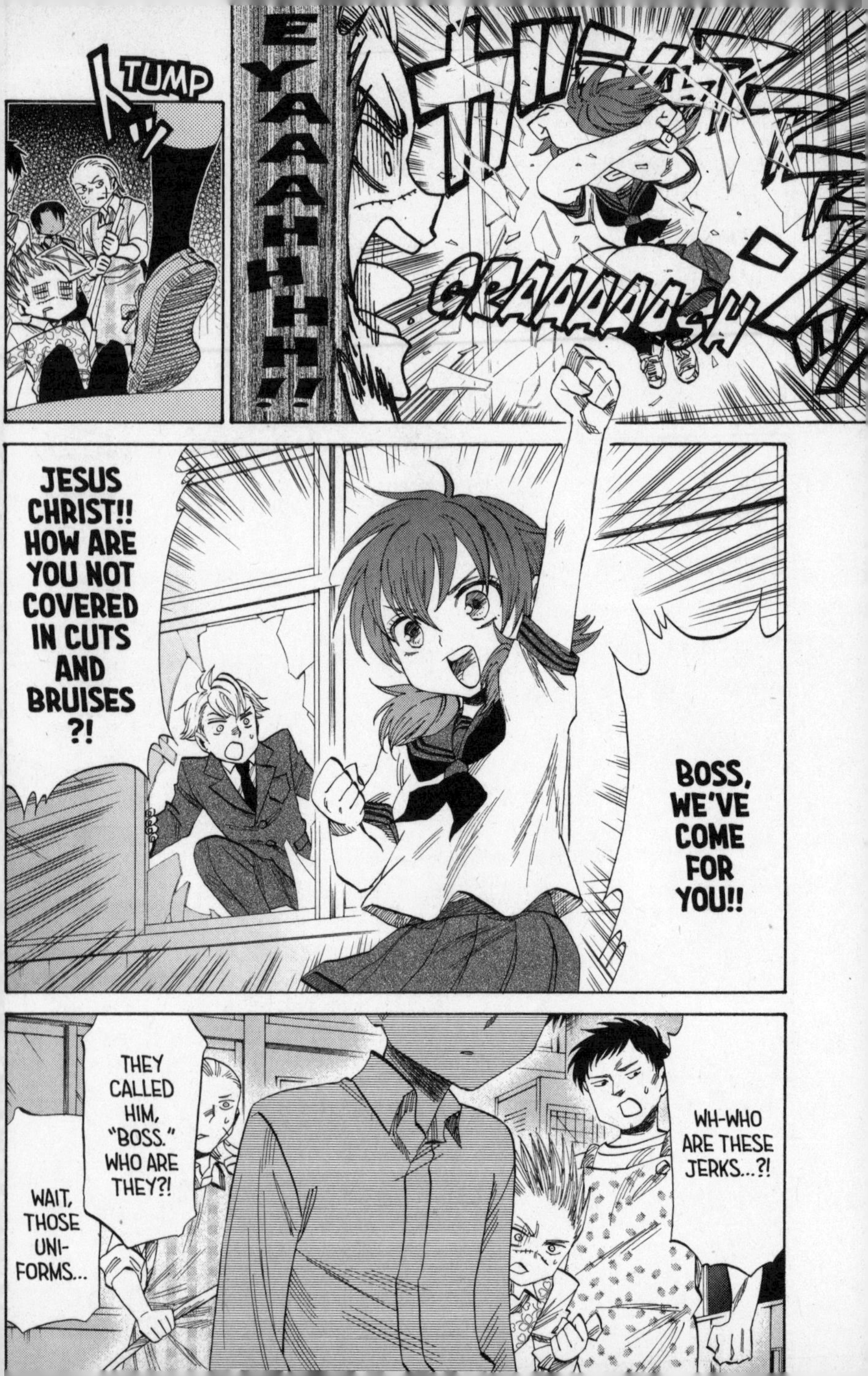

CRAAAASH
EYAAAHHHH!!
TUMP
BOSS, WE'VE COME FOR YOU!!
JESUS CHRIST!! HOW ARE YOU NOT COVERED IN CUTS AND BRUISES?!
WH-WHO ARE THESE JERKS...?!
THEY CALLED HIM, "BOSS." WHO ARE THEY?!
WAIT, THOSE UNI-FORMS...

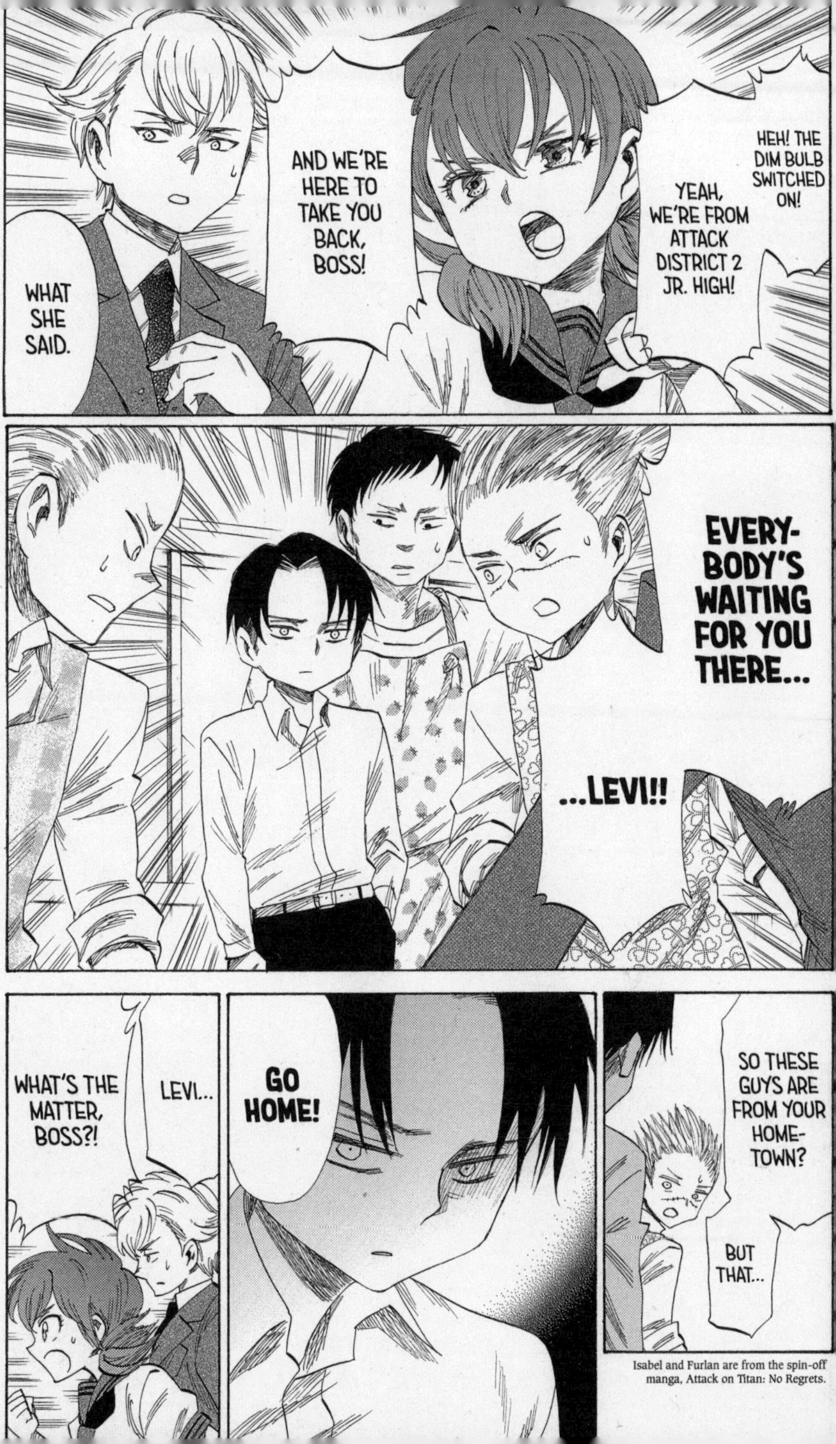
HEH! THE DIM BULB SWITCHED ON!
YEAH, WE'RE FROM ATTACK DISTRICT 2 JR. HIGH!
AND WE'RE HERE TO TAKE YOU BACK, BOSS!
WHAT SHE SAID.
EVERY-BODY'S WAITING FOR YOU THERE...
...LEVI!!
SO THESE GUYS ARE FROM YOUR HOME-TOWN?
BUT THAT...
GO HOME!
LEVI...
WHAT'S THE MATTER, BOSS?!

Isabel and Furlan are from the spin-off manga, Attack on Titan: No Regrets.

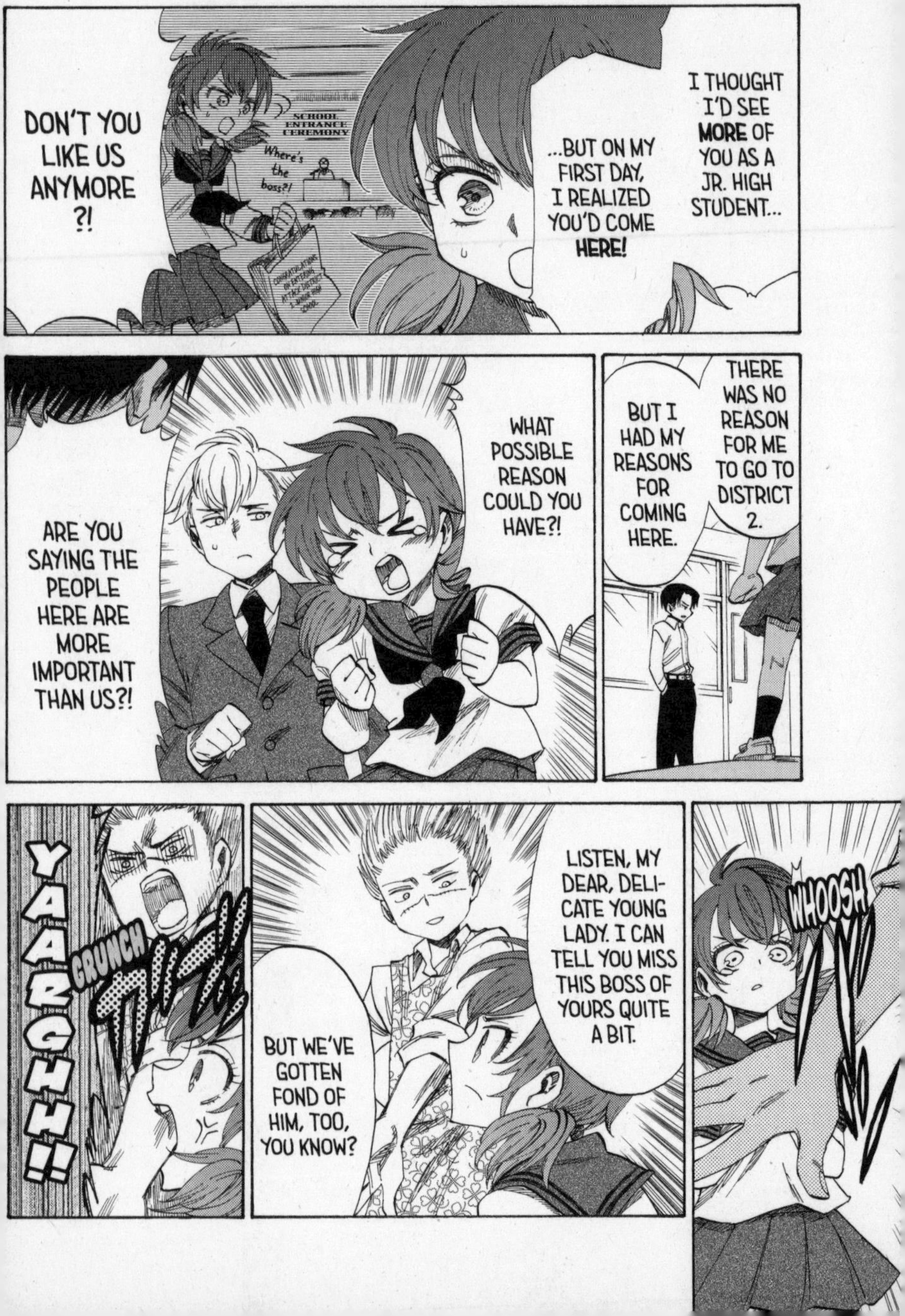
I THOUGHT I'D SEE MORE OF YOU AS A JR. HIGH STUDENT...
...BUT ON MY FIRST DAY, I REALIZED YOU'D COME HERE!
SCHOOL ENTRANCE CEREMONY
Where's the boss?!
DON'T YOU LIKE US ANYMORE?!
THERE WAS NO REASON FOR ME TO GO TO DISTRICT 2.
BUT I HAD MY REASONS FOR COMING HERE.
WHAT POSSIBLE REASON COULD YOU HAVE?!
ARE YOU SAYING THE PEOPLE HERE ARE MORE IMPORTANT THAN US?!
WHOOSH
LISTEN, MY DEAR, DELI-CATE YOUNG LADY. I CAN TELL YOU MISS THIS BOSS OF YOURS QUITE A BIT.
BUT WE'VE GOTTEN FOND OF HIM, TOO, YOU KNOW?
GRUNCH
YAARGHHH!!

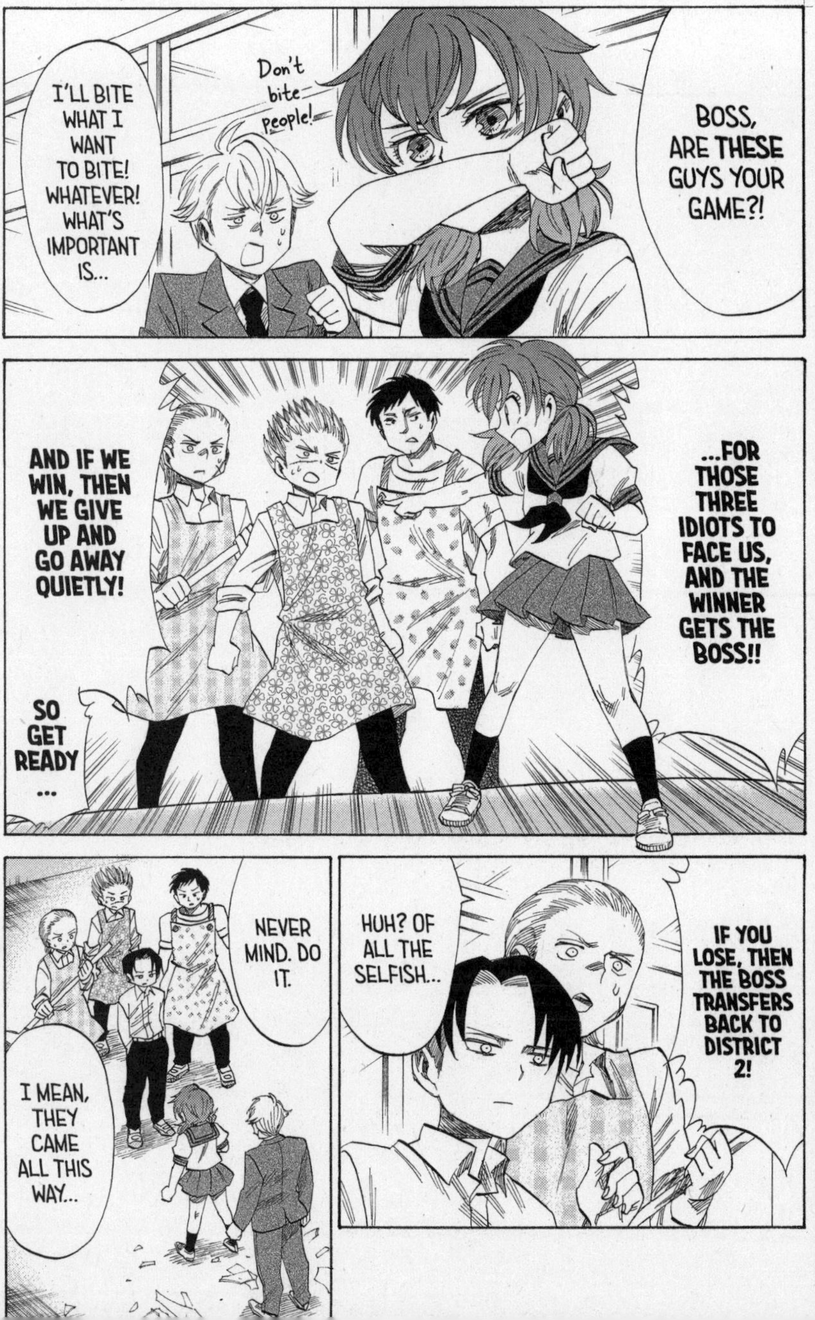
BOSS, ARE THESE GUYS YOUR GAME?!
Don't bite people!
I'LL BITE WHAT I WANT TO BITE! WHATEVER! WHAT'S IMPORTANT IS...
...FOR THOSE THREE IDIOTS TO FACE US, AND THE WINNER GETS THE BOSS!!
AND IF WE WIN, THEN WE GIVE UP AND GO AWAY QUIETLY!
SO GET READY ...
IF YOU LOSE, THEN THE BOSS TRANSFERS BACK TO DISTRICT 2!
HUH? OF ALL THE SELFISH...
NEVER MIND. DO IT.
I MEAN, THEY CAME ALL THIS WAY...

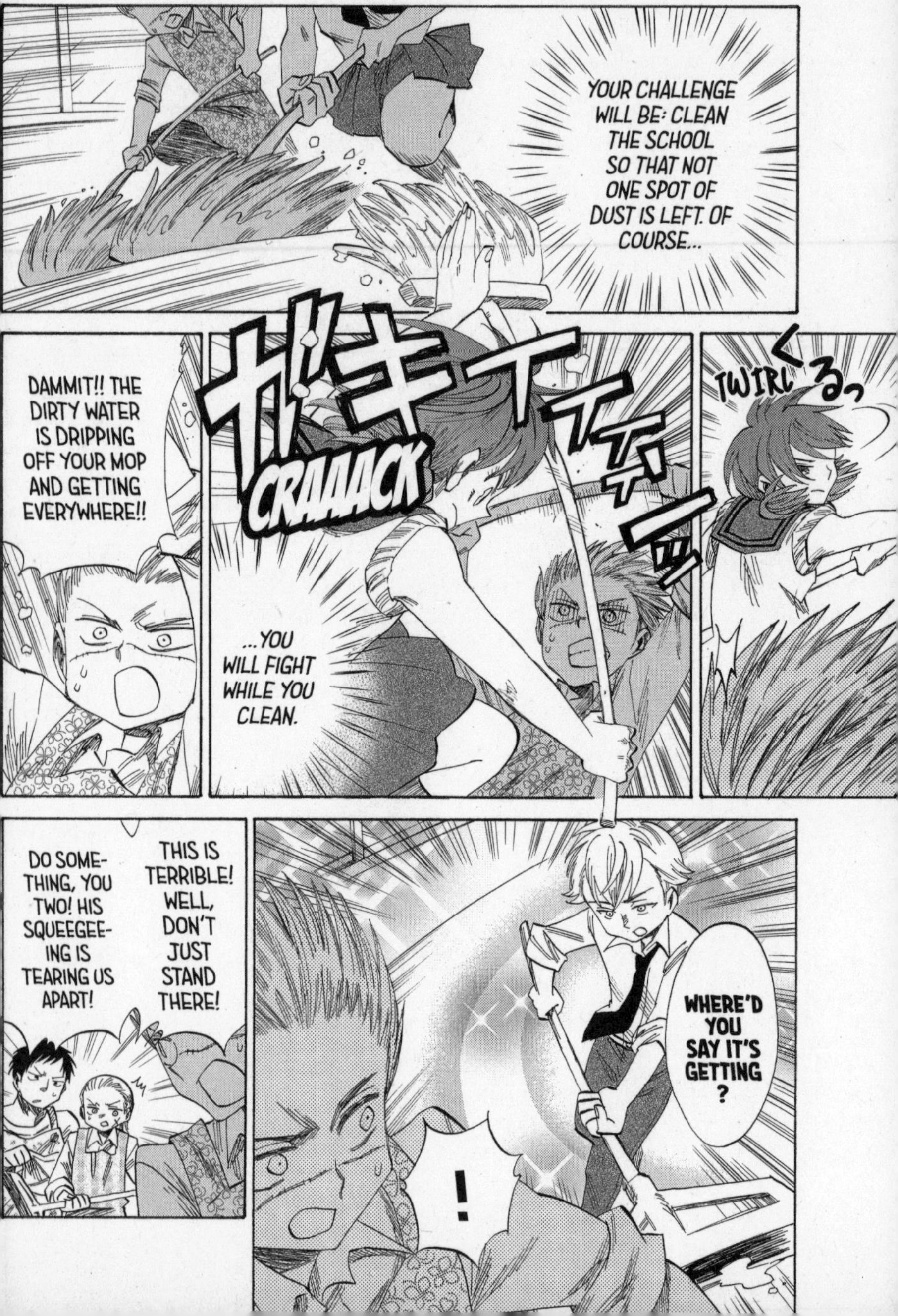

YOUR CHALLENGE WILL BE: CLEAN THE SCHOOL SO THAT NOT ONE SPOT OF DUST IS LEFT. OF COURSE...
TWIRL くるっ
ガキイイイーッ!!
CRAAACK
...YOU WILL FIGHT WHILE YOU CLEAN.
DAMMIT!! THE DIRTY WATER IS DRIPPING OFF YOUR MOP AND GETTING EVERYWHERE!!
WHERE'D YOU SAY IT'S GETTING?
!
THIS IS TERRIBLE! WELL, DON'T JUST STAND THERE!
DO SOME-THING, YOU TWO! HIS SQUEEGEE-ING IS TEARING US APART!

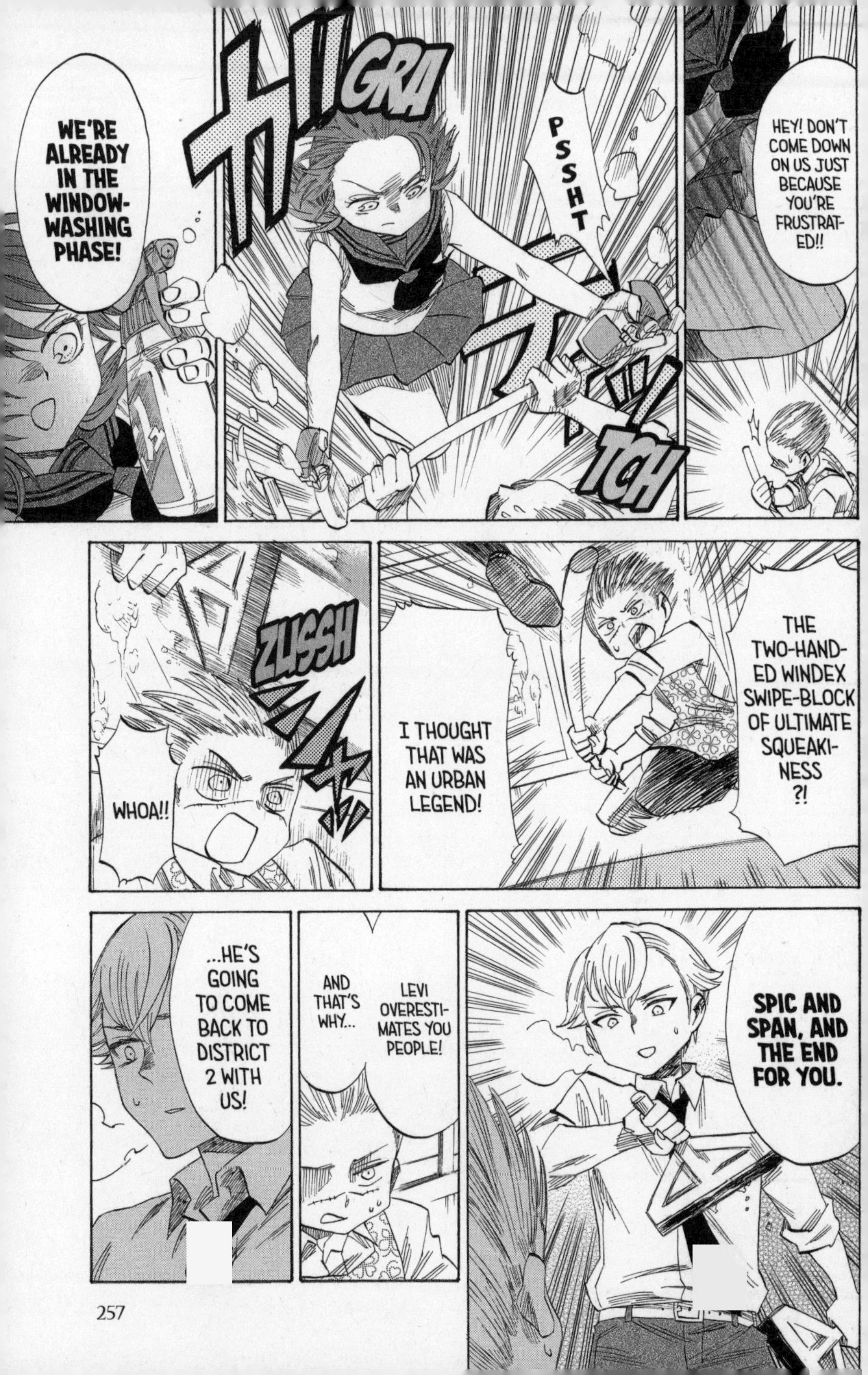
HEY! DON'T COME DOWN ON US JUST BECAUSE YOU'RE FRUSTRATED!!
GRA
PSSHT
TCH
WE'RE ALREADY IN THE WINDOW-WASHING PHASE!
THE TWO-HANDED WINDEX SWIPE-BLOCK OF ULTIMATE SQUEAKINESS ?!
I THOUGHT THAT WAS AN URBAN LEGEND!
ZUSSH
WHOA!!
SPIC AND SPAN, AND THE END FOR YOU.
LEVI OVERESTIMATES YOU PEOPLE!
AND THAT'S WHY...
...HE'S GOING TO COME BACK TO DISTRICT 2 WITH US!

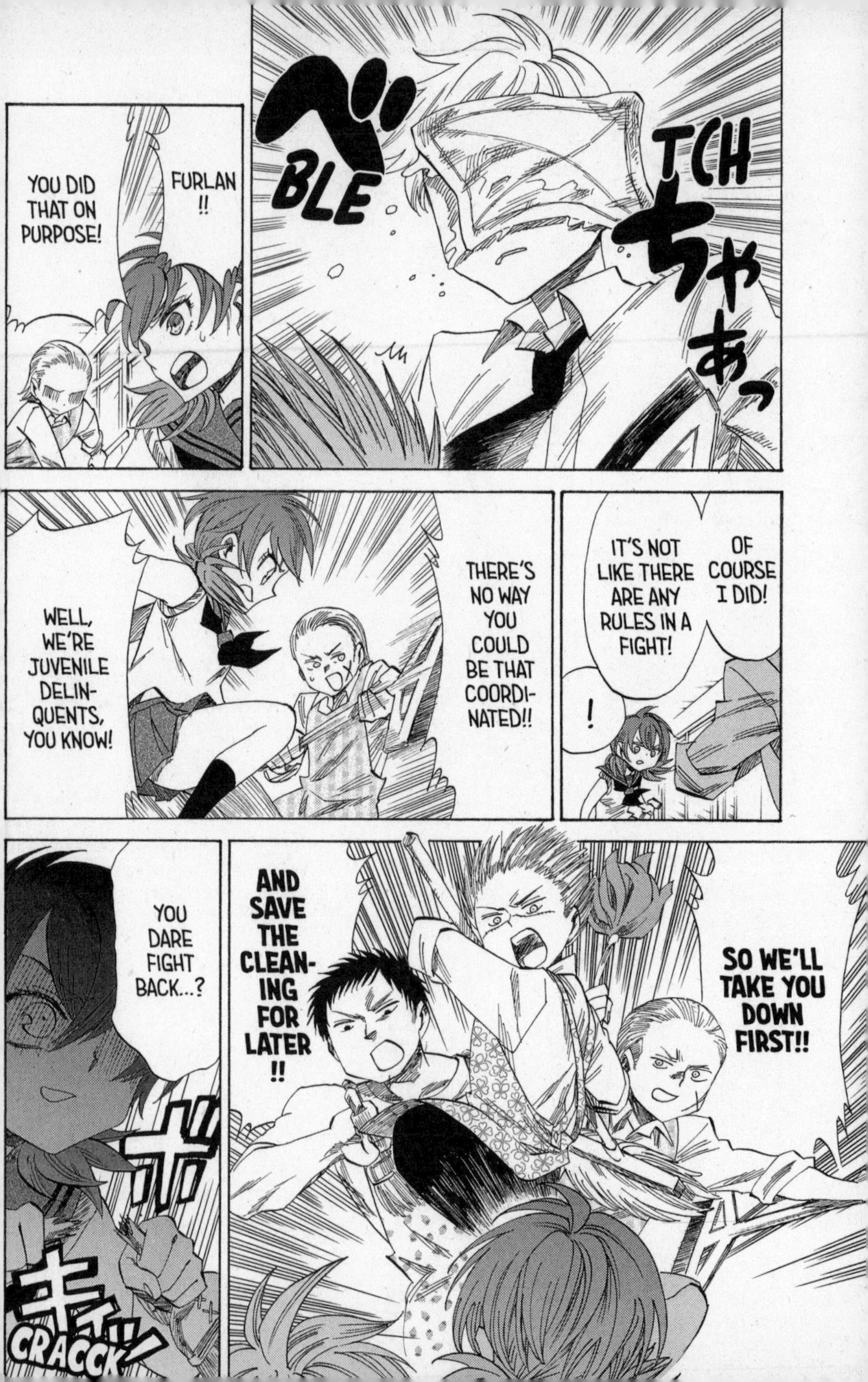

べ
BLE
TCH
ちゃあっ
FURLAN !!
YOU DID THAT ON PURPOSE!
OF COURSE I DID!
IT'S NOT LIKE THERE ARE ANY RULES IN A FIGHT!
!
THERE'S NO WAY YOU COULD BE THAT COORDI-NATED!!
WELL, WE'RE JUVENILE DELIN-QUENTS, YOU KNOW!
SO WE'LL TAKE YOU DOWN FIRST!!
AND SAVE THE CLEAN-ING FOR LATER !!
YOU DARE FIGHT BACK...?
CRACCK!

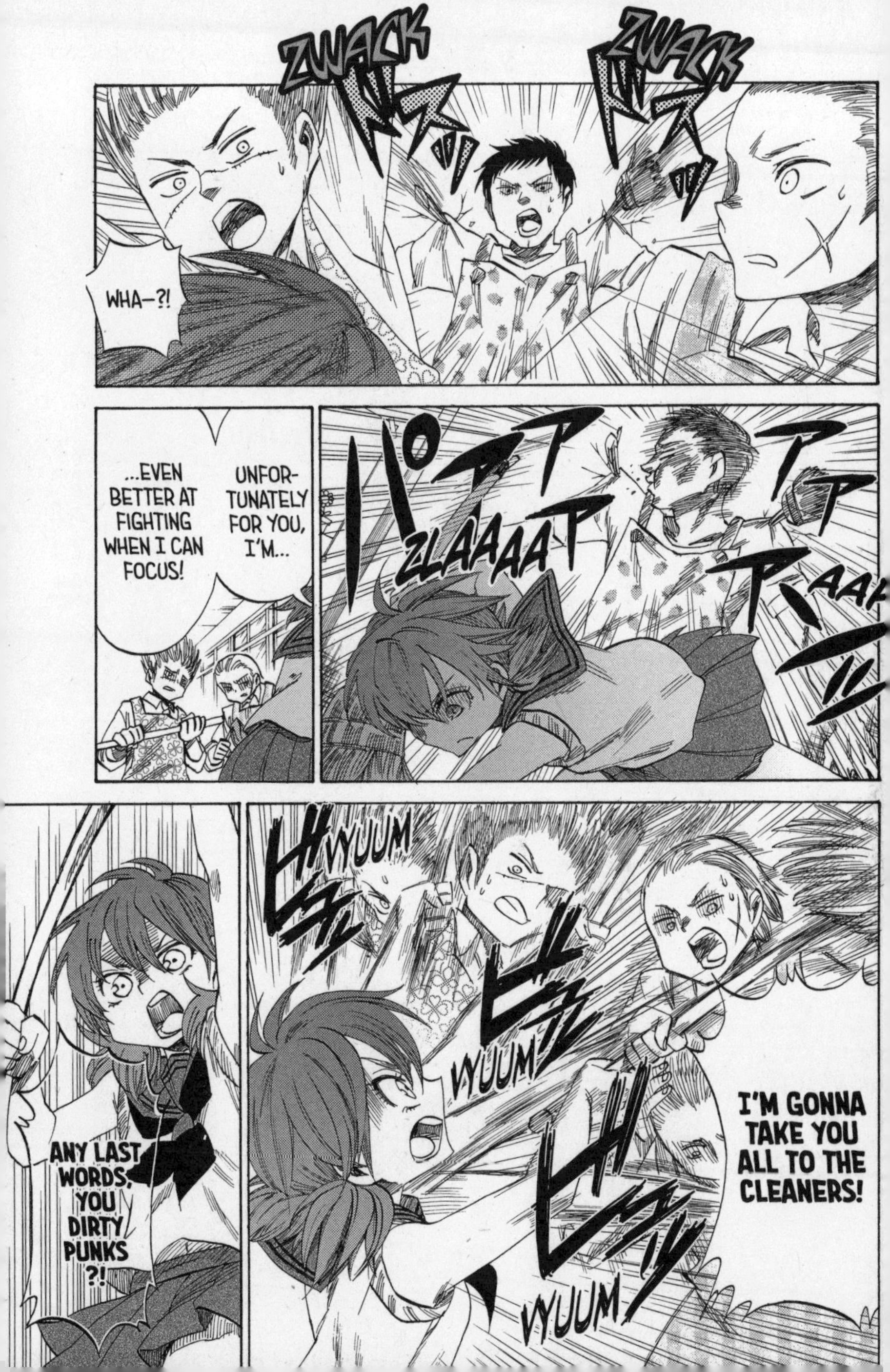
ZWACK
ZWACK
WHA–?!
ZLAAAAAT
UNFOR-TUNATELY FOR YOU, I'M...
...EVEN BETTER AT FIGHTING WHEN I CAN FOCUS!
VYUUM
I'M GONNA TAKE YOU ALL TO THE CLEANERS!
VYUUM
VYUUM
ANY LAST WORDS, YOU DIRTY PUNKS?!

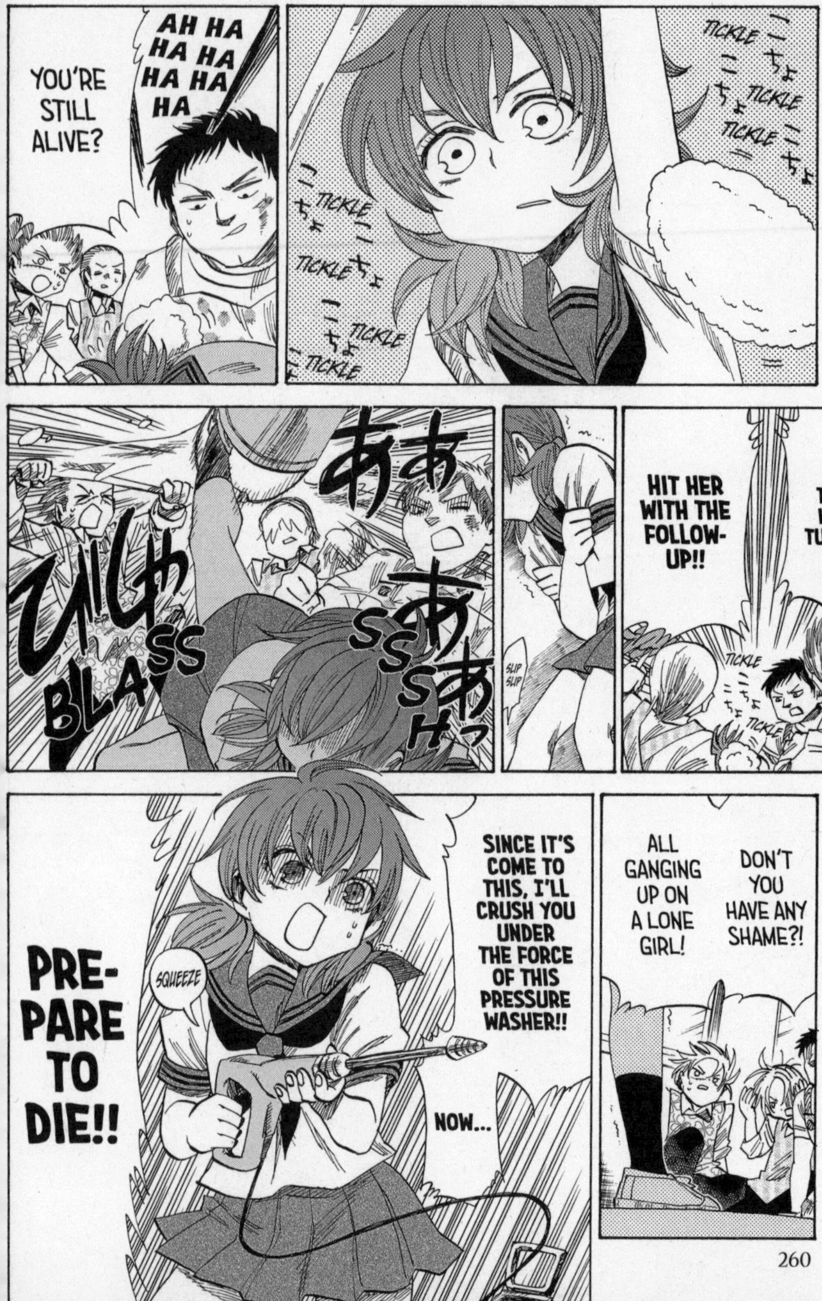
TICKLE
こちょ
TICKLE
こちょ
TICKLE
こちょ
TICKLE
こちょ
TICKLE
TICKLE
こちょ
TICKLE
TICKLE
AH HA HA HA HA HA HA
YOU'RE STILL ALIVE?
THE TIDES HAVE TURNED!
HIT HER WITH THE FOLLOW-UP!!
TICKLE
こちょこちょ
TICKLE
SLIP SLIP
ああああっ
SSSSH
ぴしゃ
BLASS
DON'T YOU HAVE ANY SHAME?!
ALL GANGING UP ON A LONE GIRL!
NOW...
SINCE IT'S COME TO THIS, I'LL CRUSH YOU UNDER THE FORCE OF THIS PRESSURE WASHER!!
SQUEEZE
PRE-PARE TO DIE!!

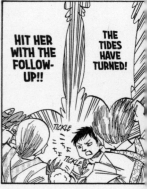

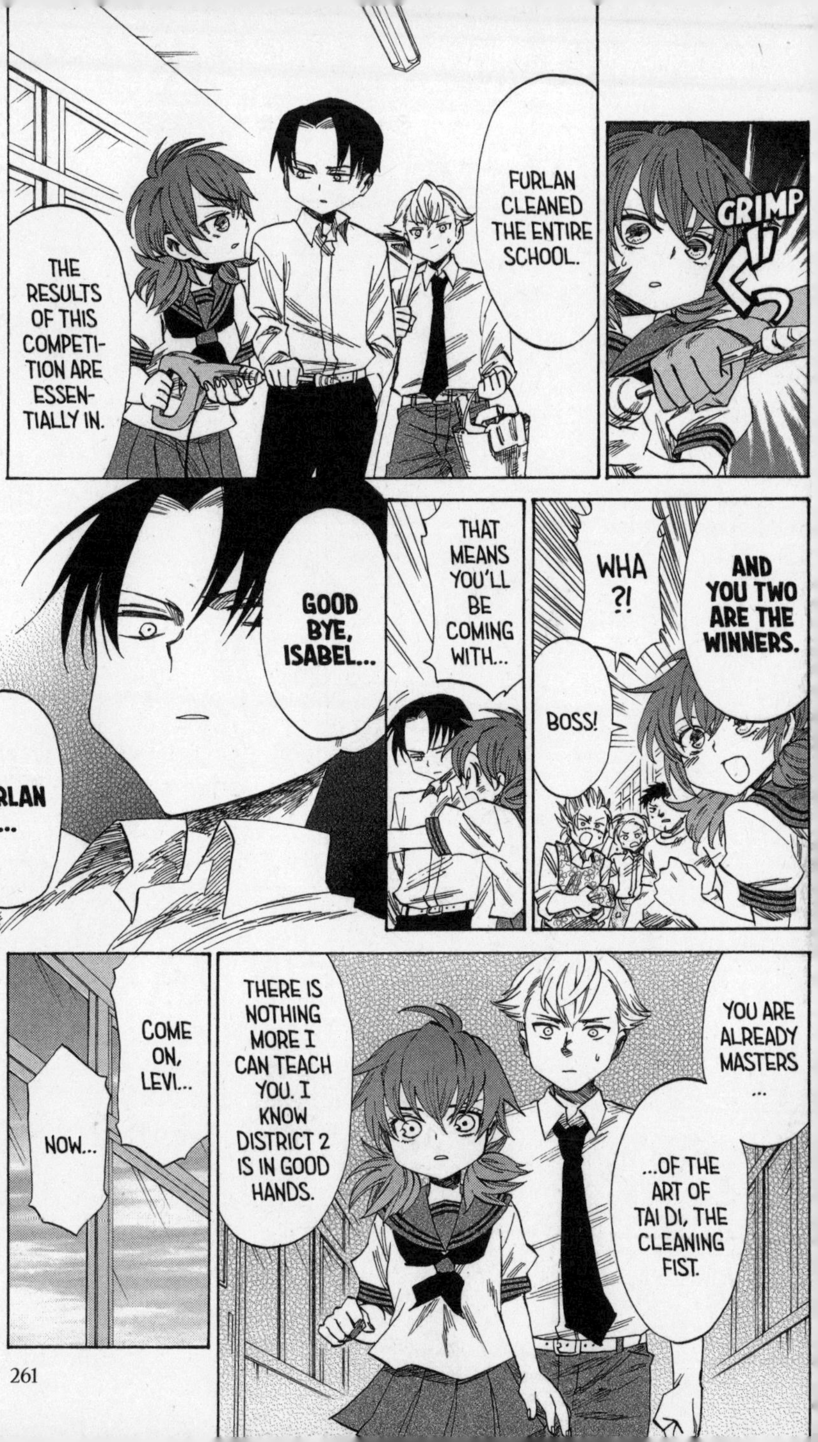
GRIMP
FURLAN CLEANED THE ENTIRE SCHOOL.
THE RESULTS OF THIS COMPETITION ARE ESSENTIALLY IN.
AND YOU TWO ARE THE WINNERS.
WHA ?!
BOSS!
THAT MEANS YOU'LL BE COMING WITH...
GOOD BYE, ISABEL...
FURLAN ...
YOU ARE ALREADY MASTERS ...
...OF THE ART OF TAI DI, THE CLEANING FIST.
THERE IS NOTHING MORE I CAN TEACH YOU. I KNOW DISTRICT 2 IS IN GOOD HANDS.
COME ON, LEVI...
NOW...

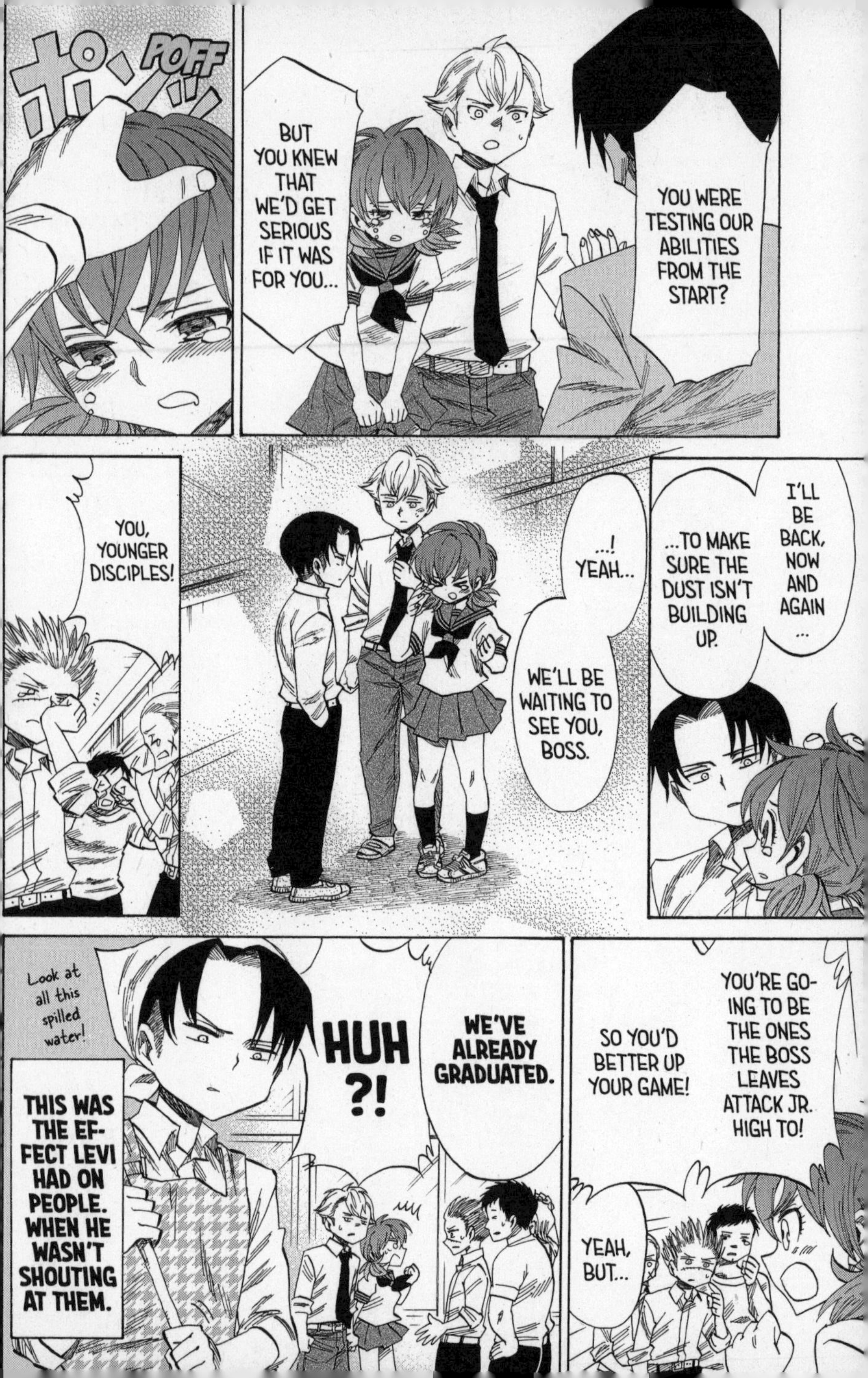
YOU WERE TESTING OUR ABILITIES FROM THE START?
BUT YOU KNEW THAT WE'D GET SERIOUS IF IT WAS FOR YOU...
ポン
POFF
I'LL BE BACK, NOW AND AGAIN ...
...TO MAKE SURE THE DUST ISN'T BUILDING UP.
...! YEAH...
WE'LL BE WAITING TO SEE YOU, BOSS.
YOU, YOUNGER DISCIPLES!
YOU'RE GOING TO BE THE ONES THE BOSS LEAVES ATTACK JR. HIGH TO!
SO YOU'D BETTER UP YOUR GAME!
YEAH, BUT...
WE'VE ALREADY GRADUATED.
HUH ?!
Look at all this spilled water!
THIS WAS THE EFFECT LEVI HAD ON PEOPLE. WHEN HE WASN'T SHOUTING AT THEM.

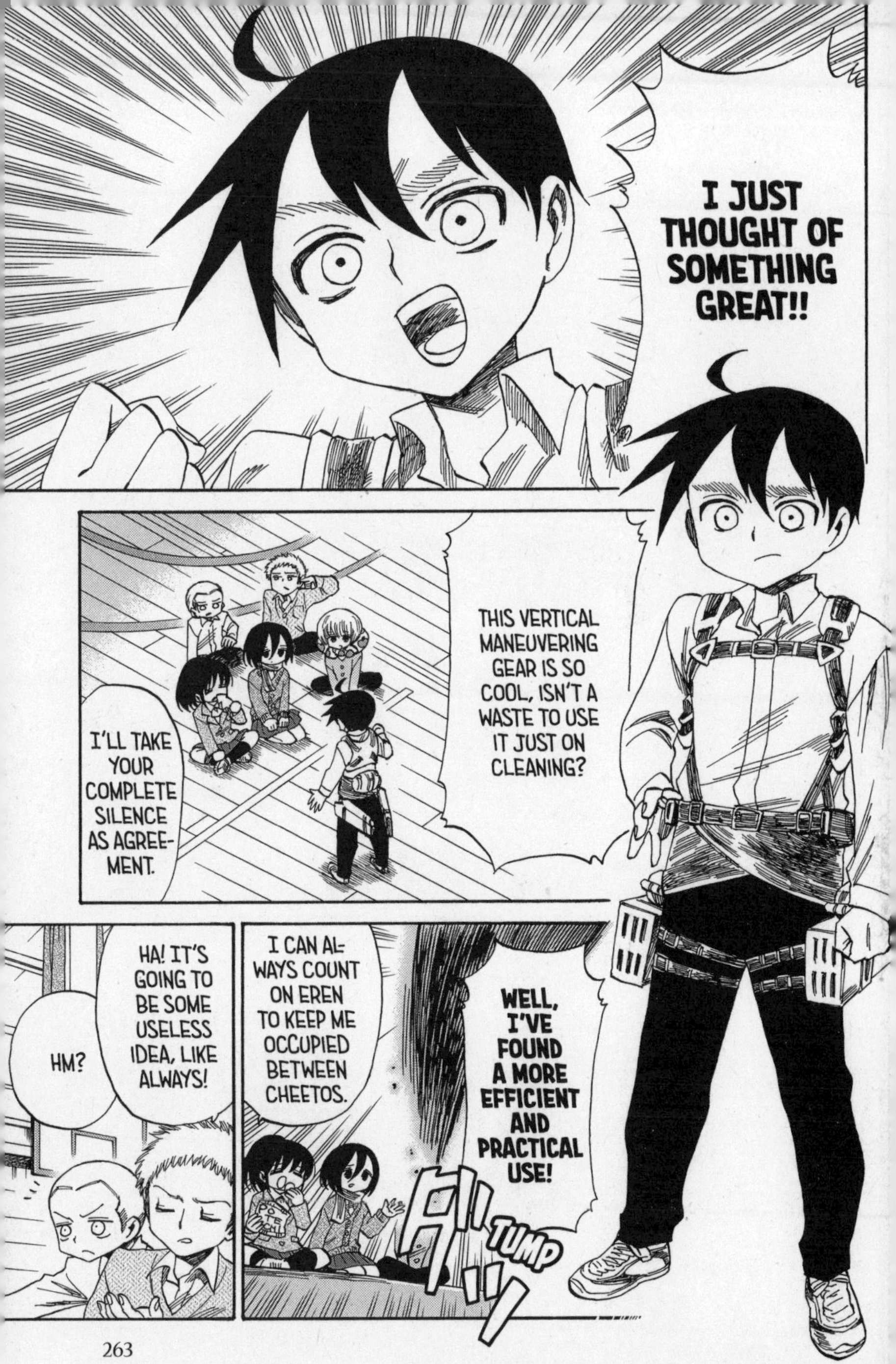
I JUST THOUGHT OF SOMETHING GREAT!!
THIS VERTICAL MANEUVERING GEAR IS SO COOL, ISN'T A WASTE TO USE IT JUST ON CLEANING?
WELL, I'VE FOUND A MORE EFFICIENT AND PRACTICAL USE!
I'LL TAKE YOUR COMPLETE SILENCE AS AGREE-MENT.
TUMP
I CAN AL-WAYS COUNT ON EREN TO KEEP ME OCCUPIED BETWEEN CHEETOS.
HA! IT'S GOING TO BE SOME USELESS IDEA, LIKE ALWAYS!
HM?

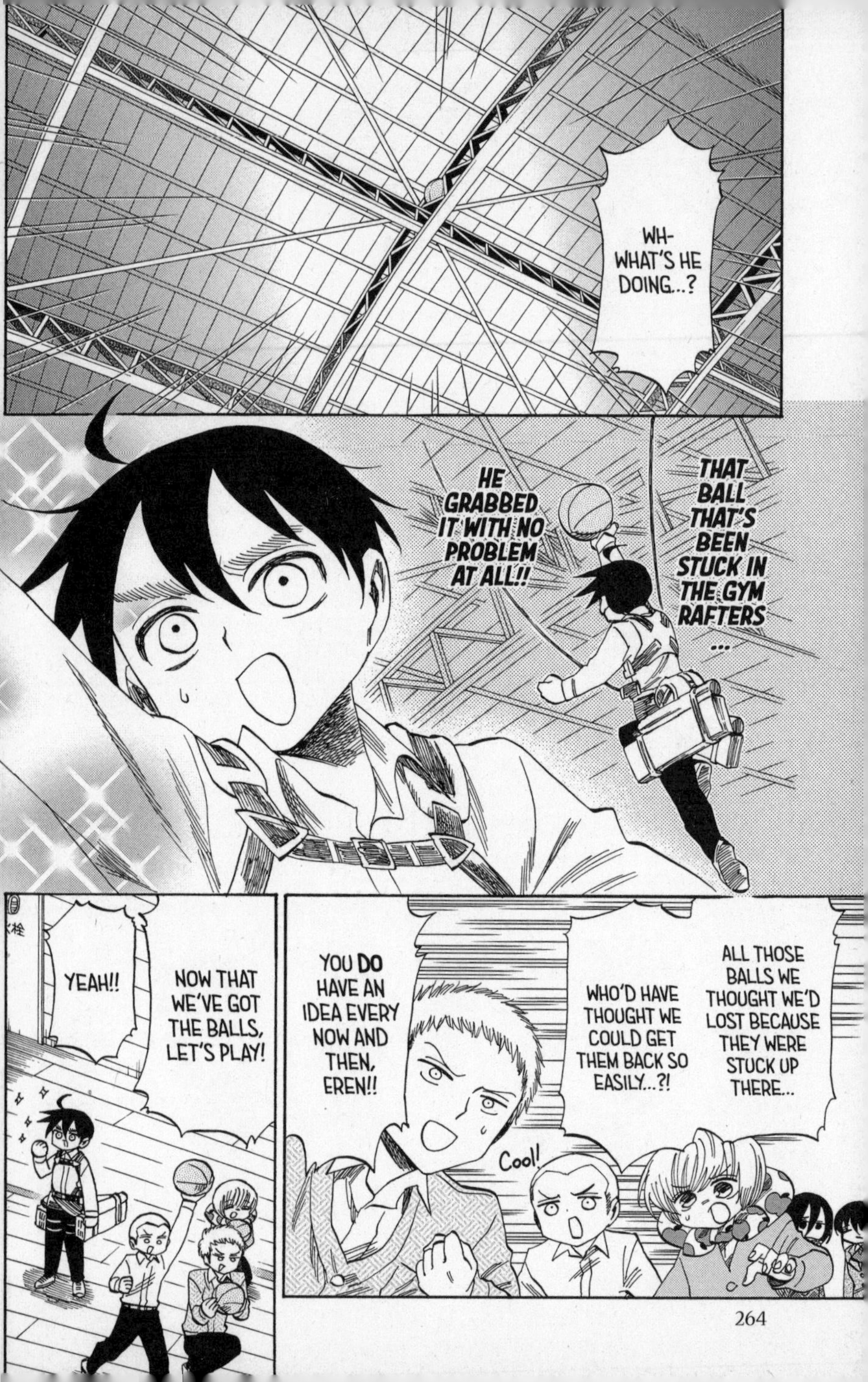
WH- WHAT'S HE DOING...?
THAT BALL THAT'S BEEN STUCK IN THE GYM RAFTERS...
HE GRABBED IT WITH NO PROBLEM AT ALL!!
ALL THOSE BALLS WE THOUGHT WE'D LOST BECAUSE THEY WERE STUCK UP THERE...
WHO'D HAVE THOUGHT WE COULD GET THEM BACK SO EASILY...?!
YOU **DO** HAVE AN IDEA EVERY NOW AND THEN, EREN!!
Cool!
NOW THAT WE'VE GOT THE BALLS, LET'S PLAY!
YEAH!!

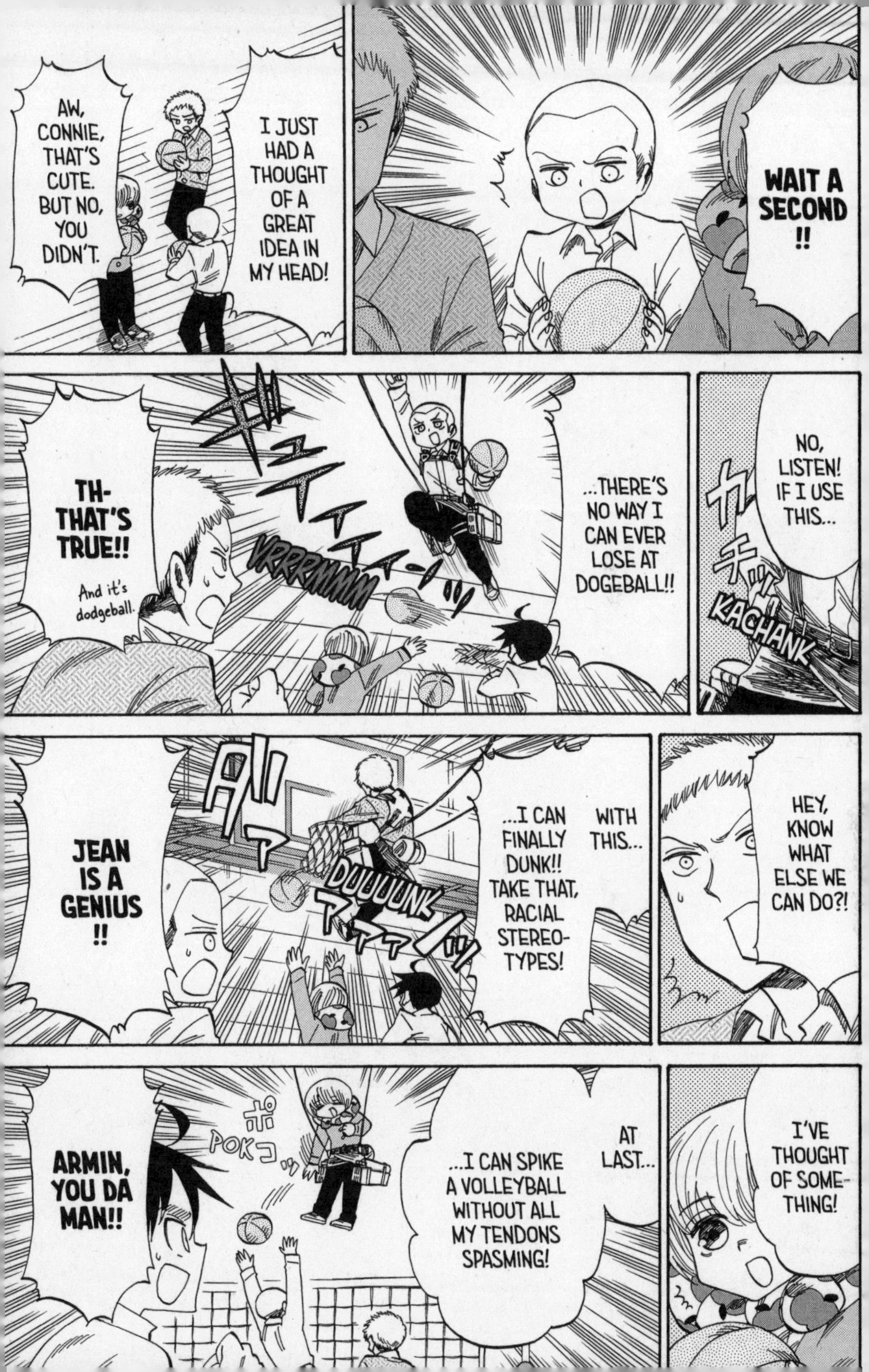
WAIT A SECOND!!
I JUST HAD A THOUGHT OF A GREAT IDEA IN MY HEAD!
AW, CONNIE, THAT'S CUTE. BUT NO, YOU DIDN'T.
NO, LISTEN! IF I USE THIS...
KACHANK
...THERE'S NO WAY I CAN EVER LOSE AT DOGEBALL!!
VRRRMMMM
TH-THAT'S TRUE!!
And it's dodgeball.
HEY, KNOW WHAT ELSE WE CAN DO?!
WITH THIS...
...I CAN FINALLY DUNK!! TAKE THAT, RACIAL STEREOTYPES!
DUUUUNK
JEAN IS A GENIUS!!
I'VE THOUGHT OF SOMETHING!
AT LAST...
...I CAN SPIKE A VOLLEYBALL WITHOUT ALL MY TENDONS SPASMING!
POK
ARMIN, YOU DA MAN!!

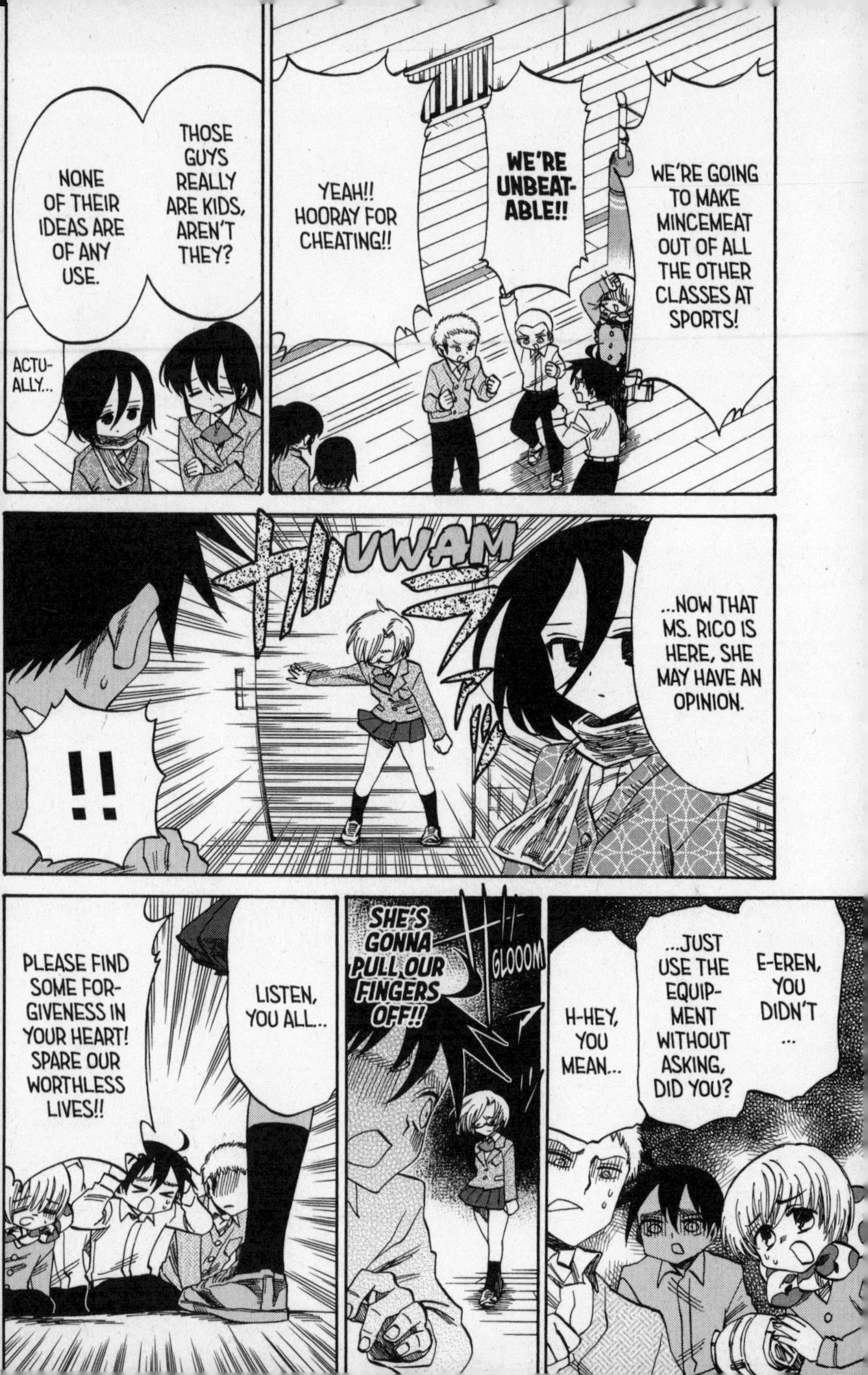
WE'RE GOING TO MAKE MINCEMEAT OUT OF ALL THE OTHER CLASSES AT SPORTS!
WE'RE UNBEATABLE!!
YEAH!! HOORAY FOR CHEATING!!
THOSE GUYS REALLY ARE KIDS, AREN'T THEY?
NONE OF THEIR IDEAS ARE OF ANY USE.
ACTUALLY...
...NOW THAT MS. RICO IS HERE, SHE MAY HAVE AN OPINION.
VWAM
!!
E-EREN, YOU DIDN'T ...
...JUST USE THE EQUIPMENT WITHOUT ASKING, DID YOU?
H-HEY, YOU MEAN...
GLOOOM
SHE'S GONNA PULL OUR FINGERS OFF!!
LISTEN, YOU ALL...
PLEASE FIND SOME FORGIVENESS IN YOUR HEART! SPARE OUR WORTHLESS LIVES!!

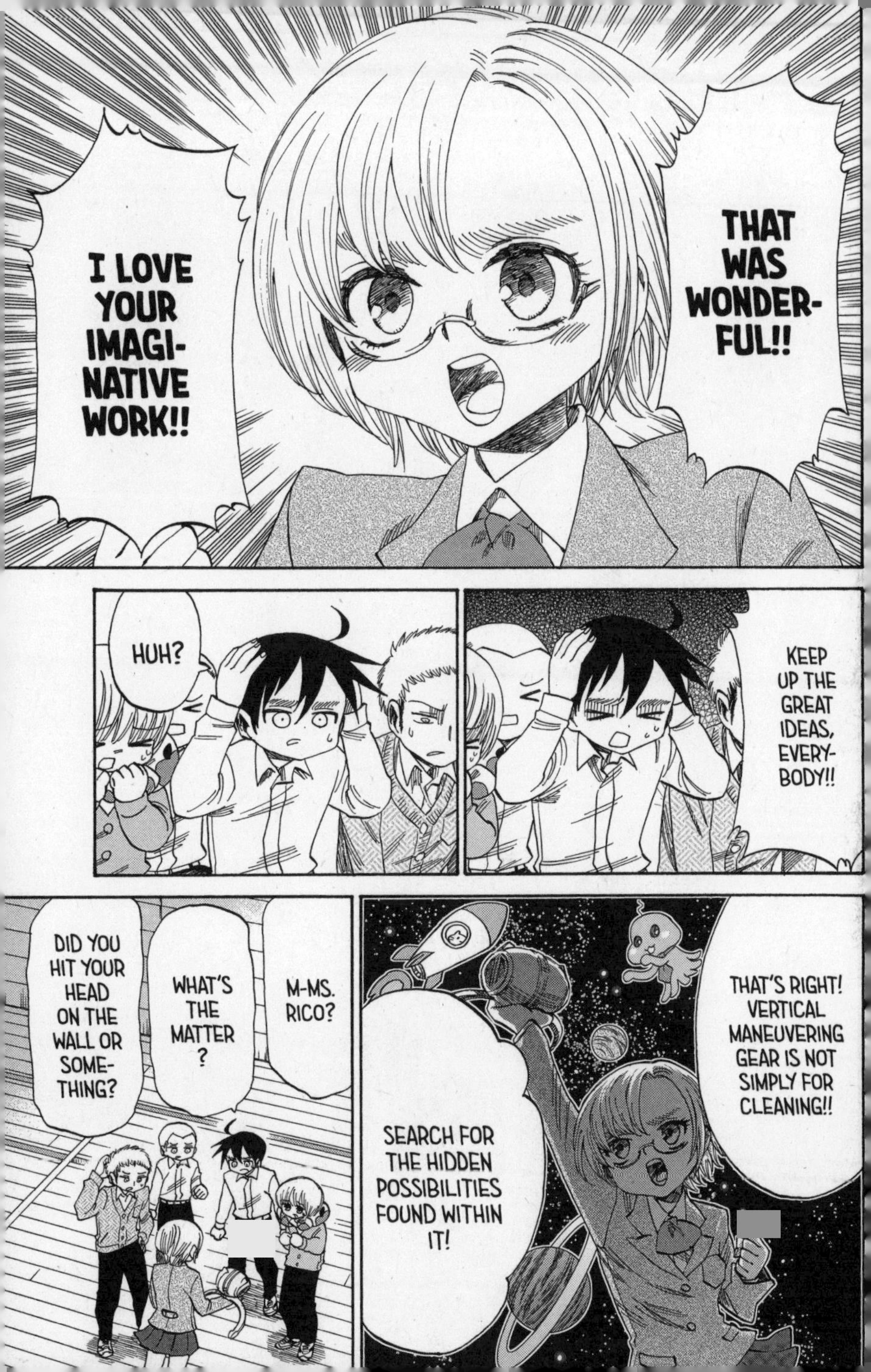
THAT WAS WONDERFUL!!
I LOVE YOUR IMAGINATIVE WORK!!
KEEP UP THE GREAT IDEAS, EVERYBODY!!
HUH?
THAT'S RIGHT! VERTICAL MANEUVERING GEAR IS NOT SIMPLY FOR CLEANING!!
SEARCH FOR THE HIDDEN POSSIBILITIES FOUND WITHIN IT!
M-MS. RICO?
WHAT'S THE MATTER?
DID YOU HIT YOUR HEAD ON THE WALL OR SOMETHING?

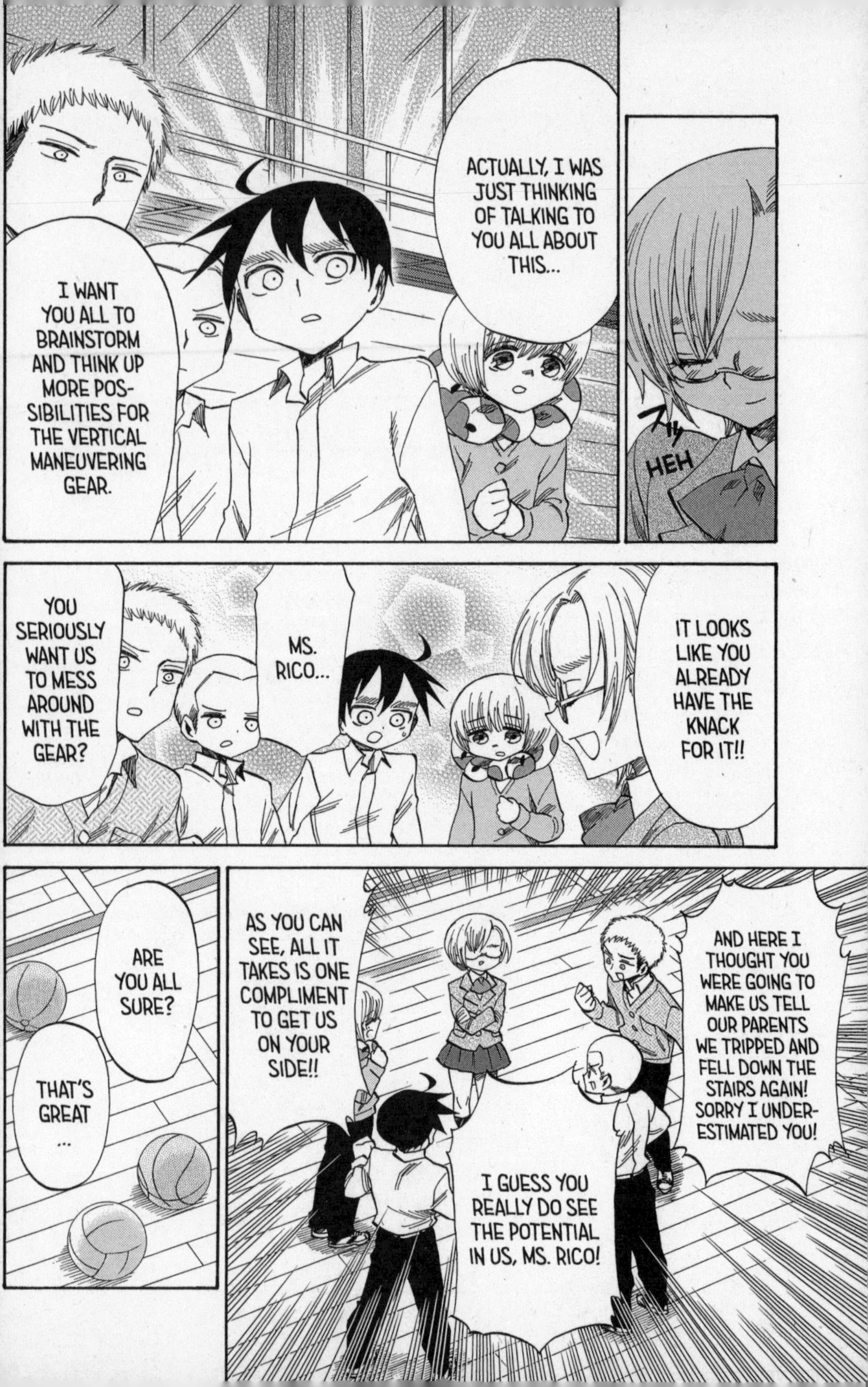
HEH
ACTUALLY, I WAS JUST THINKING OF TALKING TO YOU ALL ABOUT THIS...
I WANT YOU ALL TO BRAINSTORM AND THINK UP MORE POS-SIBILITIES FOR THE VERTICAL MANEUVERING GEAR.
IT LOOKS LIKE YOU ALREADY HAVE THE KNACK FOR IT!!
MS. RICO...
YOU SERIOUSLY WANT US TO MESS AROUND WITH THE GEAR?
AND HERE I THOUGHT YOU WERE GOING TO MAKE US TELL OUR PARENTS WE TRIPPED AND FELL DOWN THE STAIRS AGAIN! SORRY I UNDER-ESTIMATED YOU!
AS YOU CAN SEE, ALL IT TAKES IS ONE COMPLIMENT TO GET US ON YOUR SIDE!!
I GUESS YOU REALLY DO SEE THE POTENTIAL IN US, MS. RICO!
ARE YOU ALL SURE?
THAT'S GREAT ...

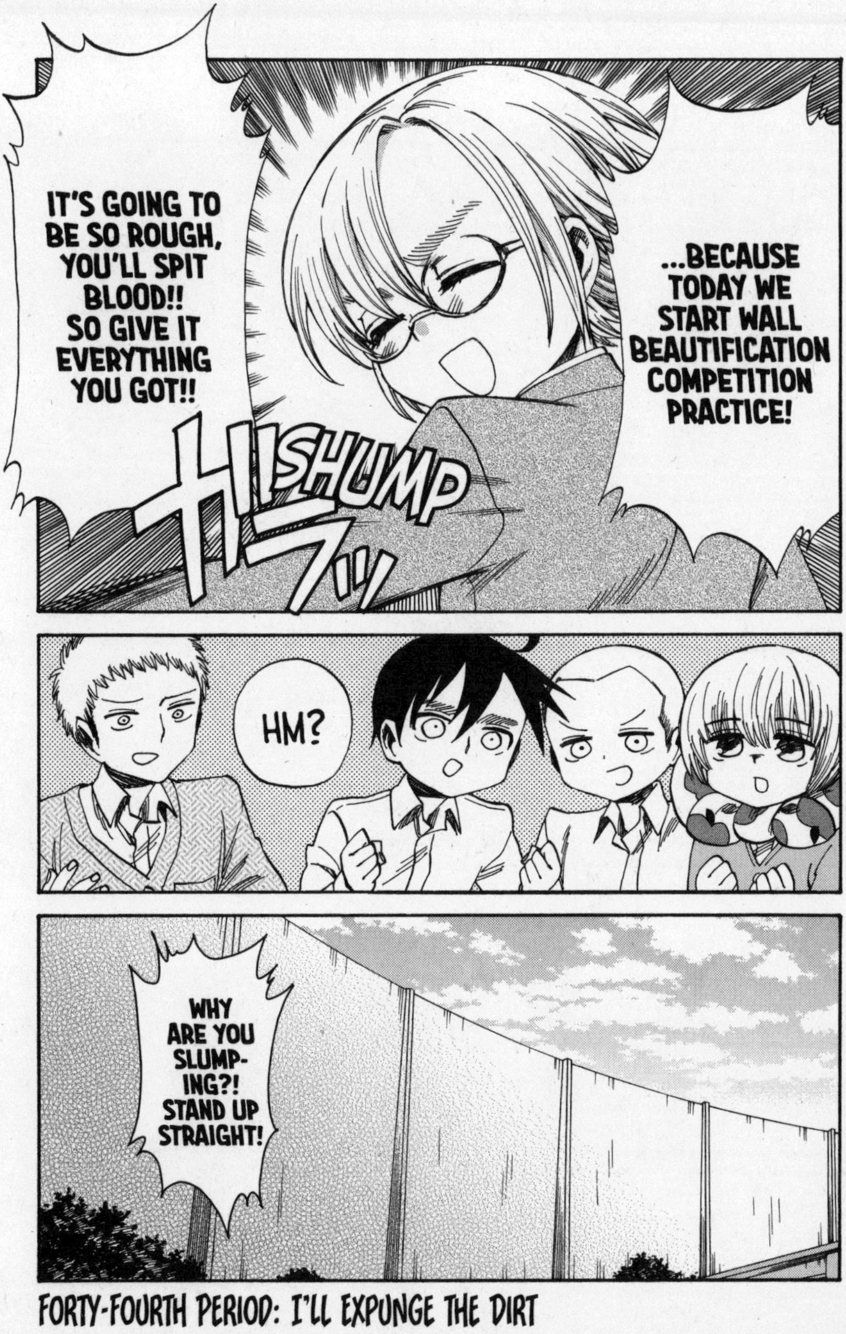
...BECAUSE TODAY WE START WALL BEAUTIFICATION COMPETITION PRACTICE!
IT'S GOING TO BE SO ROUGH, YOU'LL SPIT BLOOD!! SO GIVE IT EVERYTHING YOU GOT!!
SHUMP
HM?
WHY ARE YOU SLUMPING?! STAND UP STRAIGHT!

FORTY-FOURTH PERIOD: I'LL EXPUNGE THE DIRT

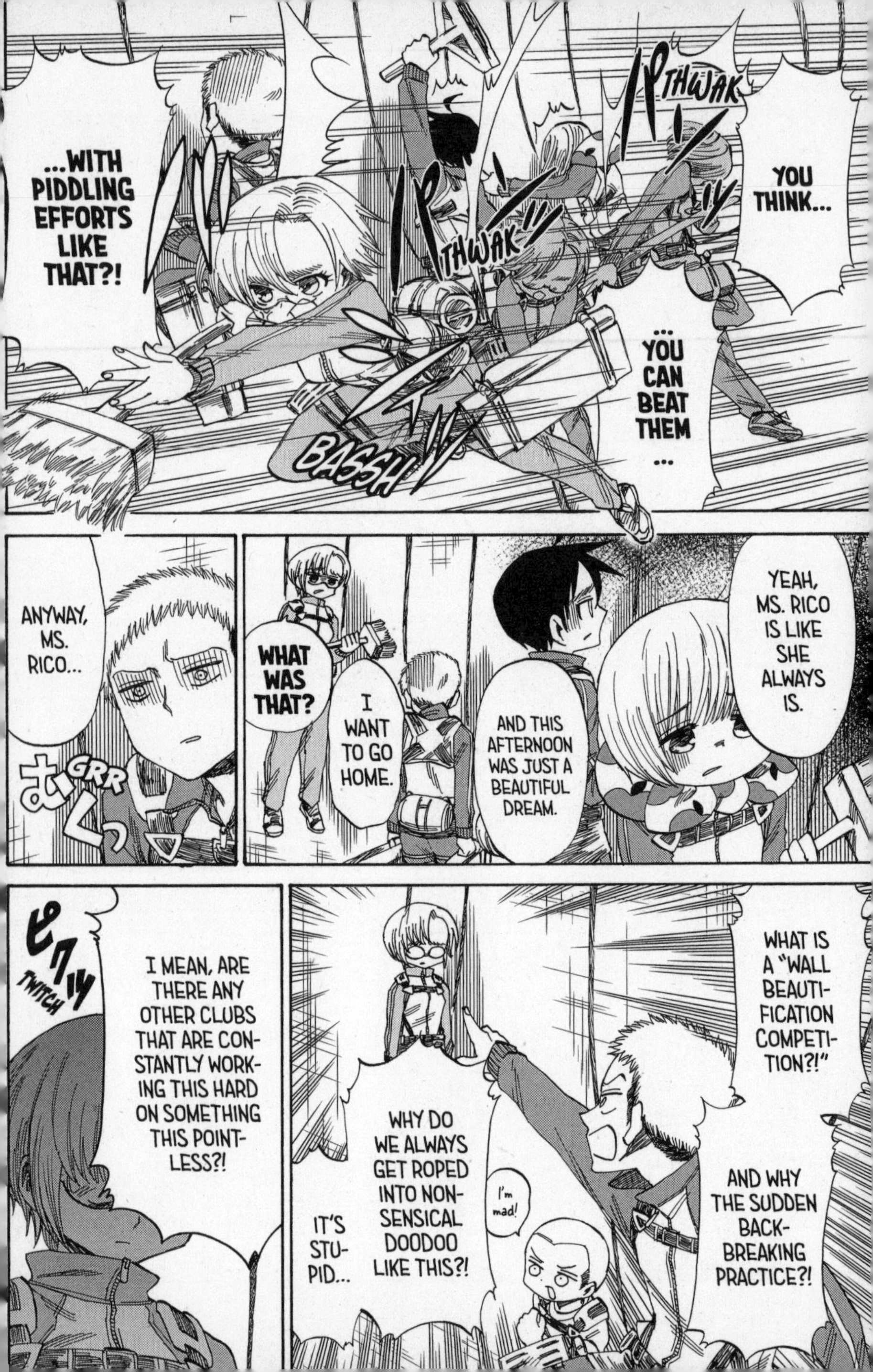

THWAK
YOU THINK...
THWAK
...YOU CAN BEAT THEM...
BASSH
...WITH PIDDLING EFFORTS LIKE THAT?!
YEAH, MS. RICO IS LIKE SHE ALWAYS IS.
AND THIS AFTERNOON WAS JUST A BEAUTIFUL DREAM.
I WANT TO GO HOME.
WHAT WAS THAT?
ANYWAY, MS. RICO...
むくっ GRR
WHAT IS A "WALL BEAUTIFICATION COMPETITION?!"
AND WHY THE SUDDEN BACK-BREAKING PRACTICE?!
WHY DO WE ALWAYS GET ROPED INTO NONSENSICAL DOODOO LIKE THIS?!
I'm mad!
IT'S STUPID...
I MEAN, ARE THERE ANY OTHER CLUBS THAT ARE CONSTANTLY WORKING THIS HARD ON SOMETHING THIS POINTLESS?!
ピクッ TWITCH

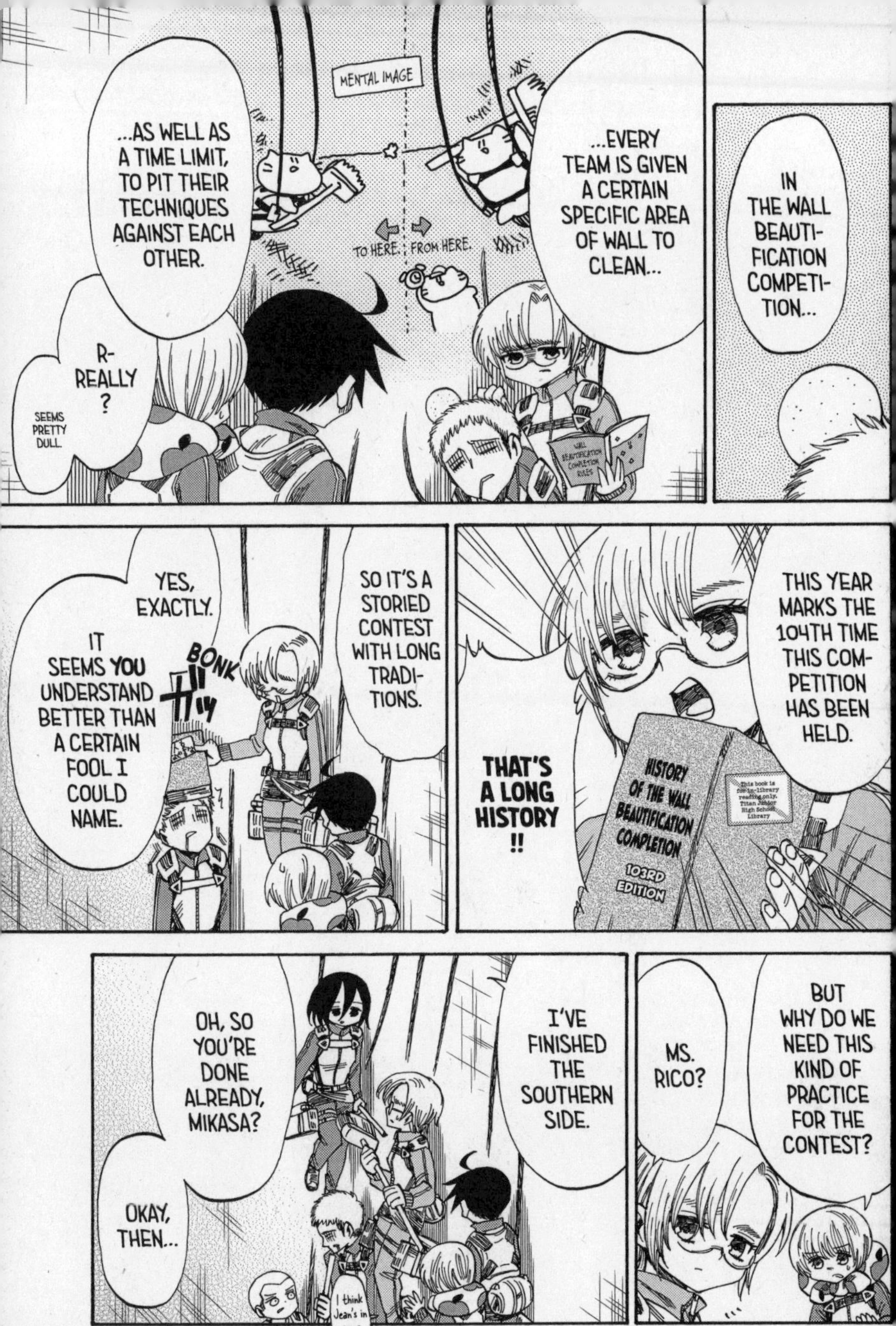
IN THE WALL BEAUTIFICATION COMPETITION...
...EVERY TEAM IS GIVEN A CERTAIN SPECIFIC AREA OF WALL TO CLEAN...
MENTAL IMAGE
FROM HERE.
TO HERE.
...AS WELL AS A TIME LIMIT, TO PIT THEIR TECHNIQUES AGAINST EACH OTHER.
WALL BEAUTIFICATION COMPLETION RULES
R-REALLY?
SEEMS PRETTY DULL.
THIS YEAR MARKS THE 104TH TIME THIS COMPETITION HAS BEEN HELD.
HISTORY OF THE WALL BEAUTIFICATION COMPLETION
103RD EDITION
This book is for in-library reading only. Titan Junior High School Library
THAT'S A LONG HISTORY!!
SO IT'S A STORIED CONTEST WITH LONG TRADITIONS.
YES, EXACTLY.
BONK
IT SEEMS YOU UNDERSTAND BETTER THAN A CERTAIN FOOL I COULD NAME.
BUT WHY DO WE NEED THIS KIND OF PRACTICE FOR THE CONTEST?
MS. RICO?
I'VE FINISHED THE SOUTHERN SIDE.
OH, SO YOU'RE DONE ALREADY, MIKASA?
OKAY, THEN...
I think Jean's in a coma...

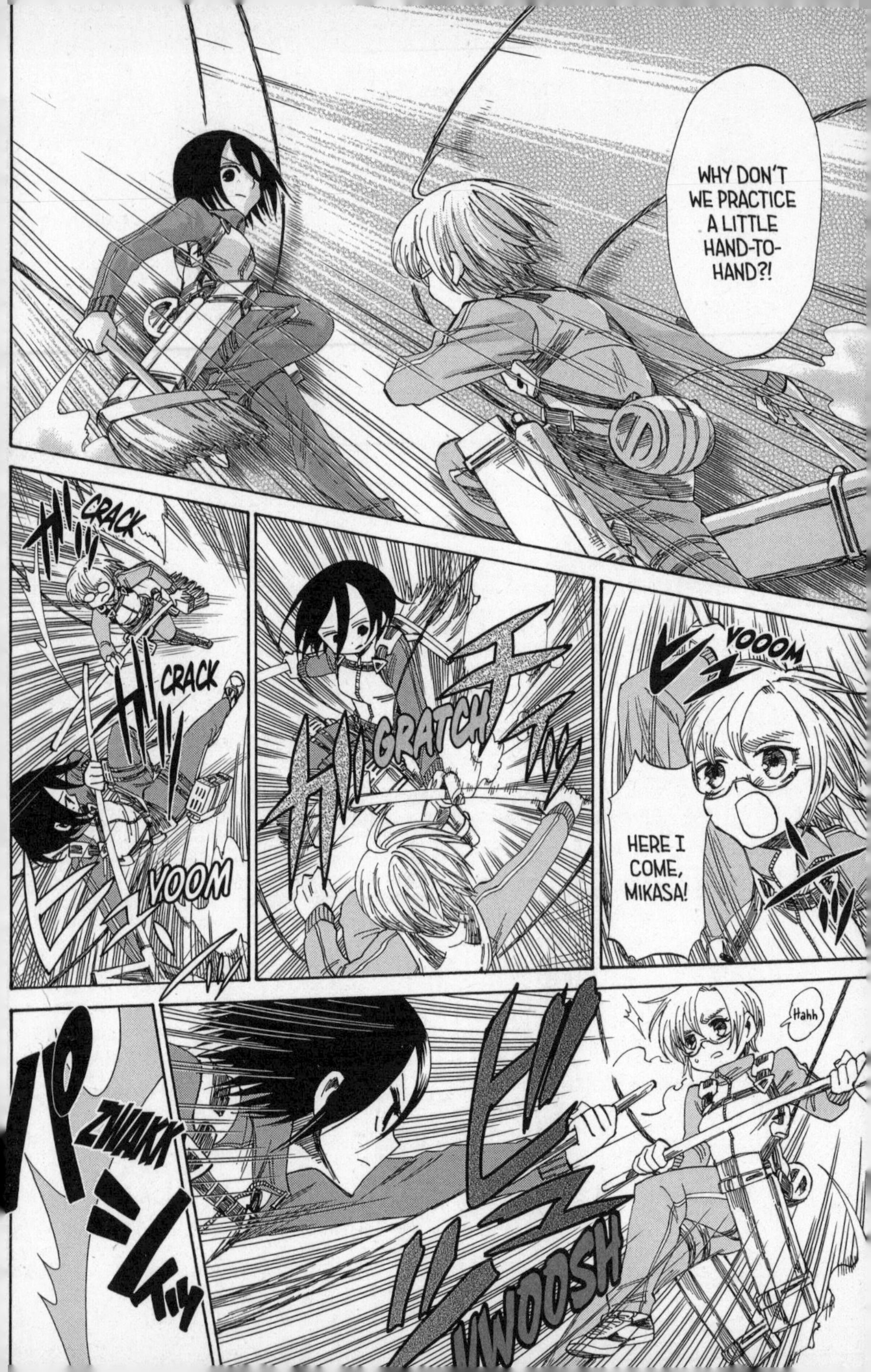
WHY DON'T WE PRACTICE A LITTLE HAND-TO-HAND?!
VOOOM
HERE I COME, MIKASA!
GRATCH
CRACK
CRACK
VOOM
Hahh
WOOSH
ZWAKK

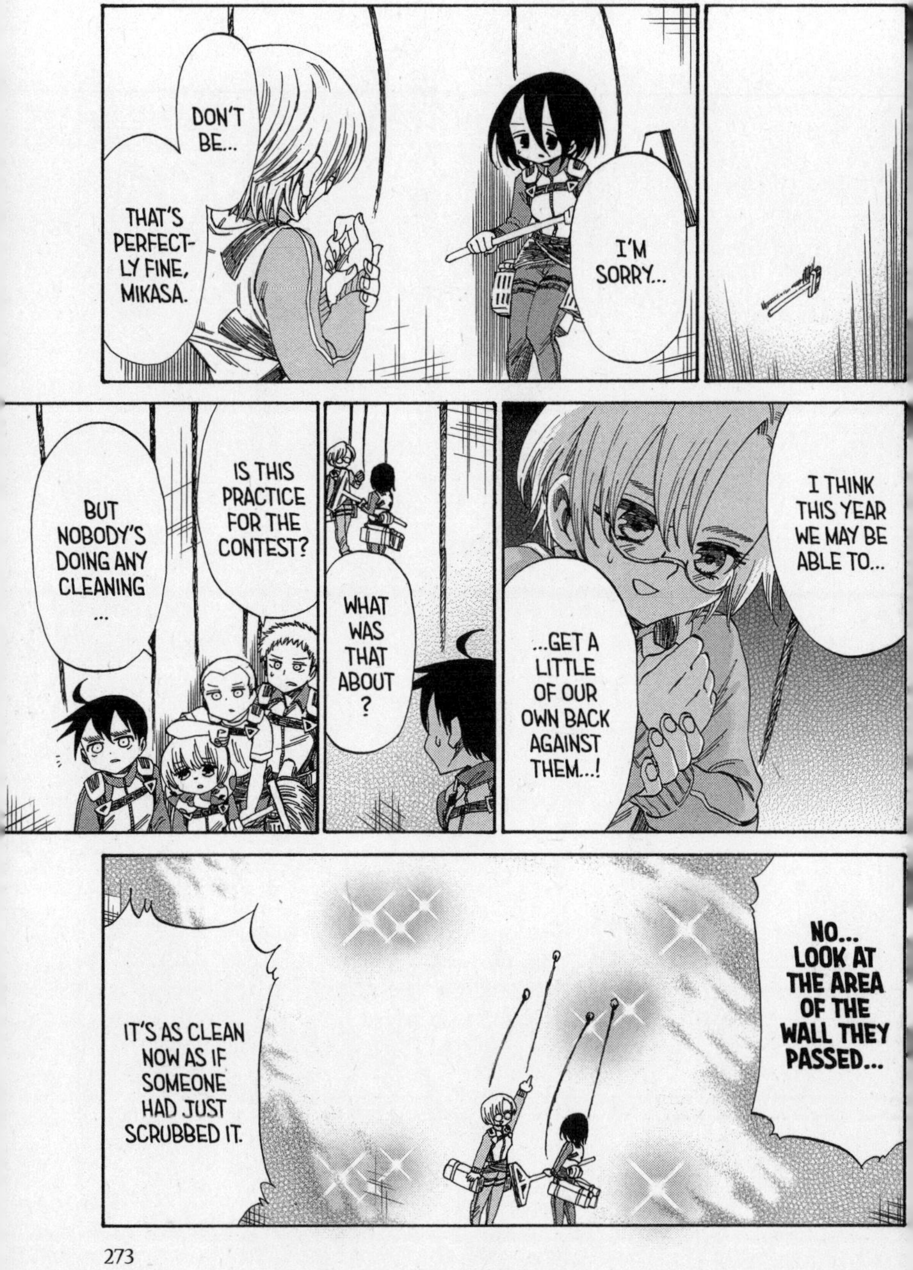
I'M SORRY...
DON'T BE...
THAT'S PERFECTLY FINE, MIKASA.
I THINK THIS YEAR WE MAY BE ABLE TO...
...GET A LITTLE OF OUR OWN BACK AGAINST THEM...!
WHAT WAS THAT ABOUT?
IS THIS PRACTICE FOR THE CONTEST?
BUT NOBODY'S DOING ANY CLEANING...
NO... LOOK AT THE AREA OF THE WALL THEY PASSED...
IT'S AS CLEAN NOW AS IF SOMEONE HAD JUST SCRUBBED IT.

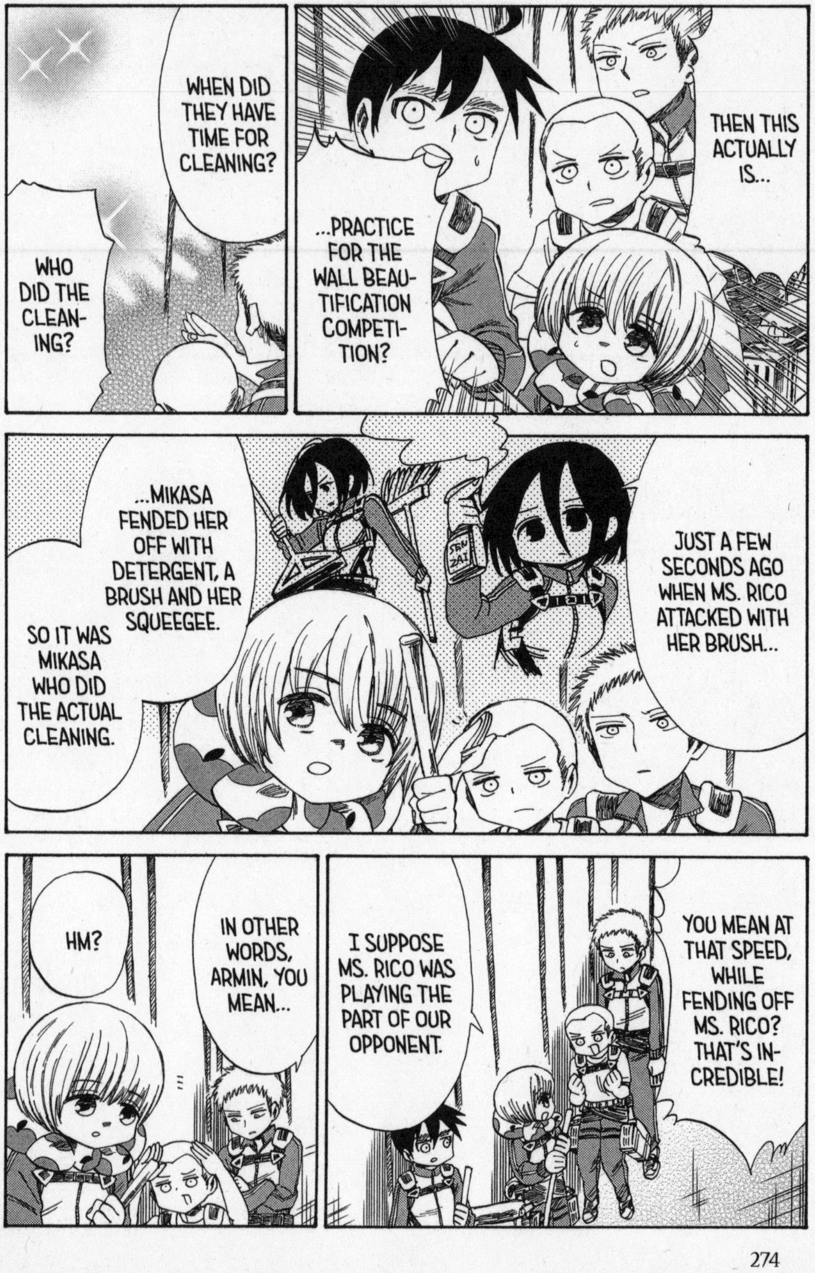
THEN THIS ACTUALLY IS...
...PRACTICE FOR THE WALL BEAUTIFICATION COMPETITION?
WHEN DID THEY HAVE TIME FOR CLEANING?
WHO DID THE CLEANING?
JUST A FEW SECONDS AGO WHEN MS. RICO ATTACKED WITH HER BRUSH...
...MIKASA FENDED HER OFF WITH DETERGENT, A BRUSH AND HER SQUEEGEE.
SO IT WAS MIKASA WHO DID THE ACTUAL CLEANING.
YOU MEAN AT THAT SPEED, WHILE FENDING OFF MS. RICO? THAT'S INCREDIBLE!
I SUPPOSE MS. RICO WAS PLAYING THE PART OF OUR OPPONENT.
IN OTHER WORDS, ARMIN, YOU MEAN...
HM?

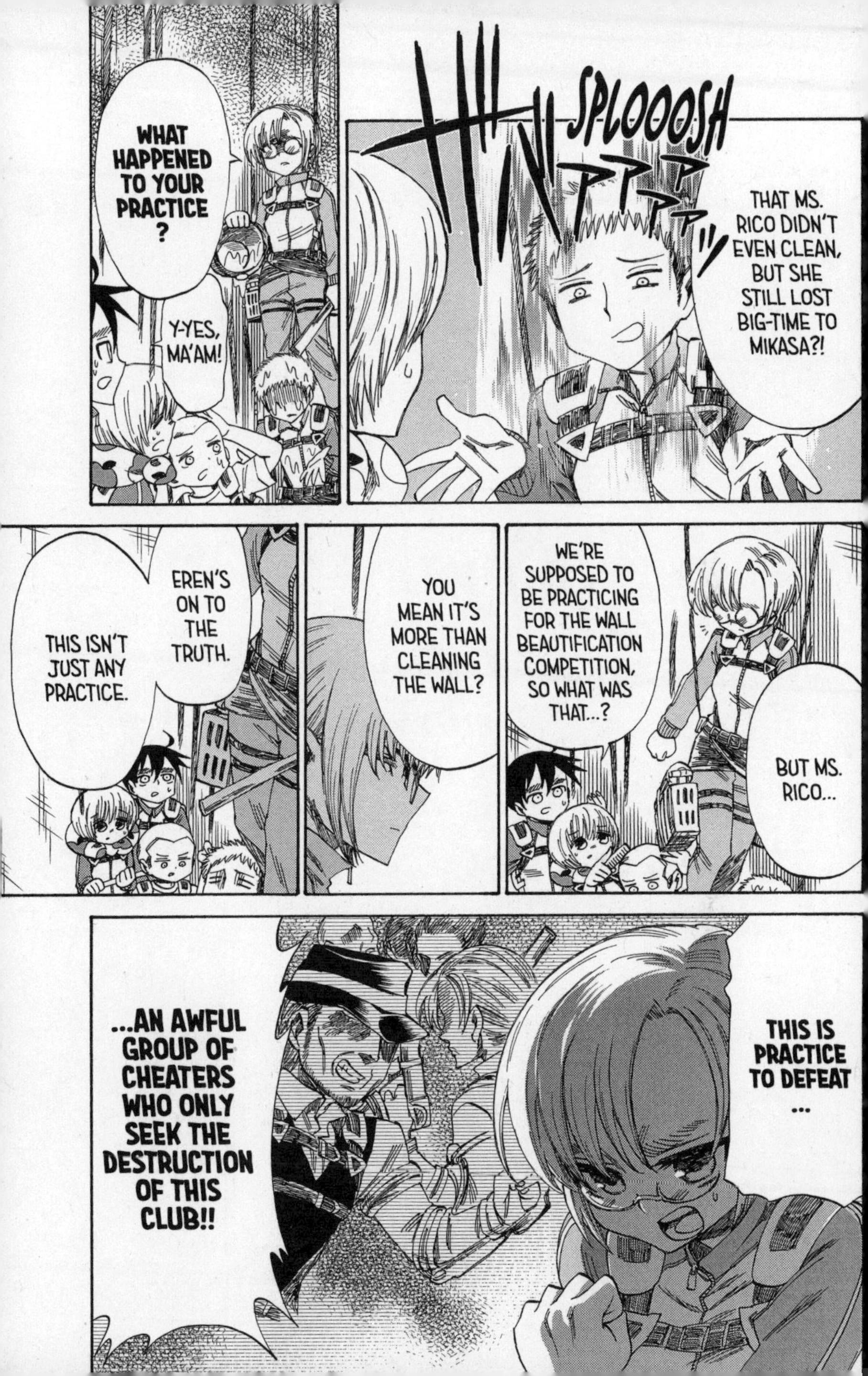
SPLOOOSH
THAT MS. RICO DIDN'T EVEN CLEAN, BUT SHE STILL LOST BIG-TIME TO MIKASA?!
WHAT HAPPENED TO YOUR PRACTICE?
Y-YES, MA'AM!
BUT MS. RICO...
WE'RE SUPPOSED TO BE PRACTICING FOR THE WALL BEAUTIFICATION COMPETITION, SO WHAT WAS THAT...?
YOU MEAN IT'S MORE THAN CLEANING THE WALL?
EREN'S ON TO THE TRUTH.
THIS ISN'T JUST ANY PRACTICE.
THIS IS PRACTICE TO DEFEAT ...
...AN AWFUL GROUP OF CHEATERS WHO ONLY SEEK THE DESTRUCTION OF THIS CLUB!!

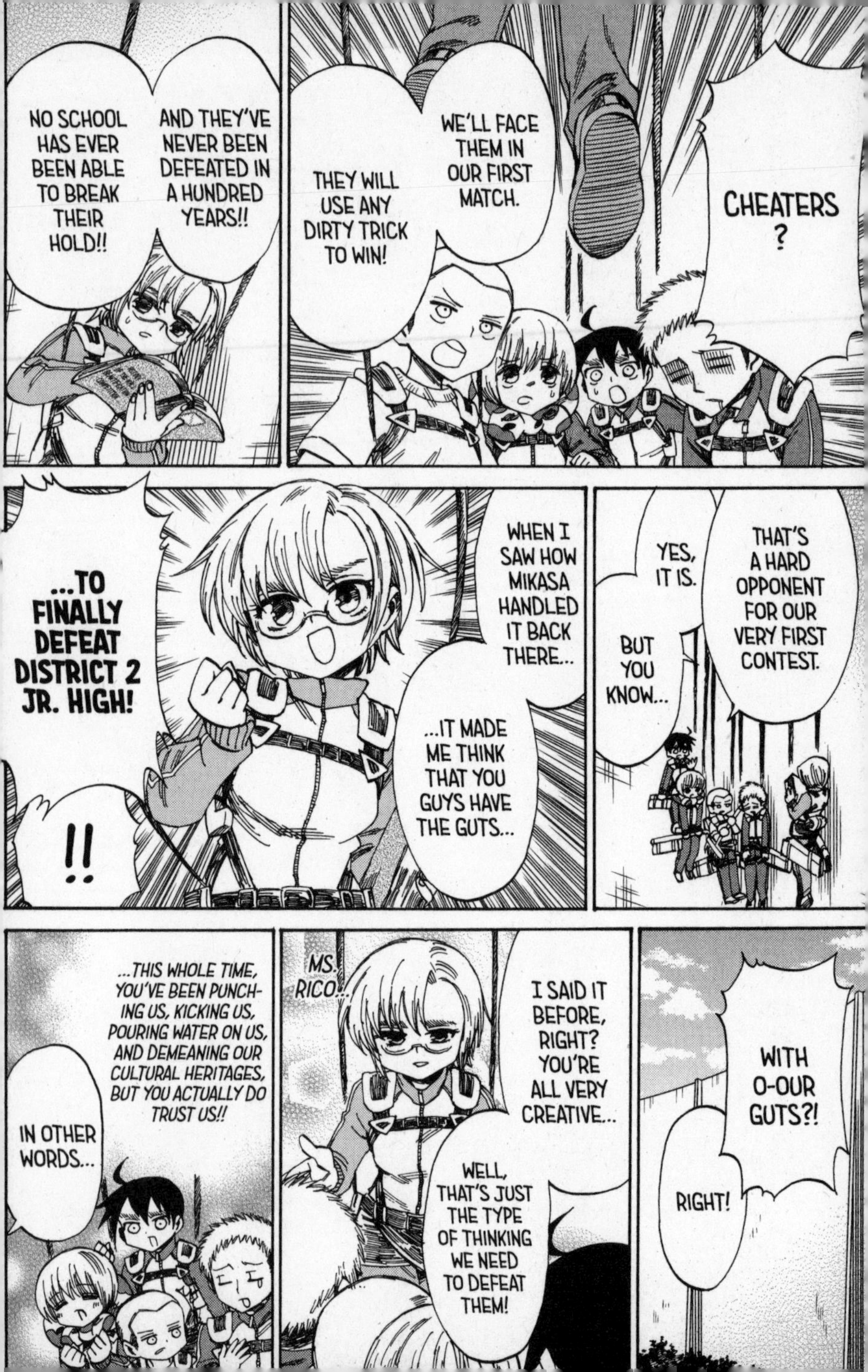
CHEATERS?
WE'LL FACE THEM IN OUR FIRST MATCH.
THEY WILL USE ANY DIRTY TRICK TO WIN!
AND THEY'VE NEVER BEEN DEFEATED IN A HUNDRED YEARS!!
NO SCHOOL HAS EVER BEEN ABLE TO BREAK THEIR HOLD!!
THAT'S A HARD OPPONENT FOR OUR VERY FIRST CONTEST.
YES, IT IS.
BUT YOU KNOW...
WHEN I SAW HOW MIKASA HANDLED IT BACK THERE...
...IT MADE ME THINK THAT YOU GUYS HAVE THE GUTS...
...TO FINALLY DEFEAT DISTRICT 2 JR. HIGH!
!!
WITH O-OUR GUTS?!
RIGHT!
I SAID IT BEFORE, RIGHT? YOU'RE ALL VERY CREATIVE...
WELL, THAT'S JUST THE TYPE OF THINKING WE NEED TO DEFEAT THEM!
MS. RICO...
...THIS WHOLE TIME, YOU'VE BEEN PUNCHING US, KICKING US, POURING WATER ON US, AND DEMEANING OUR CULTURAL HERITAGES, BUT YOU ACTUALLY DO TRUST US!!
IN OTHER WORDS...

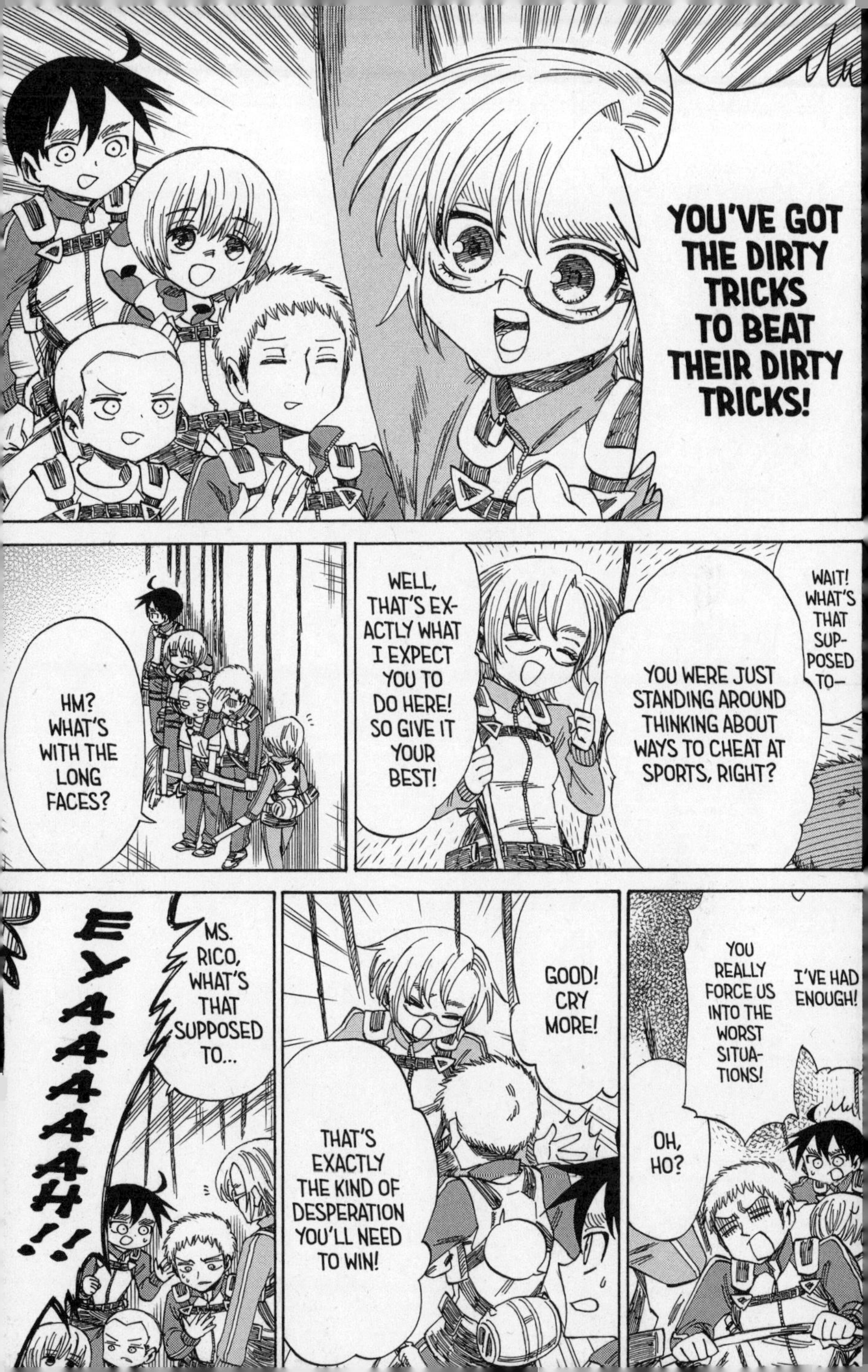
YOU'VE GOT THE DIRTY TRICKS TO BEAT THEIR DIRTY TRICKS!
WAIT! WHAT'S THAT SUP-POSED TO—
YOU WERE JUST STANDING AROUND THINKING ABOUT WAYS TO CHEAT AT SPORTS, RIGHT?
WELL, THAT'S EX-ACTLY WHAT I EXPECT YOU TO DO HERE! SO GIVE IT YOUR BEST!
HM? WHAT'S WITH THE LONG FACES?
I'VE HAD ENOUGH!
YOU REALLY FORCE US INTO THE WORST SITUA-TIONS!
OH, HO?
GOOD! CRY MORE!
THAT'S EXACTLY THE KIND OF DESPERATION YOU'LL NEED TO WIN!
MS. RICO, WHAT'S THAT SUPPOSED TO...
EYAAAAAH!!

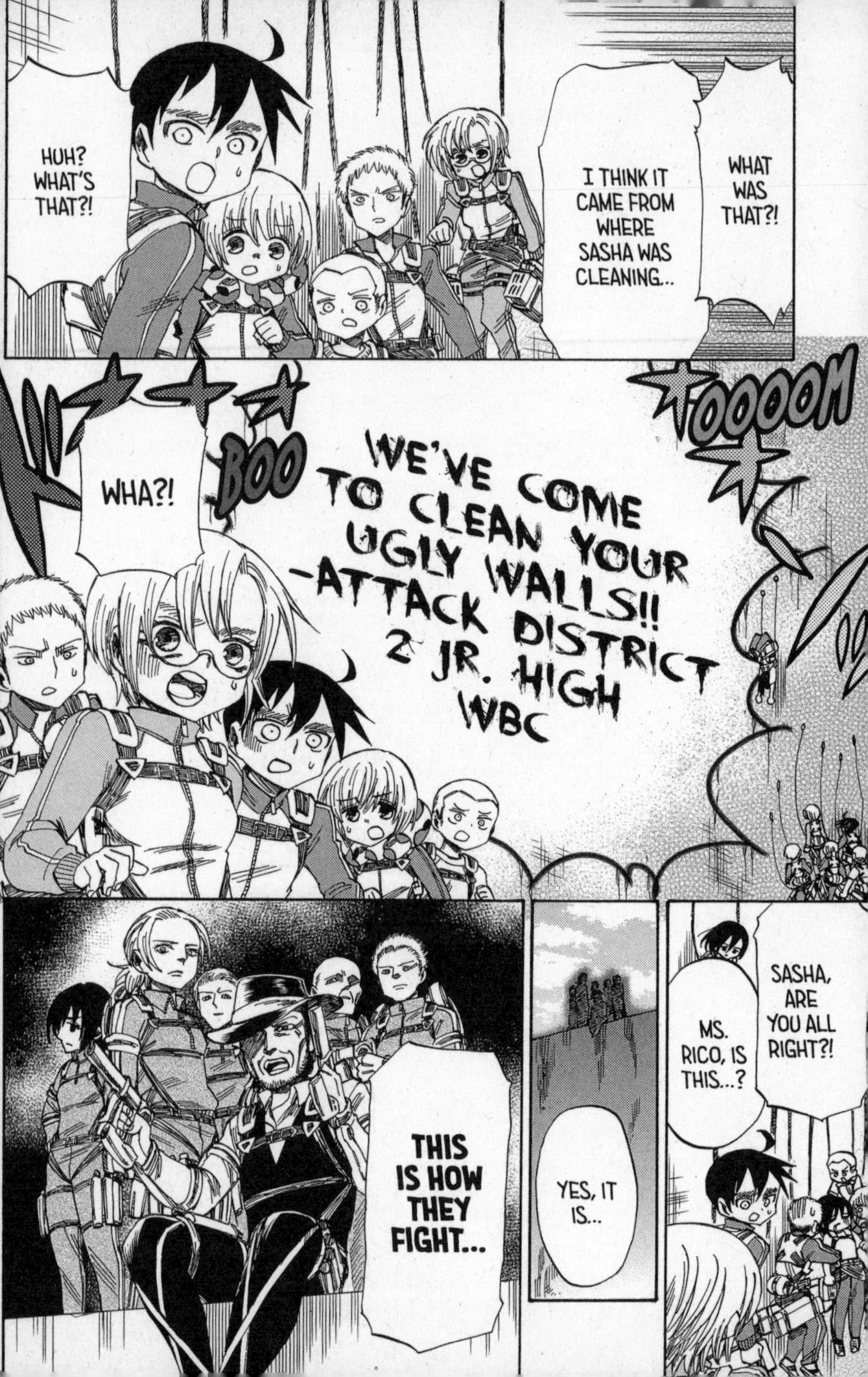
WHAT WAS THAT?!
I THINK IT CAME FROM WHERE SASHA WAS CLEANING...
HUH? WHAT'S THAT?!
OOOOM
BOO
WE'VE COME TO CLEAN YOUR UGLY WALLS!! -ATTACK DISTRICT 2 JR. HIGH WBC
WHA?!
SASHA, ARE YOU ALL RIGHT?!
MS. RICO, IS THIS...?
YES, IT IS...
THIS IS HOW THEY FIGHT...

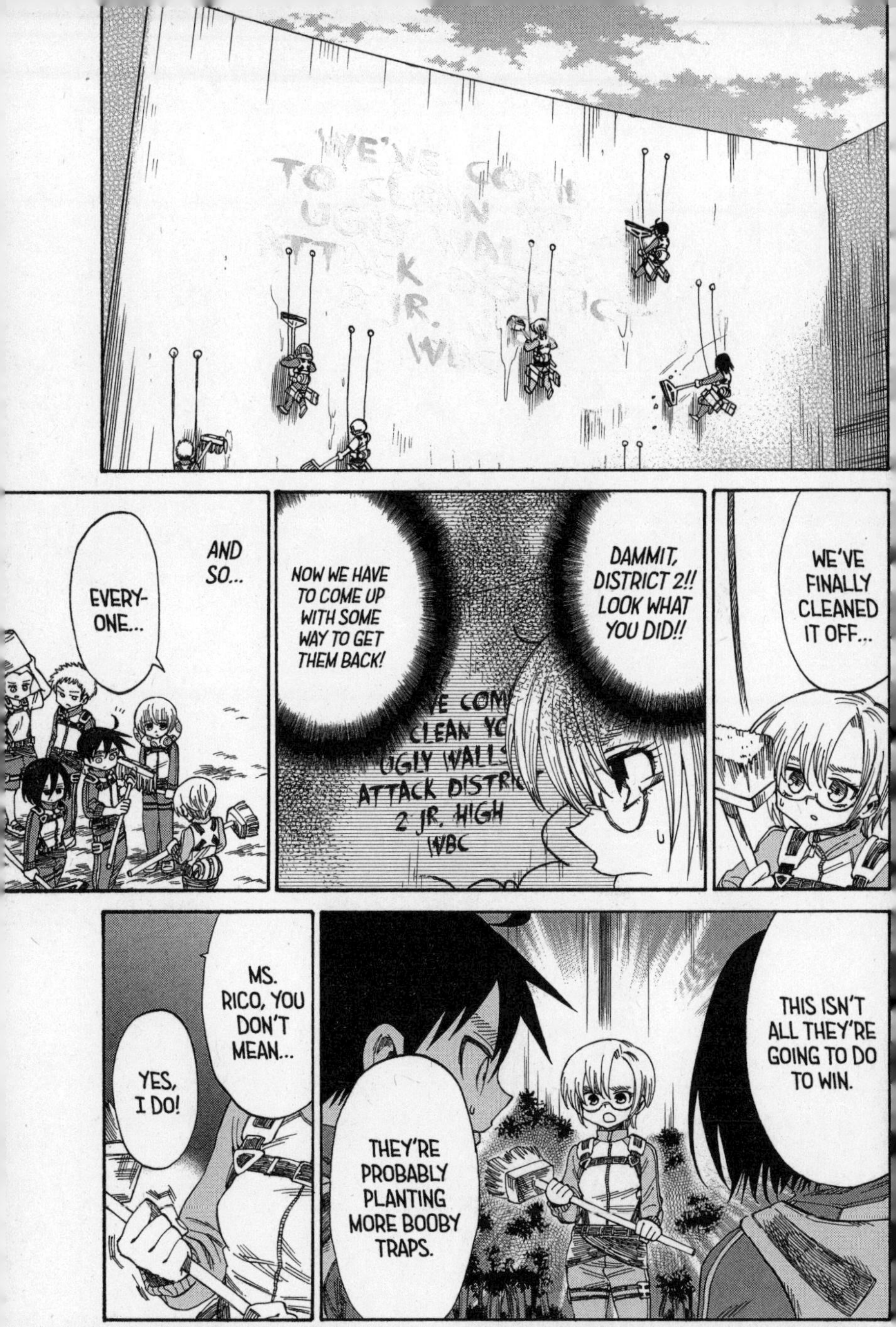
WE'VE FINALLY CLEANED IT OFF...
DAMMIT, DISTRICT 2!! LOOK WHAT YOU DID!!
NOW WE HAVE TO COME UP WITH SOME WAY TO GET THEM BACK!
2 JR. HIGH
WBC
AND SO...
EVERY-ONE...
THIS ISN'T ALL THEY'RE GOING TO DO TO WIN.
THEY'RE PROBABLY PLANTING MORE BOOBY TRAPS.
MS. RICO, YOU DON'T MEAN...
YES, I DO!

FORTY-FIFTH PERIOD: FINAL BATTLE! THE WALL BEAUTIFICATION COMPETITION

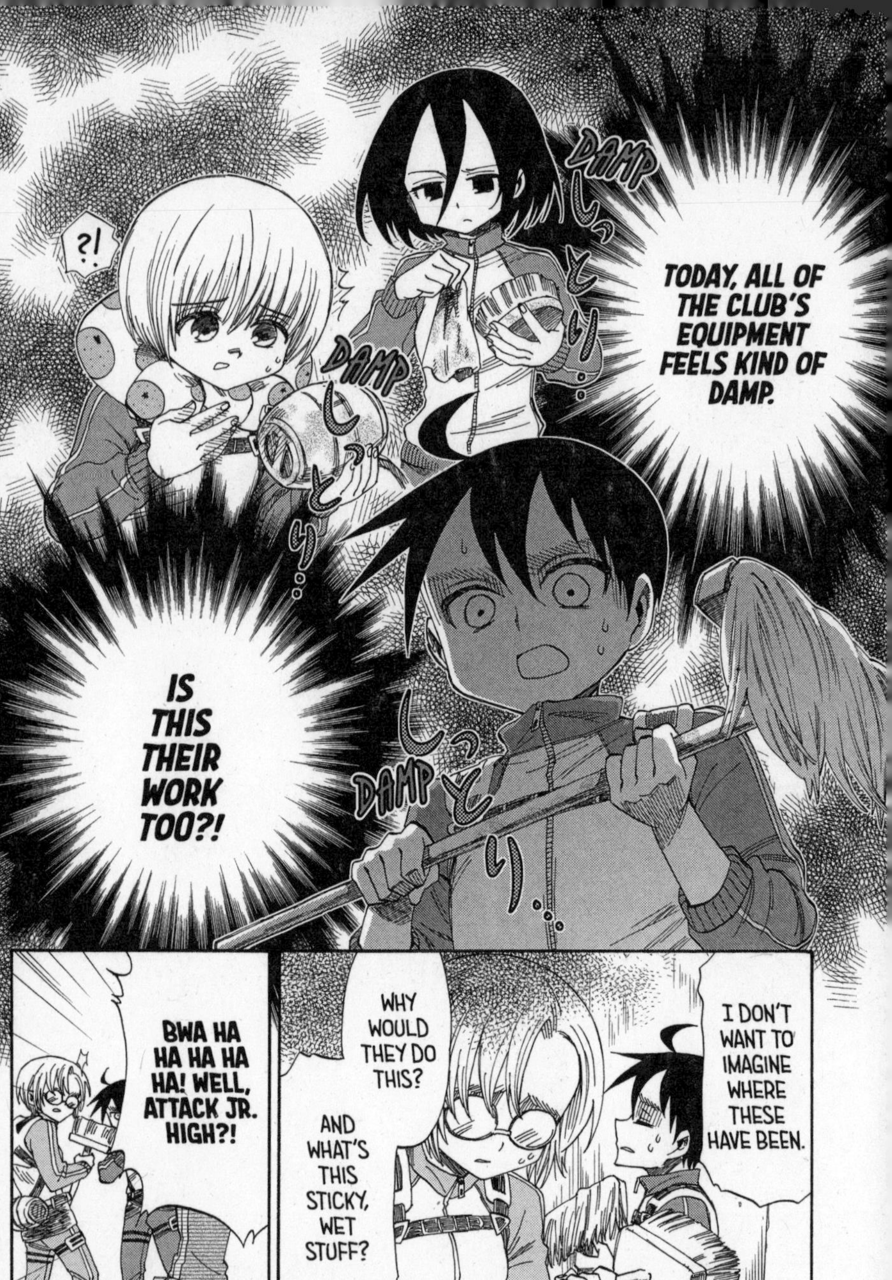
DAMP
しっとり!
TODAY, ALL OF THE CLUB'S EQUIPMENT FEELS KIND OF DAMP.
?!
DAMP
しっとり…
IS THIS THEIR WORK TOO?!
DAMP
しっとり…
I DON'T WANT TO IMAGINE WHERE THESE HAVE BEEN.
WHY WOULD THEY DO THIS?
AND WHAT'S THIS STICKY, WET STUFF?
BWA HA HA HA HA HA HA! WELL, ATTACK JR. HIGH?!

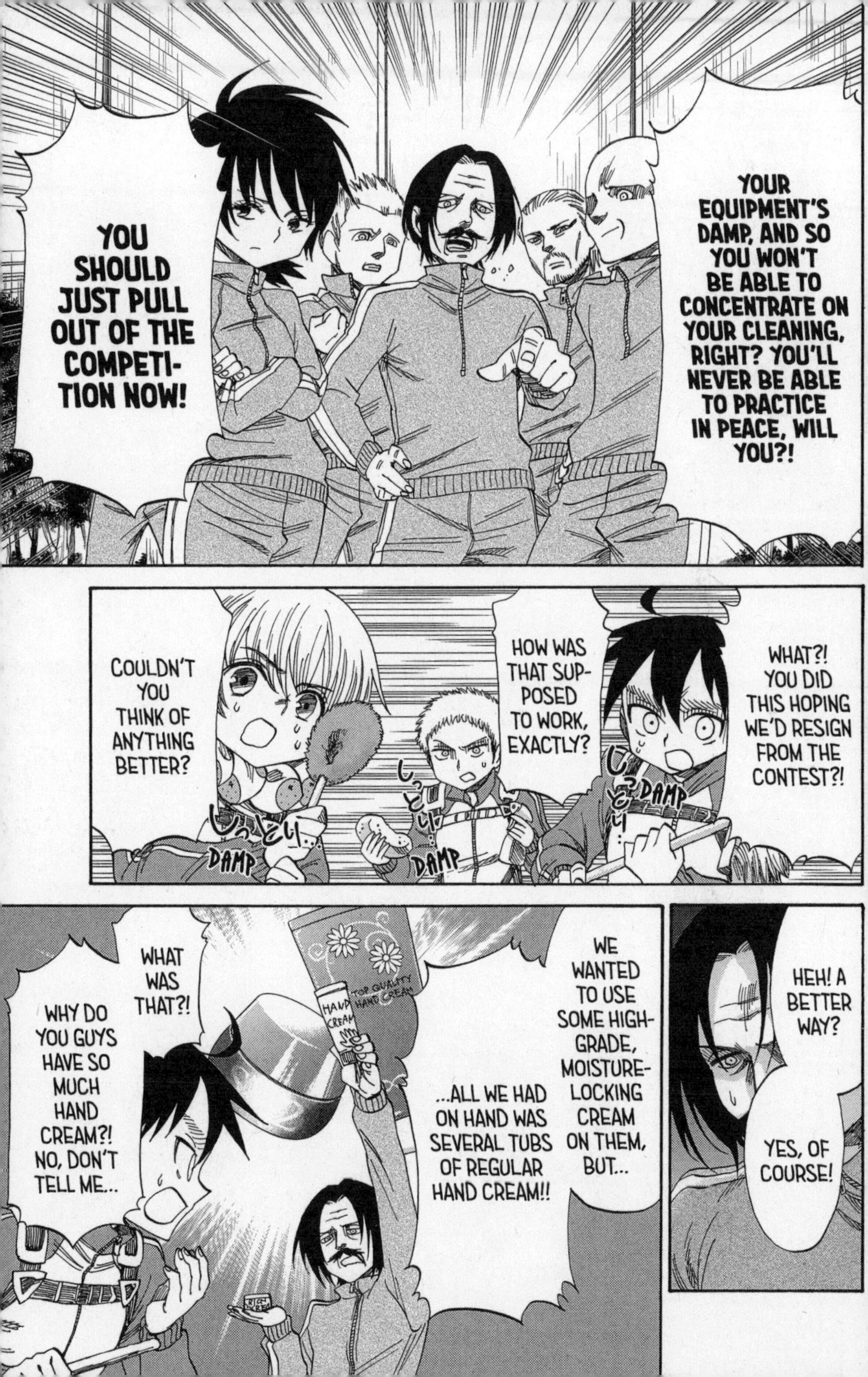
YOUR EQUIPMENT'S DAMP, AND SO YOU WON'T BE ABLE TO CONCENTRATE ON YOUR CLEANING, RIGHT? YOU'LL NEVER BE ABLE TO PRACTICE IN PEACE, WILL YOU?!
YOU SHOULD JUST PULL OUT OF THE COMPETITION NOW!
WHAT?! YOU DID THIS HOPING WE'D RESIGN FROM THE CONTEST?!
DAMP
HOW WAS THAT SUPPOSED TO WORK, EXACTLY?
DAMP
COULDN'T YOU THINK OF ANYTHING BETTER?
DAMP
HEH! A BETTER WAY?
YES, OF COURSE!
WE WANTED TO USE SOME HIGH-GRADE, MOISTURE-LOCKING CREAM ON THEM, BUT...
...ALL WE HAD ON HAND WAS SEVERAL TUBS OF REGULAR HAND CREAM!!
TOP QUALITY HAND CREAM
HAND CREAM
WHAT WAS THAT?!
WHY DO YOU GUYS HAVE SO MUCH HAND CREAM?! NO, DON'T TELL ME...

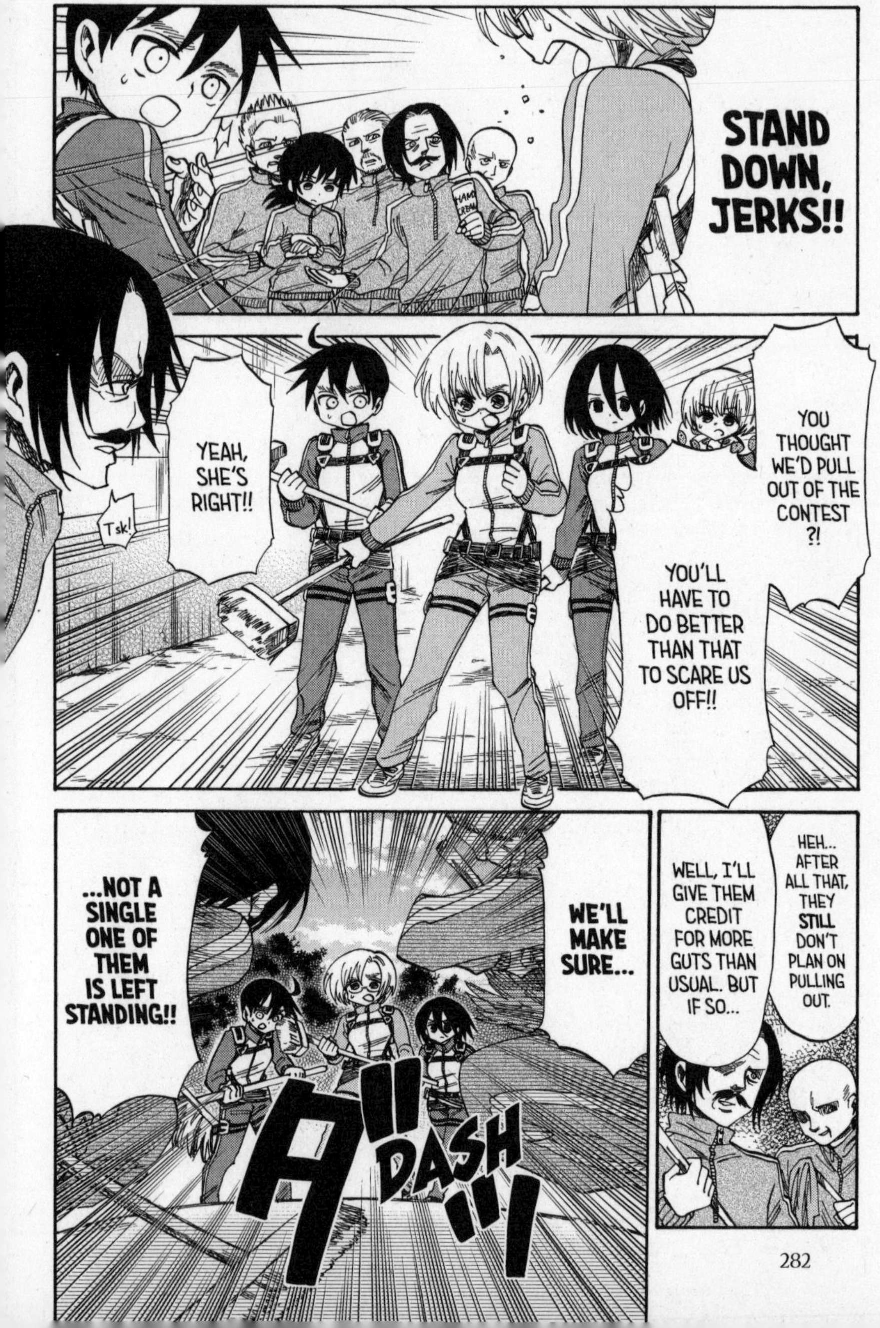
STAND DOWN, JERKS!!
YOU THOUGHT WE'D PULL OUT OF THE CONTEST ?!
YOU'LL HAVE TO DO BETTER THAN THAT TO SCARE US OFF!!
YEAH, SHE'S RIGHT!!
Tsk!
HEH... AFTER ALL THAT, THEY STILL DON'T PLAN ON PULLING OUT.
WELL, I'LL GIVE THEM CREDIT FOR MORE GUTS THAN USUAL. BUT IF SO...
WE'LL MAKE SURE...
...NOT A SINGLE ONE OF THEM IS LEFT STANDING!!
DASH!!

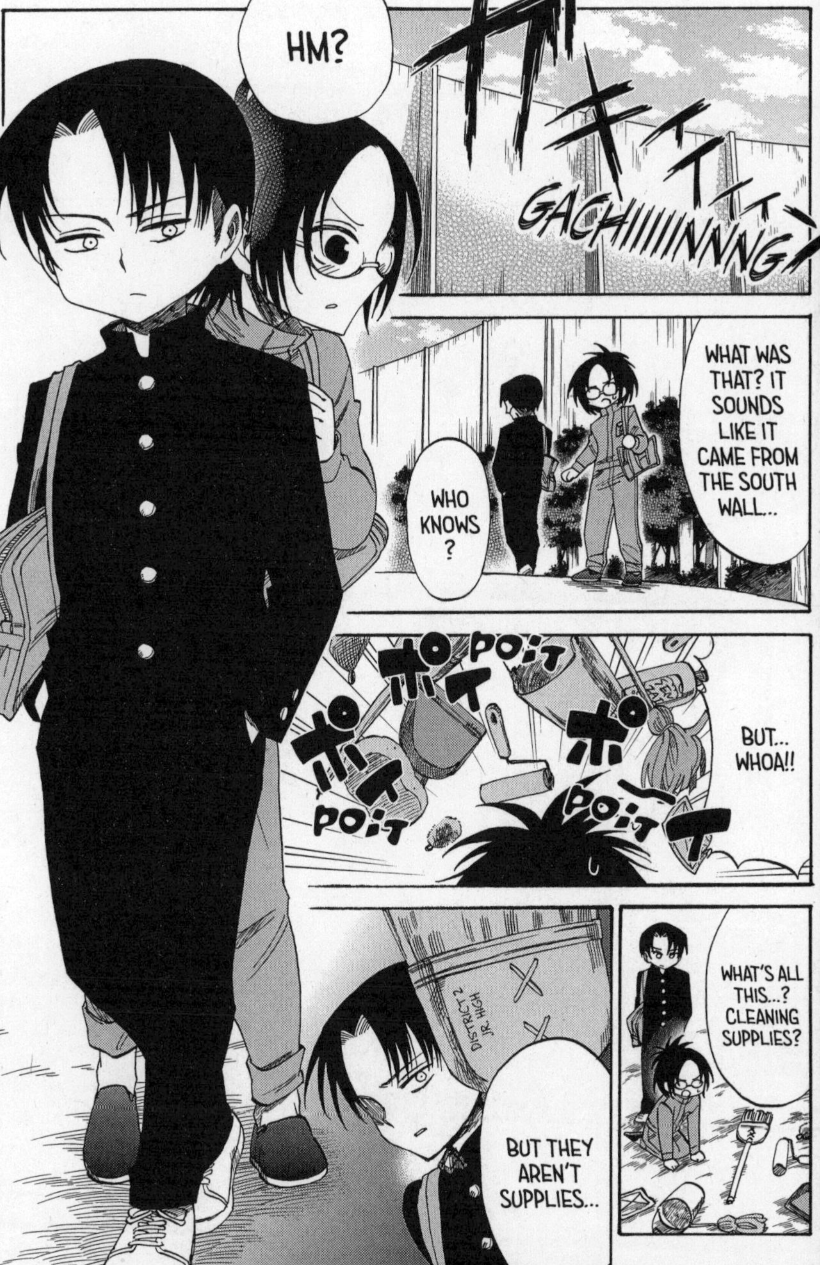
GACHIIIIINNNG!
WHAT WAS THAT? IT SOUNDS LIKE IT CAME FROM THE SOUTH WALL...
WHO KNOWS?
BUT... WHOA!!
POIT
POIT
POIT
POIT
WHAT'S ALL THIS...? CLEANING SUPPLIES?
DISTRICT 2 JR. HIGH
BUT THEY AREN'T SUPPLIES...
HM?

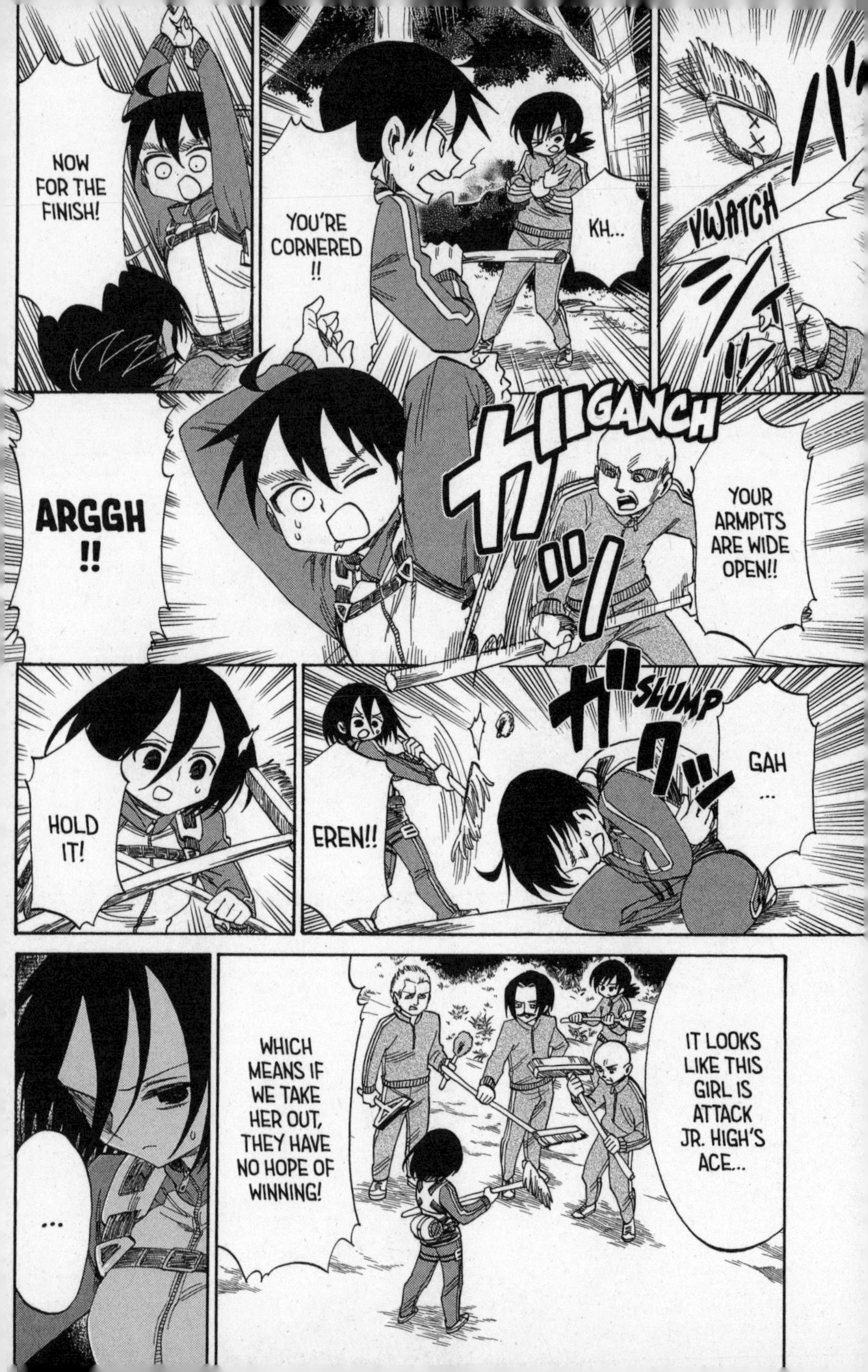
YWATCH
KH...
YOU'RE CORNERED!!
NOW FOR THE FINISH!
YOUR ARMPITS ARE WIDE OPEN!!
GANCH
ARGGH!!
GAH...
SLUMP
EREN!!
HOLD IT!
IT LOOKS LIKE THIS GIRL IS ATTACK JR. HIGH'S ACE...
WHICH MEANS IF WE TAKE HER OUT, THEY HAVE NO HOPE OF WINNING!
...

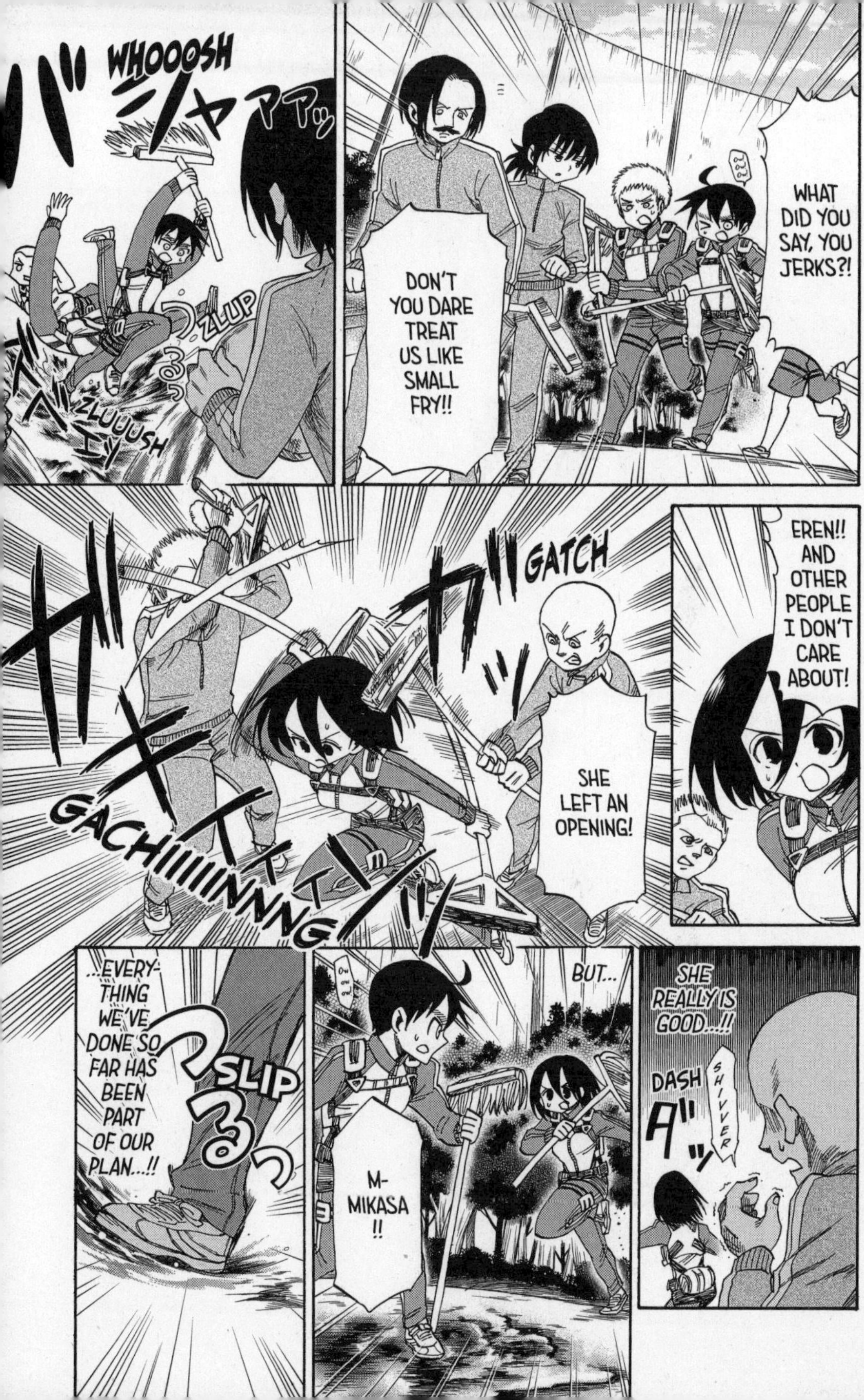

WHAT DID YOU SAY, YOU JERKS?!
OW OW OW
DON'T YOU DARE TREAT US LIKE SMALL FRY!!
WHOOOSH
ZLUP
ZLUUUUSH
EREN!! AND OTHER PEOPLE I DON'T CARE ABOUT!
GATCH
SHE LEFT AN OPENING!
GACHIIIIIINNNG
SHE REALLY IS GOOD...!!
SHIVVER
DASH
BUT...
OW OW OW
M-MIKASA!!
...EVERYTHING WE'VE DONE SO FAR HAS BEEN PART OF OUR PLAN...!!
SLIP

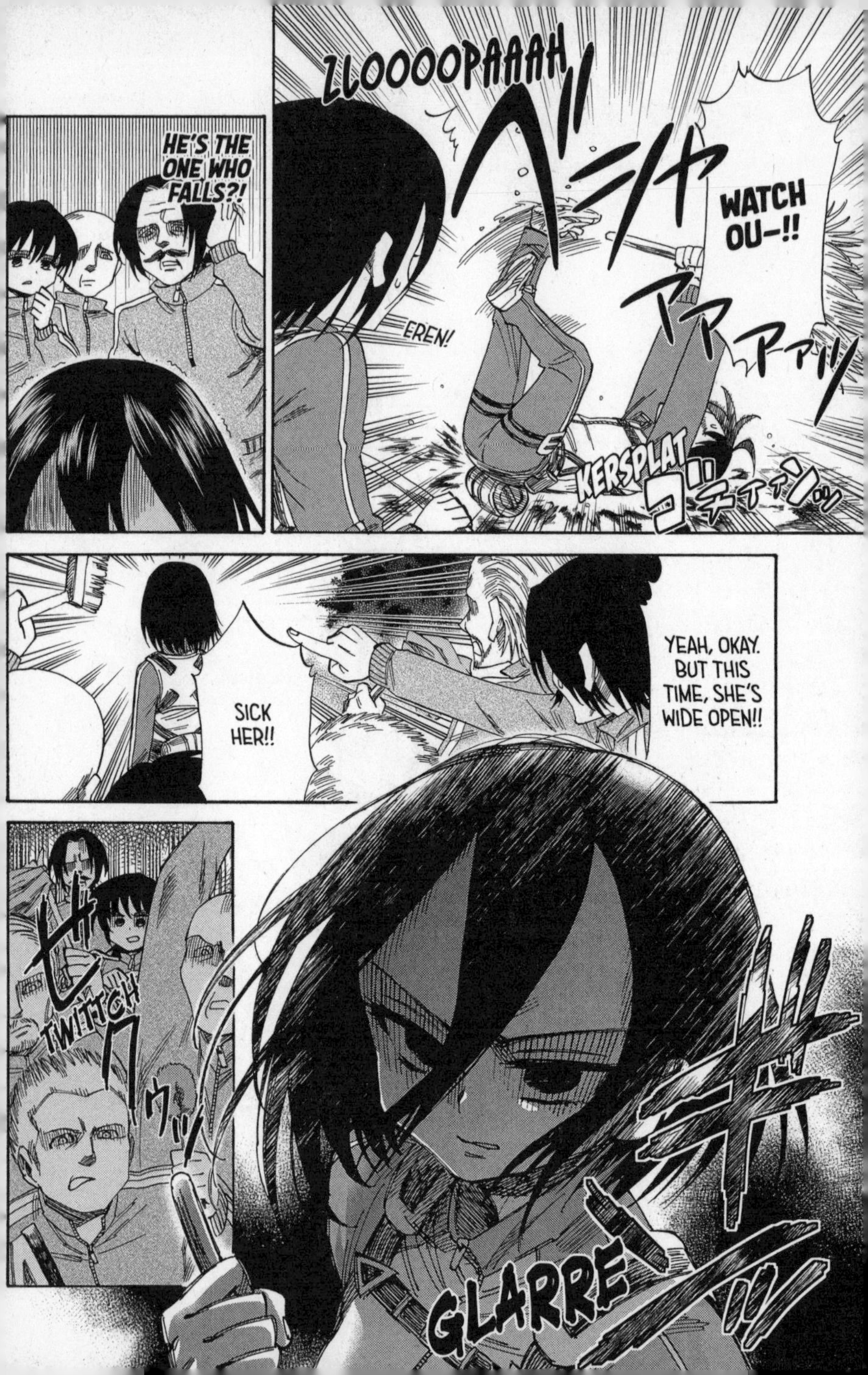
ZLOOOOPAAAH
WATCH OU-!!
EREN!
KERSPLAT
HE'S THE ONE WHO FALLS?!
YEAH, OKAY. BUT THIS TIME, SHE'S WIDE OPEN!!
SICK HER!!
GLARRE
TWITCH

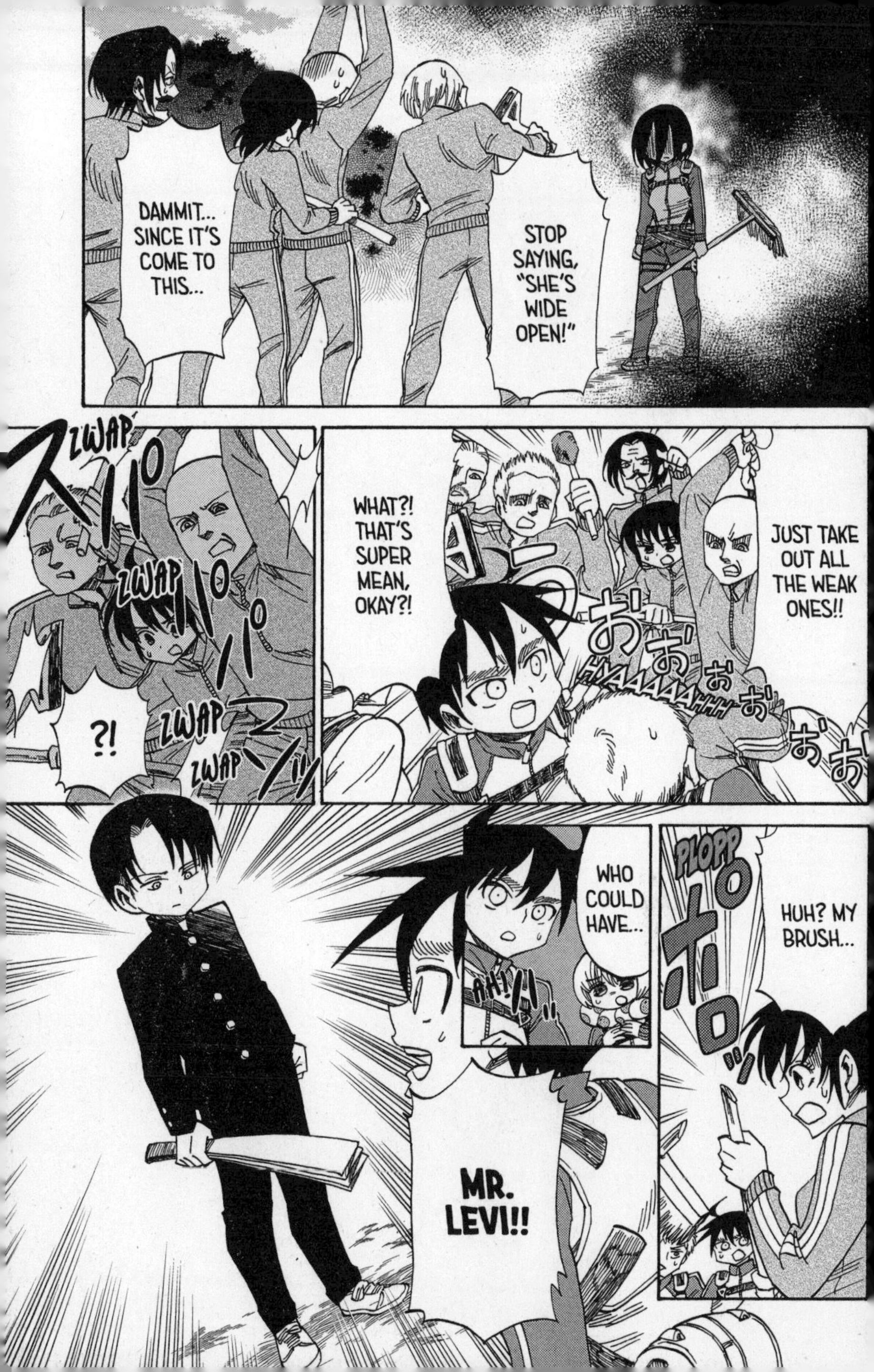
STOP SAYING, "SHE'S WIDE OPEN!"
DAMMIT... SINCE IT'S COME TO THIS...
JUST TAKE OUT ALL THE WEAK ONES!!
HYAAAAAHHH
WHAT?! THAT'S SUPER MEAN, OKAY?!
ZWAP
ZWAP
ZWAP
ZWAP
?!
PLOPP
HUH? MY BRUSH...
WHO COULD HAVE...
AH!
MR. LEVI!!

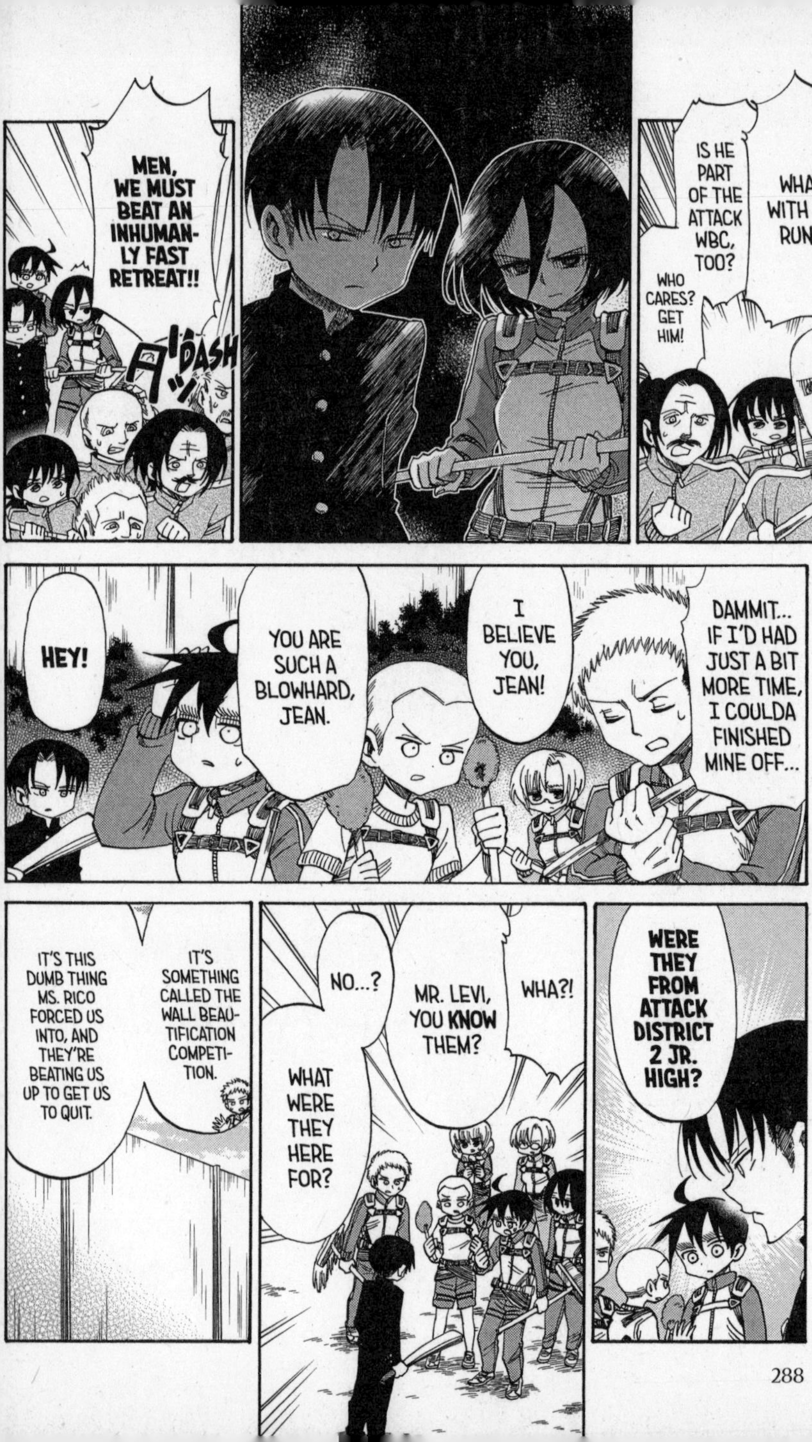
WHAT'S WITH THIS RUNT?!
IS HE PART OF THE ATTACK WBC, TOO?
WHO CARES? GET HIM!
MEN, WE MUST BEAT AN INHUMANLY FAST RETREAT!!
DASH
DAMMIT... IF I'D HAD JUST A BIT MORE TIME, I COULDA FINISHED MINE OFF...
I BELIEVE YOU, JEAN!
YOU ARE SUCH A BLOWHARD, JEAN.
HEY!
WERE THEY FROM ATTACK DISTRICT 2 JR. HIGH?
WHA?!
MR. LEVI, YOU KNOW THEM?
NO...?
WHAT WERE THEY HERE FOR?
IT'S SOMETHING CALLED THE WALL BEAUTIFICATION COMPETITION.
IT'S THIS DUMB THING MS. RICO FORCED US INTO, AND THEY'RE BEATING US UP TO GET US TO QUIT.

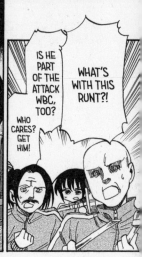

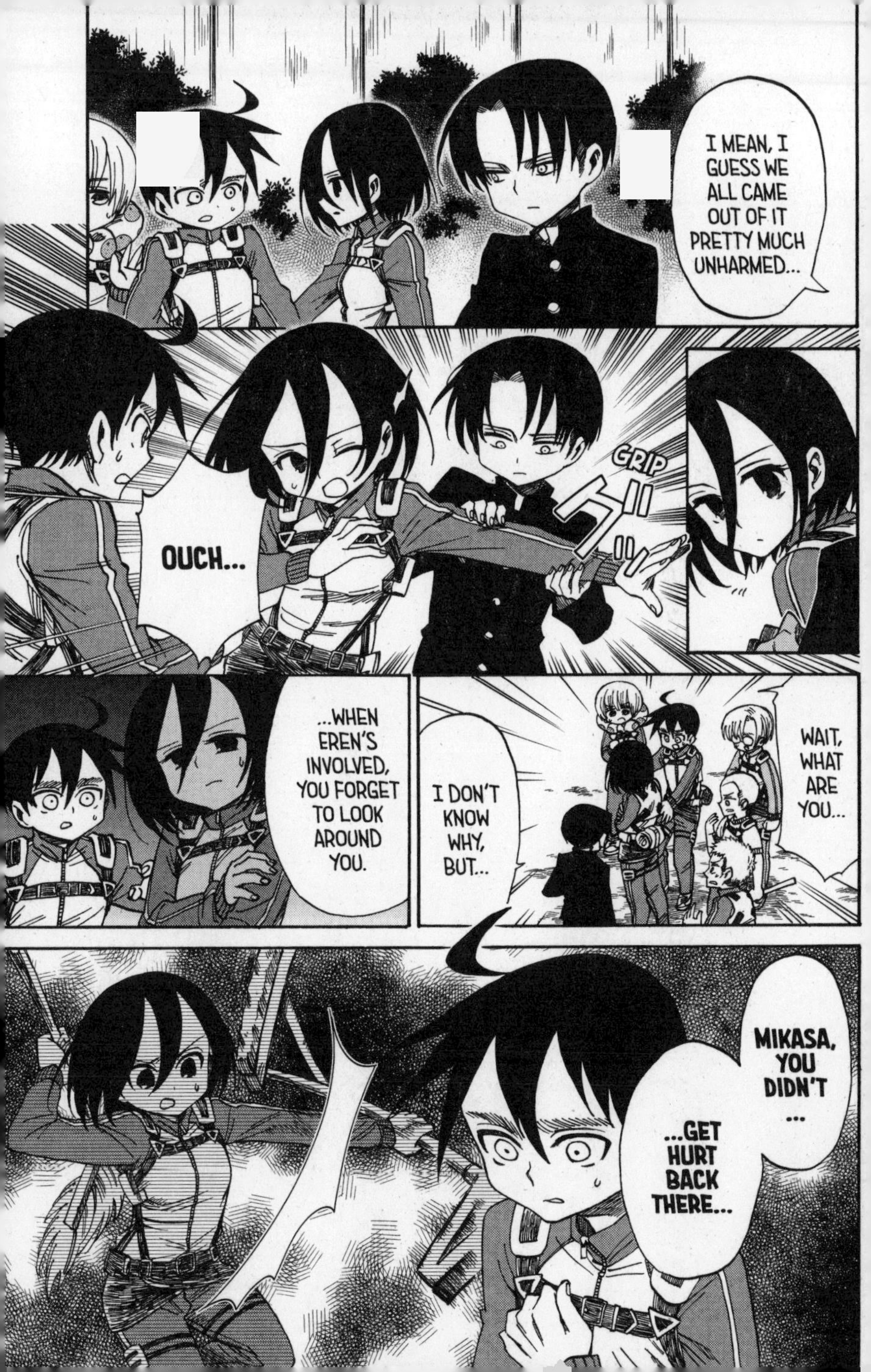
I MEAN, I GUESS WE ALL CAME OUT OF IT PRETTY MUCH UNHARMED...
GRIP
OUCH...
WAIT, WHAT ARE YOU...
I DON'T KNOW WHY, BUT...
...WHEN EREN'S INVOLVED, YOU FORGET TO LOOK AROUND YOU.
MIKASA, YOU DIDN'T ...
...GET HURT BACK THERE...

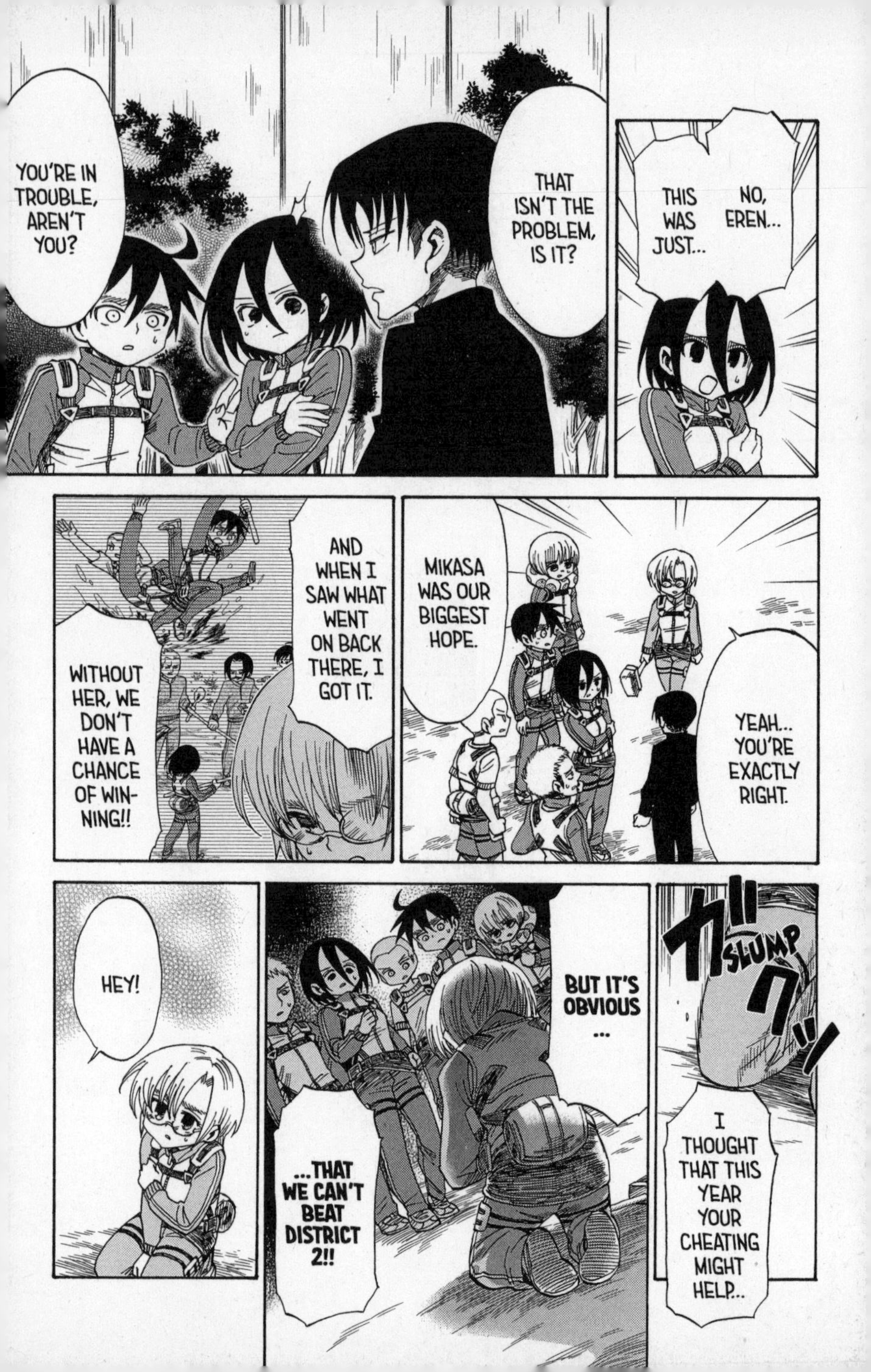
NO, EREN... THIS WAS JUST...
THAT ISN'T THE PROBLEM, IS IT?
YOU'RE IN TROUBLE, AREN'T YOU?
YEAH... YOU'RE EXACTLY RIGHT.
MIKASA WAS OUR BIGGEST HOPE.
AND WHEN I SAW WHAT WENT ON BACK THERE, I GOT IT.
WITHOUT HER, WE DON'T HAVE A CHANCE OF WIN-NING!!
SLUMP
I THOUGHT THAT THIS YEAR YOUR CHEATING MIGHT HELP...
BUT IT'S OBVIOUS ...
...THAT WE CAN'T BEAT DISTRICT 2!!
HEY!

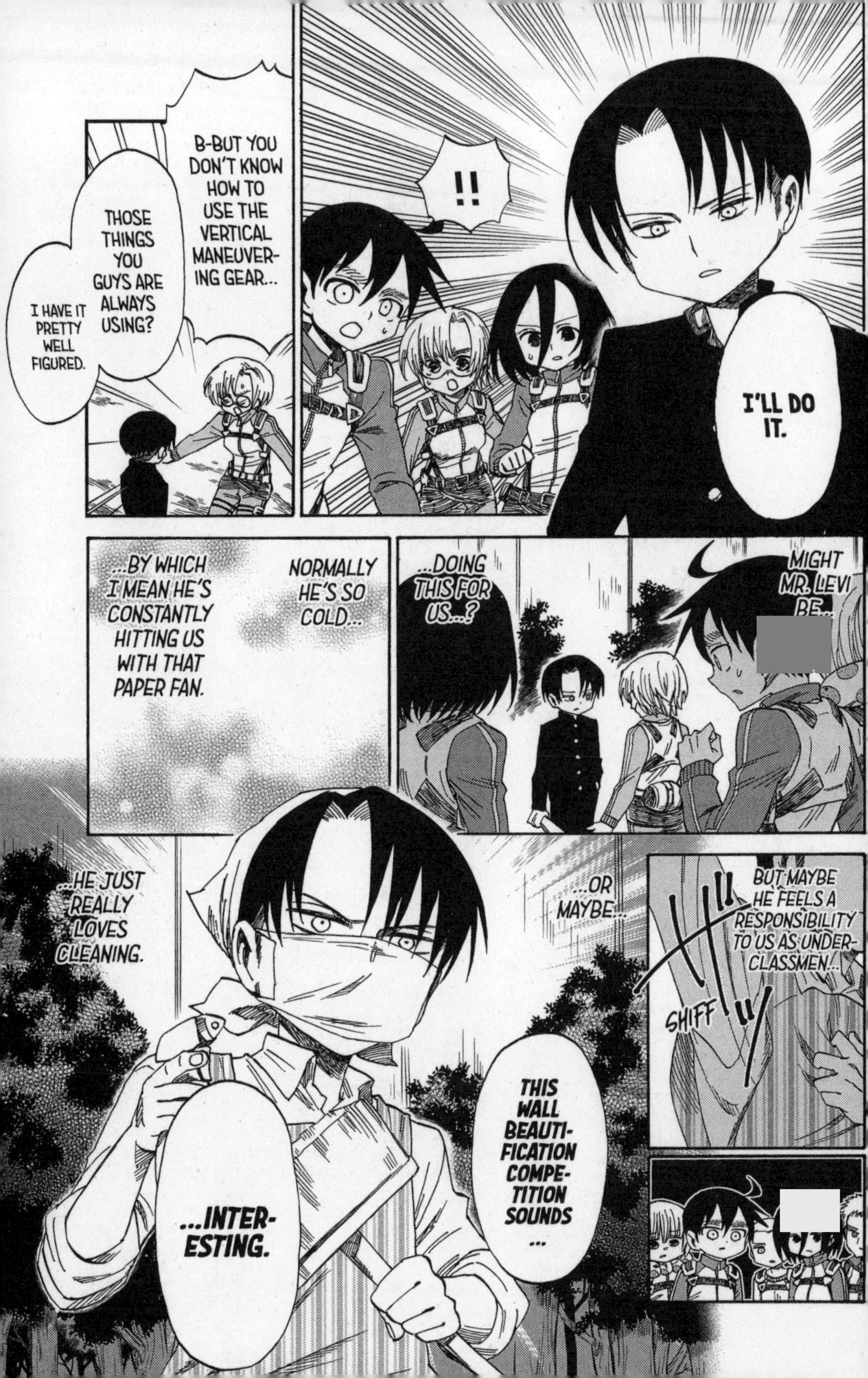
I'LL DO IT.
!!
B-BUT YOU DON'T KNOW HOW TO USE THE VERTICAL MANEUVER-ING GEAR...
THOSE THINGS YOU GUYS ARE ALWAYS USING?
I HAVE IT PRETTY WELL FIGURED.
MIGHT MR. LEVI BE...
...DOING THIS FOR US...?
NORMALLY HE'S SO COLD...
...BY WHICH I MEAN HE'S CONSTANTLY HITTING US WITH THAT PAPER FAN.
BUT MAYBE HE FEELS A RESPONSIBILITY TO US AS UNDER-CLASSMEN...
SHIFF
...OR MAYBE...
...HE JUST REALLY LOVES CLEANING.
THIS WALL BEAUTI-FICATION COMPE-TITION SOUNDS ...
...INTER-ESTING.

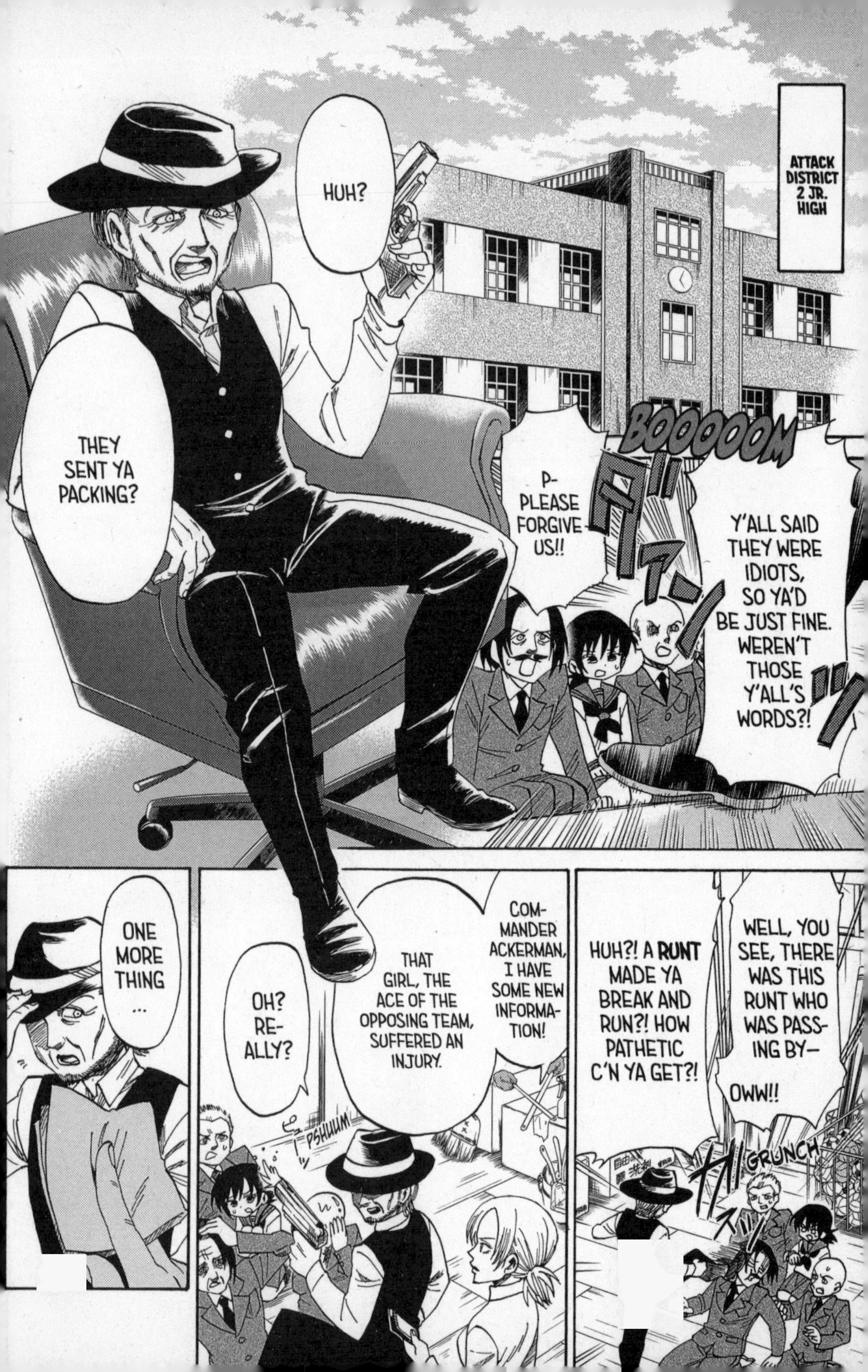
ATTACK DISTRICT 2 JR. HIGH
BOOOOOM
Y'ALL SAID THEY WERE IDIOTS, SO YA'D BE JUST FINE. WEREN'T THOSE Y'ALL'S WORDS?!
P-PLEASE FORGIVE US!!
HUH?
THEY SENT YA PACKING?
WELL, YOU SEE, THERE WAS THIS RUNT WHO WAS PASSING BY—
HUH?! A **RUNT** MADE YA BREAK AND RUN?! HOW PATHETIC C'N YA GET?!
OWW!!
GRUNCH
COMMANDER ACKERMAN, I HAVE SOME NEW INFORMATION!
THAT GIRL, THE ACE OF THE OPPOSING TEAM, SUFFERED AN INJURY.
OH? REALLY?
PSHUUM
ONE MORE THING ...

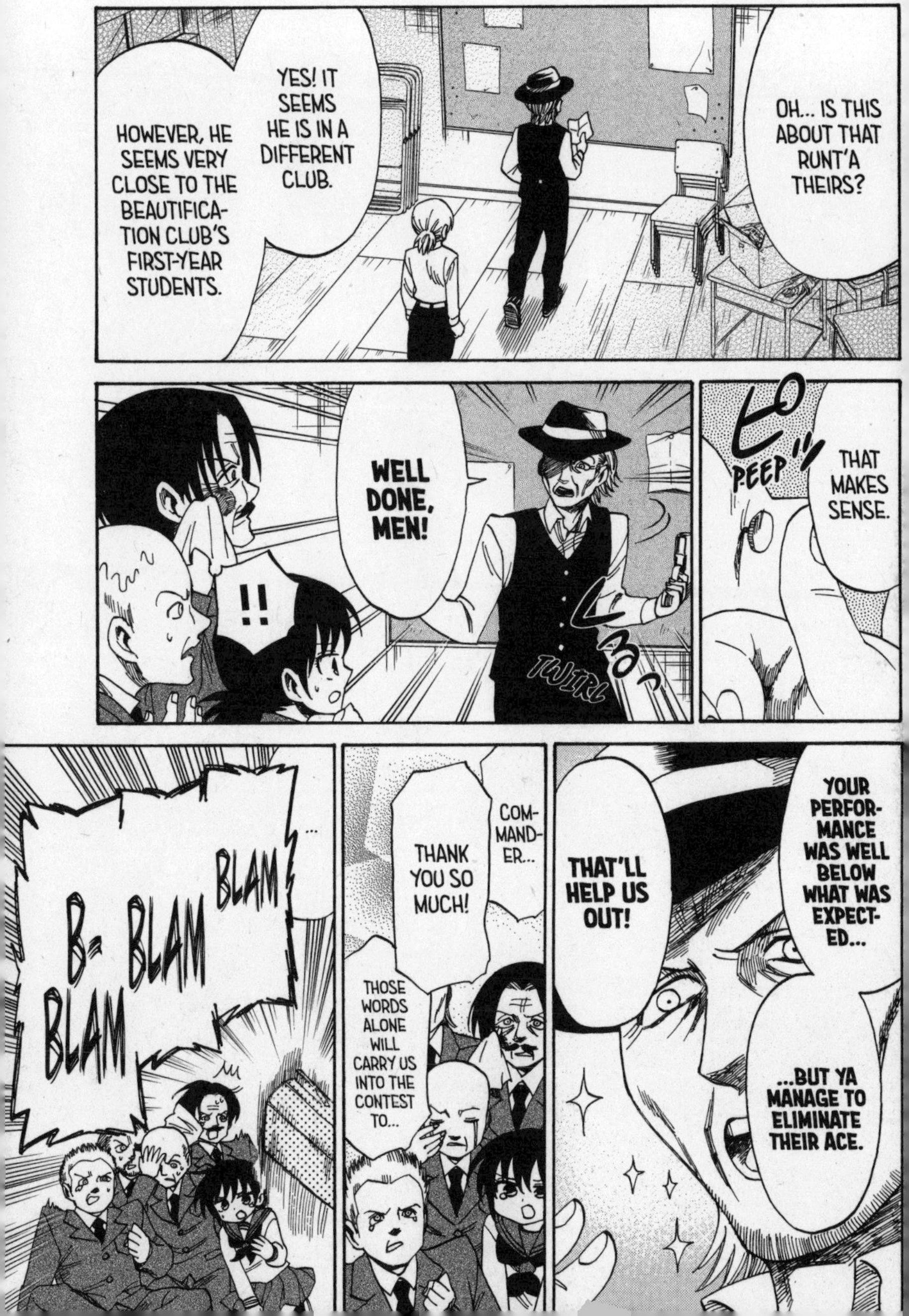
OH... IS THIS ABOUT THAT RUNT'A THEIRS?
YES! IT SEEMS HE IS IN A DIFFERENT CLUB.
HOWEVER, HE SEEMS VERY CLOSE TO THE BEAUTIFICATION CLUB'S FIRST-YEAR STUDENTS.
PEEP
THAT MAKES SENSE.
WELL DONE, MEN!
TWIRL
!!
YOUR PERFORMANCE WAS WELL BELOW WHAT WAS EXPECTED...
...BUT YA MANAGE TO ELIMINATE THEIR ACE.
THAT'LL HELP US OUT!
COMMANDER...
THANK YOU SO MUCH!
THOSE WORDS ALONE WILL CARRY US INTO THE CONTEST TO...
...
BLAM
B-BLAM
BLAM
BLAM

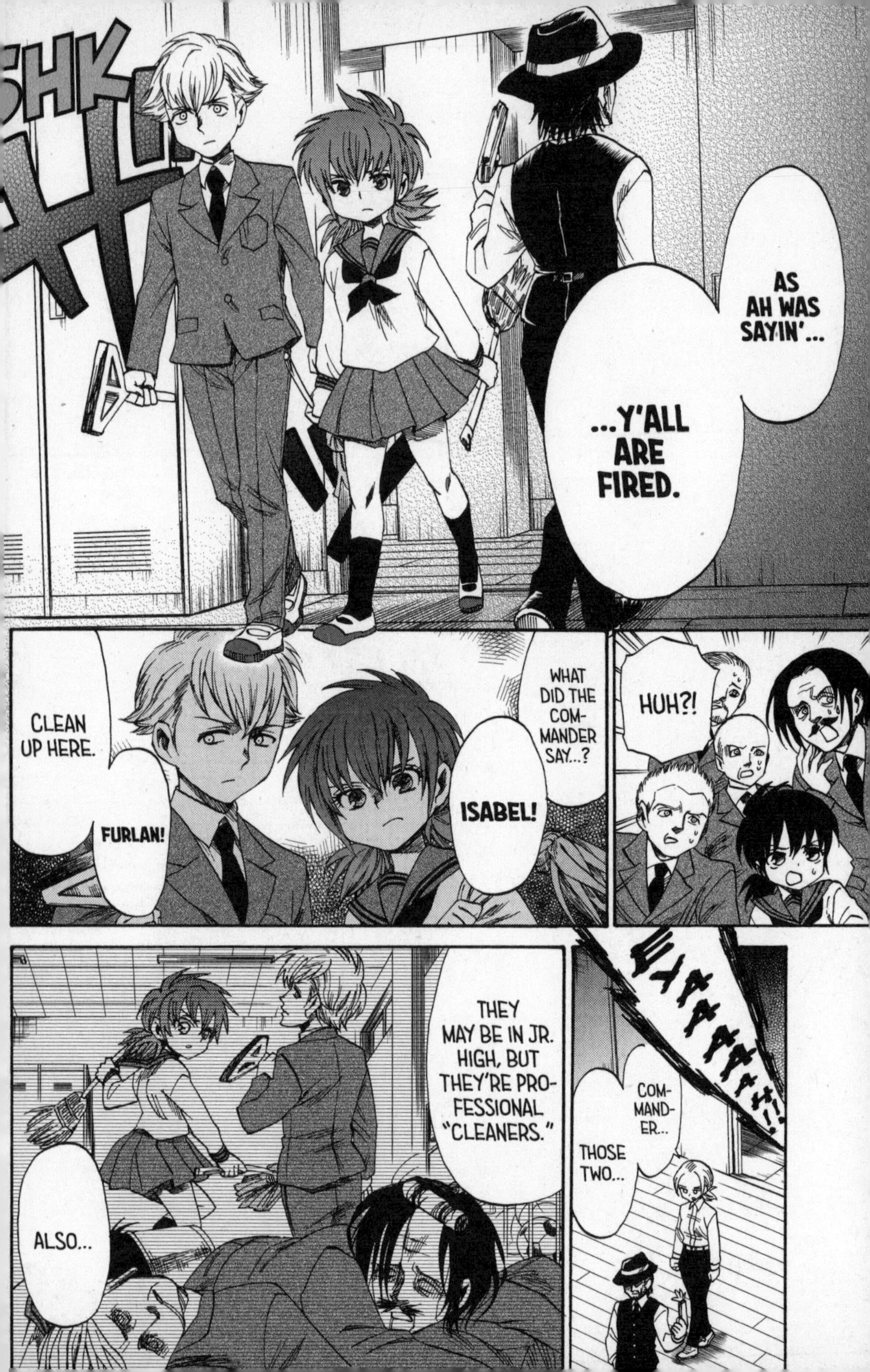
AS AH WAS SAYIN'...
...Y'ALL ARE FIRED.
SHK
HUH?!
WHAT DID THE COM-MANDER SAY...?
ISABEL!
CLEAN UP HERE.
FURLAN!
KYAAAAAAH!!
COM-MAND-ER...
THOSE TWO...
THEY MAY BE IN JR. HIGH, BUT THEY'RE PRO-FESSIONAL "CLEANERS."
ALSO...

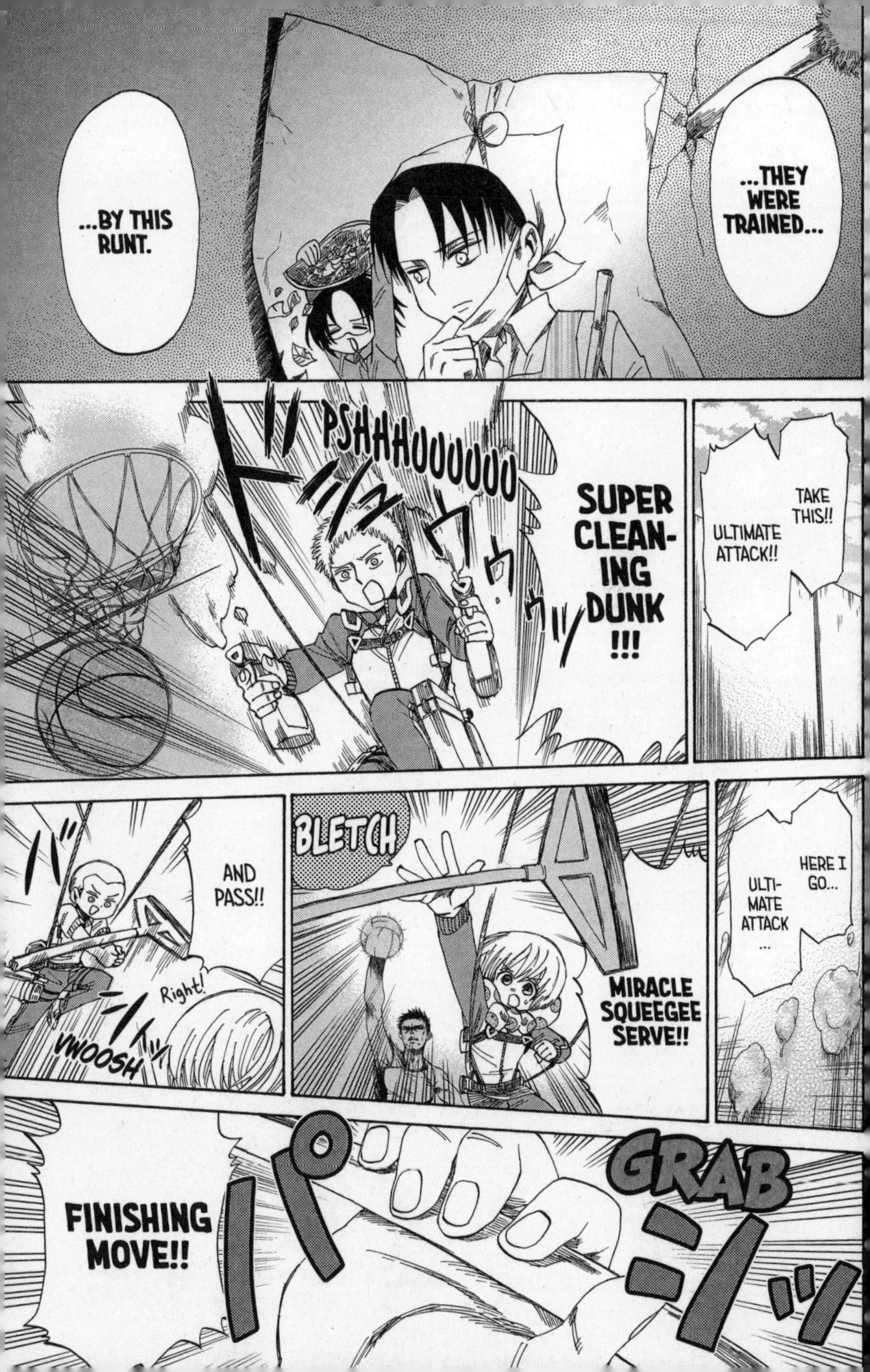
...THEY WERE TRAINED...
...BY THIS RUNT.
TAKE THIS!!
ULTIMATE ATTACK!!
PSHHHOUUUUUU
SUPER CLEAN-ING DUNK!!!
HERE I GO...
ULTI-MATE ATTACK...
BLETCH
MIRACLE SQUEEGEE SERVE!!
AND PASS!!
Right!
VWOOSH
GRAB
FINISHING MOVE!!

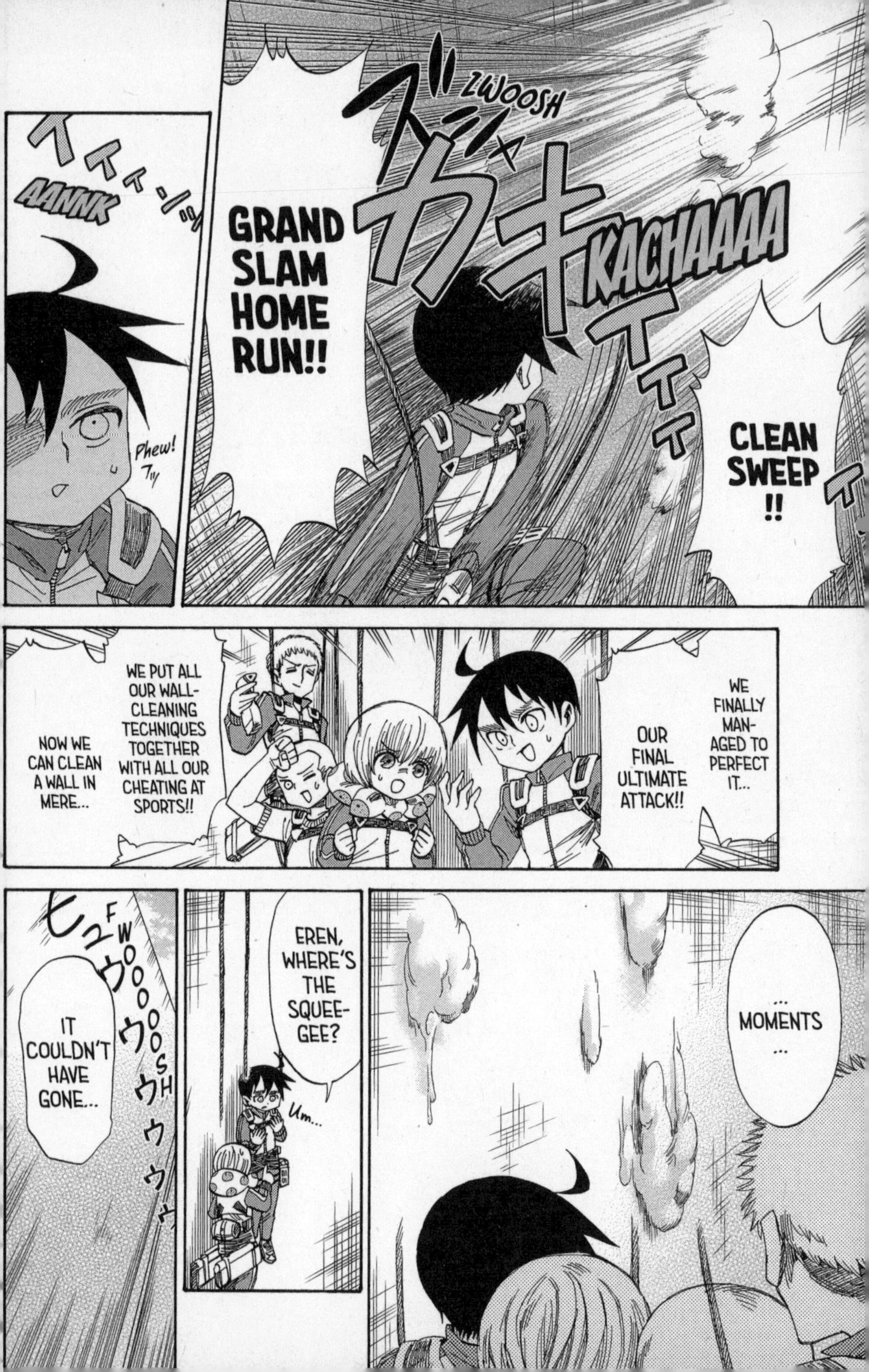
ZWOOSH
KACHAAAA
CLEAN SWEEP!!
GRAND SLAM HOME RUN!!
AANNK
Phew!
WE FINALLY MAN-AGED TO PERFECT IT...
OUR FINAL ULTIMATE ATTACK!!
WE PUT ALL OUR WALL-CLEANING TECHNIQUES TOGETHER WITH ALL OUR CHEATING AT SPORTS!!
NOW WE CAN CLEAN A WALL IN MERE...
...MOMENTS...
EREN, WHERE'S THE SQUEE-GEE?
Um...
FWOOOOOOOSH
IT COULDN'T HAVE GONE...

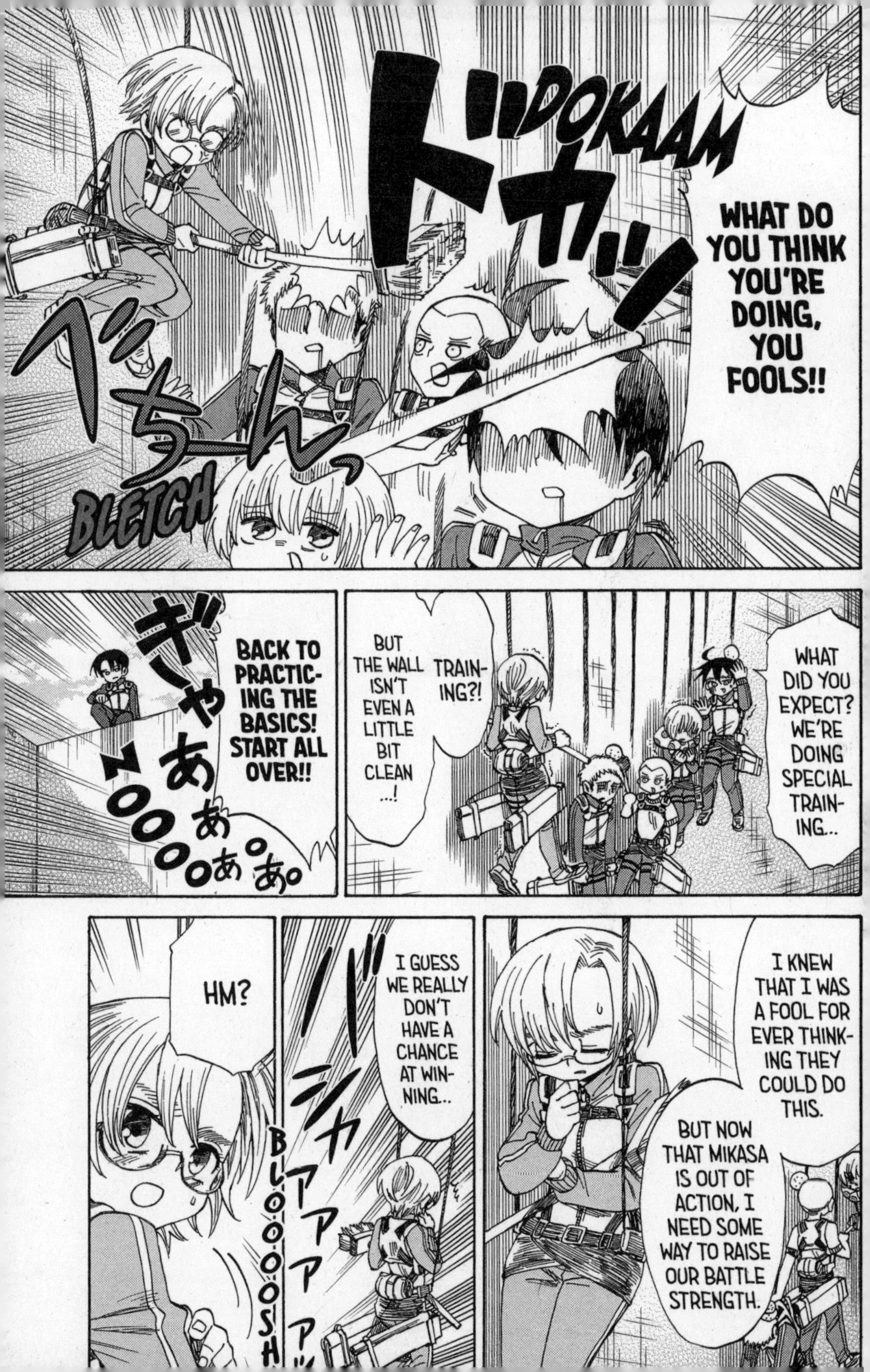
ドカッ
DOKAAM
WHAT DO YOU THINK YOU'RE DOING, YOU FOOLS!!
べちーん
BLETCH
WHAT DID YOU EXPECT? WE'RE DOING SPECIAL TRAIN-ING...
TRAIN-ING?!
BUT THE WALL ISN'T EVEN A LITTLE BIT CLEAN ...!
BACK TO PRACTIC-ING THE BASICS! START ALL OVER!!
ぎゃあああ
NOOOOOO
I KNEW THAT I WAS A FOOL FOR EVER THINK-ING THEY COULD DO THIS.
BUT NOW THAT MIKASA IS OUT OF ACTION, I NEED SOME WAY TO RAISE OUR BATTLE STRENGTH.
I GUESS WE REALLY DON'T HAVE A CHANCE AT WIN-NING...
ズシャアアア
BLOOOOOSH
HM?

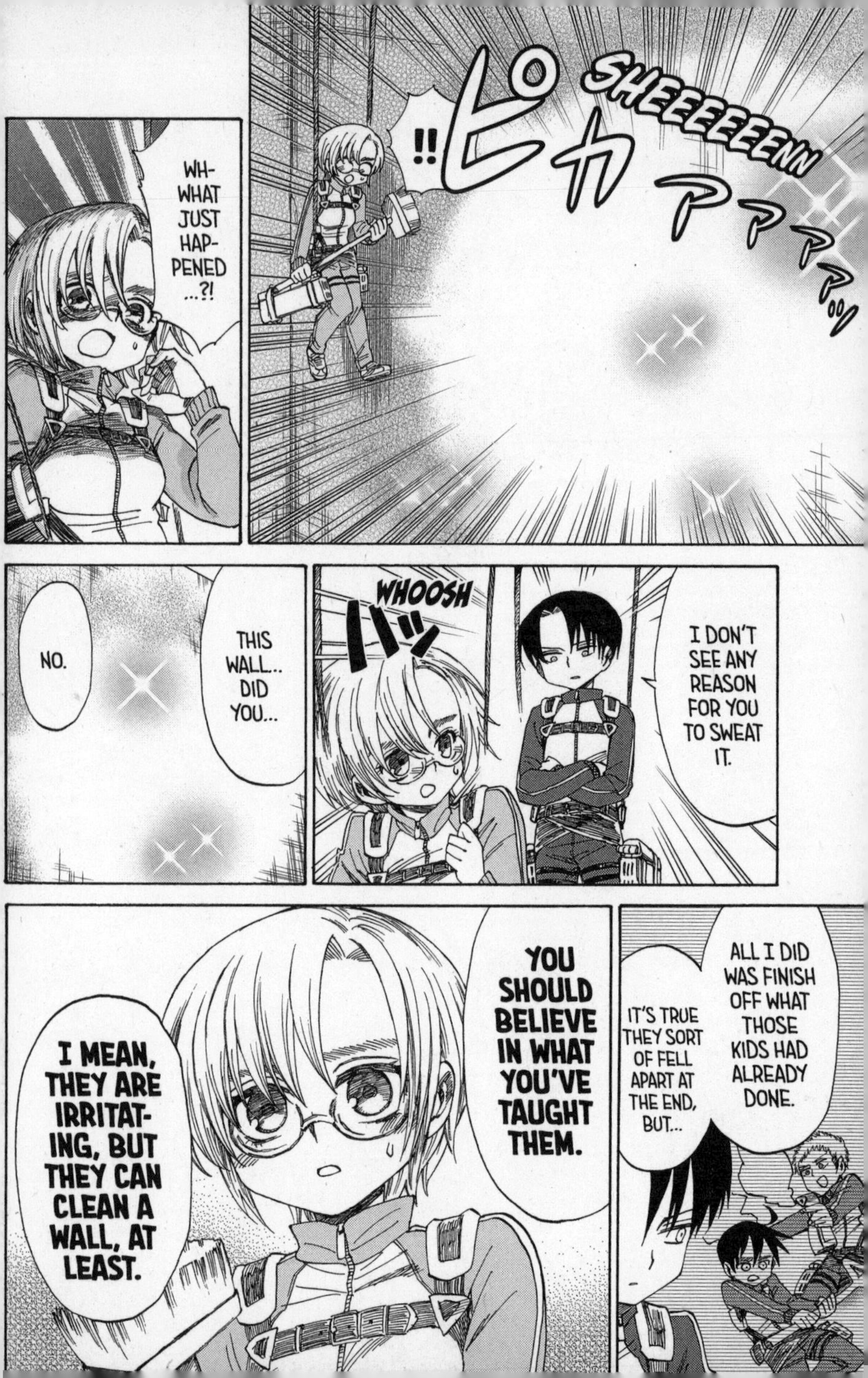
SHEEEEEEENN
ピカァァァァ
!!
WH-WHAT JUST HAPPENED...?!
WHOOSH
I DON'T SEE ANY REASON FOR YOU TO SWEAT IT.
THIS WALL... DID YOU...
NO.
ALL I DID WAS FINISH OFF WHAT THOSE KIDS HAD ALREADY DONE.
IT'S TRUE THEY SORT OF FELL APART AT THE END, BUT...
YOU SHOULD BELIEVE IN WHAT YOU'VE TAUGHT THEM.
I MEAN, THEY ARE IRRITATING, BUT THEY CAN CLEAN A WALL, AT LEAST.

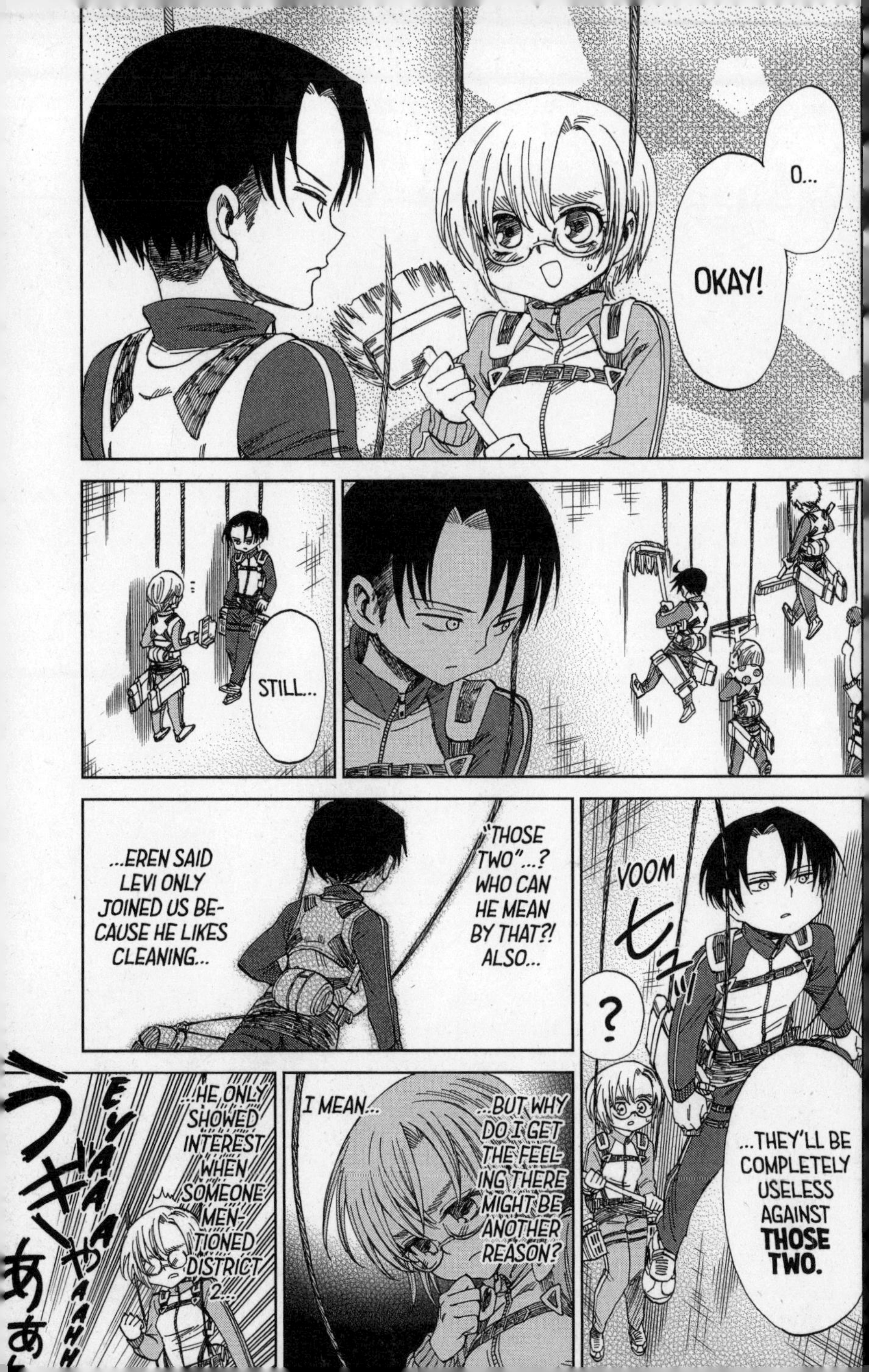
O...
OKAY!
STILL...
VOOM
?
...THEY'LL BE COMPLETELY USELESS AGAINST **THOSE TWO.**
"THOSE TWO"...? WHO CAN HE MEAN BY THAT?! ALSO...
...EREN SAID LEVI ONLY JOINED US BE-CAUSE HE LIKES CLEANING...
...BUT WHY DO I GET THE FEEL-ING THERE MIGHT BE ANOTHER REASON?
I MEAN...
...HE ONLY SHOWED INTEREST WHEN SOMEONE MEN-TIONED DISTRICT 2...
EYAAAAAHH

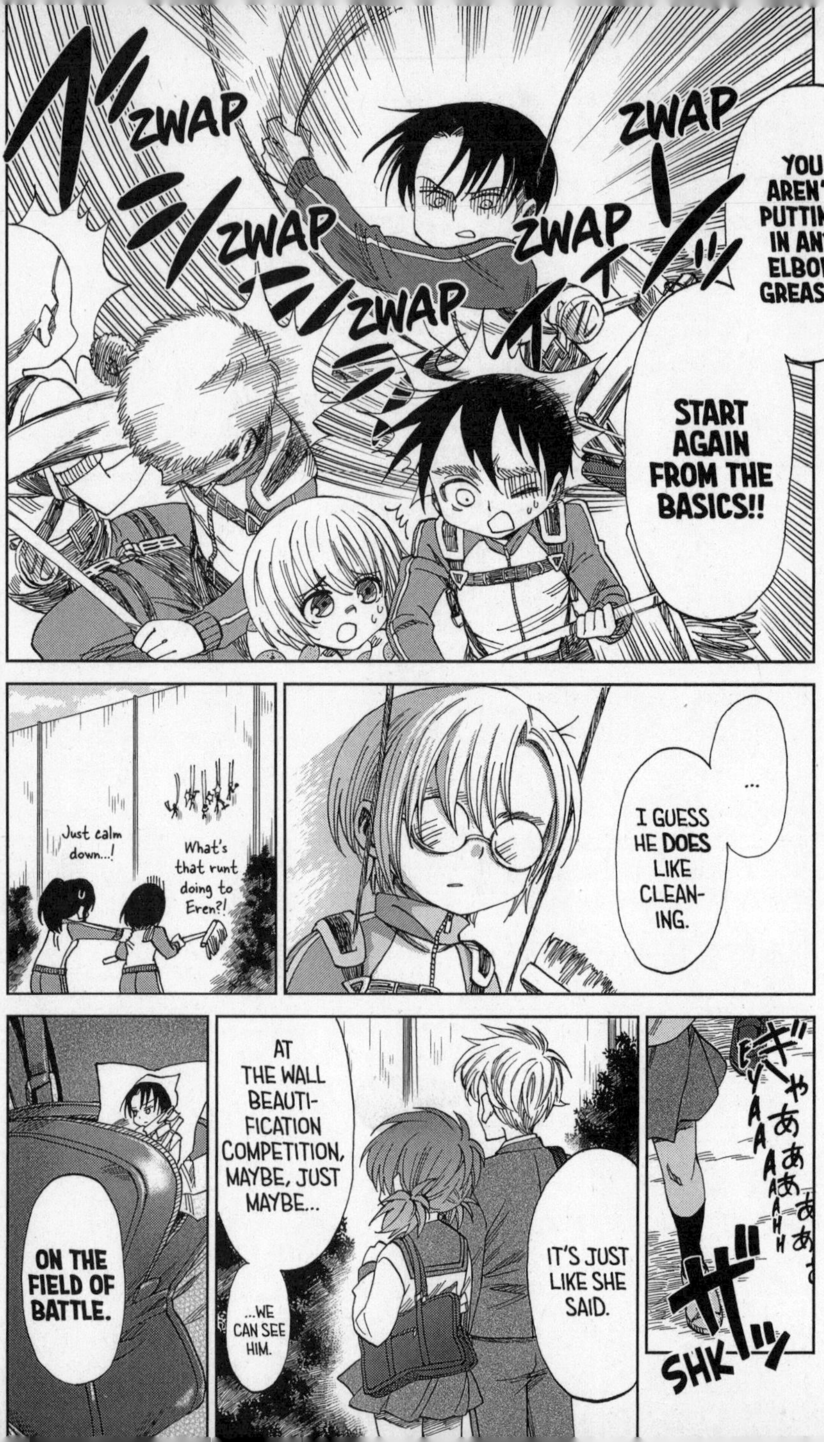
YOU AREN'T PUTTING IN ANY ELBOW GREASE!
ZWAP
ZWAP
ZWAP
ZWAP
ZWAP
START AGAIN FROM THE BASICS!!
...
I GUESS HE DOES LIKE CLEANING.
What's that runt doing to Eren?!
Just calm down...!
YAAAAAAHH
SHK
IT'S JUST LIKE SHE SAID.
AT THE WALL BEAUTIFICATION COMPETITION, MAYBE, JUST MAYBE...
...WE CAN SEE HIM.
ON THE FIELD OF BATTLE.

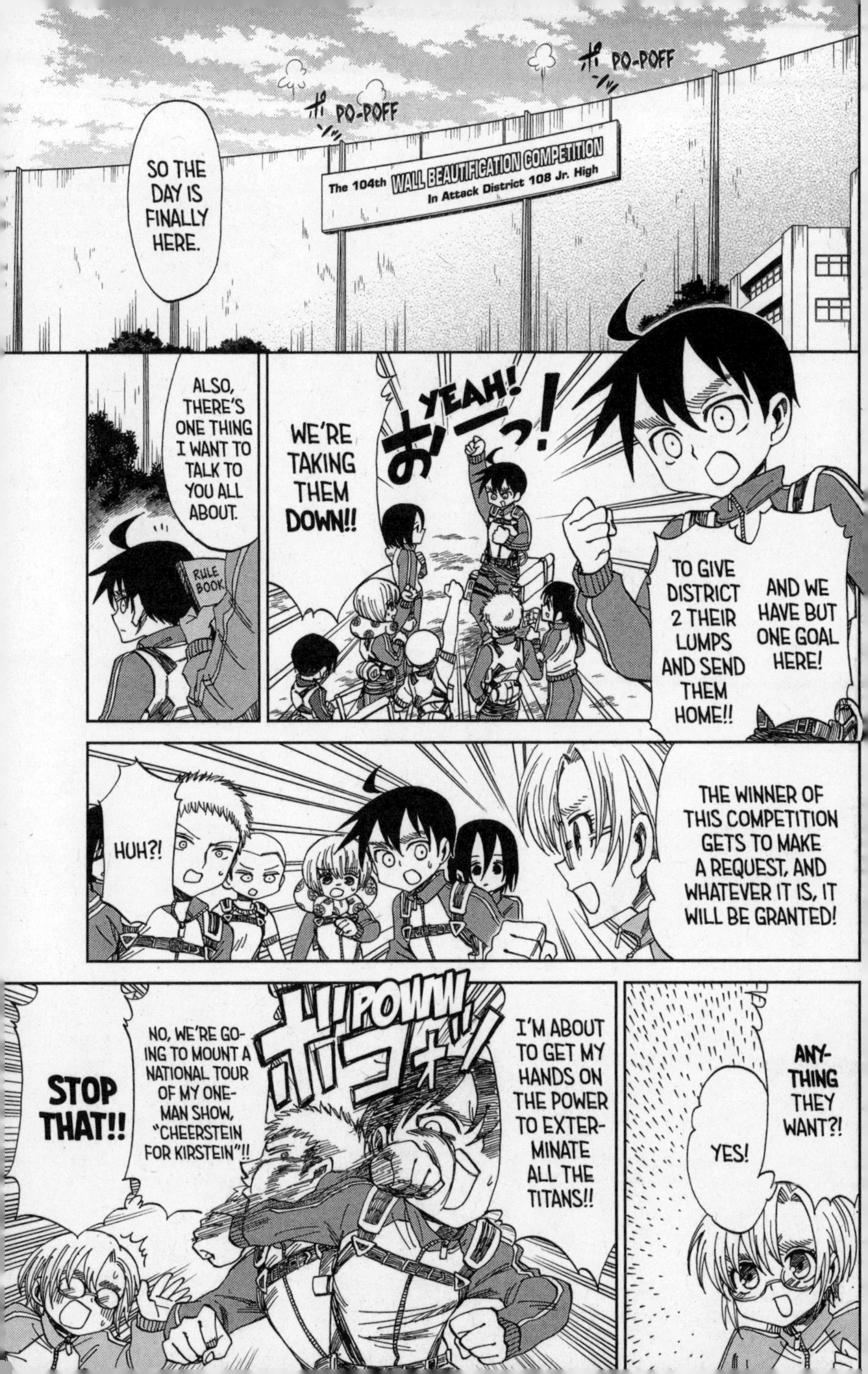
PO-POFF
PO-POFF
The 104th WALL BEAUTIFICATION COMPETITION In Attack District 108 Jr. High
SO THE DAY IS FINALLY HERE.
AND WE HAVE BUT ONE GOAL HERE!
TO GIVE DISTRICT 2 THEIR LUMPS AND SEND THEM HOME!!
YEAH!
おーっ!
WE'RE TAKING THEM DOWN!!
ALSO, THERE'S ONE THING I WANT TO TALK TO YOU ALL ABOUT.
RULE BOOK
THE WINNER OF THIS COMPETITION GETS TO MAKE A REQUEST, AND WHATEVER IT IS, IT WILL BE GRANTED!
HUH?!
ANY-THING THEY WANT?!
YES!
I'M ABOUT TO GET MY HANDS ON THE POWER TO EXTER-MINATE ALL THE TITANS!!
POWW
ボコォッ!!
NO, WE'RE GO-ING TO MOUNT A NATIONAL TOUR OF MY ONE-MAN SHOW, "CHEERSTEIN FOR KIRSTEIN"!!
STOP THAT!!

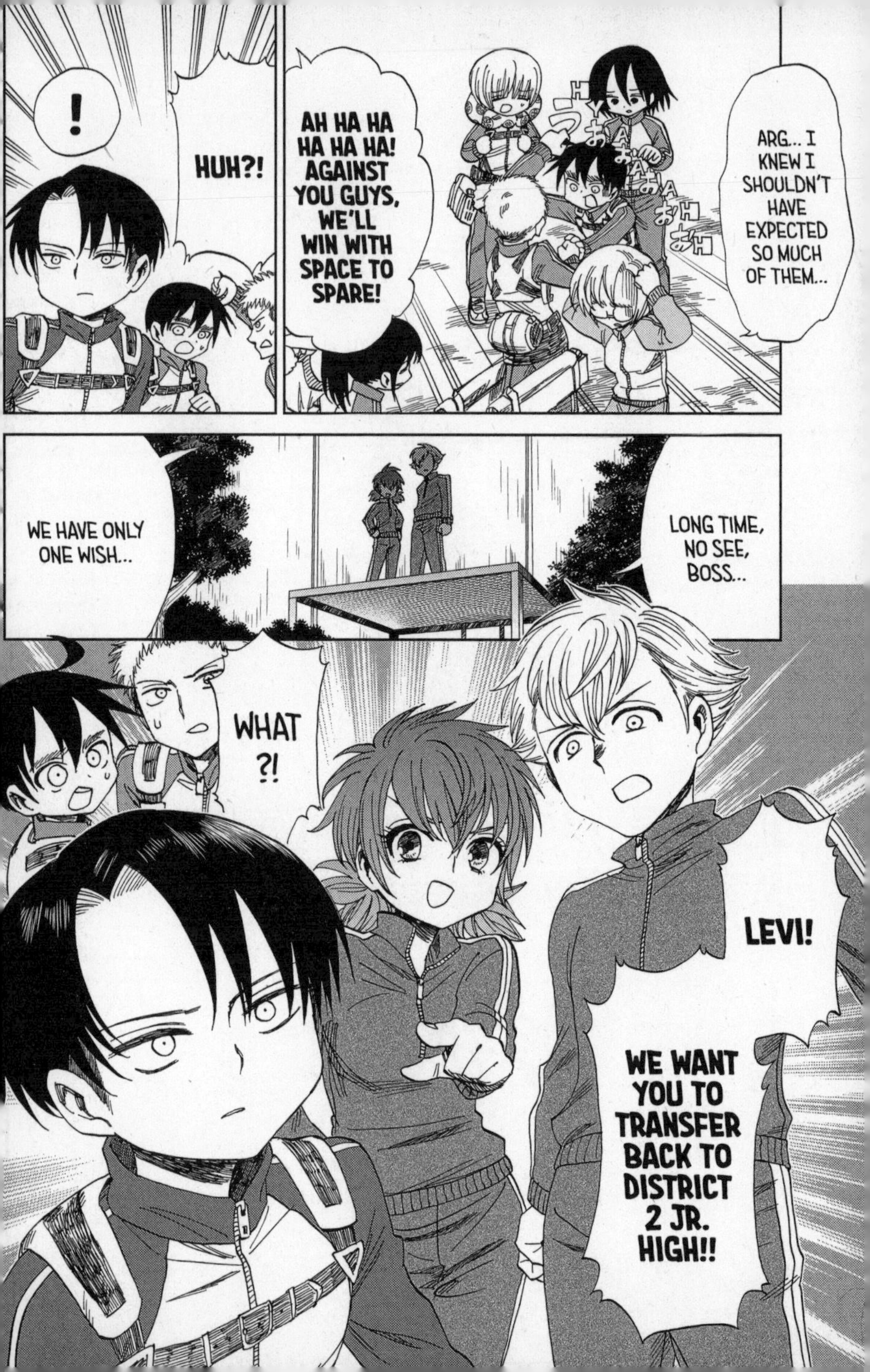
ARG... I KNEW I SHOULDN'T HAVE EXPECTED SO MUCH OF THEM...
HYAAAHHH
うおおおおお
AH HA HA HA HA HA! AGAINST YOU GUYS, WE'LL WIN WITH SPACE TO SPARE!
!
HUH?!
LONG TIME, NO SEE, BOSS...
WE HAVE ONLY ONE WISH...
LEVI!
WE WANT YOU TO TRANSFER BACK TO DISTRICT 2 JR. HIGH!!
WHAT ?!

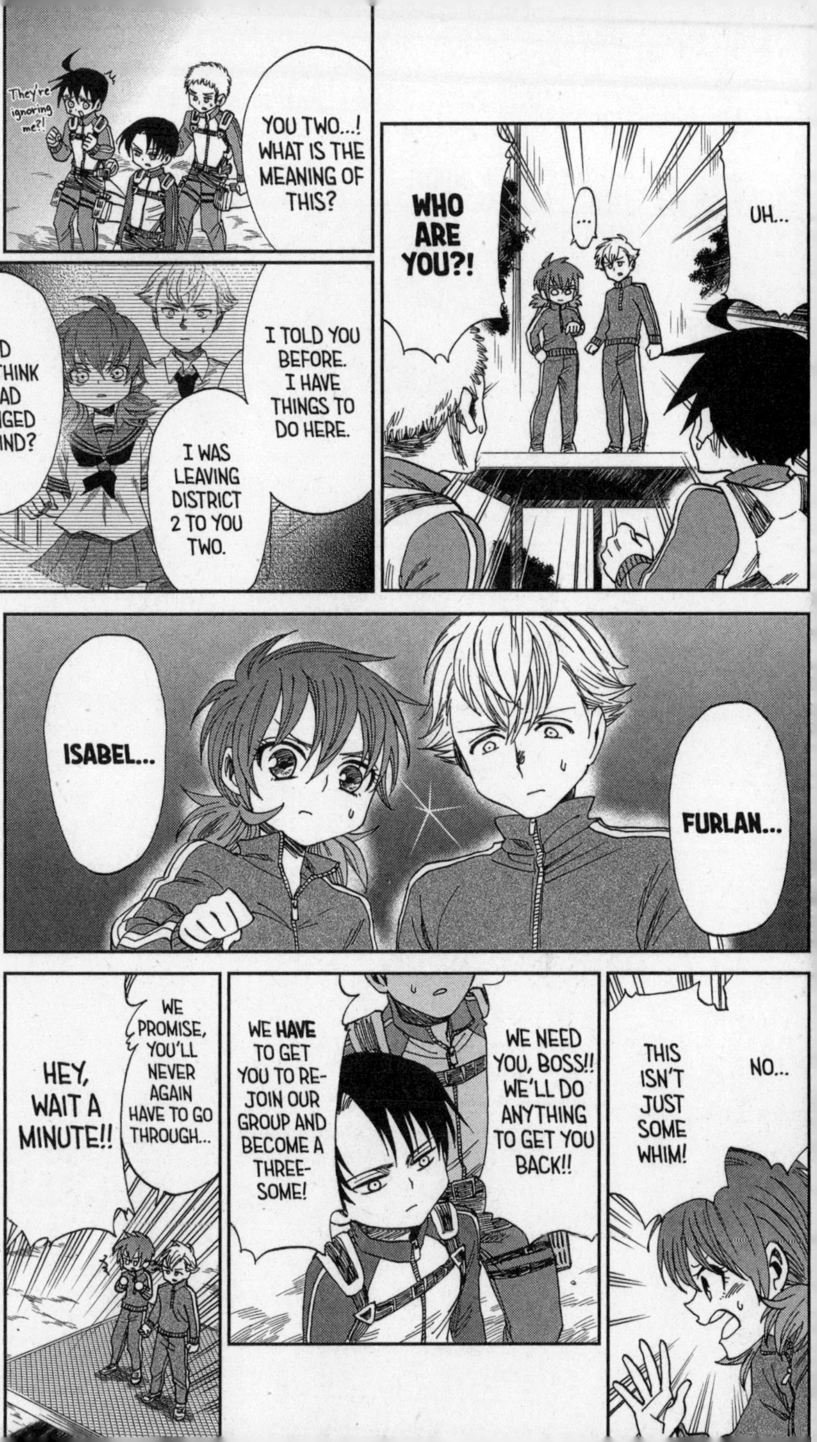
UH...
...
WHO ARE YOU?!
They're ignoring me?!
YOU TWO...! WHAT IS THE MEANING OF THIS?
I TOLD YOU BEFORE. I HAVE THINGS TO DO HERE.
I WAS LEAVING DISTRICT 2 TO YOU TWO.
DID YOU THINK I HAD CHANGED MY MIND?
FURLAN...
ISABEL...
NO...
THIS ISN'T JUST SOME WHIM!
WE NEED YOU, BOSS!! WE'LL DO ANYTHING TO GET YOU BACK!!
WE HAVE TO GET YOU TO RE-JOIN OUR GROUP AND BECOME A THREE-SOME!
WE PROMISE, YOU'LL NEVER AGAIN HAVE TO GO THROUGH...
HEY, WAIT A MINUTE!!

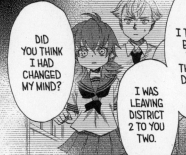

FORTY-SIXTH PERIOD: THE FINAL, NO REGRETS

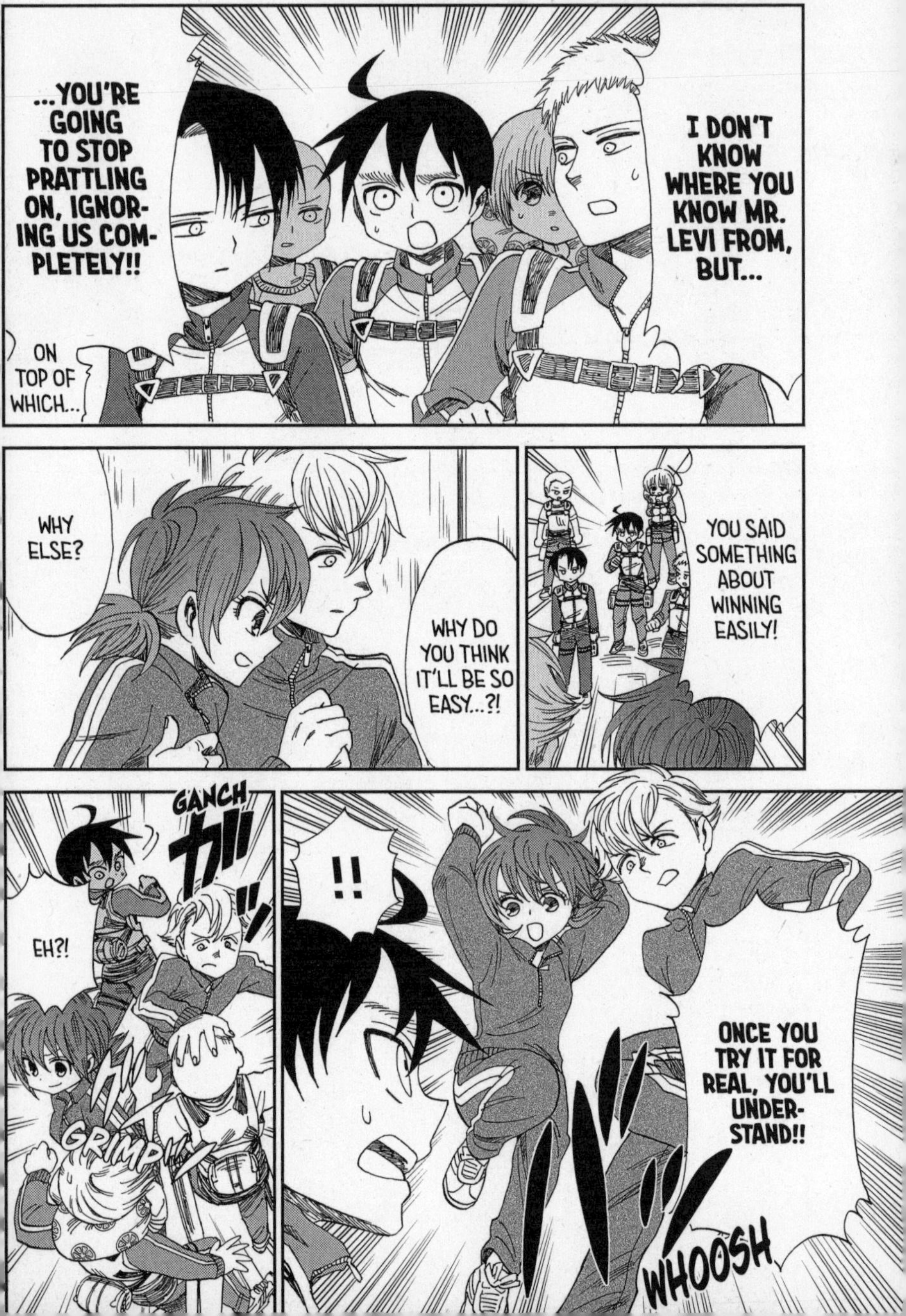
I DON'T KNOW WHERE YOU KNOW MR. LEVI FROM, BUT...
...YOU'RE GOING TO STOP PRATTLING ON, IGNORING US COMPLETELY!!
ON TOP OF WHICH...
YOU SAID SOMETHING ABOUT WINNING EASILY!
WHY DO YOU THINK IT'LL BE SO EASY...?!
WHY ELSE?
!!
ONCE YOU TRY IT FOR REAL, YOU'LL UNDERSTAND!!
WHOOSH
GANCH
EH?!
GRIMP!!

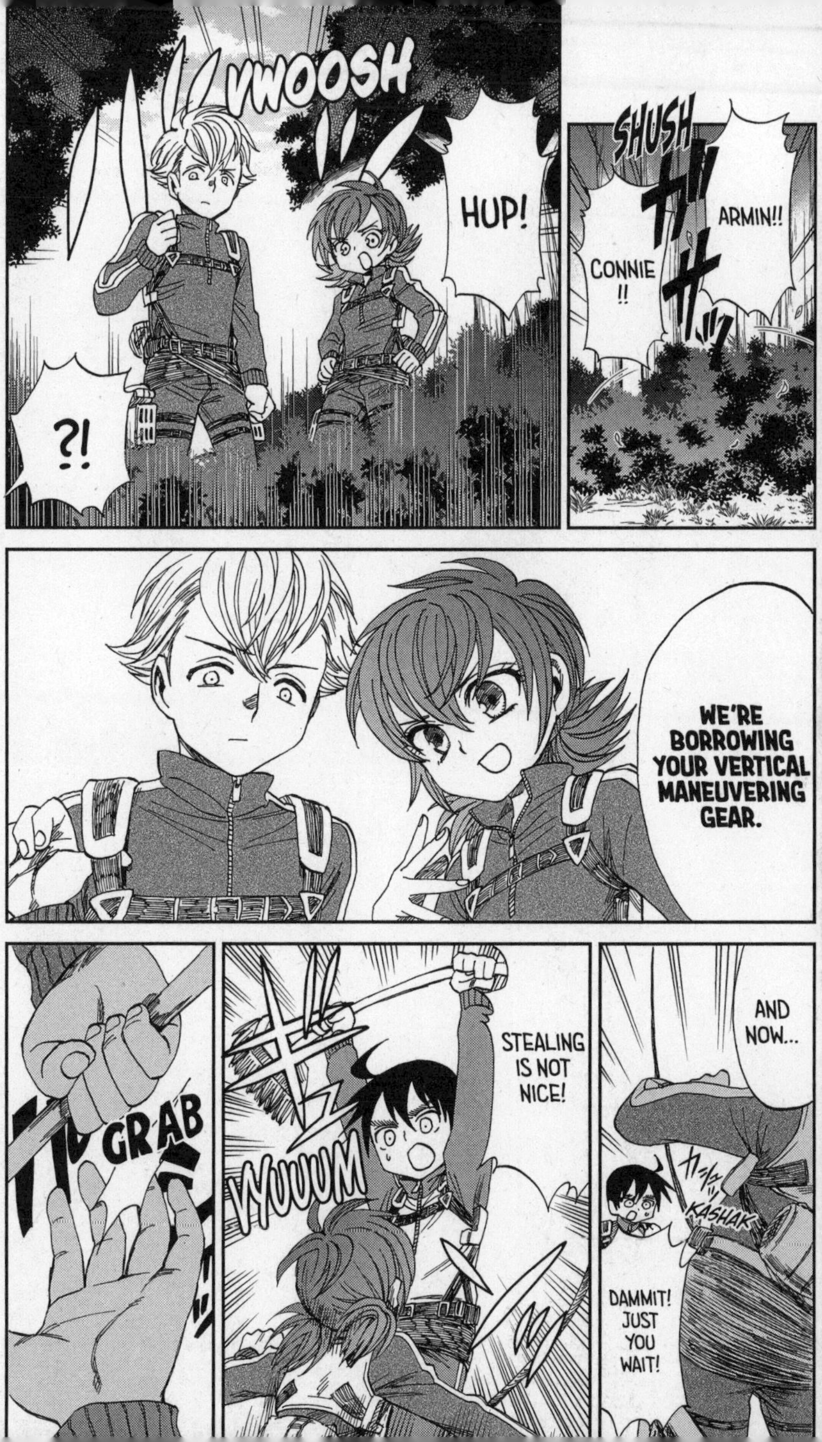
ARMIN!!
SHUSH
CONNIE !!
VWOOSH
HUP!
?!
WE'RE BORROWING YOUR VERTICAL MANEUVERING GEAR.
AND NOW...
KASHAK
DAMMIT! JUST YOU WAIT!
STEALING IS NOT NICE!
VYUUUM
GRAB

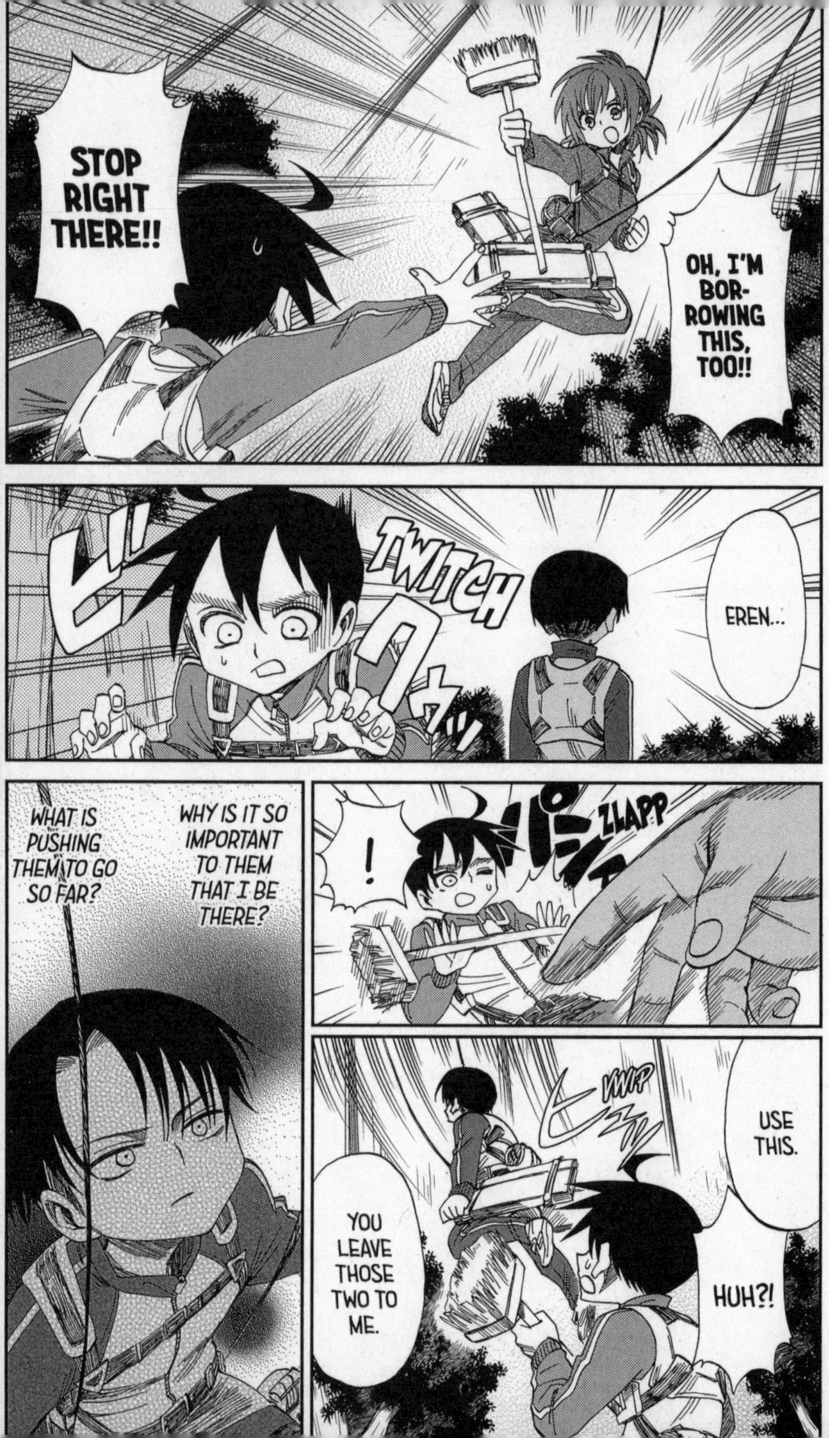
OH, I'M BOR-ROWING THIS, TOO!!
STOP RIGHT THERE!!
EREN...
TWITCH
ZZAPP
!
USE THIS.
VWIP
HUH?!
YOU LEAVE THOSE TWO TO ME.
WHY IS IT SO IMPORTANT TO THEM THAT I BE THERE?
WHAT IS PUSHING THEM TO GO SO FAR?

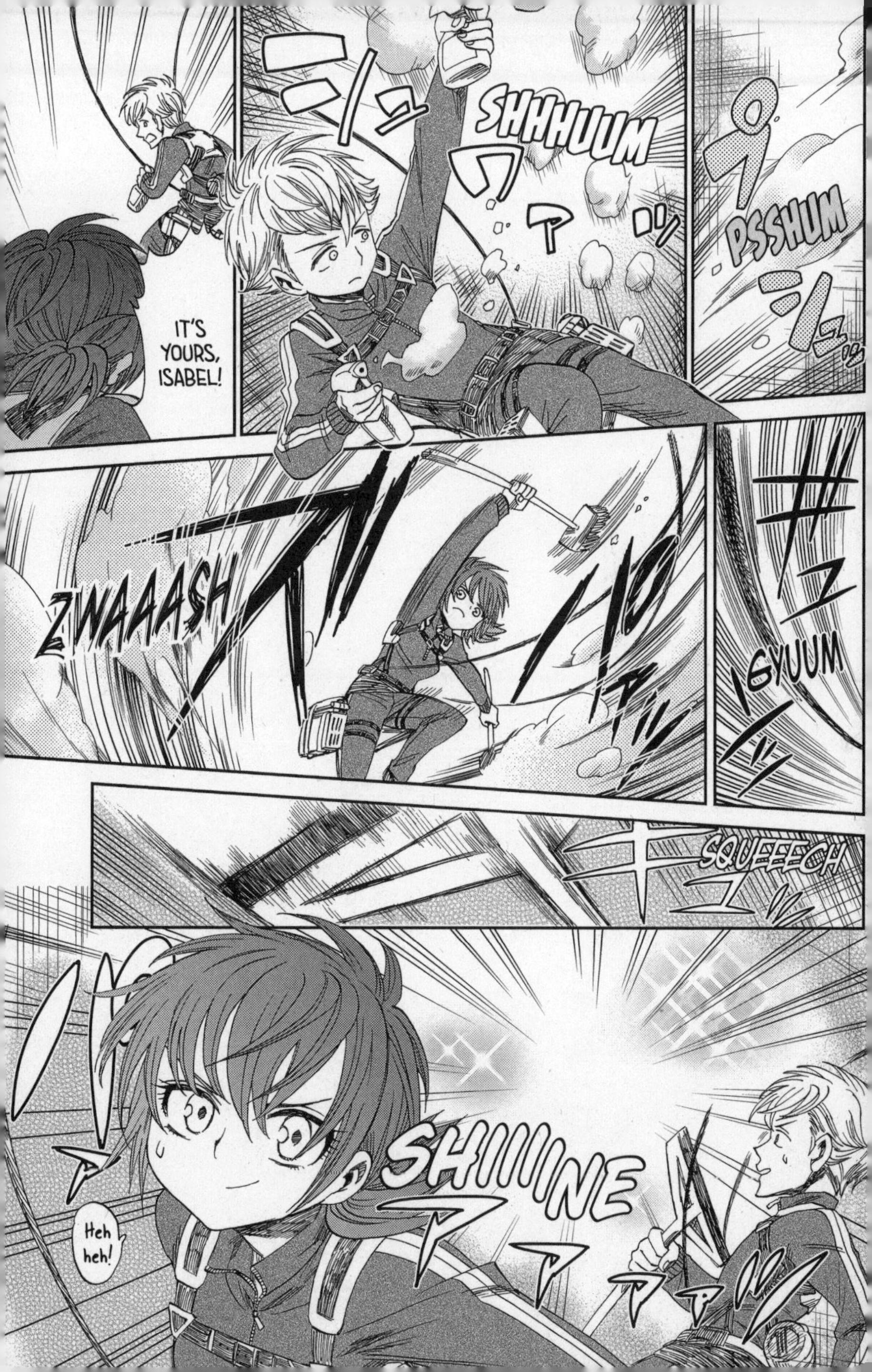
PSSHUM
SHHHUUM
IT'S YOURS, ISABEL!
GYUUM
ZWAAASH
SQUEEECH
SHIIINE
Heh heh!

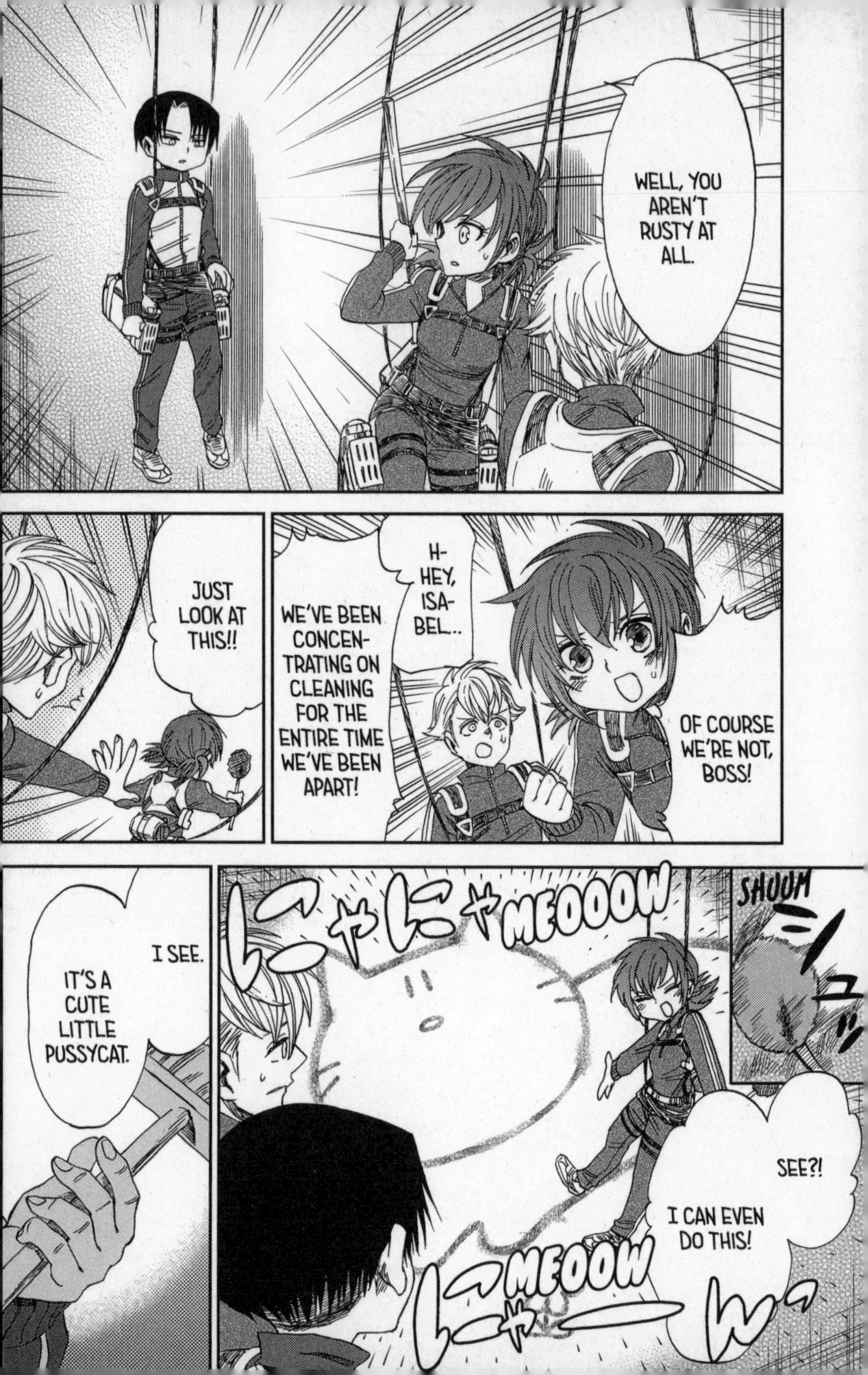
WELL, YOU AREN'T RUSTY AT ALL.
OF COURSE WE'RE NOT, BOSS!
H- HEY, ISA- BEL...
WE'VE BEEN CONCEN- TRATING ON CLEANING FOR THE ENTIRE TIME WE'VE BEEN APART!
JUST LOOK AT THIS!!
SHUUM
MEOOOW
SEE?!
I CAN EVEN DO THIS!
MEOOW
I SEE.
IT'S A CUTE LITTLE PUSSYCAT.

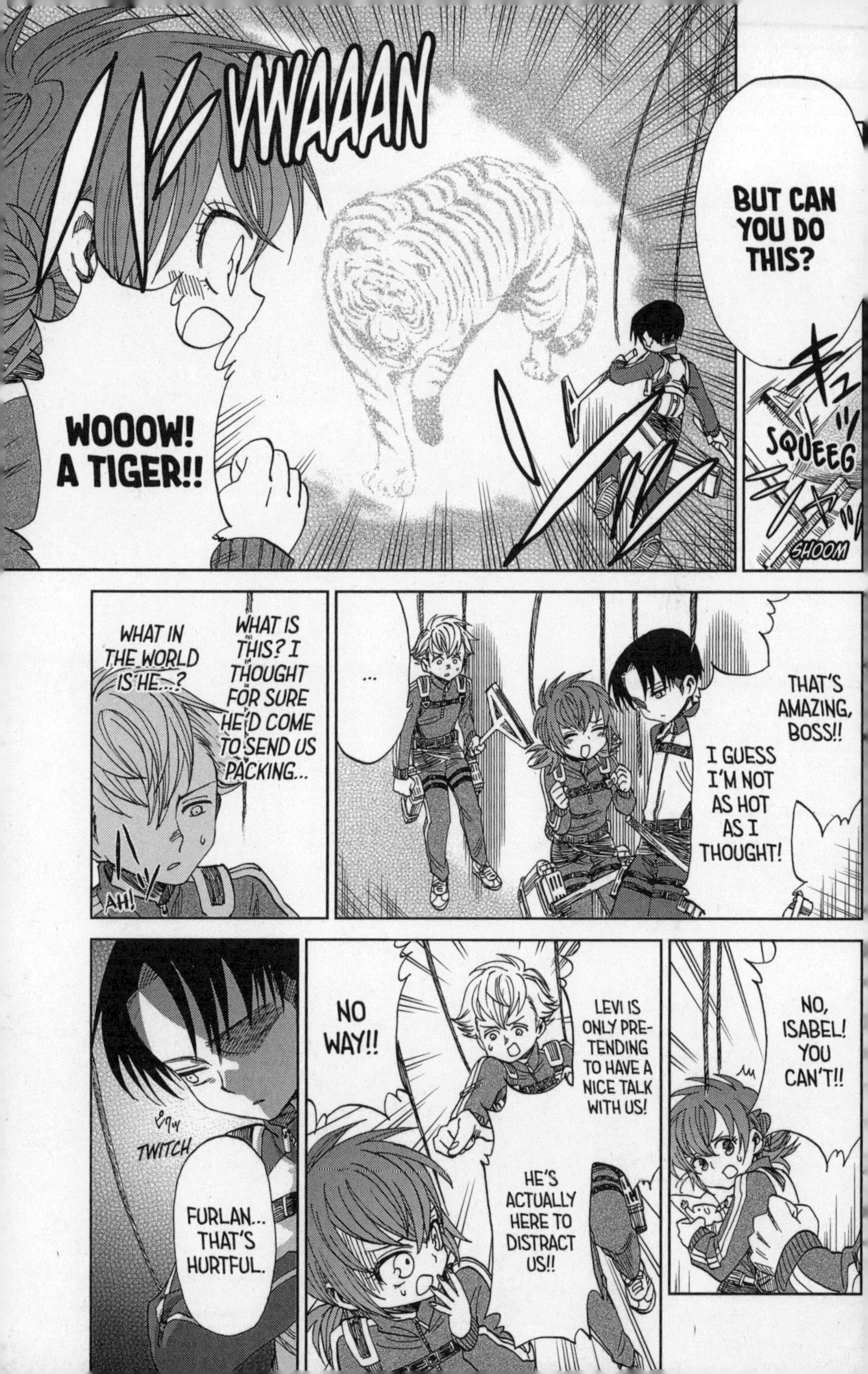
BUT CAN YOU DO THIS?
SQUEEG
SHOOM
VWAAAN
WOOOW! A TIGER!!
THAT'S AMAZING, BOSS!!
I GUESS I'M NOT AS HOT AS I THOUGHT!
...
WHAT IS THIS? I THOUGHT FOR SURE HE'D COME TO SEND US PACKING...
WHAT IN THE WORLD IS HE...?
AH!
NO, ISABEL! YOU CAN'T!!
LEVI IS ONLY PRETENDING TO HAVE A NICE TALK WITH US!
NO WAY!!
HE'S ACTUALLY HERE TO DISTRACT US!!
TWITCH
FURLAN... THAT'S HURTFUL.

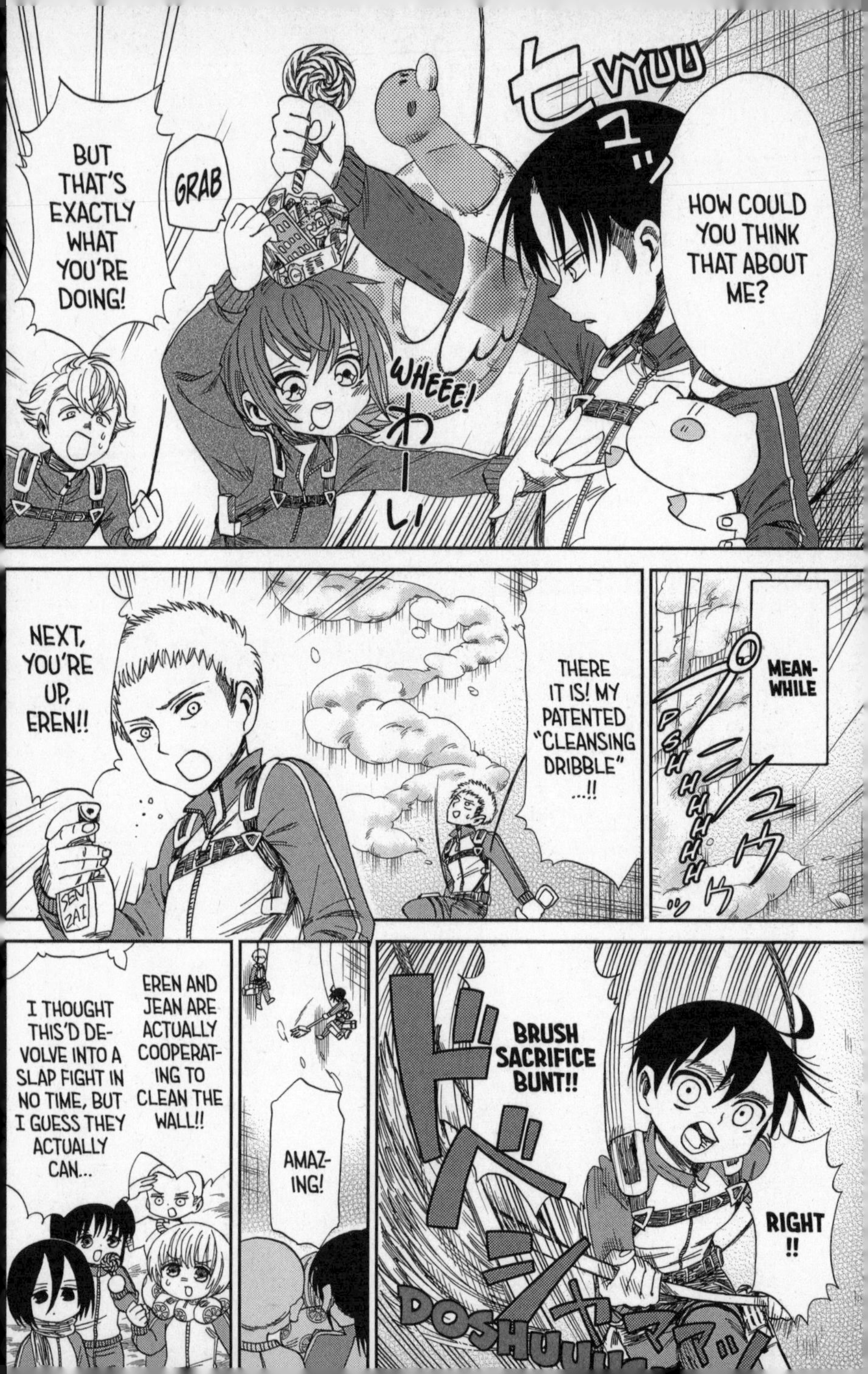
VYUU
HOW COULD YOU THINK THAT ABOUT ME?
WHEEE!
わーい
GRAB
BUT THAT'S EXACTLY WHAT YOU'RE DOING!
MEAN-WHILE
PSHHHHHHH
THERE IT IS! MY PATENTED "CLEANSING DRIBBLE" ...!!
NEXT, YOU'RE UP, EREN!!
SEN ZAI
BRUSH SACRIFICE BUNT!!
RIGHT !!
DOSHUUU
AMAZ-ING!
EREN AND JEAN ARE ACTUALLY COOPERAT-ING TO CLEAN THE WALL!!
I THOUGHT THIS'D DE-VOLVE INTO A SLAP FIGHT IN NO TIME, BUT I GUESS THEY ACTUALLY CAN...

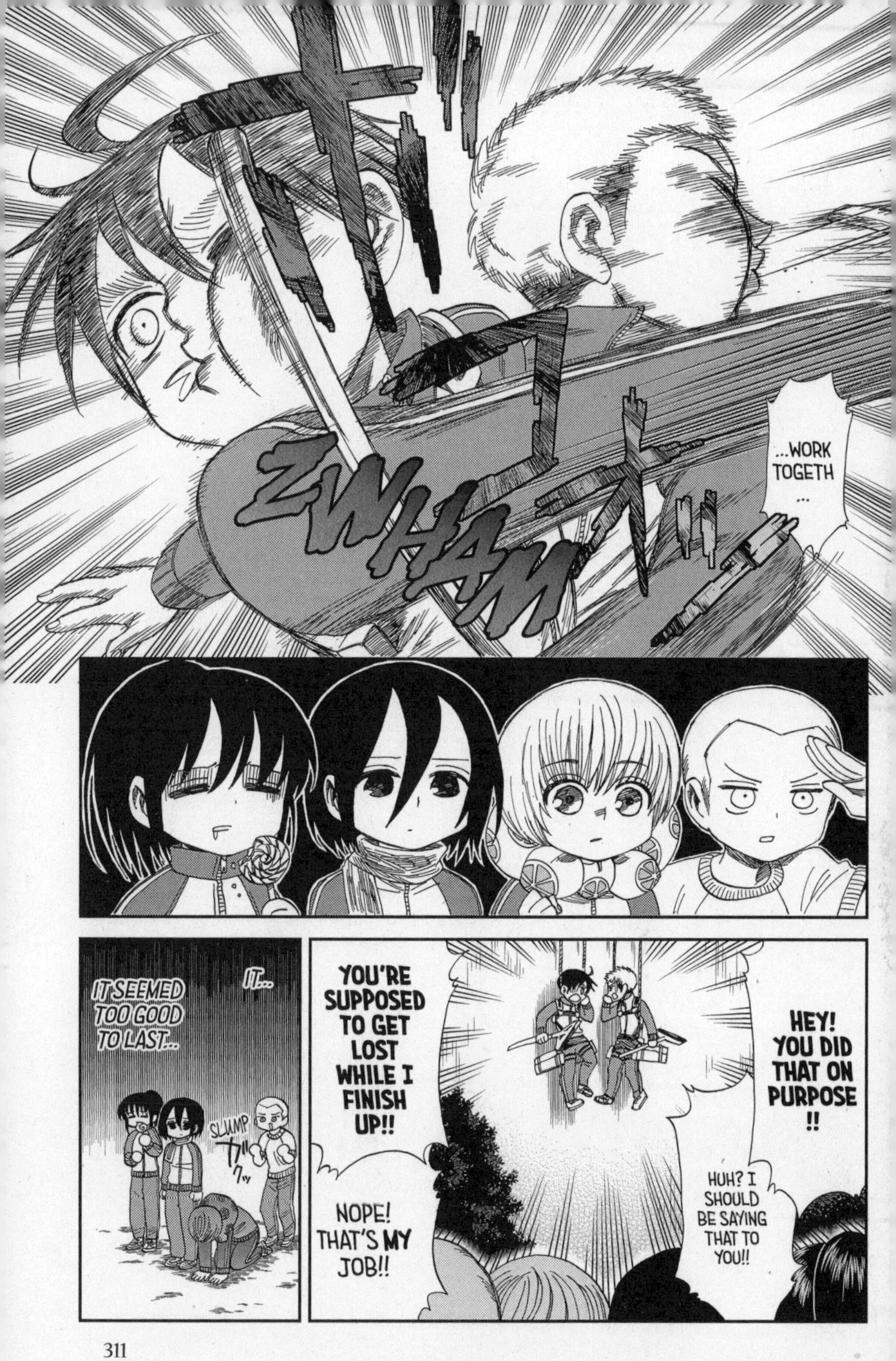
...WORK TOGETH ...
ZWHAM
HEY! YOU DID THAT ON PURPOSE !!
YOU'RE SUPPOSED TO GET LOST WHILE I FINISH UP!!
HUH? I SHOULD BE SAYING THAT TO YOU!!
NOPE! THAT'S MY JOB!!
IT...
IT SEEMED TOO GOOD TO LAST...
SLUMP

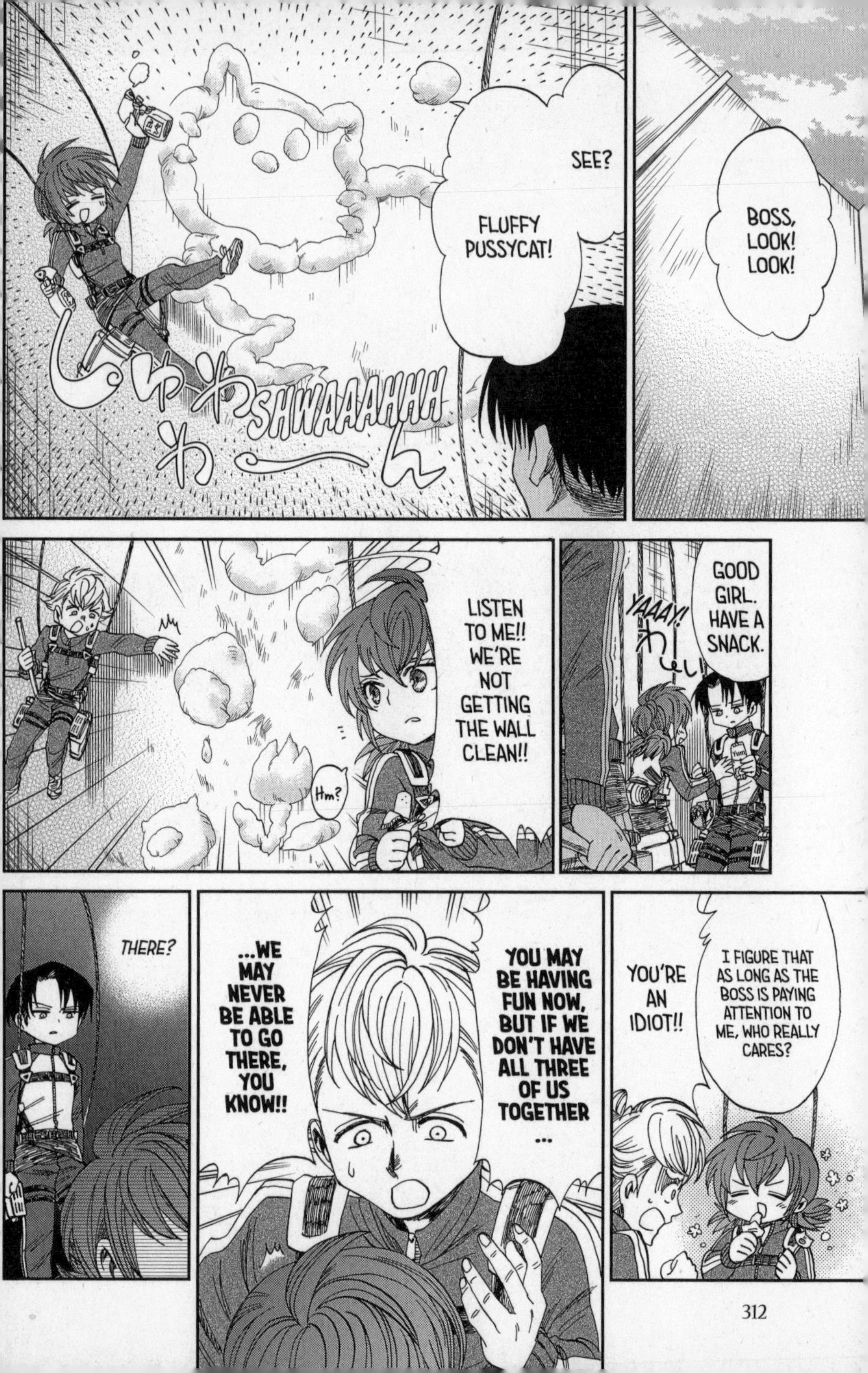
BOSS, LOOK! LOOK!
SEE?
FLUFFY PUSSYCAT!
SHWAAAAHHH
GOOD GIRL. HAVE A SNACK.
YAAAY!
Yum
LISTEN TO ME!! WE'RE NOT GETTING THE WALL CLEAN!!
Hm?
I FIGURE THAT AS LONG AS THE BOSS IS PAYING ATTENTION TO ME, WHO REALLY CARES?
YOU'RE AN IDIOT!!
YOU MAY BE HAVING FUN NOW, BUT IF WE DON'T HAVE ALL THREE OF US TOGETHER...
...WE MAY NEVER BE ABLE TO GO THERE, YOU KNOW!!
THERE?

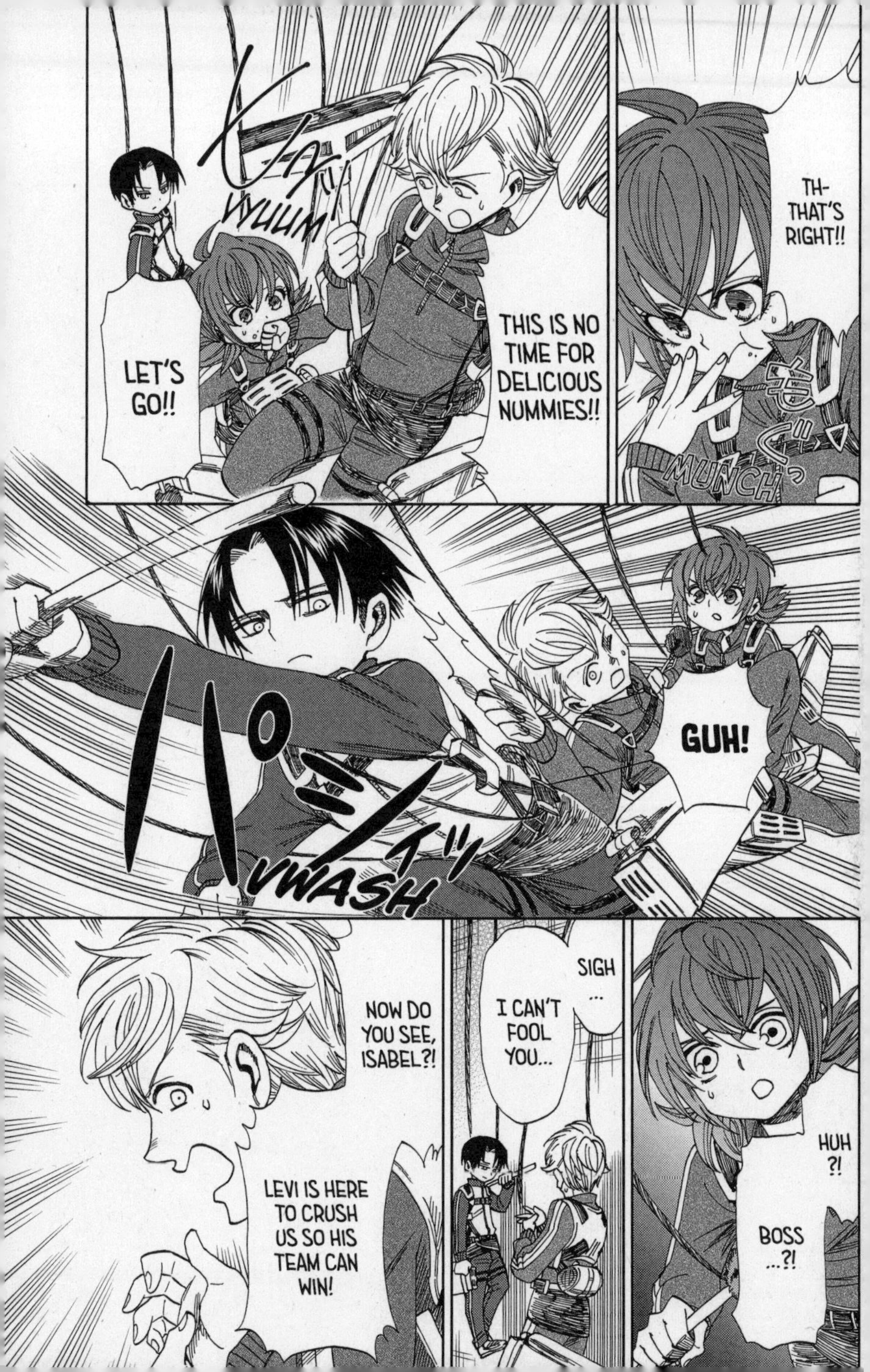
TH- THAT'S RIGHT!!
MUNCH
VYUUM
THIS IS NO TIME FOR DELICIOUS NUMMIES!!
LET'S GO!!
GUH!
VWASH
HUH ?!
BOSS ...?!
SIGH ...
I CAN'T FOOL YOU...
NOW DO YOU SEE, ISABEL?!
LEVI IS HERE TO CRUSH US SO HIS TEAM CAN WIN!

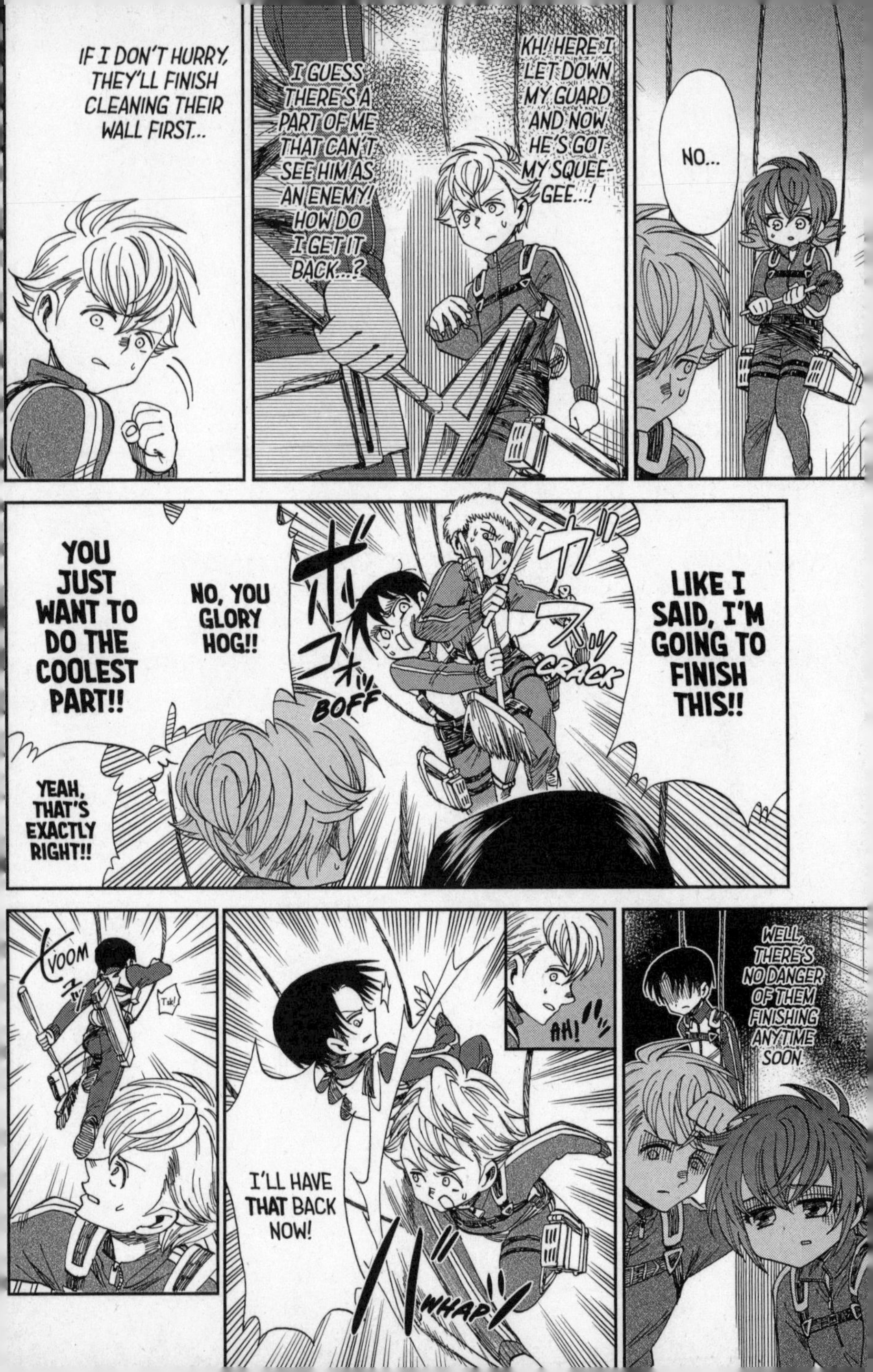
NO...
KH! HERE I LET DOWN MY GUARD AND NOW HE'S GOT MY SQUEE-GEE...!
I GUESS THERE'S A PART OF ME THAT CAN'T SEE HIM AS AN ENEMY! HOW DO I GET IT BACK...?
IF I DON'T HURRY, THEY'LL FINISH CLEANING THEIR WALL FIRST...
LIKE I SAID, I'M GOING TO FINISH THIS!!
CRACK
NO, YOU GLORY HOG!!
BOFF
YOU JUST WANT TO DO THE COOLEST PART!!
YEAH, THAT'S EXACTLY RIGHT!!
WELL, THERE'S NO DANGER OF THEM FINISHING ANYTIME SOON.
AH!
I'LL HAVE THAT BACK NOW!
WHAP!
VROOM
Tsk!

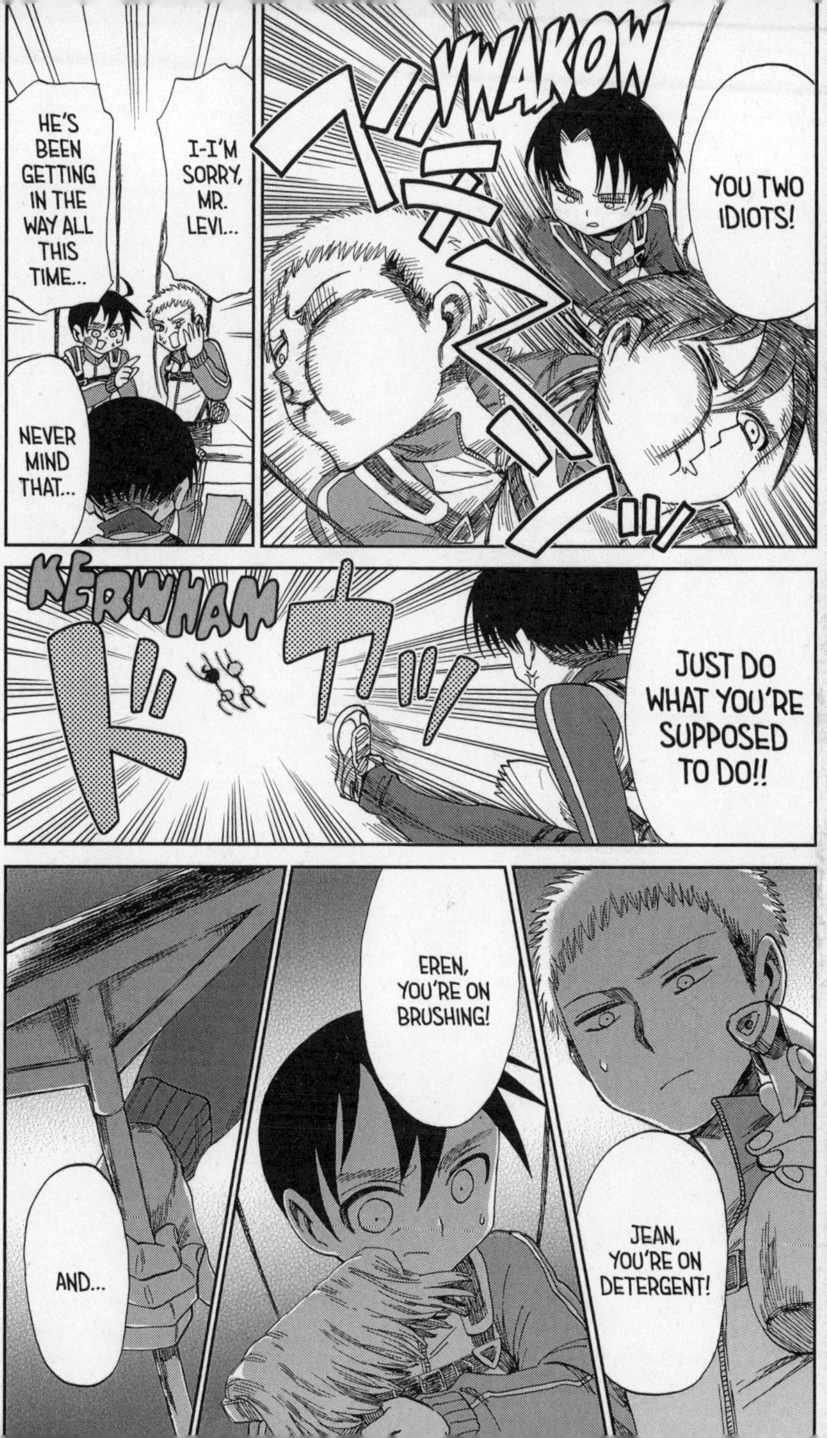
YOU TWO IDIOTS!
I-I'M SORRY, MR. LEVI...
HE'S BEEN GETTING IN THE WAY ALL THIS TIME...
NEVER MIND THAT...
JUST DO WHAT YOU'RE SUPPOSED TO DO!!
KERWHAM
JEAN, YOU'RE ON DETERGENT!
EREN, YOU'RE ON BRUSHING!
AND...

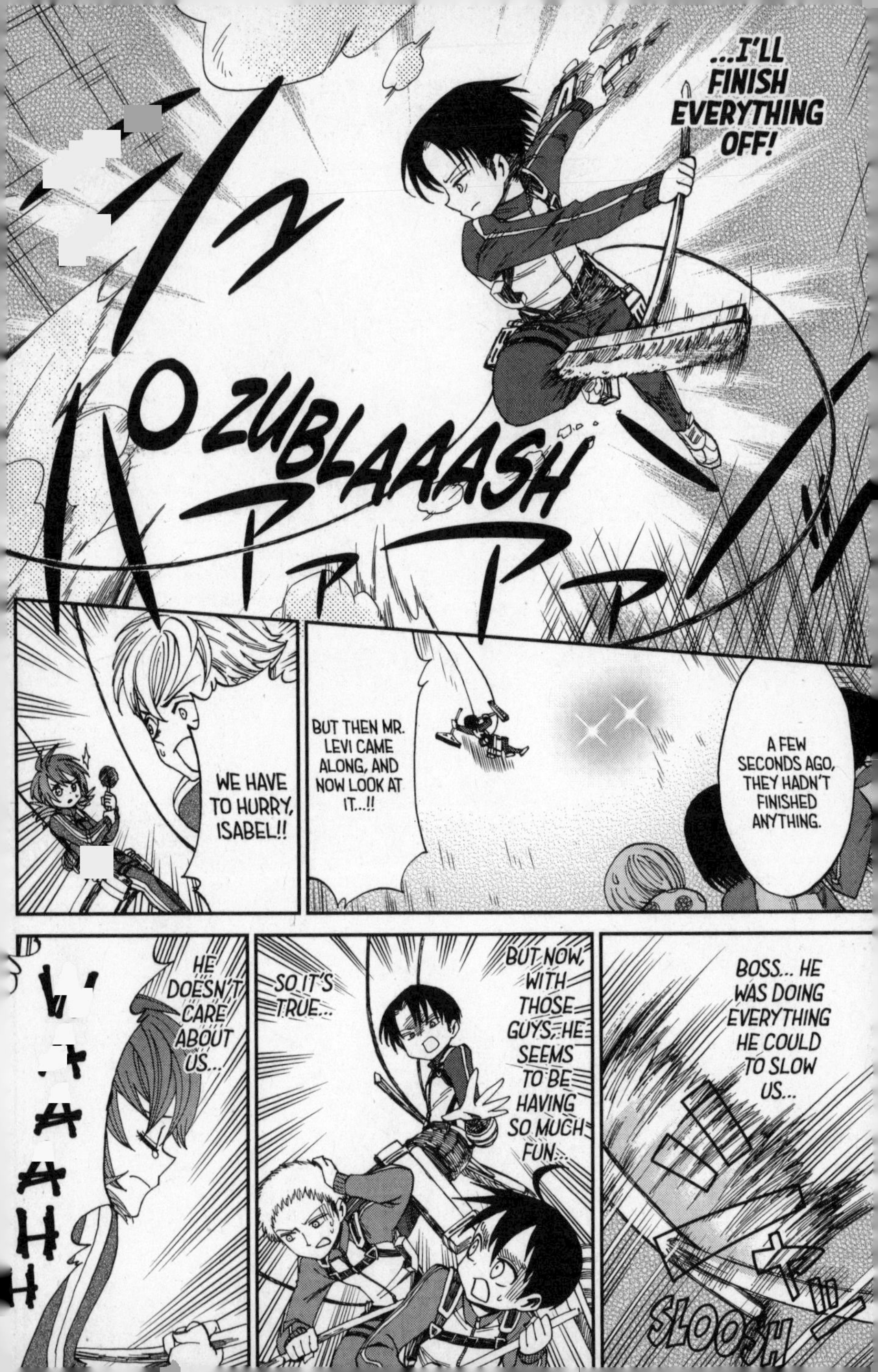
...I'LL FINISH EVERYTHING OFF!
ZUBLAAASH
A FEW SECONDS AGO, THEY HADN'T FINISHED ANYTHING.
BUT THEN MR. LEVI CAME ALONG, AND NOW LOOK AT IT...!!
WE HAVE TO HURRY, ISABEL!!
BOSS... HE WAS DOING EVERYTHING HE COULD TO SLOW US...
SLOOSH
BUT NOW, WITH THOSE GUYS, HE SEEMS TO BE HAVING SO MUCH FUN...
SO IT'S TRUE...
HE DOESN'T CARE ABOUT US...

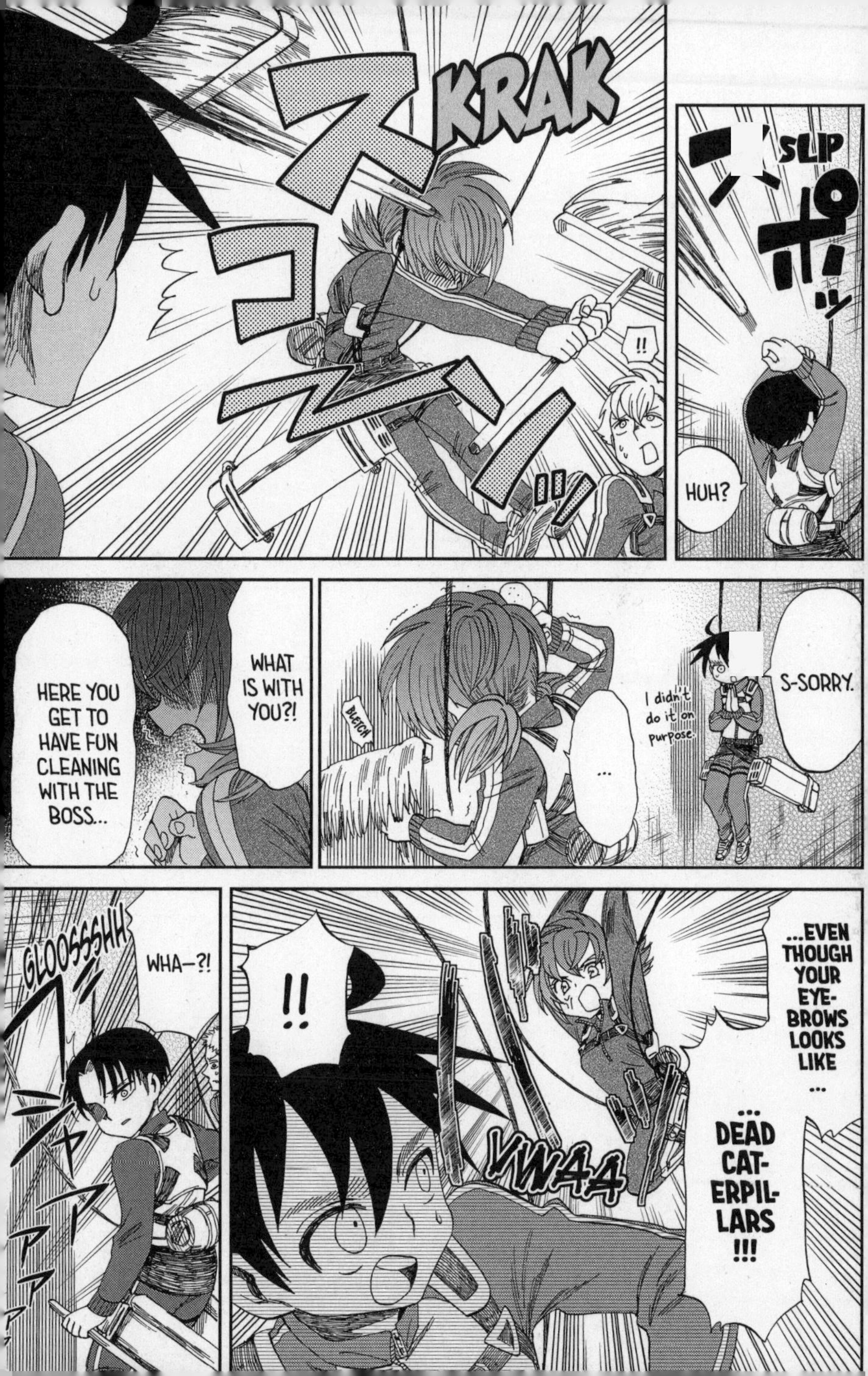
SLIP
HUH?
KRAK
!!
!!
S-SORRY.
I didn't do it on purpose.
...
BLETCH
WHAT IS WITH YOU?!
HERE YOU GET TO HAVE FUN CLEANING WITH THE BOSS...
...EVEN THOUGH YOUR EYE-BROWS LOOKS LIKE...
...DEAD CAT-ERPIL-LARS!!!
VWAA
!!
GLOOSSSHH
WHA—?!

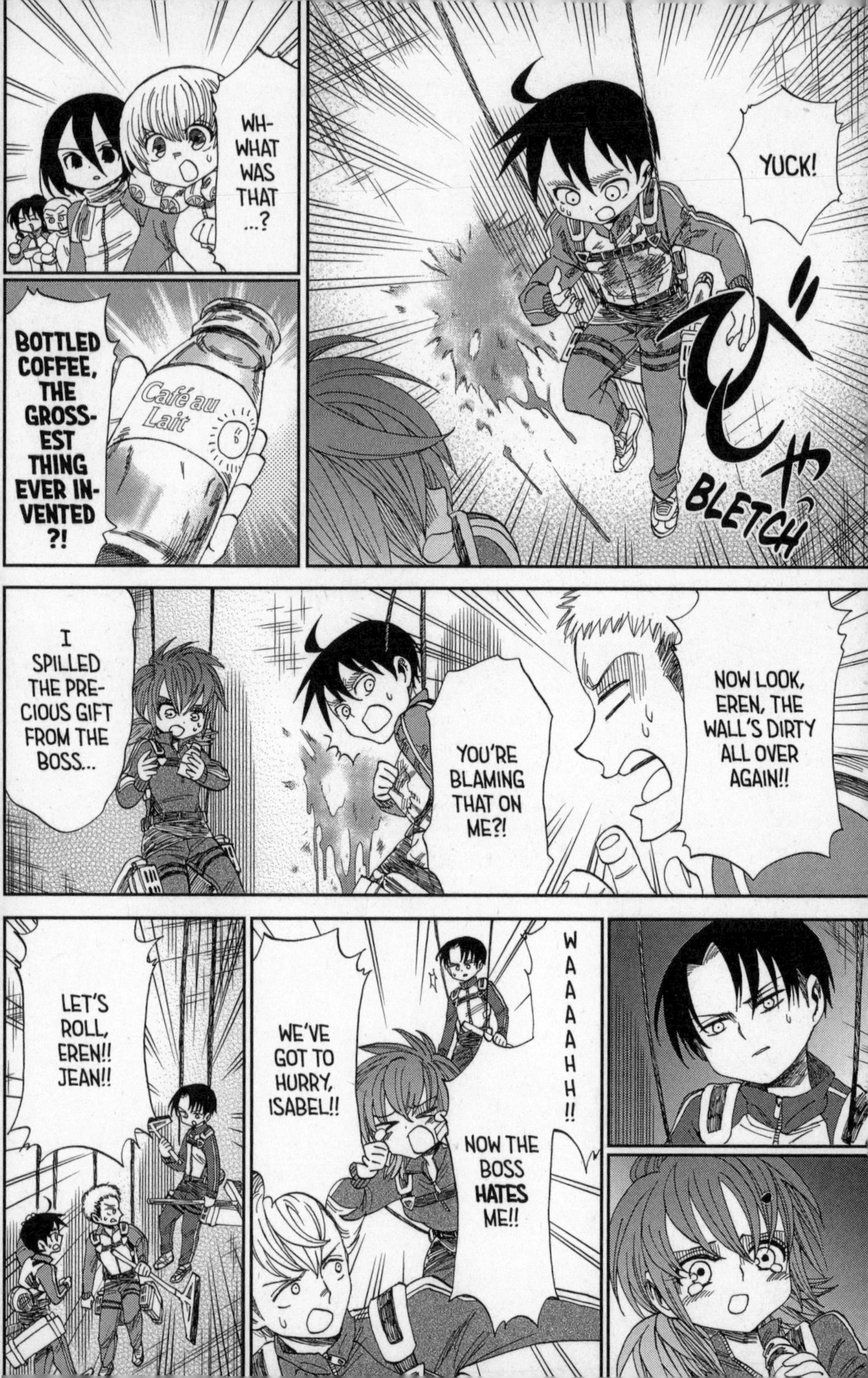
YUCK!
BLETCH
WH-WHAT WAS THAT ...?
BOTTLED COFFEE, THE GROSSEST THING EVER INVENTED?!
Café au Lait
NOW LOOK, EREN, THE WALL'S DIRTY ALL OVER AGAIN!!
YOU'RE BLAMING THAT ON ME?!
I SPILLED THE PRECIOUS GIFT FROM THE BOSS...
WAAAAAAHH!!
NOW THE BOSS HATES ME!!
WE'VE GOT TO HURRY, ISABEL!!
LET'S ROLL, EREN!! JEAN!!

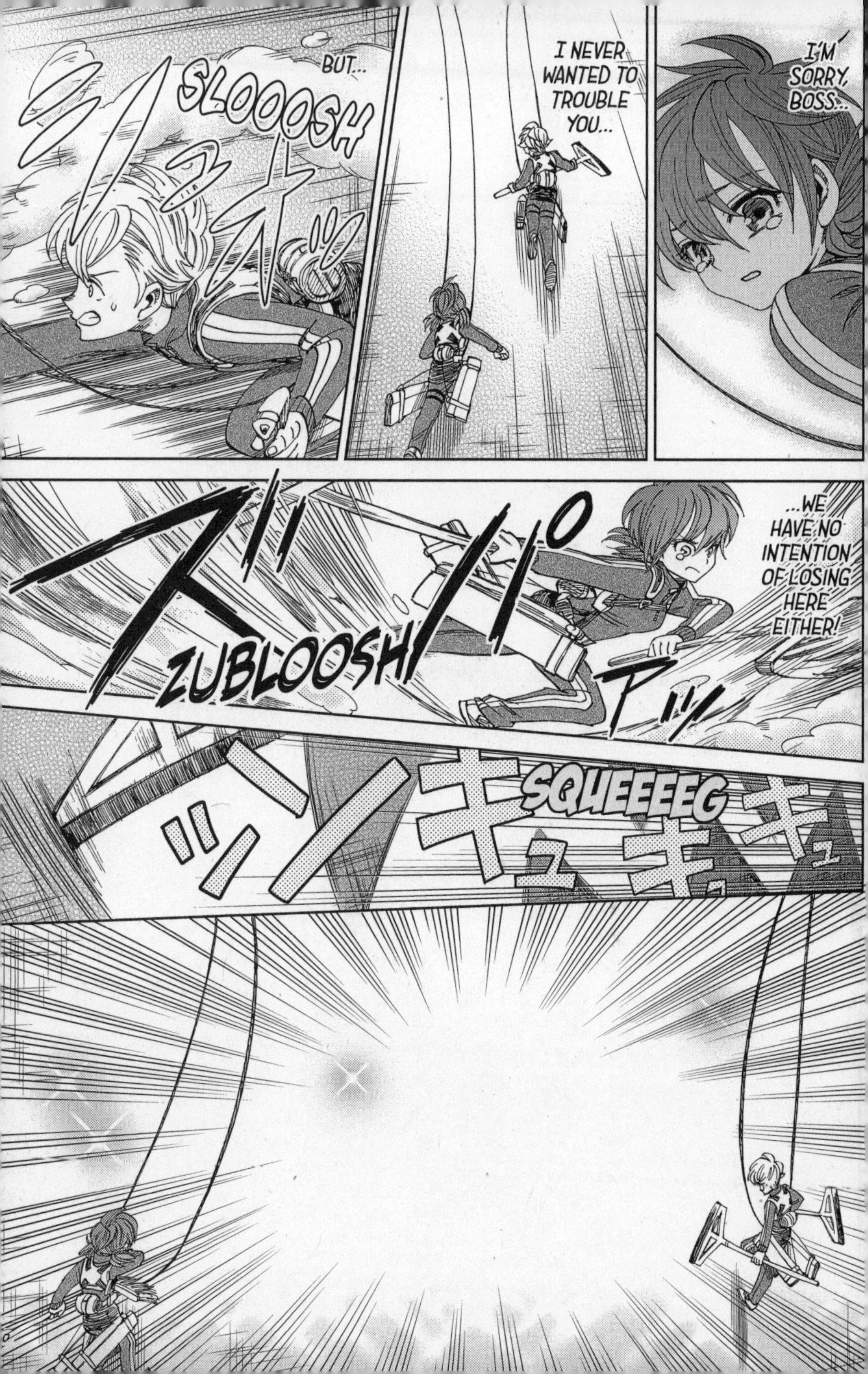
I'M SORRY, BOSS...
I NEVER WANTED TO TROUBLE YOU...
BUT...
SLOOOSH
...WE HAVE NO INTENTION OF LOSING HERE EITHER!
ZUBLOOSH!
SQUEEEEG

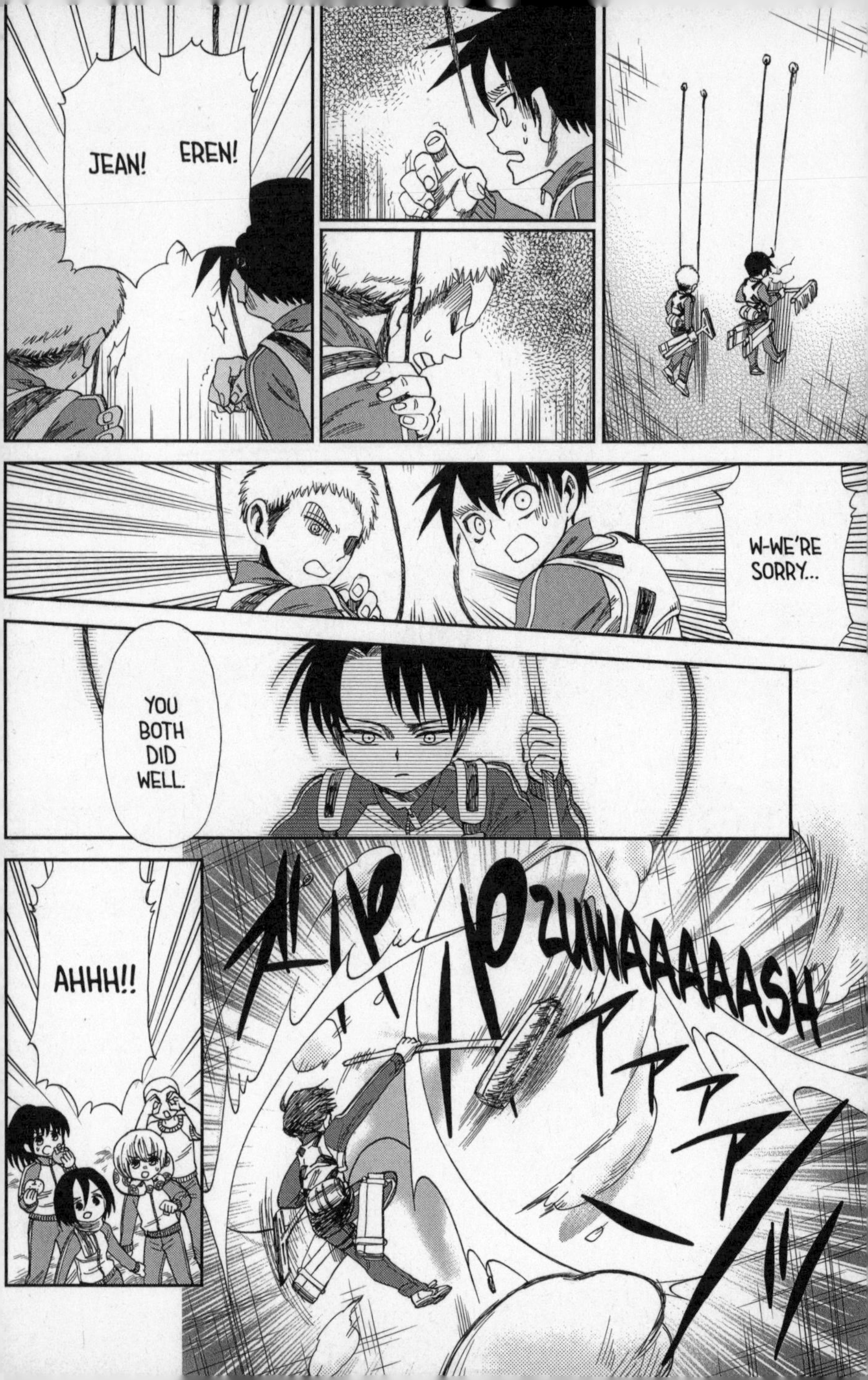
JEAN! EREN!
W-WE'RE SORRY...
YOU BOTH DID WELL.
ZUWAAAAAASH
AHHH!!

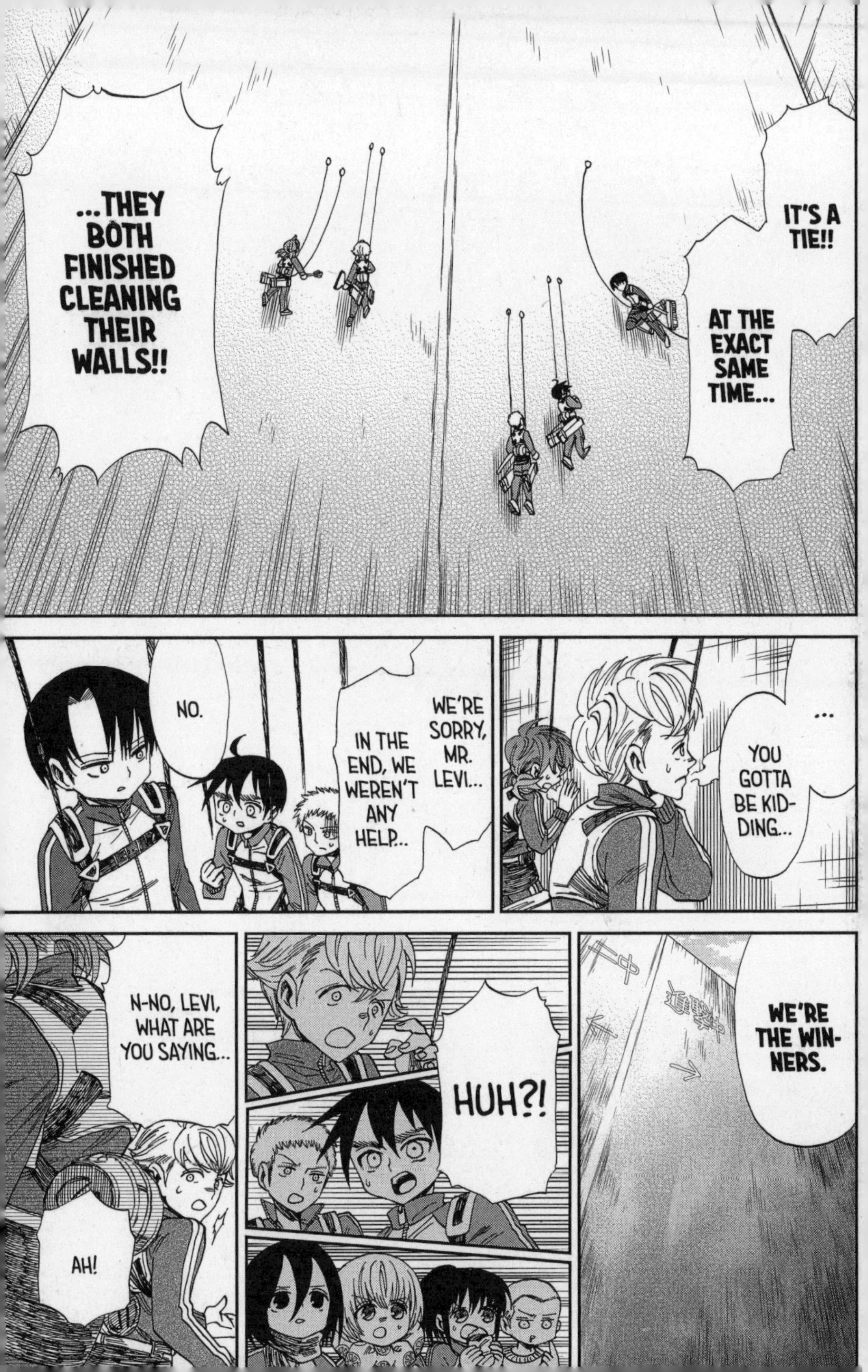
IT'S A TIE!!
AT THE EXACT SAME TIME...
...THEY BOTH FINISHED CLEANING THEIR WALLS!!
...
YOU GOTTA BE KID-DING...
WE'RE SORRY, MR. LEVI...
IN THE END, WE WEREN'T ANY HELP...
NO.
WE'RE THE WIN-NERS.
HUH?!
N-NO, LEVI, WHAT ARE YOU SAYING...
AH!

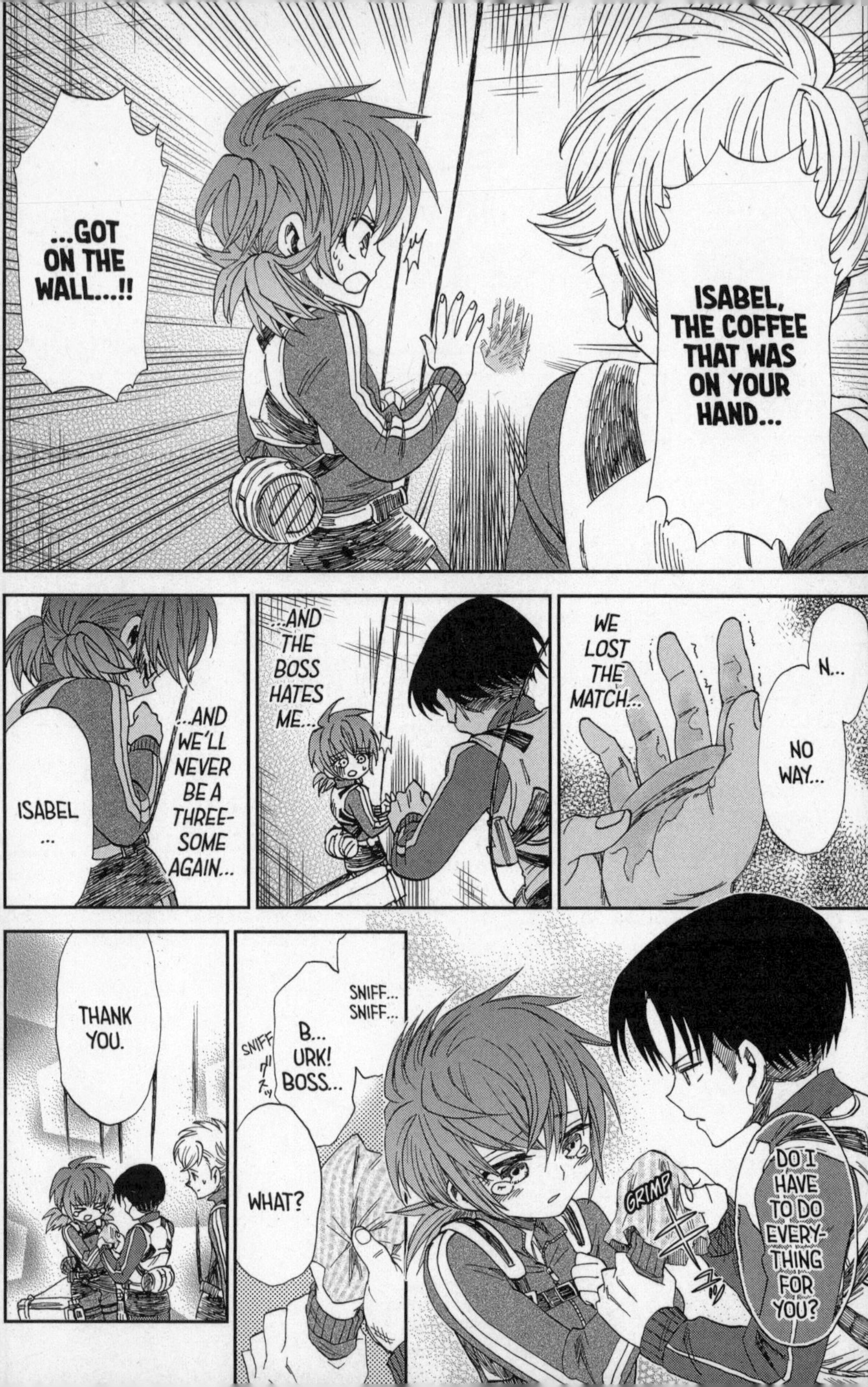
ISABEL, THE COFFEE THAT WAS ON YOUR HAND...
...GOT ON THE WALL...!!
N...
NO WAY...
WE LOST THE MATCH...
...AND THE BOSS HATES ME...
...AND WE'LL NEVER BE A THREE-SOME AGAIN...
ISABEL ...
DO I HAVE TO DO EVERY-THING FOR YOU?
GRIMP
SNIFF... SNIFF...
B... URK! BOSS...
SNIFF
WHAT?
THANK YOU.

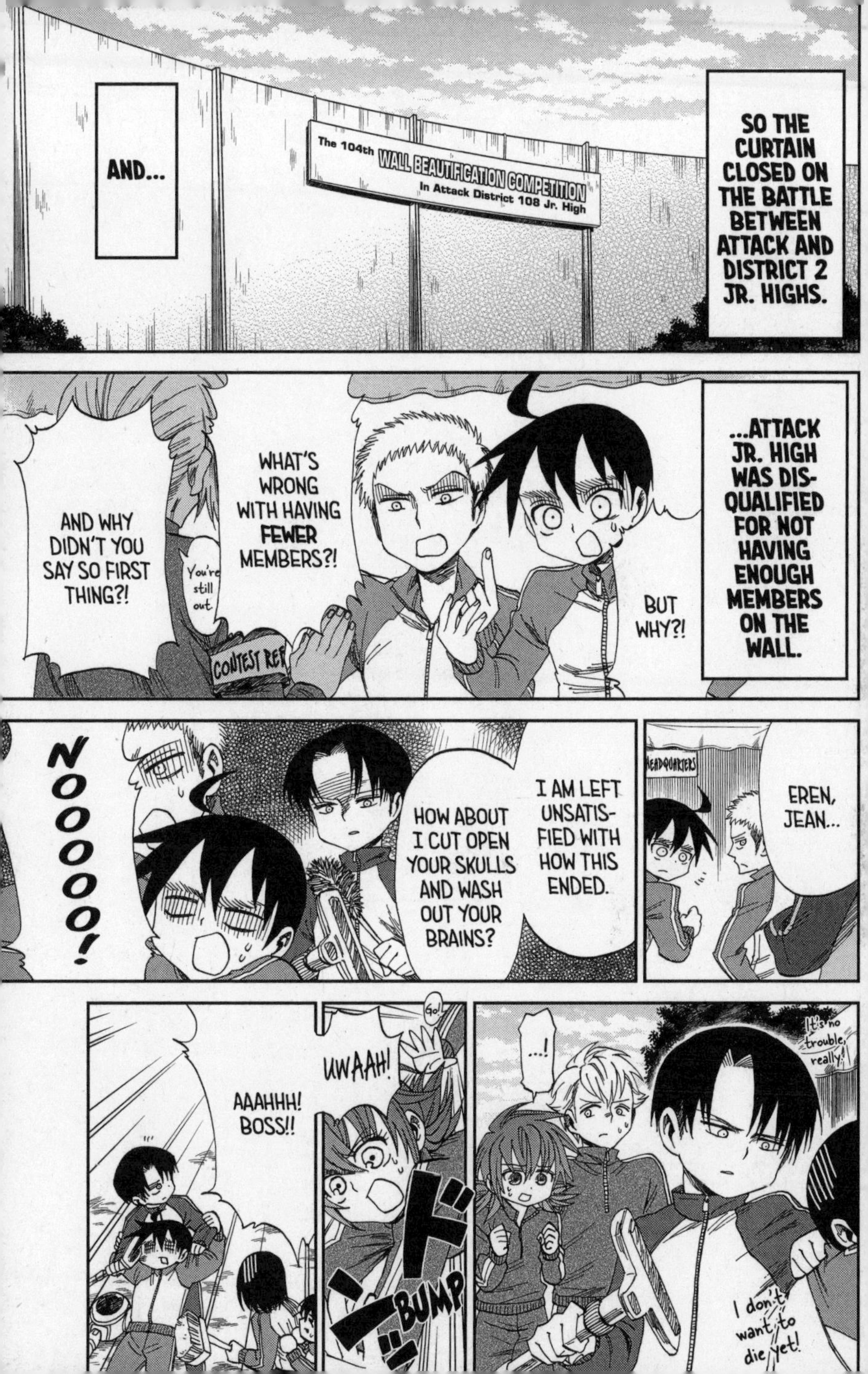
SO THE CURTAIN CLOSED ON THE BATTLE BETWEEN ATTACK AND DISTRICT 2 JR. HIGHS.
The 104th WALL BEAUTIFICATION COMPETITION In Attack District 108 Jr. High
AND...
...ATTACK JR. HIGH WAS DIS-QUALIFIED FOR NOT HAVING ENOUGH MEMBERS ON THE WALL.
BUT WHY?!
WHAT'S WRONG WITH HAVING FEWER MEMBERS?!
You're still out.
CONTEST REF
AND WHY DIDN'T YOU SAY SO FIRST THING?!
EREN, JEAN...
HEADQUARTERS
I AM LEFT UNSATIS-FIED WITH HOW THIS ENDED.
HOW ABOUT I CUT OPEN YOUR SKULLS AND WASH OUT YOUR BRAINS?
NOOOOOO!
It's no trouble, really!
...!
I don't want to die yet!
Go!
UWAAH!
ド
BUMP
AAAHHH! BOSS!!

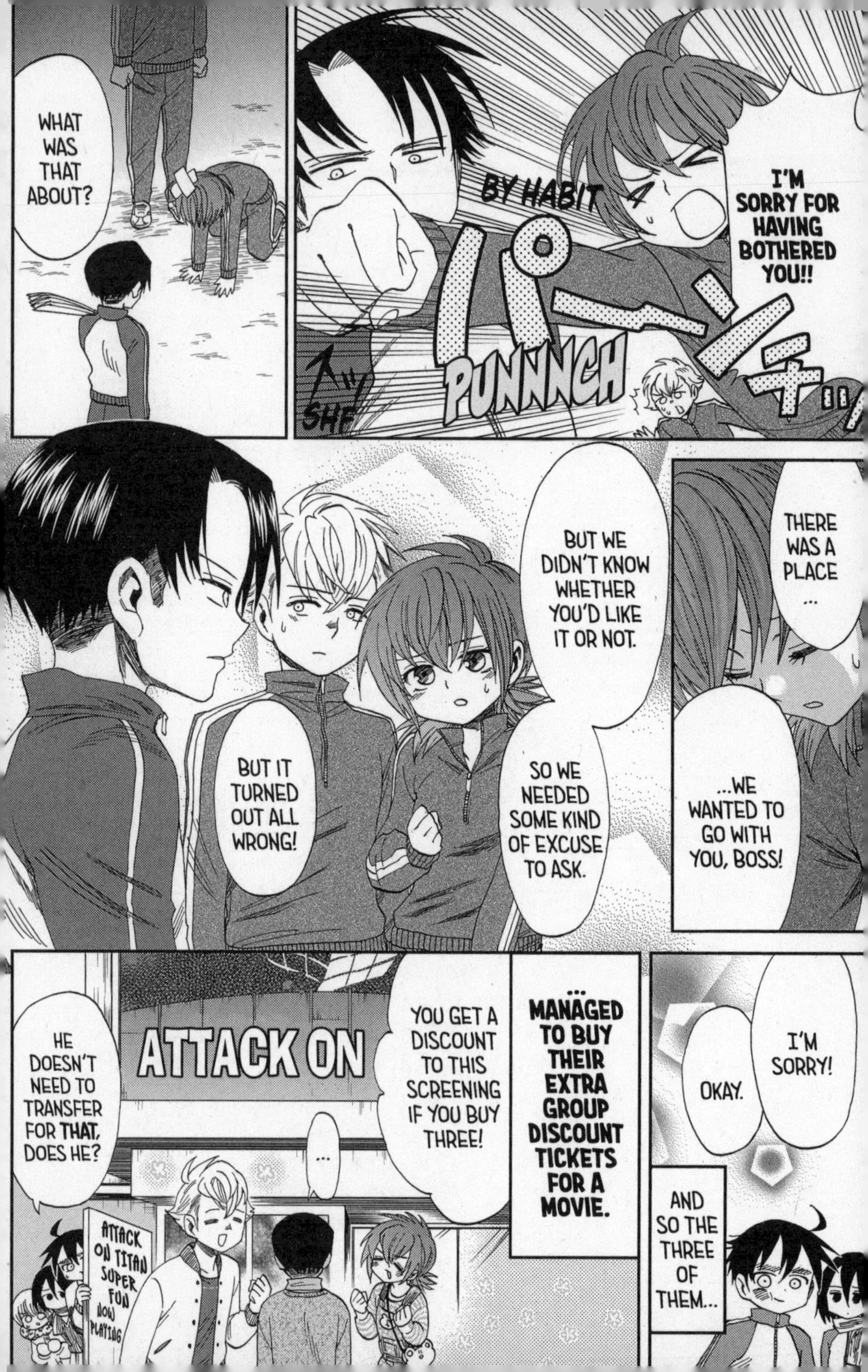
I'M SORRY FOR HAVING BOTHERED YOU!!
BY HABIT
パーンチッ!
PUNNNCH
SHF
WHAT WAS THAT ABOUT?
THERE WAS A PLACE ...
...WE WANTED TO GO WITH YOU, BOSS!
BUT WE DIDN'T KNOW WHETHER YOU'D LIKE IT OR NOT.
SO WE NEEDED SOME KIND OF EXCUSE TO ASK.
BUT IT TURNED OUT ALL WRONG!
I'M SORRY!
OKAY.
AND SO THE THREE OF THEM...
... MANAGED TO BUY THEIR EXTRA GROUP DISCOUNT TICKETS FOR A MOVIE.
YOU GET A DISCOUNT TO THIS SCREENING IF YOU BUY THREE!
...
ATTACK ON
HE DOESN'T NEED TO TRANSFER FOR THAT, DOES HE?
ATTACK ON TITAN SUPER FUN NOW PLAYING

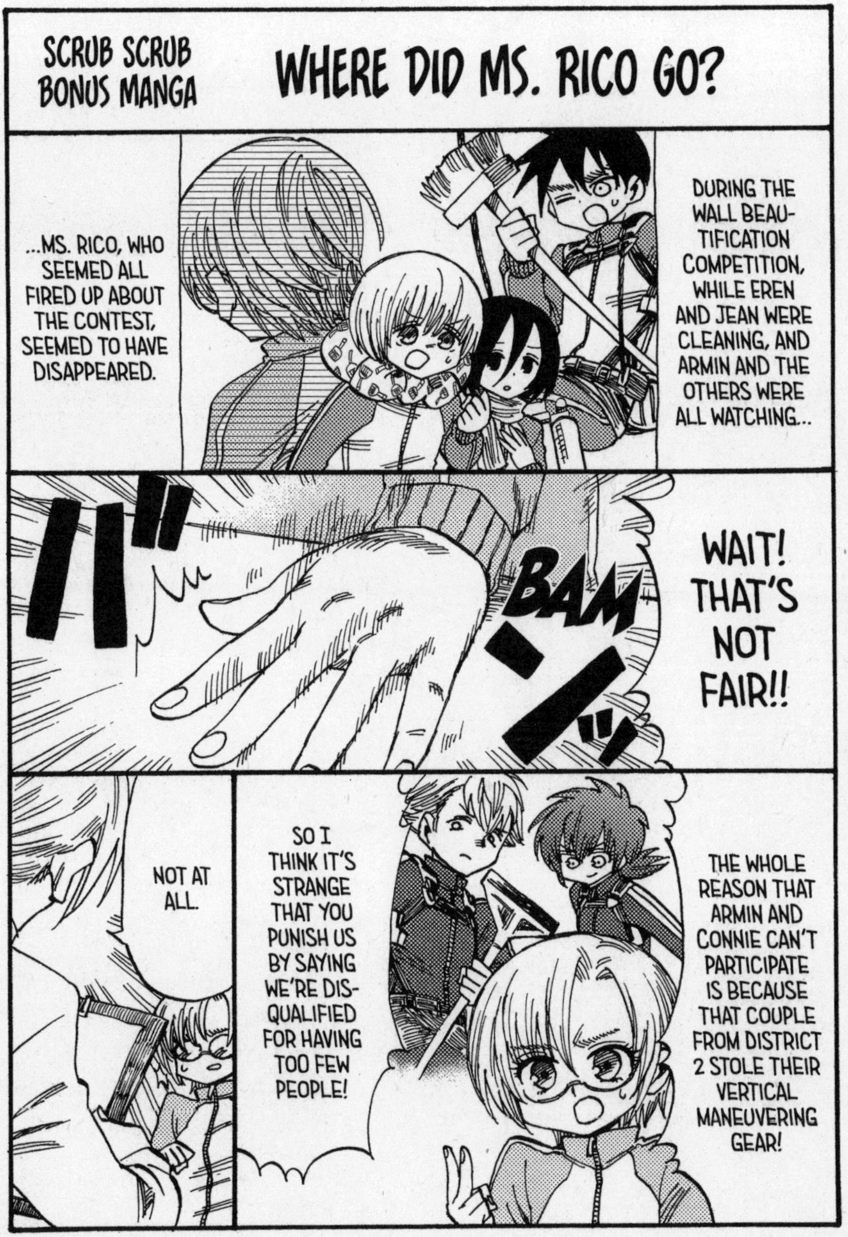
SCRUB SCRUB BONUS MANGA
WHERE DID MS. RICO GO?
DURING THE WALL BEAUTIFICATION COMPETITION, WHILE EREN AND JEAN WERE CLEANING, AND ARMIN AND THE OTHERS WERE ALL WATCHING...
...MS. RICO, WHO SEEMED ALL FIRED UP ABOUT THE CONTEST, SEEMED TO HAVE DISAPPEARED.
WAIT! THAT'S NOT FAIR!!
BAM
THE WHOLE REASON THAT ARMIN AND CONNIE CAN'T PARTICIPATE IS BECAUSE THAT COUPLE FROM DISTRICT 2 STOLE THEIR VERTICAL MANEUVERING GEAR!
SO I THINK IT'S STRANGE THAT YOU PUNISH US BY SAYING WE'RE DISQUALIFIED FOR HAVING TOO FEW PEOPLE!
NOT AT ALL.

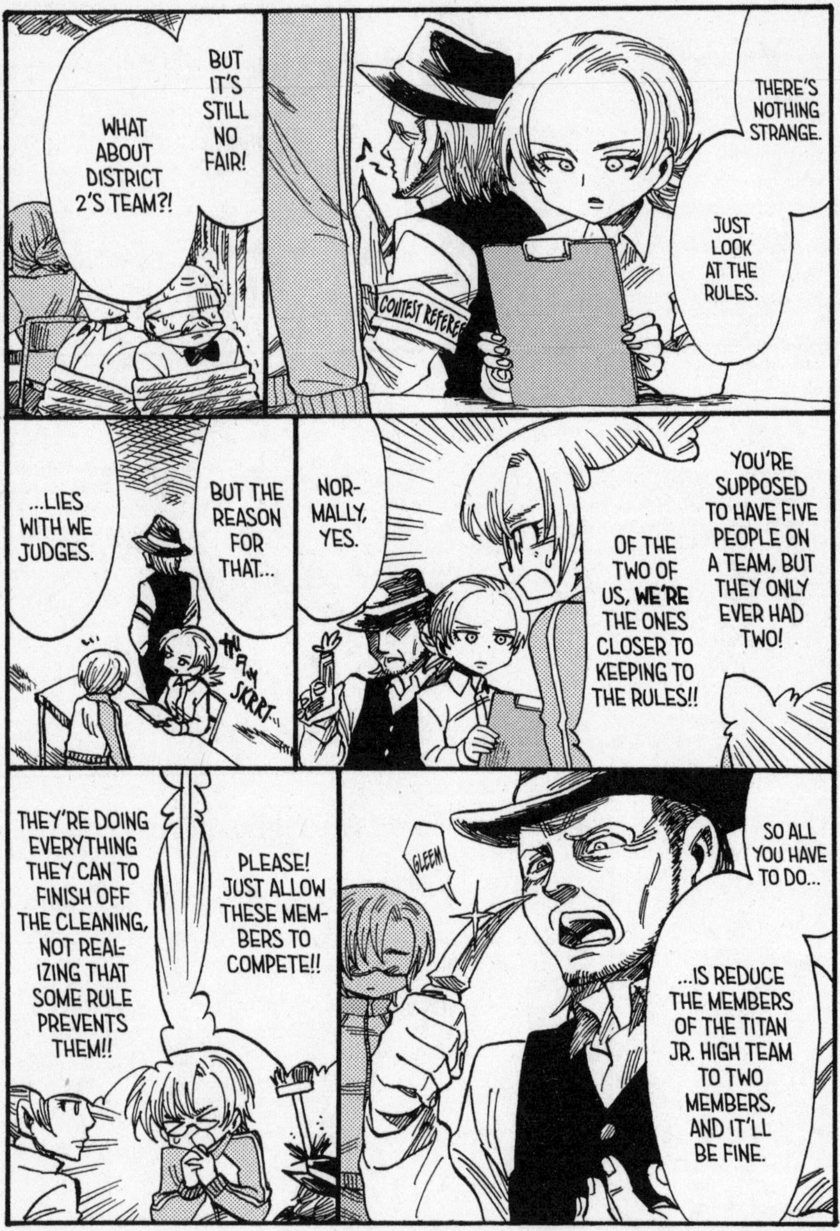
THERE'S NOTHING STRANGE.
JUST LOOK AT THE RULES.
CONTEST REFERE
BUT IT'S STILL NO FAIR!
WHAT ABOUT DISTRICT 2'S TEAM?!
YOU'RE SUPPOSED TO HAVE FIVE PEOPLE ON A TEAM, BUT THEY ONLY EVER HAD TWO!
OF THE TWO OF US, **WE'RE** THE ONES CLOSER TO KEEPING TO THE RULES!!
NOR-MALLY, YES.
BUT THE REASON FOR THAT...
...LIES WITH WE JUDGES.
SKRRT
SO ALL YOU HAVE TO DO...
GLEEM
...IS REDUCE THE MEMBERS OF THE TITAN JR. HIGH TEAM TO TWO MEMBERS, AND IT'LL BE FINE.
PLEASE! JUST ALLOW THESE MEM-BERS TO COMPETE!!
THEY'RE DOING EVERYTHING THEY CAN TO FINISH OFF THE CLEANING, NOT REAL-IZING THAT SOME RULE PREVENTS THEM!!

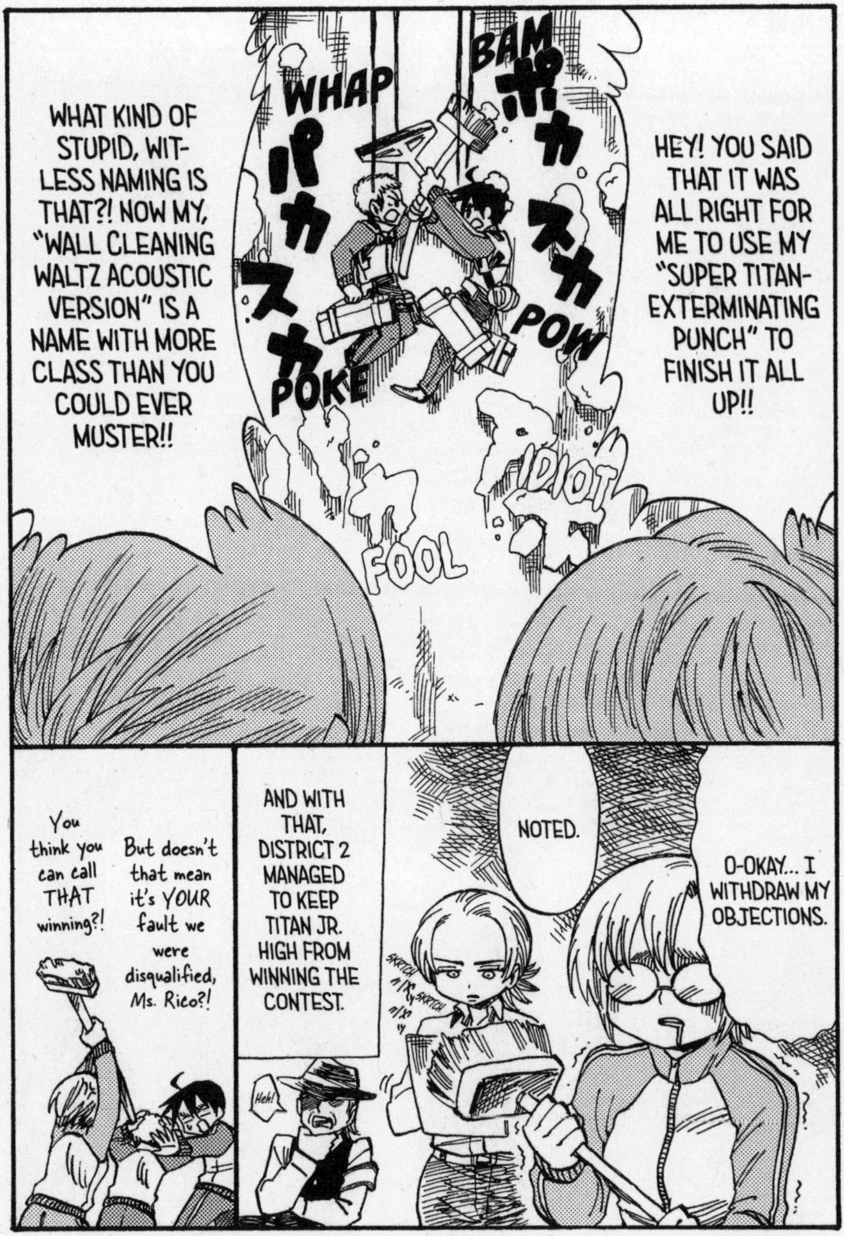
HEY! YOU SAID THAT IT WAS ALL RIGHT FOR ME TO USE MY "SUPER TITAN-EXTERMINATING PUNCH" TO FINISH IT ALL UP!!
BAM
ポカスカ
POW
WHAP
パカスカ
POKE
WHAT KIND OF STUPID, WIT-LESS NAMING IS THAT?! NOW MY, "WALL CLEANING WALTZ ACOUSTIC VERSION" IS A NAME WITH MORE CLASS THAN YOU COULD EVER MUSTER!!
IDIOT
FOOL
NOTED.
O-OKAY... I WITHDRAW MY OBJECTIONS.
AND WITH THAT, DISTRICT 2 MANAGED TO KEEP TITAN JR. HIGH FROM WINNING THE CONTEST.
SKRTCH
SKRTCH
Heh!
But doesn't that mean it's YOUR fault we were disqualified, Ms. Rico?!
You think you can call THAT winning?!

WHY IS THIS HERE?

AFTER THE CULTURE FAIR

READ THE MAIN STORY FIRST!!

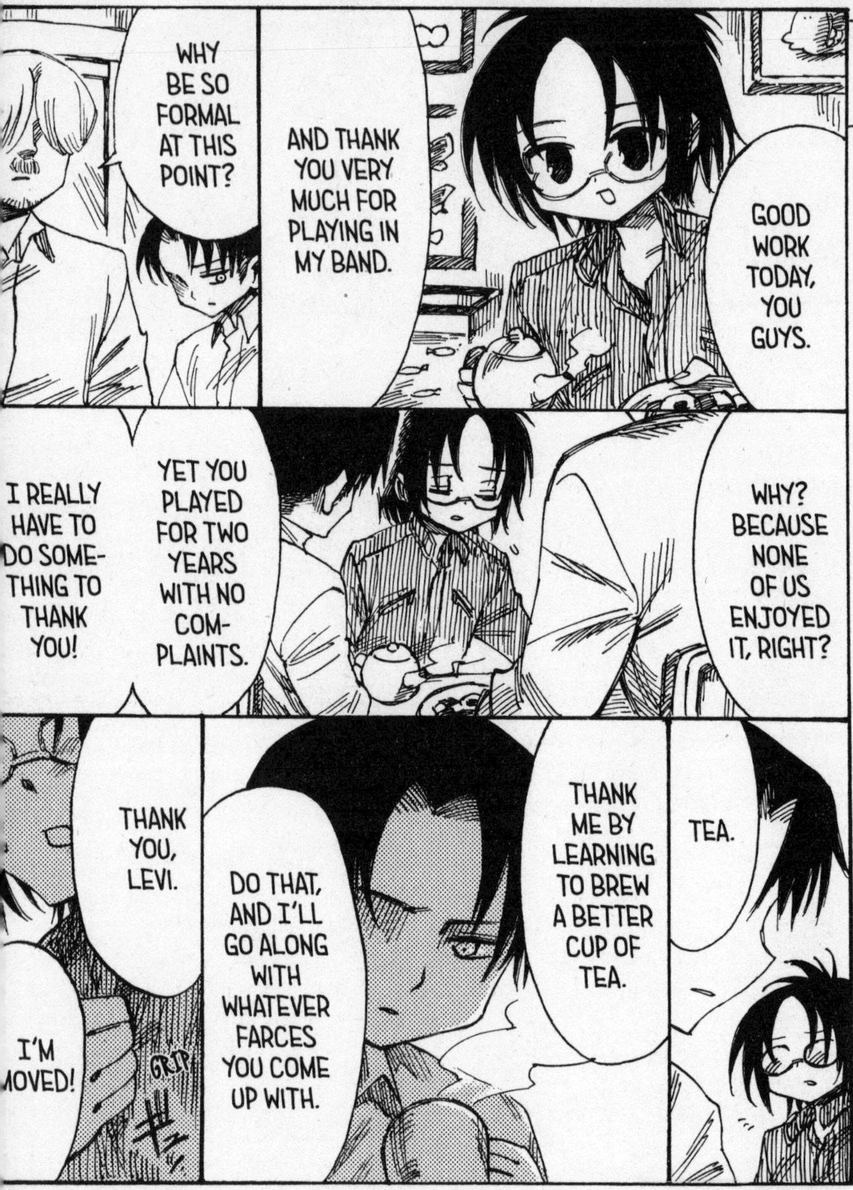
GOOD WORK TODAY, YOU GUYS.
AND THANK YOU VERY MUCH FOR PLAYING IN MY BAND.
WHY BE SO FORMAL AT THIS POINT?
WHY? BECAUSE NONE OF US ENJOYED IT, RIGHT?
YET YOU PLAYED FOR TWO YEARS WITH NO COMPLAINTS.
I REALLY HAVE TO DO SOMETHING TO THANK YOU!
TEA.
THANK ME BY LEARNING TO BREW A BETTER CUP OF TEA.
DO THAT, AND I'LL GO ALONG WITH WHATEVER FARCES YOU COME UP WITH.
THANK YOU, LEVI.
I'M MOVED!
GRIP

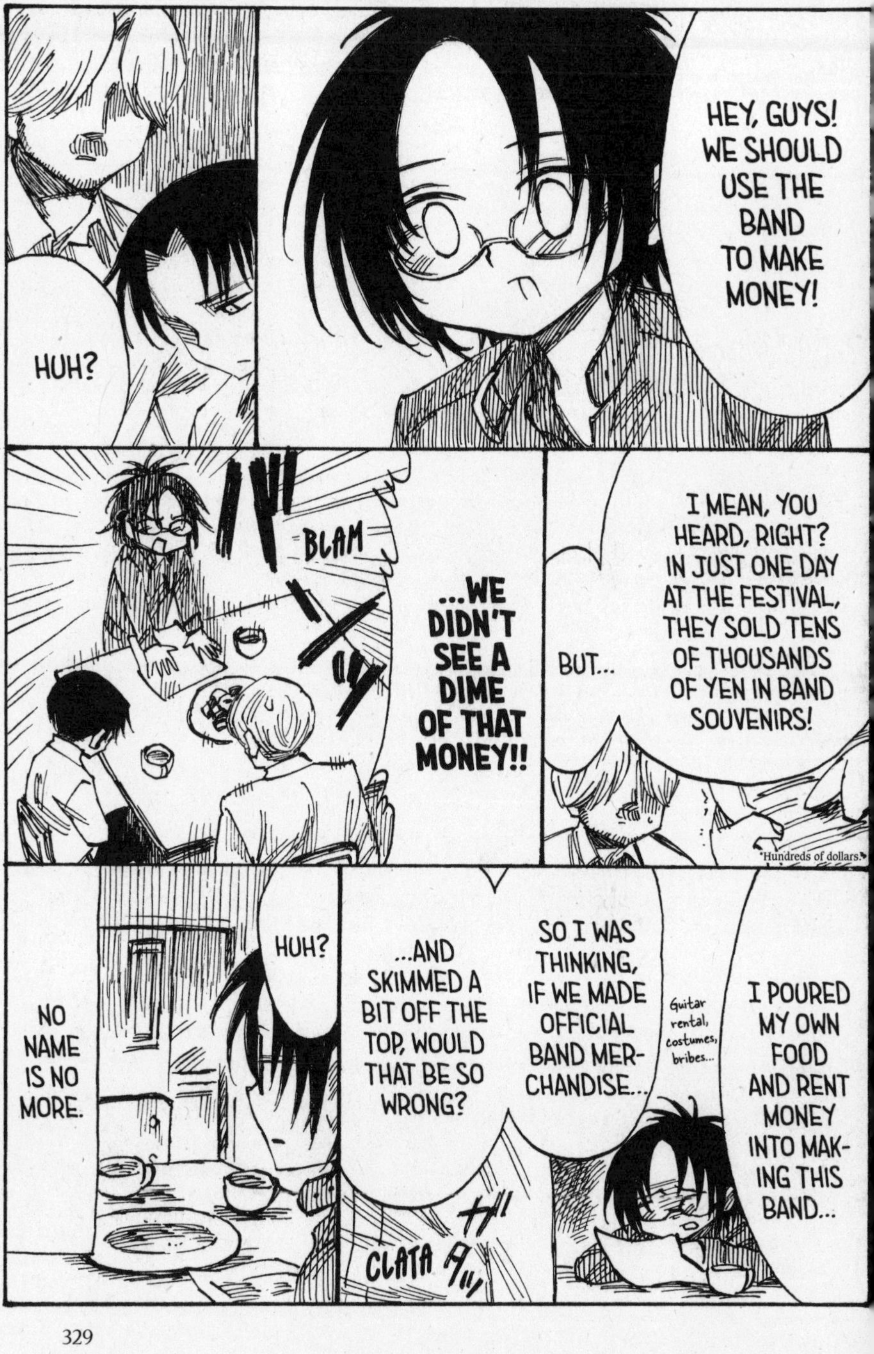
HEY, GUYS! WE SHOULD USE THE BAND TO MAKE MONEY!
HUH?
I MEAN, YOU HEARD, RIGHT? IN JUST ONE DAY AT THE FESTIVAL, THEY SOLD TENS OF THOUSANDS OF YEN IN BAND SOUVENIRS!
BUT...
*Hundreds of dollars.
...WE DIDN'T SEE A DIME OF THAT MONEY!!
BLAM
I POURED MY OWN FOOD AND RENT MONEY INTO MAKING THIS BAND...
Guitar rental, costumes, bribes...
SO I WAS THINKING, IF WE MADE OFFICIAL BAND MERCHANDISE...
...AND SKIMMED A BIT OFF THE TOP, WOULD THAT BE SO WRONG?
CLATA
HUH?
NO NAME IS NO MORE.

Translation Notes:

Page 17, Challenge menu

This is a common type of business promotion for inexpensive mom-and-pop-style restaurants all over Japan (chain restaurants and expensive restaurants generally avoid this kind of promotion). The general idea is that the customer is given some amount of food that would normally be impossible for a single person to eat in a sitting, and is given a short time, such as thirty minutes, to eat it. If the customer is able to eat everything served, then the massive meal is free. If the customer is unable to eat it all, then the customer must pay full price for the food. Examples of real-life challenge menus include eating 2 kg (nearly 5 pounds) of curry and rice in 20 minutes; eating a seven-person serving of pasta in 30 minutes; and eating ten bowls of ramen in an hour.

Page 18, Fashionable pancake restaurant

In Japan, pancake restaurants are foreign food. Far from being low-priced filling breakfast eateries, pancake restaurants are presented as classy European-styled bistros catering generally to a female clientele. Considering that most of the Challenge Menu challengers are men, it makes sense that pancake restaurants in Japan do not often use this method of promotion very often.

Page 23, Wei Ting for Si Ting

Whereas most western Chinese food restaurants sport names using terms like "Golden" or "Dragon" or the names of famous Chinese cities, Japanese Chinese restaurants tend to use names made up of two or four *kanji*. Usually they are fortuitous *kanji* such as "luck," or "prosperity." But in this case, the four *kanji* spell out, "All Chinese, All Seats Filled," which we translated somewhat insensitively as "Wei Ting for Si Ting."

Page 34, Culture festival

In Japan, most schools have a fair in which nearly every homeroom and club find something to sell or exhibit for the day. In most cases, they choose some kind of food or restaurant theme and sell snacks that are popular in other kinds of fairs and festivals throughout Japan. Others put on plays or demonstrations, still more have midway-style games or exhibits. Although most classes and clubs sell something, the entire fair is more of a social event than an attempt to make money.

Page 139, Campaign posters

In Japan, there are specific places where one can post election posters. Usually, in communities, there are specific boards with a number of open spaces (marked with a number) just the same size as an average-sized election poster. That is the designated place for each candidate to place his or her own election poster. Since Oluo's posters cover the entire poster area, we can assume that school election posters are not quite as regulated as general election posters.

Page 176, Roll cakes

As the name suggests, a roll cake is rolled. They have a layer of sponge cake and a layer of sweet whipped cream, and it is rolled into a circular cake that looks like a spiral when cut. The diameter tends to run from about 5cm to a little over 10 cm (from about two inches to a little over four inches). Like donuts, the sweet sponge cake and whipped cream make roll cakes unusually sweet for Japanese tastes (which tend toward less sweet items).

Page 184, Be-Bop Junior High

Due to the immense popularity of a manga/anime/live action/video game series called Be-Bop High School, the musical style bebop has been forever associated in Japanese minds with young toughs and punk-style violence. The manga series not only produced an OAV (original animation video) series and a popular video game, but also seven live-action movies in the late '80s and early '90s. It also saw a revival in a live-action TV series in the mid-2000s. The manga itself was a long-time bestseller, running from 1983-2003.

Page 209, Pucker

In Japanese, the sound of a kiss is *chu*, and the sound of a sparrow call is *chun*. The close sound and the way a person's lips pucker up when one says *chu* or *chun* makes Bertolt think of a kiss rather than a birdcall. Of course, since in English-language areas, the birds say, "cheep," "chirp," or "tweet," none of those would remind an English-language speaker of a kiss. So we hope that "pucker" lets you know what Bertolt was so excited over.

Page 209, Splurt

A nosebleed in Japan is indicative of a sexually immature boy getting excited. It is such a well-used (overused?) trope that the manga didn't even see a need to illustrate it directly. It just showed a black splotch coming from the bottom of the panel, and the classic Japanese sound effect for the action, *dopiii*.

Page 231, Ordinary cooking

A fish, miso soup and rice is about as average and ordinary a meal in Japan as bread, meat and potatoes is in most Western countries. In this case, it's like going to a demonstration of cooking prowess, and only seeing them make the same thing you eat at home every single day.

Page 232, Western food

As opposed to "ordinary cooking" mentioned above, Western-style food is considered a bit of a treat, like certain ethnic foods in Western countries. Since most Japanese people who cook are mostly familiar with Japanese cuisine, Japanese people who are good cooks of Western cuisine are rare, so a good Western meal is looked forward to with anticipation.

Page 251, *Harisen*

As mentioned in the notes for Volume 1, a *harisen* is a folded paper (or sometimes metal) fan that is used to punish lazy students or others in a position lower than oneself. The folded nature lessens the impact, but it still hurts.

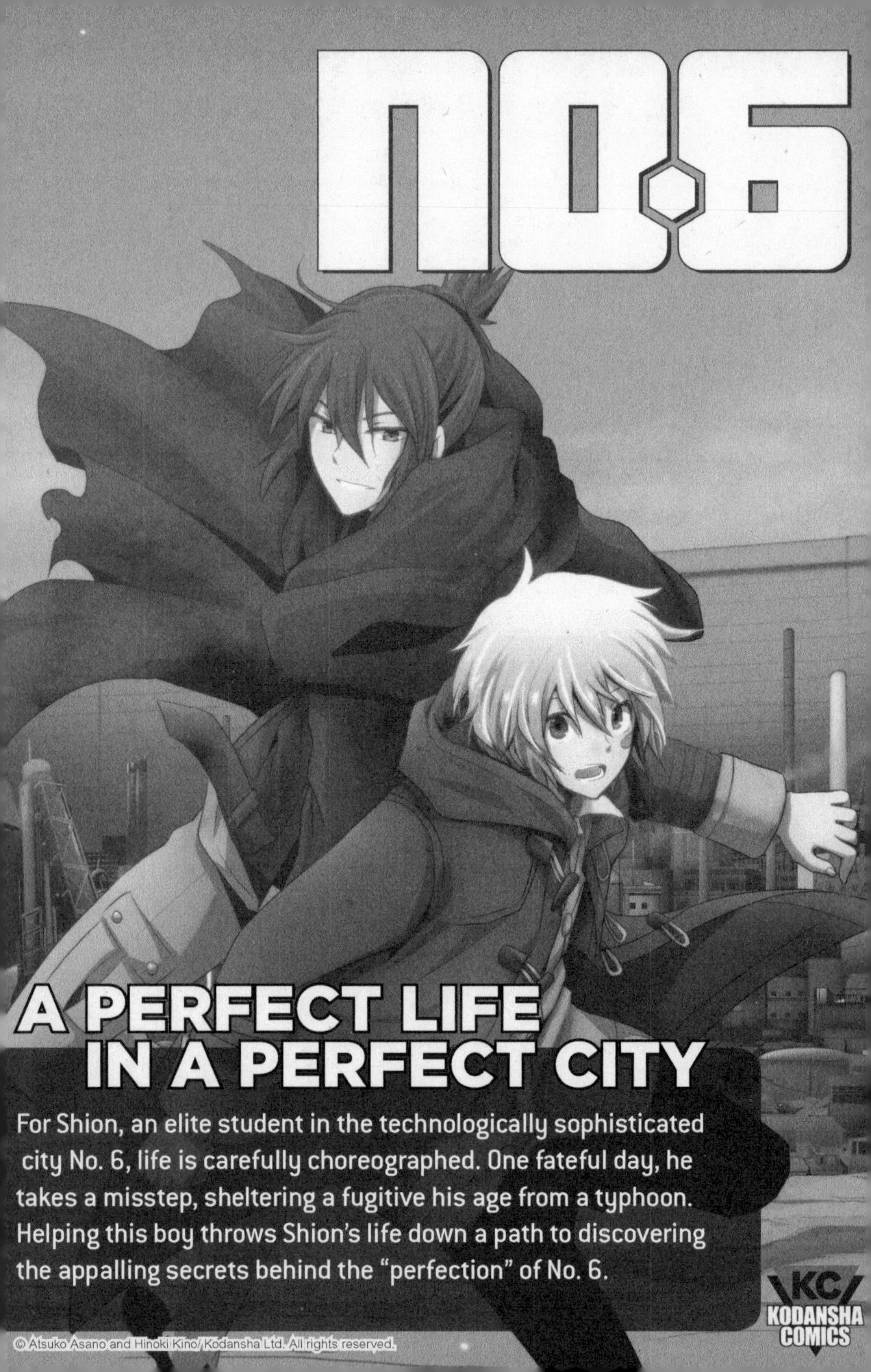
NO.6
A PERFECT LIFE
IN A PERFECT CITY
For Shion, an elite student in the technologically sophisticated city No. 6, life is carefully choreographed. One fateful day, he takes a misstep, sheltering a fugitive his age from a typhoon. Helping this boy throws Shion's life down a path to discovering the appalling secrets behind the "perfection" of No. 6.
KC
KODANSHA COMICS
© Atsuko Asano and Hinoki Kino/ Kodansha Ltd. All rights reserved.

Attack on Titan: Junior High volume 3 is a work of fiction. Names, characters, places, and incidents are the products of the author's imagination or are used fictitiously. Any resemblance to actual events, locales, or persons, living or dead, is entirely coincidental.

A Kodansha Comics Trade Paperback Original

Published in the United States by Kodansha Comics, an imprint of Kodansha USA Publishing, LLC, New York.

Publication rights for this English edition arranged through Kodansha Ltd, Tokyo.

First published in Japan in 2014 by Kodansha Ltd., Tokyo as *Shingeki! Kyojin chûgakkô*, volumes 5 and 6.

ISBN 978-1-61262-961-2

Original cover design by Takashi Shimoyama/Saya Takagi (Red Rooster)

Printed in the United States of America.

www.kodanshacomics.com

9 8 7 6 5 4 3 2 1
Translation: William Flanagan
Lettering: AndWorld Design
Editing and adaptation: Ben Applegate
Kodansha Comics edition cover design by Phil Balsman

You are going the *wrong way!*

Manga is a *completely* different type of reading experience.

To start at the *BEGINNING,* go to the *END!*

That's right! Authentic manga is read the traditional Japanese way--from right to left, exactly the opposite of how American books are read. It's easy to follow: just go to the other end of the book, and read each page--and each panel--from the right side to the left side, starting at the top right. Now you're experiencing manga as it was meant to be.